FIRST LADY OF THE SOUTH

First Lady of the South

The Life of Mrs. Jefferson Davis

By Ishbel Ross

Illustrated

GREENWOOD PRESS, PUBLISHERS
WESTPORT, CONNECTICUT

Library of Congress Cataloging in Publication Data

Ross, Ishbel, 1897–
    First lady of the South.

    Reprint of the 1st ed. published by Harper, New York.
    Bibliography: p.
    1. Davis, Varina (Howell) 1826–1906. 2. Davis,
Jefferson, 1808–1889. I. Title.
[E467.1.D27R6 1973]   973.7'13'0924 [B]   73-7381
ISBN 0-8371-6927-5

Copyright © 1958 by Ishbel Ross

Originally published in 1958 by Harper & Brothers, New York

Reprinted with the permission of Harper & Row, Publishers, Inc.

Reprinted in 1973 by Greenwood Press,
a division of Williamhouse-Regency Inc.

Library of Congress Catalogue Card Number 73-7381

ISBN 0-8371-6927-5

Printed in the United States of America

CONTENTS

ILLUSTRATIONS

The following are grouped in a separate section after page 148

Mr. and Mrs. William Burr Howell
Varina Anne Banks Howell as a young girl
Judge George Winchester
Margaret Graham Howell
William Francis Howell
Becket Kempe Howell
Jefferson Davis Howell
The Briers at Natchez
A room at The Briers
Varina at eighteen
Varina and Jefferson Davis in 1845
Some of Varina Davis's jewelry
Varina in her early thirties
Joseph Emory Davis
Mr. and Mrs. Jefferson Davis before the Civil War
The Jefferson Davis children
Kate Davis Pulitzer
Mrs. Clement C. Clay
Mrs. Mary Boykin Chesnut
Lydia Johnston
The first White House of the Confederacy, Montgomery, Alabama
White House of the Confederacy at Richmond, Virginia
Brierfield after the fall of Vicksburg
Varina during the Confederacy
A cartoon of Jefferson Davis
Varina and Jefferson Davis in 1868
Varina's two daughters, Margaret and Winnie
Mrs. Jefferson Davis at Beauvoir

ACKNOWLEDGMENTS

I am much indebted to descendants of Mr. and Mrs. Jefferson Davis for aid in the preparation of this book, and I should like to thank in particular their grandson, Mr. Jefferson Hayes-Davis of Colorado Springs, and their granddaughter, Mrs. Lucy Hayes Young, of Colorado and Arkansas, for personal reminiscences, anecdotes, and material bearing on the history of Mrs. Davis, and for checking vital facts.

No one has been more helpful in rounding up intimate family memorabilia, portraits, and inherited recollections of Mrs. Davis than her great-granddaughter, Mrs. John W. Stewart, of Santa Barbara, California. I am indeed most grateful to her for the interest she has shown in this biography and for her assistance in all respects.

Mrs. Young, Mr. Hayes-Davis, and Mrs. Stewart are all directly descended from Mrs. Jefferson Davis through her oldest daughter, Margaret Davis Hayes, the only one of Varina's children to marry and leave survivors. There are 141 Davis descendants in all, scattered across the country, including twelve great-grandchildren, twenty-nine great-great-grandchildren and three great-great-great-grandchildren. There have been several Varinas since the original Varina Davis, and both Mrs. Stewart and her mother were named after Mrs. Jefferson Davis.

I have also been generously aided by other branches of the family, and wish to express my indebtedness to Mrs. Ralph Wood, of Biloxi; Mrs. Stamps Farrar of New Orleans; Mrs. William McL. Fayssoux, of New Orleans; Mrs. Thomas Stone Howell of Alexandria, Louisiana; and Mrs. M. B. More, of New York City.

A wealth of excellent material was placed at my disposal by Miss India W. Thomas, House Regent of the Confederate Museum in Richmond, and Miss Eleanor S. Brockenbrough, her assistant. I am much indebted to both for their interest and co-operation, as I am to Miss Haydée M. Fortier and Miss Dora L. Pool, curator and assistant curator of Confederate Memorial Hall in New Orleans, where many of the Davis papers and relics may be found today.

Mrs. Marguerite M. Murphy gave me splendid assistance on my visit to Beauvoir, the Jefferson Davis Shrine on the Gulf Coast, which has many reminders of the years spent there by Mrs. Davis. And in Montgomery, Mrs. Daniel W. Troy showed me the treasures of the beautiful White House of the Confederacy in Alabama. These four centers have Davis documents and memorabilia indispensable to the biographer, and are evocative of the atmosphere in which Varina Davis passed some of the most crucial years of her life.

In New Orleans, Mr. and Mrs. F. G. Strachan received me most hospitably in the mansion where Jefferson Davis died and where Winnie Davis made her debut. In Natchez, Mrs. William Winans Wall showed me over The Briers, where Varina Howell grew up and where her marriage took place in 1845. Skilfully restored by Mrs. Wall, it is now one of the show places of Natchez.

I talked to a number of persons in Natchez who had family reminiscences bearing on the Davises and Howells, and among them were Mrs. Harry Winston, Mrs. J. Balfour Miller, Mrs. Charles H. Stone, Mrs. Arlie C. Warren, Miss Florence Harper, and Mrs. Edith Wyatt Moore. I am specially indebted to Miss Pearl Guyton, teacher and historian, for many suggestions and contacts.

Mrs. Eva W. Davis, director, and her assistant, Miss Zaidee Nield, were most helpful to me at the old Courthouse Museum in Vicksburg. Among others in the South to whom I am specially indebted are: Mrs. Julia Arnold, of Vicksburg; Miss Flora Walthall, of Jackson, Mississippi; Miss Mary L. Railey and Mrs. Carleton King, of New Orleans; Mrs. Mary G. Billups, of Columbia, Mississippi; Mrs. H. J. Leake of Tuscaloosa, Alabama; Mrs. Malcolm J. Triche and Mrs. W. A. Whitaker, both of Baton Rouge, Louisiana; T. W. Crigler, president of the board of directors of The Sons of Confederate Veterans, Macon, Mississippi; and Ray M. Thompson, executive editor of *Down South*, Biloxi, Mississippi.

I am much indebted to Miss Florence M. McIntyre, of Memphis, Tennessee, for personal recollections of Mrs. Davis and anecdotes bearing on the summers she spent at the Humberstone Club in Canada. Mrs. Merrill Parrish Hudson and Stephen Rice Phelan, both of Memphis, gave me enlightening material on the Davises involving the years they spent in Tennessee, and Bouvier Beale, of New York, recalled the close friendship of his grandmother, Mrs. J. D. Beale, and Mrs. Davis during the closing years of Varina's life.

Robert Douthat Meade, author of *Judah P. Benjamin*, Margaret

Leech (Mrs. Ralph Pulitzer), author of *Reveille in Washington,* and Burke Davis, author of *Gray Fox,* all gave me helpful information, and I should also like to acknowledge with much gratitude the co-operation of Mrs. D. A. DeVore (Margaret C. DeVore), of Vicksburg, who has special knowledge of Winnie Davis's blighted romance. In this same connection I am indebted to Miss Nannie Mayes Crump, of Washington, who threw further light on this little known story, and whose collection of papers in the Library of Congress supplies the key to the role played by Mrs. Davis when the Daughter of the Confederacy fell in love with the grandson of a famous abolitionist.

Mr. Robert Garrett of Baltimore was good enough to give me permission to study the John W. Garrett material in the Library of Congress which shows how Mrs. Davis worked to have her husband freed from Fortress Monroe. Mr. Charles Day Burchenal of Brooklyn, and his sisters, Miss Emma and Miss Elizabeth Burchenal, gave me intimate material on the life of the Davis family at Fortress Monroe.

I can scarcely begin to acknowledge all the assistance I have received in the university libraries, general libraries, and historical societies in various parts of the country, where Varina Davis correspondence may be found. But I should like to mention the help given me by John Melville Jennings, director, and H. W. Cole, curator of manuscripts, Virginia Historical Society, Richmond; Richard B. Harwell, director of publications, Virginia State Library, Richmond; Mrs. Ralph Catterall, Valentine Museum, Richmond; Francis L. Berkeley, Jr., curator of manuscripts, Alderman Library, University of Virginia; Miss Mattie Russell, curator of manuscripts, Duke University; Professor Robert Moody, Department of History, Duke University; James W. Patton, Director of Library, University of North Carolina; Mrs. Carolyn A. Wallace and Miss Anna Brooke Allan, both of the University of North Carolina.

Farther south I was greatly helped by Mrs. William J. Griffith, archivist, Howard-Tilton Memorial Library, Tulane University; V. L. Bedsole, director, and Mrs. Elsa B. Meier and Miss Marcelle F. Schertz, all of the Department of Archives, Louisiana State University; Peter A. Brannon, director, and Mrs. Allene McMillan and Mrs. Reynolds Mills, of the Alabama Department of Archives and History, Montgomery; Mrs. Julius Melton and Carl A. Ray, Mississippi State Archives, Jackson; Mrs. Sarah A. Verner and Miss Lucille Crutcher, University of Alabama Library, Tuscaloosa; Forrest Palmer and Miss Willie D. Halsell, Mississippi State College, Starkville; Mrs. Ellen Prowell of the Cabildo

Museum, New Orleans; Miss Rosa M. Oliver, of the Louisiana State Library, New Orleans; and Miss Eleanor Grayloe, Fisk Public Library, Natchez.

I am also much indebted to Miss Helen S. Mangold, assistant curator of manuscripts, Henry E. Huntington Library, San Marino, California; Mrs. Mary R. Davis, and Miss Ruth Walling, both of Emory University; Mrs. Lilla M. Hawes, director Georgia Historical Society, Savannah; Miss Virginia Rugheimer, Charleston Library Society; Robert H. Brannan, the Newberry Library, Chicago; and Mrs. W. Edwin Gledhill, Santa Barbara Historical Society, California.

I found much valuable material for this biography in the Manuscript Division of the New York Public Library, particularly in the papers of Walter L. Fleming and Dr. Robert McElroy, and am most grateful to Robert W. Hill, Edward B. Morrison, and Miss Jean McNiece for their tireless assistance, as well as to Leon Weidman and Mrs. Shirley Spranger, of the American History Room. I was aided, too, by Dr. James J. Heslin, of the New York Historical Society.

As always, the Manuscripts Division of the Library of Congress proved to be a fountainhead of essential documents and friendly co-operation, and I wish to express my most sincere gratitude to David C. Mearns, chief of the Division, and to Dr. Elizabeth G. McPherson, Dr. C. P. Powell, Wilfred Langone and Miss Kate Stewart for all the aid and courtesy accorded me in assembling material for this biography. I should also like to acknowledge the assistance of Dr. Carl Lokke and Mrs. Julia Bland Carroll, of the National Archives.

I. R.

PART ONE

1

A CHRISTMAS ENCOUNTER

VARINA ANNE HOWELL was seventeen when Jefferson Davis first crossed her path at the garden gate of his niece's home in Mississippi. She had stopped off at Florida McCaleb's house on her way to spend the Christmas holidays of 1843 at The Hurricane, the large plantation owned by Joseph Emory Davis, Jeff's older brother and idol. Varina had come from her home in Natchez and had paused for a night at David McCaleb's place, which was some miles distant from the family headquarters on lonely Palmyra Peninsula. Jeff was asked by his brother to deliver a note to Varina, telling her that his niece, Mary Jane Bradford, would arrive next day with horses to take her to The Hurricane.

It was only a brief encounter, a mild exchange of courtesies and a family chat, as he went on his way to a political caucus in Vicksburg. Varina was magnetized by the handsome planter with the soldierly bearing, although his stiff manner chilled her at first. They were widely different in age and experience. Davis had just taken his initial step along the political path that would lead to his ultimate destiny as first and only President of the Confederate States of America. Varina had recently completed her studies with a Whig tutor from New England.

Davis was eighteen years her senior, a widower who had isolated himself on his plantation for eight years, dwelling with persistent melancholy on the memory of Zachary Taylor's daughter who had died three months after their marriage in 1835. The legend of his love for Sarah Knox Taylor was to spread with his fame, casting a shadow at times over Varina's possessive spirit. Yet this second romance, touched off at the McCalebs', would flower eventually into one of the rarer idyls of American history.

Joseph may well have invited Varina to share his Christmas hospitality in the hope of diverting his younger brother from his morbid preoccupation with the past. The Howells and the head of the Davis clan were old friends, and Varina was already showing the kind of wit and intelligence that impressed the worldly Joseph, who had political aspirations for his brother and had stirred him into action for the Democratic party. She was better educated than the average girl of her generation, and even at seventeen displayed some of the strength and originality that were to distinguish her all through life, tempered at this time by a deferential manner and the soft accents of Mississippi.

Varina was of more than average height.* In her youth she was shapely and well proportioned, moving with grace and freedom. Her dark hair, glossy and thick, framed a long face, smooth in contour, firm in its planes. She had abandoned her dangling schoolgirl strands in favor of a more adult effect for the Christmas festivities. Her hair was sleekly groomed from a center part and fanned out in a high swirl on the crown of her head. Then and later Varina's eyes were the feature that people remembered. They were uncommonly large, full, and dark, settled deep under heavy lids. Many who watched her commented on the way they could blaze with anger, shine with friendly interest, or flash with amusement. Her mouth was large and freely chiseled, suggesting petulance in her early years, and vigor in later life. She already had the sultry look that matched her powerful, driving nature. Varina was intense in all her emotions, and the years were to prove her a woman who could love and hate with equal vehemence. There were few points of similarity between her and the small dark beauty with spiraling ringlets who had been Jefferson Davis's first wife, except that both were vivacious, sympathetic, and intelligent.

Because of the isolation in which he lived, Varina was scarcely conscious of the existence of Jefferson until this encounter, although Joseph Davis frequently visited their home, The Briers, outside Natchez. She had arrived in a state of high excitement after a trip up the Mississippi in the steamboat *Magnolia* which seemed a "floating palace of ease and luxury." She was impressed with the cuisine and diverted by the exchange of wares at each landing—fresh fruits and plantation flowers for ice, new books, and luxury items ordered from New Orleans.

When Mary Jane joined her at the McCalebs' with a groom and a carriage for her luggage the two girls galloped off in high spirits under a bright blue winter sky, their horses' hoofs scattering the dry leaves that strewed the forested path to the Davis home. Although used to planta-

* Notes will be found in section beginning on page 421.

tion ways, Varina was impressed with The Hurricane, which had taken its name from a cyclone in 1827 that had battered the property, eroded the peninsula, injured a Davis brother named Isaac, and killed one of his sons. There was strength, if not grace, in the massive building. Varina was conscious at once of its solid dimensions and the close spacing of the thick colonnades that ringed the house. It lacked the grace and unity of the Natchez mansions familiar to her, but she looked around her with keen interest as she entered the wide hall, noting the low ceilings in the main building, the narrow windows and massive walls.

Christmas greens were looped against cream paneling. She was conscious of a blur of rose brocatelle and polished wood through the dim light of the drawing room and the "tea room" where the feminine members of the family gathered to embroider, read, and chat. Heavy walnut pieces and French period furniture mingled harmoniously in the various rooms. Lace and satin curtains blew at the windows. The prisms of glittering chandeliers stirred faintly in the breeze. Outdoors, a pergola led to an annex where the family dined en masse in a long paved room at a table set with fine crystal and silver. Varina was struck by the abundance of game, the gargantuan roasts, the exotic foods from the New Orleans markets. But upstairs in the annex she found her favorite spot—an arched music room and study where the young people "sang and played, acted charades, gave mock concerts, and improvised games, while the family portraits looked stolidly down upon our antics." [2] The stern, handsome face of Samuel Davis, whose sons, Joseph and Jefferson, so closely resembled him, was of particular interest to Varina.

Doors paneled halfway with glass led to the grounds, which Joseph had cultivated to a high degree but which still vaguely suggested primitive forest land, although he adorned them with statuary, fountains, and arbors. Varina wandered happily in the huge rose garden and noted the pergolas and pathways; the imported trees and shrubs that blended with the native oaks and walnut trees; the China and tulip trees richly festooned with their own wild vines. Peach, fig, and apple trees covered eight acres of land. From the house the Mississippi could be glimpsed through wide clearings artfully contrived for vistas. A border of close-cut sward edged the open fields leading down to the river. Yet the plantation had a feeling of remoteness from civilization, in spite of all the modern conveniences that Joseph had introduced, and the sophisticated manner in which his household was managed. The Davis domain covered an area of more than five thousand acres on the peninsula, and land had been parceled out to various members of Joseph's far-reaching clan. The McCalebs were a case in point. His niece Florida had married young David McCaleb, and he liked to see all of his relatives established in comfort. As long as he had money and land to give away, he shared them freely.

Joseph had given up his law practice in 1827, the year after Varina was born, to develop the uncultivated land he had acquired on Palmyra Peninsula, increasing his holdings gradually by buying out the small settlers who had already done some forest clearing. His brother Isaac helped him at first, but after a clash of wills the younger brother had moved to Canton. When Jeff, who was graduated from West Point in 1828, resigned from the army after seven years of frontier service in order to conciliate Zachary Taylor, who did not wish his daughter to marry a soldier, Joseph offered him eighteen hundred acres of uncleared land to cultivate, and slaves to work it. Although a novice at farming the young soldier gave it the same concentrated and technical interest that he applied to military tactics. He became invaluable to Joseph as he developed his own acres and ran The Hurricane for him while the elder Davis toured the spas in summer. Their land lay cupped in a bend of the Mississippi, with the river running almost all around it. Today the river encircles it completely. It was thirty miles below Vicksburg. Mail arrived several times a week at a landing three miles down the river. When passengers were headed for the larger Mississippi boats they were taken by skiff to the landing through thick underbrush.

Joseph had more visible warmth and geniality than his brother ever displayed, but he was an autocrat of the first order. He was a man of extraordinary force and energy, more than six feet tall, with a close resemblance to Jefferson—the same aquiline nose, the classically carved lips, the suggestion of a sensitive and ardent spirit. In his early years he looked more poet than planter, but by the time Varina met him he was becoming patriarchal, a sarcastic, dynamic man sustaining various family offshoots on his acres.

He had amassed his vast fortune from next to nothing, and he spent it according to prevailing plantation standards. He had blooded horses, fine equipages, and his cellar was stocked with well-chosen wines. He summered at the fashionable resorts and traveled in style with his own coaches and servants. Joseph was potent in regional politics and public affairs. He was a familiar figure at the cotton depot and slave market in Natchez, and he had helped to draw up the code of honor for the local duelists, of whom there were many. With little formal education he had become one of the best read men in the South. He fluently discussed politics, books, law, science, the legends of the Mississippi, and the history of New Orleans. He was thought to rule his plantation with a sense of equity, according to the standards of his day, but he was an autocrat in his home, except where his wife Eliza was concerned.[3] She was a pliant figure in his large hierarchy, gentle, quiet, sickly, humoring him in his whims and never raising her voice in protest over his complex family relationships. Cousins and nieces abounded at the family board. His brothers and his sisters were always warmly welcomed, and the hospitality of The Hurricane was notorious in the region.

Varina quietly took stock of the assorted family circle. She had been invited a year earlier for the Christmas festivities but was busy then with her studies, and her mother thought her still too young for gaiety away from home. Actually, Varina hungered for wider experience and was ready to meet it halfway. Most of her travels up to this time had been "*autour de ma chambre*," she bleakly confessed, except for two terms spent at Madame D. Grelaud's Female Seminary in Philadelphia. Her politics, her education, even her character, had been molded for the most part by her tutor, Judge George Winchester, a New England jurist from Salem who had settled in Natchez in the early 1820's and was a true believer in Henry Clay.

Varina had just completed a stiff grounding in Latin and the English classics with the Judge. He was still so much a part of her life that her mother had asked him to escort her along the Mississippi as far as Diamond Head, where the McCalebs had their plantation. There he had left her to face the unknown. Joseph made her feel at home at once. As he strolled with her through his rose garden, he probed lightly for her political beliefs and found her ready to discuss them. Judge Winchester had accustomed her to debate and she was well informed on national politics. She read the *National Intelligencer* regularly and shared the prevailing distaste in her region for Martin Van Buren. Joseph noticed that she wore the Subtreasury cameo brooch that many Southern women affected by way of reproach. The symbol was a little bloodhound chained to a strongbox. Before leaving she took it off for Jefferson's benefit, but it appears in a contemporary portrait of Varina taken shortly before her marriage.

To her delight there were books everywhere—in the study, in the office shared by the two brothers, in the small columned library on the grounds. Varina must have seemed a little pedantic to the worldly planter who kept her well entertained until his brother returned from Vicksburg, exhilarated by the success of his speech there. But her searching mind was to be a strong factor in her relationship with her husband. After his first wife's death Jefferson Davis had read systematically and with purpose, and in the years to come each would feed this interest in the other. But for the time being he was conscious chiefly of her youth and freshness, her emotional warmth, her pride, and her keen response to her surroundings.

It was a family custom to read to Joseph in the evening. He followed the Congressional debates in this fashion, and kept abreast of the new books on politics and economics. Jefferson usually read to him until his eyes grew tired. Then the women of the household took turns. Varina picked up the thread with real enjoyment. Jeff noticed the ease with which she handled French idioms and Latin quotations, and her sharp awareness of what she read.

The days that followed were to be remembered always by the Jefferson Davises for their swift plunge into a deep and lasting love. Characteristically, Varina's infatuation for the quiet thoughtful man so much older than herself was almost instantaneous. She had quickly dismissed her first doubts about him. His response was slower, but he listened attentively when Joseph remarked after an evening of reading, "She will take high rank in the world of femininity when she blossoms out and comes thoroughly to herself." Then he added in a quick burst of admiration, "By Jove, she is as beautiful as Venus."

Jefferson made no comment for several minutes. He was always more reserved than Joseph in his judgments. Did he perhaps feel some hidden drive on his brother's part? It had always been Joseph's habit to influence his younger brother, in politics, in plantation affairs, in family matters, in so far as Jeff could be swayed by another.

"Yes," he finally conceded with cool reserve, "she is beautiful and has a fine mind." [4]

It was a swift-moving romance, and the large family party, seeing how things were going, left Varina and Jeff strictly to themselves. Joseph saw that at last his brother was conscious of another girl besides Knox, the name by which Sarah Knox Taylor had always been known. They passed much time together in the music room, Varina playing the piano, Jeff singing his favorite Scottish ballads. Or they sat with their heads close together over a book while they argued its merits by firelight. The mornings were devoted to long rides around the plantation, and although Varina accepted good horsemanship as a matter of course, she noticed that Jefferson Davis on his white Arabian horse "rode with more grace than any man I have ever seen, and gave one the impression of being incapable either of being unseated or fatigued." Although approaching thirty-six in 1844, he seemed to Varina as "erect, well-proportioned, and active as a boy." She approved his lean, handsome features, the way his fair hair curved around a high, wide forehead, the intensity of his blue-gray eyes, sunk deep beneath jutting brows, and not yet marred by the infection that later would destroy the sight of one. It was a taut, reserved face, with a look of sternness that was habitual with him, even in the prewar days. His chin was rounded and cleft, at odds with the disciplined line of his compressed lips.

Jefferson, in turn, watched Varina admiringly as she galloped beside him in a dark blue riding costume with plumed hat. She had ridden from childhood and handled with easy grace the bay he had picked for her. They toured the stables together, while he indicated the horses with special history, such as the vicious-tempered Medley, who had kicked his groom to death, and Black Oliver, sire of the Davis pacing stock. One of his foals would be seized by Federal soldiers and later become a favorite in General Ulysses S. Grant's stables. After parading past all thirty stalls and seeing many of the horses in action, Varina came to the conclusion that the riding horses at The Hurricane as a whole were "fast rackers, broken with care and ridden enough by the stablemen and the innumerable guests to make them gentle."

She was shown the office on the ground floor where the brothers discussed plantation affairs and worked over their agricultural experiments, for they were scientific farmers, trying to make the best of their land. She explored the storeroom and found that "this little closet was an ark," [5] packed with candy, shoes, farm implements, saddles, bridles, guns, knives, and bolts of linsey and calico. It enabled the planter to meet emergencies of different kinds.

Jefferson took Varina to see Brierfield, his own plantation nearby. There she met James Pemberton, his Negro overseer, who had been his cook and companion in the early 1830's, nursing Davis devotedly during a serious illness while they were stationed in the West. He now handled plantation affairs with skill and understanding. Varina was an object of immediate interest to Jim, for it was clear to him, as to others at the plantation, that Knox Taylor at last would have a successor.

By the end of January, when the time had come for Varina to return to Natchez, she had a quiet understanding with Jefferson Davis. Regardless of the difference in their ages, and his known love for Knox, he had become a romantic figure in her eyes—handsome, scholarly, reserved in manner but ardent with her, a combination of fire and ice that she was to understand and handle well in the years to come. She approved his obvious devotion to his family, his engaging way with the younger generation, and his kindly relations with the slaves on his own and his brother's plantations. His political faith was another matter.

Before returning to Natchez, Varina had already appraised him in an illuminating letter sent to her mother immediately after she met him. It was salted with sharp observations and contained some tentative judgments on Jefferson Davis that history amply confirmed. He had impressed her as being a "remarkable kind of man but of uncertain temper and has a way of taking for granted that everybody agrees with him when he expresses an opinion which offends me, yet he is most agreeable and has a peculiarly sweet voice and a winning manner of asserting himself."

He suggested age and youth to her at the same time, but she soon learned that he was "old"—only two years younger than her mother, Varina explained with some naïveté. She was not sure that she could ever like him as well as she did his brother Joe; in fact, she found him the kind of man she would expect "to rescue one from a mad dog at any risk but to insist upon a stoical indifference to the fright afterward." She had made better soundings than she was aware on her new acquaintance, but she finished her note with a strong regional inflection: "Would you believe it, he is refined and cultivated and yet he is a Democrat." [6] He could scarcely have been anything worse in the Natchez region at that time. The Howells, like most of the planters around them, were ardent Whigs and Episcopalians. Their political philosophy was cherished by the wealthy and aristocratic families among whom Varina had grown up. She could scarcely accept the fact that a man as presentable as Jefferson Davis should belong to the Democratic party then mustering strength in Mississippi.

But after a few days spent with him at The Hurricane Varina's cool reasoning was swept away in a tide of infatuation. On her return to Natchez all her young friends heard of the distinguished man she had met in the river country. Judge Winchester listened with close attention, but some concern for her Whig principles. Her mother quickly dashed her spirits by injecting several doubts into the situation—the difference in their ages, his early romance, his political faith, and her own youth and inexperience. Both families were proud. They had sturdy ancestry and were of good social standing, although Varina's father, William Burr Howell, was more impecunious and easygoing than his forebears. Joseph had helped him when he first settled in Natchez and had often befriended him since then. Mrs. Howell had known the older brother from her girlhood days, and when he visited The Briers the children all addressed him as Uncle Joe. She remembered Jefferson vaguely as a pleasant-mannered young cadet who had greeted her once when she visited West Point.[7] Like everyone else in the region, she had heard of his deep and enduring passion for his lost bride, but he had never visited them. Now she wanted Varina to wait and be sure that she was not being carried away by a passing fancy.

Shaken by this unexpected opposition, Varina wrote to Jefferson imploring him not to visit her family yet. He replied with some bewilderment on March 8, 1844: "But why shall I not come to see you? In addition to the desire I have to be with you every day and all day, it seems to me but proper and necessary to justify my wish to marry you, if you had not forbidden me I should have answered your letter in person and let me ask you to reconsider your position." [8]

Varina's hesitation was chilling and inexplicable to proud Jefferson Davis. Her father favored his suit. Judge Winchester had been Jefferson's advocate throughout and he was a strong force in the family counsels where Varina was concerned. "I am truly obliged by the defence put in for me by my friend the Judge," Davis wrote to Varina. "He would have a poor opinion, I doubt not, of any man who having an opportunity to know you would not love you. . . ." [9]

This letter brought a definite response from Varina, assuring him that her mother had agreed to the marriage, but by this time Jefferson, always conscientious where his family was concerned, was settling affairs for his sister Amanda and helping her to move her children to The Hurricane. Her husband, Judge David Bradford, a lawyer in Madison Parish, Louisiana, and former president of the New Orleans Mint, had been killed by opposing counsel in a case he was defending.[10]

When Jefferson finally arrived at The Briers, he won Varina's family with ease, if indeed the opposition had been anything more than a social ruse, or uncertainty on her part. She now became formally engaged, but other complications developed. Love and political pressures had come

into Davis's life simultaneously after a long period of introspective de-
tachment, and he was forced to go out campaigning. In the autumn of
1843, before meeting Varina, he had run for the Legislature in Warren
County and had been defeated because of the local preponderance of
Whigs. But his eloquence and fine presence had made an impression and
he was now an elector at large, canvassing for James Knox Polk and
George M. Dallas.

It was a rowdy campaign, with barbecues, cock fights, brass bands,
horse races, occasional brawls, and much heavy drinking. Davis went his
austere way, traveling by horseback or driving his roached ponies over
rough roads, making nighttime stops at planters' homes along the way.[11]
He worked with the choleric Henry Stuart Foote, a fiery little politician,
effective in debate but prone to fight duels. They were fellow electors at
large. Davis put his faith in facts and logic rather than noise and
fulmination. They made an unlikely pair, but shared the same degree of
abuse from the Whigs.

Varina squirmed over the newspaper attacks that attended the progress
of her Democratic lover. Her Natchez friends were astonished that she
had given her devotion to a political renegade whose opponent, the
lyrically eloquent Seargent S. Prentiss, worked in traditional fashion for
Henry Clay and a Whig victory. Foote, Prentiss, Senator Robert J.
Walker of Mississippi, and John Anthony Quitman, who had advocated
nullification with John C. Calhoun in 1834, had all migrated from the
North and stayed to enjoy the luxurious life of the plantations, and to
become noted politicians in the South. But at this time Varina learned
a lesson she was to absorb more thoroughly later on—that Jefferson Davis
was not easy to sway in any direction. Nearly half a century later she
would write:

If ever a man was "rooted and grounded" in his political faith my husband was. . . . Though no man was less open to the accusation of saying
all he believed, he sincerely thought all he said, and, moreover, could not
understand any other man coming to a different conclusion after his
premises were stated. It was this sincerity of opinion which sometimes gave
him the manner to which his opponents objected as domineering.[12]

Varina would reach these conclusions by degrees. At the moment she
was an anxious girl, unsure of the situation into which she had plunged.
She worried because she heard so little from her traveling suitor. She
sent him importunate letters, reproaching him for not writing more

often. She followed the news and labored to keep informed on every issue with which he had to deal. As the summer advanced she became intensely nervous, developed an illness which may well have been a climatic fever, and collapsed in a state of acute weakness and depression.

Davis wrote to her in affectionate terms, calling her his angel, his wife, and signing himself her husband. But these were anxious days for Varina, and her restlessness became a matter of concern in her home. Joseph and Eliza cooled a little in their zest for her as a suitable wife for Jefferson. Already she had developed the deep sensitivity where criticism of her lover was concerned that she was to exhibit all through life. She was bewildered by the mud-slinging of a particularly abusive campaign. Nor did she like her friends' disapproval of Jeff's politics. "Oh, he is so noble, so high-minded and good and I love him so," she protested desperately when the point was raised.[13]

The Howells were a well-known family in Natchez and their handsome children were recognized by all the planters, although they lived on a less elaborate scale than many of their neighbors. At the time of Varina's birth her father was none too prosperous, but her maternal grandparents, Colonel and Mrs. James Kempe, were always ready to provide luxuries for their daughter, Margaret Louisa Kempe, who had married Howell in 1823. Although she passed most of her premarital life at The Briers, Varina was born on her grandfather's plantation Marengo in Louisiana on May 7, 1826.[14] After their marriage her parents had lived at Kempton, the rambling family homestead on the outskirts of Natchez. When it burned down they moved into The Briers, given them by Mrs. Kempe, who lived with them after her husband's death.[15]

Varina was a baby at the time and remembered no other home. She was the second child born to the Howells, who had eleven children in all, six of whom grew up. She was named for Mrs. George Banks, a friend of her mother's. Her forebears ranged from quiet Quakers to rebel Celts, with strains of English and Welsh blood on her paternal side, and a dash of Virginian blood mingled with Irish ancestry in the Kempes. She was the granddaughter of Richard Howell, Governor of New Jersey from 1793-1801. During the war it was frequently said that Varina had Northern blood and Northern sympathies, just as Mary Todd Lincoln was linked with the South through her Kentucky family ties. Three Howell brothers had migrated from Glamorganshire in Wales to the United States late in the seventeenth century.[16] One settled in

Delaware, another in Louisiana, and a third in Kentucky. Richard Howell belonged to the Delaware branch. He bought land in New Jersey, practiced law at Mount Holly, served as clerk of the Supreme Court, and eventually became Governor. During the War of the Revolution he raised a company and served with gallantry under George Washington, both as a soldier and secret agent. In 1774, disguised as an Indian, he led a party that raided a storehouse at New Castle, New Jersey, and burned an importation of tea.[17]

Varina was an accomplished storyteller and frequently entertained her friends with anecdotes about the robust Governor. She described him as a man of "unbounded benevolence, a temper easy and equable, and manners polite and engaging." He was also a convivial soul who liked to pitch quoits in the ball alley attached to a Trenton tavern. He had a taste for poetry, too, and wrote verses welcoming General Washington at Trenton Bridge when he was on his way to his inauguration in New York. The Governor's daughter Sarah scattered flowers in the General's path. His wife was a Quaker, Keziah Burr, related to Aaron Burr.

Their third son, William Burr Howell, was Varina's father, who left home at an early age and served in the War of 1812, nine years after the Governor's death. He, too, had tales to tell of his service with the navy, and Varina often recalled that a steel stool was shot from under him and a rocketing ball dashed a tin cup of water from his hand. In 1815 he moved South, seeking a fortune in the planters' paradise. When he sailed along the Mississippi in a flatboat to Natchez one of the first persons to befriend him was Joseph Davis, then practicing law and selling land. He offered Howell one of the small holdings he was rapidly acquiring on Palmyra Peninsula, since he sought congenial neighbors for the stretch of land later known as Davis Bend. But Howell distrusted the Mississippi bottoms as a source of income and considered the region a "hotbed of malaria," so he settled in picturesque Natchez instead. Joseph Davis was his groomsman when he married one of its more noted belles, Margaret Louisa Kempe, and their first child was named after him.

They remained close friends, and both Joseph and Jefferson Davis were to help him from time to time, for he floundered badly in making a living. He was an easygoing, handsome, and affable man with considerable charm of manner and a fund of stories he had picked up in his wanderings. His wife adored him and gave him boundless loyalty in his downward slide to penury. Jefferson Davis became genuinely fond of

Varina's attractive and sweet-natured mother and she loved him as she did her own sons. After he had entered national politics he found small government jobs to keep his father-in-law going.[18] Later in life Varina was to resent the scathing remarks sometimes made about her ancestry on her father's side. "I could face any truth about my lineage but am very restive under imaginary possibilities or wilful scandals for detraction's sake," she wrote.[19]

The Kempes were Whigs, Episcopalians, and had considerable local influence. They had prospered greatly as planters after rocky beginnings by Colonel Kempe, a Trinity College student from Dublin who had found himself in trouble at the time of the Emmet Rebellion and had left Ireland for the United States. He settled first at Manassas, but a duel there led to his departure for Natchez, where he founded his family and a substantial fortune. Varina always described him as a man of classical education, who played the flute, was something of a poet, and had many good tales to tell of fighting at Pensacola and New Orleans with Andrew Jackson. These were legend to her, since he died soon after her birth. But her grandmother, Margaret Graham, a Virginian girl with a subtle, reserved face, a hot temper, and an imposing manner, was highly skilled in the domestic arts and graces, and was to be her lifelong model when it came to entertaining and running a home. Her own mother had much of Mrs. Kempe's worldly charm but she lacked the biting wit and temperamental vigor that were common both to Varina and her grandmother. It was the matriarch's judgment that counted in the final analysis when Jefferson Davis arrived to ask for her granddaughter's hand in marriage. She gave him her full approval, and Mrs. Kempe was hard to please. Varina had been her particular care from birth.

Natchez was a small and beautiful town during Varina's girlhood, gracefully laid out with six streets set at right angles to the river, intersected by seven others. It had a mixed population and a distinguished air all its own. French and Spanish were spoken in the streets. Settlers from Europe, New England, and the Southern states chaffered in Cotton Square when the teams loaded with cotton bales came in to the market place.[20] The town had a theater, open three months of the year, and here Varina watched artists from New York and New Orleans. Justice was dispensed in a cupola-topped courthouse, and of its several churches the Presbyterian had the most commanding site, overlooking the public square. The planters swaggered about in Parker's Hotel and duels were common. A verdant esplanade, used both as promenade and parade ground, ran close to the edge of the bluff. Shade trees fringed its precipitous side, and here the fashion parade took place day after day.

The white colonnaded homes, to become known as among the most beautiful in America, were situated on the outskirts of town. Their gardens, grottoes, and summerhouses, surrounding the white towers and spires high up on the bluff, had the quality of a mirage when seen from the river. Varina in later life often recalled the picturesque quality of Natchez, with its rainbow-tinted palisades, the mighty flow of the yellowish Mississippi, the somber forests of Louisiana stretching darkly into the mists, and the assorted types that gave vivid life to its shady streets.

The Briers stood high on the bluff, with red clay ravines making wide gashes down to the bayous at either side. One dry bayou to the west, fringed with pines, oak, and magnolia trees, made a playground where Varina turned cartwheels in happy play with her elder brother, Joseph Davis Howell. Pine cones and the shiny leaves of the magnolias provided a slippery foundation on which to skid and tumble, and she frolicked in the sun in her early years, becoming a healthy, vigorous little girl. Large as the Howell family became, they were able to live in style and comfort at The Briers. As new babies were born the elder sister became maternal in spirit and helped her mother to care for them. She was always brave and resourceful, and she saved the lives of her little sisters and brothers when she was eight years old.[21] A fire broke out in a house where the family were staying. The servants who had been left in charge had gone to a wedding, except for one twelve-year-old girl. When the flames flashed up she ran off for help, but Varina picked up the baby, rounded up the other children, and led them out of the house, which was burned to the ground.

Her hours of play were sharply curtailed in her teens when Judge Winchester intensified his instruction and spent long hours reading with her in the little tree-shaded annex alongside the main house. In Varina's own words:

He taught me for twelve years gratuitously and in the hard methods that a learned man is apt to adopt who has no experience in the art of pedagogics. During that period the most valuable lessons I learned were not from the Latin or English classics—in the former of which he was a proficient scholar, and remembered them well because he loved them—but from the pure, high standard of right of which his course was the exemplar.[22]

Next to her grandmother Judge Winchester was undoubtedly the greatest single force in Varina's early years and prepared her well for the demanding intellectual life she would share with Jefferson Davis. Not even her grandmother Margaret Kempe surveyed her suitor with more interest than did the aging and keen-eyed Judge, who had pled his case *in absentia* and for Varina's sake was willing to break bread at The Briers with a prominent Democrat.

Although the Howell home was simple by prevailing plantation standards, it was harmonious and delicate in design, the work of Levi Weeks, who built it in 1812.[23] Its restoration by Mrs. William Winans Wall has made it one of the show places of Natchez today. The original cornices and chandeliers are back in place. The pillar hit by a shell from Hobson's gunboat during the war has been replaced after many repairs. The drawing room to the right of the entrance hall in which Varina and Jefferson were married, and the sixty-foot room upstairs where their wedding breakfast was served, are authentic echoes of the past.

The house was named for the Cherokee roses that grew around it in great luxuriance, tangling with the magnolias, the cedars, the pecan trees and oaks. Varina welcomed their flowering, as she did the camellias that bloomed from October to March, the white clematis of August, the sweet olive of March, and the yellow jessamine and white hyacinth of February, her wedding flower. From earliest childhood she chose to wear a rose or camellia in her dark hair. She spent many introspective hours reading in the garden behind the house. On wet days she could view it through great picture windows, glazed to the floor, and extending all the way across the drawing room. The rooms were spacious and cool. Eight large dormers, glinting like pointed spires in the sunlight, were used as roomy closets in Mrs. Howell's day. Green shutters outlined the many-paned windows against snow-white walls. Mrs. Kempe's soft-cushioned lounges and fine furniture gave the Howells a gracious setting.

Jefferson Davis was to remember these surroundings all the days of his life. Shortly before he died he wrote: "In the winter season when the leaves have fallen off the trees, it is visible from the river and I often look at it from the steamers passing to and from because of the interest which attaches to it as the house in which I was married." [24]

❧ 2 ❧

WEDDING AT THE BRIERS

THE image of Knox Taylor was to haunt Varina, even on her wedding day. After Polk's election, Jefferson Davis, on his way to Natchez to claim his bride, had a chance encounter on the steamboat with Zachary Taylor, whom he had not seen since their days together at Prairie du Chien when he had opposed his courtship of Knox. The sturdy General approached him now with a friendly gesture. They shook hands and a historic feud, which their marriage and the bride's subsequent death had not ended, was over at last. It was a strange moment for this encounter and must have flooded the sensitive planter with painful memories. From this point on their course would be one of the utmost friendliness—almost the devotion of a father for his son, and Varina would be warmly welcomed at the White House during the Taylor administration.

But at the time the meeting made her uneasy. It revived old memories and emotions. Three weeks earlier Jefferson had found her still too weak to stand on her feet for the wedding. She had been so ill and nervous for months that neither her parents nor Joseph and Eliza felt she was well enough to go through with the ceremony. But now her own will prevailed. She mustered strength, so that when Jefferson returned to see how she was she told him she would be married at once. She would not let him leave without her.

Varina was no longer the happy, vigorous girl he had met at Diamond Head, but a thin, trembling figure, certain only of the great love she had for the man she was marrying. There was no time for formal preparation, or even for a traditional wedding dress. She wore a white embroidered Indian muslin with touches of lace, and a dark silk for her departure.

Margaret Sprague, her bridesmaid and cousin, went out to the garden and plucked a rose for Varina to wear in her dark hair. Her grandmother Kempe gave her the jewels that became family heirlooms—a bracelet, necklace, brooch, and pendant earrings of cut glass with antique gold settings. Her engagement ring was a large emerald with diamonds, set in gold.[1]

Varina's huge dark eyes looked startling against the pallor caused by her long invalidism. The house was scented with white hyacinth when she took her wedding vows on February 26, 1845. The Rev. David C. Page, of Trinity Church, where her father was a vestryman, performed the ceremony. Weddings were simpler in those days and Varina agreed that it was neither an "elaborate nor expensive" wedding, but she hoped it was "elaborate enough for the bride of a farmer." [2]

Only Margaret Sprague and Maria Wade, another Natchez friend, attended her.[3] The small Howells lined up to watch their sister being married. Afterward they had a wedding breakfast in the large room upstairs, which was heavily scented with masses of white flowers from the garden. For the second time in his life Jefferson Davis was being married in a more or less impromptu fashion. Knox had worn a bonnet and traveling dress on the June day in 1835 when she became his bride. Her parents were not present and she wept because of all the complications that marred the occasion. Knox was smaller and more delicately fashioned than tall Varina.[4] She, too, was considered witty, fascinating, and accomplished. Her successor had picked up all the knowledge she could about her but she may not have been wholly prepared for a honeymoon that included a trip to Knox's grave, or the chilling tale that years after his first marriage Jeff had fainted at the sight of one of Knox's slippers as he rummaged through an old trunk.[5]

They journeyed by river boat to Bayou Sara in Louisiana to visit Jefferson's sister, Mrs. Luther L. Smith, at the house where Knox had died. They went together to Locust Grove Cemetery, and Varina stood quietly by her bridegroom's side at his first wife's grave in a somber grove where forest birds sang, then kneeled and laid white flowers upon it. She may have planned this melancholy rite herself, out of her great love for her husband. But the evidence seems stronger that it was his idea and that it wounded her. Long after his death she wrote to a friend, William H. Morgan, whose daughter Belle was about to marry a widower:

I am not pleased with the widower prospect. It is as you know but a burnt out vessel offered to a fresh young creature like Belle after a successful love has been identified with one's soul life, and removed by death. I gave the best & all of my life to a girdled tree, it was live oak, & was good for any purpose except for blossom & fruit, and I am not willing for Belle to be content with anything less than the whole of a man's heart.[6]

Was this Varina's way of saying that she had never had the best of Jefferson Davis's love? Was it the clue to her most intimate feeling in this matter that she never discussed? In the last analysis could that brief and shadowy romance have weighed more heavily with Jefferson than Varina's forty-four years of unfaltering love, the strength she gave him, the obsessive care and devotion which may have worn upon him at times but was a never-failing solace during the desolate hours of defeat and abuse? Some of his descendants today feel that Knox was the real love of his life. Her romantic story has become legend. Varina herself fed this flame. She taught her children to honor the memory of their father's early love. They were all familiar with the tale of Knox dying in his arms after singing "Fairy Bells" in her delirium. Actually, Varina handled this difficult situation with tact from the first days of their marriage, however hurt she may have felt about it. She wrote of her predecessor rather stiltedly in her *Memoir*.

She was represented to me, by members of the Davis family, as refined, intelligent, sincere and very engaging in her manners. Though a woman of great decision of character, she was devoid of the least trace of stubbornness; her judgement was mature, her nature open and faithful, and her temper affectionate and responsive.[7]

Varina was happier when they stopped at Woodville, a hamlet in Mississippi, to visit her husband's mother, Mrs. Jane Cook Davis, at the family home known as Rosemont. She was in her eighties and could not leave her chair, but she studied Jeff's young bride with bright eyes, and Varina in turn observed that "her hair was a soft brown, and her complexion clear and white as a child's." She found his sisters—Mrs. Smith and Mrs. William Stamps—"spirited intelligent women" with inborn dignity and a strong conviction of duty.[8] Mrs. Smith was the clever and good-looking Anna who had practically brought him up, since his mother was seriously ill after his birth. In his early years he had slept in a large crib on rockers that eventually went on exhibition in Confederate

Memorial Hall, New Orleans. It was kept in Anna's room and she nursed him through all his childish sicknesses.[9]

Lucinda Stamps was a silent, composed girl, almost as tall as Varina, and she was to understand her sister-in-law better than any of the others. She was intelligent, gentle, and quiet. Varina was eager to please all of her new relatives, although they were different from the girls she knew in Natchez. She was already familiar with the history of her mother-in-law, a girl of Irish and Scottish descent who had married Samuel Davis soon after the Revolutionary War, in which he had served as one of the "mounted gun-men" [10] and afterward as captain of infantry at the Siege of Savannah. He was a striking-looking man, sinewy and stern, Welsh in origin. He rode with the style and dash afterward shown by his son Jefferson.

Jane had pioneered with him on various farms in Georgia and Kentucky before the birth of their most famous child in 1808, in a log cabin not far from the birthplace of Abraham Lincoln, a name not yet known to Varina or her husband, a man of destiny whose giant shadow would blanket them in the march of history. Jeff was one of ten children, and the family had trekked eight hundred miles through wild forest land with all their belongings before settling in the peaceful little community of Woodville. The house in which the frail old lady now lived had been built of solid cypress by her husband and she had planned the garden. It was called Poplar Grove at first because of its surrounding trees, but as Jane's roses flourished and made a solid hedge between orchard and garden she named it Rosemont. Varina noted the fig and pear trees and the old-fashioned jumble of flowers with borders of pinks. Matted ramblers framed the brown cottage, picturesque with gabled roof, wide porch, and heavy walnut doors. Jane Davis and her daughters were affluent now, because of the fortune made in cotton by Joseph and the free-handed way in which he spent his money and helped his family.

With their duty visits completed, and Varina properly introduced, the Davises proceeded to New Orleans. She knew the city slightly but not as she now viewed it by the side of a husband just beginning to attract political attention. They stayed at the St. Charles Hotel. Recovering fast from her depression, Varina sparkled with excitement as she took her place among the smartly bonneted women and worldly men who strolled through the lobby of the hotel. Her health improved rapidly. She attended a hotel soirée and met General Edmund Pendleton Gaines, who had fought with her husband in the Black Hawk War, and his wife, Myra Clark Gaines, whose family lawsuits would last for thirty-five years and make history. They jested a little over General Winfield Scott, who was not well liked by either soldier. Varina, who would play a masterful game in the future with generals, was responsive and enthusiastic. She made an instantaneous impression and "we found each other mutually agreeable," she noted.[11]

After six weeks of carefree enjoyment she returned eagerly to take up her married life at Brierfield, proud of her new status, and profoundly stirred by the more abundant life she now enjoyed. But the way was not altogether easy for Varina at first. She was still uncertain of herself, and at times felt like an intruder in the life of the proud, sensitive man she had married. He had grown accustomed to his lonely vigils, to his alligator hunts, his solitary rides and hours of melancholy brooding. The thought of Knox was still fresh in her mind at this particular time, and Varina suffered as she handled Knox's china and moved in her setting. She watched her husband with apprehension and worried over her own inadequacies.

Years later she was to describe herself as a "loving but useless wife" at this time. Sometimes her moods were difficult for her reserved husband. She was ardent and impetuous and she wept readily over the slightest offense. But she was so glowingly in love during these early days at Brierfield that she was to look back on the "cat and clayed" home to which Jefferson Davis first took her as the most beloved of many dwellings. He was its architect. It was chinked with clay, and it had so many structural flaws that they talked constantly of building another house, but they dawdled over the task, Joseph interfered with Varina's plans for it, and it took them five years to finish it. Although much more pretentious—"indeed for that day a fine house—the other always seemed 'home' to me," Varina noted.[12]

She laughed over the awkward windows placed too high, and the doors six feet wide that Jefferson and Jim Pemberton had designed to keep the house cool. Actually Varina felt when they were opened as if she were living in the outdoors. The deep fireplaces were Elizabethan in their dimensions and seemed designed for roasting sheep. But in the hours of stress that lay ahead of her she was often to look back with longing at its more romantic aspects and think nostalgically of the "wild-geese that passed over it in great flocks, fattened by the waste corn of the fields; at the wild ducks and the blue and white cranes standing perched among the lily-pads with lemon blossoms as large as coffee cups." [13]

Familiar though she was with plantation life, Varina had much to learn from the Davis operations. She assumed the customary duties of supervising servants and interesting herself in the women and children of the slave quarters. She took quite naturally to this life, for she loved children, the outdoors, flowers, and horses. She was energetic, rising early, and finding many outlets for her restless spirit. She rearranged the furniture. She added heirlooms from Natchez. She gave many feminine touches to a home that had long been bachelor quarters. She sewed. She rode. She read. She was always ready to wait on her husband and share in his interests. But she missed the fluid life of The Briers, her sisters and brothers, and the companionship of her young friends. All her life Varina was to be gregarious, depending on human friendship, seeking good companionship wherever she went.

She soon found the plantation absorbing, however, and got on well with Pemberton, who came to the drawing room for his daily orders and often conferred with her. To her last hours she was to uphold according to her lights the way in which the Davis brothers handled their Negro help, the training they received, the courtesy accorded them, their devotion when demoralization set in, and the record they made for themselves after the war. Joseph kept a tight rein on the overseers. They were not allowed to give corporal punishment.[14] The slaves had their own hierarchy—the upper set and the lower set, each with its own overseers. On Sunday mornings Joseph would preside like a judge at his own front door, calling the roll of the field hands, hearing complaints from both sides, and handing down his rulings. The two plantations were within easy riding distance of each other and their interests were joined.

Little Lise Mitchell, his granddaughter who lived at The Hurricane as a child and later became Mrs. M. E. Hamer, wrote as late as 1908 that her grandfather was extremely kind to the slaves, who were "well fed, well clothed and were supplied with comfortable beds and bedding." They were often referred to as "Mr. Davis's free Negroes," and when hoops came into fashion it was jestingly said that "Mr. Joe Davis would have to widen his cotton rows to allow the women to get through."

The slave cabins were plastered and some had little galleries of their own. Varina pictured them as having chickenhouses, peach trees by their doors, and a sweet potato patch for their exclusive use. They fed their chickens from a corncrib that was never locked and could sell their produce at a little store run by Benjamin T. Montgomery, the best educated Negro on the plantation. Varina soon appreciated Ben and his two

sons, Thornton and Isaiah, a remarkable trio who took over both plantations after the war and managed them on easy buying terms set by
Joseph.

Ben was the son of a slave who had been brought from Virginia to
The Hurricane. His white master, almost his own age, had taught him
to read when both were boys. In the mornings the master would be
tutored. In the afternoons he would go to the beach with Ben and go
over his lessons with him, tracing letters and figures in the sand with a
stick. When Varina first met Ben he had a library of his own, and his
technical skill was put to many uses around the plantation. Joseph saw
to it that his boys were educated. Isaiah sorted his papers, copied documents, kept accounts, and usually met the mail and rowed visitors to
the big boats on the Mississippi. Thornton prospered greatly and after
the war was a well-off planter in his own right for a time. All three kept
in touch with Varina, and Isaiah called on this "consecrated Christian
woman" in New York four years before her death.[15] They exchanged
letters when there were births or deaths in either family. The Montgomery trio remained loyal to their old employers to the very end.
Varina valued their friendship, as she did the devotion of James Pemberton.

Through watching him with the Negroes, Varina quickly became
familiar with one of the fundamentals of her husband's character—his
need to be approved. "He could not bear anyone to be inimical to him,"
she noted, observing his efforts to conciliate his servants when he
thought they were annoyed with him. She took pains always to picture
him as a just master on his own plantation, with a fixed policy that the
Negroes "should not be whipped, and that they should be kept healthy
and satisfied." For her own part she was deeply interested in their family
problems and pursued the young relentlessly with the medicine bottle
for worms, herbs for colds, and good injunctions for their conduct. It
was all part of the business of being a planter's wife in the prewar days
and she fulfilled her duties to the letter, taking small comforts to the
sick, seeing that special clothing and foods were provided for weddings,
baptisms, and funerals, and that they went to see the dentist Joseph
brought to The Hurricane once a year.[16]

The free outdoor life suited her and she grew steadily stronger. There
were velvety moors checkered with occasional patches of rough tufted
grass to traverse when she and Jeff rode far afield. Nearer at hand
the land was pastoral. The pioneering work had been done on the

plantations. The land had been cleared, fenced, and drained. Roads had been built and crops planted. Now the work was mainly that of cultivation. There were twenty-five hundred acres under tillage and fifteen hundred acres in woods. As they rode Varina was alert to the diverse beauties of their property—to the scarlet trumpet and monkey cap, the wild lilac and red woodbines, the blackberry bushes, the honey locusts, and greenbrier vines. Jeff frequently drew her attention to the rabbits and wood rats that scuttled from under the horses' hoofs; to the partridges and other bright-plumaged birds that flashed from the somber woods.

Their days ended peacefully with the resources of two libraries at their command. On hot summer evenings they read together in a room looking out on a paved brick gallery enclosed by latticework. This became one of the enduring pleasures of their married life—to study together and compare notes on what they read. It was the life for which Judge Winchester had trained Varina and it suited her temperament. She soon found that her husband's interest in governmental law and economics was reflected in his reading; so was the sensitive inner core of the nature that she was gradually getting to understand. His tastes ran from the most sentimental poetry to John Locke, Adam Smith, Prescott, Gibbon and Hume, the writings of Thomas Jefferson and Elliott's Debates. Varina persuaded him to read Henry T. Buckle's *History of Civilization in England* as a change from "governmental practise and he seemed to greatly enjoy the stately fragment," she observed.[17] But she soon detected something purposeful and deliberate about his reading, and became his ally in helping to build up political background. They borrowed the English magazines from Joseph and regularly saw the *National Intelligencer*, the Richmond *Enquirer*, the Charleston *Mercury*, the *Congressional Globe*, and the Mississippi papers.

Her husband all his life showed a great fondness for the poems and novels of Sir Walter Scott, whose romantic fiction was in high vogue in the South at this time. During his lonely years he had memorized long stretches of verse. Robert Burns and Tom Moore were other favorites. He had an excellent memory and would recite Burns in dialect, a habit picked up by Varina, who sometimes surprised her friends in Richmond with a flurry of broad Scots. The fight at Coilantogle's Ford and Fitz-James's interview with Blanche of Devon were standard fare for the Davis children and they could glibly recite long stretches from

"The Lady of the Lake" and "The Cotter's Saturday Night." In her later years Varina reviewed some of her husband's other likes and dislikes. Byron, Shelley, Longfellow, Addison, Steele, Swift, and Shakespeare were prime favorites, but he had strong aversions:

> Milton to him was a dreadful bore, while he was very familiar with Virgil, and loved to quote from him. He read parts of Tennyson, and a little of Browning, but had little sympathy with the latter. Of heroic songs, he had memorized a great number, and quoted them in intimate intercourse with his friends with appositeness. I never saw anyone who could resist the charm of these recitations, when he was in the mood. He had a lovely, high baritone voice in song, no musical culture, but a fine ear; and if he heard a song rendered accurately and well, sang it afterward very sweetly.[18]

Varina soon found that he liked to sing as he worked with his papers and he had a curious Indian song which was to become a lullaby for their children. He had learned much about the Indians at trading posts in the Northwest and he was familiar with the customs of the different tribes. He could differentiate between the Sioux and the Comanches, the Kickapoos and the Chickasaw. Although he had studied French chiefly to read books on military tactics, she always felt that he spoke it precisely as if it were English. He had some knowledge of Spanish too, and she considered him a "fair classical scholar."

The new books reached them from New Orleans, and Varina prided herself on keeping abreast of the latest works. She enjoyed a good contemporary novel, much lighter than anything her husband would tolerate, but she had a sharp taste for satire, too. Her fresh indoctrination in political theory at this time had its effect on her outlook and she veered by slow degrees. The change did not show clearly until her husband was well established in Washington but her old Whig instincts would still emerge from time to time. She was always to show a flexibility that was completely lacking in her husband. The degree to which Varina influenced him during their long life together remains open to question. In the early days of their marriage, when her judgments were still unformed, it is plain that she was swayed by him. But after they settled in Washington and she became an active factor in her husband's counsels, she developed considerable political acumen of her own.

Varina's letters show deference to his judgment and his wishes in matters large and small, yet contemporary commentators and some of her own descendants suggest that she was an overbearing and sometimes disturbing element in his affairs. Davis's own letters reveal a steady strain of respect for Varina's opinion, and they indicate the courtesy and consideration he seems always to have accorded her. He refrained from criticizing her, even to their close relatives, and in the early days of their marriage begged indulgence for her when she was unreasonable, as she often was.

He needed to show forbearance at this time, for a heavy shadow was already falling on their married life through the interference of Joseph. Varina had no conception of the influence that his elder brother exercised over Jefferson until she became a regular visitor at The Hurricane. She was to break its force, but not without much family suffering. "Materially and intellectually, I was more indebted to him than any other person in the world," Jefferson Davis noted at one point in his career. His older brother had paid for his education, given him his land, and guided him into the political field. Varina was fair enough to concede that her husband's swift political rise was due to "years of continuous study and calm comparison of opinions with a wise and prudent man like his older brother, which gave him the certainty of thought that led to the fluency that flows from it." Joseph was disposed to prove a point with a homely anecdote but, like Jeff, he failed to understand how anyone could differ from him in political policy "after hearing the reasons on which his opinion was based." [19] Varina was still a stubborn Whig and they had many political arguments.

In all her writings she carefully avoided any reference to the bitter feuds that raged for years between her and Joseph, ranging from his insistence that she share Brierfield with his recently widowed sister, Amanda Bradford, to the actual ownership of Brierfield itself. In rebuilding the house, Varina insisted on two kitchens for this arrangement, which Joseph considered an extravagance.

Amanda, who was known for her scathing sarcasm, was the ruling feminine force at The Hurricane when Varina first arrived on the scene. It did not occur to her or to Joseph that the young bride from Natchez might have a will and a way of her own, and that she would exercise them strongly where her husband was concerned. Jeff was a god to them all, but his young wife had no intention of being dictated to by the masterful Joseph. A semblance of harmony was maintained at first, but she burned with rage, became ill over petty frustrations, and was obsessed with the idea that Joseph and Eliza were mentally measuring her against the incomparable Knox. Jeff carefully avoided taking sides in the squabbling, although he was the victim of some painful cross fire between these two explosive characters. The women stirred things up by reminding Varina, when she got balky, that her husband was beholden to Joseph for everything.

Jefferson now rode with Varina, where he used to gallop with Joseph through the tangled river bottom with guns and dogs, surveying their property and talking politics and agriculture. For years they had worked and studied together, building up their properties, enlarging their intellectual horizons. Joseph was ambitious for his younger brother's future. He believed he could make great headway in the political field. Varina thought so, too, and her schooling began in the first year of their marriage, with Jefferson running for Congress. Ambitious though she was for his political future, she had not counted on his frequent trips away from home, however, and she dreaded more of the abuse from which he had suffered in the previous year.

Then I began to know the bitterness of being a politician's wife, that it meant long absences, pecuniary depletion from ruinous absenteeism, illness from exposure, misconceptions, defamation of character, everything which darkens the sunlight and contracts the happy sphere of home.[20]

At this time she also developed what became a lifelong preoccupation with her husband's health. She already recognized the fact that he suffered from extreme nervous tension. He usually had a touch of malaria in summer, and his eyes troubled him constantly. In his earlier campaign he had ridden too hard and fast in the sun and had suffered an attack of amaurosis which impaired the sight of one of his eyes. He had other griefs in that first year of their marriage. He stopped at Woodville while out on a canvass on an October day in 1845 and found his mother dead at his sister's home and being prepared for burial.[21] He attended the funeral, then rode forty miles that night to spend an hour with Varina, who was at her home in Natchez. He wished to break the news to her personally. With a fresh horse, he galloped back to Woodville to keep his speaking appointment there, having had neither sleep nor rest. "His mind dominated his body in so great a degree that he was able to endure what he pleased," Varina noted.

She returned from Natchez with two of her brothers—Joseph Davis Howell and William Francis. They enjoyed the horses, the duck shooting, the hunting, and the abundant life of Davis Bend. Varina was already aware that her husband had a kind and understanding way with the young. He readily adopted her family and was always glad to welcome her sisters and brothers to Brierfield. His encompassing aid was to become a family tradition. There would always be Howells in and out of the Davis ménage from this time on, and he helped them in many practical ways. Family relationships were important to him. Years later Nannie Davis Smith, granddaughter of his sister, Mrs. Luther Smith, was to recall Varina's visits to their home during Jeff's absence. As a child, she had adored "Aunt Varina who petted me to my heart's content" and called her a "quirky little thing." [22] She recalled the "invariable tenderness with children" of Uncle Jeff.

Varina, who never felt at her best in hot and humid weather, was ill much of that summer while her husband campaigned. She was often invited over to The Hurricane but she flinched from the involved family relationships, the critical sisters, cousins, and nieces, and the subjugated wife, all watching her with appraising glances. Mild Eliza studied her with faded eyes across the flower-banked dinner table in the annex, and Varina was convinced she disapproved of her. She lost her temper at times and showed her impatience, for she was not used to being told what to do and Eliza's meekness bored her. When the new books came in from New Orleans she pounced on *Undine* and Disraeli's *Sybil*. By the middle of September she was feeling a little better, and Eliza wrote to Joseph's daughter, Mary Elizabeth Mitchell, that "Varina was up by sunrise (so Joe Howell says) cutting out garments, and is half through with the labor. She appeared to be better." [23]

But her husband's arduous campaign was successful, and by the end of the year Varina was preparing to move to Washington. Although not yet twenty she was uncommonly well equipped for the life that lay ahead of her. She was politically educated, commanding in manner, well indoctrinated in the social graces, and she had sincere belief in her husband. Her initiation came quite suddenly when she learned that she was to be hostess to John C. Calhoun when he came to speak at Vicksburg in December.

Democrats and Whigs poured in from the river towns and plantations for a radius of fifty miles to hear the great Calhoun. The rich planter and the laborer showed equal interest in this stubborn and dynamic figure. Varina marveled at the assortment of people gathered in the hall. She came under personal observation as the wife of the new Congressman from Mississippi, and was glad to be taken under the wing of William McKendree Gwin and his attractive wife since she was not yet accustomed to the limelight. Gwin was a local politician destined to make a fortune in California.

She had to bridge a large gap in her political education before warming up to her husband's idol; in fact, she felt she could only be "coolly civil to the stern zealot" until she heard him speak. But when he had finished she felt like "rising up to do homage to a king among men." [24] Varina was impressed, as much by his appearance and manner as by his speech. She noted his large head, the forehead "beetled squarely over the most glorious pair of yellow brown shining eyes" she had ever seen. They gazed steadily from under bushy brows, the pupils dark with intensity as he talked, and "he lowered them less than anyone I have ever seen." Varina left her own clear picture of Calhoun.

He wore his thick hair all the same length, and rather long, combed straight back from his forehead. This, with his brilliant eyes and unflinching gaze, gave his head the expression of an eagle's. His mouth was wide and straight; he rarely smiled, and the firm, square chin and grave manner made a personality striking in the extreme. He was tall and slenderly built, quick and alert in both speech and movement, but mind and body were so equally and rarely adjusted to each other that no dignity could be more supreme than Mr. Calhoun's.

Jeff surprised her by abandoning his carefully prepared speech of introduction and talking extemporaneously on the tariff, the currency, the annexation of Texas, and nullification. They had worked together over his address. She had copied it neatly and clearly. They had timed it to last half an hour, and he had rehearsed it with her. She did not look at him once while he spoke, for he had begged her not to attract his attention. But she realized at once that he was talking along simpler lines than he had planned. It was the first time she had heard him speak in public and she was carried away by his "beautiful voice." She felt like a "mute inglorious Columbus who had discovered a new continent," she wrote with some extravagance.

Varina had found a new friend that day in Calhoun. After both men had finished speaking he paused to talk at length to his hostess. She found his manner so "paternal and indulgent" that in her candid way she told him how saddened she was to be leaving her mother for the first time to go to Washington. He, in turn, enlarged on his longing for his family, who were at their plantation in South Carolina. He spoke with special love of his daughter Cornelia, close to Varina's age. This was the beginning of a friendship that developed rapidly in Washington and was to help bring Calhoun and her husband closer together. He not only visited them often but carried on a correspondence with Varina on government matters "written as though to an intellectual equal." It flattered her that he should address a young girl as seriously as he might a statesman. His letters were all lost during the war. Although lamenting this fact she doubted that anyone could have deciphered them. She once returned one for elucidation. He was equally puzzled and replied, "I know what I think on this subject, but cannot decipher what I wrote."

With a fresh conception of her gifted husband, Varina boarded the boat for Wheeling next day with Jefferson and his niece, Mary Jane Bradford. Their journey to Washington was one long series of hazards and discomforts. It was December, and they moved through floating ice and could not sleep for the loud grinding of the locks against the hull of their boat. Finally, as they approached the Narrows of the Ohio River, their progress was blocked completely by solid ice. They were jammed for a week, until finally a small boat took them off and managed to push its way through floes to the shore.[25]

The next stage of the journey involved a run in a crude wooden sled. Varina and Mary Jane sat precariously balanced on their trunks as they slid on the icy road. Jeff and Colonel Robert N. Roberts, Member from South Mississippi, talked politics together until the sled slipped sideways and rolled over a bank twenty feet deep. Their trunks rumbled down in a heap. Varina's scalp was cut. Colonel Roberts hit a tree and one of his ribs was broken. After this they proceeded wearily to Cresap's House, a historic inn on the Ohio River, and found momentary comfort there, but, by the time they reached Wheeling, Jefferson's feet were frozen and the elderly Colonel Roberts was in great pain.

The next stage was a coach run over the Allegheny Mountains to Brownsville, where a boat took on passengers for Pittsburg. Varina never forgot that ride. They were tossed repeatedly to the roof of the coach and banged about like puppets on the rough highway. Mary Jane and her youthful aunt choked back groans and shrieks as the wheels slipped in the snow and they rolled to the very edge of the precipice. "On several occasions the gentlemen jumped out and chocked the wheels while the coachman whipped his horses and turned them across the road to hold the stage back," she recalled. Softly brought up, she thought she would never have survived but for her husband's quiet self-control. He rounded up sweets and milk at wayside inns and soothed them. "We'll tough it out till morning," he sang during their worst moments. This was a refrain Varina was to hear many times in the years that followed.

The journey to Washington had involved three weeks of "peril, discomfort and intense cold." [26] They were all in a shaky state when they drew up at the National Hotel on Pennsylvania Avenue. Varina had none of the bloom with which she had hoped to arrive at the capital. Not for another twenty years would she appear so bedraggled in public— and then she would be a fugitive in the Georgia woods after the fall of Richmond. But she had enough presence of mind to observe the Capitol and the White House, and she walked into the hotel with instinctive assurance. The lobby was bright with gaslight, gay with fashionable bonnets, noisy with the chatter of men and women assembled for the opening of Congress. A good many glances were cast in the direction of the new Member from Mississippi, and the bonneted girl who nearly matched him in height. Varina may have seemed young and overeager to some observers, but she was physically impressive and in spirit was altogether ready for the new life that awaited her.

❦ 3 ❦

VARINA MEETS MRS. POLK

VARINA was only nineteen when she curtsied to Mrs. Polk and looked around the White House for the first time. The President's wife sat on a sofa, wearing maroon velvet, and she seemed stern to the young bride from Mississippi. Varina already knew that she was austere in her tastes and did not approve of the frivolous. "Mrs. Polk was very decorous and civil in her manner to all," she noted. "My acquaintance with her was very slight." [1]

She had a more definite impression of the President as a man "innately single-minded, of simple tastes, and unimpugnable honor" whose kind and deferential manner grew on her. His health was poor and she thought his official duties wore on him. She went to the White House receptions, but the Davises "saw but little socially of the President's family during Mrs. Polk's administration" and she was never to know Mrs. Polk as well as she did her successors.

Washington was full of surprises for Varina, but she was equal to each fresh impression and quickly picked up the tone of her surroundings. She was greeted cordially by the older members' wives as a young bride who might need social steering. But the more perceptive quickly saw that the tall young Mississippian who rattled off French and Latin so readily and took her husband's career with such deadly seriousness might well be one to watch. Although attractive, she was not coquettish. Her conversation was shrewd and witty; she was a good listener and it was soon observed that the men liked to engage her in serious conversation. She discussed agriculture, politics, or books with equal facility, and quickly covered up any lack of sophistication with disarming references to her own naïveté, just as she stripped her bonnet of its surplus

33

trimmings. She was annoyed by scathing allusions to Southern colleges and spoke up for her region.[2]

The Davises lived simply during their early days in Washington. After their first few days at the National Hotel they moved into Mrs. Owner's boardinghouse close to the Capitol and joined a political mess with kindred spirits from the South. They had neither carriage nor horses. There were no trams or omnibuses at this time and Varina, used to the finest horses, thought $1.50 an hour a shocking price for carriage hire. Few of the legislators owned homes of their own in the capital, so the Congressional messes were the gathering ground for the wits, the orators, the belles, and the frumps of the day. There were many witty and intelligent women on the scene, backing up husbands and fathers who were eloquent, picturesque, crude, fanatical, or brilliant, as the case might be. Varina had arrived in Washington at a time when politicians' wives were busy in a quiet way spreading incense—or ruin—through their parlors and salons. It was only a few years since Floride Calhoun, the spirited wife of John C. Calhoun, had broken up Andrew Jackson's Cabinet over Peggy O'Neale, and Mrs. John C. Frémont, the former Jessie Benton, now was a rising star. Varina was too forthright at this time to enjoy the subtleties of intrigue; but as the years went on she learned to hold her own in this kind of company. Some of the women were from New England. Others came from the fast-opening West. Varina turned at first to those from the South, like the Howell Cobbs, of Georgia, who shared their mess.

With no household responsibilities she was free to explore the capital, to study the nation's lawmakers from the Congressional galleries, and to become her husband's amanuensis. Used to the large mansions of Natchez, to dense and fragrant vegetation, to slaves, blooded horses, and long siestas, she adapted herself without any trouble to the more vigorous Northern atmosphere. Her first impression of Washington was of slushy winter days. The city presented an unkempt air of hovel jostling mansion, of gaps between buildings and deep fissures in the roads, of a series of shabby effects all the way from the Capitol to Georgetown. But when spring came almost overnight, she watched the rush of blossoms with delight.

Varina was one of the most effective-looking, and by all odds the most passionately absorbed, of all the wives who gathered for the opening of Congress. She watched every move as Jefferson Davis took his place in the House. Thereafter she haunted both chambers, and famous names became a living reality to her as she looked down on such men as Daniel Webster, John C. Calhoun, Thomas Hart Benton, and her early idol, Henry Clay. Some were disappointing; others moved her deeply. She made appraising observations on all and was tense with expectation when Jefferson made his first move soon after Christmas. He offered two resolutions that were wholly in character. The West Pointer suggested converting some of the American forts into schools for military instruction. The Mississippian proposed a direct daily mail route from Montgomery, Alabama, to Jackson, Mississippi.

After that he listened attentively to discussion of the Oregon boundary line and British intervention before making his first major speech in February, 1846. Varina heard him urging calm instead of precipitate action. She thought that he showed "one characteristic that was never modified and often put to crucial tests—his contempt for illiterate clamor and demagogical attempts to influence legislation." [3] Again she was struck by his musical voice.

During his early days as a Congressman, Varina became her husband's working partner, writing, reading, researching on his behalf. It was not until he became a Senator that she developed into one of the capital's most effective hostesses. During his early days in Washington, Jefferson Davis worked extraordinarily hard and Varina kept pace with him. He was a confirmed insomniac, "visited very little, studied until two or three o'clock in the morning and, with my assistance, did all his writing," she noted. She helped him frank the numerous letters and documents sent to his constituents. In fact, in his wife Jefferson Davis had found an accomplished secretary at a time when everything had to be done by hand, and copying in itself was a wearisome rite. But it was no hardship for Varina. She enjoyed these hours spent at her desk, solving problems that challenged her alert intelligence. She was always happy in a close working relationship with her husband. It was to become a lifelong habit.

New interests engrossed her, particularly her husband's defense of Daniel Webster on an old charge of malfeasance brought against him by Representative Charles Jared Ingersoll. He was accused of misusing a secret service fund of $5,460 when he was Secretary of State under President Tyler. The charges came as a shock to a legislative body not yet accustomed to charges of corruption—particularly since they affected a national idol like Webster. Davis, serving on the committee of investigation, threw his influence behind the prominent New Englander. Varina observed that the issue "stirred men deeply on both sides of the House and became almost a party question." Tyler appeared before the committee and upheld Webster. There were whisperings that Davis, the Democrat, had helped to whitewash the great man. The Websters were grateful for the faith that Jefferson had shown in him.[4] They called on Varina and invited her to visit them at Marshfield, their New England home.

During this period she had a memorable encounter with Tyler at the National Exposition of 1845. She and Jefferson were strolling along studying the exhibits when a tall, slender man with iron-gray hair and a military air tripped on a loose plank as he passed them in the rambling clapboard building. Always physically alert, Davis caught him in his arms and saw that it was Tyler, who had come to town to defend Webster. He was also exhibiting a prize Hereford from his plantation, Sherwood Forest, on the James River. He proudly showed them his entry and offered a tin cup of "unpleasantly warm but rich milk" to Varina. The two planters then found a bench in the Capitol grounds and talked over her head for the better part of an hour. Her husband's public life seemed always to impinge on their personal moments. She longed to study the wonders displayed on the cambric-covered stands. Nor was she accustomed to being ignored. At last Tyler caught the perturbed look on Varina's face.

"Have I spoiled your morning, madame, with my dull talk?" he demanded, in what she thought was a winning way.

Her husband looked at her apprehensively, knowing that Varina was prone to speak the truth. He hastily intervened, "Oh, no, my little wife is trying to be a statesman."

She next saw Tyler sixteen years later when he called on her at the Executive Mansion in Richmond, and in 1863 her sister Jane married his grandson, William G. Waller. But this encounter made so strong an impression at the time that she wrote at once to her father: "Who do you think drank out of the same tin cup with me today? Why, ex-President Tyler, and he is not the man the *National Intelligencer* made him out at all. He is not handsome, but he looks a very fine gentleman, and I am sure was not afraid to meet the question of the tariff." [5] She then told her father all that had transpired. William Burr Howell liked to pick up such tales and share them with his cronies.

Varina viewed other wonders that day. America's expanding industrial life was mirrored at the Exposition, and she drew her husband over to look at the sewing jenny. The country women pressed around it so eagerly that he had to open a lane for her so that she could study the small box with two edges of cloth showing through a slot at the top. She observed that a "needle with an eccentric motion played laterally through the cloth and sewed a pretty good seam." Neither she nor Jefferson could resist such novelties. At this time, too, she hurried out to watch "Mr. Morse's machine make the wires talk and repeat messages from one town to another." The communication was from Baltimore to Pennsylvania Avenue and Varina was skeptical. "I think it is a trick but paid my two-bits to get a message that it was a fine day," she reported.[6]

But Varina's pleasures as a Congressman's wife were shortlived, for in May she was sobered by President Polk's precipitate announcement that the nation was at war with Mexico. Zachary Taylor was already in the conflict on the border, and Jeff was in the mood to become a soldier again. But first he rose to make a speech in praise of Taylor that was to have repercussions down the years, for it led to a skirmish with Andrew Johnson that in Varina's opinion engendered his subsequent hostility to her husband. The point at issue was the value of military science and West Point training for the soldier, as demonstrated in the bastioned fieldwork done by Taylor opposite Matamoras. Could a blacksmith or a tailor have achieved the same results, Jefferson Davis inquired rhetorically. Varina always maintained that he mentioned these two trades at random, "not knowing that either tailor or black-smith was present." He was merely arguing that military tactics, like all specific knowledge, must be learned scientifically.

William Sawyer, of Ohio, who had raised the issue, took the speech in good part, although acknowledging that he was a blacksmith, but Andrew Johnson became violently angry. Varina noted that he "summoned all history, sacred and profane, beginning with Adam, who (he said) was a tailor, to do honor to his class of mechanics."[7] Johnson blasted back at Davis, and the "illegitimate, swaggering, bastard, scrub aristocracy." Varina sat appalled as rough words flew in her husband's direction. His later efforts to apologize made no impression. Davis insisted that he had cited the two occupations without intent. The incident was to weave its way through the future history of these two men and to cause Varina many sleepless nights when her husband was Johnson's captive.

Joshua R. Giddings, Representative from Ohio, sat up alertly and cupped his ear to catch this ripe exchange. John Quincy Adams moved closer to Davis to catch the drift of the debate. Varina watched his small thickset figure and glowing bald head, feeling that her husband must be doing well to merit this attention. But she later learned that he had a way of exposing every new Member to the same appraisal. If not pleased he would never listen again. Jefferson Davis had stood the test, however. As he sat down Adams remarked to his neighbor, "That young man, gentlemen, is no ordinary man. Mind me, he will make his mark yet. He will go far." [8]

She had only begun to savor life in Washington when her planter husband became a soldier again. Colonel James Roach arrived from Vicksburg with an invitation for him to command the First Mississippi Regiment, then being organized. Varina was unprepared for this separation little more than a year after her marriage. She saw that it well might be the end of her husband's political life, so auspiciously begun. When they returned to Brierfield over the trail that had seemed so dismal and menacing the previous December, they found pink laurel suffusing the mountainsides. The roads made better traveling. The air was fragrant and warm. Varina looked about her with pleasure marred only by Jefferson's preoccupation with a handbook on military tactics. The soldier was in full ascendancy, and, alert as she was to the stern absorptions of her husband's nature, she was demanding in her own need for attention. While she and Mary Jane exclaimed over the lovely vistas he left the stagecoach to talk to a youth mounted on the caisson of a battery headed for Mexico. The war now seemed real to Varina.

She was not taking his departure in good spirit, and he felt worried about her. He had asked her if she wished to stay in Washington, but she would not consider this suggestion, though she greatly dreaded a return to the stifling influences of The Hurricane. Yet Jeff did not wish to leave her alone. Varina had already proved so difficult with Eliza and his sisters, as well as with Joseph, that on his way South he wrote to the understanding Lucinda, begging indulgence for his wife's "waywardness." [9] His Winnie's weaknesses, he gently pointed out, sprang from a "sensitive and generous temper." He felt he could send her only to the Stamps family and still feel that "no waywardness would lessen kindness." He feared that a sustained stay at The Hurricane might lead to trouble on both sides. "With Eliza she could not be contented, nor would their residing together increase their good feeling for each other," he wrote.

Davis showed his own personal elation in this communication. He suggested to Lucinda that he might return with a "reputation over which you will rejoice as my Mother would have done." Obviously, it was less of a trial for Davis to leave his young bride than it was for Varina to see him go. There was not yet the mutual affection between them that the years would bring. His devotion developed with time, and the pressure of events, as did her strength and feeling for him. She was still his "little wife," clever, sociable, and industrious, but a moody girl who needed careful handling and congenial surroundings in which to thrive. He had used the utmost diplomacy with the women at The Hurricane to offset the moods and hauteur that Varina had displayed when confronted with the autocracy of his brother's plantation. From the moment she heard that he was going to war Varina, who had done so well in Washington, had sunk into one of her deep depressions, and had become quite ill again. She was in a morbid state when he left to join his regiment near New Orleans, taking his Arabian horse Tartar with him.

He found many familiar faces in the regiment. One of the volunteers was Varina's brother, Joseph Davis Howell, now six feet seven and a good target for marksmen, she thought. But the brother with whom she had played in the dry bayou was to survive this and the War between the States, too. They sailed late in July on the *Alabama* and disembarked at Brazos Island, where they camped on a sandy neck of land, covered with mounds heaped up by storms. They had to dig through these for the brackish water that gave many dysentery. The heat was intense. The sand irritated their eyes. They were novices at pitching tents, and Davis, an exacting soldier, disciplined them severely. He put officers and men through their paces according to the most rigid West Point standards. Joseph wrote to Varina: "I think, if there is anything to be done at all, that our regiment will have the opportunity of being called into service, for we are said to be the most orderly, quiet, and best-drilled regiment that has come here."

They were awaiting transportation to Camargo to join Zachary Taylor and proceed to Monterey. Taylor had sent Davis a welcoming note on August 3, saying: "I am more than anxious to take you by the hand, & to have you & your command with or near me. . . ."

They reached the Rio Grande by August 12 and here Davis wrote to his Winnie four days later: "Be pious, be calm, be useful, and charitable and temperate in all things." But apparently there had been a mutual exchange of injunctions before they parted, for he added: "I have remembered your request on the subject of profanity and have improved. Have you remembered mine on the subject of prayer, and a steady reliance on the justice of One who sees through the veil of conduct to the motives of the heart?" He ended this letter: "My sweet Winnie, Farewell wife, Your Husband." [10] Varina had written across the back: "Letters from my dearest Jeff."

Davis finally caught up with General Taylor and was warmly welcomed at his headquarters. They greeted each other with mutual respect and good will, comrades in arms again. Knox had predicted, "The time will come when you will see, as I do, all his rare qualities." [11] The breach of the years was now to be fully closed. Varina was relieved to learn that her husband would be subject only to General Taylor's orders. He had bargained for this with President Polk before leaving, having no liking for General Scott, supreme commander, who was drawing all the forces he could for the assault on Mexico City while Taylor was operating with a small force in a difficult area. Both men were Whigs and Scott was known to have an eye on the presidency. Years later, at Varina's dinner table in Washington, Brigadier General John E. Wool would recall this period as the time when "General Scott drew all our teeth and left us to meet the Mexicans." [12]

By the time the Civil War broke out, the chill between General Scott and Jefferson Davis was intense. Before going to Mexico, Davis had seen Scott in Washington and had urged the use of the Whitney rifle made at New Haven.[13] General Scott was against percussion arms as not having been sufficiently tested for the use of troops in the field. Davis argued that the Mississippians would do better with rifles than with the old flintlock muskets. They were used to hunting and were good marksmen. He proved his point and the Mississippi Regiment became known as the Mississippi Rifles. Davis's riflemen were an important factor in the storming of Monterey, which took place a few days after his arrival. He later served on the committee of three that drew up the terms of surrender.

While her husband was campaigning in the burning sun the days passed unhappily for Varina, who moped and carried his letters tucked in her bosom, as she used to do during the days of their courtship. The ultimate decision had been made that Brierfield should be closed and that she should stay at The Hurricane. She rode over constantly to see how things were going on their own plantation and to air the house. She set various plans in motion, but, although Pem-

berton was unfailingly competent in his work, Joseph watched disap-
provingly, spotting Varina's inadequacies and suggesting improvements.
She was in great disfavor at The Hurricane and frequently sulked
upstairs, while Eliza felt that she should be with the others, doing her
embroidery, sharing their chitchat in the tea room and occupying
herself with household responsibilities. It was clear by this time that
Varina had failed to become part of this tight family community. In
fact, she had stirred up animosity against herself. Moreover, she had
learned that the will Joseph drew up for Jeff before he left for Mexico,
provided that Amanda and Anna, who had been left with large families
on the death of their husbands, Luther Smith and David Bradford,
should share equally in her estate, which she then assumed would
include Brierfield. In her *Memoir* Varina glosses over the elements in
this testament that aroused her bitter resentment at the time. In the
end Joseph failed to give his brother title to Brierfield because of his
animosity to Varina, and in 1874 Jefferson Davis was drawn half-
heartedly into a successful suit with Joseph's descendants to recover
property rights. It violated all his strong family feelings and focused a
great deal of bitterness on Varina. At that time she testified that
Jefferson had forgiven his brother in 1861, when he became President of
the Confederate States.[14] "I never did," she added under oath. None of
their relatives doubted that it was only because of Varina that Joseph
failed to give his beloved brother full ownership of the property.

In the meantime she was so angry when she learned about the terms
of the will that she packed up and went at once to Natchez, but things
were not too happy there. Her father was not prospering. Their family
was large, their needs demanding. Robert J. Walker, Secretary of the
Treasury, had promised to help him get a position of some kind. Both
Mrs. Walker and Mrs. Howell, old friends, were expecting babies about
the same time, and on September 4, 1846, Varina wrote jestingly to
Mrs. Walker, who was Benjamin Franklin's granddaughter:

My poor mother's health is very bad, but her spirits are buoyed up by
the hope of Father's being able to get a support for her family. . . . I
would vote for Mr. Walker to be anything from the grade of Major General
up to President—and when I am President he shall certainly be Secretary
of State, and you shall live in the White House with me. Won't that be
fine? . . . and Lucy H. and Mary W. shall dance the polka in the east
room—but I won't forestall the fine things we will do then—just wait and
see. . . .[15]

When Varina was unhappy it was always a great relief for her to be able to talk to her old friend, Judge Winchester. She enjoyed seeing her girlhood friends again, too, for Davis Bend was an isolated community and with her husband away she had no sense of kinship with his relatives. She had become quite scrawny again. Her eyes were like deeply hollowed shells. She worried constantly about Jeff, although she learned with pride of his gallantry at Monterey and read of the desperate charge he made with Colonel Alexander K. McClung at Fort Tenería. It was some time before she heard all the details but her mother received a letter from Joseph Davis Howell, written on October 13, soon after the battle.

The degree of power his coolness, courage, and discretion have acquired for him in the army generally would hardly be believed at home. Everything difficult of decision is left to him, and I verily believe that if he should tell his men to jump into a cannon's mouth they would think it all right, and would all say, "Colonel Jeff," as they call him, "knows best, so hurrah, boys, let's go ahead." . . . I never wish to be commanded by a truer soldier than Colonel Davis.[16]

Jeff had written to her a week earlier from Monterey, assuring her in rather cool terms that his health was good and that he knew no more of his future movements than she did. Varina was again being importunate and was demanding that he take a leave and come home.[17] The extent of Davis's devotion to his young wife may be deduced from this concession, for it was a difficult and unsoldierly move for him to make at that time. Varina still had much to learn about her husband's character when she wrote: "After the battle of Monterey my anxiety and depression were so great, and my health so much impaired by this and other causes, that my husband obtained sixty days' leave of absence, which, in those days of slow travel, were required in order to spend two weeks in the United States." [18]

He left camp in the middle of October with a corporal's guard, traveled to Camargo, and roder Tartar down, lest he be lost in battle. Tartar had stood trembling, but constant, all through the storming of Fort Tenería. But at Brazos he shied away from making the jump from lighter to ship. The sailors struck him, but it was not until his master called him gently by name that he "crouched like a cat, watched for the instant when the lighter and the ship were on a level, and then sprang lightly to his master's side, amid the cheers of the sailors," Varina later related.[19]

She returned to Brierfield from Natchez to join her husband, who was surprised to find how badly things had gone at the plantation during his absence. He was flooded with complaints and problems, but the most serious one was Varina's standing with his family. The ownership of Brierfield was at stake, since Varina was increasingly concerned over Joseph's interference in her husband's domain. She gave no clue to the solution arrived at, but they worked over the will again, and provision was made for Jim Pemberton, who wished his freedom only if Varina as well as Jefferson should die.[20] Otherwise he chose to stay with her.

Jeff's visit home entailed much bitterness. He was dismayed to find Varina looking so wretched, and although he told her stirring tales of the battle newly fought he could not easily divert her. She was angry and hurt. Apparently he discussed Varina's black mood with Joseph, for Joseph kept reporting to Jeff about her and it is clear from one of his letters that she was being maneuvered without her knowledge. He was trying to check her tendency to run home at every opportunity.

Writing from The Hurricane on December 16, 1846, shortly after Jeff's return to Mexico, he said: "It gratifies me to be able to give you the most favorable account of Varina, both mentally and bodily." [21] She had been busy with some "little arrangements such as planting trees, shrubs and flowers and some additions to her cottage . . . and has still on hand some work which she seems anxious to finish." Her mother expected her home for Christmas, Joseph wrote, but he thought she would rather stay and finish what she was doing, although she did not wish to seem undutiful. He had just written to her father, suggesting that she should not be interrupted in her labors and "advising him to write to her the concurrence of her mother on the propriety of her staying and upon this answer will depend her movements, and I feel no doubt of the view he will take of it." Only Mary Jane Bradford and Varina would be at The Hurricane for Christmas, he added. Amanda and Eliza were Varina's severest critics, after Joseph himself. Mr. Howell was a ready accomplice on this occasion.

Thus Varina was jockeyed into doing his bidding, and Eliza was annoyed when she was forced to give Varina a miniature she treasured. Joseph exacted obedience from them all. Passions simmered under his rooftree and sometimes erupted in the oasis he had made for himself on Davis Bend. Varina had broken the hold he exercised in the family circle and challenged his authority. Meanwhile, Jefferson had traveled back to his regiment with Colonel Thomas L. Crittenden of Kentucky, who one day would be a general in the Federal Army. He reached his post at the foot of the Sierra Madre early in January and he wrote to Varina on February 8 that he was waiting impatiently for battle. His next letter, dated February 25, two days after the battle of Buena Vista, came from Saltillo and told her calmly that a battle had been fought and that he was wounded.[22] This was the battle in which he acquired lasting military fame. As Varina viewed it: "Jefferson Davis twice saved the day during the great battle which conquered one-half of Mexico, and made General Taylor President of these United States." [23] Here he devised the V-formation that was brilliantly effective at Buena Vista but became something of a plague to Confederate generals. Varina called it simply a "re-entering angle."

She learned the story in greater detail from Colonel Crittenden's letter to Joseph about the battle.

> The regiment commanded by your brother won the admiration of all. . . . Your brother received early in the action a very painful wound in the right foot, but did not leave the field until the battle was over, and a very glorious victory was won. . . . Your brother's wound is not at all dangerous, but in all probability he will not be able to walk for several months, at least, without a crutch. Our gallant old General has silenced all fires, front and rear, and proven himself for the hundredth time a hero.[24]

Varina worried and wept night and day, but Jefferson made light of his wound. In his own report from Saltillo, written on March 2, 1847, he told of the "richly caparisoned lancers" riding toward him in beautiful order—"the files and ranks so close as to look like a mass of men and horses." [25] His own regiment had exceeded his expectations.

A small force of four thousand seven hundred men had vanquished twenty thousand Mexicans on this occasion, and the following September General Scott took Vera Cruz and American troops entered Mexico City. By the Treaty of Guadalupe-Hidalgo in February, 1848, Mexico accepted the Rio Grande as its boundary and in return for $15,000,000 gave the United States California and New Mexico, the territory which today includes Wyoming, New Mexico, Utah, Arizona and Colorado. The Davises were deeply involved in the political problems that followed, for the application of the Missouri Compromise to the newly acquired territory became the hottest political issue of the day, and Davis was one of the leading debaters on the extension of slavery.

His return home from Mexico early in June, 1847, brought Varina sharply into view again as the wife of a national hero. She waited for him at The Briers, where echoes reached her of the great turnout in New Orleans, when the city went wild in applauding the decimated ranks of the Mississippi Rifles and its colonel. Flags fluttered from grilled balconies and flowers were tossed into his passing carriage by the beauties of New Orleans. Great crowds had gathered in the sun-splashed Place d'Armes with its semitropical trees and brilliant blossoms, where Davis's old political rival, Seargent S. Prentiss, made the welcoming address.[26]

Since then Davis and his soldiers had sailed up the Mississippi by leisurely stages, stopping at landings to leave the men close to their homes. There were flowers, speeches, band music, at every stop. Varina was greatly upset when the boat was a day late. Judge Winchester soothed her. She saw her husband first through a double file of school-girls carrying long garlands of flowers which they draped over Davis and Colonel McClung. Joseph, in a moment of good will toward Varina, jestingly whispered, "You and I come first even if we must now come last—let them have him now—our time will come."

Suddenly Jeff was close enough for Varina to see his intense pallor, his crippled state, and the great change in his appearance. She could scarcely hold back her sobs as he limped toward her on crutches, his face grim and unsmiling. Knowing that he disliked a public demonstration and that she was all too apt to show her feelings, Varina used the utmost self-control in greeting him.

Weary though he was by this time of crowds, cheers, and speeches, Natchez wished to honor him, too, and it was late afternoon before he finally drove to the wharf with Varina in a flower-smothered carriage and sailed off for Vicksburg. Again there were salutes and ovations along the way, for this was their own stretch of homeland. Both he and Colonel McClung took turns replying to speeches and acknowledging the applause, but Varina saw that her husband was desperately tired and in great pain. She was relieved to get him to The Hurricane, while Brierfield was being opened, for she saw that he was near the end of his endurance, and was in need of surgical care for his foot. The return home for him was one of sadness, too, because of all the Mississippians who had lost their lives in battle. But the warmth with which the women greeted him on his return was symbolic of the war years to come, and Varina took note of it in her *Memoir:*

One of the most comforting memories of his life seemed to be the confidence and affection bestowed upon him by the women of the South. Sometimes, when he read criticism upon himself made by disapproving Confederates, without saying why, he would ejaculate "God keep and bless the women of the South; *they* have never shot an arrow at me." [27]

He was to suffer from his wound for the next five years and to use crutches for two. Varina learned that when he was helped off his horse, almost fainting from loss of blood, his leg had swollen so that it filled his boot. Pieces of his brass spur were driven into the wound and embedded there.

The bone had splintered, and on his return home "pieces that had been shattered worked out or were extracted by a surgeon, causing dreadful nervous disturbance, not to speak of the physical anguish," Varina noted. Even after his foot had healed, the slightest misstep for years caused him pain. This was just the beginning of a lifetime of zealous care that Varina was to give her husband where his health was concerned. He suffered constantly from one thing or another—savage bouts of neuralgia, serious eye trouble, malarial fever, gastric upsets, and chronic insomnia. He was extremely nervous and sensitive; the slightest degree of criticism threw him into silent depression, yet he had a quiet strength and physical endurance that impressed many and at times seemed superhuman. Varina became expert at catering to his ills, supervising his simple diet, dosing him with her favorite remedies, surrounding him with quiet whenever possible, and reading him to sleep. But she could not buffer him against his own self-consuming zeal and the wounds that abraded his sensitive spirit.

However, there was balm at Brierfield for the time being, and Varina and Jefferson were settling down to a peaceful existence again when once more the world intruded. He had declined President Polk's appointment as Brigadier General of Volunteers, a tribute to the "valor and efficiency" he had shown in the Mexican War. But he could not turn a deaf ear to the enthusiastic endorsement he received for the Senate, following the death of his imperious old friend, Senator Jesse Speight, of Mississippi.

His name was now a familiar one across the country, and he and Varina prepared to return to Washington and take up life on a larger, freer scale. Both were ill late that summer. Davis suffered extremely with his eyes and foot. Varina was generally out of sorts. She went home to visit her mother in September before going north, and Jefferson waited impatiently for her return. He and Joseph had sent her quite different accounts of the state of his health, and on September 30 he wrote to Varina:

We are all of us poor judges of our own case, whether morally or physically considered, but if the information you received from Brother Joe was more correct than that which I gave you, the defect was of my judgment . . . I am getting on as well as surrounding circumstances and my own condition would lead you to expect.[28]

He was arranging things at Brierfield for a long absence. Their property now was extensive. They had orchards, gardens, cotton fields, pedigreed horses, cattle, and other livestock. Their shrubs and trees were a source of satisfaction to them and Jefferson praised the new shoots that Varina had proudly planted during his absence. She had not been able to please Joseph or Eliza in any respect, but she could always win tenderness and commendation from Jeff.

The coolness that had developed between Joseph and Varina was now reflected to some degree in her husband. The brothers were never again to be as close as they had been before the Mexican War. Jeff had at last thrown off Joseph's domination, politically, personally, and in all respects except where their plantation interests joined. Varina undoubtedly had been the chief factor in this, although good manners prevailed outwardly and they continued to show solidarity to the outside world. Only through the testimony of descendants, their lawsuit, and family letters, do the echoes establish the fact.

❦ 4 ❦

A ZEALOT SCALES OLYMPIA

VARINA watched her husband join Olympian company early in 1848 as he limped on crutches into the Senate. The noble heads of Webster, Calhoun, Clay, and Benton were in view, and she came to the obvious conclusion that he would be tackling giants when he engaged "one of these dignified old men in a debate."

But Jefferson Davis was observed at once as he took his seat beside Calhoun. His role in the Mexican War was fresh in the public mind. His hard work in Congress was remembered. Although Varina described him as strictly a "working member," she made note of the fact that he considered it his destiny "to attain distinction at some future day." She felt that he had found his proper sphere and a "more imposing deliberative body one could hardly find" than the United States Senate at that particular time.

As political excitement mounted during the years 1848-50 her ambition kept pace with his and she had a deeply grounded sense of the necessity of being a helpful wife. But she still had much to learn about him as he took his place in the Senate and gradually acquired influence. "There was something lofty about his bearing, for his was the natural dignity which cannot brook familiarity," she wrote of him many years later. To some his manner suggested an icy shell of coldness and hauteur, so that the more hearty of the politicians shied away from this proud, fastidious man. Few detected warmth and humor except Varina and his most intimate friends, who found a wellspring of kindness and consideration behind his stern manner. John H. Reagan, a member of his Cabinet all through the war, found he had an "austere front for the public, and a tender and considerate one" for his personal and private relations.[1] When Mrs. Clement C. Clay arrived in the capital from

Alabama and became one of its foremost belles, she soon decided that "though spoken of as cold and haughty, in private his friends found him refreshingly informal and frank." [2]

Varina's own return appearance to the national scene was made with more assurance than her hesitant debut two years earlier. She was quickly swept into the social orbit of Senate affairs. Although following the approved social pattern, she was soon committed to the more serious side of political life in Washington. Her husband's interests came first and she refused many invitations in order to help him with his work. She was noted as she sat in the gallery, animated and attentive.

The scene was lively with men who would make history and would cross her path again, some as friends, others as foes. The forces that would divide the nation were building up, with the acquisition of the new territory for which her husband had fought. She watched the interplay with keen attention, understanding the issues better than most. Stephen A. Douglas, who had entered the Senate along with her husband, "was just beginning to figure in the public eye as a leading man of pronounced opinions." Senator John P. Hale, a strong antislavery man from New Hampshire, was soon in conflict with Davis. Varina later learned that a tall figure named Abraham Lincoln sat in the House at this time, but she viewed the future cheerfully, without consciousness of all the germinating forces that surrounded her, or foreknowledge that her husband would forever stand in opposition to this uncommon man.

In the spring of 1848 she was stirred by John Quincy Adams's collapse on the floor of the House and his death two days later.[3] At this time the Davises were settled in a mess next door to the United States Hotel, and they crossed over a little bridge to have their meals. Their messmates included Senator and Mrs. Robert Toombs, of Georgia, as well as Jacob Thompson and Governor William McWillie, both from Mississippi. Toombs would become one of her husband's most violent critics and his wife in time would scoff at Varina, but in the first flush of friendship they spent a good deal of time together. She was less conscious of Armistead Burt and his wife, relatives of Calhoun. She mistook him for "simply an elegant man, formed to adorn society." Later he was to help her in her time of greatest need after the fall of Richmond.

But Toombs was irresistible to Varina, from sheer vigor and drive. He and her husband were not congenial. Davis preferred the quieter ways of Mrs. Toombs. The Senator from Georgia was more than six feet tall, with a long mane of glossy black hair that he tossed back as he talked. "His eyes were magnificent, dark and flashing, and they had a certain lawless way of ranging about that was indicative of his character," Varina wrote. "His hands were beautiful and kept like those of a fashionable woman. His voice was like a trumpet, but without sweetness and his enunciation was thick." [4] He took French lessons with his daughters, getting up at daybreak to study. Varina laughed when she found him in the early morning with the official notes of a speech in one hand and a French grammar in the other. She liked this sort of zest in a statesman.

The most impressive figure in sight to Varina at this time was Daniel Webster, who had always been godlike to Judge Winchester. She had been reading his speeches aloud for years in the *National Intelligencer*. Now she watched him in action and, studying his "massive, overhanging forehead, with those great speculative, observant eyes full of lambent fire," she could think only of the "Jungfrau, or any other splendid phenomenon." Varina, who took pride in her husband's invariably smart appearance, noticed the "delicate neatness" of Webster's attire, his well-adjusted blue coat with brass buttons, and "shapely feet in pumps and silk stockings." [5]

She found Benton one of the few great men who did not lose stature by proximity. "He certainly was a power among men," she decided. When he spoke "most people gladly listened that they might hear. I did." With her own passion for knowledge she enjoyed watching the cross fire between him and Henry Clay and left a sharp picture of their antagonism with her own pointed phrases: "Each hated the other with the most unaffected bitterness. Mr. Benton's mailed glove lay always before the Senator from Kentucky." Lesser orators stood aside to watch them in furious combat. Benton was an inveterate fact-finder who sent the handsome little pages, with their long hair and cambric collars, scurrying in all directions for reference books and maps with which to confound the flowery Mr. Clay. This appealed to Varina, who was a fact-finder herself.

She sometimes chatted with him in the Capitol grounds when he left the Senate in the early afternoon to take his paralyzed wife for her daily airing. He would seat her on a bench in the sunshine and pluck flowers for her. Varina could almost tell the time of day by this rite. When she pointed out to him on one occasion that he was late, he said his wife had been visiting their daughter, the charming Jessie Frémont. Benton's ponderous manner did not trouble Varina, because she always felt that he had "something wherewith to maintain the dignity of his tone."

But she had some reservations about Henry Clay, in spite of her early teachings. She conceded that he was impressive as he reared his tall form and made deadly thrusts at his opponents. Her husband had old associations with Clay. He had gone to school in Lexington, Kentucky, with his son Henry, who had been killed while fighting with him at Buena Vista, so that Clay associated his boy with Davis.

Varina was already familiar with Calhoun's style of oratory and by this time had come to know him well. Her husband had received his cadet's warrant for West Point from him. His seat in the Senate was by Calhoun's side and "he always seemed to take a fatherly supervision over me," Davis noted. Calhoun was the dearest of all to Varina. The Oregon question had brought him back to the Senate. Floride was in South Carolina, so he lodged with Mrs. H. V. Hill, who ran the Capitol boardinghouse. Varina often visited him there. She and Mrs. Rose O'Neal Greenhow, the greatniece of Dolly Madison and wife of Robert Greenhow, lawyer and linguist who worked for the State Department, were two of his favorite women friends. She watched his interest swing to her husband and fostered an association that was to have historic results.

She met most of these men away from the Senate, at social affairs, and enjoyed their conversation. She liked George Mifflin Dallas, the Vice-President, for his delicate sense of humor and his "benevolence in small things." She relished an encounter with him at Robert J. Walker's home, where he and Ingersoll gently baited her over Byron and Wordsworth, Dante and Vergil. Varina was well aware that they were angling "in the shallow stream for such sport as the green recesses might afford" and that perhaps she was showing off a little on literary matters. But her comments interested Ingersoll sufficiently to make him call on her several times after that. In spite of his attack on Daniel Webster and his badly fitting wig she found him a "charming old man, and *au courant* with all the polite literature of the day."

Varina was completely charmed by Robert C. Winthrop, Speaker of the House. She never knew a woman "who did not feel the implied compliment of his notice and a keen enjoyment of his society." She also felt the influence strongly of George Bancroft, the historian, who was then United States Minister to Great Britain. Having been "liberalized by extensive and observant travel, he could bear the dullness of others."[6] It made her feel brilliant simply to talk to him, she observed. But in the end Bancroft would support Abraham Lincoln, not her husband, and would write Andrew Johnson's first message as President.

Varina had the most vivid interest in all the men surrounding Jefferson, and had many spirited arguments with him about their characteristics.

She could scarcely escape the attention of six-feet-four Sam Houston of Texas, who made her his special pet.[7] Many little wooden hearts were pulled from his snakeskin pouch for the wife of the Senator from Mississippi, and all too often for her taste he said to her, "Lady, let me give you my heart." She sometimes found his attentions embarrassing, for this rite was performed with the "several motions of a fencing lesson." She thought he had a noble figure and handsome face, but she did not care for his catamount skin and scarlet waistcoats. Her sense of decorum was strong.

Step by step Varina followed her husband through his debates, his research, his committee meetings, helping him wherever she could. She found him increasingly reluctant to attend the soirees because of his inviolable sense of duty. He did not always move by the side of Calhoun although their two roads ran in the same direction. He was conspicuous in the debates on the Oregon question. In July he became a focal figure when he offered a proviso to the slavery bill and argued his point. Varina saw this as his first formal pronouncement of principles on the subject, and in this speech he foreshadowed a peaceful secession.

If the folly and fanaticism and pride and hate and corruption of the day are to destroy the peace and prosperity of the Union, let the sections part like the patriarchs of old and let peace and good-will subsist among their descendants. Let no wounds be inflicted which time cannot heal. Let the flag of our Union be folded up entire, the thirteen stripes recording the original size of our family, untorn by the unholy struggle of civil War.[8]

As the session ended the bill was passed that excluded slavery from Oregon, leaving the battle still to be fought over California and New Mexico. Davis had opposed this measure and failed. The acquisition of rich new territory had brought on a dangerous situation and turned smoldering fires into a blaze. As a planter's wife, Varina was strongly alive to the growing pressures from the South. She talked to the most distinguished men on both sides of the argument, and they paid her the compliment of discussing the political issues frankly with her, in spite of her youth. She went through a period of great development at this time. Her children were not yet born, though she longed for a family. Her husband's affairs were not yet cataclysmic. He was advancing fast on the political scene. They were busy, successful, admired.

It was a time of growth and contentment for Varina, one of the few such periods in her turbulent life. She drew sharp enjoyment from its stimulation. Her own conversational powers improved through contact with men of diverse views and great eloquence. Varina had a flashing intelligence that caught the facets of life around her, so that when she came to write her *Memoir* she could dredge up lively images of all these men. Her children and her grandchildren were to listen enthralled to her stories. By the turn of the century, as she studied the biographies of the men she had known before she was twenty-one, she could see that her own youth had given her depth of experience.

As her husband engaged vigorously in debate his fellow legislators began to look at him with interest and awareness. A new voice was speaking, more melodious in timbre than that of Calhoun, but behind it lay the same emphasis on rigid principle. The women discussed him in their messes—his tight reasoning, his unbending stand, his good looks, his heroic role in the Mexican War, his clever wife. The Southern group at this time was sending out widening ripples.

Varina's social outings were still somewhat limited in scope, except for official receptions attended by Senators' wives. Her husband was so intent on his work that he showed indifference to the claims of society. This irked Varina, who loved the gregarious life and believed that it would forward his career.

He was so impervious to the influence of anything but principle in shaping his political course, that he underrated the effect of social intercourse in determining the action of public men, and never sought to exert it in behalf of his own policy. In consequence, we went out but little, and spent our evenings together, he in making the more important corrections in the printer's proof of his speeches—after which I attended to the minor details—or in dictating letters to his constituents; and many were the jests and anecdotes he interspersed for my amusement. . . .[9]

He accepted only the invitations of those to whom he was devoted, and they were men of science and scholarship rather than politicians.

He was also partial to war talk and a West Point background. They lived on a much more economical scale than the other planters' families. Although well-off, the Davises were not among the more affluent. Joseph was the family millionaire. Varina hunted thriftily for bargains. She could stretch a dollar far. Her mother had trained her in economy, and her father's shiftlessness had made this a necessity. In March, 1848, Jefferson was urging Robert J. Walker, Secretary of the Treasury, to appoint Howell postmaster of Natchez, writing: "You can appreciate the solicitude I feel about this matter." [10] Governor Albert G. Browne was backing up Varina's genial father with equal enthusiasm, and for a time he held this post.

Davis helped to organize the Smithsonian Institution and was one of its Regents, so that visiting scientists and men of learning were entertained from time to time by Varina. Her husband was also a member of the Library Committee of Congress and an advocate of Alexandre Vattemare's scheme for an international exchange of the literatures of the world. One of their favorite associations until the war put a breach between them was the Bache family group. Varina considered them "brilliant, well-educated, and thoroughly pleasant people." She liked the entire family and visited the various branches from time to time. Alexander Dallas Bache headed the Coast Survey. George and Richard were naval men. Their daughter Mrs. William H. Emory, was perhaps Varina's most intimate friend in Washington. Emory, a West Point man, was a close friend of Jefferson. He would serve as a general in the Federal Army, but throughout the war years Matilda Emory stood up for Varina in public at the risk of her own reputation. Another sister, Maria, who married Allen McLane in 1850, was a "woman of marvellous wit, and strong, bright understanding," in Varina's estimation. And Mrs. Robert J. Walker, her mother's old friend, was Mary B. Bache before her marriage. These clever women were grandchildren of Benjamin Franklin.

To Varina all three were "*belles esprits*" and it was one of her great pleasures to spend an evening at the Coast Survey—a barracks of a house on Capitol Hill. Tiny Mrs. Bache, who looked like a child, had eccentric ways, coupled with great strength of purpose. Supper was always served in a long bare room, hung with scientific paraphernalia. There were telescopes on the walls, and theodolites in dark corners. But the fare was worldly enough—canvasback and terrapin with Rhine wine that Bache had come to like while staying with Alexander von Humboldt in Germany. Varina always enjoyed seeing her husband unbend with Bache, Walker, and Emory, and she pictures him making merry on Rhine wine, and telling stories of West Point days and his political canvassing in Mississippi until "they all went into a regular romp." [11] Ordinarily Varina was much more relaxed and exuberant than her husband, but one Christmas Eve Jeff was persuaded to sing an Indian song and Dallas Bache played Santa Claus in costume and quoted rhymed doggerel.

They were soon to be looking at each other from opposite sides of a chasm. Strange memories would haunt them in the years to come, but Varina kept some of her Northern friendships intact, in her heart at least. Many of their friends during these early days in Washington were from the North. It was not until the time of Buchanan that the Southerners formed a solid bloc, powerful, luxurious, eloquent, and determined, and Varina of necessity became an important part of it.

As a lifelong reader of the *National Intelligencer* she was glad to accept an invitation in the summer of 1848 from Mrs. William W. Seaton, wife of one of its editors, to meet Fredrika Bremer at a high tea held at her large old-fashioned house on C Street. Miss Bremer had arrived from Sweden and was stirring up talk in literary circles. Varina had studied her books. She had found her *Neighbors* refreshing and realistic at a time when *Pickwick Papers* was considered too coarse for girls to read, and George Sand was mentioned with bated breath.

It was a hot summer night. Moonlight flooded Mrs. Seaton's garden. Mrs. Daniel Webster was on the scene and several of the better known Senators were present, since Fredrika was a celebrity. But Varina was disappointed in her. She was less than five feet tall. Her nose was the one she had attributed to her character Petrea and was "red as a damask rose." Her ruddy complexion quite neutralized her small blue eyes. Her dark hair was strewn with bows of purple ribbon fixed to a *cheveux-de-frise* of white lace. The effect was startling. Her small person was enveloped in a huge lace cape, known as a cardinal. It was lined with purple silk and covered her from neck to toe.[12]

Since her English was almost non-existent, conversation was halting. After tea they sat in the gallery at the back of the house, looking down on an old-fashioned garden which combined flowers with fruit trees. The women were chatting in the moonlight, the men were smoking in the garden, when Webster walked in, resplendent in white evening dress, sporting a great expanse of waistcoat. He had been dining elsewhere and was in a conversational mood, Varina noted. He looked down with some bewilderment at the cloaked Miss Bremer who had pleased New England with her recognition of the simple verities, and boomed out:

"Madam, you have toiling millions, we have boundless area."

Miss Bremer peered up at the great man and cut across his pronouncement with a halting, "Y-e-s, very moch."

Webster had nothing further to say to the traveling sage. He sat down abruptly and stared into space until Jefferson Davis drew him off to join the smokers in the garden. Varina tactfully started a conversation on Swedish music and asked Miss Bremer to play some of the popular national airs. They all moved into the drawing room and the tiny birdlike figure seated herself at the piano. She was playing a waltz when Daniel Webster walked in, failed to see that it was the guest of honor who was making the tinkling music, and loudly called across the room to his wife, "My dear, we will say good night; whenever a young lady is asked to play on an occasion like this, it is time for us old people to be going home."

"Dear me!" said the abashed Mrs. Webster.

But Fredrika, understanding nothing, did not take offense. She knew the great Mr. Webster was a law unto himself.

By this time Zachary Taylor was on his way into office as President and had received word of the nomination at his plantation near Baton Rouge. He wrote to Jefferson, saying that he felt neither pride nor exultation in the matter. He urged him not to be influenced by their friendship but to pursue the course that his judgment dictated, "without regard to my advancement." He reminded his son-in-law that he was now entering on the stage of action "while I must soon retire from it . . . I have your own advancement more at heart than my own." [13]

Davis was in a quandary. It was a question of his party or his father-in-law, for whom he felt the utmost respect. All that Taylor had asked from him was his friendship. In the end he gave him his support, too, although they never agreed on the extension of slavery, the Cuban question, and other fundamentals.

Varina was in poor health when Congress opened that December, and while her husband was one of a small committee arranging for the National Inauguration Ball in March, 1849, she was ill in Natchez. Her physician had ordered total rest for her and she assured Jeff, who wrote solicitously, that he could not assist her in the least by being with her, "unless looking into your sweet eyes would be balm for all wounds." Varina at last was learning not to make selfish demands on her husband at awkward moments. She was also brushing up a little on social principles by studying Mrs. Ellis's *Guide to Social Happiness.*

She wrote to him rather naïvely on this occasion, or perhaps with her tongue in her cheek, that she hoped the little handbook would help "Winnie" to be "Wife." She thanked him for sending her Dickens' "pretty little Christmas tales." [14] As usual, she was following his political moves through the papers. Her husband was warning the Northern Senators against interfering in the affairs of the South, and Varina thought his response to Hale on slavery "a little violent, more so than I would have liked to hear you be, however well deserved the censure might be." This would suggest that Varina, in a tactfully worded reproach, sought to be a tempering influence, for the New Englanders had unleashed strong forces in the Senate.

A day earlier, on January 24, 1849, she had written urgently to him about his health. There was cholera in Cumberland, and she implored him to take laudanum and camphor if he felt the slightest touch of pain. She could bear all other evils, she wrote, if only he returned safe in person. She urged him to guard his health as he would his life. Her doting affection for her husband and her dependence on him is well illustrated in this letter:

Much as I have loved and valued you it seems to me I never knew the vastness of my treasure until now. If you have no fear for yourself, have it for your Winnie, your thoughtless, dependent wife. . . . Sweetest, best husband, don't go out at night, don't drink wine, don't eat any fruit. If you feel any temptation to be imprudent just recall the question to your mind if you have any right to blast my life for your gratification of the moment. You were never selfish, then be yourself now, and think of your wife.[15]

But again Varina pulled herself out of one of her morbid interludes and was a striking figure at the Inauguration Ball, in a white dress that set off her coal-black hair and brilliant eyes. She was noted in contrast to the blond and buxom Madame Bodisco, the young Georgetown girl who had married the Russian Minister, and glistened in crimson satin with diamonds on this occasion. Soon Varina was in and out of the White House like a daughter. She got on well with Knox's father, and paid due deference to her mother, the much discussed Mrs. Zachary

Taylor. Davis had backed Zachary against Lewis Cass for the presidency, although Cass and he had been working closely together. At first the President leaned heavily on his son-in-law for advice, but as the political picture shifted he was no longer in the inner counsels, although as friendly as ever with Taylor. The President was not a politician by training, and the Whig and the Democrat could not work in harness, but their mutual respect remained constant.

Varina made a point of defending Mrs. Taylor, who had never wished her husband to be President. She was now old and ill. She had spent many years in frontier life with her husband. She did not join him in Washington at first and when she came she was seen very little. There were stories that she was deliberately kept in the background; that she smoked a pipe; that she had prayed that Henry Clay might be elected President instead of Zachary.

Much of this was discounted by Varina. She never forgot that Mrs. Taylor was Knox's mother as well as Zachary Taylor's wife. The image of Knox was all too apparent in Mrs. Betty Bliss, the Taylors' twenty-five-year-old daughter, who was so like Davis's dead bride that he was startled at the sight of her. All three of Taylor's daughters in the end had married soldiers, and Betty was happy with Major William Bliss, a West Point youth who had been his aide in Mexico. She functioned for her mother with a good deal of social grace, but Varina saw to it that Mrs. Taylor was not overlooked as a hostess and wrote of her:

I always found the most pleasant part of my visit to the White House to be passed in Mrs. Taylor's bright pretty room where the invalid, full of interest in the passing show in which she had not the strength to take her part, talked most agreeably and kindly to the many friends admitted to her presence.

She always appeared at the family dinners to which a few friends were unceremoniously bidden, of which many charming ones were given during General Taylor's administration, and ably bore her share in the conversation at the table.[16]

At one of these dinners Taylor turned to Jeff, after telling an army anecdote, and remarked, "You know my wife was as much of a soldier as I was." Varina observed that his "every look and tone bespoke respect, esteem, and love." Thus she tried to scotch the rumors that surrounded Mrs. Zachary Taylor.

When Congress adjourned the Davises stayed on for some weeks at their mess, enjoying the quiet of the summer nights, with the politicians scattered.[17] Varina walked into the moonlit drawing room one evening and found General Narciso López and an associate waiting for her husband. Calhoun was backing the Venezuelan-born filibuster who was raising an expeditionary force to overthrow the government in Cuba. López wished Jefferson Davis to lead the expedition, and while Varina sat out of earshot he offered to deposit $100,000 with him in his wife's name before they left, and another $100,00c or a fine coffee plantation if the expedition succeeded.

Davis drew away, remarking proudly, "I deem it inconsistent with my duty; you must excuse me." When Varina heard what the proposal was she felt alarmed and was glad her husband had declined it. They went next to Major Robert E. Lee, who came to see Davis about the proposal, believing it would not be ethical for him to accept. This was the first time that Varina and Lee met, and she considered him the handsomest person she had ever seen—"his manner, too, was the impersonation of kindness."

Varina, who had come into prominence socially by this time, had Miss Mary Willis Cobb, the sister of Georgia's Senator Howell Cobb, as her favorite young protégée. When it was announced that the girl who carried off the honors at one of the presidential levees would be proclaimed the belle of Washington for the winter she made up her mind to back Mary. She helped her choose her dress and gave her her wedding jewelry to wear. James Buchanan, Cass, and many of the better known politicians voted for Mary, and she won the contest. Dolly Madison threw her arms around her and kissed her. But she lost the jewels from one of Varina's bracelets and was in great distress until an old woman turned up at their mess with the missing stones. However, this was less serious than the rumpus that broke out over breakfast the next morning between Davis and Henry Foote.[18]

"Mary, my pet, whom did you capture last night?" Davis asked her at the table.

She named the man.

Davis was furious. "Who introduced that man to you?" he asked. Mary blushingly said it was Henry Foote.

"You are responsible to me for this," said Davis.

On their way into the parlor after breakfast the two men suddenly began to fight. Davis swung his crutch and Foote's wig went flying across the room. Foote challenged Davis to a duel. Howell Cobb smoothed them down, and it soon came out that Shepherd, the man in question, was an unfrocked priest and an impostor who had a wife and several children, and was regarded as quite a rogue. Varina helped Miss Cobb to discourage the young man, who had been writing poems to her as the Maid of Athens, the city in Georgia where she had gone to school. She later became Mrs. John M. Johnston of Atlanta and maintained friendly relations with the Davises all her life.

Varina was pleased by the camaraderie that existed between Zachary Taylor and her husband. She often watched the President making his rounds on the south grounds of the White House, shaking hands genially with the public, and patting "Old Whitey," his war horse, who cropped grass on the lawn. His short tenure of office was packed with political excitement. Although the measure had been defeated, the Wilmot Proviso, which proposed that none of the rich new territory brought into the Union by the Mexican War should be opened to slavery, was regarded throughout the South as one of the sparks that ignited the war. It had reopened the issue that had lain dormant for years. Varina remarked that a living coal seemed to have leaped upon the floor from the fires of the Missouri Compromise. Now the riches of California were at stake. The gold rush had already established the importance of the new territory. Zachary Taylor recommended the admission of California as a free state. The new lands were rich and vast in extent.

Davis had fought the Proviso hard. Now he was in the thick of the great debates of 1850, involving Henry Clay's Compromise bills which would admit California as a free state, give New Mexico and Utah the power of self-determination, and reinforce the Fugitive Slave Act of 1793. He offered his own amendment that the Missouri Compromise line be extended to the Pacific Ocean, partitioning California into part-slave, part-free territory. Henry Foote backed Clay, abandoned his earlier extreme stand on slavery, and fought Davis. Sam Houston also attacked him in a biting speech. Night after night it was all threshed out at the Davis mess. Jefferson came home exhausted, angry, working from dusk to daybreak over notes, conferring with colleagues, preparing groundwork for next day's battle.[19] He was chairman of the Committee on Military Affairs and had much technical work to do, aside from the impassioned fight on slavery.

Varina attended the Senate sessions whenever she thought her husband might be going to speak, and she made a point of being present when Clay presented his Compromise measures in an intimately delivered speech that went on for the better part of two days, and ended with women weeping and kissing him, while the men congratulated him on a lofty performance.

Calhoun was close to death when it was his turn to speak on the Compromise measures. Because he was too weak to deliver his speech, it was read by James M. Mason on March 4, 1850. But he dragged himself to the Senate from Mrs. Hill's to defend it after it had been attacked. Vice-President George Dallas, who knew how close Varina was to Calhoun, asked her to sit on a stool between two of the Senatorial seats, within easy range of the speaker. She watched him come in, muffled up to his frosted thatch of hair. This is how she viewed the scene that followed:

I was quite near Mr. Calhoun and saw him come in, supported on each side by a senator, breathing in short gasps, emaciated to the last degree, his eyes shining with fever; but his eagle glance swept the Senate in the old lordly way. Seeing me, he gave me one burning hand as he passed, and whispered, "My child, I am too weak to stop," he passed on and dropped into his seat. Mr. Benton looked on him with a tender glance and said, *sotto voce*, "I have nothing to say"; but Mr. Foote, of Mississippi, got up to answer the speech, and baited him for over an hour. Mr. Calhoun, rising with difficulty from time to time, answered in a weak voice, but to the point, partly bending his tall form over the desk as he found his strength failing. During Mr. Foote's remarks, Mr. Benton kept up an aside. "No brave man could do this infamy. Shame, shame!" [20]

Davis tried to save him from responding when it "became clear that Mr. Calhoun would die in our presence with a little more," Varina wrote. She looked on with deep concern as he was helped out of the Senate. She was again an interested spectator when Daniel Webster made his famous speech on March 7, backing the Compromise measures, thereby angering his Abolitionist friends in the North, but cheering his friends in the South. He spoke for the "preservation of the Union," he said, not as a Northern man but as an American. Varina was part of the grouping that day, which she later described as a "parterre of brilliant palpitating colors, a solid phalanx of ladies; on the steps of the Vice-President's seat every available inch was occupied, and even between the senators, seated on the floor, the rosy faces and waving plumes of ladies made points of color against the senators' black garments."

Again Calhoun staggered in. Again he was challenged, until Webster, seeing his helpless condition, "with a truly grand gesture, stretched out both his arms to Mr. Calhoun with a voice filled with tears, and said: 'What he means he is very apt to say.'"

"Always, always," gasped Calhoun.

Benton would not bait the dying lion. Foote was silenced at last. All the Senators stood and watched him being half borne to his carriage. None was more moved at his funeral several weeks later than Webster, delivering the eulogy. "He is now a historical character," said Clay. "He is not dead," said Benton. "There may be no vitality in his body. But there's plenty in his doctrines."

Davis was a member of the escort of honor at Calhoun's funeral in Charleston, sharing in the ceremonial that ended in the quiet church-yard of St. Philip's. His bier was blanketed with "Cloth of Gold" roses as he lay in state while crowds streamed past for three days.

On his return to Washington, Davis delivered one of the eulogies in the Senate and Webster congratulated him, citing in particular his simile: "Like a summer-dried fountain when our need was the sorest." [21] Davis promptly told him that this was the only part of his speech that was not original. The author was Sir Walter Scott. Varina thought that Webster "had no rhythm in his head and no verbal memory, although fond of poetry." He was apt to misquote the poets, unlike her husband, whose record in this respect was almost perfect.

Taylor and Calhoun, two of Davis's closest and most influential friends, were now gone from the scene. Both Clay and Webster would be dead before the end of 1852, but in the meantime the battle raged on, with the Southern leaders splitting badly now that their standard-bearer was gone. After Webster's speech Clay, meeting Davis in the Capitol grounds, made a personal appeal to him to join the Com-promise men, according to Varina. He said the measure would give peace for thirty years. Turning to Senator John M. Berrien, of Georgia, who was with him, he added: "You and I will be under ground before that time, but our young friend here may have trouble to meet." Davis told him he would rather not transfer to posterity a "trial which they would be relatively less able to meet than we were."

But Davis did not follow the same road as all his colleagues from the South. William L. Yancey and Robert Barnwell Rhett, who would fight him all through the war from the editorial offices of the Charleston *Mercury*, more closely followed Calhoun's lead than did Davis, who had never favored nullification. During the long debates in the months that followed, Varina took her usual unquestioning view of her husband's stand.

> Mr. Davis took his own course, allying himself of necessity with no party—yielding to no mere sentimental view of duty, or allegiance. He conscientiously examined the Constitution of the Union as the conservator, guarantee, and limitation of his rights, and honorably abided by its authority.[22]

The more moderate elements had looked to Zachary Taylor as an ameliorating force on the slavery issue. But while the matter was still in debate a messenger had arrived in the Senate to whisper in Daniel Webster's ear that the President was critically ill. Congress adjourned and Jefferson Davis hastened to his bedside. He had sickened after attending ceremonies at the Washington Monument foundation on a hot July day in 1850. He had spent hours in blistering sunshine and then had eaten cherries and drunk ice-cold milk, a combination which was thought to have brought on his illness, but may merely have been a contributory factor.

Among the most prominent mourners were Varina and Jefferson Davis, who stood in unique relationship to this sturdy President. Varina comforted his widow "through the torture of a state funeral." [23] Mrs. Taylor was worn to a shadow and, as Varina viewed it, she lay without uttering a sound, trembling violently from head to foot as one band after another "blared the funeral music of the different military units, and the heavy guns boomed in quick succession to announce the final parting."

Varina saw little of Abigail Fillmore, the Baptist minister's daughter who brought books and maps into the White House, and had a lame ankle that made standing at levees tiring for her.[24] Davis, for the time being, was out of office. When Foote attacked him in the Senate, denying that Mississippi opposed the Compromise or favored secession, Davis answered proudly that he would not remain an hour in office if he did not believe that he truly represented his State. Foote challenged him to a running debate on the stump. Davis and Varina went south to Jackson to prepare for a series of addresses but he was suddenly precipitated into a contest with Foote for the governorship in place of John Anthony Quitman, who had withdrawn.

He resigned his Senate seat and campaigned until hard work and exposure to strong sunshine brought on one of his more severe bouts of eye trouble. He was threatened with ulceration of the cornea. Friends nursed him until he could get back by easy stages to Varina. By October she was treating his eyes with chloroform, rubbing his head with the drug, and was making him sniff soaked wads when the pain was unbearable, but not for so long as "to cause insensibility," all this by order of Dr. Samuel A. Cartwright, the Howell family physician.[25] She used vapor from burning rosemary plucked on Ship Island, and dosed him with two grains of solid opium a day, five grains of quinine, and a teaspoonful of calchocum wine, followed by castor oil.

At this time he slept by day and walked the floor most of the night, because he could not stand even a sliver of light. When a committee directing the canvass arrived with the draft of an address for his signature, it was read to him and Varina noticed that his fastidious taste was offended by the "turgid appeal." [26] He reached out, held her hand, and guided her pen through the offending sentences. "Oh, let me get at that," he exclaimed impatiently. He threw out the whole paper and dictated a fresh one to Varina. He could never stand what he termed the "spread-eagle" approach.

Finally, three weeks before the election, he left his home to campaign, wearing green goggles and with his inflamed eye bandaged. Meanwhile, the persuasive Foote, whom the Davises despised, had been stumping up and down the state with the ready wit for which he was famous. He described his opponent as being "in the same truckle-bed with Seward and Chase and Hale, the abolitionists." The upshot was that Davis was defeated by a narrow margin, a humiliating incident in his career, since he had no respect for Foote. Varina, concerned about his health, was relieved to have him back at Brierfield. New forces were already at work in Washington with Millard Fillmore, a Compromise man, in the White House. There were angry mutterings in the North when he signed the Fugitive Slave Law section of the Clay measures. Neither side was satisfied, but the war was postponed for another decade. Meanwhile California was admitted to the Union as a free state.

✻ 5 ✻

A SON FOR VARINA

FIVE days before Varina's first baby was born in 1852 Jefferson Davis was in the North campaigning for his old friend, Franklin Pierce, and she was writing to him in some distress of spirit. "Your wife's courage is giving out about your staying away for such a time—I feel the want of you every hour, though I try not to be so selfish," she wrote.

She had learned by this time that his country's affairs came first with her husband, but she still clung to him desperately in moments of need. She feared that their peaceful interlude at Brierfield was nearing an end, and that nothing now could keep him out of national politics. He had not liked the party platform drawn up by the Democrats at their convention in Baltimore in June, but the nomination of Pierce had pleased him. His own name had been mentioned tentatively for the vice-presidency but nothing had come of it. "If he lives he will I have no doubt be President some day," George H. Gordon, who would lead a charge against the Confederates at Cedar Mountain, wrote to Posey Carnot on June 9, 1852. "He possesses the kind of reputation which will continue to grow and increase." [1] Carnot was a well known Virginian who was killed at Bristol Station in 1863.

Davis was now campaigning with quiet intensity, and was attacking his old enemy General Scott with soldierly precision. He was touring New York, New Jersey, Delaware, and Pennsylvania, and had just made the point at a world scientific convention held in the newly opened Crystal Palace in New York that "the earth was given to man for his dominion," when Varina's forlorn letter, written on July 25, reached him. The heavy rains were hurting the cotton crop at Brierfield, she informed him. The Negroes all were well. The Hurricane clan were spending the summer at home instead of going to a spa. Varina reassured him about her own condition although she could not get as far as the cow pen to see how the cattle were. But her longing to have him at her side was intense. She wrote as insistently for his return as when he was in Mexico and she begged him to come home.

I see by the papers that your party are beginning to canvass with spirit and I should judge the Whigs are quite scurrilous from the quotations I see interlarding Democratic journals of Mr. Pierce's perfections. . . . Are you not turning your steps homeward, even while I write? . . . May God keep you, my own sweetest Husband, and bring you back to me once more safe and happy, for never were you more ardently longed for and expected than does now your own devoted wife V.D.
P.S. Don't think me too selfish, but can you not come home—I so long to see you, and my resolution gives out. Do come if you are neglecting nothing.
                                        Your Winnie.[2]

Five days later their first child was born to the Davises. A long procession of Negroes streamed through Brierfield, bearing gifts for the baby. There was much rejoicing, for this was the seventh year of their marriage and Varina had long wished for a child. They named him Samuel Emory after his paternal grandfather. His life was to be short, but the Negro women made affectionate predictions for his future as they kissed him one by one, an old plantation custom, and offered eggs, chickens, yams, fruit, and flowers for the newborn babe.

Varina was happy and longed for a peaceful continuation of the life they were then living at Brierfield. It was a period of quiet between the political storms that would ever be with them. Since his defeat for the governorship, except for his speeches on Pierce's behalf, Jefferson had been at home much of the time, quietly pursuing the work he enjoyed and building up his depleted physical forces. If Varina's ambitions for her husband were involved again with the nomination of Pierce, she gave no sign of it in her comments on his return to office. Their plantation had been so long neglected that there was much to put in order. "Finding we had met the usual fate of absentees, we began to rehabilitate our home and grounds as best we might," she noted. "My husband was very fond of cultivating trees and of seeing roses and ornamental shrubs blooming about us." [3]

All that spring Varina, in splendid health before her baby was born, had ridden daily with her husband, noting only thirty seconds' difference in the speed of their horses as they raced each other through air per-

fumed with wild crab apple and plum blossom. Pausing to rest by a
slough, she observed the lotus blooms floating on the surface like yellow
chalices, their flat leaves nearly a foot in width.[4] These were days of
relaxation and beauty for Varina, with her husband all to herself, and
the plantation life stirring around them. There was stock to care for,
horses to groom, cloth to be spun, cotton to be picked, plowing, sowing,
and reaping to be done. The blacksmith shop, the carpentry shop, the
gin, the stables, the barns, the neat little whitewashed cabins—it was a
familiar pattern to Varina and one that she had not yet come to
question.

By this time they were in their new house, a graceful dwelling with
Doric columns that was to stand until destroyed by fire in 1931. It was
less barren and eccentric in construction than the old "cat and clayed"
house that Varina regarded with such affection. It was unpretentious,
according to plantation standards, and was designed for comfort and
convenience. The doors and windows were large, but this time they
were also symmetrical.

Again there were large fireplaces, but now white marble mantelpieces
gave them a more finished touch. Varina had designed the house to suit
herself, overriding Joseph's demands for accommodations for his family
favorites. One of her hardest fought battles with Joseph involved the
building of her home. He considered this a man's job that he must
attend to when Jeff was away and could not be consulted. But Varina
won this battle point by point, and now ran her home with admirable
skill and much more assurance than she had had before going to
Washington. She was no longer subject to Joseph in any sense of the
word, nor did she fear him.

Motherhood had done good things to Varina. She was now a stronger,
a sounder, a happier woman than she had been before. Her spells of
depression had long upset her mother, and Mrs. Howell was now
gratified to have Jeff's assurance that Varina was the "finest" she had
ever been. Soon after little Samuel's birth she went on a tour to show
him off to all her relatives, while her husband was still campaigning for
Pierce. Her old Natchez friends noticed how well and stately Varina
looked at a picnic, wearing a cool organdy dress and with the inevitable
flower in her hair.[5] She was saddened on this visit home that she could
not show off her son to Judge Winchester, who had died in the previous
year.

Her mother was still bearing children and had a small son not much older than little Samuel. He was named Jefferson Davis Howell after his uncle and would come to be known as Jeffy D. Varina would treat him as one of her own. Both Jeff and she were intent on seeing that the Howell sisters and brothers were properly educated. By this time Davis was giving generous aid to Varina's family and was helping her father by buying from him some property he owned at Tunisberg, Louisiana. It was now quite clear to him that Howell would never have any knack for worldly success. He embarked on many ventures with recurrent hope, but in the long run was unable to cope with the practical business of supporting his ever-growing family. Nevertheless, Varina's mother, a woman of charm and ingenuity, adored her shiftless William, loyally aided him in all his chimerical plans, and kept up appearances at The Briers as long as she could. But it was a great relief to her when Varina took over the care and education of Becket Kempe Howell, now aged ten; his older sister, Margaret Graham Howell; and, eventually, of Jeffy D. On January 31, 1853, Howell wrote cheerfully to Jeff, charging young Becket "to study hard & make a man of himself while the opportunity offers." [6] There was considerable point in his injunction to Becket, since his own life had so palpably been one of wasted opportunities.

The Davis speeches had been of great aid to Pierce, particularly in the South. Foote, who was neither Whig nor Democrat at this point, was completely out of favor. At the end of 1853 he was defeated for the Senate and moved first to California, then to Tennessee, where he continued to make headlines and ply an erratic course. Meanwhile, the newly elected Pierce invited Davis in a friendly letter from Concord to join him in Washington to talk over a Cabinet post. But at this time Dr. Cartwright appealed to Mrs. Howell to get her daughter to keep him out of public life, in the interests of his health. [7] He advocated a full year of rest, with riding and gardening for recreation, and plenty of good nourishing food to build him up. He told Mrs. Howell that Jeff had a "very peculiar constitution—is not nervous, he says, but is controlled by his will."

Varina worked zealously along these lines. Under her urging, and in spite of his great affection for Pierce, Davis made it clear that he could not join him in Washington. But the death of the President's eleven-year-old son, in a railroad accident in New England just before his inauguration, touched the Davises and changed their outlook. A sad letter from Pierce silenced Varina. "How I shall be able to summon my manhood and gather up my energies for the future before me it is hard for me to see," Pierce wrote to Davis on January 12, 1853. His wife's grief was devastating. After several telegrams summoning him, Davis finally set off for Washington, arriving too late for the inauguration.

Varina did not follow her husband to Washington for some weeks. She closed up Brierfield, then traveled north with Margaret, Becket, and the baby, under the care of Major T. P. Andrews. Yellow fever was raging in Mobile as they passed through, and Betty Bliss's husband was one of the victims. He was dead by the time they reached Washington. Jeff had rented a large furnished house on Thirteenth Street, and Mary Jane Bradford, his niece who had married Senator Richard Brodhead, was keeping house for him. Varina was not much pleased with the furnishings and found that the "trumpery chairs" would not support James Guthrie, Pierce's Secretary of the Treasury.

It was her first experience of doing her own housekeeping in Washington, but by this time she had learned how to practice the domestic arts with elegance, economy, and the precision of her grandmother Kempe. She moved at once into the White House circle and became a close friend of Jane Appleton Pierce, who was not interested in politics and shrank from public notice. The President's wife was ethereal in appearance and was thought to have tuberculosis. Delicate to begin with, the sight of her mangled son in the train wreck had been too much for her. He was the third child she had lost, and she had no more desire for her husband to become President than Varina apparently had for Jefferson to return to Washington.

Mrs. Pierce was small, fragile, and could never have been pretty, but Varina found her "very well read, intelligent, and gentle . . . a person of strong will and clear perceptions." [8] Studying her pallid looks, she thought of Elizabeth Barrett Browning, but she detected in Mrs. Pierce a "keen sense of the ridiculous" that she was too ceremonious to indulge in often.

The First Lady made her initial public appearance at a presidential levee in 1853, wearing black velvet with diamonds. Mrs. Clay thought that her "jeweled apparel did not hide her sorrowing state." [9] The White House at this time in her estimation was "practically as unimposing as in the time of President Monroe." The famous gold spoons, which had caused him so much trouble as social pretension and extravagance when he brought them from Europe, were in evidence at state dinners. Stiff bouquets of wired japonicas with huge lacy frills were at every place, bringing this flower into vogue.

It was not until New Year's Day, 1855, that Mrs. Pierce appeared in full panoply as official hostess at a big reception. In the interim she leaned on Mrs. Abby Kent Means, a relative who had arrived to bolster up the social functions at the White House. But from 1855 on she was led into the Blue Room for the presidential levees and the weekly state dinners. She gave Friday receptions of her own, but Mrs. Laura C. Holloway, a social chronicler of the day, noted that "the home of Mrs. Jefferson Davis was much more the gay center of Washington society than was the White House."

During the Pierce administration Varina came to the fore as the social leader in Washington. Since her husband was regarded as a favored Cabinet officer and the President's wife could not cope with the constant social demands of her position, Varina, with her friendly warmth and social gifts, was the natural substitute. She made a point of entertaining every member of both Houses at least once during the winter. The diplomats and visiting celebrities were always welcomed at the Davis home, which was now arranged as she wished it, with furnishings to her taste.

Davis was perhaps at his best during this period of his life. In the War Office he was doing the work he liked and he was doing it well. With a man of such sensitive temperament, this made for harmony in all his relationships. Although subject to the criticism of any man in public office, and regarded with deep suspicion by the antislavery forces of the North, he was respected by his colleagues for his integrity.

Mrs. Clement Clay viewed him at this time as a man of distinguished appearance, exceedingly slender, with a springy step, bearing himself with "such an air of conscious strength and ease and purpose as often to cause a stranger to turn and look at him." [10] She thought him magnetic and eloquent when he spoke in public, but he read poorly and actually mouthed his phrases. He was almost six feet tall, with a high, broad forehead, well-cut features, and blue-gray eyes, one of which was now clouded over with a film. He had a resolute, challenging air, and the decisive manner of the army-trained man.

To Varina he was always the most handsome and engaging of men. Together they made an imposing pair when they appeared at military reviews and public functions. The difference in their ages was not immediately apparent. He was in his mid-forties and Varina was approaching thirty. She had always had physical presence; now she had authority, too. She fitted with natural ease into the frame of official life and extracted the best from the scene around her. Her husband watched the more brilliant men gathering around her in the drawing rooms of the capital. She had outgrown her overeager manner and handled social situations with skill, although her judgments could be cutting and her opinions always were freely expressed.

Varina now had a matronly look that was considered good form at the time. She wore fashionable clothes but was not determinedly chic, nor did she ever have a large wardrobe, as so many belles of the period did. Her jewelry was sparse and simple. A cameo brooch and a striking cameo bracelet were her favorite trinkets. She did not deck herself extravagantly at a time when women were festooned with garlands; bandeaux and braids adorned their heads; and tulle, lace, and feathers were the order of the day. She had an easy grace about her, a way of arranging a single flower in her hair, or of having her silks so draped as to give stateliness to her bearing. She was fond of white, which set off her jet-black hair and eyes. Her hair was simply dressed with a center part and chignon at this time. She was impressive and none took liberties with Varina. Her husband was scornful of showy attire. He observed quite closely how women dressed, she disclosed, and when pinned down about an outfit that distressed him he remarked that the lady's gown was "very high-colored, outsetting, and full of tags, and you could see her afar off." [11]

She made splendid headway on her own account with the men whom her husband had to entertain. The women were more divided about her, for Varina could at times be skeptical or bored when the spirit moved her. She had little patience with affectation and was apt to stare through the moronic with glacial indifference. She was essentially direct, sincere, and strong, and she "preferred the straight road to the tortuous bypath," said T. C. De Leon, a social commentator who knew her well. Both of the Davises were ambitious, and many thought that Varina strengthened her husband politically. She definitely broadened the scope of his social life, and made him seem human to many who had found him stiff and even haughty. She was good company and told an anecdote well. In her best moods she had great spontaneity and created an atmosphere that few could resist. It was observed that she was articulate on all manner of subjects. As the years went on she became so much a part of the Washington scene that Brierfield and the plantation setting grew dim and she entered wholeheartedly into the life of the capital. She was still not bracketed with the more sumptuous of the planters' wives, for she did not live on their luxurious scale, although she took in all the social functions, from a *fête champêtre* at the British Embassy to a review of the troops at Fortress Monroe. On this occasion Davis directed the maneuvers, and the sky at night blazed with a pyrotechnic device spelling out the names of Franklin Pierce and Jefferson Davis.

During his busy days in the War Office, Varina accustomed herself to extensive entertaining. Her husband was hospitable although he did not care to go out. He often brought home unexpected guests for meals. Both were always surrounded by relatives. When visitors arrived from the South she expertly showed them the sights of the capital—the Smithsonian Institution, the White House, the Capitol, the Patent Office, and the House and Senate. But her life was never frivolous, as it was for many of the hostesses of this era. It always had a hard core of work, of intelligent comradeship with her husband, of much reading and clerical work done on his behalf, as well as social effort. It was often two in the morning when he got home and they would work for hours after that.

Nearly all commentators on her husband's career have given Varina star rating as wife and helpmate—a woman alert to political issues, handsome, wise, hospitable, and shrewd.[12] T. C. De Leon wrote from Mobile in 1908: "This marriage was a most congenial and helpful one to the already rising young statesman. No woman of her day proved a more potent factor in the semi-social and semi-political Government at Washington than the long Davis sway at the Capitol." Clifford Dowdey has written of her: "Varina Davis was truly the helpmate of her husband in the finest sense of the word. . . . Where she failed him was in never turning her analytical gaze on the man she regarded as perfect, virtually godlike. She saw Jefferson Davis, without reservation, precisely and as largely as he saw himself."

This was a process that began during these early days in Washington and reached its crescendo in the years after his death when Varina mustered every defense and wrote and talked of him with reverence. In some respects he became a larger figure through her definition of his character than he had seemed to his contemporaries.

Most of his work at this time was of a highly constructive order.[13] He left his mark on Washington itself, in Varina's estimation. The Capitol was remodeled with the addition of two wings and its dome during his tenure. The Smithsonian Institution, one of his special interests, was furbished up. Fireproof buildings were put up for War Department records. He put fresh life into the army, largely through his own knowledge of it. Living conditions were improved. Pay was raised. The medical corps was modernized. He worked with Robert E. Lee, superintendent of the Military Academy, on various improvements for West Point. He revised army regulations. He introduced light infantry and spurred on the manufacture of rifles, muskets, pistols, and the use of the Minié ball. He had four regiments added to the army and organized a cavalry service adapted to the needs of the country. He strengthened seacoast and frontier defenses and directed a notable series of scientific and geographical surveys in connection with his cross-country railroad plans.

Varina was sometimes dismayed by the time and effort Jefferson devoted to cranks and suppliants who pled strange causes. No beggar was ever turned away and he listened patiently to the schemes of inventors, crackpot and sound. He wrote rather sadly to James Buchanan on July 23, 1855, that the Crimean War had given such impulse to "destruction that weekly, sometimes daily, projects are presented for the more rapid and certain killing of our fellow men." [14]

Davis was sternly opposed to the use of any perquisites of office. He never ordered flowers from the Congressional greenhouse, and he scolded Varina for using his messenger to send a personal parcel. "Patrick's services are for the War Department—the horse and wagon are for Government use; employ another servant if your own are not adequate to your needs," he said. She bought her own stationery, and when her father wanted a Congress knife, the best made, Davis gave up his own.

Mrs. Clay noted that it "would have been impossible for the Government to have been cheated out of the value of a brass button" while Davis was Secretary of War. Ben Perley Poore, an observant Washington correspondent who was less of a friend and more of a critic, wrote that, with the exception of a few favored ones, the officers of the army were glad when his term ended since he had acted as though he were commander-in-chief, treating the heads of the bureaus as if they were his orderlies, and directing everything from a review down to the purchase of shoe blacking.[15]

Varina was less thin-skinned than her husband in asking for favors or puncturing bores. She had not yet reached the stage of nepotism that developed during the war, but she was always ready to aid young people in romantic difficulties. When a lieutenant who had married into the Zachary Taylor family sought a postponement of a month before being moved to San Francisco, Varina asked her husband to intercede.

He told her bluntly that he could not interfere with General Scott's prerogatives and their relations were strained in any event. Varina told him laughingly that she would take the matter to President Pierce. She did, but was checkmated by her vigilant husband, who got the note and put it on file. The President found Varina sulking in her carriage the night before the young man was due to leave for the West. He asked her what was wrong. She told him, and added, "I have never asked any favor of you except this, and it was an intensely personal one to me."[16]

He said he would go at once and ask General Scott to postpone the young man's departure. Meanwhile, Varina asked her husband what had happened to her note.

"You had a right, madam, to be put on file, and there you are," he told her.

Varina has given many instances of her attempts to influence her husband, but there is little evidence that she swayed him from his course of action, beyond the atmosphere she may have created by her viewpoint. She was strong and insistent, but he was stubborn, not only with Varina but in all his associations.

After the Japanese Treaty was signed with Commodore Perry, President Pierce invited Varina to come and help herself from the bales and boxes of presents that had come from Japan—lacquer, jars, vases, parasols, jade, figurines, rugs, and tapestries. He said they belonged to no one. Davis quickly replied, "In that case my wife knows they do not belong to her." But the President insisted on giving her husband a tiny dog from Japan. It was a family joke that it could be kept in a saucer. Bonin became the family pet.

Varina was always particularly pleased to invite in a body the members of any scientific or learned gathering who might be meeting in Washington, and at this period of her life she was hostess to such men as Professor Louis Agassiz, Benjamin Peirce, the astronomer, and Professor John LaComte, whose beautiful wife she found "exquisite among the dim old savants." Dr. Robert Hare coached her on spiritualistic fraud after she had made a skeptical visit to the Fox sisters. Professor Joseph Henry, first secretary and director of the Smithsonian Institution and a good friend of her husband's, discussed physics with her and escorted her over to Alexandria on a ferryboat to visit young Becket, then attending a Quaker school run by the Rev. George Haller. The headmaster told

Varina in front of the abashed boy, "Thy brother is always seeking for a royal road to knowledge, and is dull at figures." Becket quailed, and Dr. Henry urged Varina to send the boy to him for a little coaching. She noted that her brother never forgot what he learned from this august source.

Varina favored the friendly breakfast or small informal meal for anyone giving political trouble, and she became something of a mediator for her ultra-reserved husband.[17] The chairmen of legislative and other committees would throw out trial balloons at the Davises when a plan was in the making. Jefferson particularly enjoyed what they called the generals' dinners. By this time Varina was well accustomed to technical military talk, but she also found that the generals "unbent like boys and told good campaign stories." However, General Winfield Scott was always a trial. She found him a "great-looking man, with the grandiose manner, in a less degree than his, quite common to the men of his day." She could not warm to him, although the worst she had to say about him in her *Memoir* was that "Mr. Davis and he had an unfortunate difference about a claim of General Scott's for pay, which he could not allow. This led to a correspondence painful to both, which, having passed out of sight, it is useless to recall."

The fact was that Davis had written to Scott early in 1853 with frank allusions to his "petulance, characteristic egoism, and recklessness of accusation . . . querulousness, insubordination, greed of lucre and want of truth." [18] For good measure Davis mentioned his "grovelling vices." This was strong talk from the Secretary of War to the commanding general of the armies. There could be no fair words between them after that.

But their discord had other roots. It went back to the Mexican War, and a deep contempt in Jefferson Davis for the military tactics of Winfield Scott. One of Varina's most difficult dinner parties brought together at her board the General and a young captain named George B. McClellan, who blushed when Scott roared. Her husband had assembled the diplomats of Great Britain, France, Prussia, Austria, and Russia to meet an expedition of experts he was sending to the Crimea to report back on military advances made during the Crimean War. They were to investigate organization, ordnance, and medical arrangements, the camel corps, transportation, and construction devices. He had invited General Scott, who insisted on living in New York at this time, to join them.

The expedition was made up of McClellan, Major R. Delafield, and

Major Alfred Mordecai, whom Varina considered had a "versatile, fecund mind, and a disciplined mental and moral nature." The suave Comte de Sartiges, one of her favorite diplomats, sat at her left. General Scott, the gourmet, was explaining to the French Minister the perfect way to cook terrapin, while General Joseph G. Totten and McClellan, across the table, were discussing traprock. Scott, somewhat deaf, picked up the word "trap," raised his fork, and bellowed "No, sir—I *say no*, they are *never* caught in traps." [19] General Totten blithely set the table to rights, telling the General that the subject was traprock, but by this time Scott had embarked on a monologue on buffalo. Varina was more overcome with mirth than embarrassment but she noted that young Captain McClellan "had turned a fine rose purple" under this official barrage. The Comte de Sartiges, knowing her sense of humor, mischievously whispered to her that he really felt sorry for Scott, since "according to the necessity of his nature, he had to teach the whole company at once."

Varina juggled these various interests with considerable skill as a hostess. She was rarely embarrassed, for she could save a situation with a light shaft of her own wit. There were times when she had to fight down her sense of humor, for she was irresistibly struck by the absurd, and although she is authority for the suggestion that her husband was full of fun, his gravity and reserve in public seemed formidable. His wit had a satirical edge. In Varina's opinion he was "very full of gay suggestions until the fall of the Confederacy; but never afterward." [20]

On the whole, she felt this to be a successful party and noted later that France was the one country that did not live up to the promises made that night. Russia and England co-operated handsomely, but Varina neglected to say in her *Memoir* that some of the knowledge picked up on this tour was used by McClellan in his later efforts against her husband. It was one of the ironic sequels to her contacts with the North. She was impressed by the bashful young man on this occasion, noticing his "inveterate habit of blushing when suddenly addressed." But his modesty, gentle manner, and the "appositeness of the few remarks he made, gave us a most favorable impression of him," she wrote.

These men were to stand eventually in strange juxtaposition to one another. The young West Pointer was well known to Davis from their association in the war with Mexico. Neither he nor Varina ever disliked McClellan. Quite unconsciously she frequently was hostess in those days o men who would later fight her husband, both politically and in the field.

The expedition to the Crimea also started her husband on his drive for a camel corps—one of his more ill-judged enthusiasms, but as Major William B. Lee, who worked with him at this time, said of him—he was a "regular bulldog when he formed an opinion, for he would never let go." Or, as Varina put it: "If he expressed a decided opinion, it was prefaced by 'I take it for granted you will coincide with me in the opinion.' " [21]

She became a little tired of camels during the years that Jeff gave them his attention. He had conceived the idea that they might be used to advantage in the American desert. He was struck by the great loss of horses, mules, and oxen from the emigrant wagon trains heading for the California gold fields in the early 1850's. He also noticed that camels were used by the British Army in the Crimean War. Lieutenant David D. Porter, who later would bedevil him as a Federal admiral, was commissioned to buy and import the camels. An appropriation of thirty thousand dollars was voted in 1855.

Porter arrived next year with thirty-three camels in tow.[22] They were treated like babies but they failed to thrive in America. The army hostlers detested the camel corps and turned them loose in the desert whenever possible. The animals were afraid to wade streams and shied away from muddy bands. They fed on bushes and shrubs and had none of the hardihood of the mules. Their packs kept slipping off. The horses whinnied if they were stabled near them. In the end the remaining camels were auctioned off, but in the meantime some had gone to the Mexicans; others had wandered into the Panhandle; and many had fallen victim to wild beasts. A few landed eventually in circuses. They were never anything but a novelty—and something of a headache to Varina.

Another rocket burst early in 1854 through a Sunday morning call made by Davis and Stephen A. Douglas on President Pierce. His intimates felt that the Secretary of War was caught napping when he arranged this historic interview. Douglas sought the support of the administration for the Kansas-Nebraska Bill which would give these states self-determination on slavery. He had a strong delegation from the South behind him. The Northerners felt betrayed. They saw it as a measure to force slavery on all the states. Some of the most dynamic oratory in the history of the Union followed, before the bill finally was passed in May. Douglas was accused of yielding to the South in the hope of winning the presidency. Davis, ill and with his head in bandages from recurrent neuralgia and eye trouble, appeared to talk for it. But soon he and Douglas were at loggerheads on the slave issue as Douglas shifted ground, and Pierce was left stranded between North and South. There was little further pretense after that. The way to war was open. Varina's parlors were crowded every night with arguing politicians. All talk of guns, railroads, and construction projects was secondary to the growing sweep of the slavery issue.

The antagonisms were strongly reflected among the women in the official set, where the chill between North and South intensified steadily all through the late 1850's. By this time the capital was in one of its gayest whirls. The diplomats were entertaining on a lavish scale, and the wealthy Southerners were setting new standards of luxurious living. The White House was both simple and sober in comparison with the homes of the rich Senators. There was a constant round of dinners, dances, receptions, and balls.

Varina was often at the White House and she made every effort to cheer Mrs. Pierce in her seclusion. So did Mrs. Clay, who first joined a mess at the home of Charles Gardner and later stayed at Brown's Hotel, a favorite haunt of the Southerners, and then at Ebbitt House. Mrs. Benjamin Fitzpatrick of Alabama was another favorite quartered at this mess, and Varina saw much of them at this time. Both of these wives were considerably younger than their husbands.

Mrs. Clay and Varina frequently drove with Mrs. Pierce in the presidential equipage. They went most often to Chevy Chase or Georgetown and drove along the banks of the Potomac, gay with spectators when the shad-seining began. Finally Varina discovered that the company of her little Sam was comforting to Mrs. Pierce, so she arranged for him to spend much time with her—both driving and in her private quarters at the White House. By 1854 Sam had developed into a jolly little two-year-old, who went staggering about with a merry grin. He would wait at the door to greet his father and kiss him when he came in. But that summer he sickened and "after several weeks of pain and steady decline" he was suddenly gone in June. It was an era in which small children died as readily as they lived. Mrs. Clay had borne and lost a child, too, in her first year in Washington.

At first Davis was inconsolable. Varina wrote of his misery:

For many months afterward, Mr. Davis walked half the night, and worked fiercely all day. A child's cry in the street well-nigh drove him mad, and to the last hour of his life he occasionally spoke of "the strong young man on whose arm, had God so willed it, I might have leaned and gone down to my grave." The sympathy of thousands is gratifying and acceptable as a tribute to the living as well as the dead, but one misses sorely the opportunity to mourn in secret.[23]

The Pierces persuaded the Davises to accompany them later that summer to the seclusion of Capon Springs, Virginia, and on their return they established themselves in Edward Everett's house at F and Fourteenth Street. This was to be their permanent home until they left Washington, and few celebrities of the day did not at one time or another call on Varina and Jefferson Davis in their twenty-three-roomed house. No sooner were they settled in it than Varina's mother arrived from Natchez, for by this time Varina was expecting another baby. Mrs. Howell found Jeff in excellent condition and interested in his work. Varina's health and spirits seemed improved—although she suffered from toothache, which her mother thought natural in her condition. She also had a cough, which her doctor considered purely nervous.

Varina's second baby was born on February 25, 1855, and they named her Margaret Howell Davis. She was a bright little thing from the start, looking much like her mother. These years of childbearing and of running her home made Varina feel more happy and fulfilled, in spite of the loss of little Sam. She buried her sorrow in silence, comforted her husband, and plunged more vigorously than ever into the social life. Her cuisine compared well with that of the Embassies where French chefs were in command. She had her own Southern cooks, she marketed carefully, and was never spendthrift. In this respect she differed from Mrs. Lincoln. What Varina could not afford she did not order. But she attended and enjoyed the lavish routs given by Mrs. Jacob Thompson, Mrs. Ogle Tayloe, Mrs. Robert Toombs, Mrs. Howell Cobb, Mrs. Aaron V. Brown, the Comtesse de Sartiges, Mrs. Clement Clay, and the greatly admired Mrs. John Slidell. Ben Perley Poore noted that the Pierces went out in a blaze of glory at a party given by Mrs. Davis, who now assembled celebrities at her own dinner table instead of looking down at them from the Senate gallery.

Although Varina fared well with the smooth and diplomatic types she also enjoyed the hearty exuberance of such men as Toombs and William L. Marcy, whom her husband disliked. She thought the Secretary of State "strong, honest and an adroit politician, a man of rugged abrupt manners, yet a great favorite with the ladies." Like all the other Southern women, she went often to the home of the handsome widower William W. Corcoran, whom Mrs. Clay described as the "Prince of entertainers." His weekly dinners, where the best of the old and the new could be found, were an institution, and he gave an annual ball to both Houses of Congress. Such dissonant characters as Washington Irving, General Scott, and Sam Houston, in blue coat with brass buttons and ruffled shirt, would forgather there on the same evening. The scientifically minded Matthew Fontaine Maury was a lavish host at the Naval Observatory, and Mrs. Greenhow and her beautiful daughters haunted much the same drawing rooms as Varina. But on Christmas night, 1856, Mrs. Clay, writing to her father-in-law, former Governor Clay of Alabama, expressed the prevailing apprehension: "We feel . . . as if we are dancing over a powder magazine. Everything is excitement and confusion."

By this time President Pierce would call on the Davises at unexpected hours, soon after breakfast, or perhaps late on a snowy night, his long pale face shining with friendliness. He was sensitive about the whisperings that he was under the domination of the powerful claque from the South, so he sometimes startled Varina, Mrs. Clay, or Mrs. Pryor, with his nocturnal visits. This was marked after Davis had brought Douglas to him in one of the more significant political moves of his life.

Varina was devoted to the handsome and melancholy Pierce. She found it hard to understand why he was "undervalued and spoken of by his opponents as a man of no force." [24] She considered him one of the most "genuinely honest, upright men" she had ever known, and one who never yielded a point to his Cabinet on which he had expressed an opinion, although they were all men of decisive views. On one occasion when her husband could not agree with him at a Cabinet meeting, Jefferson came home and said he would resign rather than embarrass the President, or do what he considered an injustice. But late that night Pierce sent round a note "offering to announce himself responsible for the objectionable course, and so it was settled," Varina observed.

When the Davises took a house for the summer outside Washington, the President and his wife often drove out to visit them, and engaged in "unrestrained intercourse and pleasantries." They had become as fond of little Margaret as they had been of Samuel. She was a clever child, and Varina maintained that she could walk and talk at eighteen months

The President always remembered her as the little girl who bit the dog.[25] On one of his visits to the country home of the Davises her dog had snapped at her. Instead of crying, Margaret lay down beside him until he fell asleep. Then she bit him on the nose. The President kept her secret at the time, but told her parents the story several years later.

Varina particularly liked to hear Pierce talk of his friend Nathaniel Hawthorne. He would pace up and down at their country home discussing the "shy tender ways" of the writer. Hawthorne was not only his friend but had written his campaign biography. Varina met Hawthorne, Washington Irving, and many another writer and scholar of the day. Before the war began she had a rich assortment of memories and much intimate knowledge of the men who would be on her husband's side and against him in the coming days of the great struggle.

❦ 6 ❦

TWO PRESIDENTS COME CALLING

PRESIDENT PIERCE, well used to the snows of New England, sank up to his waist in heavy drifts in a Washington street as he went to inquire for Varina on a January day in 1857. She had just given birth to her third child and was close to death. It took him nearly an hour to cover a square and a half. One blizzard had followed another and the drifts were piled high. Varina's friend, Mrs. Henry Wayne, could not cross the street to help until a path had been dug for her. The President was exhausted by the time he reached the Davis home, but he was determined to make a personal call, out of his great affection for Varina.

When well enough to know what had happened, she was even more touched by the concern of William H. Seward, whom she had not met up to this time. Hearing that her life was despaired of, and that Mrs. Margaretta R. Hetzel, a neighbor of his who was helping Mrs. Wayne to nurse Varina, could not get a carriage to take her to the Davis home, the Senator had his own fine horses harnessed to a sleigh and personally drove her to her destination. They arrived with broken harness after a bumpy run.

The Davises never forgot this gesture although they soon were aligned as enemies. Varina wrote in 1890: "After all those long years of bitter feuds, I thank him as sincerely as my husband did to the last hour of his life." [1] The child born on January 16 was named Jefferson after his father. From the day of his birth she viewed him as the "friend of my bosom, the balm of my life," and she prayed regularly that she might rear him. He was the only one of her sons whom she did see grow up, although he died at the age of twenty-one.

Two months after his visit through the snow, President Pierce said good-by to Jefferson Davis. "I can scarcely bear the parting from you, who have been strength and solace to me for four anxious years and never failed me." That same day Davis was sworn in for his seat in the Senate. The Buchanan era had begun, during which he and Varina would have even more ascendancy than during the Pierce administration. The Dred Scott decision and a host of political problems confronted the new President as he took office. Varina had long been one of his favorites. He liked the talk of clever women and was frequently a guest at her table. Like Pierce, he had been in the habit of stopping in at the Davis home. He had made a strong impression on her on his first visit to their quarters when he was Secretary of State. Varina had studied him then, noting the "spotless white cravat, faultlessly tied" and his more obvious characteristics.

His complexion was very fair and delicate, and his eyes were blue but one of them had sustained some injury that had obscured the sight. The first thought that one had in looking at him was, how very clean he was. The only drawback to his appearance was a nervous jerking of his head at intervals, but it was not so often as to render him at all absurd. His unwilling footsteps were then just upon the boundary of middle age, and a more charming man could hardly be imagined. He was particularly gifted in polite repartee, and quick as a flash in response. In those days he liked society, and to be bon camarade to thoroughly refined women. . . . He had a reticent temper, but masked it under a diplomatic frankness of speech.[2]

That summer, some months after the birth of the new baby, the Davises went South and, while Jeff made speeches and attended barbecues in Vicksburg and Jackson, Varina rested with the children in Mississippi City, where they had a clean sweep of salt air. The threat of yellow fever and malaria was always in the background, and she greatly dreaded what she called "miasmatic effects" both for her husband and children. Davis was most unwilling to make this tour and wrote to Joseph from Jackson in August: "I leave home with extreme reluctance and if superstitious would believe that some strong necessity existed for my presence." [3] At this time he was defending the Dred Scott decision and was advocating the purchase of Cuba. He made his final speech in Mississippi City, where Varina now planned to buy land for a summer home. This was their first association with the Gulf Coast, where they were later to make their home.

Davis was active in the Senate early that winter and, in spite of her family cares and social obligations, Varina was frequently in the gallery listening to the debates. North and South had moved decisively into separate camps, and the Abolitionists were hard at work, flooding the Senators with propaganda. An opposite tide of feeling was galvanizing the South, and Jefferson Davis had become a strong spokesman for his region. Some shared Varina's view that his oratory was brilliant and convincing; others felt that it reflected a rigid and prejudiced spirit. Douglas, warm-blooded, eloquent, picturesque in debate, had more of the magnetic touch of the natural orator. Varina heard both men argue the Lecompton Constitution adopted by the proslavery factions in Kansas and backed by Buchanan. Douglas voted with the antislavery men on this measure, and Varina watched the split in the Democratic ranks grow wider. The Little Giant, whose own interests lay in the West, accused Buchanan of veering to the South on this issue and attacked him hotly. Douglas sailed back into Northern favor, but meanwhile he had lost his grip on the South.

The winter of 1857-58 proved to be an unhappy one for the Davises. No sooner had Varina picked up strength after the birth of her new baby than her husband, worn out by his sustained efforts, developed laryngitis and then an exceptionally severe case of eye trouble in February. He lay blind and speechless during the heat of the session, communicating only by slate for four weeks. Varina was desperately worried about him. She wrote:

> Mr. Davis's anguish was intense—a procedenture of the pupil had taken place, and the eye was in imminent danger of bursting. My husband's fortitude and self-control had been so great that no one but I knew how much he suffered, and I only because one day I begged him to try to take nourishment, and he gave only one smothered scream and wrote, "I am in anguish. I cannot." [4]

Dr. Isaac Hayes, an eye specialist, was brought from Philadelphia to consult with Dr. Thomas Miller and Dr. William Stone of Washington. The light streamed full on Davis while he was being examined and he clung to Varina's hand in great pain.

"I do not see why this eye has not burst," Dr. Hayes commented.

Davis felt for his slate and wrote: "My wife saved it."

Varina felt that this was the best compliment that had ever been paid her. "All the triumphs of my life were and are concentrated in and excelled by this blessed memory," she wrote. He was returned to bed almost fainting, but as soon as he could talk he eluded Varina's vigilance and went upstairs to visit Jeffy D., who then had scarlet fever. She found him sitting on the bed, telling the boy stories, although he had never had the disease himself.

To her astonishment Seward called nearly every day. They made a curious combination—the wily lackadaisical Senator from New York and the stiff Mississippian. He was quite agitated when he learned that Davis might lose an eye. "I could not bear to see him maimed or disfigured," he told Varina. "He is a splendid embodiment of manhood, he must not lose his eye."

In spite of her anxiety she was struck by Seward's philosophy as she shared in their discussions. When her husband said that he hated to speak to empty benches, Seward insisted he preferred them that way and spoke only for the papers, which had a larger audience. He frequently commented on the day in the Senate with shrewd, convincing touches and would say wryly, "Your man outtalked ours, you would have liked it, but I didn't."

Varina wrangled with him amiably now and then. "Heartily liking him, and taking a good many liberties of expression with him" [5] she asked him if he really meant some of the things he said on the slavery question. He told her he did not, but his appeals were "potent to affect the rank and file of the North."

Shocked, her husband inquired, "But, Mr. Seward, do you never speak from conviction alone?"

"Nev-er," said Seward.

Varina pictures her husband raising his bandaged head and whispering hoarsely, "As God is my judge, I never spoke from any other motive."

"I know you do not—I am always sure of it," said Seward, gently pressing him back on his pillow.

Her husband recovered slowly, and before he was well he insisted on going to the Senate to speak on behalf of an appropriation for the Coast Survey. His friend Dallas Bache was involved. Varina went with him, taking beef tea and wine in a basket to sustain him during the ordeal. He made several other appearances, tangling sharply in May, 1858, with Judah P. Benjamin, the picturesque Senator from Louisiana. He was feeling ill at the time and made a cutting observation which stirred up Benjamin. There was talk of a duel, but he apologized at once and the trouble quickly subsided. Varina, who knew Benjamin only slightly at the time, later commented that "if anyone differs with Mr. Davis he

resents it and ascribes the difference to the perversity of his opponent."
And Davis himself, after this tilt with Benjamin, remarked, "I have an
infirmity of which I am heartily ashamed; when I am aroused in a
matter, I lose control of my feeling and become personal."

When Congress adjourned his physician ordered a long rest. The
Davises considered joining the Pierces in Europe. The former President
had taken Jane to Madeira for her health. In the end, they decided to
tour New England. This proved to be one of the most relaxing holidays
of Varina's lifetime. It was also an enlightening experience for her to
visit the Abolitionist stronghold. When it was all over her husband observed, "True men could effect much by giving to the opposite section
the views held by the other. The difference is less than I expected."

Davis soon felt better in the sea air. He was able to leave off his eye
shade in the late afternoons. They sailed from Boston to Portland and
he made a Fourth of July speech on the boat, urging acceptance of the
Dred Scott decision. They were serenaded all along the way, and the
ladies of New England welcomed Mrs. Davis, the planter's wife from
Mississippi, with clambakes and basket parties at Cape Elizabeth. Relatives of Mrs. Montgomery Blair entertained them and they made excursions to the little islands of Casco Bay. They attended the annual
commencement of the Portland High School and talked at length to
ministers, educators, sea captains, and men of sundry political faiths.

Later in the summer Professor Bache took them on an exploratory
expedition to Mount Humpback to watch him make astral observations.[6]
They traveled by rail to Bangor, then switched to stagecoach and did
the last stretch of the journey over the "horseback" road by oxcart.
Finally their tents were pitched on top of a plateau and there Professor
Bache played host, serving tenderloin steaks from Bangor, vegetables
from neighboring farms, good books for evening reading, and Verdi from
a musical box. Varina relaxed and listened to him singing a most unlikely
accompaniment in a cracked voice. He read aloud to them at night,
since her husband could not use his eyes. They all gathered to watch him
make observations and followed his clear scientific comments with understanding. Varina felt that the peace and quiet were doing wonders for
her husband.

In three weeks' time they returned to Boston, where little Jeff
promptly came down with membranous croup and was desperately ill at
the Tremont House. Varina was showered with kindness and out of the
night drove the famous Mrs. Harrison Gray Otis, intent on staying with

the sick child, passing judgment on the medical prescriptions and seeming "to diffuse a sense of relief and confidence about her." Much later Varina wrote: "After thirty years this memory is clear and blessed to me, and her name has always been honored in our household." [7]

She enjoyed the hours she spent looking over first editions in Edward Everett's library, the Northern politicians with whom she talked, and the stern blue light of New England. Thirty years later she wrote: "These reminiscences of Boston to this day soften all the asperities developed by our bloody war." But the big event of their tour was her husband's speech in Faneuil Hall, the fountainhead of Abolitionist oratory. He was introduced by her old Washington friend, Caleb Cushing, statesman and author, who always interested her by quoting liberally from the *Iliad*. Benjamin F. Butler, at this time an enthusiastic state-rights Democrat, but a man whom Davis would one day declare a felon, was on the platform.

Varina wore a pink shirred satin bonnet as she sat with the eyes of many Boston matrons upon her and heard Cushing say through great bursts of applause, "Here, Adams aroused his countrymen in the war of independence, and Webster invoked them . . . and who, if he were here present from those blessed abodes on high . . . would congratulate us for this scene." [8] Davis delivered what was regarded as one of the more potent addresses of his career, and one which Varina took care to include in her *Memoir*. He waded directly into a defense of slavery and said:

There is nothing of truth or justice with which to sustain this agitation, or ground for it. . . . I plead with you now to arrest fanaticism which has been evil in the beginning, and must be evil in the end. . . . The danger lies at your door, and it is time to arrest it. Too long have we allowed this influence to progress. It is time that men should go back to the first foundation of our institutions. They should drink the waters of the fountain at the source of our colonial and early history.

Davis's expedition to the stronghold of Abolitionism was received with a deep chill in the South. It closely followed Abraham Lincoln's declaration at Springfield: "A house divided against itself cannot stand . . ." And almost immediately, speaking before the Senate Legislature in Mississippi, Davis was saying: "I hold the separation from the Union by the state of Mississippi to be the last remedy, the final alternative. . . . In the language of the venerated Calhoun, I consider the disruption of the Union as a great, though not the greatest, calamity." [9] But he was derided in his own state at this point and was thought to be making a bid for New England support at the Democratic convention.

While historic phrases were being coined and the country moved with momentum toward war, the year 1858 went down in history as the "court year," the most extravagant and reckless on record in Washington, perhaps because there were so many chroniclers on the scene who later would thread their diaries with lively accounts of the frivolity, the clothes, the Lucullan meals, the jewels, the display, the parties that preceded the war. Certainly nothing like it was seen again until the New York social whirl of the 1890's. There were dinners, balls, suppers and teas, musicales and matinee dances. Private ballrooms shimmered with crystal chandeliers that illumined women laden with jewels, dancing in gossamer chiffons with flowers in their hair and garlands festooning their gowns.

The diplomats were a conspicuous part of the picture, their uniforms ablaze with decorations, their carriages the most ornate on the scene.[10] On the more intimate basis quiet little suppers spiced with mint juleps and hot toddies encouraged storms of political gossip and intrigue. Unquestionably much of the fire and sparkle was traceable to the South, as well as the extravagance, and the most imperious of the belles was Mrs. Clement Clay. She boasted that she would have nothing to do with the Republican group and she refused to receive Seward, who was quite at home in some of the best Southern parlors.

Actually, Varina was more of an onlooker than a participant in much of this display. For years she had been watching the laden coaches heading off for the spas. She was familiar enough with the hunting set, and with planters who had huge staffs, whose wives and daughters were decked with jewels, and regularly made trips to Europe. But this was not her life. Her letters reveal the unostentatious way in which the Davises lived, even though Presidents rang their doorbell at times.

In spite of her husband's illness, she circulated considerably at this time, because 1858 fell between the birth of two of her children, and the social demands were pressing. She dined frequently at the White House, where all was quiet good form in the tasteful rearrangements that had been made by Buchanan's niece and hostess, Harriet Lane. She watched new furniture being installed, portraits being hung, a conservatory being built in the English fashion, and a red brick barn being added, in Pennsylvania style. She contributed to some good conversation, as well as highly inflammatory talk around the Buchanan board, with its long mirror centerpiece edged with a hunting scene and the familiar potted palms dotted here and there around the state dining room.

Years later in prison, Davis was to remark, "The White House under the administration of Buchanan approached more nearly to my idea of a Republican court than the President's house has ever done before since the days of Washington." [11] But the New York *Herald* viewed it as a "rose-colored administration" dominated by the women of the South.

Both Varina and Mrs. Greenhow were potent figures around Buchanan. They had warm and friendly relations with Harriet Lane, a chestnut-haired girl of stately proportions who was equally smooth to the protagonists of North and South. Varina's sharp wit was lost on the bland Miss Lane, who was always serene and self-contained, the soul of tact. The only crack in her smooth façade was her deadly feud with Mrs. Stephen A. Douglas, the beautiful Adelaide Cutts, great-niece of Dolly Madison, whom some considered the belle of Washington. Addie had vowed to make all of the Little Giant's enemies her own, and she turned her back in public on Harriet Lane. She and Varina met often at the Bache homes and at all the big parties in Washington. They maintained the outward courtesies even while the feud deepened between their husbands.

Varina was inevitably much involved with the diplomatic set and was on particularly good terms with the Comtesse de Sartiges and Lady Napier, of the British Embassy.[12] The pale patrician Ninia Napier was so much admired in official Washington that when the time came for her to leave Buchanan bowed over her hand and remarked:

"Madame, I have holy writ to substantiate my warning that you are in imminent danger."

Lady Napier showed her surprise.

"Beware when all men speak well of you," he said.

She was a Scot, plain to the point of austerity in her daily rounds, but magnificent at formal affairs. Some of Varina's friends found Lord Napier's manner stiff and his cold blue eyes forbidding, but she could think only of his kindness to her husband. The Napiers kept a small staff and had the least conspicuous equipage of the diplomatic corps, but the ball they gave in 1858 on the Queen's birthday was rated one of the last great prewar parties. Lady Napier wore her famous emerald and diamond tiara. Her gold and silver plates were impressive, and the envoys had mustered the ultimate in gold lace and decorations. Varina whirled to the strains of the "British Grenadiers."

The other memorable function of 1858 was the Gwin fancy dress ball, which the chroniclers of the day have classed as the last and most extravagant social gesture before the shadows closed on the Union. Senator William McKendree Gwin, who was from Louisiana but had tied his fortunes to California, was determined it should be the most brilliant party ever held at the capital.[13] The President came in citizens' dress and Senator Gwin was Louis Quatorze. Mrs. Greenhow affected simplicity and appeared as a "most comely Housekeeper of the Old School." Soon Gwin would be arrested for espionage, and Mrs. Greenhow would be climbing the Gwin stairs under military guard for a hearing on the same charge before Major General John A. Dix.

Mrs. Clay moved among the marchionesses and the gypsies, the shepherds and the dukes, the milkmaids and the marquises, playing the rustic part of Aunt Ruthie Partingon, with snuffbox and knitting in view. On this occasion she had her one exchange with Seward. She offered him snuff with a tart gibe. Varina, playing Madame de Staël, was a dominant figure in Mrs. Clay's estimation. "So historically correct was her costume, and so notably brilliant her witticisms, sparkling but in inimitable broken English, that her admirers declared the veritable daughter of Necker lived again!" [14] But Varina, not given to narcissism, was her usual skeptical self and although she had rehearsed her part carefully in front of her husband, she reported back to him that she did not believe she had carried it off too well.

She was a veteran on the social scene by this time. She spanned two generations and had kept pace with the growth of the Southern influence. She had watched both Washington Irving and Dolly Madison grow old and feeble. She knew all the established belles and now welcomed their daughters in her parlors. She was as much at home with Harriet Lane's generation as she was with the amiable Mrs. John J. Crittenden, whom she had previously known as Mrs. William Ashley; or with Madame Le Vert, who was famous from New Orleans to Paris, and of whom Washington Irving had said, "But one such woman is born in the course of an Empire." [15]

Varina was particularly drawn to Mrs. John Slidell and her two daughters, Rosine and Mathilde, whose destiny would be closely woven with that of the Confederacy. They were to be among her most intimate friends in the days of victory and defeat. Varina was impressed by her from the start and noted: "Her features were regular, her figure noble, and she looked so dignified and was so fair and courteous with her French *empressement* of manner that the impression she made on me then was never effaced, and years after ripened into a sincere friendship that was never interrupted." Mrs. Clay, more specifically, considered Mrs. Slidell the "wearer of unapproachable Parisian gowns, the giver of unsurpassed entertainments, the smiling, tireless hostess." [16] Slidell was a gray-eyed, keen, and subtle lawyer and politician from the North, who had settled in New Orleans. He was much older than his beautiful Creole wife, Marie Mathilde Deslonde, whose sister married General Beauregard. Like his fellow Senators of the period, he wore richly brocaded vests of satin or velvet, with jeweled studs.

But however commanding some of the other Southern women were, Varina topped them all in influence and political prescience. Mrs. Pryor, who regarded her coolly at all times, was forced to observe: "Nor must we fail to acknowledge the social influence of Mrs. Jefferson Davis, one of the most cultivated women of her time—greatly sought by cultivated men and women." [17] No one could ignore Varina. Even Addie Cutts was coldly courteous. When she entered a room she readily took command, not by virtue of her looks or attire, but because of her dominating personality and bright conversation. Jefferson Davis stood aloof from it all. He worked hard and consistently; his health was indifferent; he had neither the time nor the inclination for social interchange, but there were many quiet gatherings of Southern politicians in Varina's parlors at night, particularly toward the end of the decade.

Brown's Hotel and Ebbitt's were the acknowledged meeting ground for the Southern politicians, and some of the extremists flocked to Roger Pryor's, where good mint juleps and Kentucky bourbon were served. When Louis T. Wigfall of Texas and his family joined the colony at Brown's, it was noted that the "atmosphere was as distinctly Southern as it was Northern at Willard's." L.Q.C. Lamar, loquacious and gallant to the feminine contingent, held forth at Brown's.

Seward drew his own particular group, and moved easily between the Northerners and Southerners until the final days of secession. So did Charles Sumner, until he was assaulted in the Senate and went to Europe to recuperate. Varina got on exceptionally well with the Northern politicians but she could not warm to Sumner, who devoted much time, however, to lecturing her on such assorted topics as Demosthenes, intaglios, Seneca's morals, the Indian Mutiny, the history of lace, and the Platonic theory.[18] Since she could not resist good conversation she was at first attracted, but soon decided that his talk was studied, and his effects pretentious, with too much "Greek fire" and "set pieces." She felt that his deferential manner was as false as his conversation, and as a woman she did not have the "pleasant consciousness of possessing his regard or esteem." In short, Varina dismissed him as a "handsome, unpleasing man." She was never to like him as she did Seward.

William L. Marcy's parlors were always crowded, although Mrs. Marcy was the most retiring of the politicians' wives. Her husband was an exuberant exhibitionist who read only good of himself and thereby maintained his self-esteem.[19] Their daughter, Nellie, later became the wife of George B. McClellan. All the members of the Southern group were interested when the popular Judah Benjamin took the Stephen Decatur house and furnished it with great magnificence for Natalie, his beautiful Creole wife, who preferred to live in Paris with her daughter Ninette. With Buchanan in the White House he hoped that she would settle down with him and become a member of the official set. "The arrival of the lady, after a marked absence abroad, during which some curious gossip had reached American ears, was attended by great éclat," wrote Mrs. Clay.

Varina was not yet the intimate friend of Benjamin that she later became, and she referred cryptically to Mrs. Benjamin's "unassisted human nature," presumably implying that she considered her a child of nature. Senator Clay urged the Southern women to call on her and they went in a group to the house where Van Buren had tried unsuccessfully to force Peggy O'Neale on Washington society, and had been checkmated by Floride Calhoun. Benjamin was personally very popular and was welcomed among the *bon vivants* of the capital.

The callers tempered their usual cordial manner "with a fine prudence," Mrs. Clay observed, without naming Mrs. Benjamin. "We paid our devoirs to the hostess and retired." But Natalie gave her own conclusive answer. She entertained the diplomatic corps, snubbed the official wives, and quietly returned to France. Her silver, china, crystal, paintings, hangings, and furniture were auctioned off and Varina bought lavishly on this occasion.

She would meet Natalie again, in Paris, and under vastly different circumstances, and Benjamin would become one of the mainstays of her husband's Cabinet. But the air now was getting exceedingly frosty in Washington, and it was considered better manners to discuss George

Eliot and Dickens, or the new basques with postillion backs, than it was to talk politics. Mrs. Clay interpreted things differently. It was her observation that women now talked more of "forts and fusillades than of frills and furbelows." But Mrs. Pryor and Varina insisted that the women gave politics a wide berth except when talking on their own side of the fence. Varina, who was apt to gloss over controversial matters in her *Memoir*, wrote:

Unconsciously, all tentative subjects were avoided by the well-bred of both sections; it was only when some "bull in a china shop" galloped over the barriers that good breeding had established, that there was anything but the kindest manner apparent.[20]

Actually, she felt that this restraint produced an artificial intercourse. Her own immediate embarrassment involved Mrs. Emory, who was a Bache, and the Montgomery Blairs, her closest friends. She was one of the last to draw away, although her husband was at the heart of the storm. For years she had been close to the Blairs. She had watched the young widower calling frequently on one of her favorite friends, Judge Levi Woodbury of the Supreme Court, and wooing his daughter Minna, whom she regarded as a "feminine Die Vernon—strong, tender, and beautiful in body and mind." They became intimate friends although the day was close at hand when Montgomery and his father, Francis P. Blair, would be the friends and advisers of Abraham Lincoln. She had reason later to change her estimate of some of the people with whom she now consorted, but her friendship with the Blairs survived the strain of war, and brought her some comfort even in the days of defeat.

Varina considered Montgomery "only ten minutes behind the hand-somest man present," having what the English termed a typically American face. Tired of that "most terrible scourge to society, one who listens to controvert" she found him equable, genial, and sympathetic.[21] At this time she spent many happy hours with Mrs. Blair, and it became an established custom for her to stop in at Blair House on a Saturday or Sunday afternoon and sit at the window with Minna Blair, Mrs. Clement Hill, and Mrs. Joseph E. Johnston, watching the parade of carriages and promenaders on Pennsylvania Avenue, and discussing their children. Little Maria Blair was a year older than Varina's Margaret. Woodbury was born in 1852, and her Samuel would have been his age, had he lived. Blair House was a fashionable rendezvous at this time, and

Minna often took Varina and the wives of the Ministers to Silver Spring, where her father-in-law presided in the midst of much magnificence.

Mrs. Mary Boykin Chesnut, whose husband's family owned a thousand slaves and one of the great plantations of South Carolina, was now on the scene and had begun to take notes. Senator James Chesnut, Jr., belonged to one of the most powerful dynasties of South Carolina. Mary was devoted to her husband but maintained a glib and irreverent attitude to his parents, who lived on a fabulous scale on Mulberry Plantation near Camden. She had a mordant wit and rebelled against their autocratic spirit. She was the daughter of Stephen Decatur Miller, one-time Governor of South Carolina. Like Varina, she was well educated and political-minded. She had traveled a great deal, imported her clothes from Paris, and spoke several languages.

Varina knew her only slightly at this time, but she in turn was seeing a great deal of Lydia Johnston, cementing a friendship that was to turn to deadly enmity when their husbands came to loggerheads. Lydia was the daughter of Louis McLane, a Senator who had served in Jackson's Cabinet and as Minister to Great Britain. Her family history was closely identified with Baltimore. Johnston, who had met her while doing coastal survey, married her in 1845, the same year in which Davis married Varina. She and Mrs. Davis had much in common in their devotion to their husbands and their ambition for them. There were many parallels between them, except that Lydia was childless.

After the war had raged for some time Mrs. Chesnut noted that "in Washington before I knew any of them except by sight, Mrs. Davis, Mrs. Emory and Mrs. Johnston were always together, inseparable friends; and the trio were pointed out to me as the cleverest women in the United States."

In the spring of 1859 Varina was having another baby. Again her husband was away, but this time he was at their plantation trying to salvage what he could after the most destructive floods in their history. Virtually all of their land was under water, and levees had to be built. She was keeping herself occupied sending off copies of the speeches he had made in Boston and Jackson. Varina was particularly proud of his Faneuil Hall address and franked nearly three thousand envelopes in the days preceding her confinement.

She was no longer able to cope with household matters, and Mrs. Hetzel, who usually assisted her when she was having a baby, was attending to her shopping, her banking, and the care of her children. But she was well enough to receive guests, and President Buchanan drove up to the house two days before her baby was born, and kept Varina entertained during a long visit. He was in high spirits and evidently things were quiet in Congress at the moment for she noted that he was "congratulating himself that there was no news—thank goodness."

Varina was in a nostalgic state. Writing to Jeff she remarked on a "queer annihilation of responsibility, and of time." [22] She thought much of the past and the anxious, loving—but useless—girl she had been fourteen years earlier when she married him. Here she injected one of her rare notes of regret that Knox had been first in his heart. "It saddens me to realize that there is so very much in one's being the first love of early youth," she wrote. Now she felt old, and there was gray in her hair, her feet were swollen, and her household cares weighed on her.

But Jefferson had never loved her more. Their marriage was now in its happiest phase. As he worked at the plantation, making provision for the slaves, having the furniture hoisted above the water line, removing the stock to high ground, he was in a state of uncontrollable anxiety, remembering how ill Varina had been with her last baby. The other children were thriving, Jeff was rosy with sunburn. Maggie was running wild and her mother had had to whip her for using naughty words. The talk was that Lord Lyons, who had just arrived, was "very taciturn and very stupid," Varina wrote to her husband. [23] She noted that she was in total retirement, except for short daily drives. However, she had none of the Victorian shrinking from appearing in public when pregnant and kept up her social life to the last possible moment.

Varina had changed in one important respect. Her concern now was for her husband, and she no longer urged him to get to her side, at whatever cost, as she had sometimes done in the past. His illness had turned the tide for her and although she mentioned the heart condition that had been plaguing her for some time she told him not to worry about it, but to take care of himself, and to stay out of the sun and the night air. Although he wished urgently to get to her another son was born to her in his absence on April 18, 1859. This one was named Joseph Evan, for his brother and grandfather.

Although childbirth was easier for her on this occasion, Varina went into convulsions shortly afterward when they were settled at a summer cottage in the mountains at Oakland, Maryland, close to the Montgomery Blairs. Both men wished to be near the capital, where momentous events were brewing, and Portsmouth, New Hampshire, where they had had summer cottages since the New England trip, was too far away. So they week-ended with their wives at Oakland. Jefferson was at home when Varina became desperately ill. He hurried over to the Blair home and got Elizabeth, Montgomery's daughter by his first marriage. His wife seemed to be expiring, and there was no medical aid to be had nearby. But Elizabeth showed presence of mind and administered an improvised treatment that seemed to work.[24] Varina revived and her husband always said in later years that Miss Blair had saved her life. He was so grateful that at her request he freed some Maryland soldiers from Libby Prison during the war.

Varina found that reading matter was scarce at Oakland and she ordered travel books, history or fiction, "all of which would be equally agreeable if well written." [25] She suggested Charles Reade's *Love Me Little, Love Me Long; Summer Pictures from Copenhagen to Venice; The Prince of the House of David*, and Grattan's *America*.

Jeff was again away on political business at this time and she could not refrain from writing in the old possessive way: "Do remember that you are a part of a powerful party and therefore can be spared but you are all to your wife and babes." [26] Little Joe was making her content again—"all the sweetness of our happiest hours seem to have returned with his birth and I hate to give you up even for a day. . . ."

Jefferson Davis was always a sympathetic listener where his family was concerned. At this time Mrs. Howell wrote to him from New Orleans, telling him she tried "to submit as cheerfully as possible" [27] to her privations although she sometimes wondered why things were so ordered. This was the letter in which she told him that he was as dear to her "as any child she had." As usual, she was worrying about Varina's health and feared she was concealing her true condition, to spare her anxiety.

At this time Joseph and Eliza set off on a grand tour of Europe, taking with them Lise Mitchell, his granddaughter, and the other young people who clustered around The Hurricane. But before leaving they visited Varina to see the first of her babies to be named after the great Joseph. Long a familiar figure at the Northern spas, he now appeared on the European scene, a handsome man in his sixties, open-handed, spirited in his reactions to all that he saw, and much interested in the various Parliaments.

He returned with a German doctor who installed steam baths at The Hurricane, to be used for ailing Negroes as well as for the family.[28] Lise took music lessons with the visiting physician. Joseph was still lamenting the death of a small grandson who had been thrown from his horse and killed as he rode with him. There was an element of swift tragedy in the way most of the Davis children died. Varina's sons were handsome, sturdy, and intelligent, and she was a conscientious mother. Her own large family had made her familiar with childish ills and her observations on the plantation had given her wisdom in the physical care of sick children. She had a merry wit with the young, as well as a strong sense of discipline, and devoted much of her time to them. She was extremely proud of their good intelligence, their childish sayings, and their development, and she invariably brought them forth, scrubbed and neatly dressed, to be admired. President Buchanan was called on to view her latest baby.

Varina volunteered many anecdotes about her children and they were all taught to revere their father. But they loved him, too, and were less afraid of him than they were of their mother. Maggie would turn her great dark eyes to Varina and say accusingly, "I wish I could see my father, he would let me be bad." The 1850's was a period of intensive childbearing and child rearing for Varina. Three of her children were born in this decade.

She was often to express herself on the education of the young in her later years and at one time pointed out that long before the war she had a theory for abolishing slavery which "was at least original if not practicable."

. . . that was to send the boys and girls of the North to schools in the South, and send our boys and girls to the North. The people of the two sections are not the same people, but are the complement of each other, and their extreme opinions would have thus been modified by the education of each in the other's sphere.[29]

Varina was much observed in the Senate gallery in the portentous winter of 1859. John Brown's raid in October had touched off the final explosion. The Abolitionists were creating uproar in New England. Their spokesmen were pounding away in Congress. Guerrilla warfare raged in Kansas and all factions were divided along sectional lines.

Early in February, 1860, Davis submitted a series of resolutions defending slavery, as it existed in fifteen states. In April, the National Democratic Convention met in Charleston and split. The vehement opposition to Douglas by the extreme Southern wing led to its breakup and to the subsequent convention in Baltimore at which he was nominated. Douglas denounced Davis in the Senate as having destroyed the Democratic party by forcing a proslavery plank on the platform committee, and the feeling spread that in fighting Douglas, Jefferson had opened the way for Lincoln. In the end Davis supported John C. Breckinridge but did not take an active part in the campaign. Such extremists as William L. Yancey and Robert Barnwell Rhett by this time were ready for secession, but Davis, who had favored it a few years earlier, was now counseling delay in withdrawing from the Union unless the entire lower South could unite in one plan of action.

On November 10, 1860, he wrote to Rhett that the "planting States have a common interest of such magnitude, that their union, sooner or later, for the protection of that interest, is certain," but he felt the new states, too, should be brought into co-operation before asking for a "popular decision upon a new policy and relation to the nations of the earth." [30] South Carolina was already intent on secession. Nothing could stop the tide of violent emotion that now swept North and South.

Varina lived from day to day in a state of acute tension as her husband came in, tired and distracted, and the colloquies continued in his study late into the night. There was little social interchange at this point, except for the most formal receptions.[31] Few of the women turned out for functions, never knowing whom they might meet. But they went in droves to the Senate, and sat listening anxiously to the angry debates.

Davis's fatigue was commented on by Mrs. Elizabeth Keckley who was sewing for Varina in 1860.[32] Her dresses did not come from Paris, although her patterns did, and she handed them over to Mrs. Keckley to copy. The Negro seamstress took notes on Varina, as she later did on Mrs. Lincoln. She worked for them late in the day, since she noticed that they stayed up until all hours and then slept most of the morning.

Mrs. Keckley found their house "a resort of leading statesmen from the South" and the prospects of war were freely discussed within her hearing, she said. On Christmas Eve, 1860, Davis came in late and leaned wearily against the door, watching her as she worked over a shot-silk dressing gown that his wife was giving him for a Christmas present. She had stayed to finish it, while Varina decorated the tree in the next room.

"That you, Lizzie," Mrs. Keckley quoted him as saying. "Why are you so late? Still at work; I hope that Mrs. Davis is not too exacting."

"No, sir, Mrs. Davis was very anxious to have this gown finished tonight and I volunteered to remain and complete it," she said.

By January, 1861, with Lincoln on his way in, war was being discussed by the Davises as a certainty, according to Mrs. Keckley. Varina invited her to go South with them, saying there would be war.

"And which do you think will whip?" Mrs. Keckley asked.

"The South, of course. The South is impulsive, is in earnest, and the Southern soldiers will fight to conquer. The North will yield, when it seems the South is in earnest rather than engage in a long and bloody war."

Mrs. Keckley further quoted Varina as saying: "The Southern people talk about choosing Mr. Davis for their President. In fact, it may be considered settled that he will be their President. . . As soon as we go South and secede from the other states, we will raise an army and march on Washington and then I shall live in the White House."

Later both Varina and Davis were to insist that he never had any thought of the presidency, and the facts seem to bear them out in this. In any event, Varina parted from Mrs. Keckley in a kindly way and left some fine needlework to be done, which Mrs. Emory helped Lizzie send off to Montgomery. The last garments she made for her were two chintz wrappers. Varina had told her they would have to economize for a bit when they went South.

The spring of 1860 was one of fine weather and abundant foliage. Ailanthus trees in whitewashed wooden tubs dressed up Pennsylvania Avenue and its unsightly mélange of buildings composed of everything from deal planks to marble columns. Flower borders spattered segments of color around the official buildings, and all the way to Arlington showers of crab apple blossoms lined the roadway over which Varina drove.

The city was wearing a slightly tidier air than when she first saw it in 1845, although pigs and cattle still wandered in the principal streets and slept near the White House. The gaps and fissures were always distressing in wet weather, but omnibuses of a primitive kind were now in use. The Capitol was beginning to show signs of her husband's enterprise, with derricks in view and its dome taking shape by slow degrees.

Things developed so rapidly after John Brown's raid that the Davises had stayed in Washington the following summer. Davis spoke from the White House in July in support of Breckinridge, and that autumn they were constantly in and out of the Executive Mansion as Buchanan grappled with the disintegrating Union. Davis was consulted about the final message but was not pleased with its equivocal stand when it was

delivered. Frost settled on Buchanan toward his Southern friends in the closing hours, and even Davis was cold-shouldered when he went to the White House as the *Star of the West* sailed with provisions for Fort Sumter and the South Carolinians demanded action. Varina was reported to be very angry with Buchanan, a story that she later denied. Her husband was not yet envisioned as the man who would lead the Southern forces to war, but he had taken a strong stand on several issues—the Ostend Manifesto, the Kansas-Nebraska Bill, the Compromise of 1850, the Dred Scott decision. Having half committed himself to secession, he had turned his back on it and argued against it, so that one segment of the South was against him. Varina had not always agreed with him, but when the crisis came she was ready for firm action. She had watched Rhett, Douglas, and Yancey jockeying for place. She had heard whisperings that her husband might be President. Perhaps she alone knew his true motives at this juncture, and may well have helped him to form some of his judgments.

At the very end he was appointed one of the Senate Committee of thirteen to try for a last-minute adjustment, but its members could find nothing on which to unite and secession followed swiftly.[33] President Buchanan was attending the wedding of Mary E. Parker and Congressman J. E. Bouligny of Louisiana when there was shouting in the street, Lawrence Keitt of South Carolina danced up and down like a madman, and Mrs. Pryor whispered to the chalk-white President that South Carolina had seceded.

Varina hastened to get to him with the news, but Mrs. Pryor had been first. Rear Admiral Porter told Gideon Welles four years later that he had called that evening at the Davis home and found Varina in a jubilant mood, all bonneted and ready to leave for the White House. Many of the more prominent Secessionists were in her parlors. It was a rainy disagreeable evening and he told her she would have difficulty with the muddy roads, but she said she wanted to congratulate the President "on the glorious news" and hoped to get there first. Porter, who was an intimate friend of the Davises at this time, borrowed a friend's hack and drove her personally to the White House. He asked her why she should feel so elated. According to his recollection, she said that "she wanted to get rid of the old government; that they would have a monarchy in the South, and gentlemen to fill official positions." [34]

Returning to the Davis home, Porter found the other Secessionists preparing to follow her to the White House. It struck him that they all spoke of Buchanan as being with them in sentiment, and he came to the conclusion that he "encouraged the active conspirators in his intercourse with them, if he did not openly approve them before the world." Henry Watterson, then working as a clerk in the Interior Department, had long observed that the "South was in the saddle." Varina, Mrs. Greenhow, Mrs. Clay, Mrs. Pryor, Mrs. Slidell, and other Southern women undoubtedly had kept up a steady barrage of sentiment around Buchanan in the drawing room, while their men battled things out in Congress. He had remarked himself that the women kept stirring up the slavery issue.

Davis was ill from excitement and anxiety when the day came in January, 1861, for Mississippi to follow the example of South Carolina and leave the Union. He feared, as Clifford Dowdey has pointed out, that "hate carried to the extreme of disunion would not be resolved by a peaceable separation." It was not the hour for compromise, and the men who led both factions were strong and determined.

Varina pictures the night before her husband left the Senate and sealed his destiny as a man of many sorrows. He had been ill for a week and his physician had forbidden his appearance. Neither of the Davises slept all night. With the knowledge of the years that followed at her command, she may unconsciously have colored the picture when the time came to write her *Memoir*. In despairing accents her husband had predicted war and its attendants, famine and bloodshed, and "we felt blood in the air," Varina reported. Looking at the festive exterior of the crowd assembled in the Senate to hear his farewell, she wondered if they "saw beyond the cold exterior of the orator—his deep depression, his desire for reconciliation, and his overwhelming love for the Union in whose cause he had bled." [35]

A seat had been held for her by a servant from seven o'clock in the morning. Crowds filled the Senate, and by nine there was scarcely standing room within the galleries or in the passages behind the forum. Coal-scuttle bonnets tied beneath rounded chins topped the spreading crinolines, and Varina observed that the "bright faces of the ladies were assembled together like a mosaic of flowers in the doorway." The sofas and passages were jammed, and crinolines collapsed like fallen balloons as women sank to the floor when they could not find seats. The Diplomatic Corps with their families sat in the press gallery, aware that they were looking in on history. Varina could detect several sympathetic faces among them. They had often discussed the political situation at her own dinner table.

Her husband had trouble pushing his way to his seat. He was the focus of observation. As usual, he was carefully tailored. His suit was of black broadcloth with a stiff white shirt and black satin waistcoat. A black silk handkerchief was looped stockwise at his collar. An observer thought that his gray eyes looked out with a "kind of unseeing intensity." [36] His emaciated face suggested his iron will. To some he seemed a man bent on destruction. But Varina viewed him as "graceful, grave and deliberate" as he rose in dead silence to address the Senate for the last time.

Every eye was turned upon him, fearful of missing one word. He glanced over the Senate with the reluctant look the dying cast on those upon whom they gaze for the last time. His voice was at first low and faltering, but soon it rang out melodiously clear, like a silver trumpet, to the extremest verge of the assembly. The music of his voice prevented the great volume of sound from jarring upon the ears of his audience. Unshed tears were in it, and a plea for peace permeated every tone. Every graceful gesture seemed to invite to brotherly love. His manner suggested that of one who parts from his family, because even death were better than estrangement.[37]

Varina sat pale-faced and still, taking in every word, watching every flicker cross her husband's face. Her concentration became so deep that soon she was almost unconscious of her surroundings. He spoke of Calhoun and nullification, but secession "belonged to a different class of remedies," and was to be justified on the basis that the states were sovereign.

In parting he hoped for peaceable relations. The reverse would bring disaster on every portion of the country, but "if you will have it thus, we will invoke the God of our fathers, who delivered us from the power of the lion, to protect us from the ravages of the bear," he promised. Then he made his formal adieux.

I am sure I feel no hostility toward you, Senators from the North. I am sure there is not one of you, whatever sharp discussion there may have been between us, to whom I cannot now say, in the presence of my God, I wish you well.

I go hence unencumbered by the remembrance of any injury received, and having discharged the duty of making the only reparation in my power for any injury offered . . . it only remains for me to bid you a final adieu.[38]

Varina later commented that he was "too grief-stricken and too terribly in earnest to think of the impression he might create upon others." She saw tears in the eyes of many. Of all the Senators who picked up their portfolios and walked out for all time—some, like Benjamin and

Slidell, weeping openly—the departure of Jefferson Davis had the most historic significance. He left the Senate chamber "inexpressibly sad, with but faint hope," according to Varina. They mourned in secret over the severance of friendly ties but a "cloud covered all the rest, and our hearts were exceedingly sorrowful even unto death; we could even guess at the end." [39] He was desperately upset that night, not jubilant, as Varina had been pictured on the night South Carolina seceded. She could hear him praying, she wrote, now that his course was set: "May God have us in His holy keeping, and grant that before it is too late peaceful councils may prevail."

They did not leave Washington at once. Varina packed up her things and made the rounds saying good-by to her many friends. Her husband wrote to Franklin Pierce on January 20, 1861, that saying good-by to Caleb Cushing "seemed like taking a last leave of a brother." He continued: "Civil War has only horror for me, but whatever circumstances demand shall be met as a duty and I trust be so discharged that you will not be ashamed of our former connection or cease to be my friend. . . . When Lincoln comes in he will have but to continue in the path of his predecessor to inaugurate a civil war. . . ." [40]

At this point Varina viewed her husband as nothing less than a martyr. There were others who looked at him as the disrupter of a house of many mansions. As the planters' coaches went rumbling off to the South, laden with the fine trappings of their luxurious existence, the Davises made a quiet and unostentatious departure but were greeted at many stops as they traveled South. Before Davis reached home he was appointed by the Convention of Mississippi commander-in-chief of the army, with the rank of major general. He was returning to his homeland to prepare for what he predicted would be "a long and severe struggle."

BIRTH OF THE CONFEDERACY

VARINA bears witness to the fact that she and her husband were working in their garden at Brierfield when a messenger arrived with the telegram that was to change the course of their lives and start them on their journey to lasting fame and sorrow. A Glory of France rosebush stood close to their front door, and the legend quickly spread that they were making cuttings from it when Jefferson Davis learned that he had been chosen to head the Confederate States of America.

He was taken by surprise. Varina watched him lay down his shears, read the telegram, and turn pale. "He looked so grieved that I feared some evil had befallen our family," she noted. "After a few minutes' painful silence he told me, as a man might speak of a sentence of death. As he neither desired nor expected the position, he was more deeply depressed than before." [1]

He went indoors to compose his reply while the messenger waited. Lee S. Daniel, manager of the telegraph office at Vicksburg, eighteen miles from Brierfield, had received the notification from Montgomery at five o'clock in the afternoon. Recognizing its importance, he sent a "discreet messenger with instructions to speed the distance; deliver the document, await reply and return without loss of time." [2] The office was held open, and Davis's acceptance arrived by midnight, along with a personal note of thanks for the swift delivery. It was flashed to Montgomery and soon became national news.

A different version of the notification is given by Lise Mitchell, who remembered her grandfather Joseph going over to Brierfield with Eliza and a delegation of men to persuade Jefferson to accept the presidency.[3] It is her recollection that he was not feeling well and had gone to bed, and that when Eliza went to his room he sat up, raised his hands above his head and exclaimed, "O God spare me this responsibility," then added, "I would love to head the army."

It seems likely that the telegram arrived first and the delegation followed, but Varina was never in any doubt that her husband would have preferred to head the army. The news implied an immediate upheaval in their lives. The melancholy vein in which she wrote thirty years later of his election may well have reflected her tragic knowledge of the years between, but she knew from the start that her family would be at the heart of a great storm. Yet she must have felt some momentary elation, for she was seen on the gallery of their home that evening with the prayer book in her hands, reciting the sanctus: "Holy, Holy, Holy, Lord God of Hosts, Heaven and earth are full of Thy Glory: Glory be to Thee, O Lord Most High." [4]

Varina was deeply conscious of her husband's chronic ill health and at the moment she viewed him as an exhausted man, worn out by the long and tiring sessions in the Senate, by the impassioned debates on slavery, and the climax of secession itself. She had hoped to see him regain his strength at Brierfield, where his horses, his land, his garden, and the familiar duties of the plantation might ease the tensions that bound him. But in spite of her written protestations that he had not expected office, both must inevitably have been prepared for almost any contingency at this point. Davis's departure from the Senate had been more than an empty gesture, and hot rebellion churned through all the seceding states. Years later he pointed out that the mere fact that he had not gone straight from Washington to Montgomery showed conclusively that he had no thought of office in mind. [5] By instinct and training he was a soldier, and since war was in the air it took him some time to accept the picture of himself as chief of state in the South's hour of crisis.

Varina rose quickly to the emergency, however mixed her feelings were about the public role her husband now would have to fill. The first necessity was to speed him on his way, and then to settle plantation affairs. She packed his things and stood by his side as he bade an affectionate farewell to the Negroes, who had been summoned by bell for this occasion. Isaiah Montgomery rowed him through the underbrush to catch the river boat at the landing, but they were late starting, and Tom P. Leathers, captain of the *Natchez*, who had been watching for the President-elect, took him aboard in midstream. [6] By this time it was known throughout the South that he had been chosen to head the Confederacy and a gun salute welcomed them to Vicksburg.

Varina was to follow later with the children. She selected a few of her favorite pieces to ship, for she had acquired fine furniture and many objects of art during her years in the capital. She arranged her books, silver, and china and shed some tears over the general closing up of Brierfield and the abandonment of "all we had watched over for years." Of all her possessions she found it most difficult to give up the library of "fine and well-chosen books" that she and Jefferson had assembled.

For the next few days she watched for every scrap of news on his trip to Montgomery. Word of his triumphal progress traveled back slowly to Brierfield. There were salutations and bonfires at various stops. Garlands were strung and bands played. School children cheered the new head of the Confederacy. Some of his public statements appeared in garbled form in the North and distressed him greatly. They represented him as invoking war and threatening devastation. But when he met William L. Sharkey, an old Whig friend who had been chief justice of Mississippi, he predicted war "long and bloody . . . it behooved everyone to put his house in order." [7]

Great crowds were massed in front of the portico on the February day in 1861 on which Davis drove up the hill to the stately Capitol at Montgomery in a carriage drawn by six horses. The pageant that day was of unique interest historically—the inauguration of the first and only President of the Confederate States of America. Delegations had come from all the states involved and people poured in from the surrounding countryside. The balconies and windows were jammed with belles in flounced silks who threw bunches of flowers toward the Davis carriage.

Mrs. Eleanor Noyes Jackson, a Bostonian married to a native of Montgomery, made the wreath of crimson japonicas, hyacinths, and small spring magnolias, which the President swung over his arm. [8] She noted that the levee held that night was attended by "people from town, people from country, young and old . . . men in fine clothes and men in homespun suits, belles in silks with lace berthas, girls with pearls in their hair, girls hooded in woollen shawls." The brisk new tune called "Dixie" sounded on Southern ears with reassuring tempo. The houses were all illuminated and Bengal lights spurted through the quiet and lovely town whose eight thousand inhabitants had been augmented by an excited multitude.

"I thought it would have gratified you to have witnessed it, and have been a memory to our children," the newly elected President wrote to Varina on February 20, two days after the ceremonies, when he finally had a moment to himself.[9] He described the journey south, but through all the welcoming shouts he wished constantly "to have you all with me." There was no elation in his final paragraph:

. . Upon my weary heart was showered smiles, plaudits, and flowers; but, beyond them, I saw troubles and thorns innumerable.

We are without machinery, without means, and threatened by a powerful opposition; but I do not despond, and will not shrink from the task imposed upon me.

Varina read the accounts of his inaugural speech with some apprehension. He did not refer directly to slavery but spoke of the need for an army and navy, and observed: "Obstacles may retard, but they cannot long prevent the progress of a movement sanctified by its justice and sustained by a virtuous people." Robert Barnwell Rhett, who felt he should be standing in Davis's place and would fight him every inch of the way, welcomed him to Congress. William L. Yancey, another extremist, hailed him with the proud epigram: "The man and the hour have met." There was nothing but applause for him at this point except in the Northern press.

Varina traveled to New Orleans by river boat with Joseph. They had a long talk over family affairs, but she did not soften toward her brother-in-law. Too many bitter words had passed between them. Too many family conflicts were involved, particularly the ownership of Brierfield and Jefferson's will. These two strong personalities could find no common meeting ground, even now when Jefferson, the pivot of most of their arguments, had become a national figure in a moment of great emergency.

Military bands now played in New Orleans. Captain Charles D. Dreux brought his company to serenade Varina at her parents' home, where she stopped on her way to Montgomery. He mounted the balcony and showered her with immense bouquets of violets, but the color of the dewy blossoms in retrospect suggested only mourning to Varina. "Perhaps Mr. Davis's depression had communicated itself to me, and I could not rally or be buoyed up by the cheerfulness of those who were to battle for us," she wrote.[10]

Varina would next see the young Captain on his bier. He was one of the first to die on the Peninsula. She was amazed by the good cheer

and optimism she found on all sides, "knowing our needs to be so
many, with so little hope of supplying them." As she sailed up the
Alabama River to Montgomery young men talked to her enthusiastically
of the "general's sash" they hoped to win. Some thought her husband
"a little slow." War was in the air unmistakably but war had not yet
been declared.

She arrived in Montgomery on the March day on which Letitia Tyler,
granddaughter of President Tyler, ran up the Confederate flag on the
Capitol to a mild scattering of applause.[11] She joined her husband
at the Exchange Hotel in an atmosphere of torchon lace curtains, a
Brussels rug, a Turkish lounge, and white-globed chandeliers draped
with garlands of flowers. She gave a reception that night, and Mrs
Chesnut, who had just arrived with the South Carolina delegation,
noted: "It was crowded; too many men of note to attempt to name
them." [12]

Varina had already received her with warmth, but they did not
allude to their altered status since the carefree days when they exchanged calls in Washington. They avoided political talk and discussed
Thackeray instead. It had always been their habit to exchange notes
on the current books. Varina drove up the hilly streets to view her
prospective home with a keen eye for the newer porticoed houses
flanked by catalpa trees, and the older ones more simply framed in
honeysuckle. Montgomery was still in its youth. It was founded in 1819
and became the state capital in 1847. She approved the two-story house
enclosed by a garden that had been chosen as the Executive Mansion,
a graceful home that is re-created in Montgomery today as the First
White House of the Confederacy. It is suggestive of the Davis occupancy, from Varina's moss-rose china and the Lafayette bed to the
reproduction of her husband's bedroom on the ground floor. Before
her death she drew a diagram with everything arranged exactly as it
was when the Confederacy was in its infancy—Jeff's saber and walking
stick, his rocking chair and valise, his slippers and leather hatbox, his
night table with Bible, the bed with dark draperies, and the motto
over the mantelpiece stitched by Varina: "Thy Will be Done." [13]

When she saw what was needed she returned to Brierfield to bring
back furniture, close the house, and fetch her children.[14] On her second
arrival she was greeted with a seven-gun salute when she sailed in on
the *King* with her family, but the boat bringing her furniture arrived
too late for her first reception and she was much upset.[15] Her reputation

s a Washington hostess during a particularly lush decade had traveled
before her and there was much curiosity about the First Lady of the
Confederacy. She was thirty-five and looked her stateliest. Her life in
Washington had developed her from the uncertain girl who had arrived
at Brierfield in 1845 into an assured figure with poise, wit, and self-
confidence. As she stood at the door of her parlor for the first reception
in her official home her Negro butler announced the names of Alabama's leading families. She wore a "rich brocaded silk, with wide
flowing sleeves from which drooped delicate lace." Instead of the simple
center part and chignon that had been her hairdress for years, her
dark hair was now done in braids, *à la grecque*, and she wore long
earrings. She struck some of the guests as being unnecessarily formal
until Mrs. William Knox greeted her in motherly fashion, and Mrs.
Sophie Bibb, a local favorite, threw her arms around her and helped
to warm up the scene for Varina. Mrs. Clay, whom she had known
well in Washington, had come in from Huntsville to welcome her to
Alabama.

Varina's sister Maggie, now a permanent member of the family, was
present to help. She had developed into a handsome girl, generously
curved, with expressive features. She was fair like her father and was
less striking than Varina but quite as witty, and sometimes also as sharp.
She had attended a Quaker school in Washington and then Miss
Catherine L. Brooke's for the finishing touches. Margaret, Varina's oldest child, was now a dark-haired beauty of six. Jeff was four and Joseph
had turned two. The entire family was closely observed in Montgomery.
There was much interest in the group as they walked into church, the
president in black broadcloth with a stiffly pleated white shirt and
black string tie. He wore gloves and carried a silk hat. Varina's good
looks were observed as she knelt beside him, repeating the responses
clearly, her billowing silks half filling the pew, her sleek black hair
deftly dressed beneath a smart new bonnet. T. C. De Leon, watching
her from another pew, thought that she had a "smooth and comely
look." At the same time he observed that her husband was spare to the
point of emaciation, and his mouth was grim with tension.

Montgomery, on a smaller scale, closely reflected the scene in Washington around the Lincoln family. Varina, like Mary Todd Lincoln,
was on display, but the flames of criticism that eventually consumed
Mary did little more than singe the hardier Varina. Every move was
watched and her candid observations were quickly noted. She soon

became known as Queen Varina as one reception followed anothe
while the principals of a government in the making moved throug
her parlors. In the North, George Templeton Strong noted in his diar
that "Lord Davis (they have baptized a recently launched war-sco
or canoe the 'Lady Davis' in honor of Mrs. Jefferson Davis) means t
rule the people. That prince and his chivalric pals have no notion o
submitting constitutions to a popular vote. . . ." [16]

The war had not yet begun, but there was political pandemonium
every night in the lobbies of the Exchange Hotel and Montgomer
Hall, where the planters and cattlemen in calmer times forgathered
Montgomery's fixed population was momentarily obscured by the pic
turesque inrush of politicians assembled from all parts of the South
a new and clamorous element in the suddenly crowded town. The hill
streets were overrun with statesmen, lawyers, Congressmen, planter
and merchants. Politicians and office seekers besieged the new Presiden
"This blessed freedom to go straight to the top of the tree, if you ar
built for climbing," the skeptical Mrs. Chesnut observed, watchin
them clamber for office. But Varina, in her tactful *Memoir*, writte
thirty years later, ignored the pressures brought to bear on her husban
and the expediencies employed by some. She noted that "very fev
battled for rank; they were there for service." [17] She observed that th
Cabinet was chosen "not from the intimate friends of the Presiden
but from the men preferred by the States they represented; but
would have been difficult to find more honest, capable, fearless me
than they were."

Bit by bit the Confederacy took shape. The Cabinet was appointed
The new constitution was framed, with little deviation from the ol
The Confederate flag was designed—with some reluctance on the par
of Jefferson Davis, who thought it should be used only for battle pur
poses. Correspondents and sketch artists arrived to illumine a landmar
in American history. A strong searchlight beat on Montgomery, an
Varina learned what it was to move in its beams, at the heart of
newly created state, obviously on the brink of war.

She knew that much was expected of her socially. The visitin
politicians had brought their wives with them to Montgomery. Grea
hampers of flowers arrived regularly at her back door. The new fla
was composed for her with red and white roses on a field of larkspu
and rows of white jessamine stars. She was quickly confronted wit
heavy responsibilities and was sensitive to the tormenting problems tha

beset her husband. She made a point of being near at hand to talk things over when he needed her. His new responsibilities seemed at times to be more than he could bear, and Mrs. Chesnut made one thing clear: "Mrs. Davis does not like her husband being made President. People are hard to please. She says, 'General of all the Armies would have suited his temperament better.' Actually, she thought he would not succeed as a party leader, since 'he did not know the arts of the politician.' " [18]

However, Varina did not need any coaching for her own role. She was adept in all the current usages and a little scornful of mere social observance as such. It was difficult for her at times to hide her real feelings. She was more skeptical than her husband and viewed with some dismay the pressures being applied in the drawing rooms. She set a swift social pace, although she complained privately about the sparse markets of Montgomery after the abundance of Washington. She welcomed her guests with grace and intelligence and quickly established the tradition for hospitality that she had enjoyed in the national capital and would later create in Richmond. It was noted that she entertained in a formal and sophisticated way as levees, dinners, and luncheons drew in the visiting Confederates.

Things changed radically with the fall of Fort Sumter. This event had not been unexpected in the Davis home. The President's dispatch: "Nothing remains but to reduce Sumter before the Union Fleet arrives," had brought a tide of citizens to the Battery before the first shot was fired. Business was suspended. Shops were closed. Crowds gathered in front of the Charleston Hotel. Rooftops were peopled with anxious watchers. The houses shook when finally the cannon roared, after Edmund Ruffin had pulled the lanyard for the first shot of the war. Through a telescope women watched the shots fired at the fort. They saw the masonry crumble, the spurts of flame, the columns of smoke.[19] When the white flag showed, bells pealed and cannon proclaimed a victory. After all was quiet again Mrs. Chesnut rode along the Battery in an open carriage. "What a changed scene," she noted. "The very liveliest crowd I think I ever saw. Everybody talking at once, all glasses still turned on the grim old Fort." [20]

Varina has left her own spare record of the way in which the President received the news. His first expression was one of relief that blood had not been shed. "Separation is not yet of necessity final—there has been no blood spilled more precious than that of a mule," he said.[21]

He spoke regretfully of "Bob Anderson," his old West Point friend
But the war had indeed begun and human blood soon would be staining
the battlegrounds of Virginia.

The fall of Sumter quickened the pace of life at the Executiv
Mansion as reports poured in from South Carolina, where secession
had been hatched, and its sons swarmed into town to join the Palmetto
Guards. With spurs, sashes, sabers and gold lace, they paraded along
the Battery and drilled awkwardly in camp with drummers beating
calls and ruffles. Senators showed up in uniform alongside young lads
from the farms and plantations. So far as the South was concerned
the war had begun in Charleston.

Senator Wigfall soon arrived in Montgomery with the flashy tal
told in Varina's parlor and elsewhere of his own private capture o
Fort Sumter. There were many witnesses to the fact that he had sailed
up to the Fort in a small boat brandishing his handkerchief on the tip
of his saber while the fire still blazed. He had climbed through an
embrasure and demanded the surrender of Major Robert Anderson
When the official party arrived there was little further work to be done
He was much aggrieved by Major Anderson's more prosaic report of thi
affair.

Wigfall was born on a South Carolina plantation, although by thi
time he was identified with Texas. His wife was a Charleston gir
Charlotte Maria Cross, and they had two young daughters, Mar
Frances and Louise, better known as Luly, who later became Mr
D. Giraud Wright and wrote one of the more enlightening social diarie
of the war period. A brother, Major Halsey Wigfall, was in the army
They were a spectacular family, much commented on wherever the
appeared. Wigfall's derring-do at Fort Sumter was observed by Willian
Howard Russell, of *The Times* of London. He considered the Senato
a little the worse for wear when he pulled his coup. His powerfu
stature, wild masses of hair, and eyes reminding him of the "flashing
fierce, yet calm" [22] eyes of a Bengal tiger, impressed the visiting co
respondent. On the day President Davis proclaimed a state of wa
between the Confederacy and the United States, Senator Wigfall too
Russell to call on the Chief Executive. Later in the day the Englis
correspondent visited Varina, who soon was to christen him the "Stor
Bird of Battles" and regard him with some suspicion.

He described her home as a "modest villa" standing in a small garder
The door was open and a Negro servant ushered him in. He wa

presented to Varina by W. M. Browne, the President's British-born aide who had flourished as a journalist under Buchanan's patronage. So dimly lit was the parlor that Russell could scarcely distinguish Varina at first. She was surrounded by callers, the ladies in bonnets, the men in "morning dress à la midi." He found his hostess warm, friendly, unpretentious, and grave over the fact that the war had indeed begun.

There was no affectation of state or ceremony in the reception. Mrs. Davis, whom some of her friends call "Queen Varina," is a comely, sprightly woman, verging on matronhood, of good figure and manners, well-dressed, ladylike, and clever, and she seemed a great favorite with those around her. . . . Mrs. Davis, whom the President C.S. married *en secondes noces,* exercised considerable social influence in Washington, where I met many of her friends.[23]

Russell had been told by these same friends that "Varina Davis is a lady at all events, not like the other," the "other" being the unfortunate Mrs. Lincoln, whom he had already observed with sympathy at a White House dinner. He had promptly decided that she was more of a lady than he had been led to expect and as he watched her handling "a fan with much energy, displaying a round, well-proportioned arm" he had come to the conclusion that his Secessionist friends were in error about her supposed vulgarity. Now he studied her counterpart in the South with an experienced and calculating eye.

On the whole he was more impressed with Varina. He found her stirred up over a report that a reward had been offered in the North for "arch rebel Jeff Davis." She quickly observed, "They are quite capable, I believe, of such acts." But she soon turned to less personal talk. Varina did not underestimate the importance of British good will toward the Confederate States at this juncture, and she was well aware that the correspondent of *The Times* would mirror them all quite frankly. He was fervently wooed in the North and South until his realistic dispatches came back. By September the Lincolns would give him nothing more than a cold nod.

On the day that he met Varina, Russell also had a long talk with her husband. Used to the pomp of courts, he was surprised by the simplicity of Confederate headquarters. He found Mr. Davis in a box-like red brick building with whitewashed walls, and a plain sheet of paper on his door announcing simply: "The President." Visitors were coming and going freely. The President talked to him about Sebastopol, and the Siege of Lucknow before he was pinned down with journalistic insistence to the war just bursting into flame.

Russell thought he looked anxious, haggard, care-worn, and pain-drawn. He was relieved to find that he did not chew tobacco, a fashionable custom among the nation's legislators. He was struck by his cultivated air, his emaciation, and his erect carriage. With her strong sense of form Varina must have felt some surprise over having his attire described as a "rustic suit of slate-coloured stuff with a black silk handkerchief round his neck." It always interested her to read published comment on her husband and one may be sure that she studied Russell's appraisal of him with care. He wrote:

His manner is plain, and rather reserved and drastic; his head is well-formed, with a fine full forehead, square and high, covered with innumerable fine lines and wrinkles, features regular, though the check-bones are too high, and the jaws too hollow to be handsome; his lips are thin, flexible, and curved, the chin square, well-defined; the nose very regular, with wide nostrils; and the eyes deep set, large and full—one seems nearly blind, and is partly covered with a film, owing to excruciating attacks of neuralgia and tic.[24]

While Varina played the part that was expected of her socially as First Lady of the Confederacy, her deeper concern was for her husband and the preparations he was making for the long struggle ahead. The thorns he had foreseen were already beginning to prick him. He worked long hours and returned home "exhausted and silent." He ate little, and his sleep was disturbed by the gigantic problems that he faced, the decisions that had to be made. He was in no sense of the word a politician and the rapid-fire maneuvers of some of the men around him left him bewildered. He could find no way to harmonize the self-assertive forces that crowded him.

Varina freely expressed her own views of the men who circled around her husband and figured in his decisions. Toward the end of the war she was to write quite frankly: "I know you do not like my interfering. . . ."[25] but the process had already begun. She was more observant and skeptical of other men's motives than her husband, and a little more frank in condemning them. She argued strongly for her convictions and was never his echo. It was soon apparent to those around him that one did not discount Varina. She had mustered political strength of her own during her years in Washington and she now did what she could in the drawing room to reconcile discordant elements. She smoothed over many rough spots when her husband was too busy, too tired, or too ill, to meet his colleagues in social byplay. In time she was to create political problems for him, too, but for the moment she engaged in her new duties with all the zeal and devotion of her ardent nature. Most of her own feuds were whipped up out of her indignation over criticism of him. There were smoking embers here and there among the disappointed, and the wives inevitably became involved.

This was particularly true of the families of Toombs of Georgia and Wigfall of Texas, next only in importance to the Joseph E. Johnstons in the strength of their animosity to the Davises.[26] Mr. and Mrs. Toombs were among the few to have homes of their own in Montgomery, and Varina and Mrs. Toombs renewed their Washington acquaintance, although they quickly became bitter enemies and he was out of the Cabinet by July. He was one of the most forceful men in the group around the President—huge in build, exuberant, truculent, and eloquent. Like Alexander H. Stephens, he was a Whig from Georgia, but he was unlike him in all other ways. He rode, hunted, and lived in handsome style. He had been happily married since his admission to the bar in 1831. He liked good company and at their Washington mess Varina had found him fascinating.

Toombs was devoted to Stephens, who was Vice-President, but never the friend of Jefferson Davis. Stephens was a major problem from the start, a tense and obstructive personality. To Varina he seemed like a man "born out of season." [27] His head was "unpolished and immature." He was less short than he seemed, but was ill-proportioned, with long arms and a wrinkled, beardless face. He was a bachelor who avoided social contacts, a zealot in practice, fanatical in his views, and completely at odds with the President. But Varina, in appraising his qualities, conceded a "fine, critical deliberate expression" in his hazel eyes and "a virile mind sustained by an inflexible will."

She was soon to find her own particular friend and ally in the most subtle of the group—Judah P. Benjamin, who was asked to serve as Attorney General "because of his brilliant legal record." Another of her favorites was John H. Reagan, appointed Postmaster General "because of his sturdy honesty, his capacity for labor, and his acquaintance with the territory of the Southern States." A third to stay with her husband to the finish was Stephen R. Mallory, the genial and humorous

Secretary of the Navy, who owned a great orange grove in Florida and sent baskets of oranges to all his colleagues. He entertained handsomely with his Creole wife Angela, and their little daughter Ruby was a favorite with Varina and the other Confederate wives. His operations were scoffed at, but he began from scratch and built up a navy with ingenuity. Both Reagan and Mallory had been poor boys who had worked hard for their success.

C. G. Memminger, Secretary of the Treasury, and his wife stayed obstinately outside the social circle. He was a dour, methodical man of German birth, self-educated, who prowled around the streets in a tall beaver hat, peering at passers-by, haunting old bookshops for works on economics. His wife failed to call on Varina, the other ladies noted, and the Memmingers were regarded as social debits.

After the fall of Fort Sumter the business of creating a government was augmented by the much greater problem of raising, outfitting, and training an adequate army. Writing defensively in her *Memoir* of her husband's record in this respect, Varina maintained that "all that man could accomplish he did to equip our army and navy to meet the heavy odds with which they were confronted." She felt that his reputation suffered because his cause failed, arguing that "Junius would have made a sorry figure in the place of either Lords Mansfield or Chatham." She summarized the practical measures he took:

Nitre beds were established, manufactories of arms and powder were erected with marvellous celerity, old arms were altered, men were drilled and initiated in the arts of war; in fact, his activity was unceasing and his success abnormal.[28]

Varina appraised the manufacturing resources of the North as five hundred to one compared with those of the South. In addition, the workshops of the world were open to the North, while the South was blockaded. Her husband had asked for privateers as well as volunteers, and had dispatched agents to foreign countries to buy small arms, guns, and ships. For the time being he relied on the Tredegar Iron Works in Richmond for field artillery. Only Virginia and Tennessee, of the states in the Confederacy, had the all-essential blast furnaces when the war began.[29]

While all these moves were under way Varina coped with many small annoyances. Her husband received letters threatening assassination. Their house was comparatively unprotected with its small garden enclosure and they were all startled one night when an armed man peered into her husband's room. Davis accosted him, and he bolted.[30]

At times she could find some humor in their situation. "We are Presidents in embryo here, shorn of much of our fair proportions," she wrote to Clement Claiborne Clay on May 10. He was ill at his mountain home "Cosy Cot" near Huntsville, and had refused the Cabinet post of Secretary of War, but would be in the Confederate Senate by autumn. The market was forlorn, Varina complained, but she did her best and hoped to be spared some of the criticism she had heard in Washington of the "indifferent fare of the entertainers, because our guests eat with *l'entente cordiale,* which I now find exists out of diplomatic papers, & is not a myth."

She described her husband's state in detail and pictured him wearing out his Cabinet with his industry until they "fell like leaves in wintry weather" and went home "sans Scotch cap one at a time," a gibe at Abraham Lincoln. She found he was overworking himself and "all the rest of mankind," giving up only when no one remained with whom to work. He even begrudged time for his meals.

Mr. Davis seems just now only conscious of things left undone, and to ignore the much which has been achieved, consequently his time seems all taken up with the cabinet planning (I presume) future operations. . . . There is a good deal of talk here of his going to Richmond as commander of the forces. I hope it may be done for to him military command is a perfect system of Hygiene and unless Mr. Spinola is around somewhere I don't suppose there is much danger. . . . For my part the only preference I have is to be nearer Mr. Davis. . . .[31]

Varina was finding Montgomery uncomfortably warm and she dreaded the summer heat for the children. It was enervating for her, too, and although she thought the town a charming place and its people hospitable her patriotism seemed to ooze out at the pores, not unlike Bob Acres' courage, and "I have deliberately come to the conclusion that Roman matrons did up their chores, patriotism, and such like public duties in the winter," Varina jested.

She was devoted to Clement Clay, who had been kind during her husband's serious illness, but she was known to have had some serious quarrels with him, too. He was the godfather of her last child, and in this letter she dwelt on the children in detail. Joseph was as handsome as Maggie had been when small. It beguiled her when he planted his dirty little hands on either side of her face and kissed her. He was now talking sporadically. Jeff was "beaming, blustering, blooming, burly and blundering as ever." Little Maggie was "gentle & loving, and considerate," Varina finished. "She and I are good friends."

A warm friendship was now developing between her and Mrs. Chesnut, whom she had known only slightly in Washington. At this time Mary Chesnut started the spirited diary that lights up obliquely the principal figures of the Confederacy. She had ample opportunity to observe Varina during the war years, for her husband was in turn a provisional member of the Confederate Senate, an aide to General Beauregard at Fort Sumter, a liaison officer between the White House and South Carolina, and, toward the close of the war, a brigadier general functioning in his native state.

Some of the most penetrating and, possibly, the most accurate observations on Varina came from Mrs. Chesnut. Although she showed her at odd angles from time to time she was uniformly friendly and loyal to the President's wife and championed her as long as she lived. She was Varina's most intimate Southern friend and at the same time maintained social exchanges with Mrs. Johnston and Mrs. Wigfall, taking an ironic interest in the fierce feud that developed between Varina and these one-time friends. In a sense Mrs. Chesnut was a catalyst for the hostile elements that soon enveloped the President's wife. She could laugh where Varina raged.

It was natural that their paths should run together. They had much in common. Both were intellectuals, good talkers, voracious readers. Both aired their knowledge rather freely, sometimes to the embarrassment of the less informed. Both were shrewd in their appraisal of people and had a caustic wit. Both "matronized" the young belles of the era and their cavaliers in from the battlefields. They were excellent company themselves for men who enjoyed discussion with attractive and brainy women. They had an instinct for hearty living and had zest for the parties and social interchange that evoked much criticism during the war. Varina, however, was the more practical of the two. She had grown up on simpler fare than the pampered Mrs. Chesnut. Her approach to life was more serious.

Varina seemed restless and worried when she went out driving with her. She missed her Washington friends and found "playing Mrs. President of this small Confederacy slow work," Mrs. Chesnut observed revealingly on May 19. "I do not blame her. The wrench has been

awful for us all. But we don't mean to be turned into pillars of salt." [32]
When she lunched with her the following day, however, she found
her in the best of spirits, a "charming hostess, kind, clever and
hospitable. . . . When she is in the mood, I do not know so pleasant a
person. She is awfully clever, always."

By degrees she accustomed herself to Varina's mercurial shifts of
mood, and to the light jests that often concealed her deeper emotions.
With some skepticism she watched her hemming dish towels after
lunch on this occasion. She had still to learn how versatile Varina
could be. After the next dinner party at the White House she observed
of her host and hostess, "She is as witty as he is wise."

Varina held weekly receptions and one of her Northern friends, Mrs.
Eugene McLean, who was General Edwin V. Sumner's daughter, noted
that she saw little to distinguish them from the "anterevolutionary
gatherings.

No homespuns as yet, though the more enthusiastic talk of adopting
them, and I suppose they will when everything becoming is exhausted. The
atmosphere of Montgomery is certainly much less warlike than that of
Richmond, or any other place I have been in, nor do people seem to be
half so much in earnest. . . .[33]

Mrs. McLean had just arrived. Her husband, a Marylander, had had
a difficult time choosing between North and South, and her own sympathies were strongly with the North. She drove around town with
Varina and admired the new capital. She quickly learned that the
President's wife was being criticized for saying quite openly that she
had no personal feeling against her Northern friends. In fact, she liked
to talk about them and took great interest in their welfare. Mrs.
McLean believed that this was tactless under the circumstances.
Varina's own observations were being used against her and "already
jealousies have crept into our model republic, and some, of old standing,
have been imported with congress and other respectable institutions."

Actually, Varina was criticized for spending so much time with Mrs.
McLean, and her Southern friends soon were noting that some of the
observations of General Sumner's daughter had a seditionist ring to
them. But Varina kept up their friendship right through the war. She
found Mrs. McLean clever and bookish, an irresistible combination in
her women friends. Moreover, she was grateful to General Sumner for
his kindness to her husband during his severe illness with his eyes. Mrs.

Chesnut admired Mrs. McLean's talents but she could not accept her as a sincere ally. Mrs. Joseph Johnston frankly distrusted her.

By the end of May, Virginia had seceded and the Federal Army moved into Alexandria and set up headquarters at Fairfax County Courthouse. The Confederate Congress settled on Richmond as the new seat of government, and Jefferson Davis left Montgomery quietly, traveling as unostentatiously as possible in the rear coach of an ordinary train. Varina testifies to the fact that he had worked himself into a state of prostration and left Montgomery in collapse. He was welcomed to Richmond with a salute of fifteen guns. The Spotswood Hotel, where he stayed, was draped with Confederate flags. Familiar faces surrounded him. Many were fresh from Washington. The new alignments in some cases were startling.

A week later Varina traveled with her children to Richmond through flowering countryside. The grass was uncommonly green after heavy rains. The land was rich with corn in the tassel. Blackberries were ripening on their bushes. The peonies were in bloom and verbena scented the air. But for once she was unconscious of the beauties of nature in her intensified scrutiny of the men gathering from farms and plantations, from towns, hamlets, and lonely bayous. They seemed to be of all degrees and ages, and she noted that the "country was alive with soldiers—men in butternut trousers with gray homespun coats and epaulets of yellow cotton fringe." She was touched when several companies of soldiers waiting for transportation serenaded her party at different stations.

They were easily recognized as the President's family. Although not beautiful, Varina at this time was a distinguished-looking woman who would be noticeable in any company. Already the children were known to the public. The soldiers studied their bright young faces with curiosity, and the children in turn were fascinated by the bands, the sabers, the uniforms. There were signs of a curiously mixed army. Men from the seceding states were pouring into Richmond, with strong regional inflections and assorted attire, some with new equipment, others with nothing but the will to fight. The rich young planters were heading in from their distant estates, with servants, fine clothes, and blooded horses. Their sabers, boots, and spurs were brightly polished, but many of these same young men would soon be in homespun, too. In Varina's own words: "The fury of the North was met by a cyclone of patriotic enthusiasm that swept up from the South." [34] War was still largely drilling, the rattle of drums, and clouds of dust rising from the wheels of artillery wagons. The customarily decorous streets were brisk with marching companies and uniforms as yet unstained with grime. Manassas would be fought before tears would flow. Varina saw that she had come to a city aflame with patriotic effort when she reached Richmond on a June day in 1861. The President met her with a carriage and four, and driving through the streets to the Spotswood Hotel he stopped their equipage to jump out and pick up a little bouquet of flowers for Varina that a child had tossed with faulty aim.[35]

The social and official round began all over again for her at the Spotswood, where they were quartered by the city until the new Executive Mansion was ready for use. As in Montgomery, men of talent, skill, and soldierly address, as well as maneuvering politicians, swarmed around the President. The play for position was under way and already the generals were at loggerheads. In June, General Chesnut wrote to his wife from General Beauregard's headquarters that "our generals have not a very high opinion of the efficiency of the Administration, especially the War Department."

In summer muslins, fashioned by Mrs. Keckley, Varina drove behind magnificent bays to witness the parades and cavalry displays at the Champs de Mars. Tents were pitched at the Fair Grounds, while new regiments filed into Jackson Park and the women of Richmond drove out regularly to watch the strange new maneuvers of war. Many youths who had gone to Northern colleges were in these early regiments. Their parents had summered at the Northern spas and their fathers had been eloquent in Congress. Being Southerners, they made good cavalrymen because they had always ridden. They were expert with sabers, too, because of their heritage. Graduates of West Point and the Virginia Military Institute put the young initiates through their paces, and President Davis, with General Robert E. Lee of Virginia, rode out regularly to watch them train. None could appraise the scene more expertly.

"It was a grand tableau out there," Mrs. Chesnut reported after a cavalry display at the end of June. "Mr. Davis rode a beautiful gray horse. His worst enemy will allow that he is a consummate rider, graceful and easy in the saddle."

The night before, Mrs. Chesnut, who had been invited by Varina to share their table at the Spotswood, had annoyed the President by repeating a story that North Carolina had twenty thousand men ready for action who were being held back by Leroy Pope Walker, the Secretary of War. "Madame, when you see that person, tell him that his statement is false," said the President coldly. "We are too anxious here for troops to refuse a single man who offers himself, not to speak of twenty thousand men." [36]

Mrs. Chesnut, who was wedged between Joseph Davis, the President's nephew, and Browne, his aide, looked anxiously at Varina, but her usually voluble friend did not come to her aid. "Silence prevailed," she observed. "Now when I take my seat, my grace is a prayer to God that I may not put my mouth in at the wrong place or time."

Both Varina and Mrs. Chesnut were impetuous talkers, but Varina had a stronger sense of caution than her friend, who wrote and said exactly what she thought. Time and the many bitter experiences that lay ahead of her would chasten Varina, but Mrs. Chesnut remained spontaneous to the end. She was one of a number of women observing Mrs. Davis at close range during the war years who would later write diaries with intimate observations on her conduct at this time. These included her contemporaries, Mrs. Clay and Mrs. Pryor; and two young girls, Constance Cary and Louise Wigfall, who were part of the evolving picture. Mrs. Clay as yet was neutral. Mrs. Chesnut was her protagonist all the way through. Mrs. Pryor was courteous but not genuinely friendly to Varina. She was as absorbed in her husband's progress as Varina was in the President's, and she never felt that Roger received his due from Jefferson Davis.

Mrs. Pryor was the daughter of the Rev. Samuel Blair Rice, a chaplain in the Confederate Army. At the age of eighteen she had married Roger, who came from the vicinity of Petersburg and did journalistic work. They were a conspicuous pair at social gatherings. Roger had flowing locks that he tossed back as he spoke, and he liked to make fine speeches. Mrs. Pryor had a distinctive way of doing her hair—Grecian and quite effective with her pale, classically cut features. She chose to follow her husband from point to point during his army career and at one stage camped with him in the Blackwater region. Now she was momentarily happy when Roger received promotion while the presidential party was still at the Spotswood Hotel. Varina dragged him out from behind the plants to make a speech.

"What are you doing lying there *perdu* behind the geraniums?" she demanded briskly of the newly appointed General. "Come out and take your honors." [37]

While the Davises were at the Spotswood a steady flow of celebrities surrounded the worried-looking chieftain and his vivacious wife. Visitors arrived from all quarters to see what the Confederacy was doing. On July 4 Prince de Polignac, a small fiery figure with waxed mustaches and keen black eyes, dined with them and tried to ingratiate himself with Varina. Prince Jerome Napoleon paid her the first of many calls. There was growing anxiety in Richmond about the stand that Britain and France would take in the war.

The weather was uncomfortably hot in July, and many of Varina's friends scattered. Mrs. Pryor took her boys to The Oaks, the home of her uncle, Dr. Izard Bacon Rice, who had a tobacco plantation seventy miles from Richmond. Mrs. Chesnut sparkled at Fauquier White Sulphur Springs, where some of the South Carolinian politicians were enjoying the waters, "which were making them feel young again." It would be some time before this group of sophisticates would gather at a spa again, or have any particular reason to feel young or lighthearted. The war was now about to begin in earnest.

❦ 8 ❦

WOMEN OF MANASSAS

TEN women whose men were in the field waited with Varina for news of the battle of Manassas. It was her lot to tell the wife of the Mayor of Savannah, who commanded a Georgia regiment, that her husband was dead. Mrs. Francis C. Bartow was resting on her bed in the Spotswood Hotel when Varina knocked at her door. When she saw who it was she sat up, ready to spring to her feet, but something in Mrs. Davis's compassionate face stopped her. She sank back and covered her face with her shawl.

"Is it bad news for me?" she asked.

Varina was silent.

"Is he killed?"

Mrs. Bartow later told Mrs. Chesnut that she needed no further word. As soon as she saw Mrs. Davis's face she knew.[1]

They had all been anxiously awaiting news, moving from one room to another. On the previous night they had sat up until one in the morning in Mrs. John S. Preston's room "screaming together like a flock of chickens that a hawk had scared." Both Varina and Lydia Johnston seemed to be in good spirits, which cheered the others, since their husbands were so deeply involved. But none of the women knew exactly what was happening. Neither did the people of Richmond, for that matter, nor even the Cabinet members.

On July 16, before the battle, when they had all dined together at the Spotswood, Mrs. Chesnut observed that the President looked extremely ill and Varina seemed much troubled. Mrs. McLean, Mrs. Johnston, and Mrs. Wigfall all were fluttering around, and the feeling prevailed that something was brewing. On the 19th the President telegraphed General Johnston to move to Beauregard's aid at Manassas. Lawrence Keitt had come in with reports of General Milledge L. Bonham's early skirmishing.

They soon learned that his operations entailed more than a skirmish, and Davis set off for Manassas without letting Wigfall, his aide, know anything of his movements. Apparently Varina, too, was left in the dark, beyond knowing that her husband had gone to the field of battle. Major General Irvin McDowell had marched toward Manassas, and General Beauregard, forewarned of his movements by Mrs. Rose O'Neal Greenhow, functioning in Washington as a Confederate spy, met him in a major engagement. But in Richmond all was doubt and uncertainty as the battle proceeded. Mrs. McLean, who passed these hours with Varina, later recalled:

The day dawned quietly, calmly, beautifully. Although we knew Mr. Davis had gone to Manassas Junction, we never suspected the object, but enjoyed the day as one of rest. . . . I remarked to Mrs. Davis and Mrs. Johnston, who were in the carriage, that the people in the streets looked excited and I thought there must be some news, but they laughed at my nervous fancies, and I was somewhat reassured by Mrs. Davis saying that we would certainly know if there was any news of importance.[2]

From this it would seem that Varina and her friends knew even less of what was going on than the townspeople, or else Varina was being discreet. Finally the President's wife asked a passer-by if he had any news, and he told her that there had been fighting at Manassas since six o'clock that morning. They all rushed back to the hotel, to exchange notes. One of the ten women involved had a husband, two sons, a brother, and brother-in-law in the engagement. After a wait of three hours Varina received a telegram from her husband which brought relief to some, but told of the death of Bartow and others.

Mrs. Chesnut had gone to bed, feeling quite ill, when the message arrived. Varina entered her room quietly and leaned over her, whispering that a great battle had been fought. "Your husband is all right," she assured her friend. "Wade Hampton is wounded. Colonel Johnson of the Legion is killed and so are Colonel Bee and Colonel Bartow. Kirby-Smith is wounded or killed."

For once Mrs. Chesnut was speechless and Varina went on in a desperately calm way, "Bartow was rallying his men, leading them into the hottest of the fight. He died gallantly at the head of his regiment. The President telegraphs me only that 'it is a great victory. . . .'"

At this point they all decided that Varina should be the one to break the news to Mrs. Bartow, who had been a sprightly figure among them earlier that day, wearing a white muslin apron with pink bows on the pockets. She was the daughter of Judge Berrien, and she and her husband both were very popular.

The Cabinet members, assembled at the War Department to await news, soon shared in Varina's message through Judah Benjamin. As dispatches came in he hurried over to the Spotswood to see her and returned with the President's telegram. Some of the local editors were in the group and they asked J. B. Jones, a new clerk in the War Department, for a copy of the dispatch. He made a diary entry on July 21, 1861, that read:

Mr. Benjamin said he could repeat it from memory, which he did, and I wrote it down for the press. Then joy ruled the hour! The city seemed lifted up, and every one appeared to walk on air. Mr. Hunter's face grew shorter; Mr. Reagan's eyes subsided into their natural size; and Mr. Benjamin's glowed something like Daniel Webster's after taking a pint of brandy.[3]

In Jones, a new observer had arrived on the scene who would make sharp comments on the Davises and follow Benjamin's course with relentless venom. He was Southern-born and was editing the *Southern Monitor* in Philadelphia when war broke out. Fearing imprisonment, he traveled south and deliberately chose the War Department rather than the Treasury as a better field for the diary he planned to keep.

The war had now reached Richmond in the most intimate way. The dead and wounded were brought in. All the earlier preparations took focus in a burst of nursing and solicitous care. Homes were opened freely to the wounded. The funeral dirges that were to depress the city for four years had begun. They would now go on without end. Mrs. Bartow fainted when her husband's body was borne past the hotel. She could not look at his war horse with its empty saddle.

Soon Davis returned from the battlefield, quietly satisfied with the victory, but distressed because a series of delays had kept him from reaching the scene until the fighting was over. Colonel Chesnut had arrived with fresh details. Fantastic tales were told in Richmond of the scattered army and the cavalcade of celebrities who had set out from Washington as if bound for a festival, and had rushed back in confusion. Davis made a speech at the Spotswood, using one of his more memorable phrases as a warning against overconfidence: "Never be haughty to the humble, or humble to the haughty." Jones, ever at hand, added, "Never heard I more hearty cheering. Everyone believed our banners would wave in the streets of Washington in a few days. . . ."

A thanksgiving service was held in St. Paul's the following Sunday, and Varina, who was to have a baby within three months' time, sat with the President in their customary pew near the center of the church. Congress had declared a general thanksgiving for an important victory. The first round had been won by the Confederate Army. The President shared his prayer book with four-year-old Jeff, quietly guiding him through the chants, which he was still too young to read but could repeat after his father.[4] For the first time bandages and plasters appeared in abundance in the pews. Arms were in slings, legs were bandaged and there were many bound-up heads.

A new air of gravity had settled on the soldiers. Before long the two commanding generals of Manassas, Beauregard and Johnston, were headed into serious controversy with their President. A storm of criticism blew up over their failure to pursue the enemy after the battle, and a breach was created that affected the entire course of the war so brilliantly begun under adverse conditions.

Madame Beauregard was in New Orleans far from the immediate scene, but Lydia Johnston and Varina reflected every move made by their husbands, and some thought helped to whip up the angry waves. Both women adored their husbands; neither one could stand a word of criticism where Jeff and Joe were concerned. Both expressed themselves freely, although Varina was always the more potent in debate. Her quarrels with other women in the official set were mild compared with the bruising feud that now developed between her and her old friend Lydia. They smothered it intermittently for the sake of appearances and were seen driving and visiting together, but it smoldered and broke out in ways that embarrassed their husbands. In her intimate correspondence with Mrs. Wigfall, Lydia's animosity is painfully evident, although it centered more on Jefferson Davis than on Varina, and pointed back to their Washington days before the long wrangle developed after Manassas. She had advised her husband not to join Davis in Montgomery. "He hates, you, he has power and he will ruin you," she warned him.[5]

Mrs. Wigfall was involved by this time too, since her husband was one of the loudest critics of the President. He particularly deplored the fact that the victory had not been pushed through to a finish. There was great coolness after Varina, who sometimes served as her husband's courier around the hotel, went hunting one day for Wigfall. The President wanted to see his aide. Mrs. Wigfall was insisting that he was in camp with his regiment when he appeared inopportunely in her room. Mrs. Chesnut, who was helping Varina in her quest, made a diary note: "Mr. Davis and Wigfall would be friends if . . . if . . ." [6] clearly suggesting that their wives were at fault.

But shortly after this encounter the Wigfalls and the Davises patched up their differences, and Charlotte gave Varina a Chinese Mandarin scroll as a peace offering. An official ceremony involving the Texas Rangers was scheduled, and Varina wished to preserve face for her husband's sake. They all went to the Fair Grounds to watch the presentation of the flag to the regiment. Mrs. Wigfall drove with Mrs. Chesnut, flying the Lone Star flag from their carriage. Varina's landau rolled along in front of them. The President and Colonel Chesnut galloped past on horseback with a friendly salute. They were too far away to hear the presentation speech but had a good view of the exhausting workout the energetic Wigfall gave his men. The temperature was in the nineties, and they went smartly through their paces with perspiration pouring down their cheeks. General Toombs was thrown from his horse, which dragged him up to the wheels of the wives' carriages. He hung on to the bridle, with one foot clinging to the stirrup. His purple face, upturned, betrayed more anger than alarm. But he pulled himself up in his saddle and rode off, rumpled and choleric.

In the middle of the review Mrs. Wigfall received word that her two young daughters were safely across the lines. They had been visiting her sister in Connecticut. Varina promptly invited them to spend the night at the Executive Mansion. She rarely held a grudge and, knowing the violence of her own moods, often regretted her impetuosity and tempered the storm.

But the Wigfalls continued to gibe at the Davises and Charlotte Wigfall remarked that Howell Cobb, Governor James H. Hammond, Lawrence Keitt, and other South Carolinians and Georgians were in a coalition against Davis, and that Clay alone was his friend. There was never any real warmth between them again. Mrs. Toombs was equally anti-Davis, and by the end of August would not even concede that the President was ill, when he was so reported. "All humbug," she snapped. By this time her husband had resigned his Cabinet post to become a brigadier-general and R. M. T. Hunter was the new Secretary of State.

Mrs. Toombs was equally scornful of Varina's first reception in her new home, the Brockenbrough mansion, into which they moved early in August. She remarked that even Mrs. Reagan could have done better. Since Mrs. Reagan's social vistas were thought by the other women to be limited, this was a direct slur on Varina's hospitality.

But these were trivialities in the enveloping waves of criticism that now surrounded the President. The question of food and supplies for the army was debated back and forth with great anxiety. Colonel Lucius Bellinger Northrop, the Commissary General, a West Point man who was thought to be a pet of Davis's, was held accountable for everything that went wrong with the army. The President defended him at every turn. The accepted explanation for the failure to push on at Manassas was the lack of food, wagons, and ammunition at the crucial moment. The women around Varina chattered over the message Mrs. Chesnut received from one of her Washington friends that the Confederates could have walked into the Northern capital any day for a week after the battle, such was the state of consternation and confusion there.

Varina was hurt and angry by the middle of August when the full weight of the attacks on her husband began to dawn on her. The arrows grew in number and hit hard. She had seen a dispatch in the New York *Tribune* from Augusta, Georgia, saying: "Cobb is our man. Davis is at heart a constructionist." The Charleston *Mercury* was pounding hard, because Rhett had been passed over in favor of Jefferson Davis. Mrs. Chesnut made a pact with Mrs. Preston at this time to defend the presidential family under all circumstances.

There were many pinpricks as well as major points of attack. Another of Varina's critics was Mrs. A. C. Myers, wife of the Quartermaster General, who was much older than his wife and heartily disliked the social round. She was extremely beautiful. Even Varina, who disliked her, said there was something about her eyes "which dazes even unimpressionable me." [7] She was a New Orleans belle, the daughter of General David E. Twiggs.

Mrs. Myers became as popular in Richmond as she had been at Willard's in Washington. She danced beautifully; she was young and gay; and she caused a sensation at the camps and among the men lounging in the Spotswood lobby. Mrs. Pryor noted that she had not been there long before she became aware of a "bitter feud existing between Varina, Mrs. Johnston and Mrs. Myers." As she viewed it: "Jealousy and consequent heartburning had possessed the bosom of these ladies—do they not intrude into every court and camp? And here were court and camp merged into one." [8]

In a careless moment Mrs. Myers had remarked on Varina's girth, an observation that touched off an explosion in Richmond and was reported to have had long-drawn-out repercussions in official circles and to have caused the eventual displacement of her husband. Since Varina was pregnant at the time some indignation was felt on her behalf. By this time Lydia Johnston and Charlotte Wigfall were calling her a "coarse Western woman" instead of the "Western belle" she had earlier been to them. Varina did not particularly like being described by one of the newspapers as portly and middle-aged at the age of thirty-five, but she was sensible enough to accept a tiresome fact. However, she resented this kind of talk from the inner circle of her own court.

There was no denying the fact that she had become quite statuesque. Because of her height she carried her weight with dignity and, like Mrs. Lincoln, wore her low décolletages becomingly. Governor Robert F. W. Allston, of South Carolina, reported to his wife after calling on Varina in the summer of 1861, that "Mrs. Davis has not lost any flesh since you saw her and is as animated as ever. She moves about, receives and talks, as in a triumph, and is strong in having her countrywomen about her as a sort of court." [9]

But all the members of Varina's court were up in arms when the whisper went round that her retainers were not young or pretty but ran to red frocks and "flats" on their heads, a contemporary insult in the millinery world.[10] Mrs. Chesnut ran the author of this observation to earth and delightedly reported to Varina that she wore gaudy colors and dressed badly, that she was covered with freckles, wore a wig held in place by a tiara of mock jewelry, and that her fat wrists were encased in black jet bracelets. That settled the argument forever.

Varina's wardrobe gave her little concern, then or at any other time in her life. She wore her clothes with some distinction, saw to it that the materials were good, the laces real, and the cut reasonably in the mode. She had become slightly more responsive to fashion in Washington, but she was not one of the Southern belles famous for the richness and variety of their Paris clothes, like Mrs. Clay and Mrs. Chesnut. Mrs. Keckley had sent her south with a fresh summer wardrobe. Some Godey fashion sheets dated 1861 in the Confederate Museum in Richmond today suggest that she was not wholly indifferent to the latest mode.

Her sister, Maggie, young and of marriageable age, was a factor in Varina's calculations when it came to dress. Moreover, Varina had a strong sense of dignity and would not make a hasty appearance in the public rooms until she had completed a complicated toilette, with corsets, careful coiffure, and all the impedimenta of the era. She estimated once that it took her an hour to dress and do her hair. She was fond of heavy white silk dresses and of fine laces. In fact, in spite of the legends of pretentiousness that grew up around Varina, she was fundamentally sincere and natural. No one ever questioned her authority. Lydia Johnston bitterly recalled toward the end of the war that she had carried everything before her in Richmond. But she was far from being immune to the gossip that buzzed around her ears. She was sharply criticized for sending a baby's dress to Mrs. Montgomery Blair, whose son, Gist, was born in 1860. But Minna was reported to have responded, "Even if the men kill one another, we will abide friends to the bitter end, the grave."[11]

Another of Varina's most discussed gaffes involved Mrs. Bradley T. Johnson, who had been successful in rounding up clothing and equipment for the regiment of Marylanders raised by her husband. Dining with the Davises, she told disconsolately of the mistake that had been made when the volunteer seamstresses, cutting out underpants for the soldiers, snipped them all for the right leg only. Now more material would have to be supplied and the work done all over again. Everyone at the table was politely sympathetic, but Varina thought the incident uproariously funny, and she laughed without restraint. She had forthright manners and a hearty ringing laugh when genuinely amused. But it was no joking matter to Mrs. Johnson, and most of the spectators thought that the President's wife had been needlessly callous.

Varina was never free from scrutiny and Lieutenant Colonel William Willis Blackford caught a curious flash of her at a street crossing soon after he arrived in Richmond with a company to join Colonel J. E. B. Stuart's First Regiment of Viriginia Cavalry. He was walking along, unconscious that the woman ahead of him was the President's wife, when she suddenly "burst into a fury of invective" at a groom mounted on a "beautiful, blooded horse." The youth was "fretting and jerking it" to make it prance. She made him dismount and lead the horse away. Blackford soon learned that he had been watching Mrs. Davis and that the groom and horse belonged to the President's stables.[12] Varina's tempers did indeed blow up like summer storms and sometimes reached the same tempestuous proportions.

As stories of this kind spread through Richmond, the First Lady of the Confederacy was watched with some reserve. She was conscious of a deep chill where she had expected cordiality. The established population of Richmond had received the Davis family with cool appraisal from the start. Regional passions boiled around them and the military problems were pressing. Varina, used to the expansive manners of Mississippi and Louisiana, had not counted on this barrier of ice. Busy with relief work, preparing their men for war, the women of Richmond surveyed her from the ramparts of their native conservatism and gave her what she later defined as an English welcome—cool, aloof, astringent. The old guard did not freely open their homes to her at first, although she later made excellent friends among them. For the most part her intimates were the temporary visitors from other Confederate states.

Varina was perceptive enough to make allowance for this reception when she came to write her *Memoir* three decades later. She pointed out that in the more southern and less thickly settled part of the country frontier hospitality prevailed, whereas in Virginia, where the distances were not so great, and the candidates for entertainment were more numerous, "it was of necessity more restricted." Obviously, she was realistic in this appraisal, although she felt the sting of her situation at the time. She brought some of it on herself by her outspoken habit and her sarcasm. Her sense of humor was not benign; it bit and was remembered. But she belatedly paid tribute to the women of Richmond in tactful phrases.

. . . I was impressed by the simplicity and sincerity of their manners, their beauty, and the absence of the gloze acquired by association in the merely "fashionable society." They felt the dignity attached to personally conducting their households in the best and most economical manner, cared little for fashionable small-talk, but were full of enthusiasm for their own people, and considered wisely and answered clearly any practical question which would tend to promote the good of their families or their country. . . .[13]

Although the contemporary social diaries give a somewhat frivolous and trivial view of what went on against the growing clouds of darkness, actually Varina functioned with steadiness as her usual forceful and effective self. She was vigorous, busy, viewing her role as one of social importance in which she must support the President in a new scene of operations. However much she leaned to social display and gregarious living, she viewed him as the pivot of her day's activities. She watched and comforted him during a period of great anxiety and fierce attack, and won the respect of most of the men around him.

In her new home Varina set up a smoothly running ménage. She directed her servants, kept a close eye on her children, went frequently to the Champs de Mars, and to the hospitals with comforts for the soldiers. Before long she was recognized as a strong factor in the Confederate hierarchy. She had established herself as a person in her own right. In her journal Lise Mitchell pictured the Davises intimately in their private life during these early days in Richmond. A family group had arrived from The Hurricane—Eliza, Mary Jane Brodhead, and another niece, Helen Keary, who spent much of her time at camp with her husband. Joseph appeared briefly but did not linger under Varina's roof. However, she was kind to Eliza. While still at the Spotswood, she insisted on rooms being found for the family party there, in spite of all the crowding.

When she moved into the Executive Mansion she took them all with her. The Davis family sense was overpoweringly strong. Varina made them welcome and little Lise watched her with fascination as she arranged things in her new home according to her liking and established a corps of servants. She made intimate notes on the demeanor of the President and his wife.

Every evening Uncle Jeff and Aunt Varina had their reception where we met many charming people. When there were young ladies and gentlemen among the callers Maggie, Mary and I left the rest of the family to do the honors and retired to Aunt Varina's boudoir or to the beautiful porch where we could talk and laugh without annoying the rest of the company. In the afternoons we generally rode or walked for exercise and pleasure. We had met some old acquaintances among the soldiers in the city and once or twice paid a visit to their camp.[14]

But by August 10, when Jeff was under heavy newspaper attack, Eliza noticed that he was quite unwell. She had never seen a person so sadly changed. He rarely smiled and had not spoken to her except at table to hand her something, although she sat next to him. He looked as thin as Sister Lucinda and much like her. "His hair is cut close. He has so many callers he cannot take his meals in peace. Varina is at times cheerful and then again depressed."[15] But Eliza noted that she was always agreeable to the girls. She considered the house comfortable and the housekeeping troublesome, as it was difficult to get suitable servants. The Richmond prices seemed exorbitant to Eliza.

Varina engaged Miss Augusta (Gussie) Daniel, daughter of Judge Raleigh T. Daniel, to teach her children. Their laughter rang through the house. Like the Lincoln boys, little Jeff went wild with guns. They romped in the garden and kept up a merry din on the second floor. In time visiting generals and Cabinet officers became as familiar with the Davis children as Seward, Chase, and Stanton were with the Lincoln boys. Since the children's nursery adjoined the President's study, General Lee, Jeb Stuart, Judah Benjamin, Louis Wigfall, John Breckinridge, and other Confederate figures leaned over the cradle of the baby born to Varina during her first year in the Executive Mansion. Wigfall told of going to the Davis home and finding Jeff flat on his back on the floor with the children romping over him. The older ones enjoyed the excitement, the coming and going of smart young cavalry officers, the couriers who came galloping up to the door, the din made by the bands, the bugle blasts, the large parties given by their mother with the guests chattering and moving like shadows in the garden on hot summer nights. Jeff often rode with his father, and they all said their prayers at his knee when he was at home at their bedtime.

Varina enjoyed her new home, which today is one of the Confederate show places, with authentic echoes and relics of the Davis family. The graceful, three-storied dwelling standing on high ground was designed by Robert Mills, a South Carolinian architect who had studied with Thomas Jefferson. It was built by Dr. John Brockenbrough in 1816-18. Its brick walls were covered with pale gray stucco when the Davises took occupancy, and it was sometimes known as the Gray House. Its windows looked down on Shockoe Creek, and Varina often paused in passing to look at the peaceful vista of small farms and orchards stretching toward the swamps of the Chickahominy. To the East the James River flowed toward Drewry's Bluff and Dutch Gap.

She was charmed by the high-ceilinged rooms, the full-length windows opening on a piazza and garden at the rear, and the magnificent Carrara marble mantelpieces, which were missing for eighty years after the war but were ultimately returned to their old setting. Her children often played games involving the Greek figures on the carved pilasters. The garden had cherry, apple, and pear trees, as well as flowers. It sloped down the hill in a series of terraces, and Varina was constantly reminded by Richmond visitors of the days when the house was perfection itself, with Mary Brockenbrough walking in the garden "singing among the flowers." Her image became legendary with the Davises and she remained the "titular goddess of the garden." [16] When the President complimented Varina on some new arrangement in her drawing room she would playfully ask, "Would Mary approve?" This was a reflection of Varina's feeling of being an outsider, but, independent in all her ways, she did not let it distract her. She arranged things as she wished, and on June 18, 1903, three years before her death, she recalled in a letter the use to which the various rooms were put during their occupancy. She wrote specifically to deny a charge that spies had operated from the house.

The basement of the mansion was occupied and used as breakfast room, and children's dining room, the second story as bedrooms and one of which Mr. Davis used as a private office when he was too unwell to go to his public office. It adjoined our bedroom on one side and our children's nursery on the other. No one was received there except particular friends, the generals; the senators and members of Congress and people having such claims. . . . The upper story was occupied by the staff and the housekeeper. . . . Mr. Davis was not in the third story of the mansion more than three or four times in all the years he lived there, and then he was there because I had gone there for quiet in illness.[17]

Varina made her home a place of comfort and beauty. She never hesitated to string the knickknacks of battle given her by soldier friends beside the Meissen vases on her mantelpiece. She gave fortnightly levees in the early days of the war and was at home informally every evening of the week. At this time she was never inaccessible, but she tried to protect her husband from intrusion whenever possible. However, she thought it good for him to unbend for an hour a day in his home. She forced the issue, and he finally told her that he could do either one thing or the other—attend entertainments or administer the government—"and he fancied he was expected to perform the latter service in preference," Varina noted.

So she cut down sharply on her hospitality, confining it to formal receptions, or informal dinners and breakfasts given for as many persons as her husband felt he could see at one time. The *Examiner* promptly read parsimony into this new arrangement, but Varina became used to being called wildly extravagant in her entertainments by one faction and meanly austere by another. Her own view of it was characteristic.

It would have been much better if the President could have met the Congress, and the State officials as well as the citizens, socially and often, for the magnetism of his personality would have greatly mollified their resentments; but for years his physician had forbidden him to go at all into society in Washington, and he found this disability greater in Richmond, proportionately to the burden he bore.[18]

Perhaps better than anyone Varina understood her husband's reluctance to mingle more freely with people during these anxious and busy days. But she supplemented his efforts wherever she could on the social front. At the same time she unwittingly created difficulties for him by the very vigor of her defense. De Leon considered her levees "*social jambalaya*" [19] because of their mixed character, but they were also novel and animated, with a military band usually on hand in the early days. At first Varina's fortnightly receptions for soldiers and civilians were regarded with suspicion and were somewhat snubbed. But soon Richmond's leading citizens might be seen at the Executive Mansion, not always approving, but at least paying their respects, De Leon noted.[20] Some went merely to criticize, as Washingtonians did with the Lincolns. Varina, however, could stand up more sturdily to the social barrage of disapproval, since she had no uncertainties about herself and her nervous system was now in balance. She was not unduly extravagant. She did not run her husband into debt. She did not overdress, but she insisted on punctuality, good form, good manners, good food, as long as it was to be had, and all honor paid to her husband.

De Leon commented on the "really elegant women" in Varina's drawing room at this time and the mingling of butternut with the stars and yellow sashes of many a general in process of becoming world-famous. "The private of today might be the general of tomorrow, and the younger leaders in Richmond realized the fact, and early learned to judge their new beaux rather for themselves than for their rank marks," he observed.

The insignia of the various regiments was now quite distinguishable as more equipment was forthcoming. The Louisiana Zouaves and the Texas Rangers were easy to identify and very welcome at the Executive Mansion. Varina quickly spotted the proud young planters from her own region who had left their inland empires to sail down the Mississippi and don uniform. She welcomed them as youths from home. She saw that they met the belles and that they had relaxation between stanzas of drill and fighting.

After watching this social interchange, and seeing some of the Richmond women soften to it, and others harden against it, De Leon, who was close to the Davises and fond of them, wrote of Varina:

She was naturally a frank though not a blunt woman, and her bent was to kindliness and charity. Sharp tongue she had, when set that way and the need came to use it; and her wide knowledge of people and things sometimes made that use dangerous to offenders. Mrs. Davis had a sense of humor painfully acute, and the unfitness of things provoked laughter with her rather than rage. That the silly tales of her sowing dissension in the cabinet and behind the too frequent changes in the heads of the government are false, there seems small reason to doubt.[21]

Aside from Varina's court, the tempo of social life was greatly hastened in Richmond. There were dinners, dances, receptions, naval reviews, flag ceremonies, and parades. The young went in for picnics, hay rides, and excursions down the James, and there was much flirting on the piazza of the Spotswood, as well as in less conspicuous places. Flowers were tossed at passing soldiers. Handkerchiefs fluttered endlessly, waving farewell.

Ships were named after Varina. The Lady Davis kitten bivouacked with a Kentucky regiment and was finally buried with three volleys over its grave.[22] There was the Varina camp for prisoners. The Davises were showered with gifts. Henry A. Wise gave the President two fine horses. A private added bridle bits and spurs. An old lady in Mississippi knitted him socks for Christmas. A soldier gave him a set of chessmen carved by himself.[23]

Life in Richmond became more vivid and disorderly by the day. The normal population of forty thousand persons swelled rapidly to a final score of one hundred and forty thousand. This influx obscured the quiet habits of the residents and created its own particular bedlam. The small group of watchmen assigned to keep order were overrun by the riffraff who poured into the city along with the soldiers. Gamblers and pickpockets abounded. Garroting became a popular wartime sideline. Rows of white tents dotted the countryside surrounding Richmond. Bugles blew from the heights of Chimborazo, and the fields rustled with life. The soldiers now trained with a note of urgency, and the bands played the "Dead March" in *Saul*, along with "Dixie" and "The Manassas Polka." The arsenals and blast furnaces roared through the night. A scarlet glare rose from "smutty forges and blackened shop." [24] Down in the valley at the Tredegar Iron Works dark forms moved against a background of flame, with showers of sparks surrounding them.

Although Richmond had some of the aspects of a country fair at this time, behind the walled gardens and the gleaming windowpanes of the Southern capital, women quietly sewed and knitted, and went forth to the camps and hospitals. Typhoid fever had broken out in the camps. Money, clothing, nurses all were desperately needed. In August many were visiting the battlefield of Manassas, plowing ankle deep through the mud of the red clay roads. The trampled grass was already showing signs of fresh life. Yellow flowers were pushing up around the graves. Fences lay flat. The underbrush was speckled with shot. Dead horses and bloodstained blankets lay in grisly confusion. Spiked guns, wrecked gun carriages, and cannon balls abounded.[25]

All through September and October the President was in the midst of heavy squalls. He was still being condemned for the failure to follow up the attack after Manassas. In the middle of September, General Johnston was dumfounded to learn that he was rated number four instead of number one in the official War Department list of five ranking officers of the Confederate Army, which now read: Samuel Cooper, Albert Sidney Johnston, Robert E. Lee, Joseph E. Johnston, and P. G. T. Beauregard. He thought a "studied indignity" had been offered him.[26]

He immediately wrote a long letter of protest which the President brushed off with a five-line answer, saying its language was unusual, its arguments one-sided, and its insinuations as unfounded as they were unbecoming. Varina was quickly heard from, writing to her husband, who was out of town. She regretted that General Johnston should feel annoyed, "as he was a friend and his wife was very dear to me." Davis pointed out to Varina that General Johnston "does not remember that he did not leave the United States to enter the Confederate States Army, but that he entered the Army of Virginia, where he was subordinate to Lee."

Johnston was a man who expressed his views frankly. Lee and Benjamin were more diplomatic with the sometimes testy President. The General was immensely popular with his men and was well liked in Virginia. He was small, keen-looking, with a pointed beard and a wide forehead. His manners could be engaging, although he had a quick temper, too. He was generally recognized as a highly trained, intelligent, and skilful commander, but, like McClellan, he was to become as famous for strategic delays as for victory. By this time General Scott was out of office in the North and McClellan was in command.

That autumn, in the midst of all the uproar, Johnston sent Richard Taylor, Zachary Taylor's son, to see the President, so that he might explain his views and urge their adoption. Varina welcomed him at the Executive Mansion. He was one of her favorites, an engaging person with good manners and much common sense. "My mission met with no success; but in discharging it, I was made aware of the estrangement growing up between these eminent persons, which subsequently became 'the spring of woes unnumbered,' " he wrote.[27] He did his best to remove the cloud then "no greater than a man's hand," but failed, although both men listened to him attentively.

While the discord with General Johnston on the appointment question was a matter of common talk, the Davises picked up their copy of the Richmond *Whig* and found a startling item—a synopsis of General Beauregard's report on the Battle of Manassas. The General immediately denied having authorized the publication of the report, but it was interpreted as an attack on General Johnston and the President. Soon it was a three-cornered fight with Benjamin deeply involved. By the end of his first year Davis found himself in much the same situation as Abraham Lincoln—with Cabinet officers jockeying for power; with generals wrangling among themselves; with all the new problems of a nation unprepared; with men to train, with arms to raise, with supplies to provide.

Varina, close to the date of her confinement, was much troubled by these events. Her husband became ill under all the pressures, and on September 30 the *Examiner* announced that he would rest at the farm of Adolph Dill on the Brook turnpike close to the city, but this was promptly corrected the following day with the note that he had not felt better in the past six months. There was always considerable disparity between the official announcements about the President's health and Jones's morbid notations, which sometimes suggested that he was close to death. Varina seems to have thrown up a protective screen around him when he was unable to meet officials, but he usually continued his work in his home, where she helped him with his papers.

He left the city at this time and headed for Fairfax Courthouse where he met both Beauregard and Stonewall Jackson. On October 2 he wrote to Varina that he felt quite well, although he had ridden many miles visiting encampments. He would put in another day of surveillance and then return to Richmond. There had been some misunderstanding about the selection of a house for him, but General Beauregard had taken him to his quarters. "The condition here is not as good as I expected, and the position has nothing except its comfort to recommend it," he wrote. He added the usual affectionate message for his family. "Hourly I think of you and the children. . . . Kiss the children for me, give my love to all the family and take to yourself Benjamin's portion."[28]

At the same time Stonewall Jackson wrote to his wife, Mary Anna, whom he usually called "my precious pet" or "little one," of Jefferson Davis's visit to their camp. He knew nothing in advance of his arrival and was quite surprised to see him drive up in an ambulance, with the men cheering him along the way. Next day he watched him review the troops and noted that he looked thin, but did not seem as feeble as on the previous day. "His voice and manners are very mild," Stonewall wrote. "I saw no exhibition of that fire which I had supposed him to possess." [29] Although Jackson was anxious for a command at the time, the President left without giving him any inkling of his prospects.

Jackson was less communicative with his young wife than Davis was with Varina. She paid him a few visits at different camps but when she asked for military details, he told her that it was "unmilitary and unlike an officer to write news respecting one's post." But he took her over the battlefield of Manassas in an ambulance and explained the strategy to her. Although she knew most of the generals' wives, Varina was not to meet Mrs. Jackson until long after the war ended. But she became familiar with many tales of Stonewall's affection for his wife.

During her husband's absence Varina received another shock from the Richmond *Whig*. By this time she was apprehensive about picking up the daily papers. On September 30 it published a front-page two column letter addressed to Mrs. Davis, Mrs. Wigfall, and Mrs. T N. Waul. It was signed "Caxton" and was written from Texas Camp The writer implored these three to assume the roles of Madame Roland of Madame de Staël, or Charlotte Corday, to rout out abuses in the Quartermaster General's Department.[30]

He praised the President but cited a long list of grievances and asked that the "brandy headed public robbers be thrown out of office in favor of wounded men who would do their work much better." The various bureaus, he wrote, were manned by incompetent striplings whose only claim to favor lay in a "remote connection with a lady of some honorable gentleman having a seat in the State Legislature."

Varina was in the news again four days later when she and Lydia Johnston, driving near Adolph Dill's farm, had a carriage accident. The horses' harness gave way and their carriage fell into a deep gully. The Richmond *Dispatch* reported that "both ladies were greatly shocked and sustained some cuts." [31] Lydia's arm was broken. The incident was dangerous for Varina, since her baby was almost due to be born. From this report, it is clear that these two wives still kept up a semblance of friendliness while the chill between their husbands deepened.

October was a bitter month for the Davises. The Charleston *Mercury* kept tearing away at the President and taunting his government. The *Courier* gave away the secret of the wooden guns of Manassas, disclosing a weak chink in the Confederacy. The Northern papers made gleeful use of all the dissension in the South, although Lincoln was facing the same sort of thing in Washington, and Mrs. Lincoln was faring worse than Varina.

Mrs. Chesnut pined and fretted at Camden. Her parents-in-law did not approve of her because she had not borne a child to carry on the Chesnut name. She envied Varina, who by this time had given birth to her fourth son—William Howell Davis, named after her father. In Richmond the President's wife, with her strong maternal feeling, felt that life was rich indeed, in spite of hostile influences. She was never so happy as when she had a new infant in her arms.

DISASTERS MULTIPLY

H OW I wish I were the wife of a dry goods clerk," Varina wrote to
Mrs. Chesnut from Richmond on April 27, 1862, as she suffered
over the losses and defeats of that spring, and the waves of criticism that
almost engulfed her family. "Then we could dine in peace on a mutton
scrag at three and take an airing on Sunday in a little buggy with no
back, drawn by a one-eyed horse at fifty cents an hour. The Yankees or
no Yankees, we might abide here or there, or anywhere in cheap
lodgings." [1]

The military disasters were crushing and the Davis family seemed to
symbolize Confederate defeat. Varina's only personal consolations at
this time were the improvement in her husband's health, although he
was "much chagrined at our troubles, and very anxious for the future—
though hopeful," and little Billy, whom she found "really pretty and
good" as she tucked him up in a quilt made by Mrs. George Washington
at Mount Vernon in 1804. [2] But the military outlook dismayed Varina.

I live in a kind of maze; disaster follows disaster—guns—power—numbers
fail. There is nothing seems to do its appointed work. There is nothing like
it—except Hood's old maid who went to sea. . . . I am forcibly reminded
of the Shaking Prairies in Louisiana where if one only will keep still the
Earth melts and the water swallows the intruder up. There seems nothing
certain underfoot. This dreadful way of living from hour to hour depresses
me more than I can say.

Things had been crashing around them since the beginning of the
year. There was little cheer at the official inauguration in February,
which was held in a downpour of rain. All the principals were in depressed spirits. Many of the officers had leave to witness the ceremony

which changed the government of the Confederate States from provisional to permanent status. Varina found her husband on his knees in prayer "for the divine support I need so sorely" before he left for the Capitol.[3] She was embarrassed to find that her own carriage was escorted by four men, wearing black suits and white gloves, walking two by two at either side. She asked her coachman what it meant. He reminded her that she had told him to arrange everything as it should be done, and this was the procedure for funerals and other big events. Varina dismissed her escort and proceeded with less pomp. She was already under fire for having pretentious ways and using liveried servants.

She was struck by the size of the crowd and the panorama of umbrellas, black, brown, green, and blue, mushrooming in Capitol Square. The rain came down relentlessly and Bishop John Johns was soaked as he stood on the temporary platform beside the President, close to the bronze equestrian statue of George Washington. An awning gave them scant protection. Varina felt that her husband's speech was "characterized by great dignity, united with much feeling and grace." But she was moved when he flung out his arms at the end with the exclamation: "To Thee, O God! I trustingly commit myself, and prayerfully invoke Thy blessing on my country and its cause." As he kissed the Bible a shout went up. Varina turned away quickly, later recalling in her *Memoir*:

> As he stood pale and emaciated, dedicating himself to the service of the Confederacy, evidently forgetful of everything but his sacred oath, he seemed to me a willing victim going to his funeral pyre, and the idea so affected me that making some excuse I regained my carriage and went home.[4]

As she left she could hear applause and shouts of "God Bless our President." But Varina went home in a despondent mood, feeling there was little cause to rejoice. However, by evening she had regained her composure and gave one of her larger receptions, receiving her guests with tact and warmth, and trying to muster up some laughter among them with a droll version of her pallbearer escort earlier in the day. Jones thought it a "lugubrious reception." Few were expected, since the rain still came down in torrents but soon the "crowd came . . . and filled the ample rooms." Some observers found the President stiff and ill at ease that night, but Jones considered him calm and "Mrs. Davis seemed in spirits." [5]

The weight of personal tragedy or anxiety by this time nagged at nearly every woman present. Varina was fully alive to her own vulnerable position, to the criticism that beat constantly upon her, and the cabal that worked against her husband; to the problems of his generals and the pressures of the politicians; to the invective of the Richmond and Charleston papers. To all malcontents "the blighter's hand was the President's," she commented. No one knew better than she how deeply hurt he was. She had reasoned him many times out of his melancholy.

He was abnormally sensitive to disapprobation, even a child's disapproval discomposed him. He felt how much he was misunderstood, and the sense of mortification and injustice gave him a repellent manner. It was because of his supersensitive temperament and the acute suffering it caused him to be misunderstood, I had deprecated his assuming the civil administration. . . .[6]

The formal inauguration was scoffed at in the North. "Bogus Confederacy," said the Cincinnati *Daily Gazette* in headlines. "Hypocritical and Blasphemous Inauguration of Davis." [7] Disasters now crowded one upon another. Fort Henry and Fort Donelson had fallen. Newbern in North Carolina was in enemy hands. In March the *Monitor* had worsted the *Merrimac*, or the *Virginia*, as it was known in the South. A few days earlier, on March 4, Varina had tried to put her heart into the baptismal ceremony for little Billy at the Executive Mansion. The leading generals were absent on this occasion. There was much business afoot. But she had written a conciliatory note to Mrs. Wigfall: "If you have any interest in seeing the boy christened, I will be happy to see you & the General at the house at 2½ o'clock today." [8]

On the Western front Shiloh, fought in April, spread deep mourning throughout the South and brought its own personal sorrow to the Davises in the death of Albert Sidney Johnston. A Minié ball severed an artery in his leg and he bled to death. The General's friendship with Jefferson Davis since their West Point days "had grown and strengthened, and knew neither decay nor end," his son, William Preston Johnston, wrote of these two soldiers.[9] Davis felt that he "excelled all the men he had ever known in consistency of conduct and in equanimity and decisiveness." Varina saw that her husband was deeply depressed as well as greatly angered by the disaster at Shiloh, and Beauregard was further in disgrace. "The cause could have spared a whole state better than that great soldier," Davis remarked. Years later he wrote to Northrop that Beauregard was two miles behind the lines when Johnston died.[10]

The next sharp blow was the fall of New Orleans, an event so unexpected that Varina could scarcely credit it. Her sister Maggie had gone there for safety and to be with her parents. Her father for the time being was working as a naval agent. With amazement she learned of the forts surrendering after five days of bombardment by Admiral David G. Farragut; of the wharves and cotton being burned as the Yankees took possession; of the Negroes rolling bales to the river's edge and throwing them into the Mississippi; of the gutters running with liquor from the abandoned grog shops.[11] This was homeland to Varina and she followed developments with breathless incredulity. Meanwhile, Richmond was under martial law as spring flooded the gardens with blossoms and tender greens. McClellan's tents were pitched along the Chickahominy. His trenches fanned out with mathematical precision, and the feeling of uneasiness deepened in Richmond.

By this time George W. Randolph, who was wholeheartedly behind General Joseph E. Johnston, had succeeded the unpopular Benjamin in the War Department. Benjamin had assumed the less controversial portfolio of Secretary of State. Thirty-five years later Varina disclosed in a letter to Francis Lawley, son of Lord Wenlock and correspondent of the London *Times* at the time of the war, that her husband had given him the other appointment "with a personal and aggrieved sense of the injustice done to the man who had become his friend and right hand." [12] The talk had been that he would be out of office altogether, but she testified to her husband's dependence on Benjamin, who was "calm and cheerful, capable and industrious." Their *rapprochement* had come gradually, but it was lasting, and Varina unquestionably had a large share in cementing this friendship. Although detached from the War Department, Benjamin continued to wield genuine power in the inner circle.

In May, Richmond was threatened with naval attack. Yorktown, Williamsburg, and Norfolk, with its important naval yards, were lost. McClellan was almost within sight of the spires of Richmond. Evacuation was quietly discussed. The more important archives were packed. A train was kept in readiness to convey the treasury out of town. Artillery and musketry could be heard rattling in the hills beyond the city, and some journeyed out to listen to this grim cacophony. Congress adjourned and the feeling of crisis was widespread. The President seemed to Jones to be "looking thin and haggard," and it was whispered in official circles that he was about to be confirmed in the Episcopal Church. He came of Baptist stock, but Varina had been anxious to bring him officially into her own denomination. She had urged Dr. Charles Minnegerode to visit him and persuade him to take this step. "He met me more than half way," commented Dr. Minnegerode. "From that day, so far as I know and judge, he never looked back." [13]

He and Bishop Johns officiated when Davis and his chief of ordnance, Josiah Gorgas, were baptized together at the Executive Mansion and confirmed in St. Paul's. "A peace which passed understanding seemed to settle in his heart, after the ceremony," Varina commented. "His religious convictions had long occupied his thoughts, and the joy of being received into the Church seemed to pervade his soul." This was done on the eve of her departure for Raleigh, and it gave her great comfort. All her life she was a churchgoer and turned to prayer in moments of crisis. She and Jefferson studied and read the Bible as they did their favorite classics, and their children were carefully drilled in religious observance.

She gave a reception on May 9, having already promised her husband that she would leave the city within three days with the children, "to relieve him from unnecessary anxiety." But her departure was hastened by enemy operations. While she was entertaining, a courier arrived with an urgent message. This was a commonplace at the Executive Mansion but her husband, coming quietly into the drawing room, whispered to her, "The enemy's gun-boats are ascending the river." [14] When the guests left, Davis told Varina that she must leave with the children next day, although he had some hope that the progress of the gunboats would be blocked. "Always averse to flight, I entreated him to grant a little delay, but he was firm, and I communicated the news to the family," Varina wrote. She left for Raleigh in the morning and soon others flocked to the North Carolina town. This was a needless hegira, for Richmond would weather many months of siege.

Varina settled her family at the Yarborough House, where her baby soon became desperately ill. She watched anxiously for her husband's letters, which came with regularity, and were so calm and intimate that the transition from peace to battle could scarcely be detected in their tenor. As usual, they were warm with family affection and were filled with longing for her presence. On May 13 he described a trip to General Johnston's headquarters on the previous day. The General was out, but the distance he had ridden was so great that he decided to remain over and return next day to Richmond. As usual, he commented on military affairs.

The Army is reported in fine spirits and condition. If the withdrawal from the Peninsula and Norfolk had been with due preparation and a desirable deliberation, I should be more sanguine of a successful defence of this city. Various causes have delayed the obstructions and the armament of the covering fort, whilst the hasty evacuation of the defences below and the destruction of the *Virginia* hastens the coming of the enemies' gun-boats.

I know not what to expect when our many failures are to be remembered, yet will try to make a successful resistance and if it were the first attempt, would expect to sink the enemy's boats.[15]

Ending on the personal note, Davis wrote of the loneliness of their home without her, even though some aides and relatives were with him.

I have no attraction to draw me from my office now and home is no longer a locality. Those who stay behind have double pain in parting from the loved of earth. To them everything brings remembrance of the loss. . . . Kiss my dear children, may God preserve you and them for happier days, and lives of love for each other and usefulness to the country. . . . I am here interrupted and with a deep prayer for my own Winnie I close this hasty scrawl,

Your Husband.

Three days later, on May 16, a day of fasting and prayer in Richmond, he wrote again, telling of his trip down the James and of the elation of the garrison that the gunboats had gone.[16] The emergency was over for the time being. The momentary panic had subsided. There was increasing confidence and a show of resolution to see the city destroyed rather than surrendered, but "these talkers have little idea of what scenes would follow the battering of rows of brick houses." Then, addressing himself to Varina in the more personal vein he continued:

Be of good cheer and continue to hope that God will in due time deliver us from the hands of our enemies and "sanctify to us our deepest distress." As the clouds grow darker, and when one after another of those who are trusted are detected in secret hostility, I feel like mustering clans were in me, and that cramping fetters had fallen from my limbs. . . . I have no political wish beyond the success of our cause, no personal desire but to be relieved from further connection with office; opposition in any form can only disturb me insomuch as it may endanger the public welfare. . . . I wish I could learn to let people alone who snap at me, in forebearance and charity to turn away as well from the cats as the snakes.

And on a thin sheet of blue paper, painfully inked in a moment of stress and now to be found in the Confederate Museum in Richmond, he wrote on this same date: "Good night, dear wife, may every consolation be yours until it shall be our fortune again to be united. Ever affectionately remembered when waking, sleep brings you to me in such reality that it would be happier to sleep on."

On May 19 he wrote that General Johnston had brought his army back to the outskirts of Richmond and he had been waiting all day for him to communicate his plans. "The enemy has pushed out their pickets and have found out his movements while concealing their own. We are uncertain of everything except that a battle must be near at hand. Kiss my dear children, tell them to love one another and to be good always." [17] He signed himself "Farewell dear wife, Ever Devotedly, Your Husband."

On May 28 he wrote that they were "steadily developing" for a great battle and "under God's favor I trust for a decisive victory." [18] Well aware of the sorrow that was coming to many homes he wrote:

The enemy are preparing to concentrate and advance by regular approaches. We must attack him in motion, and trust to the valor of our troops for success. It saddens me to feel how many a mother, wife and child will be made to grieve, but what is there worse than submission to such brutal tyranny as now holds sway over New Orleans. . . . God bless and protect you all.

In the Valley of the Shenandoah, Stonewall Jackson rode to success between May 9 and June 8, wiping out some of the sting of earlier defeats and easing the strain on Richmond at a time when Davis felt he faced evacuation. His dark, heavy beard and tired eyes, his rough-hewn outlines, big cavalry boots, and religious fervor, the lemons he sucked as Davis smoked his cigar, as well as his brilliant generalship, were making an impression on the public. Varina caught the echoes in North Carolina and wrote to her husband congratulating him on Jackson's success. He replied on May 31, thanking her courteously, but adding: "Had the movement been made when I first proposed it, the

William Burr Howell, father of
Mrs. Jefferson Davis

Mrs. William Burr Howell, mother
of Mrs. Jefferson Davis

(Courtesy, Mrs. John W. Stewart, great-granddaughter of Mrs. Davis)

Varina Anne Banks Howell as a young girl (Courtesy, Mrs. Marguerite M. Murphy, custodian of Beauvoir, Jefferson Davis Shrine at Biloxi)

Judge George Winchester, New England scholar and Varina's girlhood tutor, one of the major influences in her life (Courtesy, Mrs. John W. Stewart)

Margaret Graham Howell, Varina's
sister and companion in Richmond

William Francis Howell, Varina's
older brother

Becket Kempe Howell, Varina's
younger brother.

Jefferson Davis Howell, Varina's
brother, known as Jeffy D., whom
she and Jefferson Davis adopted.

(Courtesy, Mrs. John W. Stewart)

The Briers at Natchez, where Varina spent her girlhood and where she married Jefferson Davis

The room at The Briers where Varina and Jefferson Davis were married

(Courtesy, Mrs. William Winans Wall, present owner of The Briers. Knabb-Lane Studio, Natchez)

Varina at eighteen, when she met
Jefferson Davis

Varina and Jefferson Davis shortly
after their marriage in 1845

(Courtesy, Mrs. John W. Stewart)

A favorite cameo bracelet of
Varina Davis

Varina's engagement ring, emerald
with diamonds in a gold setting

Varina's wedding jewelry, made of cut glass
in antique gold setting

Diamond and ruby pin and
pendant, a gift of the Daughters of the Confederacy

(Courtesy, Mrs. John W. Stewart)

Varina in her early thirties (Courtesy, Mrs. John W. Stewart)

Joseph Emory Davis, brother of Jefferson Davis (From the Walter L. Fleming papers, New York Public Library)

Mr. and Mrs. Jefferson Davis before the Civil War. Paintings attributed to Henry Byrd (L. W. Ramsey Collection, Frick Art Reference Library)

The Jefferson Davis children—Jefferson, Margaret, Winnie and Billy (Library of Congress)

Kate Davis Pulitzer (Mrs. Joseph Pulitzer), a cousin of Jefferson Davis (Courtesy, Mrs. John W. Stewart)

Mrs. Clement C. Clay of Alabama

Mrs. Mary Boykin Chesnut (Courtesy, David Williams, Camden, S.C., and Mrs. Hendrik B. Van Rensselaer of Summit, N.J.)

Lydia Johnston, wife of Gen. Joseph E. Johnston, first friend, then foe of Varina Davis (New York Public Library)

The first White House of the Confederacy, Montgomery, Ala. (New York Public Library)

White House of the Confederacy at Richmond, Va., now known as the Confederate Museum (New York Public Library)

Brierfield after the fall of Vicksburg, with the inscription left by the Union soldiers—"The House Jeff Built" (Courtesy Old Court House Museum, Vicksburg)

Varina as hostess at the Executive
Mansion of the Confederacy during
the Civil War (Courtesy, Confederate Museum, Richmond)

Typical cartoon of Jefferson Davis
published after his capture (Library
of Congress)

Varina and Jefferson Davis in 1868 after his release from Fortress Monroe

Varina's two daughters, Margaret and Winnie, in the 1880's

(Courtesy, Confederate Museum, Richmond)

Mrs. Jefferson Davis at Beauvoir. The girl is her maid and ward, Bettie (Courtesy, Mrs. Marguerite M. Murphy, Beauvoir)

The lounge at Beauvoir where Mrs. Davis served tea (Library of Congress)

The room at Beauvoir where Jefferson Davis wrote The Rise and Fall of the Confederate Government (Library of Congress)

Mrs. Jefferson Davis in her seventies. Painting by Adolfo Muller-Ury (Courtesy, Confederate Museum, Richmond)

Sketch of Oscar Wilde done from life by Mrs. Davis when he visited Beauvoir in 1882, and his autograph in her copy of his poems (Courtesy, Mrs. John W. Stewart)

Four generations: Mrs. Jefferson Davis with her daughter, Mrs. J. Addison Hayes, her granddaughter, Mrs. Varina Howell Hayes Webb, and her great-granddaughter, Varina Margaret Webb, now Mrs. John W. Stewart of Santa Barbara, Calif. (Courtesy, Confederate Museum, Richmond)

effect would have been more important." [19] There were other bright touches, too, at this point.

> General Lee rises to the occasion . . . and seems to be equal to the conception. I hope others will develop capacity in execution. . . . If we fight and are victorious, we can all soon meet again. If the enemy retreat to protect Washington, of which there are vague reports, I can probably visit you.

In the same letter the President told Varina that he had packed some valuable books, the sword he had worn for years, and the pistols he used at Monterey and Buena Vista, as well as his old dressing case. "These articles will have value to the boys in after-time, and to you now," he noted.

At this point McClellan's forces threw a corps across the Chickahominy and the Battle of Seven Pines was fought close to a clump of pines near Fair Oaks Station. Davis rode to the field with General Lee. All day long the cannon roared and thundered and the women of Richmond watched the smoke of battle from their rooftops.[20] Next day the streets were "one vast hospital," Constance Cary noted, as ambulances, litters, carts, and wagons rolled in with the dead and the wounded. Those who could move hobbled around with their injuries. Doors were opened to receive them and women stood in the streets with baskets of food and basins of water, to give them wine and fruit and wash their wounds. Pallets could be seen through the plate-glass windows of the shops. Church pew cushions were sewn together to make couches. Warehouses, hotels, and shops were used as shelters, and the wounded lay in the halls, drawing rooms, and porches of Richmond mansions, as well as on bare boards, or on their haversacks and blankets.

Couriers ran through the streets, bumping into white-jacketed Negroes bearing trays piled with invalid fare for the hospitals. The weather was blazing hot and the mutilated men suffered unendurably without anesthetics to ease their pain. This was war at their doorstep, and the women were part of it, as they searched next day for their own among the bandaged, smoke-smudged wounded. They nursed whom they could and, white-faced, wept over the endless parade of funerals that followed. The coffin topped with cap, sword, and gloves, the riderless horse and empty boots, the funeral dirge and bowed spectator, became a continuous experience after this.

"No city in the world was sadder than our Richmond in those days," wrote Mrs. La Salle Corbell Pickett at the turn of the century. "All the miseries and woes of Seven Pines had been emptied into her fair homes and streets. She had 'no language but a cry,' an exceedingly bitter cry, that rose in its might to God on high 'if the heavens were not brass.'"

Varina was to hear much of it in the days to come. Her husband sent his Winnie his own version of Seven Pines.

On Saturday we had a severe battle and suffered severely in attacking the enemy's entrenchments of which our Generals were but poorly informed. Some of them and those the most formidable were found by receiving their fire. Our troops behaved most gallantly, drove the enemy out of their encampments, captured their batteries, carried their advanced redoubts, and marched forward under fire more heavy than I had ever previously witnessed. Our loss was heavy, that of the enemy unknown.[21]

The powerful influence of Varina in her husband's life is clearly shown in this letter as he told how he thought of her even in the roar of battle. He waited anxiously "for the hour of our reunion . . . in peace and love we may yet find recompense for present trials." He added:

I thought of you as though you were with me yesterday and the fire of the enemy's artillery did not prevent me from remembering that you were in the same hours praying for me and making sacramental communion with our Redeemer. Farewell dear wife, may every consideration attend you and your happiness be reflected back on your own devoted husband.

This was also the letter in which he told of General Joseph Johnston's being wounded. "The poor fellow bore his suffering most heroically," he wrote to Varina, all animosity wiped out for the moment in the sympathy of a fellow soldier. As Johnston was being lifted into the ambulance the President dismounted to speak to him. The wounded General opened his eyes, smiled, and gave Davis his hand. He was taken to Crenshaw's House on Church Hill where Lydia was nursing him, "deeply distressed and very watchful." Davis had offered to take them into the Executive Mansion, but this had been declined.

Meanwhile, Varina was in a state of desperate anxiety in Raleigh, walking the floor with her sick baby and stricken by the war news.[22] Only a narrow alley separated her hotel bedroom from the telegraph office and she watched hourly for news. Shouts would reach her from the street: "Tell us what you know, please." or "Do tell us it's a victory." Every word of one telegram received from her husband was publicly recorded as it arrived. When the cheering grew boisterous someone shouted, "Don't hurrah, you will scare the sick baby." One old man paused in the alley and assured Varina sympathetically, "We will pray for your poor baby; don't be downhearted."

The President's next letter, written on June 3, informed her that General Johnston was improving and would recover, although his convalescence would take time.[23] He felt that ignorance of the enemy's defenses had caused much of the loss that they had suffered. Again he injected the personal note, as if to relieve the tensions of battle. When they were all together again he would ride with little Margaret. Did little Joey talk of him? "If there be a miasmic power of communication between us he must think of me very often," he wrote, and then described his own situation in the deserted Executive Mansion.

Dearest Winnie, our separation seems to me very long. Our house is dreary at night and no loving sounds greet me in the morning. I go into the nursery as a bird may go to the robbed nest but man's tenacious memory preserved the pain.

Again may God give you to my arms and bring us peace and freedom from further sadness like that we are doomed now to bear.

Farewell wife, around you ever hovers in affectionate solicitude the spirit of your husband.

Edward A. Pollard, author and editor, was to describe Jefferson Davis as the "most uxorious of men," [24] strongly dominated by his wife. Unquestionably his attachment to Varina showed up strongly in all the crises of his troubled life. At this time Davis was giving Varina in concentrated form an account of the fighting that would be presented more fully years later in her *Memoir*—but without the personal allusions. These letters, with their mixture of war news and affectionate concern for his family, reflect in essence his emotions during these June days so significant in the history of the Confederacy.

Not only was he unhappy about the lack of intelligence observations before Seven Pines, but he felt that if the Mississippi troops "lying in camp when not retreating under Beauregard, were at home, they would probably keep a section of the river free for our use, and closed against Yankee transports." He wrote on this same occasion:

It is hard to see incompetence losing opportunity and wasting hard-gotten means, but harder still to bear is the knowledge that there is no available remedy. I cultivate hope and patience, and trust to the blunders of our enemy and the gallantry of our troops for ultimate success.[25]

All of this suggests how freely Jefferson Davis discussed military matters with Varina and shared with her his uncertainties about his generals. Lee was now in command at Richmond and McClellan was digging in "by successive lines of earth-works, that reviled policy of West Pointism and spades, which is sure to succeed against those who do not employ like means to counteract it," Jefferson wrote bitterly to Varina on June 11. "The greatest generals of ancient and modern times have won their renown by labor. Victories were the results." He was tired of gibes at West Point.

Billy, whose life had hung in the balance, now showed signs of recovery, and Davis, returning from a night spent in reconnaissance along the army lines, was vastly relieved to get a telegram from Varina on June 12 saying that the baby was recovering. He wrote next day that he had already sent Dr. A. P. Garnett to her with a specific remedy for the child. Earlier his "heart had sank within him at the news of the suffering of my angel baby."

Varina by this time was completely worn out from concentrated effort and anxiety. She suffered now from heart trouble. Jefferson, apprehending her own state, continued:

But the look of pain and exhaustion, the gentle complaint, "I am tired," which has for so many years oppressed me, seems to have been revived; and unless God spares me another such trial, what is to become of me, I don't know. . . . My ease, my health, my property, my life I can give to the cause of my country. The heroism which could lay my wife and children on any sacrificial altar is not mine. Spare us, good Lord.[26]

In this same letter he wrote of Beauregard having been "placed too high for his mental strength." By June 21 Lee's army was taking up its position for battle, and two days later he warned Varina not to be disturbed by rumors, as he felt the army was better prepared than at the beginning of the month and "with God's blessing will beat the enemy as soon as we can get at him."

He had been ailing but was feeling better, he wrote. The heat was oppressive. The wagon trains moved in blinding clouds of dust. General G. W. Smith, after the manner of Beauregard, had taken a surgeon's certificate, "and is about to retire for a season to recruit his health." [27]

Then, in a rare salutation to General Johnston, he finished his letter to Varina with an observation that may well have been his fundamental estimate of his soldier colleague: "General J. E. Johnston is steadily and rapidly improving. I wish he were able to take the field. Despite the critics who know military affairs by instinct, he is a good soldier, never brags of what he did do, and could at this time render most valuable service."

Jones in the War Office observed the President's improved health and spirits at this point. He noted on June 15 that Davis was on the field and was "very cheerful." [28] The people of Richmond were more at ease, too. The tension had diminished. "What a change! No one now dreams of the loss of the capital," he wrote.

A crisis was past but the Seven Days' Battles were about to begin. On June 25 Davis wrote to Varina commenting on Jeb Stuart's brilliant reconnaissance for Jackson.[29] He observed that General Butler had rightly been named Beast Butler in New Orleans. "How much better it would have been had the city been left a pile of ashes!" he said of the place to which both were deeply attached.

On the following day Mechanicsville was fought and the bloody Seven Days' Battles had begun, ending on July 1 with Malvern Hill. A living core of suffering now ran through the Confederacy. Military reputations were made and lost. There were moments of glory that would live on in Confederate history. Finally, at terrible cost, the enemy retreated and the Southern capital was saved.

During the first engagement vivid flashes of artillery fire could be seen from the Capitol and the Executive Mansion. The President was on the field, but did not interfere with Lee, who always knew where he was. He rode along lanes and through orchards close to the battlefields and once, when a powerful battery was directed toward a farmhouse where he stood, Lee hastily sent a courier to warn him. He had no sooner left than the house was demolished.[30]

General Lee emerged from these engagements an established hero, a reputation which he was to sustain untarnished. The Richmond *Dispatch* commented on July 19: "The rise which this officer has suddenly taken in the public confidence is without precedence. . . . The operations of General Lee in the short campaign which is just over were certainly those of a master."

But again the intelligence work done in advance was faulty. Richard Taylor later charged that there was total ignorance of the topography, and that the leaders lacked maps, sketches or proper guides. As he saw it, the dead of Gaines's Mill, Cold Harbor, Frazier's Farm, and Malvern Hill were sacrificed to ignorance. "We blundered on like people trying to read without knowledge of their letters," he wrote. "The day before the battle of Malvern Hill President Davis could not find a guide with intelligence enough to show him the way from one of our columns to another; and this fact I have from him." [31]

Varina got a close-range narrative on the battles from her husband when she visited Richmond briefly after Malvern Hill. She rode north through countryside glowing with roses, blooming its richest. It was a lavish July and the perfumed air blew warmly around her until she reached the capital, but there she noticed at once "the odors of the battlefield distinctly perceptible all over the city." She reported that the President had "slept upon the field every night and was exposed to fire all day."

Strangers poured into the city seeking their dead and wounded. Fifty hospitals of one kind or another were in operation. Varina was appalled by the changes wrought during her brief absence. She was greatly interested in the return of Mrs. Rose Greenhow, President Buchanan's pet and one of her own friends during her Washington days. Rose had just been released from Capitol Prison and, in the middle of June, Jefferson had written to Varina in Raleigh: "Mrs. Greenhow is here. Madame looks much changed. She has the air of one whose nerves are shaken by mental torture. General Lee's wife has arrived, her servants left her, and she found it uncomfortable to live without them."

The President called on Mrs. Greenhow to compliment her on her work for the Confederacy, and on August 1 he paid her twenty-five hundred dollars through Judah Benjamin for her "valuable and patriotic service." Rose studied Varina with interest, too. It was her initial view of her as First Lady of the Confederacy and she did not agree with the Richmond *Examiner* that Mrs. Davis was trying to create an "unrepublican court by being snobbish, by aping royalty, by putting her servants in livery and not returning calls."

Mrs. Greenhow quietly started a campaign against the *Examiner*, which was controlled by the anti-Davis faction and was backed by such powerful politicians as Toombs and Stephens. She had observed that the Northerners had made good use of the constant drum fire of newspaper criticism in the South. The Rhetts and their Charleston paper were a potent factor in this barrage. There had just been a strong attack in the *Mercury* on the ladies who lolled in their landaus in elegant silks and attended parties when there was hard work to be done.[32] "Why not?" demanded Mrs. F. W. Pickens, the Governor's wife, in her soft, beguiling way. "General Washington attended the Assembly Balls, and wanted everything done that could be done to amuse his soldiers and comfort and refresh them, and give them new strength for the fray."

Varina also noted with interest that Mrs. Philip Phillips, wife of the Congressman from Alabama who had briefly shared imprisonment with Mrs. Greenhow in Washington as a Confederate spy, but had quickly gained her freedom with the help of Reverdy Johnson, was again in trouble. Butler had jailed her in New Orleans for showing contempt from her balcony as a Federal funeral passed by. Eugenia Phillips was a friend of Varina's, who had received her with "great feeling" when she arrived from the North some time earlier with a plan of campaign sewn in her corsets.[33] Before the war Mrs. Phillips had been a noted hostess, recognized for her wit.

Spies were much discussed by the women around Varina at this time. In May, Belle Boyd had run over open fields under cross fire waving her sunbonnet as a signal to Stonewall Jackson to advance at Front Royal, and by the end of July she was in Old Capitol Prison in Washington and *Leslie's Weekly* was announcing that the "Secesh Cleopatra is caged at last." [34] But she was hard to hold. A month later she was back in Virginia.

Meanwhile, the Federal drive grew stiffer. Abraham Lincoln had called for fifty thousand additional men. General Henry W. Halleck was appointed commander of the Union armies and McClellan was withdrawn from his post near Richmond to join the forces in northern Virginia under the command of General John Pope. Jeb Stuart's raids and Colonel John Hunt Morgan's cavalry dashes in Kentucky were cheering the sorrowing South. Turner Ashby, another of the brilliant soldiers who swooped unheralded on the enemy, had fallen in June as he led a charge. Jackson and Lee now stood like bulwarks in the public imagination. Lee moved north to meet Pope. Jeb Stuart had snatched his dispatch book and plans, and Stonewall Jackson had destroyed his supply base at Manassas Junction. The second Battle of Manassas was fought at the end of August, and hope burned strong for the Confederates.

By this time Varina was back in Richmond with her family. The streets were filled with bandaged men and amputees. Many of the soldiers she had entertained a few weeks earlier were dead or wounded. The women were at work night and day, making comforts, visiting the hospitals, or nursing wounded men in their homes. "The exception was a woman who did not nurse at some hospital," Varina commented, frankly acknowledging that she was one of them. "I did not, because Mr. Davis felt it was best for me not to expose the men to the restraint my presence might have imposed, and in lieu of nursing I issued provisions which had been sent to me from the Governor of Virginia, and other persons charitably inclined toward the families of soldiers." [35]

Varina visited the hospitals regularly with supplies, and even the begrudging Jones was forced to admit that "always plainly but well dressed she was frequently seen driving to the hospitals to cheer the sick or wounded soldiers with a share of the dainties carried in a large basket." She and Mrs. Chesnut, who was back in Richmond, often stopped at Pizzini's and picked up confections to take to Miss Sally Tompkins or Miss Emily V. Mason for their patients. Sally ran her own hospital and had a commission in the army. She was original, old-fashioned, and indefatigable, and she welcomed the young belles who worked all day in the wards or kitchens, then doffed their aprons and caps for ball gowns and danced the night away with the soldiers. Miss Mason presided with great dignity in another hospital and squelched Mrs. Chesnut when she sought the wounded from South Carolina. "I never ask where the sick and wounded come from," she said reprovingly. Mrs. Chesnut fainted in the St. Charles Hospital when she viewed the long rows of men "dead and dying."

Varina's nerves were steadier when Mrs. James Alfred Jones, basin in hand, approached her one day in a converted tobacco warehouse and told her of a case of pyaemia that was a menace to the other patients. "We took counsel for a moment, and then I went to my husband, who had the wounded man camped out, and fortunately only one died," Varina later recalled. She did many practical things of this sort and filled commissions from all parts of the Confederacy. She distributed money from Vicksburg, sent soldiers' possessions back to their families, wrote letters, gave out supplies, aided the women in authority, and served as a sort of liaison between them and the President. She felt that each woman did what she could, in whatever way she could, and in spite of the feeling that had grown up between her and some of the women of Richmond she persuaded herself that she had dwelt with them in "mutual labor, sympathy, confidence and affection."

Varina's own hands were never idle. She was one of the most industrious seamstresses and knitters but, like Mary Lincoln, she came in for heavy criticism for spreading bounty in what seemed to be the easy way. At this time a devastating story spread through Richmond about the Howell girls that did her great harm, although like much of the other gossip it was never wholly authenticated.[36] One Sunday soon after her return to Richmond Mrs. Lee attended St. Paul's. She stood uncertainly in the vestibule and when recognized was conducted at once to the President's pew. When the Howell girls—Maggie and Jane Kempe Howell—swept down the aisle, large and handsome in light summer attire, and saw the drab figure in the pew, all Richmond said that they stood in the aisle, waiting for her to move out, which she did. Obviously they had not recognized Mrs. Lee. Hisses reportedly were heard in the church, and pew doors were flung open up and down the aisle to receive her.

Two years later Maggie was challenged about this episode while staying with Mrs. Chesnut at Columbia. "Fancy Maggie's face!" the diarist commented, hastening to label it a slander. There is no record of Maggie's response. But the episode was never cleared up. Somehow it clung to Varina, who does not appear to have been involved. Affection for the Lee women in Richmond was unbounded. The great granddaughter of Martha Washington had spent all her life at Arlington and had moved reluctantly with the help of Custis when her husband told her that the time had come to go south. The family plate and the Washington papers were sent to Richmond. On April 20, 1861, she wrote to her daughter Mildred, then in a boarding school at Winchester, that "both parties are wrong in this fratricidal war."

Since then she had moved unhappily from place to place, staying with friends, helping ailing relatives. She finally settled in Richmond and spent the last months of the war in a house on Franklin Street where today the Virginia State Historical Society has its offices. A sufferer from arthritis, she used crutches and a wheel chair much of the time. Mary Custis Lee acted as hostess on her mother's behalf, but as the months went on it was generally understood that Mrs. Lee disapproved of entertaining while her husband commanded an ill-fed army, slept in a tent, and lived on ascetic fare himself. Thus the elegance of Arlington became the austerity of Franklin Street. The Lee women labored hard for the soldiers, and Varina noted that Mrs. Lee and her daughters, "all honor to them, furnished one hundred and ninety-six socks and gloves to Posey's Brigade, and this when Mrs. Lee was confined to her chair, a hopeless victim of rheumatism, and her daughters' time was consumed by nursing in the hospitals."

By this time Maggie Howell was almost as familiar a figure in the community as her sister. She circled around Varina at all public functions and loved to dance with Jeb Stuart, Preston Hampton, Burton N. Harrison, and the other handsome young men who were in and out of the Executive Mansion. She had a vivacious air and De Leon considered her "quite the most original and one of the most brilliant women in that bright and unique society." [37] Benjamin observed with some extravagance at Gustavus Myers's dinner table that if she lived in Paris she would be a Madame de Staël.

She often took care of the younger set for her sister, who was popular all her life with this generation, although they stood a little in awe of her. But Varina chaperoned many of the belles in Richmond and watched quick wartime romances flourish, sometimes under her own roof. She sympathized with them when their lovers and husbands were killed, and attended many of the war weddings, including that of her sister Jane to William G. Waller, grandson of President Tyler, in St. Paul's; and of tiny Mollie Beirne to General William Porcher Miles, the social event of the autumn of 1862. Mourning by this time was so general among their friends that only a score of guests were present. Weddings and funerals overlapped in the churches.

One of the women Varina comforted was Mrs. Laurence O'Bryan Branch, whose husband died at the battle known as Sharpsburg in the South and Antietam in the North.[38] She was the former Nancy Haywood Blount of Washington and they were close friends of President Buchanan and of her husband. Their home was in Raleigh, and while Varina was there Mrs. Branch had done what she could to entertain her but the President's wife, refusing social engagements, had written: "Now the times are so portentous I am really not equal to seeing company, also I never know what an hour may bring forth."

But while Antietam was being fought Mrs. Branch, in a state of desperate anxiety, appealed to Varina, who was often asked by wives for news when she knew no more than the suppliants. "I wish it were possible for me to offer you some definite news," she wrote on this occasion. "We all suffer together and God grant us our friends' lives as He is granted their victory. . . . Genl. Branch must be safe else you had heard it only too soon."

But General Branch did not return from the battle that was viewed as the turning point of the war in the North and was followed by President Lincoln's proclamation on emancipation. Corinth brought gloom in October. Bragg failed in Kentucky and marched into Tennessee, where Buell was fortifying Nashville. Lee was re-forming his lines in the neighborhood of Winchester. Early in October he praised his men's achievements and reminded them that "much more remains to be accomplished." [39] They were again threatened with invasion. Stuart encircled the Federal Army that month. His brilliant raids were now a matter of deep pride in the South, and the exuberant, red-bearded warrior was enthusiastically welcomed wherever he appeared. The Stuart cloak, the Stuart plume, the Stuart swagger, the light kiss for a pretty girl, were becoming legendary.

Although Varina drove freely about the city paying calls, marketing, visiting the hospitals with supplies, her husband was seen less and less in the autumn of 1862. He was ailing again, and Varina was setting up fresh barricades to protect him from further pressure. "The President used to be accessible to all," Jones complained in his diary on November 1. "But now there are six aides, cavalry colonels in rank and pay, and one of them is an Englishman, who sees the people and permits only certain ones to have access to the President. This looks like the beginning of an Imperial court." [40]

Browne was the British aide in question and that autumn there was much talk of "alien" elements in the government. It was pointed out that General Samuel Cooper was a Northerner; that the capable General Josiah Gorgas, Chief of Ordnance, came from the North; that General Mansfield Lovell, who figured in the defeat at Corinth and had surrendered New Orleans, was from Pennsylvania. Mrs. Pickens had complained that the President was always sending Northerners to command Southern points, and a critic from North Carolina said that, when she fled from Richmond in May, Varina consorted with Northerners in Raleigh.

Meanwhile, the President rode out with his aides, looking less concerned than he felt. He was most familiar to the public as a figure on horseback, and it was generally conceded that, like General Lee, he was impressive in this role. He usually walked through Capitol Square to his office at about ten in the morning. Sometimes his wife picked him up in her carriage in the late afternoon, but again he was more likely to walk. Maggie and the older children often rode with him, but Varina rarely appeared on horseback in Richmond.

Lydia Johnston by this time had established a little court of her own, and she and Mrs. Wigfall had pulled away entirely from Varina's sphere. The two families were established together on Grace Street that autumn while the wounded General convalesced. In October he was not yet able to report for duty, and his wife nursed him with the greatest care. She kept a tea kettle handy for guests, and visitors noticed the aromatic smell of white chrysanthemums in the room.

John S. Wise considered Lydia the "best diplomatist General Johnston ever had about him, one who supplied many of the qualities in which he was so lacking." [41] Wise's mother and aunts had gone to school with her in Philadelphia and they always referred to her as "Lit" McLane. In his opinion, Lydia was a "very fine woman, very popular, very ambitious for the General, and did more to keep him out of hot water and smooth over the rough places he was constantly making than anybody else in the world." She was not a beauty, but Wise thought she had "graceful charm, and delightful endearing wit."

Neither, however, was apparent in her relations with Varina. She was furiously angry when word came in November that her husband had been ordered to command the army in the West and that Bragg would serve with him. She viewed this as deliberate exile and burned with resentment. Randolph, an ardent backer of her husband, resigned at this time and James A. Seddon became Secretary of War. The ever-watchful *Examiner* warned Davis against establishing a dictatorship: "The Executive Chief of this country is neither a French Emperor nor a Roman dictator, but a functionary of very limited powers and distinctly defined duties." [42] This came at a time when the Davises were feeling pleased because Gladstone had said in a speech at New-castle that Jefferson Davis "had made a nation." Jones noted the President's elation over this compliment and commented: "The 'nation' was made before the President existed; indeed, the nation made the President."

Snow fell early that November as the bitter winter of 1862-63 set in.[43] Fuel was scarce and dear. Flour was sixteen dollars a barrel and bacon eight dollars a pound. The newspapers were printed on half sheets. Uniforms were frayed and worn and few warm overcoats could be had for the men in the field. General Lee estimated that he had more than six thousand barefooted men in his forces, and on November 10 it was noticed that some of them marched into Richmond shoeless in the snow. Ten days earlier General Lee had walked into the War Office with his beard grown out around his face and it was entirely white. He was mustached and not noticeably gray at the start of the war.

Varina noted with satisfaction that Benjamin Butler, who had insulted the women of New Orleans with his famous Order 28, had left the city and the women had serenaded his departure with the toast: "We fill this cup to one made up of Beastliness alone." Just before Christmas her husband proclaimed him a felon and ordered that Butler and his officers, if captured, should be treated as criminals and executed.

Early in December he and General Johnston set off together for the Western front. Fredericksburg was fought in bitterly cold weather while they journeyed through Tennessee, far from the scene of action. He wrote to Varina from Chattanooga on December 15 of his anxiety when the telegram reached him there and the outcome of the battle still seemed uncertain. If necessary, he would return to Richmond at once, he wrote, and General Johnston would go straight to Mississippi. He reported that the troops at Murfreesboro were in fine spirits, and ended with the usual intimate touch.

Kiss my *dear* children for their loving Father. They can little realize how much I miss them. Every sound is the voice of my child and every child renews the memory of a loved one's appearance, but none can equal their charms, nor can they compare with my own long worshipped Winnie—

"She is nae my ain lassie
Though fair the ladies be
For weel ken I my ain lassie
By the kind light in her eye." [44]

The news from Fredericksburg proved to be better than they could have dreamed. In good spirits, the President attended the marriage of the cavalry hero, John Hunt Morgan, and Miss Mattie Ready, daughter of a Tennessee Congressman. Lieutenant General Leonidas Polk, who doubled as soldier and priest, performed the ceremony. They would soon be in flight, as Murfreesboro fell, and for the next two years Mattie would be a wanderer in Tennessee, Virginia, and Georgia.

Joseph R. Davis, his nephew, was with the President on this trip and had just been appointed a brigadier general, to Jones's disgruntlement.

Any Tom, Dick, or Harry, never heard of before, young, and capable of performing military service, could be made "heads of bureaus, chief clerks of departments, and staff-officers flourishing their stars," he commented after learning of this appointment.

Joseph had been plaguing his Aunt Varina all year to influence the President in getting him promoted. He had been at Corinth, reporting on March 23 to his uncle that General Beauregard was still in Jackson ill and unable to attend to his duty. He thought he should be removed to a place of safety, as a "daring party of cavalry could easily carry him off." He followed this up with a note to Varina from Corinth on April 22: "In my letter to Uncle Jeff, I asked him to take me on his staff, if he takes the field he must do it, and you must tell him so, if he goes into battle I want to be by his side. I think I have the right to ask this now . . . I've smelt gunpowder." [45]

By this time Varina's young brothers, Becket and Jefferson Davis Howell, were both in naval service. Commander John Taylor Wood, a nephew of Knox Taylor and a great favorite with both the Davises, was doing important work in connection with the blockade and was in and out of Varina's parlors when he came to Richmond. By his own admission the personable and jolly Richard Taylor was embarrassed by the speed with which he was elevated to high rank by the President. He was jumped over the heads of three men who had "won their spurs in battle," to replace General W. H. T. Walker of Georgia. Fearing repercussions, he went to Richmond to discuss the matter. Varina received him warmly, as always, and the President undertook to soothe the ruffled feathers of the men who had been superceded, handling the matter with such tact, according to Taylor, that he finally had their hearty support.[46]

Charges of nepotism at the Executive Mansion flourished as the war years went on. The impression prevailed that to be connected with the presidential household meant certain promotion, and that Varina was an important factor in this. Henry A. Wise, who was not a worshiper of either of the Davises, wrote: "Among us Irreverents, it was believed that Mrs. Davis possessed great influence over her husband, even to the point that she could secure promotion for us if she liked." [47] Wise viewed her as looking large and well fed. He considered her intensely loyal to her husband. "She took no pains to conceal her pride in him and was, perhaps, a trifle quick to show resentment toward those not as enthusiastic as she thought they should be in their estimate of his abilities."

But the young man who was closest to Varina during the war years and for long thereafter was her husband's secretary, Burton N. Harrison, a Louisiana youth of Virginian ancestry who was recommended for the post by L. Q. C. Lamar in March, 1862. He was the counterpart of John Hay in Washington, a handsome, literate, suave young man recently graduated from Yale. However, he got on much better with Varina than Hay did with Her Satanic Majesty, as he called Mrs. Lincoln. Burton came to know as much about Varina as anyone in her household but he was most discreet and stood a little in awe of her. She was always the Madam to him in theory and in fact. Constance Cary, whom he later married, jested lightly about how close-mouthed he was on presidential matters.[48] All he would ever tell her about Mrs. Davis was that the President had the "happiest relations with his family, by whom he was revered," but that he often had his wife in a state of great anxiety while he took his long horseback trips. Varina worried alternately about his safety and the less pressing matter of his dinner hour. Burton became a significant member of the executive entourage, helpful to Varina in all manner of personal ways, and always ready to conspire with her in saving the President fatigue or annoyance.

❧ 10 ❧

VARINA PRACTICES STATESMANSHIP

VARINA was practicing statesmanship on her own account in the year 1863. It was more than mere rumor that she and Judah Benjamin were working in close alliance in political matters. Thirty-four years later she was to acknowledge her role in letters to Francis Lawley,[1] who by that time had undertaken to write a biography of Benjamin in England and had turned to Varina for information. Her correspondence with Lawley between 1897 and 1898 opens the pages of what must have been a closed book during the war, and gives some inkling of the positive role she played where Benjamin was concerned.

Of all those who came and went at the Executive Mansion, Varina seems to have derived most support and consolation from the suave politician who was successively Attorney General, Secretary of War, and Secretary of State in her husband's Cabinet. He trusted her implicitly with state papers and used her as an intermediary to convey documents to Rosine Slidell, whose father at this time was Commissioner to France. She received cryptic answers from Rosine and gave them to Benjamin, who used a cipher based on polyalphabetical substitution. Pseudonyms were used to conceal the identity of the "high contending parties," a common practice both in the North and South. In Washington Hosanna and Husband stood for Jefferson Davis, and Happy and Hunter for Robert E. Lee, although Lincoln humorously persisted in calling them Jeffy D. and Bobby Lee.

Varina used assumed names on her own behalf. They were usually casual, friendly letters, obscure in meaning except to those who held the key. Benjamin was quite willing to have Varina read the dispatches. She wrote to Lawley:

Many of Mr. Benjamin's inimitable State papers were on account of the dangers of the blockading squadron. . . . They were most interesting reading for me and Mr. Benjamin's clear explanation of the antagonistic policy of the Duke of Morny and the Emperor made them very plain. . . . He never put on a manner of reserve towards me, nor did he caution me "to observe the utmost secrecy towards every one about their contents," as another man who knew less of secret affairs did. Of what he knew I must be cognizant he spoke freely when alone with me, but no more reticent man ever lived where it was possible to be silent.

In many respects Benjamin was the most interesting figure in the political group surrounding her husband, and toward the end he was undeniably one of the most influential. None understood Varina better than Benjamin; none played into her hands more readily. She was a strong ally when he needed one. He was unfailingly sympathetic about her family problems and showed delight in her babies and concern for her husband's health, two of her softest spots. Both he and Varina were emotional and eloquent and were fond of the company of brilliant people.

Benjamin was a cosmopolitan, of Sephardic ancestry.[2] He was born in the West Indies and had spent the earlier part of his life in New Orleans, where he built up a fortune in land and the law. He was welcomed by the sophisticated for his glittering conversation and subtle wit. His flashing dark eyes were slightly astigmatic. He was short and rotund. A brush of beard outlined his rounded cheeks and chin. He smiled constantly and his melodious voice had caught Varina's attention years earlier in Washington. She happened to be sensitive to voices and often referred to her husband's musical intonations, which she greatly admired. Now she recalled for Lawley's benefit that Benjamin's voice "seemed like a silver thread woven amidst the warp and woof of sounds which filled the drawing-room . . . whatever he said attracted and chained the attention of his audience." [3]

She watched the development of Benjamin's friendship with her husband in Richmond with approval; observers thought she encouraged it. He had never warmed to Benjamin in the Senate, nor was Varina drawn to him when she first met him at a state dinner in Washington. She had dismissed him as an "elegant young man of the world, and a past master of the art of witty repartee." His conversation suggested a frivolous turn of thought, and Varina liked substance as well as wit. Later she came to the conclusion that her husband's earlier discord with him sprang from the fact that they were much alike in temperament. Both "were ambitious," had "quick perception," "tireless mental energy," and "nervously excitable tempers," and "no shade of emotion in another escaped Mr. Benjamin's penetration—he seemed to have a kind of electric sympathy with every mind with which he came in contact. . . ."

But Varina was always slightly baffled by Benjamin's energy and buoyancy as she watched her husband wilt under pressure. Eventually a diabetic, he told her once that he revived himself with a small sweet cake when fatigue overtook him at extended Cabinet sessions. Once a decision was made he had no regrets and did not look back, whereas her husband tortured himself with afterthoughts. Although too reticent and self-controlled to betray his anxiety, Davis "suffered like one in torment," according to Varina, whereas Benjamin would jest, play games, and relax completely in the midst of stress. He was fatalistic in his outlook and believed it "was wrong and useless to disturb oneself and thus weaken one's energy to bear what was foreordained." [4] Varina felt that he had become more serious with his new responsibilities.

He could be sharp in debate, a quality that she relished in anyone. When his point was made he "dealt the *coup de grâce* with a fierce joy which his antagonist fully appreciated and resented," she observed. On one occasion, after a long argument, she lightly remarked, "If I let you set one stone, you will build a cathedral before I know it." [5]

Benjamin laughed and quipped back, "If it should prove to be the shrine of truth you will worship there with me, I am sure."

He had established himself in Richmond with his young brother-in-law, Jules St. Martin, and they entertained their friends in as elegant a manner as blockaded *bon vivants* could, in Varina's opinion. De Leon found him "ubiquitous and a most acceptable social factor of the official circle." He quoted freely from the poets and classics and was always ready to give dramatic recitations. Varina specifically enjoyed his observations on men, politics, and books. She found him a gourmet of the "most refined and abstemious model." He ate her beefsteak pie or brains *en papillotte* with equal appreciation, and toward the end told her that with "bread made of Crenshaw's flour, spread with paste made of English walnuts, from an immense tree in our grounds, and a glass of McHenry Sherry, of which we had a scanty store, a man's patriotism became rampant." [6] By that time an occasional windfall might mean real coffee after dinner, loaf sugar, preserved fruits, and perhaps some anchovy paste, which Benjamin particularly liked.

Animosity and prejudice surrounded him as well as admiration. The generals heartily detested him as Secretary of War and felt he was merely "fronting" for that inveterate soldier, the President. He was deeply involved in the early disputes between Davis, Johnston, and Beauregard. When he ruffled the feelings of the popular Stonewall Jackson, that dour warrior was on the point of resigning. But Benjamin's shift from the War Department to the Department of State brought him even closer to the Davises. His office was only a hundred feet from that of the President and he was constantly in and out.

The amount of influence Varina actually exercised in the case of Benjamin and others, will always be debatable. There are different views of her power over her husband and thereby of her role in the fate of the Confederacy and its generals. There is ample evidence that she tried to interfere but Jefferson Davis was a man notoriously unsusceptible to influence.[7] He was not given to compromise or to the ready acceptance of suggestions from anyone. In her later years Varina wrote of his "radical stand and uncompromising nature." She was strong, but had more flexibility than her husband. Where he did not bend easily to the march of events, some practical strain in her induced her to yield to changing currents. "She was politician and diplomatist in one," commented De Leon. And in his biography of her husband H. J. Eckenrode wrote: "There can be no doubt that Varina Davis was a congenial companion for an intellectual man, and that she secured a considerable influence over her husband, even possibly in political matters. Her abounding vitality would have made her predominant over the semi-invalid Davis but for a will which always kept him master of himself." The unfriendly Pollard called him a "doting and sentimental husband" who was "as wax in the hands of his wife."

Their letters suggest that he must have discussed his generals and state matters freely and fully with her and undoubtedly she helped from time to time to color his outlook. She was too emphatic in all her views, and voiced them too candidly, to have been a negligible figure in his affairs. One of her intimate friends at this time observed that she considered Mrs. Davis a "woman of splendid intellect and fine character, devoted to Mr. Davis though by no means his echo. In fact she frequently differed with him and did not hesitate to so express herself. She was gracious in manner, but on occasion could be quite abrupt, even stinging in debate." [8]

Mrs. Chesnut and other women close to her make it amply clear that the drawing-room chatter of the satellites of Queen Varina's court stirred up a good deal of trouble among their husbands and must have clouded the political picture in sundry small ways. Everyone knew where Varina stood on all issues, and she was not to be ignored. The alert liked to post themselves in the vicinity of Mrs. Davis and Mrs. Chesnut when they tossed their glittering quips, although some sneered at their French idioms and ready quotations, which embarrassed women who did not always follow their nimble allusions. Neither Varina nor her friend from South Carolina could resist the timely *bon mot*. They had sophisticated tastes and put brilliance ahead of social status and ancestry.

It was no secret to anyone in the Confederacy that the President's wife feuded openly and vigorously with Mrs. Johnston, Mrs. Myers, Mrs. Wigfall, and Mrs. Toombs, yet her letters often suggest a real desire for conciliation.[9] She could scarcely be deaf to the repercussions that followed her quick flashes of temper. Her most intimate friends informed her. At times she saw unflattering comment in the press. Occasionally she took her punishment in silence; periodically she hit back hard, particularly where her husband's interests were involved.

In the early days of the war she may well have been overbearing. Gamaliel Bradford has said that neither Davis nor his wife "had the gift of being democratically popular."[10] They had a strong sense of the dignity of their position and sometimes emphasized it in tactless ways. Varina was broad-minded up to a point, but had a stiff sense of convention, too, and was ever mindful of appearances. Benjamin detected the essentially feminine nature behind the formidable façade that she presented, and treated her with delicacy and understanding in the closing hours of the Confederacy.

Varina enthroned family life to a degree that suggested selfish absorption in a time of national crisis. Yet she was also deeply considerate of other people's children, remembering their birthdays, anniversaries, and characteristics, and helping them when she could. She unquestionably had radiant social qualities, including quick responses, kindness of heart, and genuine interest in others, although she was capable of the most wounding sarcasm, and her candor at times was considered quite destructive. It was noted that she fared best with the brilliant or the relatively simple type of person. If she seemed haughty to some in her days of social triumph, the years made Varina wiser and noticeably more tolerant. This evolution of her character may be traced quite clearly through her letters.

It was not in her nature to dissemble when she disapproved, and she disapproved of everyone who did not bow down and worship Jefferson Davis. Since the Confederacy contained a number of dissidents she was often in hot water. She detested his enemies and loved his friends with all the strength of her wholehearted nature. When she came to write her *Memoir* General Jubal A. Early begged her as a friend not to criticize any of the Confederate generals.[11] He tactfully tried to steer her clear of the more obvious pitfalls, but some of her memories were so searing and her defenses were still so strong that echoes kept creeping in, and the impulse to state the Davis case was always close to the surface. She was cold to Beauregard and unforgiving to Johnston. She was less enthusiastic about Bragg than her husband was. She was partial to Benjamin and her early affection for Toombs had turned to strong dislike. She respected Robert E. Lee, like everyone else; admired Stonewall Jackson, and seemed to be fond of Jeb Stuart, although his name is missing from the list of "particular favorites" she made up before leaving Richmond—an omission which may have had no significance since she wrote sympathetically of him in her *Memoir*.

Much of the criticism of Varina was engendered by the climate in which she moved, and her prominence. She was assailed both in the North and South, much as her husband was. Every move she made was noticed and commented on. She was accused of being friendly to the North, of harboring spies in her home, of feasting when others starved, of pretentious ways, of nepotism, of not reading the books from which she quoted so freely, of extravagant entertaining in hours of crisis, and of meddling in political and military affairs. Some of the stories were true; many were not, but it is self-evident that she instinctively generated heat lightning around her. On one occasion she wrote sadly that she seemed to bring tragedy to those she loved.[12] She bore the aura of intensity that led to personal complications. This made her explode into tantrums—not the wildly hysterical scenes indulged in by Mary Todd Lincoln—but moods in which she grew ungovernably angry, and then refused to speak to people for days, having said her say but not achieved her ends.

"I never knew two people more unlike than Mr. and Mrs. Davis," Mrs. Kate Lee Ferguson wrote to Dr. Walter L. Fleming from Biloxi shortly after Varina's death. She had known them well. "*She* was the best reader of human nature and 'loved you' in spite of faults. With him it was blind faith." Varina was a good mixer in the sense that in no way did she hold herself aloof from the purely feminine preoccupations of the home, however intellectual her interests. She could sew, knit, embroider, play the piano, cook, or paint china. In her more abundant days she always pushed through with speed and efficiency whatever needed to be done. There was a primitive wisdom about her that also made her resourceful under stress. She gave support to her husband when he was ill and despondent; yet in her own moments of weakness—and there were many—she showed great dependency on him. Actually, their devotion was such that they were interdependent, and each seemed to borrow strength from the other.

By 1863 Varina had the same practical problems to cope with as many other women in Richmond—a large household to maintain, her children to feed, and all the harassments that surrounded her particular situation. The New Year opened in gloom with Bragg's defeat at Murfreesboro immediately after the President's visit there. Food prices had reached fantastic levels by this time, as the dollar fell in value. Sugar was twenty dollars a pound. Chickens were twelve dollars a pair. Meal sold for forty dollars a bushel and a ham cost three hundred and fifty dollars. Flour was three hundred dollars a barrel. Varina passed up a tough old gobbler offered her for forty dollars. "The family of the President had no perquisites, and bought their provender as they did their provisions, at the public marts and at the current prices," she wrote, adding, justly enough: "Our deprivations were far less than those of persons not holding such high official position, but they were many." [13] However, gifts flowed into the kitchens of the Executive Mansion. Mrs. Chesnut, who was boarding nearby in the winter of 1862-63, received regular supplies of food from Camden which she often divided with Varina. Mrs. James Grant, a close friend and next-door neighbor, shared a cow with the presidential household, which meant that the Davis children had fresh milk.

Varina held her usual reception on New Year's Day in the pervasive gloom of the defeat at Murfreesboro. A sharp picture of the White House entertainment at this time is provided by "Agnes," the otherwise anonymous wife of a Confederate colonel and Congressman, who lived at the Spotswood and sent Mrs. Pryor the local chitchat in a series of letters distinctly unfriendly to Varina. She found a large crowd in full regalia at the New Year's Day reception, she wrote on January

7, 1863.[14] The writer wore a gray silk dress with eleven flounces that had last done duty at Mrs. Stephen A. Douglas's final reception in Washington before secession. It seemed odd to her now that the Prince de Joinville, who had drunk rose wine with Mrs. Pryor at a reception to the Japanese in Washington, should have turned up on General McClellan's staff at the Battle of Williamsburg. "Doesn't it all seem so long ago—and far away?" Agnes commented, recalling that the Prince had taken her to one of President Buchanan's receptions and "now I attend another President's levee and hear him calmly telling some people that rats, if fat, are as good as squirrels."

Davis had indeed been discussing the palatability of rats at Varina's reception. "Agnes" further reported that there was not a bonnet for sale in Richmond at the time and the girls would be plaiting their own straws as soon as the wheat ripened. This letter was followed by another, undated, but written that same winter by "Agnes" to Mrs. Pryor. It was a serious indictment of Varina and was much quoted against her in later years.

A sort of court is still kept up here—but the wives of our great generals are conspicuous for their absence. Mrs. Lee is never seen at receptions. She and her daughters spend their time knitting and sewing for the soldiers, just as her great-grandmother, Martha Washington, did in '76; and General Lee writes that these things are needed. People here, having abundant time to find fault, do not hesitate to say that our court ladies assume too much state for revolutionary times. They had better be careful! We won't guillotine them—at least not on the block (there are other guillotines), but it would be lovelier if they could realize their fine opportunities. Think of Florence Nightingale! Mrs. Davis is very chary of the time she allots us. If King Solomon were to call with the Queen of Sheba on his arm the fraction of a moment after the closing minute of her reception, he would not be admitted! [15]

Constance Cary viewed things differently. She thought that Varina "courageously fulfilled all the social duties of her position," no matter what the immediate necessities of her family or her own personal problems. Connie observed that "all, gay, young society was chaperoned by her." She regarded her receptions more benignly than "Agnes" did.

We went often to Mrs. Davis's receptions, where the President never failed to say kind words in passing, and sometimes to tarry for a pleasant chat. Always grave, always looking as if he bore the sorrows of the world, he was invariably courteous and sometimes playful in his talk with very young women. These entertainments of Mrs. Davis, in the evening between limited hours, were attended by everyone not in deep mourning. The lady of the Confederate White House, while not always sparing of witty sarcasms upon those who had affronted her, could be depended upon to conduct her salon with extreme grace and conventional ease.[16]

In his January message the President spoke optimistically of the future. He pointed to larger armies and better supplies of arms than at any time since the start of the war. Hope was alive although the year had begun grimly enough with the Battle of Murfreesboro and Bragg's defeat, opening the way for Grant to get at Vicksburg. But the scene was changing visibly. There was less spit and polish, even in the drawing rooms.[17] Varina thought her husband looked lopsided in homespun. The yellow lacings were grimy now and boots lacked polish. The rifles and bayonets of Jackson's men gleamed but their uniforms were creased and dirty. "Men reared in luxury by this time were thoroughly hardened to camp life, to long marches in the scorching summer sun, and through winter's wind and rain," young Luly Wigfall, later Mrs. D. Giraud Wright, recalled. "The young people of Richmond managed to dance and sing and flirt. The girls did wonders with their costumes." [18]

Luly watched the promenaders on Franklin Street, the uniformed men making the most of their short leaves, with pretty girls decked out in the best they could muster. The adolescents at Miss Pegram's school were continually distracted by soldiers marching past, their flags now often in tatters. Great efforts were made that winter to raise funds for war needs and to cheer the soldiers on furlough with theatricals and charades. These were heralded as having patriotic purpose, and Varina and Maggie gave them countenance and support. The President, too, was sometimes prevailed on to attend. Women arrived from their work in hospital kitchens or wards, or from a long day of sewing in a church, changed swiftly into their best attire, and "Presto! an hour later the charity grub had fluttered into the society butterfly," De Leon commented.[19]

Soldiers fresh from victory or defeat set aside their cares for an hour or two to relax. Privates and brigadiers rubbed shoulders, both in the audience and the cast. Fitzhugh Lee cheerfully posed in the charades. Jeb Stuart, always a prize catch, would dash up on his horse, his plume waving, fling aside his scarlet-lined cloak, greet the girls joyously, and hold a ladder for Hetty Cary, sing a ballad, or play a minor role in a comedy. He was soon to die in battle but at the moment he was the very image of lusty life and courage, and the room sparkled with applause for a current hero.

The three Cary girls, known as the Cary Invincibles, were the mainspring of these affairs. Constance's cousins, Hetty and Jennie Cary, had arrived from Baltimore by this time and were among the reigning belles. Hetty was a noted beauty who had crossed the Potomac in a small boat, sitting on her trunk, after an enforced stay at Fort McHenry for flaunting her Confederate sympathies. She had Titian hair, a memorable face, and her fashionable Northern costume of violet moiré made a deep impression on the clothes-starved belles of Richmond when she came on the scene. Her sister Jennie had helped to popularize "Maryland, My Maryland," singing it first in Baltimore and many times thereafter at patriotic gatherings.[20] The Cary girls sewed the first of the Confederate battle flags.

The Davises attended the theatrical performance held at the home of Mrs. Thomas J. Semmes and watched their daughter Margaret play her first public role. "They had a right to be proud of her," Mrs. Chesnut commented. "She is a handsome creature and she acted her part admirably." Margaret was already beginning to look like her mother and was to grow up with the same striking presence. Mallory's "sparkling little Ruby" also acted on this occasion. Burton Harrison wore an authentic Indian costume given him by the President. Varina had combed her wardrobe for stage properties, supplying what she described as various "Oriental shreds and patches found about the house." As Connie put it: "Everybody borrowed; everybody lent; we had not the least reserve in seeking. . . ."

Another of the more discussed entertainments patronized by Varina at this time was staged at the home of Colonel and Mrs. Joseph C. Ives.[21] Young Ives, one of the President's aides, was a smooth-spoken West Pointer well known in Washington society before the war. His wife, who had been educated in Richmond, worked industriously for the soldiers all through the war. The Davises used this pair freely to help in social affairs, particularly in the entertainment of celebrities from abroad. The French princes, the newspaper correspondents, the military observers, all turned up at Cora Semmes Ives's table.

Mrs. Clay played the role of Mrs. Malaprop with the same flamboyant success she had enjoyed as Aunt Ruthy Partington at the Gwin ball. She was studded with diamonds, adorned with feathers, and her coiffure was built high over satin boots planted on top of her head. Mrs. Ives's sister, Clara Semmes Fitzgerald, who would die at Saratoga Springs in the same year as Varina, played the harp, as Nerissa Saunders did in Washington. Again there was the note of similarity in what went on at both capitals.

Belles abounded in Richmond at this time. Some were natives. Others had come in from Confederate states for the duration of the war. Every month there were fresh additions to the sad little army of bereft young brides. Varina followed the fortunes of all these young people with considerable sympathy. They gathered around her as they did at Mrs. Chesnut's and at the Pegram home in Linden Row, where Mrs. James West Pegram entertained for her daughters, while her sons, John and William, were in and out between battles. Varina maintained courteous relations, too, with the older generation, and in her *Memoir* specifically mentions the James Lyons, the Macfarlands, the Haxalls, Allens, Archers, Andersons, Stewarts, Warwicks, and Mrs. Robert C. Stanard.

However, as time went on she became increasingly unpopular with Mrs. Stanard, a wealthy widow from Louisville, whose "house was one unremitting salon" and who drew the wittiest men to her table. Benjamin, Stephens, Pierre Soulé, and Lamar were in and out of her house. Generals Johnston, Hampton, and Gordon all were favorites at her board, and the Davises were freely discussed there, by friend and often by foe. But toward the end the teas and dinners given by the more conservative elements of Richmond, as well as by the invaders from out of town, dwindled in number and scope.

Varina applauded Constance Cary when she helped to organize the Starvation Clubs that became high fashion at this time. Water only was served. Casino was played. A small orchestra was made up by the members, and John Pegram whistled blithely for them when he got away from camp. A committee of the founders asked General Lee if he approved of their dancing, and he responded heartily, "My boys need to be heartened up when they get their furloughs. Go on, look your prettiest, and be just as nice to them as ever you can be!" [22]

Rittenhouse's orchestra still played behind palms and potted plants —"Dixie," "Lorena," "The Bonnie Blue Flag," over and over—as well as the melodies of death and farewell. Many who danced by night were buried a few days later. Girls swinging gaily to waltz measure knew that they might soon be in mourning and tears. This third winter of the war had the last thin gloss of a dwindling hope. The dancing, the music, the songs, the charades, were the counterpoint of disaster.

At this time Mrs. Chesnut was seeing Varina nearly every day. They drove together. They exchanged and discussed the war news. They shared each other's problems. Colonel Chesnut had been appointed to the presidential staff as an aide, and Varina welcomed back his wife with cordiality.

Once for all let me say, Mrs. Davis has been so kind to me that I can never be grateful enough, yet even without that I should like her. She is so clever, so brilliant, so warm-hearted and considerate toward all who are around her. After becoming accustomed to the spice and spirit of her conversation, when one is away from her, things seem flat and tame for a while.

Mrs. Chesnut watched with horror while Wigfall snubbed the President openly at one of her own "evenings." Davis entered quietly and stood in front of the Wigfalls as he looked around. "They kept their seats—and turned their backs on him!" their hostess reported. As she moved quickly to their end of the room she heard a whisper, "Bully! the Wigfalls are trying to snub Jeff Davis!"

The President gave no sign that he noticed. The others all "made obeisance before him, as was due to his position," Mrs. Chesnut observed. "I was proud to receive him in my house as himself, Jeff Davis; the others stood up to receive the head of the Confederacy as well."

Jefferson Davis always struck her as being exceedingly courteous at their affairs, however aloof and preoccupied. But other observers sometimes thought he looked as if he were present unwillingly. They felt sure that Varina drove him into attending. He gave close attention to conversation when he was interested, but his handshake was cold, his glance distant. He demanded the utmost deference for Varina and was angry when General Mansfield Lovell, calling on Mrs. McLean at the Executive Mansion, neglected to greet his wife. She was in the room at the time but he paid no attention to her. The General later maintained that he did not mean to be rude. It was an oversight. But the President was inexorable and would not accept his apology.

On another occasion General Bradley T. Johnson, who became a warm admirer of Varina's, went charging into her drawing room after the second Battle of Manassas, booted, dirty, and straight from the cars, with a message from Stonewall Jackson. He was not altogether sure that the President liked his "soldierly unconventionality," but he had been trained to believe that promptness was the highest military virtue, "so I lost no moment in doing what I was sent to do." But Varina received him with the greatest warmth. "She was glad to see me," General Johnson remarked with satisfaction, "and I believe that night I promised to capture a Yankee flag for her; and she then and there captured my heart. I sent her the flag in '64, as she records in her memoirs." [23]

Varina used particular tact with foreign officers, diplomats, and newspaper correspondents who came and went as the Confederacy had its successes and reverses. They were an assorted lot, dividing their time between North and South. Francis Lawley was a favorite. Frank Vizetelly, the big, red-bearded Bohemian who corresponded for the *London Illustrated News,* helped Maggie and Connie Cary paint scenery, make wigs, and arrange sets for their theatricals. He would die later in the Sudan and have his name inscribed in St. Paul's.

Sir Arthur Lyon-Fremantle, a visiting English observer, was popular at Varina's board and was well liked throughout the Confederacy. He later accompanied Lee to Gettysburg and wrote a book on his American experiences. Prince de Polignac, small, animated, and usually wrapped in a long Napoleonic cloak, often took a Richmond belle home at Varina's bidding. Lieutenant Colonel Héros von Börcke, a German officer who had run the blockade and served as a volunteer on Stuart's staff, made the girls dizzy as he whirled them off their feet in the swift-circling German waltz. He was as tall as Prince de Polignac was small. He had fair hair and an impressive golden mustache. After being wounded in the throat, he spoke through a whistle.

Colonel Garnet J. Wolseley, later the Viscount Wolseley who ranked Lee with Marlborough and Wellington, and bitterly criticized Jefferson Davis, was another guest welcomed by Varina in the hubbub of war. She gave a matinee musicale that winter for some of the foreign visitors. But all this superficial entertaining was offset by constant effort and ceaseless worry. Church bells summoned the Richmond women to work on their sewing machines, to roll bandages and pick linen into balls of lint; to make tenting, flannel shirts, and sturdy garments for soldiers who had traveled far from the bullion fringe, pleated shirts and white gloves of the early days of the war.[24] Sewing societies were at work in every hamlet as well as in the cities. In country places wheels, cards, and cotton for spinning bees were hauled by wagons with bunches of lint hanging from twigs as their emblem.

Varina received many letters about the work being done in distant settlements—the indigo churnings in Alabama; the drug supplies drawn from herbs in the woods; the laudanum from garden poppies, and ashes of corncobs for raising dough. As an expert with needle, and with home remedies, she was alert to all the ways devised by the women to accomplish their ends. They used clippings of lambs' wool for knitting with needles a foot long made of seasoned hickory. They edged gloves with a vine-leaf border in bright colors. Mrs. John C. Pemberton sent Varina instructions for this pattern, and she followed it for her family. Girls made their own shoes from old felt hats, from tanned squirrel skins, from cornshucks lined with velvet. Judith McGuire in Richmond used a canvas sail taken from a wrecked vessel in the James River. Varina noted that Mrs. Mary Arnold, of Coweta, Georgia, made 1,028 yards of cloth in 1863, besides knitting quantities of socks and gloves for the soldiers. She paid tribute to these women in her *Memoir* and to all who worked in arsenals and government offices.

Varina and Maggie knitted constantly for the soldiers, and the hostile Jones observed them plaiting palmetto straw on the White House porch. Gifts arrived even in the midst of such general shortages. Articles were knitted for Jefferson Davis and his children as well as for the soldiers. Socks, flags, and food reached them from time to time. There were endless requests for pardons, for prisoner exchanges, and sometimes Varina interceded when particularly touched by a tale of difficult family conditions. She had innumerable letters to write—letters of consolation, letters of thanks, letters of explanation when she could— or could not—help someone in distress.

She saw little or nothing of Mrs. Wigfall at this time, but Charlotte and Lydia Johnston exchanged vitriolic comments about her by mail. Lydia was moving about, trying to stay close to her husband, and was bitterly chagrined over his status. She found that the people in Jackson had a "great horror of Mrs. D. & abuse her in the most unmeasured terms.'" Writing from there on January 19, 1863, she mentioned her husband's unhappiness over his situation. "He wants to have an army with the *right & power* to command it, which he has not now . . . in fact he has no position," she wrote.[25]

Mrs. McLean had visited her in Chattanooga, Lydia wrote, but she left the impression strongly in that city that "she was a spy for the D. family . . . a very smart woman, *jolie* and dangerous. . . ." By March, Lydia was writing to Colonel Wigfall of Maggie Howell's arrival in Montgomery from Richmond to nurse her desperately ill father. "This will put the Executive Mansion in mourning if he dies as they say he will," she wrote. "Mrs. McLane (sic) is indefatigable in her exertions to please that family & no doubt will succeed." [26]

Varina was summoned hurriedly to her father's bedside, and she left Richmond at once although her husband was ailing at the time. She and Jeff had done everything they could to help and encourage him as he aged and wandered from pillar to post. His final job was with an alcohol plant in Montgomery. Her mother was still active, keen, and helpful, and was often at the Executive Mansion with her daughters Varina, Maggie, and Jane. Varina now did her best to comfort her mother when her William died, for she had loved him dearly in spite of all his shiftlessness. She became seriously ill after Varina left for Richmond, but Maggie decided not to let her know, for the President was far from well. "Poor old lady, I pity *her*," Lydia wrote to Mrs. Wigfall. "She is very *agreeable*, and clever, & more in her than you would imagine. She often is very much alone, what a sad thing age and helplessness is without loving children."

Thus the gibes went on, although Varina had some civil interchanges with Lydia while she awaited her father's end. Lydia reported that her enemy had softened toward Mrs. Chesnut and they were now "bosom cronies," [27] suggesting that there had formerly been some trouble between them. On May 17 Lydia was writing from Columbia that General Preston spoke in "glowing terms of the Lady Queen." Still niggling away at her old enemy, she added: "Have you heard of any of the executive finery *being sported?* The faithful Betsy it is whispered has sold all the cast-off garments. . . . I thought the wives of aids might receive some such compensation, for services rendered." [28]

The Executive Mansion was like a house of glass, and Varina felt the pressure of moving in full view of hostile observers.

❧ 11 ❧

A PLEA FOR BREAD

VARINA had just returned from her father's funeral when all
Richmond was startled by a bread riot in April, 1863. Minerva
Meredith, a disgruntled local character, six feet tall, with a white feather
standing up from her hat, led the parade.[1] She headed a small group
that started at Capitol Square and mustered strength until men,
women, and children were marching hundreds strong past the War
Department. They headed for the shops on Main and Cary streets,
where pillaging began and drays drawn up to the curb were piled high
with their booty. Minerva later cheerfully admitted in court that she
carried a pistol.

Governor John Letcher ordered the Mayor to read the Riot Act, but
this went unheeded. A militia company from the Armory was called
out. Varina watched her husband hurrying off to Main Street, where
he jumped on a dray and addressed the mob. He was pelted with
crusts of bread when he first appeared but soon the crowd listened.
She wrote severely of what happened next.

He reminded them of how they had taken jewelry and finery instead of
supplying themselves with bread, for the lack of which they claimed
they were suffering. He concluded by saying: "You say you are hungry
and have no money. Here is all I have; it is not much, but take it." He
then, emptying his pockets, threw all the money they contained among
the mob, after which he took out his watch and said: "We do not desire
to injure anyone, but this lawlessness must stop. I will give you five minutes
to disperse, otherwise you will be fired on." [2]

Muskets were raised for action and the crowd quickly drifted off.
Storms of discussion followed this episode. The French Revolution

was recalled. The papers debated it pro and con. The Richmond *Whig* insisted that the "petticoated foray" was political in origin. But some were sympathetic to the rioters and compared their lot with that of the silk-clad beauties who danced, sang, and attended parties when misery was so pervasive.

The President was ailing badly at the time. Jones thought by April 16 that his remaining eye was failing and that total blindness might incapacitate him. "But he works on; and few or no visitors are admitted. He remains at his dwelling, and has not been in the executive office these ten days." [3] By April 22 his throat was inflamed and he was "dangerously ill." Varina applied all her favorite remedies and passed hours at his side. She read to him, sometimes until dawn broke. But early in May he was back at work and another arduous military month had begun. Congress had adjourned. The talk about the bread riot was dying down.

April had been full of excitement, and Varina had served as a buffer when she could for the ailing President, who lay speechless upstairs. There were desertions and discontent on a large scale, but all lesser matters were forgotten on the memorable night of Stoneman's Raid, preceding Chancellorsville. [4] Richmond was practically stripped of troops as the raiding party approached. Company after company of aged citizens or city employees formed at Capitol Square. Word had spread of the threat to Richmond. Pickets kept coming in, and couriers rode up to the Executive Mansion at the wildest gallop. Mrs. Chesnut sat on the marble steps with General Arnold Elzey, and he told her bluntly of the pressing danger. Varina came out and embraced her silently. She told her that the raiding party was only three miles away. Mrs. Chesnut had heard they were within forty miles.

"I went down on my knees like a stone," she related.

Varina invited her to spend the night under their roof. It was like none other they had ever experienced. Officers kept coming and going and no one went to bed. They served relays of refreshments to the soldiers, hour after hour. "There was not a moment's rest for anyone," Mrs. Chesnut reported. But the men were in a state of high exhilaration. Varina and Mrs. Chesnut took heart.

In the morning the President came downstairs, looking feeble and pale. He was scarcely able to stand. His pistols were loaded by Custis Lee and Colonel Chesnut, and he drove off in Dr. Garnett's carriage. By eight o'clock troops had arrived from Petersburg and the residents relaxed again, but Richmond had been defenseless for the time being. The raid was swiftly followed by the Battle of Chancellorsville on May 2. Again the women were in church and could scarcely hear the service for the rattle of ammunition wagons going past, soldiers tramping, and the iron gates of Capitol Square being slammed. The sexton kept going to different pews, quietly telling their occupants to go home. Deathly white, they staggered out of the church, knowing that sorrow awaited them. Finally Dr. Minnegerode was summoned. His wife, "as tragically wretched and as wild-looking as Mrs. Siddons," told him that their son was at the station, dead. This turned out to be a case of mistaken identity. The rector came back in time to give communion, but he was still trembling and remarked, "Oh, it was not my son who was killed; but it came so near, it aches me yet."

The azaleas, violets, and dogwood were in bloom in Richmond as the three-day battle raged. Joe Hooker failed Abraham Lincoln, but more than ten thousand Confederate soldiers died in action and Stonewall Jackson was felled by his own troops. The glory of the victory was almost obscured by the magnitude of this loss to the Confederacy. Jeb Stuart took up his command. "Charge! and remember Jackson," he cried, waving his saber.

Varina and Jefferson Davis prayed together for Jackson during the days that he lingered.[5] She thought with sympathy of the young wife traveling for days with her baby Julia to reach his side in time, and heard later how she sang hymns to him while he murmured battle commands in his delirium. His last words stayed with Varina as they did with many others, and she used them in her *Memoir: "Let us pass over the river, and rest under the shade of the trees."* She walked by his bier with her husband, and thought that his "face still bore the marks of the anguish he had suffered." A new Confederate flag covered him that "was snowed under by the masses of white blossoms left that day by all the fair hands of Richmond, together with laurel wreathes and palms." Although Varina had seen little of Stonewall she had intimate knowledge of his rare characteristics and his high value as a soldier. Paradoxically, he and Jeb Stuart, an unlikely pair, had come to symbolize the sturdy strength and the dashing chivalry of the Southern cause.

Jackson was buried on an excessively hot, bright day. Every place of business was closed. The city was hushed. The pallbearers all were generals. The President followed in a carriage, "looking thin and frail in health." Department heads walked two by two. "I have lost my right arm," mourned General Lee. And Varina wrote:

When at last the beloved form was taken to its last resting-place, the streets, the windows, and the house-tops were one palpitating mass of weeping women and men. The only other scene like it that I saw during the war was the crowd assembled when Mr. Davis was brought through Richmond to be bailed.[6]

But the war went on, lacking Jackson, and Grant battered ceaselessly at Vicksburg, with frightful slaughter. By degrees Pemberton's army was reduced to eating dog meat, and the people sought shelter in hillside caves. In Richmond there still were some serenades, however, and a naval review was held at Drewry's Bluff that summer. Early in June a great ball was given at Culpeper Courthouse and General Stuart came in with jingling spurs. Next day General Lee reviewed the cavalry at Brandy Station.[7] Strawberry ice cream parties were held at Pizzini's and the war marriages grew in number.

In a letter addressed to his brother Joseph, after Chancellorsville had been fought and won, Davis described his illness as diurnal fever followed by bronchitis. His cough remained and he was very weak, but his official duties had not been suspended at any time "except in the matter of personal interviews which inability to talk rendered it necessary to suspend." He was full of solicitude for Joseph and Eliza, who were now in an area of trouble, impoverished and homeless for the time being.[8]

That summer, a Northern youth, E. Macomber, writing from the *Carondelet* that lay off Palmyra Island, told of the foodstuffs the sailors were getting from the Davis plantations—tomatoes, peaches, musk and water melons, figs, pears and cabbage. He had picked up an old letter from among Jeff Davis's papers. "He has a very fine house & splendid furniture but between the soldiers & gunboatmen there's not much left," he wrote.[9]

Lee's army was strong and hopeful until Gettysburg and the fall of Vicksburg, and then the mood of discouragement set in. Varina's own health wavered as the weeks went on. Her husband was going through a crucial time with his eyes, as well as with military affairs. After Jackson's funeral General Lee wrote to him: "I cannot express the concern I feel at leaving you in such feeble health, with so many anxious thoughts for the welfare of the whole Confederacy weighing upon your mind." But early in June, Jones noticed him out riding, sitting "as straight as an English king could do four centuries ago." [10]

It was often the small hours of the morning before Varina got to bed. She frequently read for hours to her restless husband. After the fall of Norfolk she read George Alfred Lawrence's *Guy Livingstone* to him all night. Her children were spirited, happy, and sometimes difficult to handle. She strove to keep their lives on a steady keel in the midst of all the excitement. They played in the garden. They were tutored by Miss Daniel. They had their ponies and their playthings. She brought them constantly to the attention of their father, to soothe and cheer him. However impatient he might be with his generals and his aides, he always had time for his children. Their antics did not bore him, and he had more patience with them when they were naughty than their mother did.

Varina dreaded the visit of a courier, lest he bring a message of death or disaster. Looking back over the years, it seemed as if every time she gave an entertainment "the death of a relative or disaster to the Confederacy would be announced, destroying all pleasure." Pale faces and tears were a commonplace in her drawing room, and she had restoratives for sorrowing wives and mothers.

Gettysburg threw a cloud over the Davis household, as it did over the country itself. It was not recognized at the time as the turning point of the war. In the North there was more talk of Grant's victory at Vicksburg. Lee, assuming the blame, offered to resign. In her *Memoir* Varina pictures her husband's anxiety at this time, and quotes his conclusive answer to General Lee on August 11, 1863.

". . . Where am I to find that new commander who is to possess the greater ability which you believe to be required? . . . My sight is not sufficiently penetrating to discover such hidden merit, if it exists. . . . To ask me to substitute you by someone in my judgment more fit to command, or who would possess more of the confidence of the army, or of the reflecting men in the country, is to demand an impossibility." [11]

The long-drawn-out bombardment of Charleston had begun that July with a combined sea and land attack, and Varina wrote to Mrs. Chesnut immediately after Gettysburg and Vicksburg that she had "fasted and prayed fervently for Charleston" but was not sure that she was one of those whose "righteousness makes their prayers available." [12] She was angry over two articles in the Richmond *Whig* that went unreproved although they were "more than suggestive of reconstruction."

By this time Varina had moved to the country with Maggie for her baby's health and she found the calm a relief. "No terror stricken wives beseeching me, more helpless than themselves, to help their unhappy criminals out of jail," Varina wrote, and continued with some bitterness:

No good friends to tell me disagreeable truths. I was gratuitously informed the other day that "some parts of Carolina teemed with jokes upon my criticism of books half read—at lunches and breakfasts" and all things else disagreeable. Now to tell the truth I do not know anything nowadays— and never did know much and I felt so humble. I was glad to know that somebody could laugh. . . .[13]

Mrs. Chesnut had sent them *Dodds Abroad* and Davis had mustered up one hearty laugh at least in the midst of all his anxiety. But the floodgates of criticism had opened wide after these two major defeats and he suffered keenly under the barrage. He could do no right, in the estimation of the Richmond *Examiner*, which was battering away at him in August for stubbornness and disregard of the popular voice. There was growing discontent among the generals, and Joseph Johnston had been raging since January when he wrote to Wigfall deploring his situation and saying that his split command was merely nominal, and that he would rather be in charge of *fifty* men as a unit. On August 2 Lydia wrote from Montgomery to Charlotte Wigfall with great bitterness of spirit.[14] She had just spent four days with her husband in Mobile. After the fall of Vicksburg he had received a long letter of reproach from Davis, so scathing that she had urged him to resign.

"Imagine in times like these, a President writing 15 pages of rebuke to an officer commanding an army under such circumstances," Lydia wrote indignantly. Her husband had replied quite mildly that "no indignity from Davis could drive him from the service" since he was not serving him but a people who had never been anything but kind to him. She was surprised at his good spirits, as if "Jeff was throwing rose leaves at him, instead of nettles & thorns." He laughed at the President's rebukes and refused to be insulted. But Lydia could not swallow it and her ire embraced Varina.

I feel that nothing can ever make me forgive either of them, when I look at my dear old husband's grey head & careworn face, & felt how many of those tokens of trouble that man & woman have planted there, I could almost have asked God to punish them. How happy I was, until I knew them—it is not this war, that has broken up my home, & almost my heart, but the vengeance of one wicked man—& oh me thinks three years ago—I felt when I was leaving my home & family & all was beautiful, to be miserable, for I said then, "he hates you he has power & he will ruin you," and the same old reply, "He can't, I don't care, my country. . . ."

Lydia, like Varina at times, was apt to view her country's crisis strictly in terms of her husband's situation. In this same letter she wrote bitingly about Mrs. McLean and Mrs. Chesnut, both of whom had been visiting Montgomery and had avoided mentioning Varina to her directly but had made a point of extolling the President's wife to others in her hearing. Mrs. Chesnut had been distinctly frosty to Lydia on this occasion. Lydia knew she was out of favor, like her husband, and observed:

. . . to the people here, who despise Mrs. D. she spoke of the lady's cultivation, & graciousness. I am told Mrs. D. attributes her scarcity of friends to the influence of you & me—an ingratitude not to be overlooked, as "Jeff made both of their husbands." I ought not to talk of this creature, it arouses such a bitterness within me, & disgust that I ever should have cared for her—which I certainly *once* did.

A month earlier Lydia had written to Charlotte saying that she had managed to make some good friends in Montgomery in spite of Varina's warning that she was "so worldly and insincere" she should be avoided. "I think it was going out of her way to try & prejudice the people of a place where her husband's injustice to mine compelled me to live, a stranger too, to everyone, as I was, but I think it gained friends for me, certainly she has left few here. I'm told they are making great efforts to have a pleasant home in Richmond. Have you met any of them?" [15]

In this same letter Lydia said she was sick from anxiety and care. "The idea of the country blaming him for his misfortune keeps me wretched," she wrote of her husband. She assumed Richmond still was safe, since the "Royal Family had not departed." She prophesied a falling out between Varina and Mrs. Chesnut at this time and "hoped for it." Evidently she was unaware that Varina had quietly left town with her baby. Lydia seems to have regarded the President's wife as provocateur as well as accessory, although her letter of August 2 suggests that she felt Davis to have been her husband's mortal enemy even before they left Washington, at a time when she was an intimate friend of the President's wife and one of her warmest admirers.

Varina was carrying a watch that a dying soldier had asked to have sent on to his family when she remarked to Mrs. Chesnut on one of their drives that she rated Fitzhugh Lee far ahead of General John B. Hood as a commander. By this time she had a fixed view of all the generals and statesmen of the Confederacy. She made up a little bundle of *cartes de visite* of those she called her "particular favorites." They are in the Confederate Museum in Richmond now and supply some clue to Varina's likes and dislikes among the men who surrounded her husband. Joseph Johnston and Beauregard are conspicuously missing. Jackson and Longstreet are present. Neither Toombs nor Wigfall figures in Varina's list, although Howell Cobb and Judah Benjamin do.[16] She prized a youthful picture of Robert E. Lee with a mustache, as she preferred him, before he grew his beard. The notation with his *carte de visite* reads: "Gen. R. E. Lee when Mrs. Davis first knew him." Varina's list follows:

Judah P. Benjamin	General Robert E. Lee
General Braxton Bragg	General James Longstreet
General John C. Breckinridge	Colonel F. R. Lubbock
General Simon Bolivar Buckner	S. R. Mallory
James Chesnut, Jr.	General Humphrey Marshall
Howell Cobb	C. G. Memminger
General Thomas R. R. Cobb	Colonel John Pelham
General Samuel Cooper	General John C. Pemberton
Dr. John J. Craven	General A. S. Pendleton
General William M. Gardner	Colonel Henry E. Peyton
General Wade Hampton	George W. Randolph
General Stonewall Jackson	John H. Reagan
General Bradley T. Johnson	James A. Seddon
Custis Lee	George A. Trenholm
Fitzhugh Lee	Leroy Pope Walker

Chickamauga was fought in August. The casualties were heavy, the gains slight, although it was a Confederate victory. Davis considered Bragg's work on this occasion outstanding. The President toured the area to try to bring peace among his squabbling generals, but Mrs.

McLean reported back to Mrs. Chesnut that he could not reconcile them and that "Atlanta is crammed with displaced or dissatisfied Generals." He reviewed the army under the enemy's guns at Chattanooga. Colonel Chesnut was with him and thought it a splendid cavalcade. He wrote to his wife in October that "every honest man he saw out west thought well of Joe Johnston," and Mrs. Chesnut observed:

The President detests Joe Johnston for all the trouble he has given him, and Joe returns the compliment with compound interest. His hatred of Jeff Davis amounts to a religion. With him it colors all things. . . . Being such a good hater, it is a pity he has not elected to hate somebody else than the President of our country. He hates not wisely but too well.[17]

Richard Taylor, a less prejudiced observer and a staunch admirer of General Johnston as well as of Jefferson Davis, felt that Johnston's great abilities as a general "would have distinctly modified, if not changed, the current of events," but that his mind was so jaundiced about Davis "as to seriously cloud his judgment and impair his usefulness." There is ample evidence that both Varina and Lydia had helped to feed this feud.[18]

Late in November, Bragg was defeated in hard fighting around Chattanooga, where Grant captured Lookout Mountain. The West seemed lost to the Confederacy. "General Bragg felt, like Sidney Johnston, that success should be in a measure the test of a military man's merit, and he asked to be relieved," Varina wrote. "The President knew that General Bragg was both an able general and a devoted patriot, and after granting the request he invited him to be his Chief of Staff, or, in citizen's phrase, military counsel at Richmond."

Varina emphasized the point that his command was offered first to General William J. Hardee, who declined it so decisively that "there was no appeal from it," and General Johnston took over on December 16, 1863.[19] Varina left no doubt that he was second choice. By this time he did not want the command, and Lydia was more indignant than ever. Again the President's treatment of Johnston stirred up fresh criticism in Richmond. Mrs. Wigfall, meeting Mrs. Chesnut on her way to the Executive Mansion, asked her "with a sneer if the distance between Clay Street and the White House was not disagreeable to me." And her husband, at her side, immediately cut in with, "They say Benjamin wrote the President's message."

"Never!" said Mrs. Chesnut loyally. "Jeff Davis writes his own messages."

A few evenings later, visiting the Chesnut quarters, Wigfall said he wanted to see Jeff Davis hanged.[20] Just before Christmas, Mrs. Davis and Mrs. James Lyons lunched with Mrs. Chesnut at her home and on their way back to the Executive Mansion they met the President riding alone. They all thought this imprudent, but "Burton Harrison says he prefers to go alone, and there is none to gainsay him." Varina and many others thought he was taking chances, with all the hatred focused in his direction. Actually he had lightly dismissed an attempt made on his life at this time when a shot whistled past him as he rode in the neighborhood of Gillis Creek. He headed his horse straight in the direction from which the shot had come. A search was made of the shanties in the neighborhood, and a crank was discovered who was thought to be the culprit. He was not prosecuted but was sent to General Lee to be turned into a soldier. The matter was hushed up.[21]

His old enemy Henry Foote, seeking to emphasize the presidential arrogance, wrote of an encounter Davis had at this time with a young guard outside Libby Prison and the pacifying role played by Varina.[22] They had been to Drewry's Bluff. On their return their carriage was not at Rockett's wharf, so they walked home. A sentinel, not recognizing the President, challenged him as he passed the prison.

Davis told him who he was, but it was late in the evening and almost dark. The sentry would not accept the identification. He barred their way. The President angrily drew his sword cane, according to Foote. The sentinel promptly pointed his musket at Jefferson Davis. Without an instant's hesitation Varina sprang between them and with "prompt and fearless interposition" assured the soldier upon her honor that he was indeed talking to the President. The sentinel took her word for it and let them pass, but retribution followed next day for the skeptical sentinel.

Varina, who was pregnant again by the end of the year, drove nearly every day with Mrs. Chesnut. They went to the hospitals and did errands for their husbands. They attended war weddings and many funerals. They discussed the books and magazines they were currently reading, although Varina found less and less time for this diversion. *Romola* was proving diverting, and both were interested in Augusta Jane Evans's novel *Macaria*, bound in wallpaper and published in 1863. The tall young brunette, then busy in hospital kitchens, had dedicated it to the Confederacy, but she was a warm ally of Beauregard and a critic of Jefferson Davis.

Varina confided that she was angry with Ives, her husband's aide, for opening too many of her private letters "by mistake." She was also annoyed to find that only one of sixty letters arriving from women and non-combatants was shown to her husband, whereas General Lee insisted on every such letter being answered, and consolation offered to those who needed it. The letters were sad, witty, abusive, diverse in tone. There were even some from women who complained of Jeb Stuart, whose horse the girls bedecked with garlands. One said he should be forbidden to kiss one girl unless he kissed them all.[23]

Colonel Chesnut was annoyed with his wife at this time because of her numerous parties. He protested continually, but the young belles and their cavaliers sought out her worldly quarters day after day, for the bright company and also for the good fare coming in from Camden. General A. R. Lawton, too, was upset and told Mrs. Chesnut on their way in to supper one evening that all seemed too gay and too careless "for such terrible times." [24] It was out of place in battle-scarred Richmond. But Mrs. Chesnut insisted that hope and fear both were gone by this time and it was "distraction or death with us."

She turned to Varina for collusion on the day word reached her that General Johnston had assumed the Western command. The President, General Lee, Colonel Chesnut, and General Elzey had all gone out to look at the fortifications surrounding Richmond, General Lee riding on Chesnut's gray horse on this occasion. Mrs. Chesnut confided to Varina that she was in a fix. General Hampton had sent her game. Eggs and butter had come from Camden and she had brandy for eggnog and apple toddy, so she had planned a gathering for that night, although her husband had "positively ordered" her not to give any more parties and he is "decidedly master of his own house."

Varina listened understandingly and said she was giving a dinner for the party riding around the fortifications and would keep Colonel Chesnut with her as late as possible. But in the end he eluded Varina and returned home early, to find the party in full blast. He had had no advance warning and his wife "trembled in her shoes." But he weathered it well. He was courteous all round. Next day, however, his verdict was final: "No more parties. The country is in danger. There is too much levity here." [25]

With the approach of Christmas, 1863, Varina rounded up such confections as she could for the children and the limited type of present then to be had. Her husband gave Mrs. Chesnut what the recipient delightedly described as a "love of a parasol." The *Examiner's* Christmas present to the President was the blunt charge that he was becoming a dictator. Varina spread such bounty as she could before settling down with her own family for the day. Many gifts had come in from the plantations, including the game so lavishly supplied by Wade Hampton. On Christmas Eve, as snow threatened, groups of women carried baskets with sprigs of holly to the wounded.

The Davises gave a big reception on New Year's Day, after which the President's arm was stiff for days from handshaking and Varina's was tender to the touch. Colonel Browne and Colonel Ives, the two aides, in full rig with swords and sashes, were ushers, but Colonel Chesnut appeared in plain clothes and stood unostentatiously behind Varina, who was still in mourning for her father. L. Q. C. Lamar, who had not been confirmed by the Senate as Ambassador to Russia, had come home and was in the visiting line. Confederate contacts abroad were floundering badly. The North was winning the diplomatic game after Gettysburg, and Mason and Slidell were overwhelmed in their respective posts. No one jeered at Ulysses Grant any longer. "He fights to win," said Mrs. Chesnut. "And like Lincoln, we have ceased to carp at him because he is a rough clown. It doesn't take much soap and water to wash the hands that hold the rod of empire." 26

All through January there were festivities for Brigadier General John H. Morgan, whose raids had made him famous. Kentuckians were much in evidence at Varina's board and the hospitality of the city had been voted for the visiting General. The *Examiner* noted that a fine band played at Mrs. Davis's second reception in a month and the "attendance of distinguished generals now in the city, prominent members of Congress and the State Legislature, citizens generally and strangers, was larger than on any previous occasion." 27

Varina that night publicly snubbed one of her critics, a youth named Willie Munford who had been circulating a poem on her feud with Mrs. Myers, giving all the advantage to her opponent.28 While debating a matter of pronunciation as they downed oysters and sipped champagne, Varina turned to Willie and remarked, with a sharp note in her voice, "I hear you are a poet, or at least you write burlesque. What do *you* say?"

Everyone realized at once that she was jabbing with intent, and Munford was deeply embarrassed. General Preston hastily created a diversion, but Varina had had her innings. The Myers incident was recurrently quoted in official quarters. That same month James L. Orr writing to Governor James H. Hammond, referred to the "Quarter master General who was the only efficient bureau officer in Richmond turned out neck and heels because it is said his wife and the President's wife quarreled some two years ago." [29]

"Agnes" again wrote sharply to Mrs. Pryor about Varina on this occasion. She noted that she was wearing black for her father but that "all the ladies looked positively gorgeous." Continuing, she said:

> We should not expect suppers in these times, but we do have them! Champagne is $350 a dozen, but we sometimes have champagne! The confectioners charge $15 for a cake, but we have cake. . . . We have heard from dear old Dudley Mann; but of course *he* can do nothing for us in England, and he had as well come home and go with me to receptions. Mrs. Davis receives every Tuesday, and Mr. Mann is a better squire of dames than he is a diplomat.[30]

Varina did what she could for the war weddings, too. She offered the presidential carriage to titian-haired Hetty Cary, whom she "tenderly loved and admired." [31] But in the end Hetty drove up to St. Paul's Church in a broken-down old hack on an icy January day for her wedding to Brigadier General John Pegram. At the last minute the horses had reared so uncontrollably that a hack had to be summoned hastily to get them to the church in time.

One mishap followed another. Hetty tore her tulle veil at the church vestibule as she stooped to pick up her lace handkerchief. She had already broken a mirror, ill omens that were later recalled when she knelt at her bridegroom's coffin in the same chancel only three weeks later. But on her wedding day her cousin Connie commented on her glowing looks, her radiant hair. Many handsome officers had been in love with Hetty, who liked her beaux "gilt-edged," her cousin jested. Now she became a bride and a widow within the space of a month. It was only a matter of days until John was hit in the heart by a Minié ball. As he led a charge his sword was struck from his hand by the impact, its scabbard filling with blood.

Varina heard the news with a growing sense of doom. She had often watched Hetty dance with Jeb Stuart, and she had seen her romance with John Pegram develop. Hetty was sitting in an ambulance carding lint, not far from the battlefield where he died. None knew how to break the news to her. At last she was told to go back to her quarters and rest, since her husband would be late returning. She slept all night, unconscious that his body had been carried in downstairs.

Hollywood Cemetery was blanketed in snow the day they all went there to see him buried. Later his younger brother, Colonel William Pegram, fell in the retreat from Petersburg. The undertow of death ran through all the social events that winter and spring. The memory of Gettysburg and Vicksburg was fresh and bitter, but Grant had not yet begun his assault in the Wilderness. The fighting on the Virginia front had been intermittent, and most of the activity early that year was in the Mississippi Valley. Beautiful girls were still much in evidence in Richmond and young cavalry captains were always at their command.

Varina was following two romances with close attention at this time. Young Connie Cary and Burton Harrison were deeply in love and were keeping rendezvous in the woods above the canal close to Camp Winder, where Connie was helping her mother run a hospital. It consisted of a string of rude sheds of unpainted pine, "with diet kitchens and store rooms around which were gathered wards and tents." Together they had converted their roughly boarded room into comfortable quarters with bits of old mahogany, a folding screen, a matting rug, a mirror, some muslin curtains tied back with her one blue sash, and a box of ivy, geranium and sweet alyssum outside the sill. They now breakfasted on corn bread with drippings, and coffee made of dried beans and peanuts. In the evening they had corn-meal cakes with sorghum molasses and dried apples.

Burton would arrive with books and the latest news from the Executive Mansion. They would sit under shelving boughs and listen to the Negroes sing in the canal boats below, while they read, talked, and tried to forget the war for an hour. The other romance that Varina watched moved less smoothly. General Hood, who had been wounded several times and had lost a leg at Chickamauga, was infatuated with Sally Buchanan Preston, known to her friends as Buck. She had many other suitors, but Varina listened sympathetically to Hood and suffered for him when he took her in to supper at a presidential reception and they heard Buck disown him audibly as they sat talking after the meal was ended.[32]

"Absurd! Engaged to that man! Never! For what do you take me?" Buck exclaimed in a clear, ringing voice.

Varina looked at the General and hastily quoted General Pendleton's remark about him that had it been his fate to have been hit so often, "he would wince and dodge at every ball." Hood looked hard at Varina and replied in a desperate way, "Why wince, when you would thank God for a ball to go through your heart and be done with it all?"

The General received an ovation in Varina's parlors on this occasion and his crutches were like badges of honor. The President paid him great attention and gave him his arm going into church the following Sunday. Mrs. Davis treated him with unvarying kindness. His wooing was so ardent that Buck, in spite of family opposition, finally became engaged to the General who had made the Texas Brigade a strong fighting unit in General Lee's army. But the marriage never came off. Eventually both found other partners.

Things by this time had settled down at the Executive Mansion after an attempt to burn the dwelling and the sudden departure of Henry, the butler, the third servant to decamp in as many weeks.[33] The incendiary attempt was made on the day of Varina's second reception. Shavings and a bundle of faggots placed against a pile of wood in a basement room were already on fire when they were found and extinguished. The window was smashed and groceries had been stolen.

Henry's departure distressed Varina, although he had been in her service only a short time. These defections were becoming a commonplace. By this time the Emancipation Proclamation was having its effect on the Negroes. The President's personal servant, and Betsy, Varina's maid, had long since decamped. "The condition of our servants began to be unsettled," she noted, the feeling being that they were being paid to go north. Davis viewed the proclamation as an invitation to one of three consequences—"the extermination of the slaves, the exile of the whole white population of the Confederacy, or absolute and total separation of these States from the United States." [34]

Stories told by runaway servants made interesting reading in the North, and the Davises were particularly upset by their former coachman's statements, which had been reported by McDowell to Stanton on May 4, 1862.[35] The coachman quoted Varina as attacking General Johnston while she was driving with her husband and as saying that the Confederacy was about played out; that if New Orleans were really taken she no longer had any interest in the war, as all she had was there; and that it was a great pity they had ever attempted to help Virginia and the other non-cotton-growing states.

In later years Varina was to defend her servants; to insist that most of them were loyal; to deny that there were spies in her household, or any who conveyed information out of it. According to her granddaughter, Mrs. Lucy Hayes Young: "All her house servants were free, as she said she wanted to feel that all her service was willing." [36] Some of their servants stayed with the Davises to the end, and showed great loyalty under stress. Varina was liked by her maids, although she sometimes chastised them much as she did her children, and they stood in awe of her. She demanded efficient service, trained them carefully herself, and was always interested in their welfare and family problems.[37]

She coped as well as she could with these domestic contingencies. At the end of January she gave her customary Luncheon for Ladies, the best attended she had ever held, and De Leon noted that she seemed to be winning her way at last with the more conservative elements in Richmond. On this occasion she was able to serve gumbo, duck, chicken in jelly, oysters, chocolate cream, jelly cake, claret cup, and champagne, not exactly a starvation repast. Her guests sat around her oblong rosewood table and used her Sèvres china which had won a prize in Vienna. Her coffee cups were blue and gold with a rose pattern, and her silver coffee spoons were marked with the initial D. She used ruby-tinted glasses for wine. Even when the fare was simple, which it was not on this occasion, things were served with style and even General Lee enjoyed Varina's domestic touch.

Although there was little social interchange between her and Mrs. Lee, the General was frequently at their home and they always took him into the family circle when the President was not feeling well. Lee would join Davis in his private study, just as he was the only person ever permitted to walk unannounced into Cabinet meetings. When the General arrived with the President in the late afternoon, the clatter of their horses' hoofs was the signal for Mrs. James Grant to run in with some good fare from her farm on the outskirts of Richmond. Mrs. Grant was a member of the Crenshaw family, owners of the large flour mills of Richmond. She was a Quaker, and Varina admired her spirit. "The very sight of her handsome face brought comfort to our hearts," she wrote. "She fed the hungry, visited the sick, clothed the naked, showed mercy to the wicked, and her goodness, like the city set upon the hill, could not be hid." [38]

Varina gives an intimate picture of a visit Lee paid them one day when Jeff was too ill to go to headquarters. She invited him into the little morning room where her husband lay on a divan. The General bowed to Varina and apologized for the damage his splashed boots might do to her white carpet. He and the President at once plunged into army matters. "The two friends talked in a circle until both were worn out," Varina commented. Then the General noticed a little silver saucepan on her hearth. He said it was a "comfortable and pretty little thing" and asked her what use she made of it.

And then what a delight it gave me to heat the steaming hot *café au lait* it contained and hand it to him in a little Sèvres cup. When I attempted to ring for a servant to bring luncheon, he said: "This drink is exquisite, but I cannot eat; do not call a servant, it is very cozy just so;" then looking at the cup he remarked, with a twinkle in his eye, "my cups in camp are thicker, but this is thinner than the coffee." Behind the playful speech I saw the intense realization he had of the coarse ways and uncomfortable concomitants of a camp, and that he missed as keenly the refinements of life to which he had been accustomed after four years, as he did at first.[39]

At this time General Lee had meat only twice a week. A head of cabbage boiled in salt water and a pone of corn bread were his standard fare. His dinner service was of tin. However, he was not one of the critics of the manner in which other people lived, and his own tastes were shared by the President, who all his life was an abstemious eater. He did not have Varina's interest in good food, and was indifferent to what was put before him. If he had had his way, their fare would have been truly Spartan.

General Lee was always to pay tribute to Jefferson Davis and to treat Varina with great respect. There was something about his handsome presence, deferential yet aloof, kind yet direct, that spread reassurance around him, and their relations remained outwardly serene to the end. When asked after the war what kind of President Jefferson Davis had made he said in his temperate way, "If my opinion is worth anything, you can always say that few people could have done better than Mr. Davis. I knew of none that could have done as well." [40]

Varina did not hesitate to ask him for favors for her friends on behalf of their sons. She was worn down with appeals of one sort and another from women all over the Confederacy. At times she felt she must get away from the unceasing pressure. The light picture of her social doings presented by Mrs. Chesnut represented only the top layer of her existence, the outward froth that covered the turbulence of her days, and the deep passions that controlled her. There were many witnesses to her devoted attendance on her husband and her intimate knowledge of his affairs. The question of prisoner exchanges was one that often plagued them, and another diarist recalls an intimate scene, with the President lying exhausted on a divan after visiting the city fortifications, and assuring a visiting delegation that he would do what he could about a proposed exchange of prisoners, although it was not possible to help them at that particular moment.[41]

Varina, hovering around him, immediately assured the suppliants in a mollifying way that her husband was a father, and deeply sympathetic to family pleas. She promised that if the case slipped his mind through pressure of affairs she would bring it to his attention. She then served them tea and "made a very favorable impression on the minds of those gentlemen who had never seen her before, by her ease of manner, agreeable conversation, and the kindness of heart which she manifested."

Judah Benjamin was in and out of the house constantly at this time. Mrs. Chesnut noted in January, 1864, that every word he said was listened to with attention since "he is of the innermost shrine, supposed to enjoy the honor of Mr. Davis's unreserved confidence." The President still consulted him on military affairs, but Bragg was gaining ground in his counsels. The breach seemed ever to widen between the President and the Senate. By the middle of February the Davises discontinued their regular Tuesday evening receptions. The Legislature was considering a bill to suppress theatrical amusements during the war. "What would Shakespeare think of that?" ironically demanded the observant Jones.

Bacon was now ten to fifteen dollars a pound. Sugar was twelve dollars a pound and meal was fifty dollars a bushel. The meat stalls were closed, but a few carts were seen in the streets, peddling turnips, cabbages, parsnips, and carrots at fantastic prices. As much as a hundred dollars was asked for a wild turkey. Perch, chubb, and other fish sold at famine prices. The city was in a disordered state and incendiary fires abounded.

Varina drove out to view the ruins of Laburnum, the home of Mr. and Mrs. James Lyons, two of her closest friends and of whom she wrote: "A finer example of a high-bred Virginia household could not have been found." [42] A few days earlier she had taken tea with them under their shade trees. "Now—smoke and ashes, nothing more," she commented. Everybody was in trouble. Varina told Mrs. Chesnut at this time that paper money had depreciated so in value that they could not live within their income and must give up their carriage and horses. Together they went to a shop run by a mulatto to buy mourning for Mrs. Chesnut. Her mother-in-law had died at Mulberry Plantation. She paid thirty dollars for gloves on this occasion, fifty dollars for a pair of slippers, and it cost her a hundred and sixty dollars to have a shabby black alpaca dress made up.

The soldiers themselves were gay enough of spirit to have snowball fights that winter. Women worked in the government offices, to the dismay of the Secretary of War, who found they distracted him with "their noise of moving of chairs and running about." In March the city was startled by Ulric Dahlgren's raid. General Hugh J. Kilpatrick was threatening Richmond. Bragg had organized a cavalry squad to protect the city and young dragoons were in and out, squiring the belles, as well as mounting guard. Fourteen generals were counted one Sunday in St. Paul's at this crucial moment.

There were strange scenes in church, where everyone had a stake in what went on. Mrs. Clay observed that at Rachel Lyons's wedding to Dr. James Fontaine Heustis at this time, "you never saw such disorder in God's house before in your life. Mrs. Davis, Mrs. Mallory and Mrs. Most-everybody-else, stood up in the pews and you could not hear one word of the service for the noise." [43] Varina, who was about to have her baby, was intensely nervous and in spite of her strong sense of social decorum she was given to impetuous action. The city had been in an uproar for a week and she was badly shaken.

The apricot trees were just beginning to bloom when the President proclaimed a day of fasting and prayer. The last snows of a long and bitter winter had finally melted. There was ice in the gutters and misery in countless homes. Varina was greatly depressed at this time. She confided to her most intimate friends that the fall of Richmond must come, and when it did she would send her children to Mrs. Chesnut and Mrs. Preston. Mrs. Chesnut begged her to leave with them, but Varina said nothing.

She had taken into her home a small Negro boy named Jim Limber, who had been brutally beaten by his guardian. He was an orphan and was covered with wounds and bruises when she found him. She had dressed him in some of her own Joe's clothing and he was "happy as a lord." He was soon seen about with the Davis boys. Jeff was an excellent little horseman by this time. He often rode with his father or cantered along beside the carriage in which his mother drove. Sometimes small boys would run after them in the streets shouting at Jeff, who would flush but not turn around. A gang of boys on the plain below were known as the "Butcher Cats." They despised the "Hill Cats" from the large mansions up above, but Jefferson Davis had tempered the feud with tactful words.

By this time the Davises were having considerable trouble with their own well-disciplined children, and Varina was showing impatience with them. She took them all driving with Mrs. Chesnut on April 11 and the uproar startled even that worldly onlooker.

They are wonderfully clever and precocious children, but with unbroken wills. At one time there was a sudden uprising of the nursery contingent; they fought, screamed, laughed. It was bedlam broken loose. Mrs. Davis scolded, laughed and cried. . . .[44]

On another occasion the Davises started out with their children to call on the Chesnuts, but they became so unruly in the street that Varina decided they must all go home. She was finding it increasingly difficult to keep order among them with the excitement to which they were daily witnesses. The galloping courier had become a symbol in their lives. Some time earlier Mrs. Henry S. Foote, the wife of Davis's traditional enemy, had written a letter which appeared in the Washington Daily Morning Chronicle with the headline "Mrs. Davis Rules Jeffie," and caused much talk. It reflected on Varina's care of her children. "Mrs. Jeff is not pretty, but a fine-looking woman who dresses badly, in no taste," she commented. "She is not much liked here and is said to control 'Jeffie,' as she calls her husband. She has several children. She takes but little notice of them. They go about with their clothes tossed on in any & every style. She has public affairs to attend to . . . The President looks *care-worn* and *troubled*. He is very thin, and looks feeble and bent. He prays aloud in church and is a devout Episcopalian." [45]

Mrs. Foote was the only one of Varina's many critics to think that she neglected her children. Most of her friends considered her over-absorbed in family matters and all too ready to discuss and quote her offspring. But she was constantly torn between the need to be at her husband's service and the demands of her growing boys and little Margaret. Whichever way she turned she encountered trouble or criticism. She was due to have a baby in two months' time, and the children were reacting to all the excitement and uncertainty around them. They could see that their father was silent, their mother worried. Officers were in and out of the house at all hours of the day and night. For once, Varina's grip on her family affairs was giving her trouble. She was distracted by the complexity of her duties.

⚜ 12 ⚜

A SMALL BOY DIES

ON THE last day of April, 1864, five-year-old Joe was playing on the piazza outside the servants' quarters. He clambered up on the railing, fell to the brick pavement below, and was killed. Varina had gone to her husband's office with a basket lunch, and the child died a few minutes after they reached him. He never regained consciousness or recognized them.

Davis had been ailing greatly all through April. He could not sleep. He did not care to eat. Varina had resumed her old Washington custom of preparing a tempting lunch for him and going to his office with it. Sometimes she would stay to see that he ate it. She had been engaged in this mission on the last day of the month when word of Joe's accident reached her. Varina has left her own comment on her son's death.

I left my children quite well, playing in my room, and had just uncovered my basket in his office, when a servant came for me. The most beautiful and brightest of my children, Joseph Emory, had, in play, climbed over the connecting angle of a bannister and fallen to the brick pavement below. He died a few minutes after we reached his side. This child was Mr. Davis's hope, and greatest joy in life.[1]

"Not mine, oh, Lord, but thine," Davis kept exclaiming over and over again, sorrowing as Lincoln did for his Willie. In the midst of his grief a courier arrived with a dispatch. He stood staring at it for some moments, then turned to Varina with a fixed expression and asked, "Did you tell me what was in it?"

"I saw his mind was momentarily paralyzed by the blow, but at last he tried to write an answer, and then called out, in a heart-broken tone,

'I must have this day with my little child.' Somebody took the dispatch to General Cooper and left us alone with our dead."

Maggie had gone down the James that day with Mrs. Chesnut, the Lees, and the Mallorys, to watch the exchange of prisoners. On their return, as she reached the Davis carriage, she screamed suddenly when someone whispered in her ear that Joe was dead. She sobbed all the way home. Burton Harrison met them at the door. Their neighbors, Mrs. Semmes and Mrs. George Barksdale, were already there. All the windows were wide open. The curtains blew softly in the spring air. The house was lit up but everything was deathly still. Mrs. Semmes told Mrs. Chesnut that when she first got there little Jeff was kneeling by his brother and he called out to her in great distress, "Mrs. Semmes, I have said all the prayers I know how, but God will not wake Joe." [2]

Mrs. Chesnut saw him before she left the house that night, lying surrounded by flowers, but she did not get to his parents. Catherine, his Irish nurse, lay prone on the floor beside him, wailing. Jeff had run to her, too, to say that Joe would not wake up. Burton Harrison made all the funeral arrangements. He told Connie a "pitiful tale of the mother's passionate grief and the terrible self-control of the President who, shutting himself in his own room, had paced the floor all night."

A large crowd, touched by the sorrow that had darkened the President's home, turned out for Joe's funeral. Hundreds of school children marched up the hillside to the cemetery, each carrying a green bough or a bouquet to throw on his grave, which was already massed with white flowers. The President was pictured "straight as an arrow, clear against the sky, by the open grave of his son," [3] while Varina's tall figure drooped and her great dark eyes were mournful and still. Stories about Joe were now heard on all sides. He was a gentle child, the most docile of the boys, and devoted to his father.

Now the sum of Varina's woes came close to that of Mrs. Lincoln. Their lives had been forced into the final parallel, in the death of a young son. Both, however, had the inestimable gift of tenderness and understanding from the men to whom they were married. When Mary Todd Lincoln lost this enveloping support, her life collapsed. Varina, stronger and more resilient by nature, had a quarter of a century more to pass with Jefferson Davis.

Meanwhile, she went on in a daze, awaiting the birth of her next baby. The President had little time to think of his sorrow, for immediately after Joseph's funeral Sherman started his march to Atlanta, Grant crossed the Rapidan, and Butler sailed up the James toward Richmond. When Davis hurried into the Executive Mansion for his pistols one morning on his way to the field, where an attempt was being made to check General Sherman's raiders, Varina called the children together for prayer. This was often her custom when she knew her husband to be entering a battle area. But seven-year-old Jeff, sobered by his brother's death and the audible small arms going off in the vicinity "like the popping of firecrackers," got up from his knees and turned to his mother with the remark, "You had better have my pony saddled, and let me go out to help father; we can pray afterward." [4]

This skirmishing was the prelude to the death of Jeb Stuart at Yellow Tavern. He was forming his troops to repel the raiders when he was recognized and peppered with shot. Varina noted that he asked his staff to support him in the saddle, so that the enemy might not see that he was wounded. In this fashion he rode back to his own lines to die. He was delirious and his mind wandered, as Jackson's had done. He fought battles and was occupied with the details of his command. He urged his troops "to make haste."

When he was dying Davis took his hand and asked him how he felt.

"Easy, but willing to die, if God and my country think I have fulfilled my destiny and done my duty," he replied in a firm, cheerful voice. He sang "Rock of Ages," prayed, and passed away an hour and a half before his wife arrived at his bedside. Varina could scarcely accept the quenching of this robust spirit. Her tribute to him was born out of intimate knowledge of the dashing soldier who had been in and out of her home.

He had attained a noble fame, and no one dissented from the praise bestowed upon "Beauty Stuart." He had lived void of offence toward his fellow-men, and life was for him one long feast of good-will toward them. . . . He sang, laughed, fought, and prayed throughout all the deprivations and hardships of the Confederate service, never daunted, never carping at the mistakes of others.[5]

Stuart left Mrs. Lee his golden spurs as a dying memento of his love and esteem for her husband. He gave his horses to his staff officers and his sword to his son. "They fought in better cheer for the memory of such sainted leaders as Stonewall Jackson and Beauty Stuart," said Varina of the men then facing one of the supreme engagements of the war.

The concentrated fighting that now developed between Lee, with a third as many men, and Grant, who had moved in from the west with heavy reinforcements, kept North and South breathless with suspense. The violence of Grant's assault and the brilliance of Lee's strategy were high drama. But when Grant, repulsed after staggering losses, shifted his attack to Petersburg he had found the key to Richmond. Meanwhile, the people in the capital lived from day to day, going about the streets, the hospitals, their kitchens and gardens, dimly sensing as the weeks went on that the end must be in sight, in spite of the confident statements of the President.

The hostile beam of the press was still focused on the Davis family, and Pollard noted that as Grant's army approached Richmond "not for a day did Mr. Davis change the unpopular routine of his household, abate the luxury of his table, or his allowance of Havana cigars, or neglect his evening ride on his shabby horse, while his more pretentious wife gathered on the wheels of her equipage the dust through which Lee's barefoot soldiers might have trudged an hour before." [6]

In actual fact, there was little about Varina that was pretentious at this time, with Joe's death fresh in her memory and a new baby about to be born. White and silent, deeply saddened by her child's death and the sorrows of the country, she moved about the house in abject misery, wearing a gray calico dress with lavender flowers, still to be seen in Richmond. True, her husband still rode every day for exercise. He had invited F. R. Lubbock of Texas to become an aide that summer, saying he wanted someone familiar with the trans-Mississippi country on his staff. Day followed day with keen anxiety and a growing sense of disaster in spite of the President's outward optimism.

The funeral march reverberated constantly in Richmond. Women everywhere were in turmoil, and on June 26, the day before Varina's baby was born, Lydia Johnston wrote to Charlotte Wigfall from Atlanta, as Sherman marched South, that many were leaving the city "in confusion and fright." [7] But she had no fears, she added, and even if she had, her place was close to her husband so long as she did not cause him anxiety. "Comforts I have long since ceased looking for, don't want them, & feel really luxurious if I can keep near my husband."

But the Johnstons, too, were soon on their way out of Atlanta and not of their own free will. The General was standing on the city fortifications when he received a message from Richmond in the middle of July informing him that he should "immediately turn over the com-

mand of the Army and Department of Tennessee to General Hood."
Wigfall wrote to Johnston that Hood was much embarrassed when he
read his notification from a telegram lit by a guttering candle on top
of a barrel. Johnston promptly joined Lydia at her home outside
Atlanta, then proceeded to Macon by freight car. Howell Cobb entertained them there and Mrs. Clay rushed over to him as he came out of
church and kissed him in public, fond though she was of Jefferson
Davis.[8]

On June 27 Varina had borne her second daughter, Winnie (Varina
Anne), who one day would be known as the Daughter of the Confederacy. She was born in the large bedroom on the second floor. Billy
was born on the top floor "looking towards the railway," Varina recalled
in 1898.[9] She was now thirty-seven and the war years had aged her
greatly. Her glossy black hair was strongly threaded with gray. The guns
pounded at Petersburg during these early weeks of the baby's life, but
Richmond was safe for the summer, with the pressure centered elsewhere. The long slow siege was under way and the crater blown up at
the end of July seemed to rock the entire Confederacy. But the mine
exploded under the Southern defenses by the Federal troops proved to
be even more disastrous to themselves. Roses, magnolias, and jessamine
were riotously beautiful in Petersburg while its people hid in caves,
there was no food to be had, and only the aged and the very young
remained to guard the beleaguered city.

The death of little Joseph had created sympathy for Varina and had
broken down some of the antagonism toward her. Her own pride had
been softened by sorrow. In a letter to Mrs. Chesnut she wrote with
bitter irony: "People do not snub me any longer, for it was only while
the lion was dying that he was kicked; dead, he was beneath contempt.
Not to say I am worthy to be called a lion, nor are the people here
asses." [10]

When Atlanta fell at the beginning of September after a five-week
siege, the Confederacy was faced with a new horror in Sherman's march
to the sea. Wide columns of smoke swirled over a sixty-mile track as
the land was burned and homes were destroyed. Soon Mrs. Chesnut
was moving from point to point ahead of Sherman's bugles. Early in
autumn she was in Columbia, predicting "fire and swords" for that
picturesque town, an expectation soon fulfilled. Lydia Johnston was
there too, and Mrs. Chesnut was forced reluctantly to pay tribute to her
manner. "It is the day of her triumph," she noted. "In the small matter

of good manners, Mrs. Johnston is a notable example to her understrappers and followers." The General, too, was present, taking a gloomy view of the future.

Varina was still weak and languid when the President went south to visit his troops after the fall of Atlanta, but she had occasional flashes of hope as her strength returned. She had sent Maggie to stay with Mrs. Chesnut and she wrote to her friend that although she did not "snuff success in every passing breeze" she was so tired of hoping and fearing and being disappointed that she had "made up her mind not to be disconsolate." Another attack on Richmond was expected, but "I think the avalanche will not slide until the Spring breaks up its winter quarters." She finished on a strongly personal note: "I generally let out my crazy bone to you, so I must tell you how exquisite my little baby is. She looks like a little rosebud. It is the only point upon which I feel not very sane."

With Atlanta fallen to the enemy, Davis was roundly abused for removing General Johnston. There were demands for the restoration of his command. There had been trouble with Governor Joseph E. Brown of Georgia over reinforcements, so the President tried to build up confidence by making patriotic speeches in Alabama and Georgia. Varina was shocked to learn that he headed into fresh criticism at once for disclosing Hood's plans. Sherman sent to Washington, a transcript of his remarks indicating the plan to invade Tennessee and Kentucky.[11]

He stopped off in Columbia and visited the Chesnuts in the small trim house they had taken for the time being. Mrs. Chesnut was now peddling her butter and eggs for two hundred dollars a month and the last of her silks and satins were being sold off. But she adorned her new home for the presidential visit with mirrors that had belonged to the first Wade Hampton, prerevolutionary relics; fine old carpets that her father had owned, and curtains to match. "It is the wind-up, the Cassandra in me says: and the old life means to die royally," said Mrs. Chesnut.[12]

She had always liked to bask in the President's favor, to sit in his pew at church, to engage his attention in long conversations at the receptions, and to walk or drive with him. She and Mrs. Clay were particular favorites of his. "I did all that could be done for our honored chief on this occasion," she wrote. "Besides, I like the man. He has been so kind to me, and his wife is one of the few to whom I can never be grateful enough for her generous appreciation and attention." Now she went to the gates to greet him as he arrived with Custis Lee and Governor Lubbock. He kissed her, and as people gathered in the street to stare at him he moved in from the piazza. Custis sat on the banisters smoking a cigar while she whipped up the dessert. He told her how serious he thought things were. She entertained the President with sixty-year-old Madeira from Mulberry, boned turkey with truffles, stuffed tomatoes and peppers. Maggie eagerly questioned him about her sister and the new baby.

Varina wrote to Mrs. Chesnut on November 6, 1864, thanking her for her kindness to Maggie and for entertaining the President so royally. It is evident that by this time she was losing all hope.

> We are in a sad and anxious state here now. The dead come in, the living do not go out so fast. However we hope all things, and trust in God. . . . Strictly between us, things look very anxious here. *Verbum sap.* I am so constantly depressed that I dread writing, for penned lines betray our feelings despite every care.[13]

General Wade Hampton, who commanded the Confederate Cavalry after Jeb Stuart's death, and his two sons had just been involved in a tragedy of Shakespearian proportions. "I was dreadfully shocked at Preston Hampton's fate," Varina continued. "I know nothing in history more touching than Wade Hampton's situation at that supreme moment, when he sent one son to save the other, and saw them both fall, and did not know for some moments whether both were not killed."

Preston had ridden into the hottest fire, ahead of the line. His father, in command, had sent young Wade galloping after him. As the youth reached his brother, Preston fell from his horse, mortally hit. Stooping to raise him, Wade was hit, too. The General rode up, to find one son dead, the other bleeding while he tried to support his brother. Hampton lifted his dead son in his arms, handed him over to the soldiers nearby, and ordered them to take care of Wade. He rode off to his command, not knowing the fate of his second son.

In this same letter Varina wrote of her own children—of little Margaret dancing the toes out of her shoes; of the new baby, already nicknamed Piecake or Li Pie, "so soft, so good . . . white as a lily, and has such exquisite hands and feet, and such bright blue eyes. She is Piecake still. . . . She seems conscious who I am, or rather, that I am her supply store, but she is an immense source of comfort to me."

As a family the Davises were addicted to pet names, some of them rather incomprehensible, like Li Pie and Banny, which first was applied to her husband by Varina and after his death was used for Varina by her grandchildren.[14] Margaret was Polly, the name Jeff had also used for his sister Anna, and Varina was sometimes jocularly known as "Waafe." There was a good deal of family fun among the Davises in their happier moments, stiff though Jeff was with his colleagues. Nicknames were part of the game. They were sometimes confusing to strangers and were the more surprising because of the outward dignity always maintained by Varina and Jeff.

There were occasions when Varina impatiently remarked that the President's children needed some attention too, when she was accused of making herself scarce. She was always responsive to family demands, and between the close attention she gave her husband, the hours she read to him in the night, her hospital visits, the management of her household, the supervision of her children, and the social and clerical demands made upon her through a large correspondence, she was as busy as any woman in Richmond.

Varina was a good neighbor. She was always ready to help with a remedy for a sick child, or to supply broth or arrowroot for an invalid. Emma Lyon Bryan, who had a house close to the Executive Mansion, where first the Browns and then the Chesnuts boarded, recalled that she was always "exceedingly genial and pleasant without any airs of superiority and walked in upon my mother who was arranging the dining table and upon invitation partook of the food when she and Mrs. Chesnut were going shopping." [15]

At this time Varina gave up her carriage and horses, feeling that she could no longer afford them. They were promptly bought back for twelve thousand dollars (Confederate money) and returned to her by James Lyons and the other men who had made the purchase for her originally. She still did not know how she would manage their upkeep, and she planned to sell a green satin dress to bring in some ready cash. She did not feel at this time that she would ever again wear anything but mourning, and indeed she was rarely seen thereafter in anything but black or white.

Congress convened on a dark wet day in November and at once a storm broke loose over Davis's proposal to use the slaves in the army and emancipate them after the war. Both Houses held many secret sessions. Wigfall raged in the Senate. There were stormy scenes, with Davis under fire, and Foote assailing him so violently that the papers did not dare to quote him. Varina watched her husband come in, gray and wilted after his daily battles, and finally he became extremely ill in December. He was even reported dead, but Jones finally concluded that perhaps he had not been ill at all, a favorite deduction of his when he could not understand what was going on. But Varina knew better. His neuralgic pains were plaguing him again with their seasonal visitation. Even the most skeptical could see that he was ill, whereas General Lee, appearing in town on December 20, was "looking robust, though weather worn." [16]

The sound of guns down the river could be heard clearly in Richmond. Fog, rain, and dismal weather threw a pall over the suffering and hungry city. Christmas Eve was clear and cold, as rumors spread that Savannah had been evacuated. The North was rejoicing over General Sherman's message to Lincoln: "I beg to present you as a Christmas present the city of Savannah, with 150 heavy guns and plenty of ammunition, and also about 25,000 bales of cotton."

There was no occasion for rejoicing at the White House of the Confederacy, but Varina did her best for the sake of the children. The family rations had shrunk by this time to rice, corn meal, and an occasional piece of meat. When she had the ingredients for a pie she would invite Governor Lubbock for his favorite dish. This Christmas rice, flour, molasses, and small pieces of meat had been sent to her anonymously to be dispensed to the needy. She made her rounds with these supplies, then helped her family assemble toys and confections for the orphans of the Episcopalian home. She urged her friends to strip their homes of such toys as they could spare, and appealed to her own children, "who rushed around the Mansion picking up eyeless dolls, three-legged horses, tops with the upper peg broken off, rubber toys, monkeys with all the squeak gone silent, and all the ruck of children's toys that gather in a nursery closet." [17]

Robert Brown, one of their most valued servants, made a doll house to give as a prize. Maggie Howell painted the mantel, shelves, door panels, grates, picture frames, and other adornments. Varina directed the making of furniture with twigs and pasteboard, and her mother, then staying with them, made pillows, mattresses, and sheets for the two little bedrooms. On Christmas Eve young people were invited in to string apples and popcorn for the tree. A neighbor made candle molds. Mr. Pizzini gave love verses to wrap with the candy he had sold them at the nominal price of $1.50 a pound. The tree was set up in the church. The President shared in the distribution of the toys on Christmas Day.

Varina managed to round up some substitute ingredients for their own mince pie and plum pudding. Their cook made a spun-sugar hen, life-size, on a nest full of blanc-mange eggs. All the servants filed in to wish them a Merry Christmas, according to custom, and each received a gift. Stockings were stuffed with molasses candy, apples, small whips plaited by the family, worsted reins knitted at home, woolen gloves for each, paper dolls, and small tops.

The President received a pair of chamois-skin riding gauntlets, embroidered and monogrammed under the guns of Fortress Monroe. The children had written him little letters with their grandmother's help. For Varina there were six cakes of soap made from the grease of a ham, a skein of fine gray linen thread spun at home, a pincushion made by "some poor woman and stuffed with wool from her pet sheep," a baby bonnet and handmade dress for Piecake, selections from Swinburne's poems bound in wallpaper, and a chamois needlebook left her by one of the visiting English correspondents.

The family all walked to church on Christmas morning. They never used the carriage for this purpose or drove out on Sunday. While they were attending the Christmas tree festivities for the orphan children, General Lee called at their home. He had received a barrel of sweet potatoes which had been sent to him by mistake. "He did not discover the mistake until he had taken his share (a dishful) and given the rest to the soldiers!" wrote Varina. "We wished it had been much more for them and him."

The day ended with a starvation party at a neighbor's home. There was dancing to the familiar war tunes. Officers rode into town with their long cavalry boots pulled up over their knees. They were splashed to the waist with mud, Varina noted, but they put up their horses, rushed to where they kept the remains of their dress uniforms, and did their best to celebrate the last Christmas of the Confederacy with good cheer and brave spirit.

Meanwhile, in Paris the Confederate chieftains gathered at Corbin's on New Year's Day, 1865. Slidell and General Randolph, among others, solemnly drank a toast: "The new year opens in sorrow. May it close in joy; God grant it." In Richmond the President sat in St. Paul's on that same day, with Varina in black by his side. He was wearing a woolen cap she had knitted for him, since he was again plagued by neuralgia. A few inches of snow had fallen in the night and the morning was clear and frosty. The Confederacy was in its closing hours and apathy had gripped Richmond. Even General Lee seemed despondent. Talk of evacuation was in the air and on January 12 he reported that he had only two days' rations for his army.[18]

The *Examiner* was pushing hard for the removal of Davis. Howell Cobb was opposed to arming the slaves. The women of Richmond were pressing their plate and jewels on the Treasury Department for the subsistence of the army. At this juncture Francis P. Blair walked into the Executive Mansion early in January, a self-appointed emissary of peace. Varina could not restrain herself but impulsively threw her arms around the neck of her old friend. This story soon took wings in Richmond and, in the opinion of the ever-watchful Jones, "was injurious to the President." She followed with the closest interest and apprehension the negotiations conducted by Blair during his two visits to Richmond that month.[19] He stayed unregistered at the Spotswood Hotel, rode around town with his old friend Robert Ould, a *bon vivant* of the Washington days, and dined at Mrs. Stanard's, where he heard talk by Stephens and others that was far from friendly to the Davis family.

Varina was unfeignedly glad to see him, both because she was devoted to all the Blairs, and because she felt that his coming might mean a glimmer of hope. The President received him cordially, too, assured him of his full confidence, and said he would never forget his obligations to the Blair family. But there was no compromise with the North at this point. All the talk led nowhere, and the Richmond *Examiner* commented as Blair left for the North again that it "looked with distrust and disgust upon his private interviews with Mr. Davis. . . . What right had Mr. Davis to allow the whispering old humbug to come here, spreading rumors and insinuating false suggestions."

Varina was again on the alert when the peace mission made up of Judge John H. Campbell, Alexander Stephens, and R. M. T. Hunter went north to confer with President Lincoln at Hampton Roads. The papers were filled with rumors of their "secret" mission as they drove off in a carriage for Petersburg, accompanied by the Mayor of Richmond. Varina listened in an adjoining room when they reported back to her husband on their two days of fruitless fencing with Lincoln. She knew now that they were *in extremis*; that all the hopes and fears, the gallantry and terrible losses; the victories and defeats; the bitter attacks and desperate frivolities of the last four years would soon be resolved. Every day there was fresh disaster, and she was torn by the more personal pain at this moment that her husband was being pushed into giving up his command of the armies to General Lee.

Desperate as was the situation, and undeniable her respect for General Lee, Varina was deeply wounded for her husband's sake.[20] She tackled Senator George M. Henry, of Tennessee, who had always defended Davis under attack, and said to him: "So, you, too, Mr. Henry, have turned against my husband." She listened attentively while he told her that he had voted to make General Lee commander-in-chief, not because he had lost faith in her husband or respect for him, but because the people demanded it. "At least Mr. Davis may console himself with the consciousness that he has not deserved the condemnation which the people wills," said Senator Henry.

"I think," retorted Varina tartly, "I am the person to advise Mr. Davis; and if I were he, I would die or be hung before I would submit to the humiliation that Congress intended him." [20]

A few days later Senator Henry wrote to the President that "next to Lancashire, Mincing Lane, and Lombard Street, the Queen is our most formidable enemy in England." [21] In December, A. Dudley Mann had written from Brussels: "From the Emperor of the French we never had nor have now, anything favorable to expect." The President had clung tenaciously to the hope that France and the Confederacy might find a common link through Mexico.

By February 1 General Lee was in full command of the armies, by act of Congress and the clamorous demands of the people. The President's neuralgia seemed to leave him at this time, and he was able to use his disabled right arm again. On February 19 Jones observed him riding past with three of his aides "seemingly as cheerful as if each day did not have its calamity." General Lee had appeared at the War Department three days earlier, spreading reassurance with his large and equable presence. His face was ruddy, his manner cheerful as he settled down to work. Everyone felt better with Lee in command, except perhaps Varina.

Wade Hampton and Hood, Lovell and Joseph Johnston, all were at Columbia in January. "Generals are as plentiful as blackberries, but they have no one to command," Mrs. Chesnut noted with truth. She thought General Johnston unduly joyful as he mulled over the mistakes made by General Lee and Stonewall Jackson. General Hampton wrote to Wigfall on January 20, begging him to re-establish the intimate relationship that once had existed between Jefferson Davis and himself. "*You* can aid him greatly and you can serve the country by giving him counsel." [22]

But the chasm between Varina's drawing room and the Wigfall quarters at the Spotswood was unbridgeable now. A few days later

Lydia wrote to Mrs. Wigfall, who was still in Richmond, saying she longed to be there too, but she feared the ghost of Varina would haunt her.

I have had some very pleasant days there, in the infancy of our confederacy—but its dingy old corridors now would be filled with ghosts to me. I'd almost be afraid of meeting the skeleton of "Varina" flourishing—as of yore, carrying everything before her. She and her "Jeff" are certainly my *skeletons*, would they were their own! ! ! ! [23]

Varina had not been able to hold her peace about Lee's appointment and Wigfall wrote illuminatingly to General Johnston on February 27:

Lee I believe fully sustains you and is now I understand hated by Davis as much as you are. Mrs. Jeff is open in her denunciations. They all feel that the attempt to supercede you with Hood has resulted in Jeff's being superceded by you. Lee's support of you too has given great offence. . . . Lee does not hesitate to say that he was consulted and disapproved of your removal. [24]

But General Johnston took it with good grace and wrote to Wigfall from Raleigh, on March 14, 1865, taking note of Varina as well as of her husband: "Be assured, however, that knight of old never fought under his King more loyally than I'll serve under General Lee. . . . I regret very much that he put me into this position so late. . . . I have a most unchristian satisfaction in what you say of the state of mind in the leading occupants of the Presidential Mansion. For me it is very sufficient revenge." [25]

Varina's closest friend and her most consistent foe fled simultaneously when Columbia fell to Sherman's men. While maintaining outward courtesy Mrs. Chesnut had sparred bitterly for weeks with Lydia Johnston over the Davises. She noted that General Johnston actually believed Jefferson Davis would "sacrifice wife, children, country and God" to satisfy his hate for him. As the General left Columbia for Charlotte, Lydia was stricken and wrote to Luly Wigfall: "I'll never forget his pale face & moist eyes, & never will I forgive the man that has crippled such a true soldier."

Mrs. Chesnut got to Chester, stripped of the last of her finery when a real lace veil—the only one she had left to wear—was lost along the way. There she slept in a public drawing room with people parading through, and became desperately ill when given an overdose of morphine. [26] Mulberry House was saved by a Negro who told the invaders that if it were burned the slaves would suffer. Davis's Arabian horse, which he had left with Colonel Chesnut, was lost in the evacuation of Columbia.

Things now looked hopeless in Richmond. The city itself was shabby, stripped, and dismal, its curtains gone, its windows blurred, its flagstones muddy, its shops empty, its people hungry and poorly clad. In nearly every home there were crutches or empty chairs. But the harried soldiers were entertained, even in the closing hours of the conflict, and several parties were given during January and February, notably the last ball of the Confederacy held at the Welford home. Luly Wigfall recalled that "grandmothers' satins and brocades were worn and the fiddles scraped and the music swelled . . . while they shut their ears and would not hear the minor key that wailed the ruin of our hopes." [27] Inevitably this ball was compared to the one that preceded Waterloo.

Meanwhile, the Davises kept up front. The President went riding with his aides, looking serious and haggard. Varina went about her business, although the gloom and despair around her were marked. She soothed her children, for the older ones by now were well aware of what was happening. She nursed her new baby. Above all, she sought to comfort her husband when he came home each night. The spurred couriers still arrived at their home. There were many conferences. The tiny newspapers revealed little, but the atmosphere of death and sorrow was overpowering. No one tried to flatter or delude her any longer. The end had come, although her husband was less willing to concede it than some of his generals. There was still self-delusion on his part. Varina was more realistic. She had planned to send the children to Mrs. Chesnut and possibly go herself, but her friend now was in flight. Anticipating her own departure, she gradually disposed of many of her things. The last of her silks and laces, of the feathers and flowers and gloves that remained in her wardrobe, were sold and were promptly spotted in the shops as belonging to Mrs. Davis. Books, china, silver, glass, imported objects of art, and some of her furniture were auctioned off.

She was so pressed for cash that she tried to sell fifty barrels of flour she had set aside to carry her family through the siege. The market price at the time was eleven hundred dollars a barrel. Her husband peremptorily forbade its sale. When she was leaving Richmond she planned to take the flour with her for the children, but again he stopped her, reminding her that he could not have flour taken from the city when the army needed it. Her total sales came to twenty-eight thousand dollars in Confederate money. She left this sum in Richmond to be converted into gold, and Judge Reagan brought it to her in his saddlebags when he left the city with the President.

Varina dated the beginning of the end from the day her husband's last message was delivered to Congress in March, even though he held out hope that in spite of reverses they still might win. Writing for *Spare Moments* shortly before her death in 1906 she recalled that he still believed the army could fight on, that "Lee was opposing to the limit of his endurance the crushing power gathered to oppose him, and was generally believed to be perfectly competent to hold in check the army that had as its objective point, Richmond." [28]

But he thought the time had come for Varina and the children to leave, and as she recalls this significant moment in her *Memoir:*

> Darkness seemed now to close swiftly over the Confederacy, and about a week before the evacuation of Richmond, Mr. Davis came to me and gently but decidedly, announced the necessity for our departure. He said for the future his headquarters must be in the field, and that our presence would only embarrass and grieve, instead of comforting him. Very averse to flight, and unwilling at all times to leave him, I argued the question with him and pleaded to be permitted to remain, until he said: "I have confidence in your capacity to take care of our babies, and understand your desire to assist and comfort me, but you can do this in but one way, and that is by going yourself and taking our children to a place of safety." He was very much affected and said, "If I live you can come to me when the struggle is ended, but I do not expect to survive the destruction of constitutional liberty." [29]

He still talked of setting up government in another place; of shifting the military focus. He gave her a purse with all the gold he had, but for one five-dollar piece. He handed her a pistol which may be seen in the Confederate Museum in Richmond today, and showed her how to load, aim, and fire it. He feared she might fall into the hands of marauders. If reduced to the last extremity, she could force her assailants to kill her by producing the pistol "but I charge you solemnly to leave when you hear the enemy are approaching; and if you cannot remain undisturbed in our own country, make for the Florida coast and take a ship there for a foreign country."

The streets were almost empty when Varina left during the last week of March, 1865. Red flags hung along Clay Street, indicating the sale of furniture, and houses for rent. The apricot blossoms were bursting into bloom as she drove to the depot, no longer an ostentatious figure, no longer Queen of the Confederate Court, but a sorrowing, trembling woman, about to part from the man she adored, not knowing if she would ever see him again, or what fate might await the Confederacy and its President. She was well aware that capture would mean punishment and that he would be the inevitable focus for revenge. The future must have looked black and uncertain to her at that moment. "With hearts almost bowed down with despair, we left Richmond," she noted.

Jefferson Davis was deeply affected during their last moments together at the train. Little Jeff did not want to leave him and cried to stay behind. Maggie "clung to him convulsively, for it was evident he thought he was looking his last upon us." The President sent his secretary, Burton Harrison, with them as escort. Connie, returning from a walk that evening, found a note from Burton, who had called in her absence, saying he had been asked unexpectedly to take charge of Mrs. Davis, her sister Maggie, and the children on a "visit" to Charlotte, North Carolina. He hoped to be back in town quite soon, "well and happy and light of heart." But Connie did not see him again until the following autumn, and then he was behind prison bars.

The train puffed out at ten in the evening with Varina, Maggie, the four children, Ellen the mulatto maid, James Jones, the coachman, and the daughters of George A. Trenholm, Secretary of the Treasury, on their way to South Carolina. It was a short train, consisting of only two or three cars. Varina's carriage horses were in one. The engine gave out on a grade after they had gone less than a dozen miles. They stayed there all night, Varina soothing her children and trying to justify their separation from their father. The cars leaked and since it was a wet night their bedding was soaked through.

Late the following day they got to Burkesville Junction. On the Sunday that Richmond was evacuated, they arrived at Danville, Virginia, and Burton called on Major W. T. Sutherlin, who had the largest house in town, presumably to make future arrangements for the President. They finally reached Charlotte in North Carolina, on Tuesday, where a house had been rented for them, but all the furnishings were packed up and they would have fared badly but for a kindly merchant, A. Weill, who did everything possible for Varina and her family, sending them their meals for several days and helping them in sundry ways.

It was a strange hegira, with Varina keeping a cool front but wondering every hour what was happening in Richmond. They knew nothing of the evacuation of the capital until a telegram arrived on Wednesday from the President at Danville, merely announcing that he was there. Harrison hurried back to join him after seeing Varina settled, and it was some time before she heard the full story of her husband's summons in St. Paul's on April 2 and all that followed.

The crisis had come on a blossoming Sunday, fragrant, warm, and drowsy. The weary residents of Richmond flocked to church. Bells pealed and the guns, for a change, were silent. The streets were almost deserted except for the churchgoers, and no vehicles were in sight. The President was alone in his pew when a courier clattered down the aisle and the congregation watched as he read the message handed him. Lee was withdrawing from Petersburg and urged the immediate evacuation of Richmond. Mrs. Josiah Gorgas thought the courier seemed greatly excited. She noticed the President turn pale, then control himself before he got up to leave with his "usual dignity of bearing." [30] Connie Cary, sitting immediately behind him, saw a "gray sort of pallor" creep over his face as he read the scrap of paper thrust into his hand. "With stern set lips and his usual quick military tread, he left the church," she observed. Everyone felt that something was wrong. Many got up and went out. The rector moved to the altar rail and asked the congregation to stay.

When summoned out of church the President went direct to the Capitol where he found General Breckinridge, his Secretary of War, and broke the news to him. [31] They worked together on arrangements for the evacuation. He assembled the heads of the various departments "so far as they could be found on a day when all the offices were closed." Preparations had already been made for departure, but the last of the executive papers were arranged for removal. As he walked toward the White House in the late afternoon Jefferson Davis was accosted by many who wished to know what was happening. He worked for some hours at his home, making final disposition of papers and other belongings. The train bearing the archives and all the official remains of his shattered government awaited his departure. Judge Campbell elected to remain in Richmond, but most of his colleagues left the city with him on the departing train.

The fall of Richmond was an electrifying experience. Burton later told Varina that Connie cried until no more tears would flow. Few went to bed. The residents roamed the streets like lost spirits. The night "was full of farewells as if to the dead." Fires broke out, with the Shockhoe Warehouse going first. Soon flames were hissing and crackling in all directions, as cotton and tobacco were burned, fired by the Confederates before the invading Union troops could reach them. Jets of flame shot up from the War Department and archives lay abandoned in the gutter. Shells exploded in the Confederate Arsenal. Gunboats were blown up in the river. Shock after shock rocked the city. Glass was shattered. Chimneys fell to the street. A considerable area was burned and some of the old mansions as well as the business section had been destroyed by the time the Federal troops took possession next day. The Custom House and the Spotswood Hotel were the only important buildings saved in the burned district. The Lee house stood unharmed, and "Agnes" wrote to Mrs. Pryor on April 5 that Mrs. Lee had sent out a breakfast tray to the Federal guard posted at her door. "Mrs. Davis was gone and out of harm's way," she wrote. "The Lees were sacred from intrusion." [32]

The hope persisted that General Lee would make a stand somewhere, but wild scenes continued in the morning as the tired citizens faced the uncertainty of a new day. Government bakeries were thrown open and food was dispensed. Many fled from the city; others stayed and quietly watched the blue-coated men of the North march in with "new and glittering arms, good boots, good hats, a whole suit of clothes to every man—a long, bright, prosperous-looking procession."

Connie walked past the Executive Mansion later and took notes. The porch was crowded with Union soldiers and politicians. The street in front was filled with gaping spectators. The young leaves were "just shaking out, the fruit trees a mass of blossoms—the grass vividly green, the air nectar," she noticed. [33]

Finally Abraham Lincoln arrived, under a veil of smoke, leading Tad by the hand. [34] The day was warm. The streets were dusty. The air was acrid and choking. The President seemed hot and tired. He fanned his face as he looked around. It was not a jubilant entry, but a quiet arrival in a stricken city. Both the North and the South had suffered too much for exultation. He went straight to the Executive Mansion, where he sat at Jefferson Davis's desk and surveyed Varina's parlors. Within a matter of hours their Richmond home was the headquarters of General Godfrey Weitzel, in command of the Federal troops.

The Davises had already faded from view, fugitives headed for nowhere, strangely forgotten in the crash of their empire. Only their love remained to sustain them at this bitter moment in their lives.

PART TWO

☙ 13 ☙

FLIGHT

Dear Wife, this is not the fate to which I invited [you] when the future was rose colored to us both; but I know you will bear it even better than myself and that of us two I alone will ever look back reproachfully on my past career. . . . Farewell, my dear, there may be better things in store for us than are now in view, but my love is all I have to offer and that has the value of a thing long possessed and sure not to be lost. . . .[1]

In the midst of all his anxiety Jefferson Davis wrote with depth of feeling to Varina from Charlotte, North Carolina, on April 23, 1865, as he watched the last remnants of the Confederacy dissolve around him. Burton Harrison bore this love better to her at Abbeville in South Carolina and at once she responded with equal warmth.

It is surely not the fate to which you invited me in brighter days, but you must remember that you did not invite me to a great Hero's home, but to that of a plain farmer. I have shared all your triumphs, been the *only* beneficiary of them, now I am but claiming the privilege for the first time of being all to you now these pleasures have past for me.[2]

At this point the Davises were two fugitives, traveling separately along country roads, constantly in danger, neither knowing what fate awaited the other, exchanging messages by courier, longing to be together yet missing connections, sunk in misery and hopelessness. To Varina it was like a flight before furies, jouncing along muddy lanes and through forest land in an ambulance, pitching tents, living like gypsies, with her younger children happy and unconcerned, and the older ones saddened over the role of their father.

There were hectic stops in little towns as she pushed southward in the general direction of Florida, and at each stop the exchange of notes took place—letters from her husband that conveyed historic bits of news hastily scribbled on odd scraps of paper, and always ending with a note of love and concern for her and their children. Thus she learned of the evacuation of Richmond, of the surrender of Lee to Grant, of her husband's fluctuating plans, of the dispersal of the Cabinet, of the assassination of Lincoln.

She in turn tried to comfort him, as his empire crumbled around him, friends deserted him, the armies collapsed, and the cavalry disbanded. These notes make a disjointed narrative of one of the most significant flights in American history. Written in moments of desperation, they also illumine the true natures of Varina and Jefferson Davis and bear testimony to the strength of their personal relationship. But the note of despair did not show until after Lee's surrender. Their earlier letters suggest that Davis at least still believed the struggle might continue in another area.

Varina received her first message from her husband penciled on grayish paper while she was quartered in the house that had been taken for her at Charlotte.[3] He wrote from Danville on April 5, where he was trying to pull together the remnants of his government. He had not heard again from General Lee, he wrote, and had postponed writing to Varina in the hope that he would be able to speak to her of the future with some confidence. He told her how the call to evacuate had reached him in St. Paul's. He described his hurried trip to his office to make final arrangements. Then, with meticulous detail, he reviewed what he had done at their home before leaving. Varina had left many instructions, but nothing had been done after her departure, and little could be accomplished in the few hours before his train left, he wrote. After dark he had packed some things and given them to John Davis where they would "never be found by a Yankee." One of the items he mentioned was a favorite painting named "Heroes of the Valley." The furniture was left, and few of the things he had ordered put up, including bedding and groceries, were saved.

He rode to the depot on horseback, leaving the servants to follow with the boxes. He sent a messenger back for the silver spoons and forks but nothing more was heard of them. He was so often interrupted and had such short notice that the "results were very unsatisfactory," he wrote, apologizing for things left undone in this moment of crisis. "I weary of this sad recital and have nothing pleasant to tell," he finished. "May God have you in His holy keeping is the fervent prayer of your ever affectionate Husband."

On the following day he wrote to her again from Danville.[4] He still had no word from General Lee and "having to conform my movements to the military necessity of the case" he was setting up an executive office where current business could be transacted but he had not yet decided on a definite point for the seat of government. He had no wish to leave Virginia but did not know where within its borders the "requisite houses for the Departments and the Congress could be found."

Clearly Jefferson Davis still believed that things could go on, and Varina in a letter written from Charlotte on April 7 tried to bring influence to bear on him even at this climactic moment.[5] Her letter illumines the tentative way in which she sought to sway her husband. It also suggests that she was not accustomed to easy success in having her way, and it specifically makes the point that he did not like her interference. Nevertheless, she was advising him earnestly in this moment of crisis, fearing that he was about to make a tactical mistake. It was too late now for him to use Bragg in any event, but Varina wrote:

> Though I know you do not like my interference, let me entreat you not to send B. B. to command here. I am satisfied that the country will be ruined by its intestine [sic] feuds, if you do so. If your friends thought it best I should feel helpless, but resigned; but even those who hope for favors in that event deprecate it for you. If I am intrusive forgive me for the sake of the love which impels me, but pray long and fervently before you decide to do it. . . .

Addressing him as "My Dear Old Banny," Varina wrote that the news of Richmond had come upon her like the "abomination of desolation, the loss of Selma, like the 'blackness thereof.'" She had heard nothing but wild rumors since his telegram sent immediately after his arrival at Danville. She could not judge of the moral effect of the fall of Richmond, she wrote, although the people with whom she talked were already so low in spirits that she did not think the shock was as great for them as might have been expected.

She had seen a digest of the statement he had made to the people of the Confederacy but "could not make much of it, except an encouraging exhortation." She was anxious to see it in full. All kinds of surmises were being hazarded about his future, but "I know that wherever you are and in whatever engaged it is in an efficient manner for the country." She felt that the trans-Mississippi might be their ultimate destination. Varina wrote:

I, who know that your strength when stirred up is great, and that you can do with a few what others have failed to do with many, am awaiting prayerfully the advent of the time when it is God's will to deliver us through His own appointed agent. I trust it may be you, as I believe it is. . . .

Varina reported that Lydia Johnston was living at the home of the bank cashier and kept a "pretty fancy carriage and horses." She had not seen her but she heard she was moving on to a watering place. The Wigfalls were with her. Mrs. Semmes had just left for farther South. The Trenholms had pushed on to Chester, South Carolina. Mrs. Chesnut had written her affectionately from there, saying she was quartered in two badly furnished rooms and was being fed by friends. Varina thought she would invite her to her little home in Charlotte, which had carpets, curtains, some window shades and three pictures, some excellent books, a marble table, brocatelle chairs, nice china and good kitchen utensils, plus the "utmost delicacy and hospitality" extended to her by Mr. Weill.

Burton Harrison also had surprised Varina with the stamina he had shown. The elegant and cultivated Burton had been "more efficient and attentive than I thought he could be and very affectionate and kind." At the end Varina reported lovingly on their family.

Our little ones are all well, but very unruly, or else the small house "makes me sensible" of it. Li Pie is sweet and pink and loving, her hands and gums are hot and swollen and I think she is teething. Billy is well but bad. Jeff is unremunerative, but behaves well in the main. Jeff is very much exercised about his pony—Maggie about her saddle—Margaret about her saddle—Ellen about her child—Washington (who is a fine boy) about his $2000 left in his master's hands with his clothes, I about my precious old Ban, whom I left behind me with so keen a heartache.

Write to me, my own precious, only love, and believe me as ever your devoted wife. . . .

Varina finished with a long list of questions for her husband to answer about the final moments at their home in Richmond. Had Ives turned up? Did Johnston leave his family? Had Mrs. McLean got off? Did Dr. Minnegerode come out? Had he brought the brandy? Had he brought anything with him? Where was Joe? Actually, their nephew,

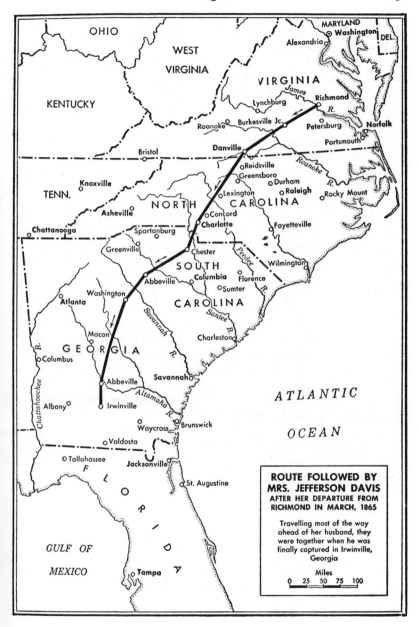

ROUTE FOLLOWED BY
MRS. JEFFERSON DAVIS
AFTER HER DEPARTURE FROM
RICHMOND IN MARCH, 1865

Travelling most of the way
ahead of her husband, they
were together when he was
finally captured in Irwinville,
Georgia

Miles
0   25   50   75   100

Joseph R. Davis, had lost his command.[6] All of his brigade but twenty men had been captured. He had gone to Richmond to join the President but was too late.

By this time Jefferson Davis was lodged at the home of Major W. T. Sutherlin in Danville, and after a Cabinet meeting had issued the proclamation to which Varina referred, calling on the people not to yield. "Let us meet the foe with firm defiance, and with unconquered and unconquerable hearts." [7] Mrs. Sutherlin found him in an "anxious frame of mind, but always pleasant and agreeable and self-possessed." He spent these troubled nights in a room overlooking a lawn with noble trees, and he told her one morning that the song of the mockingbirds refreshed him. She served him her best pickles, sweetmeats, and preserves, but he was indifferent to food.

Word of Lee's surrender reached him by courier on April 9. Young Robert E. Lee was in the room with him as he studied this significant message. "After reading it, he handed it without comment to us; then turning away, he silently wept bitter tears." [8] Burton Harrison busied himself getting a train put together for full evacuation and within seven hours they were on their way south, fully aware of their plight at last, and of the menace of Sheridan's cavalry. They received a cold reception in Greensboro, North Carolina, where Harrison took a few moments to send off the latest news to Varina. She had begged him to keep her fully informed of every move and he wrote on April 12 that since his return to Danville he had "been in such a turbulent uproar all the time that he could not write, although he had sent her telegrams along the way." Burton was still a little in awe of the Madam and wrote apologetically that he felt like a ruffian for not having communicated the many events that had befallen them, and "stand in awe of your disapproval for my apparent forgetfulness." He had relieved his feelings by "hectoring everybody else with denunciations of your wrath for their uncommunicativeness."

They had all been lulled when the sounds of battle ceased in the country roundabout and they inferred that matters had improved.

Imagine then our astonishment and dismay when the President was summoned from dinner on Monday, to be informed of the surrender by Genl. Lee of himself and all his Infantry on the 9th at or near Appomattox C. H. . . . The same information as to the result reached us from several other sources before night. A cabinet council was held immediately and a march on this place decided on.[9]

At this point Varina realized to the full that they were not heading toward a new government but into chaos. William Preston Johnston, one of the aides most dear to her and her children, wrote to her on the same day from Greensboro:

> The disaster to Genl. Lee's army is extensive. . . . The people you will see and hear are utterly demoralized. Do not be discouraged by them. The loss of an army is not the loss of the cause. There is a great deal of fight in us yet. The President is as collected as ever. He is with Mrs. Wood and comfortable, there is no personal danger here to him. We have troops enough here to beat any raid.[10]

Mrs. Wood was the wife of John Taylor Wood, who had moved his family from Richmond to Greensboro. Since no one in the town would open a door to the presidential party, the others lodged night and day in their railway cars while Mrs. Wood entertained the President. Varina was to learn with great distress of the council of war held at Greensboro in Colonel Wood's room, with her husband's two arch enemies, Johnston and Beauregard, coldly watching him in defeat. Both must have felt that but for him their own fate might have been different. Beauregard had evacuated Charleston without approval, and Johnston was fiercely resentful of his immediate command. Breckinridge, Benjamin, Mallory, Reagan, and George Davis listened attentively on the sidelines while the generals explained the military situation.

Jefferson Davis talked at length in a cold, strained manner. Finally he asked General Johnston for his opinion. "Sir," said the General, "my views are that our people are tired of the war, feel themselves whipped and will not fight!" He drew attention to the desertions. General Beauregard concurred with him in all respects. The suspension of hostilities was suggested, and the President agreed that General Johnston should treat with General Sherman for terms. If they were not satisfactory, he said, a stand would be made in Charlotte and, if forced to yield, he would seek Texas as the final goal.[11]

Knowing now what he faced, the President immediately sent Varina a note from Greensboro written as General Bonham waited on horseback at the door to deliver it.

Dear Winnie,

I will come to you if I can. Everything is dark—you should prepare for the worst by dividing your baggage so as to move in wagons. If you can go to Abbeville it seems best as I am now advised. If you can send everything there do so. I have lingered on the road and labored to little purpose. My love to the children and Maggie. God bless, guide and preserve you, ever prays

Your most affectionate

Banny.[12]

General Johnston at this point began his negotiations with General Sherman, and Davis and his cavalcade traveled toward Charlotte, making stops at Lexington, Salisbury, and Concord in North Carolina, where they were received with the same chill as in Greensboro. Benjamin did not like to ride, so Burton rounded up an ambulance, in which the Secretary of State, Jules St. Martin, George Davis, and General Samuel Cooper rode together. The wagons frequently stuck in the red mud, but Benjamin kept them all diverted. Burton could hear his "silvery voice as he rhythmatically intoned, for their comfort, verse after verse, of Tennyson on the death of the Duke of Wellington."

The President, who galloped along on horseback, surprised Burton by his cheerfulness under such adverse circumstances. He had much to say, and ranged from subject to subject, as if to keep his thoughts from dwelling on the immediate moment of desperation. Burton, used to the moods of his sensitive chief, noted:

> During all this march Mr. Davis was singularly equable and cheerful. He seemed to have had a great load taken from his mind, to feel relieved of responsibilities, and his conversation was very bright and agreeable. He talked of men and of books, particularly of Walter Scott and Byron; of horses and dogs and sports; of the woods and the fields; of roads and how to make them; of the habits of birds and of a variety of other topics.[13]

At Lexington Burton decided that Davis had given up the last vestige of hope. As they bivouacked in a pine grove outside the town, dispatches reached them from General Johnston, telling of his negotiations with General Sherman. Breckinridge and Reagan were at once sent off to Johnston's headquarters. Meanwhile, Wade Hampton had offered to fight on.[14] He wrote to the President on April 19 from Hillsboro urging that a small organization be kept in the field "to give Europe the opportunity of aiding us." He added: "I think it far better for us to fight to the extreme limit of our country, rather than to reconstruct the Union upon *any terms*." He volunteered to bring to Davis's support "many strong arms and brave hearts—men who will fight to Texas, & will seek refuge in Mexico, rather than in the Union."

The news of Lee's surrender hastened Varina's departure from Charlotte.[15] She decided to push on at once with the treasure train, which was heavily guarded by midshipmen, one of them being her own brother Jefferson. She put her family on the extra train that had been provided to go as far as Chester. Beyond that point the railroad line was impassable.

Her husband was bitterly disappointed when he reached Charlotte and found that Varina had moved ahead, although he understood the necessity. He was coldly received again and was just entering the house that had been found for him when a courier rode up with a message from General Breckinridge, who was then at General Sherman's headquarters, saying that President Lincoln had been assassinated.

Davis quietly conveyed the news to those around him. He handed the message to a local citizen to read to the crowd. Someone shouted and Davis checked the outburst. Burton Harrison later recalled that there was no expression on the part of the President other than "of regret and grief." In 1876 Davis wrote to his old West Point friend, Crafts J. Wright, recalling the manner in which he received the news of Lincoln's death and said, "The fact was that without any personal regard for Mr. Lincoln, I considered him a kind hearted man and very much to be preferred to his successor, Mr. Johnson." [16]

Next morning they all went to church in Charlotte, and the President remarked, "I *cannot* feel like a beaten man." But he worried constantly about Varina and the children and urged Burton to go toward Abbeville in the hope of catching up with them. He would make his own way as fast as possible to the trans-Mississippi Department to join the army of General Edmund Kirby-Smith, who was in command in that region, and actually did not capitulate until the end of May. But the Confederacy was crumbling fast at its very base and the President was to hold his last Cabinet meetings at Abbeville and Washington, Georgia, in turn. Before leaving Charlotte, Varina had heard through a courier that Johnston's army was going the way of Lee's and that, he, too, was surrendering his forces.

She was welcomed in Chester by Mrs. Chesnut and three generals, all old friends—Preston, Hood and Chesnut. "If I have lost my leg and also lost my freedom, I am miserable indeed," said General Hood.[17] "Anything that man can do I will for you or the President," added

General Preston, and General Chesnut assured her, "Let me help you if I can, it is probably the last service I can render." Clement Clay was there and showed as much devotion to Varina in her adversity "as if they had never quarrelled in her prosperity," Mrs. Chesnut remarked. They discussed the fall of Richmond and exchanged such snatches of news as they had heard. Varina was "calm and smiling," but the skies were so altered that a member of the staff did not even rise when she entered the room. "There were people here so base as to be afraid to befriend Mrs. Davis," Mrs. Chesnut observed, and when Varina had gone she was laughed at for making such a fuss about the "Royal Family in Exile."

Before learning of Lee's surrender Varina had invited her friend to stay with her in Charlotte. "One perfect bliss have I," she wrote in this moment of extremity. "The baby, who grows fat and is smiling always, is christened, and not old enough to develop the world's vices or to be snubbed by it. The name so long delayed is Varina Anne. My name is a heritage of woe." [18]

Varina paused at Chester only long enough to get an ambulance and wagon with which to follow the treasure train when night fell. She sent her husband a penciled and frantic note on a rough scrap of paper, telling him she would travel with the specie train because it had a strong guard. They might go to Washington in Georgia, or perhaps only to Abbeville, depending on how the children bore the journey. She felt "wordless, helpless," she wrote, and added: "Would to God I could know the truth of the horrible rumors I hear of you. One is that you have started for Genl. Lee, but have never been heard of. Mr. Clay is here and very kind. . . . May God have mercy upon me and preserve your life for your dear wife. . . ."

Varina was now beginning to realize how desperate her husband's situation was. It had been hard for her to accept the fact that he was now a friendless outcast, a fugitive with no power to order or organize. But the full force of it caught up with her after a perilous journey had been made to Abbeville. For the rest of her life Varina would recall that trip over muddy roads, with her family huddled in an ambulance, their belongings in a wagon, and the drivers trying to keep within sight of the treasure train ahead. The road was a quagmire of soft sticky mud after an uncommonly wet spring. The ambulance was overburdened, and Varina got out and "walked five miles in the darkness in mud over my shoe tops, with my cheerful little baby in my arms." Her nurse was too ailing to walk; her maid refused to wallow in such mud; so she tramped along herself with little Piecake in her arms. By some miracle all the children enjoyed the excitement of keeping up with the government treasure train, which also was having trouble with the mud.

There were alarms along the way, for Yankee pickets and scouts abounded. Marauders were watching for the train, still believing its contents had value, but there was no direct encounter on this stretch. At one o'clock in the morning they reached a little church where the guardians of the train had taken refuge. They were sprawled out on the floor, but the communion table had been saved for Varina. She had no wish to commit sacrilege, she said, so she settled herself on the floor, her tired children fell asleep, and she lay awake all night, staring into the darkness, plagued by a thousand worries.

At daybreak they moved on again. Her children were hungry now. A biscuit or a glass of milk cost from fifty cents to a dollar, and they were glad to get them at any price. "More dead than alive," Varina related, "we reached Abbeville, where our welcome was as warm as though we had something to confer." [19] The treasure train moved on without a halt, and she and her children were taken into the home of Armistead Burt, who had shared their early mess in Washington. Although he knew his house might be burned for sheltering a Davis, he and his wife treated Varina with great consideration. She had begun to feel the sting of being an outcast and was grateful now for every friendly gesture. "People call promptly and seem to feel warmly," she noted in a letter to "My Dear Old Banny."

The fearful news I hear fills me with horror. This is that Gen. Lee's army are in effect disbanded, Longstreet's corps having surrendered, Mahone's also saving one brigade. I do not believe all, yet enough is thrust upon my unwilling credence to *weigh* me to the earth.

Where are you? How are you? What ought I to do with these helpless little unconscious charges of mine are questions which I am asking myself always. Write to me of your troubles freely for mercy's sake. Do not attempt to put a good face upon them to the friend of your heart.[20]

Varina gave him news of their entourage. Jeffy D. had been quite ill on the cars and was staying across the street with Mrs. Helen Trenholm. The children were well and happy and played all day. Billy and Jim Limber were fast friends. Little Winnie was "the sweetest little angelic thing in the world—she rode along in the wagon as we bumped over the

horrible roads, making noses at everything." Actually the children
seemed to improve with the excitement of the trip, Varina observed.

Next day she received the startling message from Burton Harrison
that Abraham Lincoln had been assassinated. He was shot on the 14th.
It was now the 20th, showing how cut off Varina was from vital news.
"I burst into tears," she noted, "the first I had shed, which flowed
from the mingling of sorrow for the family of Mr. Lincoln, and a thor-
ough realization of the inevitable results to the Confederates, now
that they were at the mercy of the Federals." [21] The same message told
her of the general suspension of hostilities.

On the 24th Varina sent a note to "My own dear old Banny,"
saying she was very wretched; she longed for one word from him; she
would try to get to him for a day or two if the truce that was being
discussed meant anything, or if he could not get to her. "May God in
His mercy have you in His holy keeping prays your devoted wife," she
finished.[22]

Up to this time Varina had had an understanding with her husband
that he would join her "when he felt he could do so without danger
to the Cause." But now she realized that she must not interfere with
his plans for reaching the trans-Mississippi. Those around her had
persuaded her that he could move more freely and easily without his
family and their impedimenta. Everyone involved was well aware of
the danger of capture, and the full weight of the catastrophe was
finally clear to Varina.

In Charlotte, meanwhile, her husband had just completed his classic
love letter of the "rose colored future." [23] It was many pages long and
included a general summing up of the military situation. He did not
know where she was but "deeply felt the necessity of being with you, if
even for a brief time, under our altered circumstances." Governor Z. B.
Vance, of Greensboro, and Wade Hampton proposed to meet him in
Charlotte, and General Johnston had asked him to remain at some
point where he could readily communicate with him. Under these
circumstances he had decided to send Burton Harrison again to her
aid. He believed her to be at Abbeville. Then he summed up the military
situation, with a good deal of underlying misery for the general collapse
of all his hopes.

Your own feelings will convey to you an idea of my solicitude for you
and our family, and I will not distress by describing it. . . .

The dispersion of Lee's army and the surrender of the remnant which remained with him, destroyed the hopes I entertained when we parted. Had that army held together, I am now confident we could have successfully executed the plan which I sketched to you and would have been today on the high road to independence. Even after that disaster, if the men who "straggled," say thirty or forty thousand in number, had come back with their arms and with a disposition to fight we might have repaired the damage, but all was sadly the reverse of that. They threw away theirs and were uncontrollably resolved to go home. The small guards along the road, have sometimes been unable to prevent the pillage of trains and depots. Panic has seized the country. J. E. Johnston and Beauregard were hopeless as to recruiting their forces from the dispersed men of Lee's army and equally so as to their ability to check Sherman with the forces they had. Their only idea was to retreat. Of the power to do so they were doubtful and subsequent desertions from their troops have materially diminished their strength. . . .

Davis expressed the view that the terms of pacification were hard enough, "though freed from wanton humiliation." He had asked each member of the Cabinet that day to give him a written opinion on them. He conceded that the issue was one which it was very painful for him to meet personally. "On one hand is the long night of oppression which will follow the return of our people to the "Union"; on the other, the suffering of the women and children, and carnage among the few brave patriots who would still oppose the invader and who, unless the people would rise en masse to sustain them, would struggle but to die in vain." Resuming the personal note, he went on:

I think my judgment is undisturbed by any pride of opinion or of place. I have prayed to our Heavenly Father to give me wisdom and fortitude equal to the demands of the position in which Providence has placed me. I have sacrificed so much for the cause of the Confederacy that I can measure my ability to make any further sacrifice required, and am assured there is but one to which I am not equal—my wife and my children. How are they to be saved from degradation or want is now my care. . . .

At this point he urged Varina to try to get to Mississippi during the suspension of hostilities, and then either sail from Mobile for a foreign port or cross the river and proceed to Texas. If their land could be sold, there would be a little money. For himself, he hoped that a devoted band of cavalry would cling to him, so that he could force his way across the Mississippi and proceed to Mexico. The enemy might well decide to banish him, he said.

In conclusion he gave further details of the disposition of their household goods. Mrs. Omelia, their housekeeper, had behaved strangely at the end. She had removed groceries from the mess chest as he was leaving. Little Maggie's saddle was concealed and was not with the saddles and bridles he had ordered put together. He was also told that Varina's saddle had been sent to the saddler's and left there. He was struck by the fact that "everybody seemed afraid of any connection with their property." He had told Mrs. Omelia to sell what she could and he asked Mrs. Grant to observe her, but realized to his astonishment that "she, too, probably under the influence of her husband, was afraid to be known as having close relations with us." The only "yearning heart" at the end was poor old Sam, wishing for Piecake—"and thus I left our late home, no bad preparation for search for another," he commented bitterly.

"Dear children, I can say nothing to them, but for you and them my heart is full, my prayers constant and my hopes are the trust I feel in the mercy of God. . . . Once more, and with God's favor, for a short time only, farewell. Your husband."

The following day Davis telegraphed to Varina from Charlotte, saying that Burton had left to join her and he expected to see her himself "at the earliest practicable moment." The longing between them now was intensified by their desperation and showed clearly in their communications. On the 28th Varina responded in kind to his affectionate letter of the 23rd which Burton had brought to her. She described it as a "sweet letter." [24] and one that had brought her great relief.

She sent Colonel Henry Leovy to meet her husband at the Saluda River with her reply, in which she begged him for his own safety to make no more attempts to join her, even for an hour. "Let me now beseech you not to calculate upon seeing me unless I happen to cross your shortest path toward your bourne, be that what it may," she wrote. She was grateful for his guidance and told him her own plans, "subject to his approval." They seemed confused and conflicting; obviously Varina was casting about in all directions. She would leave in the morning with the wagon train going to Georgia. Washington would be the first stop for unloading. Then she might continue to Atlanta or thereabouts—"and wait a little until we hear something of you." She hoped to be able to raise enough money to put the two eldest children in school. She would go to Florida if possible, and from there to Bermuda, or Nassau, and then to England, "unless a good school offers elsewhere." In that case she would join him in Texas with the two youngest children—"and that is the prospect which bears me up, to be once more with you—once more to suffer with you if need be—but God loves those who obey Him, and I know there is a future for you."

The Burts had urged her to stay with them and had "offered to take the chances of the Yankees with us." "Here they *are all your friends,* have the most unbounded confidence in you," she wrote reassuringly to her forsaken husband. She doubted that a military stand could be made in the region, however. Of all the soldiers she had watched pass through, none had talked fight. "Things might be different in the Trans-Mississippi," she wrote, but there was little conviction any longer behind Varina's protestations.

She had a painful thumb which ached as she wrote. Maggie sent him a "thousand loves." Piecake had become "too playful to suck— Billy and Jeff are very well. Limber is thriving but bad," she finished, with the usual family bulletins. "God bless you, keep you—I have wrestled with God for you. I believe He will restore us to happiness." In a sense Varina felt that this was farewell. She had little hope of seeing her husband soon. She had no doubt by this time that the last hope for the Confederacy was gone.

Colonel Leovy broke the news to Davis at the Saluda River that Varina had moved on again. The Burts and Harrisons had tried to persuade her to stay. They felt she would be safe there. Abbeville was peaceful and friendly. There was no antagonism to the Davis family. It was glowingly beautiful at the time, its pillars draped with vines and roses, its gardens massed with scented blossoms. The children had played happily at the Burts but Varina had been determined to push on to the coast, feeling that she menaced her husband's safety by staying in his vicinity. She was adamant, until finally Burton had agreed to head toward Madison in Florida and there determine how best to get to the coast.

Varina set off again in a large wagon with an escort of young Kentuckian cavalrymen who were on sick leave—among them Lieutenant Winder Monroe, Lieutenant Messick, and Lieutenant Hathaway, with whom her sister Maggie fell in love.[25] Before they reached the Savannah River they learned there was smallpox in the vicinity. The baby had not yet been vaccinated, so Varina halted at a likely-looking house close to the road, and, according to Burton, "heroically had the operation performed by the planter, who got a fresh scab from the arm of a little Negro called up for the purpose."

"Every letter, I thank God for anew," she wrote as she journeyed with Harrison. "Do not try to meet me, I dread the Yankees getting news of you so much, you are the country's only hope, and the very best intentions do not calculate upon a stand this side of the river. Why not cut loose from your escort? Go swiftly and alone with the exception of two or three. Oh! may God in His Goodness keep you safe, my own. The children send pipes—Maggie dearest love, says she has your prayer book safe. May God keep you, my old and only love, as ever Devotedly, your own Winnie." [26]

They met the treasure train of the Virginia banks returning from Washington when they were half an hour out of Abbeville. There was much confusion between this train and the specie train with Confederate funds which Varina had been trailing. The little town of Washington, in the heart of Georgia's plantation country, was a strange sight as she arrived with her cavalcade through the dust and confusion. Eliza Andrews, the young daughter of Judge Garnett Andrews, a man devoted to the Union cause although several of his sons had fought for the Confederacy, has left a picture of Mrs. Jefferson Davis upon her arrival in the town of 2,200 inhabitants that had become pandemonium as the shattered remains of General Lee's army streamed through it.

The poor woman is in a deplorable condition—no home, no money, and her husband a fugitive. She says she sold her plate in Richmond, and in the stampede from that place, the money, all but fifty dollars, was left behind. I am very sorry for her, and wish I could do something to help her, but we are all reduced to poverty, and the most we can do is for those who have homes to open our doors to the rest.[27]

General Toombs, ignoring the bitter exchanges they had had, called on Varina and offered help. Mrs. Andrews and many of the women welcomed her, and here Varina held what might be called her final reception. "To the honor of our town," Eliza wrote, "it can be truly said that she has received more attention than would have been shown her even in the palmiest days of her prosperity."

General Arnold Elzey and his wife, who had been in town for a week, called on her. Washington had become the last Confederate stronghold for the moment. The remains of the naval and medical depots had been moved there. Jefferson Davis was expected. Eliza wrote excitedly that the "whole world seems to be moving on Washington now," repeating its Revolutionary history all over again when George Washington, traveling in the opposite direction from Jefferson Davis, rested there and gave the picturesque little town its name. Now the vaults of its bank held what remained of the Confederate treasury, and they had just disgorged the funds of the Richmond banks that Varina had seen being conveyed back to the fallen capital. She found the town a visible proof of the dissolution of the Confederacy. Handsome General Elzey wished he had died in battle rather than live to see it.

The village was crowded with disorganized troops, all hungry, many in rags and without a penny piece, vaguely moving about, hoping to reach their homes, or talking uncertainly of reorganized forces under Kirby-Smith "and a final stand for liberty in the trans-Mississippi." But not even a flicker of genuine hope was alight any longer, and many of the Confederates themselves had become raiders and looters. Their cavalry ranged the country roads, picking up horses, mules, and forage. Bands were looking for the specie train from Richmond. Eliza noted a silver cake basket tied to the pommel of a saddle and a ruffled pillowcase filled with plunder. Varina wrote to her husband of their own soldiers being "unruly" and taking mules and horses from camp.

The Andrews home was like a hotel, with soldiers pouring in and being fed on cornfield peas. The son of the richest man in New Orleans trudged through, with no coat to his back, no shoes on his feet. General Wigfall, who had started for the West, was back because his mules had been stolen.[28] He was frantic with rage and disappointment. His family had left Richmond a week before the evacuation. After the capitulation of Lee and Johnston, he disguised himself as a private soldier, shaved off his beard, and got hold of a borrowed parole. His family traveled in a large covered wagon packed with their belongings. Luly rode on a saddle horse. She was clad in homespun and wore a poke sunbonnet. They headed for Montgomery, while Wigfall made tracks for Texas. He had called on Burt the week before Varina arrived and had traveled on with General Hood.

Eliza Andrews was able to give Varina some news of her mother and sister, Mrs. Waller, whom she had recently encountered in the Milledgeville Hotel, on the road from Augusta to Macon. Jane Waller, who had a good voice, had sung songs in the parlor to cheer them all. Mrs. Howell, plump and handsome, with a "rather determined face, and pretty, old-fashioned gray curls falling behind her ears" had been loud in denouncing Governor Joseph Brown of Georgia, Eliza thought, and had "paid her compliments to everything and everybody opposed to Jeff Davis."

The countryside was wonderful to behold—palmettoes and bright flowers growing along the way; magnolias, willow oaks, and myrtle linked with smilax and jessamine vines. The Cherokee hedge close to the Andrews home, flinging its white festoons around the sycamore tree at the gate, reminded Varina in the midst of all her misery of The Briers. Campfires burned at the gateway, and shadowy figures moved like restless spirits in all directions.

Official confirmation of General Johnston's surrender caught up with Varina in Washington. His army had been her ultimate hope, although the rumors had prepared her for the worst. On June 6 after her husband's capture she gave her views in a letter to Francis P. Blair written from Savannah.[29] Years later, in her *Memoir*, she summed up the family view of this event. Her husband insisted, she wrote, that Lee "surrendered to overwhelming force and insurmountable difficulties." But the surrender of Johnston "was a different affair . . . he put everything at the mercy of the conquerors, without making a movement to secure terms that might have availed to protect the political rights of the people and preserve their property from pillage when it was in his power."[30]

In any event, the Davises felt betrayed by Johnston at the end, and Wade Hampton's offer to escort the President to the trans-Mississippi with the cavalry escort lost all point with the general surrender of forces, and became a matter of controversial comment. This definitely was the end. Even before the official notification of Johnston's surrender, Burton Harrison had decided on a change of route and had rounded up a strong cavalcade for the journey. He roused Judge W. W. Crump, Assistant Secretary of the Treasury, and had him go to the bank vault for a few hundred dollars for Mrs. Davis and $110 for himself, to be charged to the President and himself out of their accounts.

Just before leaving Washington he sat squeezed in a doorway between Toombs and General Humphrey Marshall, a huge Kentuckian. They discussed the sudden collapse of the Confederacy.

"Well, Harrison, in all my days I never knew a government to go to pieces in this way," said Marshall.

Burton next saw him in New Orleans in the spring of 1866. Marshall had escaped from Georgia across the Mississippi River. Varina's last glimpse of Toombs showed that exuberant figure in an "ill-cut black Websterian coat the worse for wear" and a broad-brimmed shabby hat. He was standing beside an old buggy drawn by spavined horses and the atmosphere was "murky with blasphemies and denunciations of Yankees," Burton observed.[31] When he saw him again, it was at the Théâtre du Châtelet in Paris in the autumn of 1866. The Texan was sitting in an orchestra chair, fashionably dressed, and looking pleased with the world.

Before leaving Washington, Varina, watching the débâcle around her, wrote bitterly to her husband that she could not refrain from expressing her intense grief "at the treacherous surrender of this dept." [32] She felt strongly that he would now be safer "without the country than within it, and I so dread their stealing a march and surprising you." She was fleeing Washington, she said, because of the danger of being captured and deprived of their transportation. She had given up all hope of seeing him "but it is not for long." Burton proposed following a line between Macon and Augusta, and going from there to Pensacola, hoping for a ship to Europe. She was short of funds but "I think we will make out somehow." The children had been more than good. "Oh, my dearest, precious husband, the one absorbing love of my whole life, may God keep you from harm," she finished.

At the same time Burton wrote to his chief on May 2, assuring him that Mrs. Davis was anxious to see him if she could do so without embarrassing him in his movements, but that in the meantime he had rounded up good drivers, teams, and seven wagons, a supply of forage and provisions, and they were prepared for a long and continuous march "to a place of safety in or beyond Florida."

His aides were concerned for the President, but the President was concerned only for Varina and his children. A council of war had been held at Abbeville before he rode on to Washington. Five brigade commanders were present and General Bragg, his military adviser. They all assured him that the continuation of hostilities would be futile, but that they would not disband their men until the President had been escorted to a place of safety. He brushed off their solicitude for his personal safety, and appealed to their patriotism. But reading the expression on their faces, he raised his hands to his head and cried in full realization, "All hope is gone! I see that the friends of the South are prepared to consent to her degradation." [33] He swayed as he left the room, supported by General Breckinridge.

After that he continued on his way to Washington and rode into town on a sunny May morning several hours after Varina had left. A group of men sitting on the bank piazza recognised the erect figure in Confederate gray, jumped to their feet, and bared their heads. Dr. J. J. Robertson, who was cashier of the bank and lived on the premises, was his host. Dead tired, Davis went straight to bed and slept until evening. Later, crowds flocked to see him. General Elzey wiped the dust from his eyes and his wife burst into floods of tears. Judge Andrews, in spite of his Federal sympathies, told Eliza his manner was "so calm and dignified that he could not help admiring the man."

After the crowd left they held a private meeting in his room, and again next day there was a Cabinet meeting—the last. The various members had already given him their opinion in writing, each one conceding formally that the moment for disbanding had come. Reagan's statement was later found in his saddlebags when he was captured with the President. The Cabinet was already partly dispersed. Two members had been missing from the Abbeville conference and four had scattered before the final one held at Washington. There Secretary of the Navy Mallory left to join his family at La Grange, Georgia. Breckinridge, with a remnant of cavalry, rode west from Washington, and John H. Reagan followed the President South, overtook him the following day, and was with him when he was captured.[34] G. A. Trenholm, pleading illness, had left the cavalcade on April 27 and had gone to Fort Mills. Attorney General Davis had returned home to his motherless children near Charlotte. Judah Benjamin, who had said he would never be taken alive and had abandoned his trunk at Abbeville, finally left them on May 3 as they breakfasted in the Vienna Valley, a few miles out of Washington.[35] Disguised as a Frenchman, he traveled south by horse and buggy, wearing goggles, with his hat pulled down over his familiar face and a huge cloak covering his paunchy figure. He pretended he knew no English and adopted a French name. In Florida he changed his disguise to that of a farmer, wearing homespun. He journeyed perilously down the Florida coast and finally sailed for the Bimini Islands in a little sloop that foundered. But his luck held. He transferred to another boat, reached Nassau, then went on to Havana and finally reached Southampton by the end of August.

In later years Varina never liked to have it said that her husband was deserted by his Cabinet at the end. She had a careful explanation for the departure of each one, and pointed out that Benjamin found it impossible to keep up the pace on horseback. He was not used to riding. Varina viewed this excuse as his way of saying that all was lost—"like Samson's lion after his strength was sped, he sent forth sweetness," she wrote to Francis Lawley, adding: "Thus these two master minds which seemed to be the complement of each other parted with mutual respect and affectionate esteem. . . ."

Reagan, who stayed to the end, was a frontiersman who could match her husband in the saddle. She also pointed out:

> The Confederate President neither asked nor received of General Johnston or anyone else a guard to accompany him to a place of safety, nor did he seek for himself any immunity for the part he had taken in the Confederate government. He was willing to the last hour of his life to give it for his country if he could serve her.[36]

It was obvious to his associates that the President was bitterly disappointed when he learned he had missed Varina by such a narrow margin of time. He looked gray, tired, strained, but kept his composure. Before riding off he gave away some of his personal effects to those who had been kind to him. Mrs. Robertson treasured the books, inkstand, and dressing case that he left with her.[37] She held some papers for him for two years, then sent them to England. He was urged to be more prudent about his personal safety at this point. His large escort of cavalry proclaimed his identity all too clearly, and his friends considered that he was in great danger. Finally he left Washington with his personal staff and a small escort only. This time he was determined to find Varina and his children. His professional duties were ended. His armies were gone. His Cabinet was scattered. He seemed no longer to care what befell himself.

Meanwhile, Varina's party had been making headway through the woods. The young cavalrymen from Kentucky had been joined by Captain George Moody of Mississippi and Major Victor B. Maurin of Louisiana, who gave Varina his light wagon. She was now a fugitive along the back roads of Georgia, seeking to escape identification. All the teamsters were warned not to talk, and when questioned Mrs. Davis became Mrs. Jones in their responses.

They went ten miles the first day and pitched their tents by the roadside. As they were trying to get their tea in the "awkward manner of townspeople camping out," Varina related, Richard Nugent, her husband's nephew, arrived with a note from Davis of bitter regret over not seeing them for consultation at Washington, and offering a few words of advice. "The ground felt very hard that night as I lay looking into the gloom and unable to pierce it even by conjectures," Varina wrote.[38]

All along the way they encountered footsore and ragged Confederate soldiers "plodding along depressed and sorrowful, in the direction of their homes." Varina was literally seeing the Confederacy in process of disintegration. On their third night out from Washington a company of paroled Confederates invaded their camp under the impression that they were part of the "treasure train." But the Captain recognized Varina at once and recalled that she had dressed his arm wound in Richmond. He apologized and left, after giving her a safe-conduct slip to take her past the group he had assigned to waylay her party at the crossroads.

With this threat behind them another developed in the vicinity of Milledgeville. When Jim Jones, their coachman, went into town for milk for the children, his mule was seized, and he learned that a raid was planned on the camp for that night. Cavalrymen from Alabama were supposed to be the culprits this time. It was a bright moonlight night, and Burton directed defensive operations. The animals were enclosed in a stockade made by the grouped wagons. Guards were posted, and Varina produced the Colt revolver and a fine Adams self-cocking revolver given to her husband by its maker. She then retired to wait for the moon to set, believing that the attack would not be made until it was completely dark.

When horsemen did ride up, Varina was prepared for the worst. Instead, Jefferson Davis had reached her at last.[39] Burton Harrison spotted his familiar figure in the moonlight, hailed him, and heard his musical voice establish his identity. He was accompanied by Colonel William Preston Johnston, Colonel John Taylor Wood, Colonel Frank R. Lubbock, Colonel Charles E. Thorburn, John H. Reagan, and Robert, his servant. He explained that Colonel Johnston had heard from a man at the roadside that an attempt would be made in the night to capture the wagons, horses, and mules of a passing party that sounded much like Varina's cavalcade, as he had heard it described in Washington.

Davis instantly changed his course and rode rapidly across country to overtake them, trying several different roads before finding them. Varina clung to her husband on their reunion. He was exhausted, but he reviewed all that had happened for her benefit. He was as relieved to see his wife and family as they were to welcome him. The children jumped with joy when they saw him. Varina and he discussed their plans for the future. Jeff still talked of trying to get to General Kirby-Smith "and it was arranged that I should follow out my original intention of getting to Nassau and then joining him where I could," Varina recalled.

There was no attack on the camp that night. It had been a false alarm. The President rode with them the following day, camped with them the next night, then rode off after breakfast, "in deference to our earnest solicitations to pursue our journey as best we might with our wagons and encumbrances," Varina wrote.[40] That night he camped at another Abbeville, this time in Georgia, and slept in a deserted house outside the village. There was a terrific downpour, and Varina's miseries were greatly intensified by the storm. To get the wagons through the "difficult bottom lands on the Eastern side of the Ocmulgee River was a severe ordeal." They crossed the ferry eventually and camped on the western bank. In the middle of the night Harrison was roused by a courier sent back by Davis with the report that the enemy was at Hawkinsville, twenty-five miles to the north. He urged them to move southward, and Harrison spurred on his party again through a driving storm of thunder, lightning, and rain.

They passed through Abbeville first, and there he found his chief lying on the floor in the old house wrapped in a blanket. He urged them to keep moving, and said he would overtake them when his horses had had some rest. They moved south all through the night, "the rain pouring in torrents most of the time, and the darkness such that, as we went thro' the pine woods, where the road was not well marked, and wound about to accommodate the great trees left standing—the wagons were frequently stopped by fallen trees and other obstructions and we were then obliged to wait until a flash of lightning enabled the drivers to see the way," Burton reported.

Finally the President caught up with them in the storm and darkness and rode with them until five that afternoon, when they decided to camp after crossing a little creek north of Irwinville. Again Varina was relieved to be with her husband. Floodgates of talk opened between them each time they met, Jefferson unburdening himself of some of the frustration and anxiety bottled up behind his proud reserve.

But the aides were all agreed that he must move independently of his family and the cumbersome wagons. Seemingly indifferent to his own fate, he docilely promised Wood and Thorburn that he would leave the party for good that night. As soon as a meal had been cooked for him "he would say farewell for the last time and ride on with his own party, at least ten miles further, before stopping for the night," Burton reported.

Although Varina clung to him she saw the wisdom of this and added her persuasion, but Burton always felt that had it not been for his wife Jefferson Davis might not have been captured. Had he continued his journey "there is every reason to suppose that he and his immediate party would have escaped through Florida or elsewhere to the sea-coast, as Mr. Benjamin escaped, as Genl. Breckinridge escaped, and as others did," Burton maintained in his personal narrative written for his family. "It was the apprehension he felt for the safety of his wife and children which brought about his capture. And, looking back now, it must be thought by everybody to have been best that he did not then escape from the country."

Thoroughly exhausted from anxiety, strain, and a bout of dysentery, Burton arranged the tents and wagons for the night, refused food because he felt ill, and threw himself on the ground under a little canvas cover. The next part of the drama took place as he lay in a deep sleep.

🕊 14 🕊

A PRESIDENT IS CAPTURED

SHORTLY before dawn, as stifling mists rose from the nearby swamps, shots crackled through the stillness that enfolded the camp where Varina and Jefferson Davis slept. Their tents were pitched close to a little stream bordered with a narrow thicket and some trees that shut them off from the road. Wagons, horses, and the other tents were some distance away, across the road.

Jim Jones, who was on guard as he washed Winnie's things at the campfire, roused the President, who had intended to leave the night before. His horse waited by a tree. His pistols were in their holster attached to his saddle. Varina explained that he had been bilious and was so worn out from constant traveling that he had decided to stay where he was until morning.[1]

Since they were all on the alert for the expected marauders, Varina's first thought was that they were being raided. But when the President stepped to the tent flap and watched the movements of the horsemen, his experienced military observation persuaded him, even through the morning mists, that they were enemy cavalry and not raiders. He turned back and told Varina that he believed them to be Northern troops. Actually two detachments of Union men, Wisconsin and Michigan cavalry, were on the scene, unconscious of the prize awaiting them.

Varina reacted at once in her impulsive way, and begged him to flee. She instantly saw the menace to him, but did not believe that she or the children would be in danger if they stayed. Unwilling to leave his family, Davis hesitated, "and lost a few precious moments before yielding to her importunities," he later commented.[2]

There are many versions of what occurred after that, but a letter written by Varina to Francis P. Blair from Savannah on June 6, 1865, gave her most immediate impressions of the agonizing hours that followed. She wrote:

Knowing he would be recognized I pled with him to let me throw over him a large waterproof which had often served him in sickness during the summer season for a dressing gown, and which I hoped might so cover his person that in the grey of the morning he would not be recognized. As he strode off I threw over his head a little black shawl which was round my own shoulders, seeing that he could not find his hat and after he started sent my colored woman after him with a bucket of water, hoping that he would pass unobserved.[3]

It was an impulsive act and one for which both paid dearly. It led to national ridicule, to cartoons of Jeff Davis in petticoats and poke bonnet, to gibes that wounded them deeply. In the last year of her life Varina was still protesting that her husband had no intention of disguising himself, and that in throwing the shawl over his head she was doing no more than any wife might have done under similar circumstances. "Could the tortures wantonly inflicted when he was a helpless prisoner, have been averted from my husband by any disguise, I should gladly have tried to persuade him to assume it; and who shall say the stratagem would not have been legitimate?" she wrote. "I would have availed myself of a Scotch cap and cloak, or any other expedient to avert from him the awful consequences of his capture."[4]

After relating her own share in the incident in her letter to Blair, Varina added: "He attempted no disguise, consented to no subterfuge, but if he had, in failure is found the only matter of cavil." There is no doubt that she hoped he might escape through the morning mists. Her Negro maid carried a bucket, and the impression created in the dim light was that of an old woman accompanied by an attendant on their way to the stream for water. It developed later that the cavalry had no idea on their arrival that Jefferson Davis was there, although several soon laid claim to recognizing him—one when he spoke, another noticing his cavalry boots under the long waterproof.

The Northern papers pounced on this item as an essential part of his capture. "Jeff in Petticoats" . . . "Jeff Davis captured in Hoop Skirts. . . ." It made brisk reading throughout the Union, and the cartoonists made rare use of it. Gideon Welles entered it in his diary as an established fact. George Templeton Strong commented on the "universal guffaw" over Davis's "new character of comic gentleman, running through bush and briar, in the cumbrous disguise of hooped skirts that were the property of Mrs. Davis." [5] P. T. Barnum telegraphed Stanton offering five hundred dollars for the "petticoats" in which he was captured and later made money on a life-sized figure of Jefferson Davis in feminine attire, resisting Union soldiers.

In the long run even his captors toned down their stories. Davis met the issue with quiet dignity and described Varina's hasty act as a piece of "thoughtfulness." His own account of the capture differs slightly from hers.

My horse and arms were near the road on which I expected to leave, and down which the cavalry approached; it was therefore impracticable to reach them. I was compelled to start in the opposite direction. As it was quite dark in the tent, I picked up what was supposed to be my "raglan," a waterproof, light overcoat, without sleeves; it was subsequently found to be my wife's, so very like my own as to be mistaken for it.

As I started, my wife thoughtfully threw over my head and shoulders a shawl. I had gone perhaps fifteen or twenty yards when a trooper galloped up and ordered me to halt and surrender, to which I gave a defiant answer and, dropping the shawl and raglan from my shoulders, advanced toward him; he leveled his carbine at me, but I expected, if he fired, he would miss me, and my intention was in that event to put my hand under his foot, tumble him off on the other side, spring into his saddle and attempt to escape. My wife, who had been watching, when she saw the soldier aim his carbine at me, ran forward and threw her arms around me. Success depended on instantaneous action, and, recognizing that the opportunity had been lost, I turned back, and the morning being damp and chilly, passed on to a fire beyond the tent. [6]

It developed that the two separate parties of cavalry had approached the camp from opposite directions, and after some reconnoitering had commenced firing, each believing the other to be Confederates. Both groups were working at cross purposes, quite unaware of the prize catch within their reach. It was some time before Lieutenant Colonel Benjamin D. Pritchard, who led the party that captured the President, reached his side, so busy was he investigating the clash of the two detachments and the casualties that followed. On riding into camp he had noticed three "wall tents" to the right of the road, but there was no sign of life, or any guards posted. He had started out to find Varina's train and bring it into Macon, but was wholly unaware that the President of the fallen Confederacy was with her.

The first shots stirred the whole camp to life, and soon a shadowy figure was noticed emerging from one of the small shelter tents. This was Jefferson Davis. Lieutenant Julian G. Dickinson and Andrew Bee, a Norwegian who had difficulty making himself understood, both claimed to be first to recognize him. They were assertive afterward about their share in his capture. Dickinson quoted the maid as saying, "Please let me and my grandmother go to the brook to get ourselves washed." Bee observed that the "old woman" was wearing boots, and instantly cried out, "There goes a man dressed in woman's clothes." [7] Another version had him saying, "See, that is Jeff himself. That is no woman." Bee stuck obstinately to his story, although it was later challenged.

In any event, the President was halted in his tracks. Varina recalled in her letter to Blair that she told the soldier to shoot her if he wished as she clung to her husband, and that he retorted that he "would not mind a bit." Her husband murmured, "God's will be done."

The various stories told about the capture never quite tallied in minor details. Even Varina's version changed slightly between 1865, when she wrote to Blair, and 1906, when she was writing for *Spare Moments* on the last hours of the Confederacy. Her recollection of details may have faded by then, but the main points remained unchanged and nothing outraged her more than any slur on the gallantry of her husband. There is no doubt she felt that her own impulsive act had led to a misunderstanding and she suffered accordingly. Many times Davis took up the issue himself, quietly answering the attacks that came from different quarters. He explained that he had stayed on that night when word reached him that marauders were in the vicinity.[8]

Dickinson pictured Varina as coming out of the tent after the capture and demanding to know what was to be done with her husband. He said she warned them not to make any trouble as he was a dangerous man and would hurt someone. She asked if she and the children might accompany him, and Dickinson said he would have to talk first to Colonel Pritchard. His story in large part was denied by Captain James H. Parker, who also claimed recognition of the President, and whose statement hangs today in the Confederate Museum in Richmond.

I defy any person to find a single officer or soldier who was present at the capture of Jefferson Davis who will say upon honour that he was disguised in woman's clothes. . . . His wife did not tell any person that her husband might hurt somebody if he got exasperated. She behaved like a lady, and he as a gentleman, though manifestly he was chagrined at being taken into custody.[9]

Although Varina always found it difficult to speak with restraint of the various cavalrymen involved in the capture, she later conceded that Pritchard showed "an obliging temper." When he and Jefferson Davis stood face to face, the President proudly pled for his family and his aides. He told Pritchard he supposed that his orders had been fulfilled in arresting him and that there would be no interference with the women or children. He asked that they be permitted to pursue their journey. But the Colonel said he had orders to take everyone found in his company to Macon. Davis protested the pillaging that was already under way.

Sitting shivering beside the campfire because of the cold and the damp, he watched the cavalrymen round up saddles and horses with great dispatch. He was wearing the clothes in which he was captured, Varina reported later—a long frock coat with velvet collar, breeches, riding boots, soft felt hat, and an upstanding collar and tie. His own horse was promptly seized and his waterproof cloak, similar to the one Varina had thrown across his shoulders, was taken from the saddle.

"You are an expert set of thieves," Davis remarked to one of the men.

"You think so. Do you?" the man replied.

But the thing that angered him most was their interference with the preparation of the children's breakfast. The food was snatched from the fire when only partly cooked and "*this* was the thieving which provoked my angry language to Col. Pritchard when he at length came and told me he was a commanding officer," Davis later wrote to his old West Point friend, Crafts J. Wright. "We were prisoners subjected to petty pillage . . . and the annoyances such as military *gentlemen* never commit or permit."

Varina wrote to Blair that trunks were broken open, clothing was scattered on the ground, their gold was confiscated, the children's clothing was taken—even the baby's tiny garments—and the prayer books and Bibles were scattered about. "These latter articles were easily recovered, as being of no use to the robbers," she wrote. The few things that were returned had wet leaves and grass clinging to them. A hoop skirt from Paris that she had never worn was dragged out, to be flourished later as part of the Davis "disguise." Her gold and her carriage horses were seized at once.

The surprise capture had stunned the various aides. When Jim Jones roused Harrison he was dismayed to find that the President was still in camp. He got into action at once, but "we were taken by surprise and not one of us exchanged a shot with the enemy," he reported. He later claimed to have been the only witness, besides Jones, to what actually occurred around the Davis tent. He heard the violent language of the raiding party. He observed Varina's consternation. He expressed his astonishment at Davis's presence.

Wood and Thorburn tell me that, after the President had eaten supper with his wife, he told them he should ride on when Mrs. Davis was ready to go to sleep; but that when bed time came, he finally said he would ride on in the morning—and so went to sleep in the tent. He seemed to be entirely unable to apprehend the danger of capture. Everybody was disturbed at this change of his plan to ride ten miles further—but he could not be got to move.

Harrison's $110 in gold disappeared. Colonel Lubbock and Colonel Johnston had one thousand five hundred dollars apiece, which became part of the loot. Johnston's money was in his holster since he had found it heavy to carry. He particularly mourned the loss of his horse, saddle, and pistols, all of which had been used at Shiloh by his father, General Albert Sidney Johnston.

While the cavalrymen were arguing over the booty Burton emptied the contents of his haversack into the fire where breakfast was being cooked. He watched a photograph of Connie, some of her love letters, and a few telegrams and letters of public interest go up in smoke. In the midst of all the confusion, Colonel Wood and Colonel Thorburn, who was a naval purchasing agent for the Confederacy, quietly walked away from the camp and disappeared. They had been classmates at Annapolis and were blockade runners. Thorburn had a small vessel in Indian River, Florida, with which he had hoped to convey the President around to Texas. The plan was for him to ride on in advance, make all the necessary arrangements, and return to Madison, Florida, to meet the President there and see him safely aboard this vessel.

Both Varina and Davis were devoted to Wood. He had captured and sunk many enemy vessels and was regarded in the North as a dangerous pirate. The Davises realized that things would have gone hard for him had he been captured. Writing of their departure in *Spare Moments* Varina noted that "they walked out of camp, which was perhaps as well, as they could have been of no assistance to us had they been captured." Wood subsequently made his way to Florida, where he joined Breckinridge. Together they sailed down the east coast in a small open boat. They lived on turtles' eggs found in the sand, as they traveled close to the shore. Finally they overhauled a more seaworthy boat, seized it, and eventually reached Cuba.

It must have surprised the Davises, nevertheless, to watch the various moves made by those around them in the final débâcle. They were becoming used to desertion by this time. Davis retreated into icy pride and silence. Varina was inconsolable and angry. Maggie and the children were in a second tent when the capture took place. The President was calm, but his wife was greatly excited, and Wood later made a diary entry that Varina "by her appeals, the children by crying, the servants by fear howling, destroyed all," and added that only Varina's distress could ever have induced the President to wear the garments she thrust on him.

Wood had been surprised to see how well the Davises had taken to the primitive life of the woods. "The P. & Mrs. D. have accommodated themselves to this way of living very quickly. I saw them at the branch washing 'al fresco' this morning," he noted a few days before their capture.

Now the entire party was taken prisoner and in due time they all marched to Macon. The men who would later be paroled were allowed to ride their own horses for the time being. The period that followed would be a searing memory to the last day of Varina's life.

Only a firm belief in the wisdom of an omnipresent and merciful Providence upheld us at this time, and Mr. Davis did not lose heart. . . . If I can speak thus calmly of those awful days, it is because the finger of Time has used its healing influence upon the scars and wounds inflicted during the previous months and the two years that were to follow. Even after the lapse of this period, it is next to impossible to think of those days and nights without some of the horror that stamped every moment for its own.[10]

It was a march to jeers, to insults, to an uncertain fate. Davis was ashen, quiet, and proud in the shelter of the ambulance. Varina tried to control her emotions, but Maggie sobbed hysterically, and the children were upset. The Davises were objects of the greatest interest, for the news of the President's capture was fresh and startling. Their dismay was augmented by the sight of some of General Johnston's soldiers straggling along the roads. They encountered a brass band playing Northern airs. It was "Yankee Doodle" now, no longer "Dixie."

Burton Harrison, John H. Reagan, Jefferson Howell, Colonel Johnston, Colonel Lubbock, and the young cavalrymen who had been protecting Varina, rode in columns of two. Burton cantered beside Major Victor Maurin. At a cavalry camp along the way word reached them of the proclamation offering a reward of $100,000 for the capture of Davis for alleged participation in the plot to assassinate Lincoln. Colonel Pritchard handed Davis a printed copy of the proclamation. Burton noted that he read it quietly, "unruffled by any feeling other than scorn."

Andrew Johnson, who had long hated Davis, seemed to be having his innings now, although it later developed that Stanton and Joseph Holt, Judge Advocate General, were the instigators of this move. But the attitude toward the prisoners changed subtly after news of this proclamation spread. It became venomous and threatening. Varina later disclosed that she was much shocked but her husband was not disturbed, merely remarking, "The miserable scoundrel who issued that proclamation knew better than these men that it was false. Of course, such an accusation must fail at once; it may, however, render these people willing to assassinate me here." [11]

Their escort became extremely rude. Captain Charles T. Hudson threatened to take Jim Limber away, and "solicitude for the child troubled us more than Hudson's insults," said Varina. On the outskirts of Macon two regiments were drawn up in double file, and as they passed between them they were "subjected to every coarse jest and word unfit for women's ears that can well be imagined." Varina was deeply offended. Her husband remained calm, but when little Margaret, terrified, crept into his arms for protection, he repeated psalms to her in a soothing voice. "Of the horrors and sufferings of that journey it is impossible to speak," Varina noted. "All that we could bear was heaped upon us."

They stayed at the Lanier Hotel in Macon where General James H. Wilson had his headquarters. They had a large and comfortable room and were served a good dinner. Varina was touched when the Negro waiter who brought it removed a cloth from "one corner of the tray and exposed a bunch of flowers." She saved one of the roses, a memento of an "act of kindness done in an hour of darkness."

After dinner her husband was interviewed by General Wilson, whom he had known in the past and whose troops had made the capture.

Davis inquired for old West Point friends and spoke feelingly of Lee, declaring him to be the "ablest, most courageous, most aggressive and beloved of all the Confederate generals." He referred to Mr. Lincoln and his "untimely death in terms of respect and kindness."

They discussed the proclamation. Although knowing that anything he might now say could be used against him, Davis was determined to register his opinion of Andrew Johnson. He told General Wilson that there was one man in the United States who knew the proclamation to be false, and that was the man who signed it. "He at least knew that I preferred Lincoln to himself," Davis noted.[12]

He then asked if his family might travel north by water, since he thought it would be easier for the children. At the time he believed they were heading for Washington. "He manifested a courteous, obliging temper," Davis observed. "My preference as to the route, was accorded." He asked that the men with him who were on parole should be allowed to keep their horses. This was granted, too, but was not carried into effect.

The troops were boisterous and rude as the Davises left the hotel for the station in what Mrs. Clay viewed as a "jimber-jawed wobble-sided barouche, drawn by two spavined horses." Maggie, the children, and their nurses followed in a carryall. Harrison was not allowed to ride with the President, but the Davises were deeply touched when he resolved to follow their fortunes, "as well from sentiment as from the hope of being useful." The trees were in full foliage. May blossoms scented the air. Macon was overrun with soldiers. Crowds had gathered around the station to stare at Jeff and Varina as they set off for Augusta. The President's pallor matched the gray tone of his Confederate suit. Varina looked white and strained. There were Rebel and Union clashes within their hearing.

"Hey, Johnny Reb, we've got your President."

"And the devil's got yours!" was the swift reply.

Mrs. Clay noted the President's gray look as he rose to embrace her in the train. "This is a sad meeting, Jennie," he said, offering her a seat beside him.[13] Varina was already deep in conversation with Mr. Clay, who had also been taken prisoner. His wife had insisted on accompanying him, but as the train moved off and she heard the thud of musket butts on the floor she realized that she was in custody, too.

At Augusta they rode to the river after dark, their carriages bumping over rough ground. Here they were joined by Alexander Stephens and

General Joseph Wheeler. The former Vice-President was ill and upset, and presented a strange appearance with his greatcoat, his shawl, his carpetbag, his cane, and umbrella—as Lincoln had said of him when he saw him unswathe himself at Hampton Roads—"the biggest shuck and the littlest ear that ever you did see." [14] Stephens had parted coldly with Davis after the Hampton Roads conference, and he was apprehensive about the meeting in his weak and wretched state. Both the Davises bowed to him as he drove past on his way to the wharf and he caught a glimpse of little Winnie in her nurse's arms.

Their conveyance at this point was a river tug without a cabin, bound for Savannah. There were a few bunks below and Davis settled there as a chill wind blew in from the ocean. Stephens looked so wretched that Varina, dropping all animosity, gave him a mattress and arranged for a good dinner to be served the prisoners from the ship's supplies, for which she paid. He and the luxury-loving Mr. Clay shared a shawl for covering and used carpetbags for pillows. All the servants were sick. When Davis and Stephens met on deck they shook hands in their common misery. Their greetings were polite, if not warmhearted.

They were greeted with fresh jeers at Port Royal, where tugs brought out Federal soldiers and small groups of women who had come to stare. Varina watched them sadly; she had ceased to care for appearances, but their scrutiny angered her husband. By this time she was beginning to fear for their lives. She had no idea what fate awaited them, and her husband tried to comfort her in her extreme distress. At the same time she tried to minister to him for his physical ills. He was suffering from neuralgia, his eyes were giving him trouble, he was desperately in need of sleep. He paced the deck restlessly and sometimes held little Winnie in his arms.[15]

Here Varina parted company with Jim Limber. She had appealed to General R. Saxton, a friend, to take charge of him, lest he fall into Captain Hudson's hands. When Jim learned he was leaving the Davis children he "fought like a little tiger," in Varina's words. Years later she saw in a Massachusetts paper that he would bear to his grave the marks of the stripes he had received from the Davis family. Varina was never to believe that he had made these charges, "for the affection was mutual between us, and we had never punished him." [16] Her maid Ellen had been like a mother to him.

At this point they were transferred to the *William P. Clyde*, an oceangoing steamer, and sailed up the coast under the guns of the

Tuscarora. "Once on board, he seemed to be the observed of all observers," noted the *New York Times* of May 22, 1865. "He was seated in a corner, his wife, a plain-looking lady, dressed in black, by his side and the two were engaged in perusing papers which had been brought them. . . ." [17] Their children "were about everywhere, seemingly unconscious of the intense interest concentrated upon their sire."

The trip north was rough, but Varina stood it bettter than the servants, most of whom were seasick. Finally on May 20 they sailed into the waters of Hampton Roads, and saw the British and French ensigns flying from many mastheads alongside the Stars and Stripes.

Soon the partings began. Her young brother, Jefferson Davis Howell, a paroled midshipman, threw his arms around Varina and bade her good-by. General Wheeler, Governor Lubbock, and Colonel Johnston set off under guard for Fort Delaware. Davis was deeply affected when Stephens and Reagan were transferred to the *Tuscarora,* bound for Fort Warren. Reagan had been faithful to the end, and, although Davis and Stephens had been enemies, at the last moment he "squeezed the frail hand that was laid into his, and then turned away." It was hardest of all to part with blithe young Burton Harrison, who had done so many personal things for the President and Varina, who was "Pudding" to little Piecake, who had escorted Maggie to so many parties and listened to so many tales of her romances. He was headed first for Capitol Prison, then for Fort McHenry.

At last the summons came for Davis. There was little warning when he was taken off with Clay for Fortress Monroe. Jeff ran to his mother, white with terror, and exclaimed, "They say they have come for father, beg them to let us go with him." Davis walked up to Varina by the side of an officer, and announced, "It is true. I must go at once." As his wife's ravaged face showed fresh consternation he whispered to her, "Try not to weep, they will gloat over your grief." She did her best to keep her emotions in check until he had gone, then gave way afterward. His own demeanor was like steel as he headed for the tug, and Varina recalled in her *Memoir* that as "he stood with bared head . . . and as we looked, as we thought, our last upon his stately form and knightly bearing, he seemed a man of another and higher race, upon whom 'shame would not dare to sit.' " But she wrote sharply to Blair a few days later:

Without five minutes' warning we were separated. With a refinement of cruelty worthy of savages we were not told we were to meet no more.

and when I begged to be allowed to separate from my children and share Mr. Davis' imprisonment, since I had been thought worthy of so large an expedition for my capture, if denied this boon, to write a word of farewell to be handed to him open, or to send a verbal message—all were refused.[18]

Charles A. Dana, watching his arrival with a cooler and more impartial eye, wired to Stanton from Fortress Monroe on May 23, 1865, that Davis on landing bore himself with hauteur. His face was flushed but his features were composed and his step firm. Clay's manner showed less "bravado & dramatic determination." Both were dressed in gray with drab slouched hats. Davis wore a thin overcoat, and Dana observed that his hair and beard were not so gray and he seemed "much less wan & broken by anxiety & labor" than Blair had reported on his return from Richmond. Dana's report on his parting from Varina was somewhat paradoxical.

From his staff officers Davis parted yesterday shedding tears at the separation. The same scene has just been renewed at his parting from Harrison, his private secty. who left at one o'clock for Washington. In leaving his wife and children he exhibited no great emotion though he was violently affected. He told her she would be allowed to see him in the course of the day. Clay took leave of his wife in private & he was not seen by the officers. Both asked to see Genl. Halleck but he will not see them.[19]

Only Varina knew that his flush was caused by a high fever as he left; that his body trembled as he embraced her silently, that he paused when little Jeff said he would kill every Yankee in the country when he grew up. Varina went down to her cabin, and Mrs. Clay noted at this point that "the bitter wailing of women and children told them everywhere that he had left the ship."

Mrs. Clay and Varina were searched before the *William P. Clyde* sailed off. Varina reacted with rage and tears, Mrs. Clay with ridicule. She showed her contempt for the two women "garishly dressed, rouged, powdered, and befrizzled with huge chignons, bustles of the largest size, high-heeled shoes, conspicuous stockings, and gay petticoats," who were their guards.

When she went to Varina's room she found her in deshabille and in tears. "What humiliation!" the President's wife exclaimed.

"But I would die before they should see me shed tears," said Mrs. Clay.

"Ah, but you haven't four little children about you."

Before leaving port, Colonel Pritchard, whom Varina credited with according her courteous treatment on the whole, asked for her waterproof which she thought "would disprove the assertion that it was essentially a woman's cloak." She gave it to him at once. Later Captain Hudson, whom she detested, arrived with a raiding party and their trunks were opened and some of the contents were seized. Little Jeff hung on to his suit of Confederate gray by handing it over to Varina to keep. The flag that General Bradley Johnson had sent her as a trophy was taken from her trunk. Her shawl was extracted next, to be added to this collection of Davis exhibits.

Mrs. Clay, meeting her coming out of her cabin in tears, with Winnie in her arms, asked Varina what was wrong. She told her that Hudson was taking her shawl, saying it was part of her husband's disguise.

"You're not going to let him have it," Mrs. Clay protested.

But capable Varina seemed to be the more helpless of the two at this juncture. Mrs. Clay was carrying things off in a highhanded way, twirling her pistol mischievously in the face of the women who searched them and advising Varina to confuse Hudson by giving him both their shawls. When he returned with a coarse, cheap shawl as a substitute, she handed over her own and Mrs. Clay's.[20]

"Puss-in-Boots," Varina quipped, with a flash of her old spirit as she watched him walk away with the shawls.

Before leaving port Varina had her first look at General Nelson A. Miles, the man who would order her husband shackled and incur her lifelong enmity. She observed that he seemed quite young and was "not respectful," but she considered that he knew no better. He refused to tell her anything about her husband, or where she was headed, and added that " 'Davis' had announced Mr. Lincoln's assassination the day before it happened and he guessed he knew all about it." [21]

Davis had urged the authorities to send his family to Richmond or to Washington. This was refused. He had asked that they be allowed to board one of the vessels lying in Hampton Roads. This also was denied. He then urged that they be put off at Charleston, where they had friends. But they were headed now for Savannah, after a fruitless effort made by Varina to persuade the captain of a British man-of-war to take her aboard.[22] Her letter was intercepted. It was a note scrawled in pencil, describing the capture, her immediate plight, the fact that she had been robbed of all her money and even of the children's clothing.

"Mr. Davis' family from wealth have been reduced to poverty as have been mine by the Federals," Varina wrote. "They have burned our two plantations and stolen our property. . . . I cannot pay my passage to England if I could find a ship to go. May God grant your domestic life may never be invaded as has been mine, and fill your heart with pity."

Varina now abandoned all pride, becoming a suppliant, begging where once she had commanded, battering at doors that would not open, assailing ears that would not listen. All her servants had left her at this point, except the faithful Robert who went with her to Savannah. "He was too true and brave a man to abandon women and children so desolate and oppressed as we were," Varina commented.[23] The boat trip was one of terror but faced with her family's necessities she pulled herself together and acted as nurse and chambermaid to Mrs. Clay, to her children, and to her sister Maggie, who was desperately ill. A great gale blew up. The upper deck was awash with water, so that no one could keep a footing, but "as I felt as wretched as could be, I did not fear a future state," Varina recalled many months later, when she had recovered from the experience.

The *Clyde* was a weather-beaten vessel, not designed for women and children. Their quarters were infested with insects. Water poured into Varina's stateroom, so that she caught a severe cold and lost her voice. Mrs. Clay and Maggie by this time were helpless. Varina had to hold Winnie in her arms much of the time lest she be injured by the tossing of the ship. The soldiers and crew were helpful with the children, and let her get some sleep when she was too exhausted to hold up any longer. Small Margaret was "quite like an old woman," looking after Winnie in the early morning. "Little Jeff and I did the housekeeping; it was a fair division of labor, and not unpleasant, as it displayed the good hearts of my children," Varina wrote.

At Charleston they all began to recover. They obtained some ice and milk, and felt better with the rolling ship at anchor. Maggie alone was in a serious condition when they reached Savannah. They had been unable to get medical aid for her, since all outside communication had been denied them. By this time Varina was desperately anxious about her husband's fate.

❧ 15 ❧

SAVANNAH

PALE, drawn, and disheveled, the First Lady of the fallen Confederacy trudged "quite in emigrant fashion" [1] to the Pulaski Hotel in Savannah. Lacking a carriage, Varina shepherded Margaret, Jeff, and Billy, "keeping all straight and acting as parcel-carrier." Her sister Maggie, faint though she was, carried little Winnie. Robert handled the heavy luggage.

The President's family were observed with close attention as they passed through the streets. Varina walked proudly, in spite of her inner wretchedness and a cold that made her voiceless. After her nights of camping in the woods, and rolling at sea, the hotel seemed a haven.

Gideon Welles, traveling south on an inspection trip after the great review in Washington of the triumphant armies of the North, noted her presence at the Pulaski Hotel when he visited Savannah. Needless to say, he made no effort to see her, but fished on the Savannah River and was serenaded in traditional fashion. Touring Fort Fisher, he studied the formidable defenses which had given him "exceeding annoyance for several years." [2] He stopped also at Fortress Monroe, walked around the ramparts, and noted that "Jeff Davis was a prisoner in one of the casemates, but I did not see him."

Welles held the key to the official disposition made of Varina and her children. He had protested as "too general" Stanton's ruling that they should be sent south. Mrs. Davis might pick an awkward spot such as Norfolk. " 'True,' said Grant with a laugh. Stanton was annoyed, but I think altered his telegram," Welles noted. Savannah, where she had no friends, was chosen.

Varina was virtually a prisoner in the lovely Georgia town. A guard was posted at her hotel. She was forbidden to leave the area or communicate by letter with officials or friends, except through the Provost Marshal's office. Many of the residents were kind to her, however. Their homes were thrown open in welcome, and her children were provided with the clothing they needed after all the looting. Meanwhile, she entered on one of the most painful phases of her troubled life. For the first time in twenty years she was cut adrift from the man she loved, and was not allowed to communicate with him in any way.

There was little sympathy for Varina at this time and less for her husband, who was lampooned, caricatured, and reviled. It was as if he, and he alone, had plunged the country into war. The wounds and scars were at their sorest. Too many families had suffered for the Davises to be regarded as anything but the symbol of their sorrows. They were the focus of the fires of hate that a civil war had stirred up throughout the country.

Proud and tempestuous, Varina had never practiced humility. Every insult made a deep scar. A look of permanent sadness settled in her great dark eyes, which were sunken now from sleepless nights. She did not mind the physical hardship for herself, since she had stamina to meet a practical challenge. It gave her no concern that she was shabby, well attired though she had always been. All the women of the South were shabby and bruised at this time. But her husband's fate was a daily nightmare and when she read of his shackling at Fortress Monroe in the Savannah *Republican*, she shut herself in her room and gave way to hysterical outcries. Maggie regretted that she had ever seen the paper. She had to be kept under opiates for a week.

This indignity was an incurable wound for both of the Davises. Varina would never cease to assail General Miles for his treatment of her husband. Stanton hastily ordered the irons removed. There was indignation in the North as well as in the South, and Thurlow Weed wrote to Stanton that he thought it "an error and an enormity, a dreadful cloud that would obscure the glory of other attainments." [3] Davis, in turn, worried about the effect the shackling would have on Varina. Late in May, feeling weak and despondent, he interlocked his fingers over his eyes and exclaimed, "Oh, my poor wife, my poor, poor girl! . . . I wish she could have been spared this knowledge. . . . I can see the hideous announcement with its flaming capitals, and cannot but anticipate how much her pride and love will both be shocked." [4]

But Varina was spared nothing, for she insisted on reading every line, over and over again. She lived through it all. Her husband sitting

on his cot reading his prayer book. Captain Jerome B. Titlow walking
in with a group of soldiers, a blacksmith, and the irons. Her husband's
protest, his demand that top officials be consulted. Titlow's reply: "Mr.
Davis, you are an old soldier and know what orders are," and her husband's response that he was a soldier and knew how to die.[5] "Let your
men shoot me at once," he demanded. Then a fierce struggle as the
blacksmith bent to shackle him, and four guards forced him into submission. "The prisoner showed unnatural strength," Titlow observed.
And when it was over, and his manacled feet rested on the floor, his
breakdown, head in hand, and his muttered exclamations: "Oh, the
shame, the shame!" He later told Dr. John J. Craven, the prison
physician, that he would have welcomed death at that moment.

I never sought my death but once, and then when completely frenzied
and not master of my actions. When they came to iron me that day, as a
last resource of desperation, I seized a soldier's musket and attempted to
wrench it from his grasp, hoping that in the scuffle and surprise, some one of
his comrades would shoot or bayonet me.

Varina, picturing it all, grew frantic. She wrote to Dr. Craven on
June 1, saying that she had been driven to addressing him by the
"terrible newspaper extras issued every afternoon, which represent my
husband to be in a dying condition." She added: "It seems to me that
no possible harm could accrue to your government from my knowing
the extent of my sorrow. If you are only permitted to say he is well,
or he is better, it will be a great comfort to me, who has no other left."
Even to think of it stopped her "heart's vibration," she added.

But as she read she applied her common sense and her knowledge
of her husband to the situation. On June 14 she wrote again to his
medical attendant. "Can it be that these tales are even in part true?"
she asked.

That such atrocities could render him frantic I know is not so. I have so
often tended him through months of nervous agony, without ever hearing
a groan or an expression of impatience, that I know these tales of childish
ravings are not true—would to God I could believe that all these dreadful
rumors were false as well![6]

However, Jefferson Davis was in worse condition than she imagined.
He was deeply despondent and was plagued by the familiar neuralgic
pains in his head. He even feared he might be losing his sanity. "His

memory, vision and hearing seemed to be impaired," Dr. Craven noted. The glaring whitewashed walls of the casemate irritated his eyes. The ceaseless tramp of the twenty-four-hour guard made him nervous. The constant surveillance kept him awake. He could not eat the coarse food served him on tin plates, without knife, or fork, lest he attempt suicide.

Dr. Craven did not respond, but Varina persisted in her attempts to get some word from him. She could tell from the newspaper accounts that he was treating her husband sympathetically, and that soon his wife and daughter Annie were preparing special delicacies for him. "How I love them for their goodness," she wrote,[7] as she poured out all the family news in a series of letters to the doctor, hoping and believing that he would relay it to her husband, since she could not communicate with him in any other way. She made things sound more cheerful than they were, not wishing to depress him further. Dr. Craven noted that he had worried about them all at sea and could not rest until he heard that they had landed safely.

She now pictured the children praying for him at meal time. Her daughter Margaret had made up a little grace but actually would run from the table crying after she had repeated it. However, Varina wrote cheerfully: "Will you tell him that we are well—that our little children pray for him, and miss his fatherly care—that his example still lives for them." But various problems about the children had arisen. They, too, were singled out for gibes and contempt.

Varina refrained from showing herself on the street in the daytime but went out at nightfall, accompanied by the faithful Robert. She walked under the orange trees on the bluff, catching their fragrance, or sat by the stone fountain in the park, with roses, camellias, geraniums, and verbena scenting the air. Although she could keep out of sight she was forced to let her children mingle with their contemporaries, and soon they were coming in with tales that frightened and appalled her. Jeff, then eight, was told he was rich and that his father had "stolen eight millions." Billy, nearly four, was taught to sing "We'll hang Jeff Davis on a sour apple-tree," and Varina sorrowfully noted he "made such good friends with the soldiers, that the poor child seemed to forget a great deal of his regard for his father" and would parrot off "I am a Yankee every time."

Finally two women from Maine threatened to whip Jeff when they found out who he was, and a captain's wife in the hotel dining room told him his father would soon be hanged.[8] He ran to Varina in tears, and next day she asked leave to go to Augusta but was refused. She felt that the children's lives might not be safe, as there were violent scenes in the streets at this time. In the end she decided to send them to Canada, where a number of Confederate familes had taken refuge. She entered Jeff in a grammar school near Montreal and Maggie in the Convent of the Sacred Heart. Varina sent her mother north with the children, and the faithful Robert accompanied them as courier, valet, and guardian of their safety. She kept only Winnie with herself.

Varina now made many desperate moves on her husband's behalf. Since she was more or less a prisoner herself, letters were her only medium and she sent out a tormented flow, spending hours over their composition, worrying ceaselessly about her husband's condition. She was ingenious about getting them past the inspectors, who found her a formidable captive. She had been told that she must not go north, or leave the country, or communicate with her husband, or live near him. If she tried to leave she would not be allowed to return.

Burton Harrison had written to F. P. Blair on May 22 urging passports that she might go abroad with her children. He described the woes she had suffered and appealed to Blair's old-time friendship for Varina. "Whatever may be done with the President I cannot consider it to be the purpose of this Government to subject his wife and sister and little children to wilful and extreme discomfort and painful mortification," wrote Burton.[9]

Varina wrote several times to Blair in the same vein, first from the *Clyde*, then from Savannah, but it was some time before any of her letters reached him. Plainly, he was touched. He also showed surprise that she should think of leaving the country, "knowing that your feelings could not prompt it." He assumed she was following her husband's counsel. This was indeed the course that Davis had advised before leaving her, with the underlying hope that he might eventually join his family. On June 6 Varina addressed Blair in her most fervent vein.

Shame-shame upon your people! While a felon's gyves were being fastened upon a soldier, and honest gentleman, did not the limb which was shrunken from a wound received in defence of your country arrest the work of his tormentors? They need have taken no precaution against his suicide. He never has taken aught which was not his own. His life is his wife's, his children's, his country's, his God's. . . . They may kill but can never degrade him. . . . May God except you from the curse which He will surely visit upon such sin. . . .[10]

Varina charged in this letter that the manacles were the "tardy vengeance of Mr. Johnson for an offence offered him years earlier." He had "bided his time," she wrote with scant logic. And how should she "characterize the conduct of a young brute like Genl. Miles, who could not have been born when my husband was striving, and fighting for the country whose flag his tormentor now disgraces by such atrocities?" But the people of the North as well as the people of the South knew Jefferson Davis, Varina added. She took pains to give Blair a minute account of the flight and the capture, carefully explaining the circumstances of the waterproof and shawl because "I value your opinion as much as I love you."

Turning to her own predicament, she asked why she should be a prisoner at large in a strange place surrounded by detectives who reported every visitor? Why was she kept in a garrisoned town bereft of home, friends, husband, and means of support? As a family they were treated with less consideration than she had seen her "knightly husband show to the beggars who came to our doors for alms," Varina wrote. "I never knew him to stand covered in the presence of a woman or allow one to be persecuted." She also pled for the aides and her husband's secretary, urging him to see that they had a fair trial.

Blair replied from Silver Spring on June 12 that this "sad letter" had finally reached him through Seward's office, and "no man mourns over your swelling overflowing sorrow more than I do." [11] He told her that her earlier letter and Harrison's had induced him to go to President Johnson about a passport for her, and that there seemed to be a chance of getting it if she would make the request to him personally. "There is nothing that I can do for you or your little ones that will be wanting to them or you," he finished affectionately.

Varina's next move met with a deadly chill. Two days after writing to Blair she addressed a letter to General Montgomery C. Meigs, who had been a close family friend in Washington. She asked him to use his influence to have her moved with her children to a more moderate climate and for permission to correspond with her husband. "Johnny" Meigs had been one of Varina's favorite young men. He had died in battle. Varina recalled many a dinner party at which Meigs and her husband had discussed the Capitol dome and the work he was doing on it. But now he was forgetful and unforgiving. He did not reply to her directly but wrote to the Commanding General at Savannah a letter sent through the Secretary of War, in which he bracketed her with her husband as having "inaugurated rebellion and civil war." He gave Varina one crumb of comfort—her husband was better, he wrote, but the rest of his letter dumfounded her.

I was under obligation to Mr. and Mrs. Davis for kindness and courtesy received before they inaugurated rebellion and civil war.

The effect of that war, *my personal loss* in the death of my eldest son, murdered by one of Mr. Davis's assassins, called guerillas, my *position as an officer of the Government*, makes it altogether improper for me to enter into any correspondence with Mrs. Davis or to attempt to interfere in the course of justice.[12]

Varina next tackled Horace Greeley, who had written many a sharp word about her husband. But the erratic sage of Park Row was known to have a tender heart, and to champion lost causes. She enclosed an article from the Savannah *Republican* assailing her husband. "How can the honest men and gentlemen of your country stand idly by to see a gentleman maligned, insulted, tortured and denied the right of trial by the usual forms of law?" she wrote. "Is his cause so strong that he must be done to death by starvation, confined air, and manacles?" Varina, who wrote extravagantly and sometimes ungrammatically when under stress, continued:

With all the archives of our government in the hands of your government, do they despair of proving him a rogue, falsifier, assassin and traitor— that they must in addition guard him like a wild beast, and chain him for fear his unarmed hands will in a casemated cell subvert the government? Shame, shame—he is not held for the ends of Justice but for those of torture. . . . Is no one among you bold enough to defend him? . . . I have also important evidence which I could give if summoned—*I demand to be summoned* upon Mr. Davis' trial, if the means used to slay him do not succeed before that time. . . . Let me implore you to cry aloud for justice for him, with that I shall be content.[13]

Greeley was interested. He showed Varina's letter to George Shea, a well-known lawyer, and solicited his professional services. Shea talked to Henry Wilson, Thaddeus Stevens, John A. Andrew, Gerrit Smith, and other strong party men, but before Greeley would go into the matter wholeheartedly Shea went to Canada, met Breckinridge there, and examined such archives of the Confederate Government as had been saved.[14] He reported back so favorably on the stand that Davis had taken on prisoners of war—being against retaliation—and on other controversial issues in the counsels of his government, that eventually Greeley did some editorial pounding on the subject of bringing him to trial without further delay. Shea now joined forces with Charles O'Conor, known to Varina as a dinner guest in the distant past. He had already become chief counsel for the prisoner in Fortress Monroe.

In the meantime, Greeley answered Varina's letter publicly through the War Department. It was a sympathetic note but noncommittal. Long accustomed to working with the press, she pursued this line and on July 9 addressed herself to the *Metropolitan Herald and Vindicator* which had spoken in defense of her husband. Again she recited the family woes and detailed the story of the flight and capture. She told of her financial embarrassment. She had thirteen hundred dollars left in the world, and did not know how she would pay her bills when this amount was finished. "If the cry of an oppressed woman ever appeals to the heart of man, does not mine stir the heart's blood of the brave and true of your people. . . ." [15]

The following day she sat down in great anger to write to Seward protesting the publication of some of their personal correspondence. The Savannah *Republican* had reprinted a Boston dispatch and headed it "Glimpses into Jeff Davis' desk. Interesting Correspondence." This was unjustifiable, Varina argued, although she conceded the right of the government to examine these papers. But they should never have been shown to the "newsmongers" to be paraded as "readable matter." [16]

The only legacy the government had left her children, Varina wrote, was the record contained in these letters of their father's love for them and the "constant unpremeditated exhibition of his moral rectitude." She had hoped to get them back when the government had finished with them. Varina signed herself to the man who had always interested her, and at times had shown her kindness, "Very respectfully, Your old servant, Varina Davis."

"How long oh Lord, how long!" she wrote to George Shea four days later, still burning with anger about the letters. "Quidnuncs are polluting with their unhallowed gaze the precious records of my few happy hours, and turning an honest penny by selling garbled extracts from my husband's letters, and mine, to those papers whose readers needing a gentle excitement, are willing to pay for 'readable matter.'" [17]

Varina was well aware from the papers by this time that the Cabinet was having much internal discussion on the fate of her husband, and that there was disagreement among them about the course they should pursue. She felt they were "mousing among the Archives" for something on which to support accusations. By this time she was going into the legal aspects of her husband's case with Shea. She gave him practical suggestions as to where he might find evidence—from the letter book she was harboring if she could get it to him, from the files of the Richmond papers, from persons she would indicate, from material in Canada, as well as from her own knowledge.

"Living in the closest friendship with Mr. Davis, I am cognizant of a great deal relating to his official conduct, and where I cannot speak from personal knowledge, could tell you in most instances where to apply to those who participated in his action," she wrote with the authority born of her knowledge of her husband's affairs. Varina commented that public opinion had compelled Mr. Johnson and Mr. Stanton to feed her husband's body better, but that "his mind was given over to their tender mercies." She felt "unhinged by sorrow." She had been robbed of everything except memories—"God has kept them green."

The summer of 1865 passed like a nightmare for Varina. From the weakness and despondency that she had read about in May, her husband had passed into a worse phase. By the middle of July, while the Cabinet was discussing what to do with him, his eyes were in such trouble that he was seeing all objects double. By the end of the month he was critically ill. His prostration was so complete that Dr. Craven feared he would die. By August he had a carbuncle and high fever, a matter of Cabinet discussion in Washington.[18] On September 1 Dr. Craven notified General Miles that his health was "rapidly declining" although he showed "all the evidence of an iron will." But he had become "despondent and dull, a very unnatural condition for him."

Bit by bit various conditions that had maddened him were corrected and he received better treatment. Dr. Craven was a large factor in this, and Varina's letters had been illuminating about her husband's particular sensitivities. The two guards were removed from his cell. The lamp that had burned night and day in his room finally was screened at night. He was permitted to walk for an hour on the ramparts and to read some books and magazines, subject to official approval. Dr. Craven ordered tobacco for him. "This is noble medicine," said Davis as he packed his meerschaum with it, a pipe he later gave to the doctor as a souvenir.

By this time Varina was close to a breakdown, and at the end of July she was permitted to go to Mill View, the home of George Schley, a friend who lived five miles outside Augusta. She wrote a bright letter soon afterward to Dr. Craven, obviously hoping it would cheer her husband. Winnie had grown "fat and rosy as the 'Glory of France,' a rose which Mr. Davis recollects near the gate of our home." The fine country air and the privacy were doing her good, too. She could now sleep and eat and she felt alive again. Winnie was taking hominy and drinking fresh milk. She grew in "grace and weight." She talked a little and was a great pet with everyone. The next paragraph was an obvious attempt to make things seem much better than they were.

The difficulty is to accept all the invitations I get, or to refuse them rather . . . the whole Southern country teeming with homes, the doors of which open wide to receive me; and people are so loving, talk with such streaming eyes and broken voices of him who is so precious to them and to me, that I cannot realize I do not know them intimately. Mr. Davis should dismiss all fears for me. Money is urged upon me—everything, I only suffer for him. I do not meet a young man who fails to put himself at my disposal to go anywhere for me. I cannot pay a doctor's bill, or buy of an apothecary. "All these things are added unto me." [19]

On August 3 she was thanking Octavus Cohen of Savannah for eight hundred dollars which had been raised by friends for her use. "I would it were in my power to give to our powerless and impoverished people instead of from he 'that hath little' taking 'the little that he hath' away," Varina wrote.[20]

Although her health improved at Mill View her restlessness and anxiety were clearly expressed in a sequence of letters she wrote at this time to Mrs. Martha Phillips of Savannah. She adopted a light and almost flippant note, and sometimes even seemed hysterical as she discussed their friends, books, and her new circumstances. Obviously, she was casting about for interests to fill the empty, anxious hours. Torn with worry, she had small outlet for her abundant energies, physical and intellectual. It was a new experience for Varina to be in an ignominious position and she could not quite get used to it.

"Are you sick or sad, dull or mad, light or airy?" she asked Mrs. Phillips rhetorically on August 18.[21] She was starved for a chat, she said, for news of friends and events. She conceded that General James B. Steedman, the new commandant, whom she had known in Washington, had shown some sympathy and a desire to help her in her troubles. He had followed General H. W. Birge, whom she despised. Had there been any word from her mother, she asked. She worried constantly about Mrs. Howell and the children in Canada, as well as about her husband. She also wondered about Maggie, who was visiting Joseph Davis at Canton, Mississippi, and was considering marrying young Hathaway. "I do not think she will marry that man," said Varina of the girl who had had so many beaux in Richmond during the war years.

Soon after this Varina sent Maggie north to Canada to join her mother and the children. Her sister had not been feeling well. She was unhappy over her love affair as well as the disordered state of the country. Varina felt she would be a help and support to their aging mother, who was inclined to be spontaneous in her observations and had made some public statements that her daughter, weighing the effect of everything on her husband's fate, thought ill-judged. "I am sorry to see the notice of Ma's conversations," she wrote to Martha Phillips. "I begged her so to travel quietly that I am the more astonished at the result. . . . Nothing is more insane than to crush out the sympathy of the North by violence. I have heard but once from her since my arrival here. I cannot imagine what she can be doing." [22]

On August 9 Varina wrote to President Johnson, asking if she might join her children, if not her husband. She said she had been forced to send them out of the country because of the abuse showered on their father, and his career, which "His Excellency could well understand must form to me, as to them, the proudest memory of our lives,—the crowning grace of our honest name." [23] She added that she was conscious of no crime, "save the unrepented one of being his wife for twenty-one years."

The President did not answer. "The worst criminals wait on the order of the Styx for a ferryman who never comes," Varina wrote to Mrs. Phillips on August 22. Meanwhile she read Sydney Smith, and studied Dr. C. Schley's "highly colored plates upon obstetrics" but decided that "exact science does not charm when brought to bear upon oneself." [24] She longed for news of all her friends. "Tell me Savannah news and scandal—if it is not naughty scandal," she implored, "who marries, who dies, who steals, who enjoys his own, who lives and loves, who wakes and does not love but weeps—drag your nets, and send me the miraculous draught." She asked for the Savannah papers. She was bored, restless, frantic with worry. Her full life had become one of aching emptiness and uncertainty.

I lead a very humdrum life, eat, sew, don't sleep particularly much, and occasionally go to Augusta. . . . I buy a yard of ten cent calico, look drearily at my diminished well thumbed greenbacks, and with a pathetic sigh mount the family carriage and hie me home talking platitudes with my tongue & with my heart following my soul's laboring in some dread extremity.

In another letter to Martha Phillips, Varina's pain was self-evident. "I am well nigh worn out with the heart sickness of hope deferred," she wrote.[25] She needed tears that would not flow to cool her "burning tearless eyes." She read ceaselessly to quell her longing for her husband. She was finding *Our Mutual Friend* a charming book, although not one of Dickens' best. She had been reading Charlotte Yonge and liked her "twilight unexceptional misty style." She had dipped into Robert Burton's *The Anatomy of Melancholy* and considered it the "dirtiest book" she knew, yet at the same time she "felt meritorious for reading such a scientifically filthy thing." However, she was not given to the enjoyment of such books, Varina added. She preferred Mrs. Browning. But in her present mood she did better with "Miss Braddon or Miss Somebody who did not delve down deep." She thanked Martha for sending her writing paper and sugarplums. The sweets kept her "unwilling to die for days—now I am resigned for they are gone," she wrote. "I am a voracious as well as a veracious creature and the only tooth I have is sweet."

Clearly, Varina's mood at this time was one of desperation masked in irony, and her letters to Martha Phillips were an outlet for her frustrations. But her tone changed quickly when she heard at last from her husband on September 4, 1865. It was his first direct communication and she wrote at once to his brother Joseph, quoting excerpts. Jeff had urged her to write to his Brother and his sisters "in such terms as you can well understand I would use if allowed to write to them myself." [26] The door now was open for communication, with two restrictions: they must deal only with family matters, and all letters were to be submitted to the Attorney General before being sent on to Varina. He impressed on his impetuous wife the need for caution in their correspondence, but was reassuring in tone.

The confidence in the shield of innocence with which I tried to quiet your apprehensions and to dry your tears at our parting sustains me still. If your fears have proven more prophetic than my hopes yet do not despond.

"Tarry thou the Lord's leisure, be strong and He will comfort thy heart."
. . . Be not alarmed by speculative reports concerning my condition. You
can rely on my fortitude and God has given me much of resignation to His
Blessed Will.

Davis discussed his situation with Varina, and directed her to turn
to Joseph for advice about plantation affairs if he should not regain his
freedom, but he urged her not to attempt to do anything personally in
the matter. Discussing his plantation interests, he wrote:

It is to be inferred that you have decided, and I think wisely, not to
return to our old home, at least not in the disturbed condition of society.
Should I regain my liberty before "Our people" have become vagrant, there
are many of them whose labor I could direct so as to make it not wholly
unprofitable. Their good faith under many trials and the mutual affection
between them and myself make me always solicitous for their welfare and
probably keeps them expectant of my coming.

Comforted by this communication, Varina's accompanying letter to
Joseph was almost warm in tone, in spite of the breach between them.
She suggested that she might be able to pay both his and her husband's
property taxes from the money coming in to her. She had two hundred
dollars in gold on hand, besides greenbacks and "as my kind friends
insure me from want I am well able to share with you." Varina said that
it would make her happy to contribute to his comfort in any way. "The
deep sense of obligation Jeff and all of us must feel to you for your
kindness to him of so many long years makes me very anxious to do
anything in my power for you," she wrote, adding that she had not
wanted for friends or money—"the Federals offering service as well as
our own people." She was telling him all this "not from egotistical
vanity," Varina explained, but so that he would understand why she
could not attend to their business affairs.

Joseph did not respond, but Varina deposited two hundred dollars
in gold for him in Charleston, writing to Lise Mitchell on December 7
that it seemed strange "for us to be able to give to him who has conferred so much upon my dear, grateful husband, who so wishes he was
able to work for him." She added that her husband now had dainties,
wines, spirits, brandies, and everything that she and her friends could
send, and had near him a man "who loves him devotedly and is able to
help him." This was Dr. Craven. She had made Jeff two "splendid
flannel nightgowns." The commandant, she added, was "a beast, a

hyena and only twenty-five years old." She expressed the hope that the
Lord would reward him according to his iniquity. Varina sent Lisa a
photograph of herself with this letter, pointing out that she had
changed very much. If it was a "hideous thing" she had to acknowledge
that it was a "pretty fair likeness of the original."

At this time Varina was corresponding with Mrs. Howell Cobb in a
characteristically candid vein. They were old friends and understood
each other well. Referring sarcastically to the restrictions placed upon
her, she wrote: "Think what a roaring lion is going loose in Georgia
seeking whom she may devour—one old woman, a small baby, and
nurse; the Freedmen's bureau and the military police had better be
doubled lest either the baby or I 'turn again and rend them.' " [27] The
extent to which she leaned on her husband's advice and guidance may
be deduced from this letter. The permission to write to him had relieved her of the "dreadful sense of loneliness and agonizing doubt and
weight of responsibility. . . . I may ask his advice instead of acting
upon my own suggestions, and above all I may know from him how he
is. . . . He writes in such a spirit of pious resignation and trust in God's
faith with those who rest their dependence upon Him that he has
comforted me greatly."

A few days later Varina wrote to her old friend Mrs. Chesnut, who
by this time was back at Camden, still making diary entries with spice
and point. One of Mrs. Chesnut's friends, Isabella Martin, had just
drawn her attention to an item in the New York *Herald* describing Mrs.
Davis and Maggie as "coarse—not delicate and refined like the northern
ladies—" "Mrs. Lincoln, *par exemple!*" snapped Mrs. Chesnut. She had
written twice to Varina before receiving the following letter from
her:

You give me a sad picture of your life, but *you* have your husband—so
do not murmur lest he be taken away. As for me I have nothing—but my
own little ewe lamb—my baby. I will not go through the weary form of
telling you how I have suffered—But enough to content any enemy, be he
ever so bloodthirsty—you know I bleed inwardly—and suffer more because
not put in the surgeons' hands as one of the wounded—I never report unfit
for duty. . . . What do I do all day long? I dream—I do not even sew—
I cannot read. I dream—"sweeter to rest together—dead—Far sweeter than
to live asunder." [28]

Varina discussed the failure of health that both she and Mrs. Chesnut
seemed to have experienced with their misfortunes. "I never feel well—
my health as well as yours seems gone," she wrote. Her old friends

in Washington had followed her with "tender letters." So had "Mrs. Lee and the dear Richmond people." Although she and Mrs. Chesnut had often thought they suffered from an icy reserve in Richmond, she now wrote warmly: "I will give you an instance though it slays me. They have sent to me for my boy's age. They mean to put a monument over him. This has filled the cup of love I offer them to the very brim."

But Varina wrote with bitterness of South Carolina, which had "genteelly refrained from petitioning for Mr. Davis, or from showing the least interest in his affairs . . . after precipitating secession by hasty action." She would no longer sorrow as she had for its people— "now indeed that fountain of bitter tears is sealed—I'll weep no more." Discussing the future of the Southern people Varina continued:

Mr. Chesnut must take heart, and know that the true believers in states rights must eventually receive their own peoples suffrages again. Except such scapegoats as my dear husband—a sin offering for a nation, upon whose devoted head the ban is placed, and whose very immolation lightens the heart of the ransomed people, I do not think the future so dark to the statesmen of the South. . . . With a free press and speech even though in our bitter "cup an Union shall be thrown"—our men may write and speak themselves free again—*perhaps equal.*

Varina switched abruptly from the serious note and injected a wry thought that she knew Mrs. Chesnut would appreciate. "However, women are always insufferable upon politics—I think I see the beard sprout as they generalize in their weak way so I do not propose to treat you to a dose of political suppositions—When all is vain and clouded—'all we know is that nothing can be known.' "

At this point she reviewed the fate of their old friends. John Taylor Wood and Johnston were in Canada. Browne had written affectionately to Varina from Athens. Custis Lee was now a professor. She had written both to him and to Robert E. Lee about her husband's defense. Burton Harrison, "poor boy," was still in prison, and she did not know anyone who could get him out. "I am extremely unhappy about him and the other true men imprisoned for their faith," Varina wrote. "Benjamin is reciting the Princess—I suppose—or 'I slip—I slide—I gloom—I glance—etc. etc. For men may come and men may go but I glide on forever.' "

Varina asked Mrs. Chesnut what she thought of "Jordan's manifesto in the interests of Beauregard and Joe Johnston" printed in *Harper's*

New Monthly Magazine. It had made her very angry, and it evoked
a torrent of discussion both in the North and the South. Colonel
Thomas Jordan, who had played a significant role as Beauregard's
right hand and amanuensis, had written an article sharply critical
of Jefferson Davis, calling him "censorious, imperious and narrow."
A. H. Mason, an aide to General Hood, wrote to Beauregard from
Washington as soon as the manifesto appeared, saying he deprecated
any attack at that time "on that fallen man—and oh, how low a fall!
from a Southerner." He thought that on the whole it would do Davis
good with the Northern people, but he believed he would rather be
hanged than thus defended.

Varina's most revealing letter, however, was addressed from Mill
View on October 3, 1865, to William Preston Johnston who had gone
to Montreal after two months' imprisonment at Fort Delaware. She
had quarreled badly with him during their distracted flight along the
Georgia roads, and she now took occasion to apologize, reluctantly,
painfully, apparently having realized that she was in the wrong. Varina's
self-knowledge of her sometimes violent nature shows in this letter.

Have you thought of our quarrel on the road? I have, and it had made
a painful impression, a longing to be forgiven. I was unjust, but so goaded
I could not tell the difference—a touch seemed a stab. When I am ill at
heart I am wild, and vagaries possess me. "Forgive them where they fail in
truth, and in Thy wisdom make me wise." This apology comes hard, value
it . . .[29]

She was hurt because Johnston had taken so long to write to her.
She had arraigned him in her "aching heart." She craved a line from
those she loved. The uncertainties of her position had swept away all
her familiar landmarks and she did not know how high the tide of
loneliness might swell. He was seeing her children in Montreal and
she now wrote thankfully:

Your message was the first tidings of my children since the week after
they left. . . . I had wept myself ill, written another imploring letter to
Mr. Johnson to let me go. . . . Know that I have been torn like Prometheus
bound, without his divine power to endure. I have been "purified, yet as
by fire." . . . No man of my kind or even of my friends came to me until
the last three weeks, when Joe Davis came announcing that I could not be
found before—it cut me to the quick. Billy slandered and belied me and
never wrote me one line even of comfort. Clarke did come, and affectionately urged upon me his services, he is the only man who has that I ever
saw before—so much my dear Friend for the sympathy of friends. . . .

Joe Davis was Joseph R. Davis, her husband's nephew and aide-de-camp. Billy was her brother, William Francis Howell, who had fled to Montreal. Clarke was M. H. Clarke, last Treasurer of the Confederacy. At this point Varina disclosed that her husband "was evidently a little hurt that no one has defended his good name." His letters breathed "the utmost resignation, a holy peace, and grand fortitude . . . but he wondered why no one answered the 'fictions' published about him." She pointed out that she had offered repeatedly to take up quarters with him in prison and to take a parole not to discuss public matters with him, but "Hog Birge"—I write the name with gusto—the Hog told me if I escaped, I should never be allowed to come back—that he had been officially so informed—think of being advised by the Hog. . . . He went away and wrote me a fierce note, the wretched porker. . . ."

Varina wrote without restraint of her own and her husband's enemies. She was given to using strong terms when moved, and she lashed out now with all the force of her formidable nature. But many of her letters went unanswered. Even as late as October she had not received a response from Dr. Craven, in spite of all the letters she had sent him. It was like writing to a shadow, she sometimes thought, yet she knew that all she wrote was conveyed to her husband and that every kindness was being shown him by the Craven family. "Though you remain irrevocably dumb I am sure you hear me, and in addressing you, feel as if writing to one of my oldest and most reliable friends," she wrote from Mill View on October 10. "Every letter from my husband comes freighted with good wishes for you."

At this time he was suffering from an obstinate case of erysipelas. He was unable to sleep. "I dread paralysis for him, his nerves have been so highly strung for years without relief," Varina wrote.[30] She begged that his eyes be protected from light, but she knew it was useless to advise Dr. Craven about her husband's constitution since he must have become aware of its peculiarities "in the long and kind watches" he had kept over him.

By this time she was raging over comments made by Andrew Johnson on her conduct when the South Carolina delegation visited him. He deplored her letters and called her an angry woman. Writing to Armistead Burt on October 20 from Augusta, she denied she had ever sent him a discourteous letter "although his unmanly persecution of me has been very often a great temptation."[31] She detailed all the "humiliating circumstances" of her circumscribed activities, her efforts to break these bonds by writing to men in authority, her desire to leave the country, and her protest to Seward about the garbled publication of their personal papers. But Varina insisted that her letters to Andrew Johnson were uniformly respectful and added:

I have been vilely persecuted, and would have tried the issue of right long ago but for my husband. Mr. Johnson's theories about my character are of small importance, because I have never been in the same room with him in my life, unless unconsciously. It is the wolf and the lamb repeated . . . I pray God I may bear all the insults, and agonies of the life to come with the same quiet fortitude which I have evinced in the past . . . What Mr. Johnson confers in future he will offer, for so misrepresented, I will appeal no more. . . .

Varina ended on a note of defiance. She did not acknowledge the right of the government to keep her a prisoner, she wrote proudly, and she would not bind herself not to try to escape, provided this would not be prejudicial to her husband's case. Mr. Johnson had both the power and the will to torture her, she charged, and "he has done so until my heart seems to beat only from the impetus of terror and agony." She was not insane enough to provoke a man with despotic power over her husband's life, she assured Mr. Burt. "I must think that had you been there you had not stood by, in however small a minority, and heard a countrywoman so coarsely criticized for the benefit of a mixed company without a remonstrance."

Varina could not understand the bearing of the South Carolina commission on this occasion. In a sarcastic postscript she reviewed the case they had made before the President. They were glad that Mr. Trenholm was paroled. They hoped Mr. Johnson would not execute Mr. Davis for his "traitorous conduct." They conceded that Mrs. Davis was a "woman of strong feeling, and strong temper." Varina was deeply wounded by this personal affront, and wrote passionately to Mr. Burt:

If to despise moral cowards, and to loathe a man capable of insulting a defenseless sorrowing woman to unresisting listeners, is to justify this characterisation, I acknowledge its justice—and rather ten thousand times rather would I go into the wilderness with the sinless scapegoat, fainting under his load of vicarious sin, than be one of those who breathe freer in the assurance that he is their proprietary sacrifice.

"Oh who be he would be the King
Of such a many-headed monster thing."

Varina also wrote bitterly to Mrs. Clay about this incident, after sympathizing with her on the pending release of her husband. She assumed that Mrs. Clay had seen the "gentlemanly attack which Mr. President Johnson made upon me to the South Carolina delegation." [32] She assured Mrs. Clay that she had never written him a line without consulting Mr. Schley and General Steedman on the tenor of her letters, and receiving their approval.

Mrs. Clay had been having more success than Varina in her efforts on her imprisoned husband's behalf. She had seen President Johnson a number of times, and although he kept putting her off with excuses of helplessness she finally pinned him down until he gave her a copy of Joseph Holt's report containing the charges against Davis and Clay. This was so compromising a document that Holt promptly issued a pamphlet justifying himself.

Mrs. Clay met Horace Greeley in the lobby of the New York Hotel and showed him these documents. The upshot was that in December the President gave her a permit to visit Clay at Fortress Monroe. She found Miles polite, although she was left to simmer for hours. When she finally reached her husband she learned that he had virtually no communication with Jefferson Davis, except for passing glances on the rampart. When they exchanged greetings in French on one occasion they were promptly separated. But in sending the former President cigars on her subsequent visits, Mrs. Clay tucked little paper lighters into them with messages about Varina and the children. And when the time came for her husband to leave the Fortress, Davis managed to give him a note in tiny script naming friends "whose influence might be awakened" on his behalf. On one of her visits she caught a glimpse of him on the ramparts and she reported to Varina that his beard and hair were white, and he was thin to the point of emaciation, "but walked like a President still." [33]

Mrs. Stephen A. Douglas had gone with Mrs. Clay to President Johnson in the first instance. She literally went down on her knees and with tears streaming from her eyes begged him to help Clement Clay. She urged his wife to follow her example. "This, however, I could not comply with," said Mrs. Clay. "I had no reason to respect the Tennessean before me. . . . My heart was full of indignant protest that such an appeal as Mrs. Douglas's should have been necessary; but that, having been made, Mr. Johnson could refuse it, angered me still more. I would not have knelt to him even to save a precious life." [34]

She went to Stanton, who was "gravely polite"; to Judge Holt, whose wife had been one of her intimates at the Ebbitt House; to General Grant, who received her courteously and said that if he had the power he would release every prisoner in the land—"unless Mr. Davis might be detained awhile to satisfy public clamor."

The following April, Clay took the oath of allegiance and was released on parole. These various moves made Varina more determined than ever, regardless of the rebuffs she suffered. Mrs. Clay commented on the fact that President Johnson's remarks about Mrs. Davis to the South Carolina delegation "became the talk of the country." [35] Their feud was out in the open. She was not a woman who could knuckle under, and her pride was deeply involved. In another undated letter, written to Burt about this time, Varina seemed to be deeply depressed. Quoting from *Uncle Tom's Cabin* she wrote: "Like poor Tom 'I'm aweary—I'm a-cold! I would not live alway.' " [36]

At this time the lawyers were assuring her that her husband might be expatriated, and that his health was better. But she was feeling "too wretched to guess." She was trying to assemble her "debris" in Savannah so that when final action was taken she would be ready, with her things put together—though by this time they were "pitifully small." But Varina still had a long way to go. The doors were not opening yet, and she would write many more letters, and badger many more men in public office, before her husband would recover his freedom. On September 19 she wrote to Shea: "I look forward to a trial as a boon."

By the end of the year Dr. Craven had been removed from his post. He had shown too much friendliness to the prisoner, and a black pilot cloth overcoat he had ordered for him created a crisis. He had already been told by General Miles to confine his conversations with the prisoner to professional topics. The doctor had engaged in many long talks with Davis and had learned his views on diverse things, from his attitude toward women to his reactions to the war. He astounded the physician with the depth and variety of his knowledge—"a mind as active as his could not suddenly lie fallow." He was always ready to talk of the war. He said it was a rule of his life never to express regret over the inevitable. "Fire is not quenched with tow, nor the past to be remedied by lamentations." He summed up his own history in a phrase: "Success is virtue and defeat crime." [37]

He inquired about the fate of the plantations along the James River. He discussed the generals of both armies and paid tribute to Grant as a "great soldier, beyond doubt, but of a new school." He considered McClellan the ablest officer of the Federal Army but thought his caution so extreme as to suggest timidity—"moral timidity, for he was personally brave." There were only seven thousand troops to meet him when he landed on the Peninsula and he should have rushed upon them and overwhelmed them at whatever cost, in Davis's opinion.[38]

He praised Lee, Bragg, Jackson, Pemberton, and Albert Sidney Johnston among his own generals, and considered Bragg's victory at Chickamauga "one of the most brilliant achievements of the war, considering the disparity of the forces." Assessing other men close to him, he described Toombs as a "man of great natural force and capacity, a man of restless nature, a born Jacobin, though with honest intentions." He had found Benjamin "the ablest and most faithful member of his advisory council" and Reagan a "plain, strong man, of good common sense and a good heart, faithful to the last." [39]

He spent a great deal of time with his Bible and prayer book, and favored Job and the Psalms. He seemed to have a "clear almost passionate grasp in his faith." [40] He asked for books on conchology, geology, and botany. He discussed the shellfish family, after watching the oysters on the slope of the moat opposite the fort. He analyzed the flight of the fish hawks and was well informed on dogs, Dr. Craven observed. He was preoccupied with the subject of vision, discussed his ulcerated cornea with scientific interest, and made it the starting point of a technical discussion on optics and acoustics. He talked politics and hoped for a constitutional trial. He compared his own plight with that of Lafayette in the dungeons of Magdeburg and Olmütz, but he did not complain about anything save the restrictions imposed by General Miles on his correspondence with Varina, when he was finally allowed to communicate with her. It irked him to think that young staff officers or clerks in Washington might mull over his expressions of pain, or his terms of endearment for Varina.

His thoughts dwelled often on his wife. One day he told Dr. Craven it was rarely, save in man's hours of deepest infliction, "that he realized how much he stood in need of the support of his gentle counterpart." [41] He expressed the opinion that unfaithfulness in marriage was usually the husband's fault, either through neglect, or by throwing his wife into association with dissolute men. "No woman will err if treated properly by a husband worthy of the name, but she is the weaker vessel and must be protected," he declared.

Varina tried to draw cheer from his statement in a letter written on October 11, 1865: "I have not sunk under my trials . . . and trust I shall be sustained under any affliction which I may be required to bear." [42] The critics were noisy, he commented. The multitude was silent but "my own heart tells me the sympathy exists, that the prayers from the family hearth have not been hushed. . . ."

He described the new quarters in Carroll Hall into which he had moved early in October, on the second floor of a house built for officers. The dry air, the good water, an occasional fire, were helping him already. His room was eighteen by twenty feet. He had a fireplace, an iron frame bed, a water bucket, basin and pitcher, and a folding screen which enabled him to wash unobserved. At last he had a shelf for books, pegs on which to hang his clothes, and a closet. He had breakfast at nine, dinner at four, tea if he wished it. The food now suited him well. His chair was more comfortable than the one he had had, and Varina soon would send him a better one, which is on view today in Montgomery.

She could picture it all, as she read his letters over and over, carrying them about in the bosom of her dress, an old custom dating back to the days of their courtship. They were sprinkled with historical allusions. They referred to books they had been reading shortly before his capture. There was much religious feeling in his letters, some homilies, and the tone of restraint that suggested he knew they were to be read by unfriendly eyes. "Misfortune should not depress us, as it is only crime which can degrade. . . . Our injuries cease to be grievous in proportion as Christian charity enables us to forgive those who trespass against us, and to pray for our enemies."

Varina did not share her husband's humility or his charity, although she also offered him spiritual consolation. His letters at this time, characteristically courteous and restrained, suggest a certain degree of resignation to his fate, whereas hers overflow with a passionate sense of injustice, and a frantic beating against the bars. As in their former relationship, he tried to hold her impetuous nature in check. "To make the best of the existing condition is alike required by patriotism and common sense," he wrote on November 21, 1865.[43] He discussed public issues in these letters, took note of the reconstruction policies, and added: "Though neither a spectator nor an actor, a life spent more in the service of my country than in that of my family, leaves me now unable to disengage myself from the consideration of the public interests. . . ."

He warned his wife strongly not to be affected by any of the statements made about him by correspondents. To calumniate a state prisoner was an old device and "never was a fairer opportunity presented to do so without the fear of contradiction than is offered in my case." On November 22 he wrote that the six months of their separation seemed as many years, measured by his "painful anxiety" about her and the children. But his confidence in her was strong. He thought of her with "increased pride and fully sustained confidence," and added: "Shut out from the everchanging world, I live in the past with a vividness only thus to be accounted for. . . ."

Varina took note of the "heavy erasures made in his letters under official scrutiny." There was much she could read between the lines of the personal suffering as well as the front of resignation shown by her husband in the long days of his captivity. On December 7 he wrote revealingly that, although his prison life did not give him the quiet of solitude, its isolation enabled him to look inward and "if my self-love, not to say sense of justice, would have resisted the reckless abuse of my enemies, I am humbled by your unmerited praise." It taught him what he ought to be, he observed. And again the optimistic note broke through: "I live and hope. . . . There is an unseen hand which upholds me, save when my thoughts are concentrated on the objects of my dearest love and greatest solicitude." [44]

Thus Varina and Jefferson Davis communicated back and forth through a veil of darkness, each comforting the other in spite of the binding strings that confined them.

Their status changed suddenly in the spring of 1866. Varina finally was permitted to visit her children in Canada during April. While there she got dismal news of her husband's condition and telegraphed to President Johnson from Montreal: "Is it possible that you will keep me from my dying husband? Can I come to see him?" (Signed) Varina Davis.

This message brought a measure of relief. The President referred her appeal to Stanton, who ordered General Miles to let Varina visit her husband. By this time Clay was free. She hurried with Winnie to Fortress Monroe and had an emotional reunion with Jefferson early in May. She was shocked by his "shrunken form and glassy eyes; his cheekbones stood out like those of a skeleton." She noted that he had a horse bucket for water, a chair with one short leg that rocked it, a copy of the New York *Herald* for a tablecloth, and that his bed was infested with lice. At first she could spend only short periods with him. General Miles fixed the hours. When she arrived with silver, table linen, and some delicacies, he told her that the fort could not be made a "depot for delicacies, such as oysters and luxuries for Jeff Davis."

Varina got angry and told him that she was not his prisoner and that the law would not protect him if he infringed on her private rights. He looked at her thoughtfully and remarked, "I guess it wouldn't."

Miles was still protesting the issue when Varina reached the President in person and had a chance to state her case, after she had sent him two more imploring letters early in May. Their tone, for Varina, was humble. She thanked him for letting her visit her husband at last. She reported on his condition and urged him to take her husband's case in his own hands and "give him the freedom of the fort—*both of night and day*, so that his mind and body may have *natural rest*." [45] Varina continued:

Please Mr. President do not refuse me—it is far more than life to me for which I plead. Will you not grant it? If Mr. Davis could be in a quiet dark room at night, relieved of the agony of knowing that so many watch around him, with power to walk about at will all day, he would I think in a few months be better. Will you not have quarters assigned to him, and let us try the experiment?

Varina followed up this letter with another on May 12, in which she urged the President to suspend opinion and action on any information given him by General Miles until he could summon Dr. Craven's successor, Dr. George E. Cooper, "who is not the less zealous in the Union cause that he is a humane and an upright man." [46]

By the end of May she was in Washington and face to face with Andrew Johnson, a man who had publicly reviled her but who now received her with some degree of courtesy and kindness. None could plead the cause of Jefferson Davis more eloquently than Varina. She could even spare some sympathy for the man she faced. The tide had turned for him, too, and he stood on the brink of impeachment proceedings.

❦ 16 ❦

WASHINGTON REVISITED

WASHINGTON sparkled with postwar energy when Varina returned to it late that May, and drove through the streets, no longer the honored wife of a prominent Cabinet officer, but the harassed advocate of the world's most famous prisoner. The scars of war were in view, as in the South—men without arms and legs, many women in black. The Civil Rights Bill was the big issue in Congress.

As she passed through the streets, a saddened woman, her drooping, weary eyes noted the changes that the war had wrought in the capital. She drove past her own old house and others where she had attended brilliant parties. Many of her former friends called to welcome her. Some, like Senator Reverdy Johnson of Maryland and Senator Willard Saulsbury of Delaware, were bold enough to appear with her in public. A Washington item headed "A Sensation" appeared in the New York *Tribune* on May 28.

> The great sensation of the Capitol today has been the appearance of Senator Saulsbury at the Church of the Ascension "clothed and in his right mind" as an escort for Mrs. Jeff Davis. After church a noted Rebel procured an open buggy, and took a Sunday evening drive with Mrs. Davis about the principal streets of the city. Mrs. Davis has received very marked attention, and many distinguished personages have made unseemly haste to pay their respects to her. Senators Johnson and Saulsbury were among the many other callers upon her Saturday.[1]

Varina looked around her with the keenest interest—studying the buildings, the homes, the people. She habitually wore black now, but she noticed that many of the Northern women were blossoming forth in rich and flattering fashions, after the Spartan days of the war. In the South there was no money for clothes, nor much heart for them either, but in Washington she noticed the lush silks, the gigot sleeves, the looped-back skirts revealing braided petticoats. Hats were airy trifles, tip-tilted bonnets with narrow ties, known as the Watteau, the Pamela, the Mary Stuart, a change from the coal-scuttle bonnets of plaited straw trimmed with corn-shuck rosettes that had made a virtue of necessity. There was much false hair—puffs, frizzes, curls, and braids. Hoops were gone with the war. So were the berthas that Harriet Lane had introduced and Varina had worn becomingly on her rounded shoulders. In January she had noticed with interest the news of the marriage of Harriet Lane to Henry Elliott Johnston at Wheatland. It had brought back mixed memories of White House days and the era of James Buchanan, when the clouds were gathering that now enveloped her.

It was no new thing for Varina to enter the White House and confer with a President, but she had never crossed the threshold with such qualms as when she went to call on Andrew Johnson. Only her desperation could have driven her to take this step with a man who had publicly affronted her. To her surprise he greeted her without malice and with the same air of helplessness that Mrs. Clay had reported. She found him civil, even friendly, but he told her, "We must wait, our hope is to mollify the public toward him." [2]

Varina told him bluntly that there would have been no need to mollify the public but for his proclamation that her husband was an accessory in the assassination of Lincoln. "I am sure that, whatever others believed, *you* did not credit it," she added.

He assured her he did not, but was in the hands of wildly excited people, and was forced "to take such measures as would show he was willing to sift the facts."

Varina told him that he owed her husband a retraction as public as his mistake on this particular charge. She pointed out that there was never the slightest intercourse between him and John Wilkes Booth. Then, to her astonishment, the President told her that he was "laboring under the enmity of many in both Houses of Congress, and if they could find anything on which to hinge an impeachment, they would degrade him; and with apparent feeling he reiterated, 'I would if I could, but I cannot.' "

Johnson then asked Varina if her husband had thought of requesting a pardon. She said he had not. He told her he could not withdraw the proclamation at that time and she felt she could not press the matter further. Watching him being harassed by a Senator who had interrupted their interview, she actually felt sorry for him. She later told Burton Harrison that the President said he had never believed her husband had anything to do with the assassination of Lincoln, and that he had been compelled by Stanton and Holt to issue the proclamation after they had assured him that they had conclusive evidence of complicity. His own position was so insecure and the popular excitement so great at the time that he had fallen in with their wishes.

She had been counseled not to ask for a parole, so that she merely sought permission to establish the family group at Fortress Monroe and urged the range of the fort for her husband.[3] She also proposed the removal of General Miles, arguing that he did not respect the person or feelings of Jefferson Davis. Dr. Cooper backed her up with a letter to the President about the prisoner's health. It set forth that he had done all in his power to maintain Mr. Davis's health, but that he was becoming weaker by the day. The only thing left, wrote Dr. Cooper, was to give him "mental and bodily rest and exercise at will." This could only be effected by letting him have the freedom of the fort "with permission to remain with his family." [4]

All of her Washington friends and the men who once had worked so closely with her husband studied Varina with the greatest interest. They knew that she had suffered deeply in the intervening years, and she showed it. The eyes once commented on so much were wells of sorrow. There was a sharp downward droop to her mouth. Henry Wilson, who had succeeded her husband as chairman of the Committee on Military Affairs and who had never taken the assassination charges seriously, called on Varina and deplored the "infamous party assaults" [5] on her husband's character. They all saw that her sorrows had embittered Varina; it would be many years before the final mellowing came. But her zeal, her eloquence, her wit, remained with her still and the men who talked to her now were aware of new depths in Varina.

While she was petitioning President Johnson for the betterment of the conditions under which her husband lived, the two lawyers, Charles O'Conor and George Shea, were at Fortress Monroe, interviewing him for the first time. Miles was angry over Dr. Cooper's full confirmation of Dr. Craven's estimate of the prisoner's condition. He, too, had found his nervous system deranged, his appetite failing, his muscular strength diminishing, and "every sentient nerve" being flayed by minor annoyances. Miles soon wrote to General E. D. Townsend, Assistant Adjutant General, that Dr. Cooper was "entirely under the influence of Mr. and Mrs. Davis, that the surgeon's wife was a Secessionist and one of the F.F.V.'s of Virginia, and that Dr. Cooper was exceedingly attentive to Varina, escorting her to Norfolk and back." Mrs. Elva Jones Cooper was a beauty from Point Comfort, tall and graceful, with startlingly white skin and dark hair and eyes. Her mother was a Virginian and she whispered to Mrs. Clay on her first visit, "We are all rebels of the first water." [6]

In short, "since Mrs. Davis's appearance at this place there has been a determined effort made that as he could not be a hero to make a martyr of him," General Miles summed up. Varina would have been the last to deny this statement. She was making headway with the idea, too. Some of the Northern papers were showing sporadic signs of sympathy. The New York *World* in May drew attention to Dr. Cooper's reports on the prisoner's health, commenting that they could not be read by "any honorable and right-minded American, no matter what his sectional feelings or his political opinions may be, without a sickening sensation of shame for his country."

President Johnson sent Hugh McCulloch, Secretary of the Treasury, to Fortress Monroe to talk to Jefferson Davis and make a report on him. Varina insisted on seeing him, but General Miles would not leave them alone together. However, she spoke up before him without any hesitancy, mentioning the "thousand little stabs he gave his emaciated, gray-haired prisoner," and his interpretation of the word "luxuries." Oysters, and green chartreuse sent to Davis by the Bishop of Montreal were discussed. McCulloch turned to Miles and remarked, "General, oysters are hardly to be classed as luxuries on the sea coast, are they?"

General Miles was so nettled that he showed Varina on this occasion his orders from Washington to shackle the prisoner at the time of his capture, if necessary. He insisted he had given him all that a gentleman should require, but Varina was far from satisfied. McCulloch reported back to the President that Jefferson Davis seemed "to be neither depressed in spirits nor soured in temper . . . he said nothing in the way of justification or defence." He considered that he had the bearing of a "brave and high-bred gentleman."

But Varina, knowing him better than anyone, saw that his repose was close to inanition. He could sleep only when read to, and "many times the day broke on me as he slept under the sound of my voice, with my hand on his pulse; at times it would stop, and then he was wakened and a glass of chartreuse given him, with one of half a dozen things kept ready for him to eat. . . . Never during this extreme torture and harrowing anxiety did his dignity give way, or his high bearing quail before the torment."

In coping with every aspect of the charges against her husband, Varina wrote to General Lee about the treatment of the prisoners at Andersonville, but he replied that controversy of all kind would "only serve to continue excitement and passion," and he therefore refrained from answering accusations.

During the first week of June, 1866, while the graves of Jeb Stuart, the Pegrams, little Joe Davis, and many others in Hollywood Cemetery were being decorated with flowers, O'Conor's move for the release of Davis on bail failed. Application for an immediate trial was rejected. Varina was bitterly disappointed. It was a week of significant news and her husband's case got little public attention. General Scott, touching eighty, had died on May 29. On the following day Sumner introduced a Negro enfranchisement bill, and the Freedmen's Bureau Bill passed the House over Johnson's veto.[7] The report of the Congressional Committee on Reconstruction reviewed the course of the President and defined his powers. Andrew Johnson, as well as Jefferson Davis, was in deep trouble.

On June 16 Varina wrote to the group in Richmond whose boys and girls were putting a tablet over little Joe's grave. She was deeply touched and had sent to Canada for the Bible record of his dates— "so many dreadful events have swept over us in the past two years, that we were afraid to trust our heart's memory," she wrote, and indeed Varina in her great distress was a year out in calculating the birthday of one of her own children. "I become so unhinged when I think of our boy that my power of expressing my gratitude seems to be swallowed up in grief," she wrote on this occasion.[8]

Money was still being raised for the Davises. On May 9 Mrs. Henrietta Y. Cohen of Savannah sent Jefferson Davis a fund from the ladies of Savannah for his wife and family.[9] Varina promptly returned a gold dollar sent by a little girl for Joe's grave and told the child to use it for a doll and name it Varina Anne Davis, after her baby Winnie, who was at Fortress Monroe with a nurse. She was showered with food supplies for her husband from well-wishers in Norfolk, now that the channel of communication had been opened and so much of his story had come into public view. Her visit to the President had brought immediate results in the way of greater freedom for the prisoner. The New York *Tribune* reported on June 9 that his health was better, he rambled around the fort at will, and was served "epicurean food." The Davises now lived virtually as a family unit at Fortress Monroe.

Burton Harrison was again at large and was advising Varina on the course she should follow. He was also of great aid to the Davis lawyers. He had further endeared himself to Varina by saying he would never testify for the government "if it is possible for me to injure him by doing so—let the consequences to myself be what they may, because of the affection I bear him & because of the peculiar and intimate relations we have sustained." Salmon Portland Chase, who had liked his father, helped Burton get his release. General Grant had come to his rescue, too, as well as Francis P. Blair. Even the President had "shown the most good-natured disposition to help." The upshot was that, by June, Burton was in New York, a free man working on behalf of Jefferson Davis.

By this time strategy was being planned around Horace Greeley, who was now definitely interested in the case.[10] There was talk of a bail bond to be signed by prominent Republicans. Burton wrote to Varina on June 28, urging discretion on her, as of old. He had often warned her to be careful of what she said. He did not think that she could always control her feelings.

In her headstrong way, she was being too importunate with O'Conor in her anxiety to further her husband's affairs and Burton tactfully told her: "Mr. O'Conor has received a letter from you within a few days—& asks me to say that he thinks it better that he should not write to you again for the present."

By August, Burton was going abroad to see his Connie, who was in Europe with her mother. Varina gave him letters to General George Magruder, whose daughter Ella was Lady Abinger in London, and to A. Dudley Mann in Paris. She sadly told Burton that her husband could not write for him, since a point of honor was now involved. She, too, felt she could only approach those she knew to be *friends*. The essentially proud Varina added: "We do not occupy a position which admits of our taking liberties." She confessed to being low-spirited because Mr. O'Conor was at as much of a loss "as we are to see Mr. Davis' way out of this living tomb." [11]

But a week later, in much better spirits, Varina was again writing to "My dear Boy," [12] her usual salutation for Burton, this time from the South. Thanks to Andrew Johnson she was now free to move about and with Winnie was making her first tour of her homeland since the war, visiting Mrs. Howell Cobb in Macon, then proceeding to Vicksburg, Canton, and New Orleans. She told Burton that she had seen his mother and sisters in Oxford, and it had brought back the time four years earlier when her husband had spoken to the students as he passed through and "I had him between the world and me."

"The trail of the serpent is over them all here," Varina wrote. Maggie, back from Canada, was ill and nervous. The railway between Jackson and Vicksburg was in such a shocking condition that it took three days to make the short trip. Varina was heading up the river to see Joseph Davis, her brother-in-law, as she wrote. At Coffeyville Mr. and Mrs. Lamar came down to the cars to see her and Mr. Lamar went with her as far as Canton. The *bon vivant* was in a sad way. "I can but pray for him," wrote Varina, "for I am very sincerely attached to him—and too poor to help him."

She wrote about this trip in greater detail to Mrs. Cobb as she sailed on the *Virginia* toward Vicksburg. With her usual frankness where her women friends were concerned, she gave her impressions with great spontaneity. Old schoolmates had thronged into New Orleans to see her and "would you believe it—I looked younger than they," Varina wrote. "This is a beatific memory to me though their careworn faces, as not compared with mine, were painful." [13] They overwhelmed her with kindness. Many came "with streaming eyes, shook hands and left me." She was refreshed, comforted, "a wordless sympathy silently offered is inexpressibly grateful to me."

Winnie was ill in New Orleans, and she feared measles for her. She saw Dick Taylor and quarreled with him and then made up. It was strange to see what her husband's former generals were doing. Beauregard did not call, she noted. Longstreet was engaged in a commission business. "Little Wheeler"—formerly General Joseph Wheeler, of the cavalry command—was in a small hardware shop—measuring out nails, and tacks, "and such like things, smiling and deft with his fingers— he has a sweet little shy pink-faced wife—just bearing the same relation to the body social, as he did to the cavalry service, presentable, but neither influential, imposing or efficient." However, Varina wished these two babes in the wood safe-conduct to their haven. Otherwise they "would eat blackberries and die." Then, with a flash of self-revelation that explains much about Varina's character, she shows how she used mockery as a self-protective device.

I am glad too, more than glad, that I went to see you—though I have long understood you. As for me, I am like a wild animal about trouble—I can better afford to lick the lance which rankles in my heart than bear the surgical examination which may teach the mode for its extraction. I take refuge in mocking—you in silence. We fit each other—always did and you are very dear and precious to me.

Mrs. Cobb was a Lamar. She and Varina were in close intellectual sympathy, although of different temperaments. Mrs. Clay thought her "highly cultured, modest as a wild wood-violet, inclined, moreover, to reserve . . . and a conversation with her was ever a thing to be remembered." [14] Her husband, bland, worldly, had been one of the wealthiest and most genial of the planters before the war.

On this trip Varina had a chance to observe the devastation that the war had brought to the regions most familiar to her. She found Joseph nearing eighty and very feeble, living near Vicksburg. She looked with misery in her heart at the familiar outlines of Davis Bend. The Hurricane, once so flourishing and busy, was in ruins. Most of the books had been stacked on the lawn and burned. China and glass had been piled in heaps and smashed with muskets. Paintings had been ripped with bayonets and flames had completed the ruin of the massive mansion. However, Lise was able to make her home for some time afterward in the library which stood by itself in the grounds.

Brierfield had a different fate. The Federal soldiers streaked the phrase "This is the house Jeff built" across the portico. The furniture was destroyed but the house stood until 1931, when it burned down. Varina felt like a visitor from another planet as she viewed familiar scenes and talked to old friends. She was observed on all sides with the greatest interest. She was now a public character in a wholly new sense—no longer a social queen, but an unhappy woman, beating her wings against a cold front of officialdom. Her interest in people was as keen as ever, however, and her observations as she moved around had their former pungency and the note of mockery which she herself conceded.

Before going south, Varina had written to Reverdy Johnson, imploring him once again to try to induce the President to give her husband the *entire* parole of the Fort, or have him transferred to one of the

forts in New York Harbor where he would be nearer his counsel.[15] Now
that she was seeing him constantly, she was burningly aware of his
altered condition. Although he had fewer harassments, better fare, and
more freedom of movement, it broke her heart, she wrote, to find him
"so entirely acquiescent in this death in life."

Such was the agitation she had stirred up about General Miles that
he was transferred to another post that summer, and Mrs. Montgomery
Blair promptly wrote to her on September 9, 1866, from the summer
home at Portsmouth, where they had spent some carefree days together:
"I see by the *Herald* Genl. Miles is removed. If so I congratulate you
upon it—if he is only mustered out there is an end of him."

But it was not the end of General Miles. He went on to further
glory and wound up as senior commander of the United States Army
in 1895. He was the nephew-in-law of General Sherman, but Varina
was never to give up the battle against him. Now she read Mrs. Blair's
letter with the greatest interest. Her old friend gave a piece of news
that must have been comforting to Varina in the midst of her woes.
It also suggests the strong hold she had on her friends, and the like-
lihood that the Mrs. E. in question was Mrs. Emory.

Mrs. E. is a cautious woman but no one ever kept a truer friend than you
did when you went South and she has never swerved. I know for I have
heard her called on to express her opinion over and over in trying positions
and she has always had the same reply of the kindness she had received
from your husband and her affection for you—which was often brought up
against her by those ill-minded people who were sweet at her face and
envious at her back. . . . Write me soon and tell me all about your baby
and yourself—Remember me kindly and sympathizingly to your husband.
. . . Believe me to be

As ever yr. friend

Minna [16]

In a significant postscript Minna wrote that Blair was making great
changes in their home, "having it raised up a story and a half till
it towers above its neighbors, so I hear—I wanted more chamber room,
but not quite such a display of it as he has given us, I fear."

While the wife of a Union general was in sympathetic communication with Varina at this time, the wife of one of her husband's leading
generals was writing to Louis Wigfall from Baltimore with no diminu-
tion of her old bitterness: "Varina is with him at the Fortress—in the

character of a 'ministering angel,' you can imagine her!" Lydia observed, her viewpoint still unchanged.[17]

From Vicksburg, Varina went to Canada to visit her family. She wrote to William Preston Johnston from the New York Hotel on August 29 telling him of an investment of three thousand dollars on behalf of her children.[18] By the end of September she offered him a loan of one thousand dollars. He had six children and was having difficulty supporting them. He had returned from Canada and hoped for a professorship in Virginia. "The Lees must help you in the matter," Varina wrote. By this time General Robert E. Lee was president of Washington University in Lexington, Virginia. Discussing her own restless condition, she wrote:

Nothing new, nothing certain—all as misty and anxious as ever—shuffling and truckling seem to be the order of the day—I have been reading a little, but do not remember what after it is read. Sewing a little, but rip it out, knitting a little, but ravel it out—talking a little but unsaying everything. We have a great deal of company, some of these are pleasant to take such trouble to see us—I have learned to swim very well, so as to save this eminently hopeful and cheerful life of mine in case of accident or perhaps the deluge may be after me.

Varina wrote that Brigadier General Henry S. Burton, the new commandant at the fort, had been civil and kind to both of them. His wife was a "sympathetic warm-hearted talented Mexican woman who is very angry with the Yankees about Mexican affairs, and we get together quietly and abuse them—though to say the truth since Miles' departure all here are kind to us, and considerate. . . ."

Varina wanted a piece of colored silk from one of Mrs. Johnston's dresses for a quilt she was making that was to tell the story of the Confederacy—Mrs. Clay called it her "immortal patchwork." Each square was to be a "memory of better days." Wearily she added: "This is my first symptom of the sere and yellow leaf which has been content with my body, and until now left my mind untarnished." But Varina's spirits picked up at the thought of little Winnie, and she added: "Pie is the sweetest brightest child I ever saw. She is as much company for us as a grown person."

Winnie was now a pet at Fortress Monroe. She played with her father and was his chief comfort at this time. It was the beginning of a long and loving association between Jefferson Davis and his youngest daughter. Visitors would find him sitting on the floor, building blocks with her, or reciting his favorite Walter Scott poems for her benefit. She would sometimes play with the officers' children, and she loved to listen to the band. By this time the Davis family, except for the boys, still in Canada, were installed as a family in a four-roomed apartment in Carroll Hall, a historic building with arched doors and windows, and double galleries along its façade. The upper gallery was connected with the ramparts by a little bridge, so that Jefferson Davis could go directly to and from his quarters on the second floor. Maggie had come north from Mississippi and had joined them.

Mary Day, a pretty girl from Bowling Green, Ohio, who was visiting her brother, Selden Allen Day, captain at Fortress Monroe, lived in the apartment below the Davises and often observed Varina at close range during this period. They lived very quietly in their "plain but comfortable apartment." They did not return the calls of the officers and their wives at the fort. Winnie went to the children's parties, and Mary watched Varina fashion little dresses for her out of her own clothing, taking care not to cut the laces but to maneuver the trimming so that no damage was done them.

Selden Day had been kind to Davis during the Miles regime. When Mary arrived at the Fort, Varina and she were grateful to each other for mutual kindnesses, for the prisoner's wife had nursed her brother when he collapsed during a cholera scare and had revived him with cordials.[19] Then Maggie nursed Mary when she fell ill, sending her trays trimmed with geranium leaves and outfitted with a bedside tea set, all of which made Fortress Monroe seem less like a prison. Mary's three brothers had fought for the North. Her father's ancestors had settled in Virginia. Her mother's were descended from the Pilgrim Elder Brewster.

Mary was struck by the great devotion the Davises showed for each other. "Though built of different calibre, they were equally charming, each seeming the completion of the other," she wrote. "Mrs. Davis was indeed a lady who could have graced any position." Her husband never mentioned his imprisonment or the war in Mary Day's hearing. The nearest he came to it was one day while Varina "stood stroking his head in her loving way, and she made a reference to 'our people!' This caused him to turn sharply to her and say most earnestly: 'My wife, our people *that were.*'" Varina's only answer was a toss of the head which seemed to say most plainly: "There are some of them alive yet."

Varina found much consolation in the companionship of her sister at this time. Maggie had always got on well with her husband, too, so that they had many cheerful three-cornered discussions in their semi-imprisoned state. She wrote to Martha Phillips of Savannah that spring:

> But for her companionship I cannot tell what I should do. You know it is absolutely necessary to have a woman to whom one may confide "a woman's thoughts about women" and who will be responsive. So in strict confidence we take out all the vim remaining in us at heroines of novels, and living women indiscriminately, and with an equal amount of acrimony. The Yankee male and female are very civil to us, and really some of them are quite pleasant in the sort of intercourse that we have with them. . . .[20]

Under the new regime some of Davis's old friends were able to visit him—Wade Hampton, General Gordon, General Preston, Dr. Minnegerode, Franklin Pierce, and others. Henry Wilson, who had succeeded her husband as chairman of the Senate Committee on Military Affairs, was one of his callers, a voice from the past, a strong antislavery man who wished to help him regain his freedom. When John R. Thompson arrived from England in October he brought him an English overcoat and a message from Thomas Carlyle that delighted Varina. That worthy wished Davis to know that he thought he "had more of the heroic in him than any other actor in the drama and that he was one of the very few great and good men now on this planet." [21]

Although his living conditions had improved, Davis was no closer to freedom, and Varina planned, wrote letters, and tried every expedient to force a showdown. Her lawyers were convinced that the best measure was to get a bail bond signed by prominent Republicans, and, on her way to Canada, Varina had seen Horace Greeley and had solicited his support. That autumn, when nothing seemed to move, she peppered him with a series of letters, imploring his editorial aid.

On September 2, 1866, she wrote asking if she might come to him again "in the black uncertainty of our picture, for light and help." [22] She had prayed for thirteen months, she wrote, but fruitlessly, for she now saw her husband "patiently, uncomplainingly fading away and cannot help him." Those who reported his condition good stayed a few moments and were deceived by his "spirited self-controlled bearing." In her opinion, a slight illness would kill him, "for he is patched up by the most excessive care both upon his part and mine." He lost rather than gained strength meanwhile. Their children except Winnie were in Canada, yet she was "not equal to the self-sacrifice of leaving him for their sakes." Varina ended with a fervent plea:

And now I appeal to you who always sympathize with the weak to help me—*will you not procure* signatures enough to that paper which Mr. Shea has, to arrest Mr. Johnson's attention? I cannot, my dear kind Sir, tell you all my sorrows growing out of this arbitrary imprisonment of my husband— they are legion—but I have enlisted you, I am sure, when I say that I am utterly helpless, and well nigh broken-hearted. If a nation's tears could wash out venom, then mine ought to have cleansed many a heart filled with the lust for vengeance—and for blood.

A month later she was writing again to Reverdy Johnson, fearing that her husband's case might be tried by a "Radical Congress." President Johnson's decision to postpone the trial suggested to her a further delay of two years, and on October 16 she wrote again to Greeley, beseeching him to use his influence for her husband's release.[23]

She scanned the *Tribune* anxiously every day after this, knowing that Greeley often spoke through the editorial columns of his paper. On November 9 he ran a strong editorial that brought her comfort.[24] In the meantime, he had written her a kindly and reassuring letter. In his editorial he summed up the status of Jefferson Davis. He had been a prisoner for eighteen months. The $100,000 reward for his capture had been paid. Repeated attempts had been made by his counsel to bring his case to trial, but to no purpose. One legal tangle succeeded another so that now "Congress, President and Chief Justice, were in a complete muddle on the subject." Greeley strongly urged his release and argued that President Johnson should have publicly retracted the charge of complicity in the assassination of Abraham Lincoln. He continued:

It is neither just nor wise to send forth a prisoner of state with the brand of murder on his brow; and a naked failure to prosecute is but equivalent to the Scotch verdict, "Not proven." . . . A great government may deal sternly with offenders, but not meanly; it cannot afford to seem unwilling to repair an obvious wrong. . . . We feel confident that magnanimity toward Davis . . . will powerfully contribute to that juster appreciation of the North at the South which is the first step toward a beneficial and perfect reconciliation.

Thus Varina had drawn a powerful editorial on her husband's behalf from the most influential editor in America at that time. Twelve days later she was hot on the trail, thanking him and again appealing to his easily aroused sympathies. She urged him to try such pressing recommendations for her husband's release as would move Andrew Johnson.[25] Jefferson Davis knew nothing of these appeals by Varina at the time, he indicated in a letter written from Beauvoir on April 20, 1888, to Gordon L. Ford of Brooklyn, N. Y.[26] He wished to give Greeley full credit for the role he had played in having him freed. Conceding that his wife most "zealously strove by every justifiable means" to effect his release from confinement, he pointed out that her efforts should be viewed as an "exhibition of a wife's ardent work for the relief of her husband, not as diminishing the merit of Mr. Greeley's action in the cause of right against oppression." He believed him to have been actuated by a higher motive than "friendship for me, or compliance with the appeal of my wife for his aid." He felt that Greeley was moved by his own sense of justice.

A number of the President's old friends were working for him now. Richard Taylor wrote to Varina on November 10 that he had been bringing pressure to bear on the White House.[27] He had had a three-hour talk with President Johnson about Jefferson Davis and the people of the South. He was sure at this point that Mr. Davis would be paroled to appear whenever the government was ready to try him, and that a general amnesty would be announced. But again the case was postponed.

By spring Varina was busier than ever, making trips to Baltimore, for things were coming to a head and at last she had touched a responsive key on her husband's behalf through John W. Garrett, president of the Baltimore and Ohio Railroad.[28] He was a good friend of Stanton. He had known him long before he became a member of Lincoln's Cabinet, and Stanton had served as counsel for his railroad. The link was close, and Varina was persuaded that here was someone who could aid her. All her other attempts to soften Stanton had been fruitless.

Heavily veiled, she called on Garrett with Charles W. Russell, a Wheeling lawyer and prominent Virginian politician. She went straight to the point. Her husband would die unless he were released from prison, she argued. She knew that he had great influence with Stanton. Would he be willing to give active aid in getting her husband freed? Garrett listened attentively to Varina and was impressed. He agreed to help her. She told him that Hugh McCulloch, Secretary of the Treasury, had sent her word that she could rely on his aid.

Varina wished to go to Washington with him, but he considered this impolitic and advised her to wait for word in Baltimore, where she was staying with John S. Gittings, a close friend of her husband. Garrett saw McCulloch in Washington, then was taken to Attorney General Henry Stansbery, who remembered him well. But he said the Secretary of War was home ill and refused to see anyone. Nevertheless, Garrett drove to his home, sent up his card, and was admitted. He found the Secretary of War lying on a lounge, too ill to rise and greet them. And then, as Garrett related it:

I stated firmly and frankly the nature of the matter that had brought me to disturb his sick repose. As I somewhat expected Mr. Stanton exhibited much anger and displeasure, and I told him that two at least of the Cabinet were willing for the release, and that the President was only waiting his order for the release, that the court would approve such action, and that, lastly, Davis's health was failing, and that his death in confinement at Fortress Monroe would be most unpleasant and inconvenient to the authorities of the United States.

They had a long, sharp discussion, for Garrett was determined not to be "set back by anything short of a positive refusal, and that I should have combatted before the President." Stanton finally said he would raise no objection to the Attorney General arranging for Davis's release. Garrett went back to Stansbery's office, the preliminaries were arranged, and Horace Greeley's name was mentioned as a bondsman. Garrett reported the result of his interview to Varina, who was tearful with happiness. William Prescott Smith was sent to New York to invite Greeley to the Garrett home.

Varina stayed close to her powerful Baltimore friend while the plan was being worked out. Although Stansbery would give no specific promise, he thought everything looked bright for release within two weeks' time, or at least for a change of prisons. Some of her friends favored the parole method, but Varina held out for bail, because it was "less trammelling and not dependent upon the will of an individual, and also because a *nolle prosqui* could be entered later if need be."

Varina had made real headway through persistence, but she was undergoing one of the universal ills of man and was having severe dental trouble. Her eyes were inflamed and she was quite ill. She was torn between the urgent need to have all but three of her teeth removed and her anxiety to be her most effective self during these crucial negotiations on her husband's behalf. She felt she could not see people until her plate was finished. "But I can live just as well without them, however unlovely I shall appear," she wrote to her husband. "I do hate it, however." [29]

She apologized for staying away from him so long in Baltimore. "It is not that I have been enjoying myself, for I cannot feel free, cannot bear to mark the difference between our condition and that of others. Your friends seem immensely encouraged about your case but I have been so often disappointed. May God grant us patience to wait His good pleasure."

Varina was worried about the baby too. Writing five days later from Barnum's Hotel in Baltimore she asked him to have Ellen keep "Winnieanne" in the open air, and out of the kitchen. She would bring her home a watch and a little mouse, but she had made up her mind to stay close to Garrett until she was satisfied that the plan was going through.[30]

This time it did, and Jefferson Davis learned that at last he might be on his way to freedom. Just before his release Franklin Pierce, his "beloved friend and ever honored chief," called to see him. Jane had died in 1863, and he felt very much alone without her. Burton Harrison joined the Davises at Fortress Monroe the night before they left. He had arrived from New York with the original habeas corpus writ. Burton was one of the very few who knew how much Varina had done to bring about her husband's release. They had worked closely and quietly together after Burton was released from prison. She had done all the preliminary work and had spread a net for the better part of two years that had reached right into the White House and finally smashed the stubborn front presented by Stanton. Now the strings were being drawn together, but Varina was content to stay in the background.

General Burton escorted them to Richmond. They traveled on the *John Sylvester* as a "select party of private gentlemen" [31] with no guards, or any suggestion that Davis was still a prisoner. All the landings were crowded with spectators. At Brandon Landing, Burton's sisters greeted them with flowers. A crowd waited at the wharf as the former President stepped ashore, holding on to Burton's arm. He gravely acknowledged the lifted hats and quiet greeting of the crowd who "simply and silently uncovered in token of his presence." Mounted artillerymen followed the open carriage as it drove through the streets where he had lived through triumph and defeat. Varina drove with Mr. and Mrs. James Lyons, Judge Robert Ould, and her maid Ellen.

"I feel like an unhappy ghost visiting this much beloved City," she remarked, as she watched the crowds at windows and on roofs and "not one man but bared his head." She detected a "suppressed current of feeling" rather than open excitement. Burton also thought it a serious rather than a jubilant crowd. The *Enquirer* took note of Jefferson Davis's appearance after his long imprisonment.

He wears a full beard and mustache, which in a measure conceals the ravages made by sorrow and suffering upon his face, but his countenance, although haggard and care-worn, still preserves the proud expression and the mingled look of sweetness and dignity for which it was ever remarkable. His hair is considerably silvered, but his eye still beams with all the fire that characterized it in the old time, and he seems every inch a king.[32]

At the Spotswood they were shown to the suite they had occupied when they first arrived in Richmond. The following day was a Sunday and friends flocked in to welcome Davis after church. "No stranger would suppose for an instant that the quiet gentleman who receives his visitors with such graceful elegance & dignity is the State prisoner . . . whose trial for treason against a mighty Government today attracts the interest of all mankind," Burton wrote to Connie.

Varina was under close observation, too, as she greeted old friends. Her face was worn. Her hair was silvering. Her silks were not so fashionably cut as of old. The reflection of intense suffering was visible on her face. She watched her husband closely, for fatigue, for overexcitement, for any hint of distress. She was happy enough to watch him kiss the women who passed by. "I observed that he took delight in kissing the prettiest when they went out as well as when they came in," Burton noted.

In the morning Davis left the Spotswood by a back alley to avoid the crowd as he went to court to be heard on a charge of treason in the room that had once been his own office.[33] Every angle of the courtroom was familiar to him as he walked in, stiff and soldierly, in a black cloth suit flecked with tiny gray spots, and wearing dark green kid gloves. He bowed gravely to acquaintances, and Burton Harrison was asked to take a place beside him with their counsel. General Burton had preceded them, dressed in full uniform. The most observed figure in the courtroom after Davis was Horace Greeley, who straggled in at eleven o'clock, his black silk cravat disordered, his glasses slightly askew, his movements awkward, and his pink face outlined with a fringe of whitish-yellow hair.

Varina deliberately stayed away, to pray as she used to do when she knew her husband was close to a battlefield. Her work was done. The court proceeding was cut and dried. Everything had been arranged in advance, although none could feel assured that Judge John C. Underwood would perform according to plan. O'Conor, who looked like a "demi-god of antiquity" in the courtroom, Burton wrote to Connie, had carefully briefed his fellow counsel in advance. It was understood that there should be no pretentious declamation or long speeches.

Greeley, Gerrit Smith, and others strong in the Republican party, were present to sign the bond in person. Cornelius Vanderbilt, another of its backers, had sent a representative. It was a moment of considerable significance in the life of Jefferson Davis, who had been in prison for the better part of two years. When his release was ordered General Burton and Dr. Cooper moved forward to offer him their congratulations. Others followed suit and a shout went up as he descended the stairs, shaking hands as he passed. Taking his arm, Burton pushed his way through the crowd to the waiting carriage. Robert Ould and O'Conor rode with him.

But at this point they were mobbed. The crowd had been waiting for the court verdict before letting go. Now the carriage "was beset with a crowd perfectly frantic with enthusiasm, cheering, calling down God's blessings, rushing to catch him by the hand & weeping many tears of devotion to 'our President.' I shall never see such boisterous profound joy in a crowd again," Burton reported to Connie.

As he alighted from the carriage, a voice was heard saying, "Hats off, Virginians!" and every head was bared. The Spotswood corridors were filled with friends eager to congratulate him, but Davis hurried upstairs, and they drew back with a sense of delicacy, knowing that he was eager to reach Varina, as always in the crises of his life. Burton followed a few moments later. Then Dr. Minnegerode, Miss Jenny

Ritchie, George Davis, and Burton gathered around the Davises behind a locked door and they all sank to their knees at a table while the rector offered a prayer of thanksgiving. By this time they were all sobbing "with tears of joyful emotion." When the door was opened their friends streamed in, and now there was a true celebration with toasts, kisses, embraces, and tears. "The animosities of the war were forgotten for the moment," Burton reported, "and for the first time since the war ended, Richmond people showed hospitalities to the Yankees."

But it was not until February, 1869, that the last legal move against Jefferson Davis was made, and the case finally was dismissed. Meanwhile, he was free, except for a technicality and the understanding that he would appear upon demand.

When they could break away from their friends Varina and Jefferson went quietly to Hollywood Cemetery to lay flowers on the grave of little Joseph. Some of the greatest warriors of the Confederate Army rested nearby, and their visit must have been one of profound emotion for the two Davises. Meanwhile, Burton strayed off to the spot where he had kept his early trysts with Connie. He, too, was older and graver now. He had been sobered by the grim events of the war, the fate of his chief, his own imprisonment, the sorrows of the Confederacy. But he found the path through a wooded glen and tangled briers that he and Connie had followed to get to their little beach cove near Camp Winder. She had worn a white dress with jaunty ribbons on the first of these trips, and had smiled up at him, as she leaned her elbow on the stem of a broken tree. Now Burton plucked a buttercup and some dogwood petals from the same spot, and enclosed them in the letter to Connie that told all about the court proceeding. Their release was at hand, too, for Harrison's devotion to the Davises and his long imprisonment had delayed and upset their romance. Burton was now free to go North, to practice law successfully in New York, to marry Constance Cary.

With the court proceeding over, Burton and the lawyers decided to take the "chief" away as fast as possible from the scenes of explosive excitement in Richmond. He was in an intensely nervous state. They boarded a ship for New York that same evening, but the excitement was renewed all over again as visitors crowded around him in the New York Hotel and people gathered in the streets to stare. There was also the feeling that there might be a hostile demonstration. Burton

Harrison "took bodily possession of him and (despite his half-expressed unwillingness) drove him by carriage to the home of O'Conor at Fort Washington on the Hudson," he reported to his mother. "He is looking very thin and haggard and has very little muscular strength. But his spirits are good, he has improved in appearance very greatly since he left his dungeon, and I think he will be in very good condition as soon as he gets rested."

Relieved and content for the moment, Varina took Maggie to see Ristori, playing her last night in New York. It had been a long time since she had felt carefree enough to forget her immediate troubles in opera or a good drama. During all the months of her husband's imprisonment she had never relaxed in her efforts to have him freed. It was the end of two tortured years, but the beginning of she knew not what. They now headed for Canada to visit their children and find brief sanctuary there. She knew that their scars would not be healed overnight. Ahead of them lay a period of melancholy wandering, of rootlessness, of the bitter dregs of defeat, of impoverishment, of the loneliness of a ruler in exile. By this time Varina had tasted the full measure of disillusionment. She had watched friends turn their backs on her husband, giving him wounds deeper than those dealt by his enemies. It was now her role to restore the warm family life that had always surrounded Jefferson Davis and in the period that followed she showed her greatest understanding and fortitude.

℁ 17 ℁

DISPOSSESSED

IN THE summer of 1867 Varina mopped floors, baked pies, and fed logs of wood into a balky stove in Quebec with the capable hands of a well-trained housekeeper but the restless spirit of a displaced queen. Her neighbors were kind and ignored the fact that "we were unsuccessful, *cidevant,* threadbare great folks," she wrote to Garrett from Montreal at the end of May.[1]

Young Jeff said he had "no intention of being a swell," and little Billy worried because he was the only boy in town who did not own a crossbow. "So my babies are blotted from the things that be," Varina wrote, but her husband's health was improving, her mother had a plain but comfortable house, and she was infinitely grateful to Mr. Garrett, to whom she sent a pair of hand-worked slippers as a small souvenir.

Varina's thoughts, as always, took wider range. In a postscript she "actually luxuriated" in Horace Greeley's answer to the Union Club which had called him to account for signing the Davis bond. He had refused to attend the special meeting called to discuss the matter, and predicted that "out of a life earnestly devoted to the good of human kind, your children will select my going to Richmond and signing that bail bond as the wisest act. . . ."

Varina now had the most difficult task of her lifetime—to comfort the proud and bitterly wounded man whom she loved, while he sought a place in the world for himself and his family. He was a man without a country, since he would not take the oath of allegiance. His sad, grim face was known to everyone who beheld him. Lesser figures from the shattered Confederate States had begun to live again; some of them even to prosper in distant places. But the way did not open for

Jefferson Davis. He took comfort when he heard from old friends, however. Robert E. Lee wrote to him on June 1, 1867:

> You can conceive better than I can express the misery which your friends have suffered from your long imprisonment and the other afflictions incident thereto. To none has this been more painful than to me, and the impossibility of affording relief has added to my distress. Your release has lifted a load from my heart which I have not words to tell, and my daily prayer to the great Ruler of the World is that He may shield you from all future harm, guard you from all evil and give you that peace which the world cannot take away. . . .[2]

Franklin Pierce had written to Varina from Concord urging them to rest at his cottage at Little Boon's Head in New Hampshire, after her husband's release from prison, but they felt they must join their children as quickly as possible. They headed for Montreal, but Davis stopped off briefly at Niagara to visit James M. Mason, who had a house in Toronto but was summering close to the Falls. A colony of Confederate leaders had settled for the time being in Canada. Others had gone to England. A few had moved south to Mexico.

Great was the joy of their reunion in Canada, Varina reported, "but the motion and life about us drove my husband wild with nervousness; he said the voices of people sounded like trumpets in his ears." Her own sensibilities had been affected by all these months of tension. She described her state with some perception: ". . . long restriction had stiffened and impaired my powers, I could not think clearly or act promptly, difficulties seemed mountain high, the trees and flowers sheltered and bloomed for others, I knew they were fair, but they were not for me or mine."

After a restless summer they settled in the village of Lennoxville in Quebec. By September 6 Varina was writing to Mrs. Howell Cobb in Athens, Georgia, that "after numberless packings and terrible housecleaning throes, at last behold me settled in a little Canadian village for some months to come. . . . We found housekeeping too expensive and have gone to boarding and are tolerably comfortable."[3] Varina was in deep water when she wrote this letter. She was overwhelmed by the problems she faced—her husband's depression, his poor health, their lack of funds or prospects of any kind, their uncertain status and the feeling that they had lost all place in the world. "I should be miserable if I thought I had to do anything hereafter but love and be loved again," she wrote. " 'Rest, enduring rest in Heaven' is the goal for which I run, and were I sure of going there, notwithstanding these helpless children, I should cry from the bottom of this weary heart 'Come Lord Jesus quickly.' "

They had simple pleasures with their children.[4] The boys were attending the excellent boys' school outside Lennoxville, which had drawn them there in the first place. It was attended by a number of Southern boys, and Mrs. Howell, when first staying in Toronto, had sent Jeff east to it with young Hansell Stotesbury. Wards of Lord Mountcastle—Mary, Jennie, Kate, and Stevie Cummins—lived in a large quiet house called "Rock Grove" close to the village. It was surrounded by trees and soon became a haven for Jefferson Davis, who was much upset by the village noises and the lack of privacy in the small hotel where they were quartered. To sit in the garden of "Rock Grove" was balm to his jangled nerves, and a welcome change from the clatter of the circus gymnasts quartered temporarily in their hotel.

Soon the Davis, Cummins, and Stotesbury children all gathered in the evenings there to sing and play games, and Varina felt that she was experiencing a semblance of home again. Years later Stevie Cummins recalled Winnie sitting in her mother's lap, little Margaret and Jeff squatting on the floor with the other children, and Jefferson Davis beating out the time of old plantation melodies on Cissie Stotesbury's shoulder while they all sang.

But the days passed slowly and painfully in that first year of exile, and Varina was distracted trying to comfort the shattered man whose horizons now were bounded by a village street. He called it vegetation, not life, in a note to Burton Harrison. The further delay about the disposition of his case kept him on edge, since he had promised to remain within forty-eight hours' call. "What do you think of Andy's procrastination?" Varina demanded of Mrs. Cobb. "Did you ever see a seven months so funny and ill-favored? The mountain has certainly brought forth a ridiculous mouse."

In October he was summoned to appear again in court and the *nolle prosequi* was filed. While this was pending Varina had to rush off to Bennington, Vermont, where her mother, on a visit there, had become desperately ill with typhoid fever. She wrote to Burton Harrison on November 1, 1867, saying that nothing would detain her from her husband but her mother's extreme illness. But if he had to appear in court she would join him nevertheless. "I am at my wits' end with trouble," she wrote. "Ma is very low with typhoid fever." [5]

Varina also ran into "sectarian rancor" on this visit and was much upset by it. The patient and cheerful Mrs. Howell, who had endured much with great good nature, sank rapidly and her daughter was with her when she died. Her family had gathered in strength around their mother earlier that summer, since Varina was a focus for all the Howells. Becket, who had been on the *Alabama*, and Jefferson who had been imprisoned—unjustly in Varina's opinion—had traveled north to join them in Montreal, and various other members of the family had appeared on the scene. Her brother Willie was already there. He had fled before their capture in Georgia.

"In our mother Mr. Davis lost his dearest friend, and as much of virtue as could die," Varina wrote.[6] But life went on in their old circle, and at the end of that month Burton and Connie were married in New York and spent Christmas at Morrisania, the home of Connie's aunt, Mrs. Gouverneur Morris. They settled near Gramercy Park, and Varina rejoiced that a romance that had fluctuated with her family fortunes had at last reached its consummation.

With nothing ahead of them and Davis's days a nightmare of emptiness, he considered writing a history of the painful years just ended. The need to explain and justify burned within him. Some of the letters and message books had been secretly taken to Canada in Maggie's trunk and were now deposited in the Bank of Montreal. But as he studied the messages that had meant life and death at the time, instead of settling down to arrange them, he paced the floor distractedly and then decided that he must put them aside. "I cannot speak of my dead so soon," he told Varina.[7] At this time he wrote to his brother Joseph from Montreal that he felt he had less ability to write than formerly. It tired him both mentally and physically even to write a letter.[8] He had hoped that this condition would pass, but it did not. It proved to be a long time before he could settle down to this task. Before he did, others had published their versions of the war years.

The Canadian winter was considered too severe for the worn and debilitated Jefferson Davis, and he was advised to go South after the court hearing in Richmond. He and Varina visited friends in Baltimore before sailing for Havana. They landed on the tropical island just before Christmas and found it in a festive state, with flowered arches everywhere in honor of the new Lieutenant General, Don Antonio Caballeroy Fernandez de Rodas. They stayed at a hotel run by a Southerner, Mrs. Sarah Brewster, and were soothed by the iris waters, the pastel façades of the houses, and the warm, bland air of the tropics.

They sailed on from Havana to New Orleans, where they were

warmly welcomed, not only as part of Confederate history, but because of their local links. This was their home region, and friends crowded around them at the St. Charles. But Davis's most downcast moments were experienced on his return to Davis Bend, where ruin was all too apparent. He wandered over their property, heavy at heart. Stables, gardens, roses, shrubs—all the years of labor and love were blotted out, and the weeds grew thick over neglected land. The trail of fire was everywhere. "We found our property all destroyed, our friends impoverished, and our old brother very feeble, but cheery," Varina reported. "As many of our Negroes as could came to see us, and Mr. Davis paid a few hours' visit to the rest at Brierfield and Hurricane." [9]

Joseph, aged but still spirited, was living obscurely at Vicksburg, a living symbol of the fallen Confederacy. The confiscated land on Davis Bend had been returned to him after the war and he had immediately sold it for $300,000 to Ben Montgomery on easy terms, with the understanding that he and his sons could take ten years or longer to buy it, provided they could work it successfully.[10] They were to pay 6 per cent interest on the notes. Meanwhile, he appointed Ben his agent to get the old people back to work on the familiar ground. This was how things stood at the moment, except for great changes in the physical conformation of Davis Bend. Fortifications had been built across the narrow neck of the peninsula, and there had been so much boring and drilling that in 1867 the Mississippi rushed through, making it an island, as it is today.

While in the region the Davises visited Jeff's sisters, Mrs. Luther Smith and Mrs. William Stamps, and saw many other members of both their families. They went to Canton to visit Mrs. Isaac W. Davis, and on the return trip a bevy of pretty girls boarded the cars and Jefferson Davis, in the old wartime tradition, claimed a kiss from each one of them. Varina was asked if she objected. A little sadly she retorted, "Oh, they are not always pretty girls. He has to kiss the ugly old women too, and then I get my revenge." [11]

It was altogether a painful and enlightening pilgrimage for the head of the Confederacy, and Varina suffered with him. He saw what war had done to state after state, to family after family. He had been chary of returning to Mississippi and wrote to Judge Charles B. Howry from Madison County on February 8, 1868, saying that apprehension had kept him from going there immediately after his release on bail, but that the political events of the summer and autumn "with the natural subsidence of the feeling created by my liberation emboldened me to return to my friends and the land with which alone I associate the feeling of home." [12]

The Davises were warmly received at Jackson by Governor Benjamin Humphreys, who gave them an unostentatious reception because the town was still garrisoned with Northern troops.[13] They made quiet visits to the homes of old friends there. But they returned to Canada more depressed than they had left. Both saw clearly that their future did not lie in the South at that time. The misery was widespread. Everyone had troubles undreamed of in the past, and resentment burned over reconstruction policies. The Davises had hoped that some of their property might be salvaged, but they returned without a dollar of income from it. In fact, Davis paid out money from his own limited funds to take care of "our superannuated old Negroes," Varina wrote to Mrs. Cobb. "Suffice it to say we came back with no hopes for our children's future save those we have in God's promises." [14]

Back in Lennoxville during the summer of 1868, Varina began to push hard for a trip to England. Many of their friends had gone there, both before, during, and after the war. Davis was dubious about this move. Discouraged, uncertain about his future, he stirred about for ways in which to make a living for his family. He had talked to many businessmen in the South, but this had not been encouraging. There was still a certain timorousness about being linked with his fortunes, and no one had any prospects at the time. Varina conducted some correspondence with Randolph-Macon College in the spring of 1868, but although she favored her husband assuming the presidency of the college, he felt that "he could not risk the fortunes of any institution by becoming connected with it until the odium cast upon me has been removed." [15] He was still a prisoner of state, released on bail.

Finally he made an arrangement to work for a commission merchant in Liverpool if cotton and tobacco could be assured from America. He was banking on guarantees of cotton from his old friends before going to Liverpool and thereby hoped "to be raised above the wretched sense of idle dependence which has so galled us," he wrote to Howell Cobb on July 6, 1868.[16]

But early in July, Davis had an accident that shook him badly. His foot slipped as he carried Winnie downstairs. There was just one chance to save the child, and with quick thought he took it, throwing her to a landing while he plunged all the way down himself.[17] He landed unconscious at the bottom. A surgeon was called. Jefferson's first question when he revived was about Winnie's safety. His second remark was that he did not wish Varina to see him die. Two of his ribs were broken and his recovery was slow. His condition was now such that they decided on a complete change and sailed from Quebec for England on the *Austrian*.

Just before leaving Lennoxville, Varina wrote to Mrs. Cobb, whom she called Sister Maran, that the children "were growing apace," but that her husband's soul was wearing out his body. Inactivity was killing him, and since his accident his "cough and psychic exhaustion have increased." [18] She felt sure that he would recuperate if he could once get something tangible to do, but "it is fearful to hold your earthly hopes upon an 'if.' " She could only feel thankful that all she loved were not in the same plight—"floating uprooted." Of herself she added: "I can scarcely tell you how I have languished out my time while my body worked, for I have worked with my hands in this little out of the way village, and prayed and hoped with my soul, without much expectation of release from my troubles."

It was a difficult voyage. Her husband was still in great pain from his broken ribs. He moved stiffly. The crossing was rough. Little Jeff was violently seasick, but ginger beer helped to revive him. With a strong sense of emotion Varina watched Ireland come into view through the mists.[19] They were met at Liverpool by James Spence and other Confederate agents, who had staged a welcome for them. There was much interest in Britain in the arrival of the former head of the Confederate States, and reporters were on hand to note that Davis wore a plain suit of "gray plaiding" and Mrs. Davis was essentially *"une femme jolie."* They held a reception at the Adelphi Hotel, and there were a few days of welcoming warmth and sightseeing before heavy family troubles set in.[20]

The boys were entered in a school at Waterloo, a suburb of Liverpool, and their parents went to Wales to visit American friends at Llandudno. "The Confederates everywhere tried to serve us, and from that time we did not feel like strangers in a foreign country," Varina commented. But Northerners were pouring into Britain, now that they could travel, and the war was still a live and controversial issue. Varina realistically commented: "We represented no country, and general visiting might have brought about unpleasant contretemps." [21] So they proceeded carefully.

They were at Leamington during the hunting season and "everywhere Mr. Davis attracted all who saw him." But Varina was summoned north from there in a hurry when Billy became seriously ill with typhoid fever "of a kind called gastric," Varina wrote to Mrs. Cobb on October 22, 1868. She found him delirious, his lips black, and "fighting everything in deadly fright." His physician had no hope for his life, but Varina "prayed without ceasing and poured brandy down his throat when he could no longer swallow." In three weeks' time he was convalescent.

But after her siege of nursing Varina was so spent that she could not move for several weeks. Her husband was unable to leave them and she feared he would never be able to do much again, she wrote to Mrs. Cobb. The least exertion bowled him over. Exposure brought on severe headaches, and a touch of cold weather gave him neuralgia at once. She felt sure his health was "permanently broken" and that his cracked ribs were the *coup de grâce*. He was very much of an invalid. In one of her rare allusions to the difference in their ages Varina added:

I watch over him unceasingly and pray to go first if it must be that we are to be parted. Twenty years difference asserts itself when the younger of the two is middle-aged, and I am in terror whenever he leaves me.[22]

This same letter was one of sympathy to Mrs. Cobb, whose husband had just dropped dead in a New York hotel room. Cobb and Toombs had been the two notable figures from Georgia in the Confederacy, and, although Toombs had been one of Davis's most bitter enemies and critics, the early breach with Cobb had long since healed. Aside from the loss of a close friend his death also ended the cotton link on which Davis had counted. He soon learned that the commission house with which he had planned to deal was unsound, and this led to further trouble and embarrassment.

Varina was appalled by the cost of everything in England. She felt too poor to travel, or even to buy new clothes, and was irked by "the necessity of pinching at every turn." She decided that if Jeff were summoned back to America for a court hearing, she would take the children to the continent and enter them in less expensive schools. At this point she was deeply concerned about the education of her children, which she felt had been neglected during the war years.

George Campbell and his Virginian wife were now in Liverpool, and they frequently entertained Judah Benjamin, who was just beginning to make his way at the British bar. He was specializing in mercantile cases and had much important business in the Liverpool region, where Confederate interests had been strong. By 1870 he would be Queen's Counsel for Lancashire County. The Davises saw much of him in

London that winter. He was reluctant to discuss the war after one long and exhaustive talk with Davis on the subject. "In speaking of his grief over our defeat, he said that his power of dismissing any painful memory had served him well after the fall of the Confederacy," Varina commented. She thought him more contented than he had ever been. He was enjoying the fleshpots of Victorian England. "His success at the English bar was exceptional, but did not astonish us," she noted.

When Wigfall reached London and settled his family in Portman Square, he called on all the Confederate leaders except Benjamin, whom he detested, as he did Varina and Jefferson Davis. But the Southern exiles as a whole were profoundly interested in the arrival of their former President, and most of them were curious to see how Mrs. Davis would fare in the stately social atmosphere to which they were now exposed. But she was no longer the Varina who loved pomp and circumstance. She had suffered too much, and had learned the virtues of anonymity. Although many social strings were thrown in their direction, they soon felt the financial pinch of keeping up with the peers of Victorian England. They were also well aware that tales of ostentation would be freely retold in America. But there was no escaping attention. Davis's story was well known in England, and Varina had some fame on her own account. Even the children were recognized through newspaper dispatches.

After visiting various English country homes they took rooms at 18 Upper Gloucester Place, Dorset Square, and in April, 1869, Varina wrote to Lise Mitchell: "We jog on here about as usual. We refuse all invitations to go out to fine parties, or to fine people. Lord Campbell and Sir Henry Holland, and Lord Abinger have been very civil in their pressing invitations to us to go to them for dinner, luncheon, etc., but we cannot afford to associate on those intimate terms with such rich people."

However, at one time or another in that year they were entertained by Lord Percy, Lord Lovell, Lord Lytton, Lord Lothian, Lady Brownlow, and the Duke of Sutherland. Lord and Lady Leigh had them at Stoneleigh Abbey. Lord Shrewsbury, who had been well entertained by them in Richmond, called on them in Llandudo and found them out, but subsequently invited them to Alton Towers for the "flower show for labourers," telling them that the gardens at Alton in themselves were well worth seeing. The Marquis of Westminster, a special favorite of Varina's when he visited her in Richmond before acquiring his title, now entertained them in genial fashion.[23]

Lady Mildred Beresford-Hope invited them to Barking to stay with her and A. J. Beresford-Hope in the "queer old English manor house we are living in." It was in an ugly part of the country, she said, but they gave no thought to its lack of beauty because they were preoccupied with the model farm adjoining it. Lady Marian Alford had them for dinner at Princes Gate on a bland April evening and Lady Eardley offered them her house at 4 Lancaster Street, where Jefferson Davis's portrait already hung. Her father had been dismissed from his post as consul at Mobile for "sympathy with the dear old South." Varina saw much of the Dowager Lady Abingdon and they stayed repeatedly with Mrs. C. E. Barrett-Leonard, who had a Tudor house in Essex "with secret chambers, a Cavalier hiding place and a ghost in the tapestry room." Davis became godfather to her niece, who was baptized Anne Varina Jefferson Davis and was known as Winnie, like Varina's own daughter.

Thus the Davises visited some of the stateliest homes of Britain. This was Victorian England at its most sumptuous. The Confederate cause was threshed out all over again at the dinner tables of the Englishmen who had been most sympathetic to the South. Varina would have enjoyed it all under different circumstances. It was distressing for her to forego worldly pleasure and social intercourse with spirited and eloquent people. But her husband was desperately unhappy and restless, the children were not adjusting themselves well to the English pattern after all the vicissitudes they had been through, and Varina herself felt thoroughly out of sorts.

Her main interest, as always, lay in trying to ease her husband's discontent. He now felt to the full his position as a man without a country, without occupation, without the sense of destiny that had been with him from his earliest days in Washington. Long stimulated by fame, debate, excitement, even disaster, he was now a man without a cause, without purpose, worn out in body and soul. But he showed his usual professional interest in various tours arranged for him. He received a warm welcome in Wales and went down into the collieries. He and Varina visited the Tower of London with Sir Arthur Lyon-Fremantle, who happened to be quartered there at the time and knew which chord to touch with Jefferson Davis. He warmly recalled Varina's hospitality in Richmond during the war days. He took Davis to the House of Commons, where his appearance excited interest. He put him up for the Travellers' Club. W. H. Gregory, a Member of Parliament who had long been a Confederate sympathizer, took him to hear

Gladstone make a notable speech that spring, but the demand for seats in the Commons was so overwhelming that there was no place for Varina—much to her disappointment, since she was deeply interested in statesmanship and had a special fondness for Gladstone, who had extolled her husband.

Several Fleet Street figures came forward to entertain the Davises.[24] Charles Mackay, the poet from Perth who edited the *Illustrated London News* before the Civil War and corresponded for the London *Times* in Richmond, called on them with Lord Campbell on a chilly March day in 1869. H. B. Praed, another of their correspondent friends who had also been with *The Times*, lost his post at the end of the war. "When Lee surrendered, the *Times* surrendered, but thank heaven I can afford to despise the *Times*," he wrote from the seclusion of Fern Dell in Dorking. Miss Louisa Tremlett, daughter of F. W. Tremlett, a leading figure in the English group dedicated to promoting the cessation of hostilities in America during the war, frequently invited Varina to visit them at St. Peter's Parsonage, Belsize Park. Octavus Cohen, then staying in Harrogate, asked Jefferson Davis to sit for a bust. He had done Queen Victoria and a memorial to Prince Albert for the Horticultural Gardens.

Before settling down for the winter in Dorset Square the Davises visited Paris for a few weeks. This was an interesting experience for Varina, whose bright scrutiny was focused on all the traditional landmarks. Although Americans at this time were bowing the knee quite regularly to the Emperor and Empress, official etiquette for the courts of Victoria and Eugénie was somewhat involved where they were concerned, with Northern Ministers now in full ascendancy. Varina's explanation for their failure to be formally presented was offered in her *Memoir*.

We went to Paris for a few weeks, and there the Emperor was attentive in a manner. He sent one of his staff to offer an audience to Mr. Davis, and the Empress kindly expressed her willingness to receive me. But Mr. Davis felt that the Emperor had not been sincere with our Government. He did not wish to say anything uncivil, and could not meet him with the cordiality his Majesty's kindness warranted.[25]

However, reviews were held in her husband's honor, and he received official attention. Cards were given them to attend chapel in the Tuileries, where they watched Napoleon and Eugénie worshiping with the little Prince Imperial. Varina thought he seemed so like their own

Billy that she followed his later life with interest. The Davises found some of their closest friends in Paris and were warmly welcomed by the Slidells, A. Dudley Mann, the Gwins, and other Southerners. The Gwins by this time were living in Neuilly with great elegance, and young Rosine Slidell had become the Baroness Erlanger. They stayed with Mann at Chantilly, and Benjamin crossed from England to join this little group. He was always glad of an excuse to visit his wife and daughter in Paris.

Varina was struck by the luxury with which some of their old friends lived. She felt distinctly out of the swim as she watched *"le skating"* on a pond in the Bois, and the coroneted carriages bowling past with wigged and powdered footmen in gorgeous satins. Empress Eugénie could be seen skating at times with the help of a baton held by two court attendants. Her gowns and hats were much discussed by all the American women in Paris. Cora Pearl drove along the Champs-Elysées with her lapdog dyed to match her hair, and Adelina Patti, whom Varina remembered as a young girl singing in Washington before the war, was now in her prime. They dined with the Slidells on New Year's Day, and recalled the receptions in Richmond. The *Gaulois* noted: "Mr. Jeff Davis . . . is among us, with his wife, whose heroism is equal to the harshness of her destiny."

Some time after their return from Paris, Dr. Maurice Davis ordered the former President north to Scotland for the bracing air. Charles Mackay accompanied him on a tour that was invigorating for Davis. They spent some time in Glasgow at the home of James Smith, a well-known philanthropist who had lived in Mississippi. He had given a battery to the Confederacy and his brother had died fighting with the Southern forces. They were all photographed together in a group picture that was later to hang in Davis's study at Beauvoir. Mackay's adopted daughter, present on this occasion, later came to be known to the world as Marie Corelli.

On his first trip North he visited Burns's birthplace in Ayr and found his own portrait hanging beside that of the poet. Two of the poet's nieces, knowing that he was in the country, felt sure he would visit Ayr and they were ready for him with a warm welcome. When he visited Dumbarton he astonished the Clyde shipbuilders with his technical knowledge of their work. He stayed with John Blackwood, the magazine editor, at St. Andrews in September, 1869, when the heather was in bloom and the shooting season was in full swing. He had passed through Edinburgh in July, visiting the Highland and Agricultural Society gathering there, and had climbed the hill to Holyrood. Varina had not felt equal to taking Winnie the entire way on this pilgrimage north. She was thoroughly worn out but was glad to detect the lift in her husband's spirits on his return from Scotland.

She had entered Margaret at the Convent of the Assumption close to Paris. Young Jeff and Billy were still in school outside Liverpool. Her sister Maggie surprised them all by marrying the Chevalier Charles de Wechmar-Stoëss a native of Alsace-Lorraine who was Consul in Liverpool for some of the German states. He was a widower, much older than Maggie, and had a son aged eighteen. She had met him at the home of the Campbells. He was small, mustached, and bore small resemblance to the cavaliers with whom Maggie had so blithely danced during the days of the war. Her beaux had been numerous. She had fancied herself in love a great many times. Varina arranged as fine a wedding as they could afford and invited many of their friends, including Lady Abingdon, to the ceremony held on April 26, 1869, in St. Peter's Church, Belsize Park.

Their funds melted fast. The commission house venture came to nothing. When Davis was offered a post in Memphis as president of the Carolina Life Insurance Company, he decided to go home and look into the prospects, since he was greatly worried about finances. He sailed late in 1869, and soon Billy and little Pollie were writing letters to him. Pollie, as he called Margaret, had been brought home from the convent, where she was wretched, and felt much happier with Miss Jarvis, the governess she now shared with Winnie. Shedding a swift beam on the family progress she wrote to her father:

We are living very quietly now and have very few visitors but my studies are so interesting and fill up the time so nicely that I do not mind it. . . . Winnie can tell you any place on the European map and is learning to write and read and studies spelling. First steps to knowledge, Play Grammar, tables and French. Billie is learning very fast. . . . We are all going down to Liverpool to spend the Christmas holidays with Mrs. Campbell. Your little Pollie.[26]

Young Jeff wrote in a correct and stilted vein to his mother from Waterloo, and Billy wrote cheerfully that he was as "jolly as a sand boy." [27] He wanted to know how Maggie felt, walking in Regent's Park without him, and how far Winnie had got in her primer. He wondered if the London boys had set off fireworks on Guy Fawkes Day. They had in Liverpool, but it was a rainy day and they had only two cannons.

Billy was all too familiar with the roar of cannon. "As I am just drawing a Confederate flag now, I must go to finish it," he wound up.

Varina worried constantly about the change of surroundings and schools for her children. They were well-mannered and essentially well-behaved children, but the events of recent years had had their effect on them and they had become shy of the insults that had been tossed at their father. Young Jeff met Theodore Roosevelt when he visited a cousin at his school at Waterloo. "Teddy" later reported in his diary that he had "a nice time but met Jeff Davis' son and some sharp words ensued." [28]

They had their pictures taken in Liverpool on Winnie's birthday in June. They were all handsome and bright and made an excellent impression. Varina and her husband took the greatest pride in them. The boys brushed their hair in soldierly fashion and stood erect like their father. The girls were correctly turned out by Varina in the clumsy fashions of the day. She was a martinet on manners, punctuality, tidiness, and respect for elders. Doting as she seemed at times about her children, Varina was alert to their faults. She had them all appraised. Jeff was the rowdiest, Billy the best-behaved, Margaret the hottest-tempered, Winnie the perpetually sweet child. Varina whipped them when she felt they needed it. They all treated her with the utmost respect, but they were more demonstrative with their father. She was ever the perfectionist, even in the midst of confusion.

Varina, in the dignified clothes that had been given her by friends before her departure for Europe, moved with a touch of her old hauteur among the shifting scenes around her, passionately upholding the Confederate cause to all who would listen, and still burning with resentment over the indignities her husband had suffered. The contours of her face were still firm and strong, but her waistline had thickened—a yard around, she noted—and she was no longer in any sense of the word a fashionable figure. Her face had a worn look of suffering. Her great dark eyes were slightly sunken now and suggested reserve and endurance. But her dignity was unimpaired; her pride was as strong as ever.

Varina had the most severe of shocks to her self-esteem that summer with the publication in America of Edward A. Pollard's book which attacked her husband unmercifully and made a savage appraisal of her own looks and nature. She was not unduly vain about her appearance, but when she first read Pollard's indictment, her anger knew no bounds. He wrote:

The Confederate President himself, though a recluse and haughty in his government, was democratic enough in his personal habits, simple in his social tastes, and plain and accessible to the populace. But Mr. Davis was the most uxorious of men; and it was surprising that a man of his fine nervous organism should have fallen so much under the dominion of a woman who was excessively coarse and physical in her person, and in whom the defects of nature had been repaired neither by the grace of manners nor the charms of conversation . . . a woman loud and coarse in her manners; full of social self-assertion; not the one of her sex who would have been supposed to win the deference of a delicate man like Mr. Davis, whimsical in his health, a victim of "nerves," nice and morbid in his social tastes, although she might well have conquered the submission of such a creature by the force of her character. Mr. Davis deferred to her in the social regulations she would impose upon Richmond. She demanded the etiquette of Washington, that the President's lady should return no calls. She introduced what were unknown in Richmond, liveried servants; and, when every horse was impressed in the military service, the citizens, forced to go afoot, remarked, with some disdain, the elegant equipage of Mrs. Davis, that paused much more before the shops of Main Street, than the aristocratic residences of Grace and Franklin.[29]

There were many other things in the book that outraged her, and for a time she was inconsolable. Written by an experienced newspaper editor who was bitterly critical of the Davises all through the war, it remains today the most venomous comment on the Davis family, and by all odds the most cruel commentary on Varina. They discussed it with Benjamin from the legal point of view, but he advised them to ignore it, that it would "drop into oblivion, unless advertised by your notice of it." He, too, was an object of derision in the book, but Benjamin, flourishing at the British bar, did not wish to stir up sleeping dogs. Five years later Henry Stuart Foote charged in *A Casket of Reminiscences* that Benjamin had misused Confederate funds and that by prearrangement he and Davis had planned to reunite in England.[30] Actually, there is no record that Benjamin did anything to help Jefferson Davis in England, other than to maintain pleasant social relations with him and Varina. He was anxious at this time not to become involved in any controversy about past affairs.

Even the Northern papers saw the injustice done to Varina by Pollard. Some of the most brilliant men of the day had commented on her manners, her wit and fine conversation. The New York *Tribune*, giving his book a four-column review on July 16, 1869, ended with the statement: "His remarks upon Mrs. Davis are wholly unjustifiable, and we hope in cooler moments will be expunged." [31]

But no one could persuade Pollard that she was not the power behind the throne. Redirecting his camera lens at her after acknowledging her husband's scholarship, cultivation, and studious habits, he wrote that Davis was "ready to make a quarrel of State for the whim or distemper of his wife" and that the man who could remove the most important officer in his government—his Quartermaster General—"because a female member of the family of the latter had presumed to criticize Mrs. Davis's figure . . . who gave himself up to social frivolities in the midst of a great war, and amused himself with intrigues and shows in Richmond when the enemy was making his vastest preparations, was clearly not the one to rule and direct the struggle of eight millions of people in a cause of life or death." [32]

Both friends and foes were now at work on books about the war and Jefferson Davis's role in it. Frank H. Alfriend's book pleased Jefferson and Varina. She eagerly read all appraisals of her husband as they came out, and smarted over the critical ones. On his return to America in the summer of 1870 Davis visited his brother Joseph in Vicksburg and found him in poor condition with a dislocated arm. He considered taking him and Lise back with him to England for the trip, but in the end sailed alone on the *Russia* in August. His family were all quite ready to return home with him. He had satisfied himself about the position in Memphis and, although business seemed an alien occupation to him, and he had little heart for it, he was concerned now with the need for making a livelihood.

The great homes of England, the men's clubs to which he had been invited, the gardens in which he was perpetually interested, the literary landmarks that touched him, the Welsh mines, the Scottish hills, the House of Commons—all would have absorbed him in other days, but now he was like a ghost moving among them. Neither he nor Varina could find contentment. Although their friends were kind and sympathetic, their cause was lost. They had no resting place and were tired of furnished rooms. Their welcome had a forced ring that Varina was the first to detect. It was intolerable to her proud husband and disconcerting to her. They longed to be home—yet where was home? What was the future? For the moment they sought it in Memphis.

❦ 18 ❦

MEMPHIS

"THE town looked very small after London," Varina noted, as she settled in Memphis in the winter of 1870. She was warmly received, but she was no longer the leading feminine figure of a wartime administration. The Davis family was in total eclipse. Things did not go well with her husband. "Don't laugh at the idea of my having business relations," he wrote to Mrs. Cora Semmes Ives that year. He was a planter, a soldier, a statesman, never a businessman. Although the mathematical problems of life insurance were an open book to his scientific mind, the human equation eluded him. His pride would not let him go begging at other men's doors.[1] The company policies had been issued recklessly. The percentage paid on renewals was excessive. Yellow fever in the area had increased the risks, and he ended by sinking much of his own capital into the stock to save the company. By this time he was getting some revenue from his lands in Mississippi.

Their stay abroad had cost them a great deal of money. Although Varina was not a spendthrift, and had learned in her youth to economize, she had grown accustomed to affluence. Like the other women of the planter generation, she now buckled down to a simpler way of living, and applied her genuine homemaking skill to a modest house on Court Street. She made a strong impression on all around her and kept up a lively correspondence with friends at home and abroad.

Although not universally liked in Memphis, the Davises put down deep roots and retained friends from this region in later life. Davis was called the Chief and was so dignified and aloof that few tried to make small talk with him. Varina, on the other hand, dominated any gathering and talked with force and purpose. Some of their Memphis neighbors thought that she talked too much and tired her weary husband.

Her health was poor and the climate did not seem to suit her. The heart affection she had long had made her uncomfortable in heat and humidity. She and Winnie both were ailing in 1872, but Davis noted that she "persisted in her purpose to remain with me during the summer." The Davises were close friends of Mr. and Mrs. William R. Hunt, who had a fine library which they both enjoyed. Jefferson Davis spent many of his spare hours in it, relaxing from the irksome details of his business. Mrs. Hunt, who had lived on a plantation, had much in common with Varina. She found her a "veritable encyclopedia about flowers and invariably at once went with me into the garden, while her husband made for the library here and browsed over interesting books in deep content." Stephen Rice Phelan, their great-grandson, later recalled: "Their concern was as much with the fish and birds of the air and the seeds of the field as with social life." [2]

On their return from England they had entered the boys in a church school in Maryland. There was still the fear that they might be exposed to political animus. Margaret was left in Liverpool with her Aunt Maggie. Winnie by this time was a clever imaginative little girl, much beloved by her father. Varina felt that the normal pattern of life for her children was gradually being restored when the boys came home for their holidays and were again under the influence of their father.

General Robert Ransom, who had known them since Davis was Pierce's Secretary of War, recalled Billy's bursting in with half a dozen boys whom he had unexpectedly brought home to dinner. He had gathered them up in the streets to help him finish a gardening project and now wanted dinner for his co-workers. His father showed great pride and satisfaction as he helped Varina entertain the boys and put them at their ease. Both were instinctively hospitable to the young. General Ransom considered his relations with his wife and daughters those of "knightly chivalry" and to his sons he was a "loving mentor and wise companion." The Davises seemed to him to enjoy the "perfection of domestic existence." [3]

The children at least appeared to be settling down, when suddenly Billy developed diphtheria late in 1872 and was dead within a few days' time. He was then eleven, the first of Varina's children born in the White House of the Confederacy. He had always been the most docile of her sons, and would sit quietly in his father's office and watch him work. When Varina noted his absence Jeff would say,

"You will not grudge me our grave little gentleman's company when you know how I enjoy his presence." Varina recalled him as a "perfect model of statuesque beauty" in writing about him a decade later to Dr. Robert P. Myers, an old Savannah friend.[4]

Fresh troubles beset them. Nothing went right. Soon after Billy's death the insurance company failed and they began to cast about for some other means of livelihood. Things had become so difficult for them that their niece, Mrs. Helen M. Keary, wrote to Jefferson Davis from her plantation on Red River, asking them to move in with her. "My heart aches to think you are in actual need of money and cannot get it and dear Varina not well and obliged to remain in Memphis, when it is so warm and disagreeable," she wrote. Helen was the daughter of Samuel Davis, another of the Davis brothers.

In the summer of 1874, with her husband's business in ruins and his debts mounting, Varina tried a gentle maneuver to focus his attention on writing his memoirs.[5] She sounded out Davis's former aide, William Preston Johnston, to see if he would initiate collaboration. She did not wish her husband to know that the suggestion had come from her. Unless urged into it he would never start, she felt sure, although he had a mass of material that needed only to be arranged. She thought her husband would find Johnston "the most pleasant person with whom he could cooperate in writing a history," and added: "I think that now is the accepted time for Mr. Davis to write out his recollections of the war, yet know that he has not the strength to perform the labor, mental, or physical."

By this time Johnston was established at Washington University as professor of history and English literature. On his return from Canada he had received his appointment from Robert E. Lee, president of the university. Now Lee was dead. The South had gone into deep mourning in 1870 for one of its greatest.

Varina's plans for a book came to nothing at this time, and her husband looked around for some more immediate means of livelihood. In 1875 he visited Texas, where he was offered a tract of land and stock to go with it, but he felt this was too much of a gift and declined it. He was feted all along the way—at Galveston, Houston, Austin, and Dallas. By this time he had embarked on a family lawsuit to recover Brierfield and other lands which he thought rightfully belonged to him.

News of Joseph's death in 1870 had reached the Davises in England just as they were about to sail for home. This was a great blow to Jefferson Davis, for his older brother had been a dominant force in his life as far back as he could remember. It developed that he had made Jefferson executor of his will and had divided his property between Lise and Joe Mitchell, his two grandchildren; and Jefferson's four surviving children, who were to receive twenty thousand dollars each. But once again Joseph had failed to give Jefferson title to Brierfield.

The lawsuit was a painful proceeding for so close-knit a family. After assisting his fellow executors, J. H. D. Bowmar, Hugh R. Davis, and Joseph D. Smith, in carrying out the will for more than three years, Jefferson Davis sued in 1874, losing his case in Chancery Court.[6] He appealed to the Supreme Court and finally won in 1878, Brierfield becoming legally his after four years of litigation. Thirty years' possession had made it his "by prescription," the court ruled. He also established his claim to another part of the land on Davis Bend as part of his children's inheritance, so that he ended up with one-half instead of one-quarter of Joseph's estate.

Varina testified by deposition that in the spring of 1844, before her marriage, Joseph had told her that he had given Jeff part of a tract of land and that he had cultivated it with success. She revealed at this time that while her husband was in Mexico she was wounded by remarks made by the family suggesting that Jefferson was dependent on his brother. She had gone directly to Joseph and asked him point-blank if her husband owned Brierfield. He assured her, Varina testified, that he had given Jeff the land, that he stood in the place of a son to him, and that she must not mind ill-natured remarks on the part of the family.

She told of the "ungenerous" will made by her husband in 1847 at his brother's behest, and of the dispute about the two kitchens. There was further testimony that Varina had said to Joseph in 1861, "I owe you nothing and am perfectly aware of your hostility to me," and that she had indicated that her husband would not have left the army had not Joseph promised him Brierfield.

A former Congressman named John Perkins testified that in 1855 Joseph expressed much affection for his brother to him, but was "very determined . . . that no portion of the Hurricane estate or Brierfield should come under the control of his brother's wife, or any member of her family. . . . The brothers were not on friendly terms at the time,

because of a misunderstanding originating through Jeff's wife."
During the war the Freedmen's Bureau had the property, but in
1866 Joseph applied for its restoration. At this time he took the oath
of allegiance and received a pardon. The plantations were returned
to him while his brother was at Fortress Monroe and he promptly sold
them to the Montgomerys, but by the time the suit came up the
situation was complicated by the fact that they had been unable to
meet their payments. Floods, the falling price of cotton, and the
restlessness of the tenants were defeating them in their efforts. Brierfield
was valued at seventy-five thousand dollars when Davis regained possession of it. Throughout the suit he was unable to feel anything but
friendliness for Lise.

On March 21, 1873, some months before he brought the action,
he wrote to her that he had known nothing of his brother's intentions
about the property except what he gathered from his will. "He never
spoke of it to me, or of any disposition of property, except the sale
made to Ben Montgomery, and that I find was very imperfectly understood. . . . I have not sought to find what should have been the provisions of the will, but only to execute them as they stand."

But Lise, who had been in occupancy, was bitter over the suit and
blamed Varina entirely for it. Years later she wrote:

The Davis relations believed he was influenced by his wife to bring the
suit, and it always caused me more sorrow than anger for I valued our
mutual affection more than the property I lost by the suit. I think he deeply
regretted it afterwards for though I begged him "to let bygones be bygones"
and never to allude to it again he would not do so but would write and talk
about it as if trying to convince me that his suit was not an unjust one. . . .
I think my grandfather's reason for not giving his brother a title to Brierfield
was that he disliked Mrs. Davis and did not wish her to inherit the property.
She quite as heartily disliked him, but on Uncle Jeff's account they kept on
apparently good terms. As head of the Davis family he was sometimes rather
"brutally frank" in reproving her and others.[7]

On their thirtieth wedding anniversary—February 26, 1875—Jefferson
Davis made Varina happy with the gift of a huge tooled-leather Bible
which may be seen today in Confederate Memorial Hall, New Orleans.
She was particularly touched by the inscription:

*Thirty years of married life have under many trials been solaced by fidelity
and love, and your husband offers this tribute as due to his wife.*[8]

Varina's fidelity had perhaps been her outstanding quality during all these troubled years. But fresh family grief struck her within the next few months. In November her brother, Jefferson D. Howell, who had always been known as Jeffy D., was drowned when his steamship the *Pacific*, plying between Seattle and San Francisco, was hit by a sailing ship and wrecked. Jeff saw the three hundred passengers removed safely, then swam to a raft with an old lady clinging to him. "The exhaustion, the cold, the hunger of four nights and three days of exposure, did not daunt his great soul," wrote Varina.[9] He comforted her till his strength failed, then he slipped off and drowned. He had been a familiar figure around the White House of the Confederacy and to many in Richmond.

In the following year Margaret, who had returned to Memphis from England and had developed into a handsome young woman closely resembling Varina, was married to J. Addison Hayes, a young bank cashier whom they were glad to welcome into the family circle. She wore a Paris dress which may be seen today at Beauvoir, and the marriage was a national news item. Later they moved to Colorado Springs for Addison's health, since he was threatened with tuberculosis. There they founded a strong family line, with many descendants, who are scattered in various parts of the country today. Margaret was the only one of Varina's children who lived to marry and have heirs. She had much of her mother's force and magnetism. Sometimes their strong wills clashed, but their deep family loyalty did not waver.

By this time Jefferson Davis was involved in a new venture, ambitious in scope but also doomed to failure. He helped to found a company known as the International Chamber of Commerce and Mississippi Valley Society. Its aim was to build up international trade through the port of New Orleans, by linking North and South American interests with European ports. English and American branches were to work simultaneously on an interchange of commodities, using ships built in England. In 1877, immediately after Margaret's marriage, he and Varina went abroad to make further plans for the new company. They took Winnie with them and entered her in a school at Carlsruhe. She was now thirteen, a shy and clever girl who suffered intensely from homesickness in the months that followed. They felt quite hopeful as they visited England again in a particularly lovely spring. Varina commented in her *Memoir* on the "hedgerows prinked out with pink May," but her spirits quickly drooped as she saw disaster come to her husband again.

This visit to England showed them how impractical the scheme was.[10] It was too visionary to encourage investment. The promise of ships they had hoped to get in Britain fell flat. High tariff was a stumbling block, and there were other difficulties. Jefferson Davis was bitterly disappointed and Varina became seriously ill. He nursed her devotedly and did not leave their lodgings for weeks on end. Her heart was now seriously impaired, and when he returned to America she was too ill to travel and decided to stay behind in the care of their old medical friend, Dr. Maurice Davis.

By this time Jefferson realized that there was no future for him in the business world, yet they were hard-pressed for cash. He was now close to seventy. His life had been one of phenomenal strain. Some of their friends felt that Varina had traveled too much for their means and thus had added to his anxieties. He returned to America, convinced at last that his next move must be his book. This brought a new element into his wife's life that was to prove highly disturbing to her.

She was still in England and forbidden by her physician to attempt an ocean voyage, when her husband first moved into Beauvoir, the house on the Gulf Coast between New Orleans and Mobile, which was to be their home all through the 1880's, the final haven found by Jefferson Davis for the closing days of his life. Here they were to find the only peace they knew from the day war began, but Varina settled only reluctantly on the Gulf Coast, under difficult circumstances, and with many misgivings.

More than the question of climate was at stake this time. There was also Mrs. Sarah Anne Ellis Dorsey, whom she had known from her childhood days in Natchez, but who had suddenly become an intrusive factor in her life.[11] Mrs. Dorsey was an ardent Confederate, a writer, and a collector of celebrities. Knowing Jefferson Davis to be badly off, she had invited him to stay at Beauvoir while he worked on *The Rise and Fall of the Confederate Government*.

Mrs. Dorsey belonged to two wealthy families of cotton planters and traced her ancestry back to the Percys of Northumberland. Her father was Thomas G. P. Ellis; her mother was Mary Magdalen Routh. She had properties in Louisiana, Mississippi, and Arkansas, and a home in Natchez, where she had first met Varina as a young girl. Sarah went

to Europe to finish her education, made many friends among the
British peers, and developed various social and literary interests. In
1853 she married Samuel Worthington Dorsey, a Maryland man who
was overseer on one of the family estates. He became a planter after
marrying her and managed her Louisiana properties.

She was a dark, vivacious woman, restless and ambitious. In 1871
she was in England, where she talked to Thomas Carlyle about the
Confederacy. In London she met Judah Benjamin, who was then
practicing on the northern circuit. Her literary interests were strong,
and may well have led her to suggest that she help Jefferson Davis
with his history of the Confederacy. She used the pen name Filia
and had had four books published. The last, *Panola, A Tale of
Louisiana*, came out that year. In 1866 she had written *Recollections
of Henry Watkins Allen*, a brigadier general in the Confederate Army
and former Governor of Louisiana.

Her husband died shortly before she moved into Beauvoir in 1876.
The place got its name from her exclamation when she first saw its
beautiful setting on the Gulf coast: "Oh, beautiful to see." Davis at
the moment had come to the end of his rope and was looking for
a quiet and healthy spot in which to concentrate on his book. She
offered him her hospitality, and he established himself in a separate
pavilion to the east of the main house, where he could work undisturbed with a collaborator, Major W. T. Walthall, who was suggested
by Sarah Dorsey. He paid rent, built bookshelves for his study, put
up a trellis to support the eight acres of scuppernong vines, furnished
the pavilion with his own things sent on from Memphis, and made
other improvements. He found the air bracing and liked the landscape, but he worried constantly about Varina until she finally returned
from England. Mrs. Dorsey wrote to Major Walthall on May 1, 1877,
that he was "in a very troubled condition of mind" and she had not
been able to get him to work steadily on the book but she had copied
some papers which he would send on to Major Walthall himself. "I
do not like to urge him beyond his strength . . . his movement must
be governed by his wife's health and its requisitions. He hates to make
the effort to travel—but I shall not be surprised if he finds *himself
compelled to cross over to England at any time.*" [12]

After his birthday in June, Varina sent him an affectionate letter,
now in a family scrapbook in California, although, among other ills,

she was suffering severely from eye trouble and could scarcely see to write:

The day that gave you life cannot be indifferent to me. It was a momentous, a glorious day for me, and full of promise, as the anniversaries have been of fruition. You are a year older, therefore a year dearer to me. "What care I for life or death so that thou are nigh." . . . If love has waned, and dwindled away, and died, then "memory is possession for the time" . . . Life is inexpressibly barren to me without the little tender reminiscences which render it sweet. . . . Therefore I have sought to exaggerate the value of the little things which brighten existence for each other to my children. . . .

She had drunk a silent toast to him on his birthday, Varina wrote. A few days earlier she had dined with Lord Lytton, who had invited her down to Knebworth, his country seat in Hertford, where she knew she would meet Robert Browning, Owen Meredith and other literary celebrities. Varina noted that she thought Lord Lytton handsome, with eyes like Jefferson's at the time his miniature was painted. But she did not have the strength that summer for many social outings because of the state of her health. It was late autumn before she managed the Atlantic and instead of joining Jefferson she felt compelled to go at once to Memphis to join Margaret, who was depressed over the loss of her first baby. She wrote to Major Walthall on January 6, 1878:

It was very kind of you to tell me how Mr. Davis is looking. He does not often speak of himself, and I am always more or less anxious about him. My daughter's health is so precarious that I do not feel it quite safe to leave her here alone, so I cannot say at what time I can join my husband. As you will very easily imagine, the separation from him is a sad disappointment to me.[18]

In this letter Varina recalled earlier and happier Christmases than the one she had just gone through. She was finding that anniversaries had now become "painful reminders of one's sorrows." Jeff, who had attended the Virginia Military Institute and had grown into a striking-looking young man, closely resembling his father, was working in the same bank as Addison and was "doing very well on a small salary." Her husband had come up from New Orleans to see her and she thought he looked older and "much oppressed by pecuniary losses." But the devoted Varina, for once, did not rush to be at his side. No real breach, but a slight coolness had developed over Mrs. Dorsey. She had hoped that Jeff would settle in Baltimore or return to Memphis, but he seemed to shun observation. His business failure in Memphis had led to embarrassment.

For the moment Varina was determined not to budge from Memphis. Margaret needed her at the time but deeper still lay her aversion to going to the Gulf Coast, particularly under the aegis of Mrs. Dorsey. The years had changed Varina, and her trips abroad had made her a cosmopolitan, so that she hankered less for the beauties of nature and more for the brisk interchange of city life. She had never had any aversion to being in the center of the stage. "I dearly love people," she wrote revealingly to Connie Harrison from Memphis. "They act on my dullness like steel on flint. Mr. Davis inclines to the 'gentle hermit of the dale' style of old age—so behold we are a tie—and neither achieves the desired end." [14] Yet she had no thought of fighting the issue. Pursuing the subject with her usual clear and emphatic point of view she wrote:

In the course of human events I shall go down to Mr. Davis's earthly paradise temporarily. . . . St. Paul says that when we are old we are girded up and taken where we would not be—so my time to be girded up has unquestionably come—and as unquestionably I "would not" if I could help it. The beauties of nature are for those who either have a hope of reaping the fruits of many seasons, or can make them immortal in verse, or color— or else for man-haters—I cannot do either of the former, and am not the latter.

But Varina, always a possessive and demanding wife, soon was dissatisfied with the divided life she and her husband were leading. It irked her that Mrs. Dorsey, an old friend whom she now violently disliked, should be aiding him with his memoirs. He appealed constantly to Varina for help on various points. In writing to him on April 18, 1878, answering a number of questions he had put to her, for her fine memory was ever at his service, she added courteously but unhappily:

There is only one thing, my dear Husband, that I have to beg of you. Do not—please do not let Mrs. Dorsey come to see me. I cannot see her and do not desire ever to do so again, besides I do not wish to be uncivil and embarrass you and I would certainly do so against my will. Let us agree to disagree about her, and I will bear my separation from you as I have the last six months—as best I can and hope for better times the history being once over. [15]

The rest of this significant letter was written in Varina's usual affectionate manner. In checking up on various points for him she assured him that he rightly supposed she was always willing "to bear any, or if I could, all of your burthens with a grateful sense that I am permitted to do so, even in the smallest degree." She felt a certain hopelessness about answering every criticism that arose. She did not feel that much was gained by "bandying words" with his critics. "It is the cue of the Yankees to call you and your friends out into innumerable contests, it confuses and disturbs your mind and their end is answered," she wrote.

The immediate point at issue was the behavior of the cavalry that was supposed to have covered the President at the time of his flight. Walthall had been "rebuttling the falsehoods of which a paper by Genl. Wilson was composed from turret to foundation stone." Varina studied the material and decided that Major Walthall's statements in answer were "loosely constructed." Her view of the work her husband was doing at this time may be gauged from the following paragraph:

I know you must be greatly harassed by painful things and I am mean enough to care nothing for posterity and a great deal for the peace of your declining years. So I heartily regret that you have attempted the history since it has been, and must ever be, such bitter, *bitter work.*

Varina was having a number of small family worries of her own. Jeff had fallen "heels over head" in love with Bessie Martin, and Bessie was in love with him. Varina was not too sure that she approved. Jeff was extremely popular with the belles of Memphis. Varina was not enjoying her surroundings at the moment, but one bright ray was the news from Germany about Winnie. Miss Addie Friedlander, her teacher at Carlsruhe, had written enthusiastically about her to both parents. Varina felt she was a "golden thread most sweet and fair" through all their sorrows, and went on in the somewhat unrealistic vein she sometimes used in writing about her family, that she felt as if Winnie were "anchored in a land locked bay, where the wind never blows cold, and the sun never scorches." She was thankful that she was delivered from the "curse upon our other children—idleness, constant change of residence . . . with her brilliant mind and teeming imagination, full of fair plants lying like the wheat in the mummy's sarcophagus alive, but unfruitful." Varina concluded:

If she should grow up pretty, God be thanked, if she does not, thank God—we shall not have to part from her so soon, as we did from our other darling—though I cannot find it in my heart to regret having Addison even though we have her no more as our very own. . . .

Jefferson Davis was no happier about the temporary separation than Varina. At this time he would drive over to a neighbor's home, never mention his book but discourse in a quiet voice on flowers, grapes, fishing, the sea, navigation, astronomy, or some other favorite topic. He often called on General W. S. Harney, who was staying at the Mexico Gulf Hotel at Pass Christian, and they would discuss the war, but he never spoke of it to Northerners passing through.[16]

He now had a "creole filly, with some appearance of blood, but no pedigree, she walks well, has a light elastic trot, and when broken will suffice for our sandy roads and my short trips in search of air and rest from reading and writing," he wrote to Colonel Northrop on April 9, 1879.[17] It was the first horse he had owned since the war.

Meanwhile, Varina was fuming in Memphis and was feeling far from well. When Mrs. Dorsey sent out invitations for a large party at Beauvoir, to be given in honor of the absent Winnie, she appeared suddenly and it was noted in the *Times-Democrat* of New Orleans that she "reigned supreme with queenly dignity." Few knew that this united front was preceded by a burst of anger on Varina's part that led her to go off to the woods and stay there until Mrs. Dorsey followed her and spread balm.

But the air remained chilly between Varina and Sarah, and to her dying day she harbored resentment over the proprietary interest Mrs. Dorsey had taken in her husband. She was adept at warding off worshipers of Jeff, whose handsome looks and courteous manners brought him some feminine adulation. She was reported on one occasion to have broken a stick given him by a gushing admirer.[18] But no one ever questioned his unswerving devotion to Varina, and their attachment showed great resiliency, in spite of the strains put upon it from time to time. She did not feel that Mrs. Dorsey had engaged Jeff's interest— she was too sure of herself for that—but she did resent the gossip that inevitably developed from this situation.

By midsummer Varina, too, was established at Beauvoir and was making the best of matters. She reported to Major Walthall on September 8, 1878, that her husband had not done any work on his book since his departure. It was too hot for effort, and yet there was a certain feeling of autumn in the air. "Mrs. Dorsey is busy with many things. . . . Mr. Davis and Mrs. Dorsey unite with me in many anxious thoughts of you," she finished.[19] Thus the breach ostensibly had been healed.

In this same letter Varina sent news of Major Walthall's wife and children, who were summering along the coast, while he was in the yellow fever area. In a burst of self-revelation about her feeling of responsibility for her own children, she wrote:

God grant that you may be soon restored to your little ones to guide and comfort them through their chrysalis state. I feel the responsibilities of a parent so intensely that I thank God that there is a time when the power, and consequently the onus of failure ceases—when the children grow, like Moses, to an age when they may kill a man, or lead a great nation on to victory and possession, and I be only like Moses' Father as dweller in their tents, and in no wise an indicator of anything.

Clearly Varina was torn at this time between her concern for her children in Memphis, where yellow fever was raging, and her husband at Beauvoir, who needed her help. The issue soon confronted her directly, for young Jeff was stricken early in October, five weeks after she wrote this letter, and was dead within a week. He had written to his father for the last time on September 19, saying: "I am delighted to know that my darling mother has at last found something that she likes about the Sea Coast. I felt sure she would like it after a while . . . kiss my mother many times for me and tell her I am always longing to see her dear face once more. Maggie and Addison join me in all the love your three children are capable of feeling for their dear Father and Mother." [20]

Young Jefferson had been stricken after a strange dream of death which later seemed premonitory to his friends.[21] A telegram was sent at once to his father, who was ill at the time. Margaret wished to nurse Jeff, but "she consented to wait until she hears from you before doing so," Walthall wired to Varina. He seemed to improve and on October 15 Margaret telegraphed her mother: "Oh! my darling, I feel so much for you and yet now that our boy is better I so much hope you will not try to come." [22]

Varina was frantic with anxiety but she was getting reports that he was recovering, and that Margaret was in no danger, when word cut through from Walthall on October 16: "He died quietly and peacefully at five this afternoon. Buried tomorrow at ten." Jeff was twenty-one, and the fourth of the Davis sons to die, leaving them with their two daughters. Varina received a sad letter from Bessie Martin, who had loved her son and would always be a friend of the Davis family. After Jeff's death his father could make no progress with his book. He would sit all day in silence, staring into space, and Varina quoted him as saying, "I do not know why I suffer so much, it cannot be long before I am reunited to my boy." [23]

The following February, while Varina was again in Memphis with her ailing daughter, Mrs. Dorsey made an arrangement with Jefferson for the transfer of Beauvoir. She was ill and was moving into New Orleans for medical treatment; in fact, she was in the last stages of cancer. Meanwhile, it would have retarded his work to remove his papers, and since property was selling for little along the Gulf Coast at this time they agreed on a price of fifty-five hundred dollars for Beauvoir, to be paid in three installments. When Mrs. Dorsey died a few months later it came to light that a year earlier she had willed all her property "to my most honored and esteemed friend Jefferson Davis . . . I do not intend to share in the ingratitude of my country towards the man who is in my eyes the highest and noblest in existence." [24] The property was bequeathed in turn to Winnie. Varina's name did not appear in the will. Davis was named Mrs. Dorsey's executor. [25]

The impression spread that Beauvoir was an outright gift from Mrs. Dorsey to Jefferson Davis. Actually, he had already begun making payments when she died, and eventually paid for the property in full, as well as taking care of other debts for her. Like all the planters' families, her once huge holdings had dwindled to little. As late as 1902 Varina was still indignantly explaining this situation and denying that her husband was the ultimate beneficiary in this transaction. [26]

Davis was with Mrs. Dorsey when she died and repeated to her a favorite beatitude. In a letter written soon afterward to her cousin, Mrs. Samuel W. Ferguson, he paid tribute to her "noble soul, in which there was neither hatred nor malice, her devotion to the truth, and sublime patience under injury." [27] In her tactful *Memoir* Varina, too, had praise for Mrs. Dorsey, saying that her "uniform kindness to him and deference to his wishes had endeared her to him, and he felt her death very much." [28] But she continued to wrangle with various members of the Dorsey family, and in 1902 returned "Mrs. Dorsey's silver to Miss M. R. Dorsey with great pleasure"—it had been left to Winnie. The memory of Mrs. Dorsey rankled for a quarter of a century.

Although painfully acquired, Beauvoir became a true home for the Davises and there they managed to recapture some of the serenity and grace that the war had taken from their lives. With Mrs. Dorsey's death a bitter chapter ended for Varina, although it was long before she recovered from the shock of young Jeff's death. She narcotized herself by working night and day with her husband on his book. From feeling antagonistic to this work, because of the bitter memories it stirred up in him, she now became deeply involved in the quest for records and reminiscences that would fill out the picture convincingly and justify her husband's acts.[29] All the old rancor over General Johnston welled up; the mistakes made by generals; their alibis and their triumphs; her husband's motivation at every turn of the road. There was no one who understood so well what was needed, or could better recall the facts.[30] Varina had been her husband's amanuensis from the earliest days of their marriage. She fitted naturally into the role now, when much seemed at stake, and she was desperately anxious for his vindication in the eyes of the world.

Since many of the official papers had been lost or destroyed, it was not an easy matter to put together this history. The memory of various participants was involved. An exchange of papers was effected whereby he received copies of some of the more important official documents in Washington in exchange for material he had collected from Confederate authorities. His book began with his "constitutional argument, setting forth the grounds of his faith," Varina noted.[31]

It was an absorbing but trying occupation and she was grateful for the calm of Judge W. J. Tenney, who had been sent by the publishers to help; and the zeal of Major Walthall whose fluctuating health, in her opinion, was caused by his "body sympathizing with his mind." She was ever at her husband's elbow, visiting the east pavilion where he worked at his small desk, surrounded by the bookshelves he had built himself, with his favorite pictures on the wall and a couch on which to rest.

It was enlightening to Varina to see how some of their old friends reacted to requests for information. When Davis appealed to Benjamin on the subject of Joseph Johnston, the lawyer showed obvious reluctance to be drawn into the matter. "I freely confess that it is not agreeable to mix in any way in controversies of the past which for me are buried forever," he wrote on February 15, 1879.[32] "If at any time your character or motives should be assailed and my testimony needed, I should be indeed an arrant coward to permit this feeling to interfere with my prompt advance to your side to repel the calumny." He added that he sought rest and quiet after the "exhausting labors of 68 years of a somewhat turbulent or rather adventurous life." In the same letter he conceded great gallantry on the part of General Johnston, but he expressed the opinion that his "nervous dread of *losing a battle*" caused him to miss opportunities that seemed to indicate an open path to victory.

At this time Jefferson Davis was in correspondence with Colonel Lucius Bellinger Northrop, his former Commissary General, who had survived storms of criticism in his administration, and had cheerfully gone around Richmond with copies of the *Examiner* that assailed him wrapped in flannel and used as wadding against his chest to keep out the cold.[33] Now Davis wrote to him of the "impossibility of getting men to state in a manner to be used, the truth as known to them orally." They had told him many things, he wrote, which in that "miserable spirit of harmonizing now endemic they cannot be induced to put in writing." [34]

However, the book was due on the first of May, 1880, and Varina worked with increasing intensity at her husband's side. At the last minute she was seeking a copy of his speech made many years earlier in Faneuil Hall. She had just received an issue of *Appleton's Journal* from their publishers and was delighted with its contents. She said she would like to meet its editor—"he must be a gourmet in literature, and his palate and mine have the same necessity," she wrote. "I *do get so tired* here of the sameness that when glimpses are offered of all the realm of science & art such as *Appleton's Journal* affords, I roam over the picture like a 'child at a feast.' " [35]

Finally, after three years of labor the work was finished.[36] It was four o'clock in the morning and Varina had been writing since eight the previous evening. Her husband dictated the final paragraph, acknowledging the fact that the war had shown secession to be impracticable, "but this did not prove it to be wrong." She looked up when he paused, waiting for the next sentence.

"I think I am done," he said.

"And so was finished his life's work for his countrymen," she commented. A great weight had been lifted from her own shoulders. But in the end his history was not a success. It was tepidly received in the North and with some interest in the South when it came out in 1881, but its price prohibited the impoverished Confederates from buying it freely. Both the Davises felt that it had not been well promoted. There was trouble with Appleton's and long litigation, which ended only with the author's death. According to Varina, however, her husband took the view that the book had not been undertaken for profit but for the purpose of "setting the righteous motives of the South before the world." In May of that year Judah Benjamin wrote to Francis Lawley asking if Davis's book on the Confederacy had appeared in Britain, and if so where it could be obtained.

As the book reached its closing stage Varina wrote at length to Connie Harrison on the life they were leading at Beauvoir.[37] Her old friend had sent her a picture of her son Fairfax, and she thought his head like his mother's and his eyes like Burton's. All of her friends' children had personality for Varina, who made pointed comments on them, remembered their names, their childhood diseases, and their characteristics, in a way most gratifying to their mothers and fathers. Her strong family feeling was one of her most distinguishing qualities. In this letter she gave her views on child-raising.

Nobody knows what is good for children and I am inclined to think that plenty of fresh air—porridge and love suit their early years, and later that a good example set before them, and the assiduous cultivation of the love of truth and their verbal memories will do the rest. If they love the truth, and can remember exactly what they hear and learn, they will pull through.

Margaret, still living in Memphis, was "very slender, very gentle and dignified and remarkably pretty . . . with a charming voice, given to singing old sweet ballads in the gloaming, and with one child." Her first boy had died. Now Varina was a grandmother, with a little girl named after her. . . . "I know you would be amused with the quiet little two-year-old creature . . . running around like a partridge and talking about everything like an old woman."

Winnie was still in Germany and Jeff kept promising her, said Varina, that she could go abroad and get her, but they might be delayed again by the publication of the book. Their estates brought in no revenue and "we have a Barmecides feast of possessions, and can hardly exist on the income, like all other Southern planters just now." She spoke of the loss of Jeff at the age of twenty-one, leaving her without "one strong arm on which to lean" in her old age. A glimpse of Varina's inner melancholy is caught through her final words to Connie.

And I cannot be comforted, because my children are not. I do not cry and grieve, but I do not find anything gives me pleasure or much pain—I am waiting for something, I do not know exactly what—Mr. Davis is less changed than I am. He has not grown old very fast—I write for him, and stay about in a dreary kind of fashion, that is all. This is a bright airy place—but I do not like it—As home is here, I stay here and cultivate a few roses and take care of things—I wish you and Burton would come to see us some time, then you could imagine us as we are. . . .

The Harrisons were among the "reconstructed rebels" [38] who had pitched their tents in the apartment house built by Rutherford Stuyvesant on Eighteenth Street near Irving Place. Here Connie held her own *salon* in a flat bright with cretonne and French gray walls, with pale blue medallions featuring shepherdesses, "hearts and darts, pipes and tabors." After their children were born they moved to a house at the corner of Lexington Avenue where their neighbors were Samuel B. Ruggles, James W. Gerard, Cyrus Field, John Bigelow, George Templeton Strong, Peter Cooper, and Samuel J. Tilden. Their children played in Gramercy Park.

Varina, looking out to sea, sniffing the spicy air of her garden, longed for more human communion, and for friends like Connie Harrison. She was now fifty-four and life had lost much of its savor for her. The intense purpose that had sustained and driven her through the difficult years now left her drained and restless in more placid surroundings. London had stirred up her taste for cosmopolitan life.

❦ 19 ❧

BEAUVOIR

MISS EMILY V. MASON, with round curls tumbling over her forehead, and her silks and lace fichu much as Varina remembered them from Richmond days, studied Jefferson Davis across the table at one of their Confederate gatherings in Paris in 1881, while they all played a quiz game on quotations. No matter what the epigram, quatrain, or couplet, he could supply the answer.[1]

"I am glad to have this happy memory of Mr. Davis," she observed. "Otherwise I should always be seeing him as he looked in prison."

Miss Mason, who ran a school in Paris and was coping with an endless procession of visiting Americans at this time, had brought Winnie back from Carlsruhe to meet her parents. She had been giving her a modest taste of Parisian life and some music and art classes at her school until they arrived. Miss Mason found her shy, unsophisticated, and unfamiliar with American history. Her father had stipulated that she must not be prejudiced in any way against her country in her formative years.

Confederate friends settled in Paris, and Judah Benjamin, who had crossed from London to spend some time with the Davises, observed Winnie with the greatest interest. Benjamin was now an imposing figure at the British bar and had prospered greatly financially. His milieu now was Duke Street, St. James's, instead of Richmond or New Orleans. But this was the last time Varina would see him. He died in 1884 and she did not return to Europe.[2]

A new happiness invested Beauvoir when Winnie made her home at last with her parents. She had developed into a charming girl, slim, graceful, with light brown hair curled close to her head, and eyes that ranged from gray to blue, depending on the intensity of her mood. Her health was delicate, her manner pensive. All who knew her noted a certain melancholy about Winnie. Her days in Carlsruhe had been lonely ones. It was an austere school and she had been bitterly homesick. Later she wrote for the *Ladies' Home Journal* on the folly of educating American girls away from home. It had been misery for her, and her mother later blamed her respiratory ills on the poor heating from the porcelain stoves in Germany.[3]

The seascape beauty of Beauvoir appealed to Winnie. She walked along the sands, hand in hand with her father, discussing the poets, her travels, the gardens, and literary matters. She had a high-pommeled English saddle and rode along the sandy paths, or drove with her mother in their victoria.[4] She brought fresh interest into their fading lives, helping her father with his papers, reading to him, playing backgammon. Gradually Varina let some of the burden slip from her own shoulders to Winnie's. Instead of accompanying Jeff on his various trips to ceremonies, Winnie now became his companion.

Both of her parents gave her careful indoctrination in American history "to make her breathe their atmosphere and adapt herself to their habits of thought." But although she became an ardent advocate of the Confederate cause, her years abroad had given her a more impersonal slant than theirs on many things.[5] Since she was not argumentative, like Varina, this did not bring her into collision with her parents.

Her mother soon was aware that Winnie had pronounced literary tastes and a knack for sketching. She spoke German and French fluently, and English with a faintly German accent that remained with her always. Her mother quickly saw that the deepest sympathy existed between her and her father, for she was much like him—in looks, and in her quiet courtesy and reserve. In the Victorian tradition she played the piano and sang old Scottish ballads to him at the end of the day.

Before she could read Winnie had listened to these same ballads being sung by her father, and long heroic poems being recited.[6] Sitting on his knee as a child, she had heard innumerable stories of Indian warfare, of hairsbreadth escapes, of big game hunting, horse fights, and the wild dances of the Indians. Now Winnie, like Varina, read to him—Byron, Scott, Burns, Don Quixote, the Bible, and Shakespeare. Her father still stayed awake most of the night, and on one occasion *Ben Hur* carried them from ten in the evening until daybreak. The Book of Job was especially dear to him. Varina had often heard him say that it contained much of the finest poetry in any language.

Both wife and daughter by this time knew his tastes well. His favorite songs were "Mary Dream" and "Annie Laurie." Although he continued to sing around Beauvoir into his extreme old age, as his eyes failed him he became increasingly fond of backgammon and card games. He never played for money, but he and Varina tallied the score in euchre with buttons or counters.[7] She humored him strongly in all these matters, even though she sometimes found them dull. Long accustomed to his insomnia she would waken at the slightest movement next door and slip from her yellow-painted bedroom, where she slept on the frilled, monogrammed, and paper-fine pillowcases that may still be seen at Beauvoir, to go to his side, to read to him, to fan him with her turkey feather fan, to talk to him of battles lost and won. She still had trouble getting him to eat enough for good health. He was always indifferent to food and ranked gluttony with lying as a major vice. He had trouble digesting starch and stuck to his tiny pones of hoe cake, "the only sort of bread he could digest," according to Winnie. Her mother, on the other hand, had a splendid digestion, was a hearty eater, and saw that everything was prepared in the best manner.

Maggie had returned with the Davises from her home in Southport, outside Liverpool, and she passed the winter of 1881-82 at Beauvoir. Varina thought she looked about "twenty years old and quite young in her feelings." [8] She now had a daughter Christine as well as her stepson Philip. At this time Varina was rounding up American children's books for Margaret's offspring. She wanted the Uncle Remus stories and a "series of rhythmical versions of the baby Mother Goose written by a Boston lady and published about 1860." In ordering the books she wrote: "To say that the belief in Brer Rabbit has been restored would be too much, but the interest is fresh as yesterday, and the dialect is a perfect imitation of that used by our old Mammys." [9]

A measure of peace had finally descended on the storm-tossed Davises. At Beauvoir they had the privacy and dignity that suited their natures. The storms of criticism that had whirled about them became only echoes here, with the waters of the Gulf Coast washing almost to their door, and a rough shell road discouraging visitors. Today a stream of rainbow-tinted cars sweeps past Beauvoir on a flawless road that stretches in a blue-green arc from New Orleans to Mobile. There was no road at the edge of the sea in the time of the Davises, but rough land leading down to the water.

Architecturally Beauvoir today is much as it was in the time of the

Davis occupancy, a white house with a wide gallery and a hall cutting clear through the center to make a pleasant sitting room on sultry days as the Gulf breezes sweep through. Here Varina used to serve tea to her many guests. The two small pavilions to the east and west stand in balanced perspective, and the rooms are furnished with many reminders of the Davis family, from Varina's phaeton in the museum downstairs to the bookshelves made by her husband for his study, and Winnie's blurred painting of an Italian landscape still visible on one of the mantelpieces. The pavilion where Jefferson Davis worked and wrote his book remains as it was, with his desk, his couch, 712 volumes now valued at $100,000, and Winnie's pallette with a half-finished painting.

Old newspaper clippings give many different views of the Davises at Beauvoir. Editors and reporters visited there often during the 1880's, as well as governors, generals, politicians, diplomats, and celebrities from abroad.[10] Varina was always prepared with pot luck for the visitor and her hams and seafood were famous. She had put together a substantial home again and she presided over it with her old air of authority, although she no longer had a staff of servants to help her and was known to come in from the kitchen looking hot and tired after preparing a fine meal for unexpected guests.

In those early days sheep grazed on the grass, and a vineyard of scuppernong grapes flourished to the rear of the house. These were carefully tended by Davis, and Varina sometimes felt as if she were back at Brierfield again as they worked over their rosebushes, planted new shoots, and grew vegetables as well as flowers. They spent contented hours in the garden and on the latticed gallery to the rear of the house. At heart Davis was still the farmer and planter, an instinct as deeply ingrained in him as that of soldiering. And Varina, born on a plantation and long used to its abundant life, was quite in tune with this. She could talk horses, supplies, and feed; she knew how to order seeds and shrubs and what to do with them when they arrived; she was as adept outdoors as in managing her household. She was a familiar sight in Biloxi, bowling along in her little phaeton with her horse Gladys, and being helpful to her neighbors.

Poultney Bigelow visited them on a spring day in 1881 and found Varina a "motherly and beautiful woman." [11] Margaret and Addison were staying at Beauvoir at the time, and he thought they made a happy group together as they chatted under the huge trees shading the front lawn. "I think of this family and that of Mr. Gladstone together—

particularly because of the comfort each of these men found in his wife," he wrote. "Mrs. Davis was not merely of strong character, but handsome also. . . . Like her husband, she was ever dignified, gracious and tactful."

On this occasion they all accompanied Bigelow to the little station that had been opened at Beauvoir especially for the Davis family. As they sat on a log waiting for the train a large dog attacked their New-foundland. "Davis leaped up, into the Catherine wheel, flung the combined jaws across his knee, and with bare knuckles hammered into the foaming mouths with such swiftness and force that he achieved a parting of the astonished animals," Bigelow observed.

None was more impressed with Varina in her fifties than General George W. Jones, of Iowa, who visited them in 1883. Conceding that time had wrought some changes in her, he considered her still the "same bright, genial, cultivated, domestic woman, who is equally well qualified to grace the parlor, preside at a State dinner with historic men as her guests, attend to the minutest details of her housekeeping, or visit her neighbors, or look after the needy poor." [12] He considered her one of the finest conversationalists he had ever known and was impressed with her devotion to her husband and her pride in his fame. "She strikes all who know her," he added, "as worthy to share the fortunes and comfort the declining years of our chief, as she was worthy to share his honors and reign in society at Washington and at Richmond." [13]

When Alexander K. McClure arrived at Beauvoir in 1885 he was surprised to find Jefferson Davis one of the most optimistic of the Southern leaders.[14] He had caught others in utter despair over the rehabilitation of the South. They had a long conversation in which Davis questioned him closely about Lincoln and was surprised when McClure told him that on many occasions he had heard Lincoln speak of Davis, Lee, and other prominent Southerners with the greatest respect. McClure was sure that had he lived Davis would never have been taken into custody.

Catharine Cole, visiting the Davises on behalf of the New Orleans *Picayune*, carried away distinct impressions of all three as she found them in their "cool, sweet drawing room" [15] in a house already mellow with paintings and portraits, books, lounges and ottomans, big rocking chairs and antique cabinets, a grandfather clock and open piano, a Turkish curtain separating the front parlor from the back, and flowers arranged everywhere in graceful vases. She considered Varina "a deeply learned woman . . . gracious, genial, large-minded, large-hearted . . . a woman born to a commanding position." She studied Mr. Davis as he leaned back in his arm chair, his thin white hands clasped around his knees, and viewed him as a gentleman of the old school—"tall and thin and shrunken, with silver white hair and beard, distinguished and remarkable in his appearance."

Winnie, in a dove-gray gown and wide-brimmed hat, walked down the garden path with her, snipping flowers for a small bouquet, and making an unforgettable picture as she "bent over the bushes of blue-eyed periwinkles" in an old-fashioned garden with "odd little flower-beds, and long, wandering walks, all set with mignonette." The air was sweet with the scent of damask roses. Mrs. Cole noticed the tangle of vines and brambles around the magnolia, cedar, and oak trees, in the grounds reaching down to the sea. The sprawling pent roof of the kitchen was hidden by a snow of roses. Farther away were the barn and toolhouse, the sheepshed and cornbin, a carpenter shop and the kitchen garden beyond the "sweet old-fashioned flower garden."

Varina was to become quite friendly after this with Mrs. Cole, who was Martha R. Field, a Northern writer who wintered on the Gulf Coast and in 1894 joined the staff of the New Orleans *Times-Democrat*. Other correspondents arrived from time to time and made similar observations, noting the "foostools of violets," the matted roses and Varina serving tea, English fashion, in the lounge with Sally Lunns, seed cake, preserves, sweet wafers, and sandwiches. Minnie Reese Richardson, representing the Montgomery *Advertiser*, was struck by the "flashes of intelligence that went back and forth between mother and daughter in iridescent play" [16] and by the silence of Jefferson Davis, or the brevity of his responses. And Steven S. Cummins, their old friend from Lennoxville, commented on the "charming picture of Mrs. Davis in her rose garden at Beauvoir in the early morning.[17]

Oscar Wilde was perhaps their most famous visitor, and his coming was a great event to Varina. But she did not relax the protective rules she had established for her husband's health or let him stay up late to talk. Wilde visited them in May, 1882, and to this day the portrait he gave them hangs in the east pavilion at Beauvoir. It is inscribed: "To Jefferson Davis in all loyal admiration from Oscar Wilde, May, '82." A niece recalls the day he spent under their roof.[18] There was good conversation, and one may be sure that Varina had arranged an excellent dinner. He posed for her while she made a rapid sketch of him. But when bedtime came she held them all to the rules, even though her husband might not sleep for hours. Everyone retired but Wilde, who was not yet ready for sleep. Instead, he wandered off for a walk along the beach in the warm May night.

The former President of the Confederate States relaxed and grew healthier in these surroundings, except for a severe illness in 1884. He wrote to his old associate, General Gorgas, who by that time was at the University of Alabama: "The air is soft, in winter especially the sea breeze is invigorating. The oranges are shining golden on the trees, and our pine knot fires roaring in the chimneys and in their light I try to bury unhappiness." [19]

In the summer of 1883 Varina was interested to receive a racy letter from her old friend, Mrs. Chesnut. Her husband was considering writing a book and she had finished hers. She was busy overhauling her diary, but "I must overhaul it again—and again," she wrote.[20] Her compatriots were in for some shocks from the book *A Diary from Dixie* about to be published. Her most intimate friends would wilt with horror and generals would suffer. But she was comparatively reserved about the Davises and treated Varina kindly.

"Three cheers for Jeff Davis," she exclaimed in this *non sequitur* letter, written on odd scraps of paper as if it still were wartime. "I am Davis straight out. I was—I am—and I always will be—heart and soul a good old Confederate. . . . My love to Mr. Davis—one world for the pen of Carlyle. He is a better fellow than his wife. . . . God bless you—for all your kindness to me—when you had the power to be my staff and stay. . . . You see I am a frank heathen—I love my friends—and I hate my enemies. . . ."

As of old, an avalanche of company was about to arrive at Mrs. Chesnut's—Wade Hampton, Bonham, Mary Darby—all old friends of Varina's. Mrs. Chesnut enclosed a snapshot of Mary Darby "to show how the Old Guard hold together by the heart strings." The childless Mrs. Chesnut ended on a note of envy.

How I wish I could hear your girls sing—music is the one pleasure that never dims. You thank God for your young immortals. I have nothing but Polish chickens and Jersey calves. Some of these days I will send you some wine I make—as good as Rhine wine—and it is *too* strong.

All through the 1880's a steady literary output continued at Beauvoir. Although his history was not a success, Davis had many requests for magazine articles. They sold for $250, and a number appeared in the

North American Review, which was edited by James Redpath, a news-paperman who had been lured east by Horace Greeley and was a close friend of Wendell Phillips. He first visited Beauvoir to write a critical piece about Davis, but was so won over by him that he stayed for weeks and afterward collaborated with him in some of his work.

In 1883 Mr. and Mrs. Davis carefully read and marked an article that Burton Harrison had written for Richard Watson Gilder of *The Century* on the capture and imprisonment of the former President. Gilder thought it put him in a good light and was the best account he had seen of the capture. But four years later Burton was jibbing at doing a piece on the start of the war. He wrote to C. C. Buel of *The Century* that Davis was "very sensitive to criticism or to any remark by a friend which is not all praise." [21]

Shock after shock hit the Davises in these days as books, reminiscences, and statements about war issues appeared. Varina's active mind was ever at work, remembering, checking things in old newspapers, correcting errors. Davis wrote articles on the protective tariff, which he considered unconstitutional; on Robert E. Lee; on prisoners of war, and on Andersonville. Replying to the charges that kept recurring in connection with this notorious prison, he maintained that it was "not starvation . . . but acclimation, unsuitable diet, and despondency which were the potent agents of disease and death" and that "these it was not in our power to remove." [22]

Varina always became greatly riled on the subject of the prisoners of war. This had figured strongly in the charges brought against her husband, and part of her campaign while he was at Fortress Monroe was to show that he favored leniency for prisoners at all times. More than once he wrote to friends, saying: "It would be impossible to frame an accusation against me, more absolutely and unqualifiedly false than that which imputes to me cruelty to prisoners." [23] He had learned at first hand what it was to be a prisoner of war.

Varina worried considerably about the article on General Lee. She wrote to Redpath on September 6, 1888: "I insisted upon popularizing the article as much as possible, for I thought it was not a military critique you wanted but to see the heart of the man through the eyes of one who knew and loved him. Fortunately, my husband agreed with me, and has left out everything which could suggest controversy. . . . He has written all his sunny memories of our great hero, and I think the world will hear him with eager sympathy."

A clue to the way in which Varina spared her husband's feelings is contained in her warning to Redpath: "If you do not like the articles, just preserve the graceful silence that you did when we disagreed. . . ." And the large share she took in the work may be gauged from a note she wrote to Redpath on October 1, 1888.

I am so much a part of everything Mr. Davis does, being his hand, and in Aesop's sense, one of his members, and also in the Mosaic sense, that there is only one part of his writings I do not in some sense share, and that is their composition.

In the summer of 1888 Davis was asked to write an introduction to the biographies of some of the Confederate generals for the *Review* and he felt uneasy about it. "I have written it and hope our own people will not blame me for holding the opinion now which was generally held among them in 1861, as to the sovereignty of the State," he wrote to Jubal Early. "The howl of the Northern radicals cannot exceed its past bitterness against me, and will affect me as little as it has done heretofore."[24]

He automatically bore the brunt of all attacks, as the symbolic figure of the Lost Cause. Moreover, his viewpoint did not change, however much he analyzed the situation; however deeply he studied the trend of events.[25] His position was anomalous, since he could not ask for amnesty nor would he accept a pardon. He was a man without a country, where most of his old associates had bowed to the inevitable and been pardoned.

In his last speech, delivered before the Mississippi State Legislature at Jackson on March 10, 1884, after he had been asked to run for public office again, he said, "Repentance must precede the right of pardon, and I have not repented. . . . I deliberately say if it were to do over again, I would again do just as I did in 1861." [26] But to his youthful audience he added, "Let me beseech you to lay aside all rancour, all bitter sectional feeling, and to take your places in the ranks of those who will bring about a consummation devoutly to be wished— a reunited country."

This speech had many repercussions. Davis continued to stress the non-repentance theme in personal letters, emphasizing his consistency. He remained a controversial figure to the day of his death. An invitation to speak in Illinois, Lincoln's state, brought protests.[27] After that he was cautious about the invitations he accepted.

His health improved at Beauvoir, and his eye trouble subsided. He gained some weight. He was at last free of the terrible sense of responsibility that had rested on him. At this time the Davises had some revenue coming in from their properties on Davis Bend. The Montgomerys had done their best to work the land but conditions had been against them and finally they gave up, still maintaining close and friendly relations with Jefferson and Varina. The floods of 1884 were devastating. Davis was advising Lise on the need for levees. The bitterness of their lawsuit had subsided to some extent, and he was trying to help her, but there were still many complications about the boundary lines between their properties. Varina, who had been at odds with Lise, relented sufficiently to send her a note on October 20, 1885, when she was having trouble with plantation affairs. "My dear poor little girl, do come to us, Your devoted aunt, V. Davis." [28]

Jefferson, too, invited Lise to visit them at Beauvoir. She would then see Winnie, and in looking at her would find the "chin your grandfather had." He wrote of Joseph as an "eminently handsome man," with sparkling eyes his most striking feature . . . "he was my beau ideal when I was a boy and my love for him is to me yet a sentiment than which I have none more sacred." [29]

He went to great lengths to explain to Lise that the suit about the property was brought because the co-executors of his brother's will considered a judicial proceeding necessary when he proposed taking Brierfield back and releasing Ben Montgomery from a proportionate amount of his bond. He had not anticipated any opposition to the claim, he explained, and "though disappointed in that expectation I have not felt such alienation from you as your letter indicates you believed to exist." [30] The complications revolved chiefly around the Montgomerys. Lise's husband and they had argued over the line of division. After the Montgomerys pulled out Isaiah founded a colony of Negroes in the Yazoo region in 1887 and Thornton became president of a promotion company, prospering in North Dakota. Varina took the friendliest interest in them always. She visited them from time to time when Brierfield was again their responsibility and had long talks with them about the Negroes and how they could best be helped. [31] No ill-will developed with them over the lawsuit, for they wished to be free of the responsibility they had assumed.

She had a long illness in 1883, and in the following year Jefferson was very ill with a bronchial infection. Varina nursed him with her usual devotion. He had become accustomed to her ministrations and, although from time to time he had a battery of doctors attend to his various disorders, from eye specialists to gastric experts, she was much given to dosing him with the remedies that she found worked best for him. Long before his doctors gave up on quinine, she found that it did not suit him. She dosed him freely with Dover's Powder, calomel, and soda, used hot cloths for his neuralgic pains, and kept him out of drafts. She understood him better than anyone else, but she sometimes found him as baffling as his doctors did.

He was ailing badly on an April day in 1886 when a reporter from the New York *World* appeared to get his opinion on public issues.[32] He could not leave his bed. Varina did not appear, but Winnie came out, sweet and unpretentious, and handed him a note from Davis saying that he was not in office, nor was he a candidate for official position; therefore he felt he had the right "to lead the life of retirement in which the will of others as well as my own has placed me."

Jefferson's courtesy to Varina never wavered, whether he was well or ill, and Winnie told of his insistence on dressing for dinner when her mother urged him to come to the table in a dressing gown after he had been ill.[33] They were dining alone and it did not matter, she said. But Davis replied, "I know no one for whom I have more respect than yourself. I hope I shall not take cold, but I cannot sit at dinner with you in my gown."

James Redpath thought that Jefferson Davis was as deferential to his wife "as if she were presiding at a tournament in the olden time." It amused him to note how readily Varina spoke of herself as an "old lady," although she was much younger than her husband. He thought her "quite as noteworthy a personage as her husband—a woman of large brain and great heart, highly educated, of marvellous insight into character, with the rarest conversational powers, bright, brilliant, witty and sympathetic." Although they had been married forty years he decided that "their honeymoon does not seem to have reached its first quarter yet." He found it delightful to witness their mutual affection and to hear them address each other.

But she ruled her household with a somewhat despotic hand at times. She was a stickler for form. Meals must be on time. Everyone must be present. The children were quickly shunted off to their own dining room on the back porch and noise was kept in abeyance. When little Marguerite Hayward (later Mrs. William Fayssoux), whose parents, Mr. and Mrs. William Burton Hayward, were relatives of both families and close neighbors, came over to play and banged out tunes on the piano, Varina quickly silenced her.[34]

"But how will the children ever learn?" her husband mildly interposed. He usually took their side in all such matters, answered their questions with scientific precision, and made them feel quite happy. He often stood as a buffer between them and Varina's severity, but she really loved the young, and had many pets, in addition to her own children and relatives. She lectured them at times, corrected their pronunciation, denounced their manners, and as she grew older demanded a certain obeisance, but she knew what interested them. They never forgot her or what she had to say. She was known to have her bad and good days, and one child would warn another, "Better stay away from Auntie today."

Marguerite considered her stately as she watched her move about in ruffled white wrappers with trains that became her well. Her slim, beautiful hands were never idle. Her bright mind was alert to every nuance of behavior and conversation. The child noticed that she never walked to the end of the wharf, although Winnie and her father were often down by the water. Mrs. Fayssoux recalls her as a "brilliant and imposing woman" who loved contact with people of culture and learning. When she visited her relatives in New Orleans the children gathered around her in droves, and she knew them well, down to the last attack of measles and the favorite hair ribbon.[35]

Together Winnie and her mother pressed flowers and grasses from all parts of the world into a portfolio. They restored and added to the family album,[36] which had been soiled and battered after it was stolen from one of their trunks on the way to Fortress Monroe and taken out to Independence, Iowa, by a soldier named Moore. It was returned after the war by his father. The album contained pictures of most of the European rulers, of well-known statesmen, and the great writers and scientists of the day, many of them known personally to Varina and Jefferson.

They ranged from Lord Palmerston to Garibaldi, and from the Prince of Wales to Dumas. Prince Napoleon was entered next to little Jeff, wearing a tartan sash. Kossuth was companion to blond Billy. The family pictures included Charles de Wechmar-Stoëss, whiskered and wearing a burnoose. There were few wartime subjects, but Varina included Mrs. Robert E. Lee, Jeb Stuart, and Charles O'Conor. Two Union figures were represented—Abraham Lincoln being embraced by George Washington, who held a wreath over his head, and John Brown. Jefferson Davis had been upset over the loss of this album and devoted much thought to its recovery.

Varina had a cypress cupboard built to hold her Staffordshire china and her willowware. Among her treasures were a cup and saucer that had belonged to Lord Byron. She often drew the attention of visitors to a mirror and console in the hall, brought from Paris in 1871 from the home of the first Napoleon. She treasured a mask of Napoleon given to her when she visited Maine. The Davises all prized the quilt stitched for the former President by 350 Confederate women.

Varina used hairs from her own head for the fine stitches of the bold flower pattern on a black alpaca sampler, on which she inscribed the lines:

> To heart that cannot vary
> Absence is Presence
> Time doth tarry.
>
> 1886

Two years after her death Major J. J. Hood scrawled across a clipping from the Jackson *Daily News* that gave Winnie full credit for being her father's amanuensis:

His peerless wife was his amanuensis and did nearly all his writing and copying of the manuscript of these huge two volumes and this arduous work so impaired her health as to necessitate her going out of this climate. She was a fit companion for such a man! and the world does not know what Mrs. Jefferson Davis suffered all these long, trying years at Beauvoir.[37]

Varina sadly watched the passing of the generals, but Jubal A. Early, like Jefferson Davis, lived on and they were ever the best of friends. Davis fought the battles all over again with Early and wrote that there were few "with whom he could agree so fully." In April, 1885, they were corresponding about Grant and Lee at Appomattox, and General Early was assuring Davis that "so far as Genl. Lee is concerned I have as his friend always contended that he surrendered only when it was impossible for him to continue his retreat to the mountains & carry on the war for the independence dearer to him than life."[38]

As the tides washed in and out, as the seasons changed, as Varina buffered his last years, as generals and statesmen called to see him, as letters revived old issues, he could see his life panoramically unrolled as others saw it. Charles de Wechmar-Stoëss sent him the British publications. Varina helped him to answer his critics, but as one denial followed another she tried to discourage him, feeling that it was a "work of supererogation." So much that was false and legendary surrounded him by this time that there was no catching up with the truth, and it made him silent and morose to dwell on his situation. Although she became quite as fanatical herself after his death and let nothing go unanswered, she tried to calm the waters in the 1880's.

Varina knew how to soothe her husband when the endless churning debates began in his mind, and he fought the battles all over again with her and Winnie. The mistakes that had been made. What might have been. The instinct to defend himself. His correspondence often whipped it up. She saw realistically that it was impossible to stem the tide of hate that still flowed in their direction; to offset the constant rehashing of cause and effect; or to mollify the sons and daughters of men who had fought in the Union Army. But she was relieved to see him gradually worrying less, the keenness of his pain subsiding.

Some issues stirred him up more than others. General Johnston's charges that he had failed to account for all the Confederate money. General Sherman's observation that in his Washington days he was a well-known conspirator, plotting to disrupt the Union and head the new state. Viscount Wolseley's charges in England of military incompetence on his part, a professional slur that deeply offended him. During 1888 he was not only defending himself over Andersonville but he was mustering precise military data to answer such charges as Viscount Wolseley's, that he thought ten thousand Enfield rifles sufficient to overawe the Northern forces.[39] Varina could remember well when she had entertained the young Briton in Richmond. He was now on his way to being commander-in-chief of the British Army. Her husband answered vehemently that it was a fact of ineffaceable record "that I publicly and always predicted a long and bloody struggle."

Varina now saw much in perspective that she had been too busy to take in when she was in the midst of the overwhelming events of the war. As she read and watched and listened, she had a clearer picture of these desperate years. She was disillusioned, too. "I am disheartened with popular sovereignty, still more with State sovereignty, and fear both are fallacies," she observed.[40] Many had betrayed her husband. Many had foresworn him. Blind ever to his imperfections, she knew at last who the betrayers, the deserters, and the true friends were. But now she talked less vehemently. She was slower to condemn. Winnie, too, had been a leavening influence in the lives of both her parents.

℀ 20 ℀

DEATH OF JEFFERSON DAVIS

VARINA was busy nursing a small grandson through a bout of scarlet fever in the spring of 1886 when Winnie was publicly christened the Daughter of the Confederacy at a veterans' rally in Atlanta. It was a name that caught the public fancy. She was touring the South with her father when General John B. Gordon led her to the front of the platform and introduced her by the title which became peculiarly her own.[1]

Caps were tossed in the air. Winnie listened to the strange and unfamiliar sound of the Rebel Yell, shouted by thousands of voices. The band played "Dixie." Later their carriage was mobbed, and the young daughter of Jefferson Davis had emerged in the public eye as a personality at the age of twenty-two. On this same tour she stood at his side between the Corinthian pillars of the State Capitol at Montgomery on the exact spot where he was inaugurated President of the Confederate States a quarter of a century earlier. Letitia Tyler, who had first run up the Confederate flag, now pinned a white rose in Davis's lapel. The band played "The Bonnie Blue Flag." The crowd cheered. Many of the women wept. For the first time Winnie realized to the full the intensity of feeling that surrounded her father's history. Because of her upbringing she had been less aware of it than many another Southern girl of her age.

Both fell ill on their return from Alabama. Winnie had picked up measles, and her father, aged seventy-eight and getting feeble, had acute bronchitis. Varina pictured herself going from one invalid to the other "to help whichever was in greatest need." She was greatly cheered by the "manifestations of love which Mr. Davis received on his journey, and if anything could make us love our people more we do so now," she wrote to Mrs. Octavus Cohen of Savannah on May 18, 1886.

After this the Daughter of the Confederacy began to move about freely in her own right. She was soon in Richmond staying with Governor Fitzhugh Lee. At Christmas she was in New York, visiting Bessie Martin Dew, young Jeff's former love, now married to a New York doctor. Varina was reproaching her for not visiting the Burton Harrisons. She had become immersed in a social round of teas and receptions, but Varina assured Connie that Winnie would much rather see the galleries and public buildings, attend the theater, and meet the artistic and literary set in which the Harrisons moved, and from whom she could "elicit by notes and queries enough to thoroughly formulate her opinions and aspirations." [2]

Winnie was good and wonderfully clever, Varina wrote. With rose-colored glasses she heightened the picture—"but not like the rest of the world and does not know that this mental difference separates her from most girls, and wonders why she feels lonely. She is so faithful, so delicately modest, and so conscientious, and withal has such a brilliant and responsive mind."

Apparently Winnie's trip alone to the North had been a matter of debate at Beauvoir. Varina was nervous about her because reporters now watched every move she made and "but for my knowledge of her discretion and well poised character I would summon her home at once." Apparently her father had been opposed to the trip and had given out "sybilline warnings" against it. When newspaper items came back to them Varina heard a "well-bred grumble" in which she could make out the words "your wishes were deferred to unfortunately." Winnie had fallen in with some people the Harrisons considered "seditionists."

But the Daughter of the Confederacy was having growing pains and was showing a mind of her own at this time. Varina had been urging her to pay more attention to her dress, but when she mentioned making over a half-worn gown into something more fashionable Winnie headed off "on the woes of the Irish, the labor question, or some system which she had been studying with intense interest." Varina continued in a revealing vein that she thought it good for Winnie to get away from Beauvoir, which seemed as "isolated as the Island of Elba." There her horizons were limited to "*curious* strangers, unreasoning devotees, and two discouraged failing old people." She hoped that her husband would let Winnie go to Bar Harbor with the Harrisons, but she could not be sure that he would.

It is needless to tell you, in confidence though it be, that Mr. Davis, who is, as you know, very old, dwells on the past. The shadow of the Confederacy grows heavier over him as years weigh his heart down and my child is the coming woman, not the woman of my day, still less of his. . . . You never will seem old to me and no more will Burton who I do dearly love, tell him, for the sake of our old times. . . .

In this same letter Varina commented on the death in the previous month of their old friend, Mary Boykin Chesnut, at Sarsfield, the home they had built after the war close to Mulberry, the scene of their former magnificence. Her husband had died in the previous year. She had been ill only two days and when she knew she was going to die she faced the fact in characteristic fashion, saying, "Then I must try to give my friends as little trouble as possible, and live as well as I can live to the end." Varina continued:

And so she did and died full of resignation and hope. My old friends are dropping off very fast, and infirmities are accumulating upon me so that my sixty years begin to be an acknowledged weariness and a trouble—but I most certainly do not want to die, and would see the world if I could, but only in an impersonal way—being merely a looker on. Do not let Burton work too hard—all our men live too fast—they do not grow old, hale and hearty, at least few do.

Three days later Varina wrote again to Connie, still worried because Winnie had not gone to visit her at Irving Place but assuring her that "Winnie's dignity is invincible, and she will go through better than another would less well intrenched." [3] For a cotton planter Mr. Davis was "abnormally cheerful," Varina added. "He has ceased to speculate on ruin as a contingency, and has relegated this trouble to the realm of the *fait accompli*." She felt less cheerful herself. "Nothing gives me much continuous joy and nothing ever has since I lost my good tender son," she finished, alluding to young Jeff.

The key to much of Winnie's independence and discontent at this time was the fact that she had fallen in love with a handsome young lawyer from Syracuse named Alfred Wilkinson. [4] Ironically enough, his maternal grandfather was the Rev. Samuel J. May, one of the leading abolitionists associated with Emerson, Lowell, Longfellow, and Garrison. His father, Alfred Wilkinson, a banker, had been appointed Revenue Collector for his district by Lincoln. Winnie had met him at the home of Dr. Thomas Emory, of Syracuse, son of General and Mrs. William H. Emory, her parents' old friends.

Winnie had a cool reception at some of the homes in Syracuse, and when Fred met her at the Emorys' home he championed her cause as a Confederate. They fell in love almost instantaneously. Winnie said nothing about it to her parents when she returned to Beauvoir, but a year later she visited the Emorys' home again and the romance blew stronger than ever. At this time Fred was in partnership with two other patent lawyers in Syracuse. His father's banking business had failed six years earlier.

Her secret romance with the grandson of a famous abolitionist posed a great many problems for the Daughter of the Confederacy, and her parents wakened only slowly to the fact of Winnie's being in love, and then to the depth and intensity of her feelings. On her return south she continued to correspond with Fred, while she sank back into the pattern of established life at Beauvoir and turned her attention to writing, to her painting and music, and to giving her father the close companionship he craved from her. But she soon began to pine. By the spring of 1888 she was in wretched health, and Varina wrote to General Early, expressing the hope that Winnie would spend a month with his family that summer and get built up. The general, an old friend of Jeff's from the days of the Mexican War, was now practicing law. He had refused to take the oath of allegiance.

There were few people to whom Varina could complain of the way in which she was tied down, but her bond with Jubal Early became close and confidential as Jeff aged and she felt she could discuss her husband's growing feebleness with him. Writing to him on her sixty-second birthday, May 8, 1888, she told the General that if she were in any strait "out of which a strong-hearted liberal sincere man could help me, you are the person of all the world to whom I would apply with an ever grateful sense of your willingness to serve me, and a profound confidence in your power, but the fact is I am contending with physical suffering and constant depression against heavy odds, and unless our dear Lord were here to bid my husband take up his bed and walk, no one can do much for me." [5]

Varina acknowledged at this point that Jeff was declining steadily, with occasional revivals for a few weeks, and she felt "powerless to do more than smooth his path." She believed that if she left him he would not live a month. When physical weakness detained her in town for two days he returned on the same night, got his feet wet, and had never been well a moment since. "He seems listless and exhausted all the time while he is in this condition," she added.

Varina's instincts about her beloved husband were not far astray at this time, for he was close to the end of his life and was failing gradually. He was most averse to leaving Beauvoir for any reason whatever—"and no matter how much I need change I must, as you know, stay where duty calls me," she wrote to General Early, regretfully declining an invitation for both of them to visit him. But two weeks later her spirits revived when Mississippi gave him a silver crown on his eightieth birthday. Davis was feeling much better and Varina wrote more cheerfully to General Early on May 23, 1888: "I do not know what is the matter with my head or with the world at large when Mr. Davis is ill, but I get so worried up I do not get anything right." [6]

He was unable to go to Jackson for the laying of the cornerstone of Mississippi's Confederate Monument, but Winnie represented him. Varina was anxious at this time for him to refrain from making any sort of speech until the presidential election was over. Grover Cleveland was running for the office. "If he goes to the stream, no matter how far down he may be, the wolf above him will swear he muddied the waters," she wrote to General Early. "He is too weak & excitable to make public addresses, and I deprecate his going in to such turmoil. . . . You are so much a man of business and action that I never feel as if I could do other than tire you with my country letters . . ." Varina finished, on a humble note.

However, a reporter from the New Orleans *Picayune* found few signs of the octogenarian in Jefferson Davis when he visited him to write a birthday story on his eightieth anniversary. He was "immaculately dressed, straight and erect, with the traces of his long military service still showing in his carriage, with his eighty years resting as lightly on his head as a silver crown and with the flush of health on his pale, refined face." [7] Davis showed keen interest in the topics of the day, political, religious, social. The reporter tried to break through his reserve—a difficult task. Varina was more accessible in this respect.

In his home life Mr. Davis is exceptionally fortunate. No Southerner but is proud to know the cultured, dignified mistress of Beauvoir as the best example of what Southern civilization has done for womanhood, and as for Miss Winnie, she is one to whom the tenderest and the heartiest toast is drunk at every reunion of veterans—"The Child of the Confederacy."

However, in spite of this fair picture of her husband, Varina still wrote despondently and probably more realistically to her friend and neighbor, Major William H. Morgan, about his condition. The Major was a planter and cotton statistician with the firm of Lehman and Stern in New Orleans. He had a house close to Beauvoir, and his daughter Belle was one of Varina's pets. Mrs. Morgan was an invalid and Varina sometimes took care of the child, to build her up and give her mother some rest. She dosed her with phosphates and Ducros elixir, a French preparation that had helped her husband on various occasions. Belle was attending a fashionable school conducted by the daughter of General Leonidas Polk. The Major leaned heavily on Varina for familial advice, and she sent him yeast, crabs, oysters, and other fare for his ailing wife. She shopped for them at the Christian Woman's Exchange in Biloxi.

With the balmy breezes "fretting my grey hairs into a fringe which impartially hangs as much in my eyes as on my head" Varina sat in the lounge on a hot June day writing to Major Morgan about the birthday celebration. Letters had reached her husband from many quarters, but the drawings of his grandchildren and the lemons sent by Milo Cooper, one of their former slaves, had pleased him most of all. Milo was now settled in Orlando, Florida, and from time to time sent plants, pineapples, and full-grown citrons to Beauvoir.

Varina's sense of desolation crept into this letter, too, and her realization of their place in the social structure.

. . . and altogether he did not suffer from the sense of having no place among the "men that be." It is a frightful thing to drop out of one's place and never find it again. I try very hard to keep my memory green and thus by sympathy live anew, or if not anew, aright, which is more to the point, much more. People come and go as usual, stay and go out of my life with pleasant & very few with bitter memories.[8]

But the Davises had not been forgotten by the outside world, and Varina received a letter that summer that brought the drawing rooms of Europe close to Beauvoir. It came from General John M. Read, a cousin, who was making up the family genealogical tree and wanted her aid. He had homes at Fontainebleau and on the Champs-Elysées and belonged to the fashionable set in Paris. He had been dining with Mrs. Joseph Pulitzer, "who looked bewitching in a most becoming dinner dress" and they had discussed Varina and her husband.

After dinner Mr. Pulitzer took me aside in the smoking room and spoke of you in terms which delighted me for they responded to my own feelings. He then related many interesting characteristics of Mr. Davis which made me wish to sit down in your hospitable home and have a long talk with him. He and myself would agree to disagree about the war—and then I would proceed to draw upon the treasures of his rich experience. . . . Mr. Pulitzer told me the other evening that your letters in his estimation should be placed in the highest rank. He valued them more than any in his possession.[9]

Mrs. Pulitzer was Kate Davis, a distant cousin of Jefferson Davis. Winnie had been visiting them in New York and they were fond of her. Varina was much relieved to have her daughter join the Jubal Earlys at a Virginia spa that summer, with her cousin, Mary Stamps, of New Orleans. She wrote to the General on August 6, 1888, that she felt perfectly at ease about Winnie when she was with him "in dear blessed old Virginia 'where duty is pleasure and love is law.' " [10] But there was no hope of getting Jeff to join them, much as Varina longed to go. "He thinks this place the best for him, & sink or swim the catastrophe must be here." He now disliked going in to New Orleans, even for a day, and was happiest sitting on the porch, looking out to sea.

But no sooner had Winnie returned from Virginia than Fred Wilkinson arrived at Beauvoir to ask for her hand in marriage. This was a sensational event in Varina's life, for it was her first glimpse of the man over whom her daughter had been pining. Since he was a Northerner she did not know how her husband would stand the shock of this encounter. Varina had not realized how committed Winnie was to Wilkinson, for she had cherished her romance in secret. But her mother was quite bowled over when he walked into the house, displaying the "most splendid manners." He was six feet tall, with dark eyes and good features. Varina quickly appraised him—"not enough nose, but enough chin—is lithe and energetic, & has fine teeth & small feet and hands, & as tender and boyish a heart as I ever saw & a very good mind as well as exquisite manners," she wrote to Major Morgan.[11]

This letter, like many more of Varina's that have survived, was marked "Private, please burn when read." Better than anything else it illumines the Davis parental approach to Fred and, in particular, to Winnie's future.

He came having announced he could no longer be put off—he looked like an undertaker just announcing an impending commencement of "the procession," but also like a handsome gallant young gentleman faultlessly dressed, and very refined in manner, but evidently dreadfully depressed & urgently anxious. I determined my consent never should be given to union with a Yankee—he urged the condition of health into which she had fallen, his great love—his patient waiting & forlorn hope & wound up with— "Of course, we being young can recover from the refusal, but only in years hence & with our lives broken and with a wretched substitute for the first love of each. . . ."

Fred was nearly thirty at the time. Varina listened, "purporting to be a stern parent." Meanwhile, Winnie had gone to her room "white as death, after first saying she could never love any one else, but would give him up if I wished it." At this point Varina, who had known of Winnie's love but not of its intensity, realized that she had been in a "fool's paradise." Now she saw things more clearly. Continuing the story in her letter she wrote:

When I looked at this refined well born Yankee, full of energy, spirit, and love for her, I felt for her, and decided that we had given all to the Confederacy but I could not surrender my ewe lamb upon an altar, the fires of which were not now fed by my countrymen with such rich gifts. She is a shadow of her former self—thin to attenuation & so weak a little drive tires her. Dinner & breakfast sometimes both go untasted & she looked to me to be going into a low fever.

When Varina finally broke the news of Fred's arrival to Jefferson Davis he exclaimed at once, "Death would be preferable," and added, "I will never consent." She thought he looked "quite cool and resolved" as he made these observations, but after she had brought them together things went surprisingly well. Fred stated his case and "so delicate is the essence of a cultivated, fine young creature like that," Varina wrote with a relief, "that the conversation turned quite paternal."

Fred had won Jefferson Davis's attention, if not his total approval, or else the laird of Beauvoir was being a courteous host. They could not doubt that his love for Winnie was great, and both parents had seen her drooping in the most wretched way. After the initial meeting Varina drove off in her phaeton to leave them alone together. When she returned she was astonished to find them in friendly conversation. Next day her husband invited Fred to go with him to Brierfield in October, and a day later he took him down to the bathhouse to watch the flounders, "a liberty never accorded to any other young man as the bathhouse had been prohibited at night."

Winnie was enchanted. "She is like one out of prison," her mother wrote. And each day he was there Varina thought better of him. On his first evening at Beauvoir when Bettie—the little maid from the hills whom Varina had brought in to train and now treated as a member of the family—expressed the hope that he would sleep well, he jumped to his feet and "made a dudish bow as this generation of vipers do, saying 'thanks very much'—which was repeated every night as long as he stayed." Varina liked this and found his "simple honesty and directness of purpose refreshing in those days." She decided that she had never seen anything more "unsophisticated than his devotion to Winnie," unless it was Winnie's adoration of Fred.

In the Victorian fashion Varina made careful soundings about his material prospects. He had come to Beauvoir assuming he was getting a portionless bride, she wrote, but she assured him that if she and her husband could get out of debt, there would be something left for Winnie. He made light of this and said he had life insurance and hoped to be able to settle a home on her within two years. Varina told him that Winnie had had little experience in saving and economizing, but Fred assured her, as they discussed these practical matters, that he had spent two thousand dollars a year at Harvard when his father was ill and still had managed to keep his mother and sisters in "comfort and ladylike ease" by doing outside work, and "is it likely that I would reduce this love of my life to such a squalid grind?" he asked Varina. "I can maintain her in comfort—& she & you must believe me for my life's sake."

Fred's family had been well off but had lost much of their money. At this time he told Varina that his mother had just recovered eighty thousand dollars in a lawsuit, and that this left him free to seek his own happiness.[12] But in the long run this became one of several factors that helped to break up Winnie's romance. Fred's family felt that Varina was the dominant figure in its collapse.[13] His sister was bitter. But the letters in the Library of Congress that passed between Varina and Fred, and Varina and Major Morgan, do not suggest that she was wholly the culprit, although they show that she thought he had not been frank about his family's financial affairs. Winnie's excessively sensitive spirit, her poor health, press criticism of her in the South for her romance with a Yankee, her father's death, all entered into the situation.

There is no doubt that Varina was concerned for Winnie's material well-being at this time. She had long hoped for an alliance with one of the well-off young men of New Orleans, but although Winnie had had various beaux her love for Fred was tenacious and made her indifferent to other suitors. It became a long tug-of-war, but, after Fred's visit to Beauvoir, Winnie was momentarily happy. He left her in a cheerful frame of mind, and wrote to her later: "Never mind, I have done very well to get tolerated inside the house. The rest will come. I am a States Rights Democrat & had nothing to do with the war, & he must see that I could not help being born a Yankee." [14]

In the weeks that followed Winnie softened her father. He could not bear to see her so thin, nervous, and anxious. There was deep sympathy between them, and as they walked along the beach, they talked of Fred, and by degrees she wore down his resistance. Then one day she galloped happily to the Hayward home wearing a green habit, with a long plume dangling to her shoulders. Her eyes were sea-gray that day, and little Marguerite Hayward could recall nearly seventy years later how lovely she looked and how proud she sounded when she announced her engagement to Fred.[15] The news was not made public at this time, however, but Winnie wilted gradually when she realized how unpopular her choice was among their more intimate friends in the South. Threatening letters came to their home. All the worry and excitement had worn her down, and in the autumn of 1889 she sailed for Europe in a state bordering on collapse. She was plagued by indecision about the course she should follow. Early in December the news reached her that her father was dead. This was the final blow for Winnie and she had a severe nervous breakdown.

For Varina the close association of forty-four years was at an end, and the great grief of her life was upon her, although she had slowly accustomed herself to the thought that her husband's life was fading away. In November he had gone up the river to Brierfield to collect the annual rents. He became so ill on the boat that he decided to go on to Vicksburg instead of getting off at his plantation. But next day he revived and returned, driving through a chill autumnal rain from the landing to Brierfield. He developed the acute form of bronchitis to which he was subject and developed a high fever. But he got up, dressed, and kept in motion until he had boarded the familiar *Leathers*, bound for home. Meanwhile, Varina had been notified that he was seriously ill. She set off on the *Laura Lee* to join him at Brierfield, but they met his boat below Natchez and she boarded it.

As soon as she saw her husband, she realized that he was "as low as could be," she confessed to Major Morgan in a letter written on November 30, 1889.[16] But he seemed to revive when he saw her. At Bayou Sara, which was associated forever in her mind with Knox Taylor, two doctors who had been summoned by telegraph diagnosed his illness as acute bronchitis, complicated by malaria. Varina "got ahead of the disease a little by an expectorant and calomel."

Dr. Stanford E. Chaillé, of New Orleans, and Judge J. U. Payne, his close friend and business agent, met them at the dock. "It was a cold spitting rain and Mr. D. was struggling for breath like a dying man," Varina wrote to Morgan. They got an ambulance from the Charity Hospital, and he was taken to the stately pillared home in New Orleans which today is owned by Mr. and Mrs. F. G. Strachan. It was built by Judge Payne and was occupied at the time by his son-in-law, Judge Charles Erasmus Fenner, a close friend of the Davises. Its wide front galleries extended across both floors, supported by six columns of Ionic design. Camellia bushes and orange trees grew in the lovely grounds, but Varina was much too anxious to take note of anything but the high-ceilinged room on the ground floor where her husband lay fighting for his life.

At first she thought there was hope for him. His doctors were optimistic as they gave him cordials and quinine. "I do not ignore his danger but I see many reasons for hopeful expectation," Varina wrote. In the midst of her own distress she gave thought to Mrs. Morgan, whose hours were numbered, too. In this letter she suggested the "hydrogen treatment" but ended: "You and I are in a condition now to know how little anything avails to help us when the hand of disease is laid upon our heartstrings."

Varina wanted to send for her daughters but Jefferson gently observed, "Let our darlings be happy while they can; I may get well." Margaret, reading the news in the papers, set off at once, but was delayed by a train mishap and did not arrive before her father died. Addison got up from a sickbed to accompany her. Winnie was kept in ignorance of his condition until his death, and by her father's request she was forbidden to return, "as she was then pronounced by her physician too feeble for the journey," Varina wrote.[17]

He lingered for days, with his wife constantly at his side. In a gray and black wrapper, she moved about his bed, giving him his medicine, holding his hand in hers by the hour, comforting him in his conscious moments. If she left him, he grew restless and moved uneasily until she returned to his side. He rallied several times, and on December 6 was considered convalescent. He woke at daylight and found Varina sitting beside him, as she had so often done in the long watches of his sleepless nights. "I want to tell you I am not afraid to die," he said. At another time he told her, "I have much to do, but if it is God's will, I must submit." [18]

She begged him not to speak of so dreadful a contingency, and he smiled and fell asleep. In the hours before his death he seemed to improve. Word got out to the watching public that he was free from fever and his appetite was better. Dr. C. J. Bickham felt quite hopeful about him. In the late afternoon Varina sent an encouraging message to his niece, Mary Stamps, and her daughter, Mrs. E. H. Farrar, who had been helping to nurse him, and they decided to go to the opera that night. They were called home later when the crisis came.

At six o'clock he was seized with a "violent congestive chill." Two hours later Varina tried to give him the medicine the doctors had prescribed. He took a little, but it sickened him and he weakly waved it away. Varina persisted and told him he must get it down. With the unfailing courtesy that always marked his manner to her, as to others, he said, "Pray excuse me" and turned away.[19] These were his last words. After that he lapsed slowly into unconsciousness and, as he slipped away, a gentle pressure on her hand was the only answer he could give to Varina's tearful inquiries.

Just before one o'clock in the morning he died so quietly that no one quite realized when the moment came. Varina gave one stricken cry and was led away by one of the doctors who quickly gave her a sedative, for there was apprehension about her heart condition. But she showed strength when she wakened and was able to see some friends and to discuss the funeral arrangements. Few knew until they had seen the morning papers that the head of the Confederate States was dead at the age of eighty-one.

Varina went through the next few days in a daze, as telegrams poured in from governors, statesmen, soldiers, and old friends far and near. Flags hung at half-mast in the South, but since Jefferson Davis was not a citizen of the United States, no official notice was taken in Washington of his death. But a group of Southerners, including L. Q. C. Lamar, Senator Walthall, and Senator George, met in the capital and wired to Varina "that the historian of after years, looking down the perspective of the past, will see Jefferson Davis the colossal figure of his times, and do justice to the virtues which so deeply fixed him in our hearts."

The Mayor of New Orleans issued a proclamation, and Varina consented to a public funeral and to temporary burial in Metairie Cemetery. She stipulated that her husband's body "should be removed quietly and unostentatiously from the Payne residence between ten and twelve" at night to lie in state, but until that hour "she desired to have her dead to herself." Her husband was dressed in the familiar Confederate gray. Flowers were massed around his bier. The high-ceilinged room was filled with shadows, and Varina's tears flowed without restraint in the last hours with her beloved.

Milo Cooper had hurried from Florida to attend his funeral, and when he arrived she saw to it that he was admitted to the death chamber. He fell on his knees and prayed. Thousands streamed past the catafalque in the Council Chamber of City Hall. The Confederate flag covered the coffin, which was topped with the sword he wore in the Mexican War and with flowers from Beauvoir.[20] The funeral was held on December 11, a bright and balmy day although it was close to Christmas. There were generals, Senators, judges, bishops, governors, in the procession, but it was noted that General Beauregard was not among them.

General Joseph Johnston was still alive, and by this time was United States Commissioner of Railroads, but there was no communication between the two households. Lydia had died in 1887 after forty years of marriage. Her husband worshiped her memory as he had worshiped her when she was alive. He kept their home always exactly as she had left it.

All over town church bells tolled, and the sound of muffled drums, which had haunted her for years, was heard again by Varina, this time with the strongest personal impact. People had poured in from distant points, and the streets were jammed with horsemen, carriages, and pedestrians, as when Jefferson Davis returned from the Mexican War. All the military organizations of the Confederate States were represented in the long procession to the cemetery, and again brilliant uniforms and white shakos were in view. The entire city seemed to be veiled in crepe and all business was suspended. It took an hour and a half for the procession to pass a given point.

Varina, who always found strength to meet an emergency, sat white-faced and tearless in the carriage. She rode with Judge Payne, her daughter Margaret, and her nephew, General Joseph R. Davis. Margaret fainted twice during the funeral drive, but Varina kept her frozen self-control, even when the piercing notes of "Taps" made others weep. She held herself in check until all the ceremonies were over. Then she gave way.

In the weeks that followed she was deluged with messages and letters from all parts of the world. The North and South now appraised Jefferson Davis as he stood in historical perspective, a quarter of a century after the war in which he was a central figure. With sadness and some skepticism she read what was said of him now that he was gone. Few historical figures had been so vilified. She read, clipped, and filed the editorials in her methodical way, dwelling with pleasure on the tributes paid her husband by the British press. But for her the most significant comment appeared in the New York *World*. "While the public life of Mr. Davis was in many respects one long storm, his private one was full of peace and sunshine. Than he few men have been happier in their domestic relation. . . . He was proud, sensitive and honorable in all his dealings and in every relation of life." [21]

Varina would be the first to say Amen to that.

❦ 21 ❧

DAUGHTER OF THE CONFEDERACY

O N A RAINY February night in 1890 when the sea lashed against the shore and the wind roared around Beauvoir, Varina got up after sleepless hours and wrote revealingly to Major Morgan. She was still fresh to the sorrow of her widowhood and could find neither peace nor rest. For the time being she felt cut off from life, old, unwanted, finished, and her vigorous nature could not accept this negation.

I lie night after night next my Husband's room into which an uneasy turning in his bed or a light sign would summon me at any hour of the night & long to be called & know my life is over, that no one remembers me with any charm or grace & that I am a lame old weary woman to every living soul. The testimonies of my youth are hidden in death, & I with capacity for many things have fallen into desuetude forever—I feel like an executed person swinging in chains on a lonely road—I ought not to tell you this, but it is true.[1]

Varina had returned to Beauvoir with a great sense of emptiness. Morgan had recently lost his wife, too, but she reminded him now that he was young enough to harbor hope. He had a "future and a theater of action." She was "old and infirm." Her widowhood weighed heavily on Varina. She wrote of it to Grace King, the Louisiana author who was an old friend of hers. "After the consummation of my great sorrow and long parting . . . the only thing I could do not to die or give way in an unbecoming manner was to steel myself against memory & forecast and be still." [2]

Varina received so many thousands of letters of sympathy that it was impossible for her to answer more than a fraction, but among those that particularly touched her was one from Thornton Montgomery, who wrote from North Dakota on December 7: "Would that I could help you bear the burden that is yours today. Since I am powerless to do so, I beg that you accept my tenderest sympathy and condolence." [3]

And on January 12 the old servants and tenants of Brierfield, Elija and Gus, Ned and Grant, Mary and William, Teddy and Laura, Tom and Mary, Isabel, Henry, William "and others" signed a note of sympathy, saying that they had "cause to mingle our tears over his death, who was always so kind and thoughtful of our peace and happiness." [4]

Wartime memories were revived in many of the letters she received. On Christmas Day, 1890, immediately after her husband's death, she wrote affectionately to Mary Day Burchenal, then living in Fairlee, Vermont, and recalled their friendly relations at Fortress Monroe. "I cannot realize that there is nothing left for me to do personally for him," she wrote, at the same time giving the final picture of her husband as she saw him.

Mr. Davis never lost his handsome figure, never stooped, never grew bald; his voice never changed nor did the elasticity of his step become heavy. He gained enough flesh to make him look like a well-preserved man of sixty. He grew more and more tender and gentle, was the only change I saw. But my loss is too new for me to count it now.[5]

As she mustered strength, instead of sterile brooding, Varina threw herself wholeheartedly into the task of writing her *Memoir* of her husband, an extension of the autobiography that he had already begun. Immediately after Christmas she invited Redpath to Beauvoir to look over the letters and papers she had arranged. "I am trying to get through my letters before you come, but am ready to try a beginning whenever you can come here," she wrote. "I am worried *out of heart by many things* but everything is so small beside the great woe that I do not dwell on the small troubles." [6]

Nannie Davis Smith, a great-niece of Mr. Davis, who had been living with them for some time and had helped her to nurse her husband at the end, now did secretarial work for Varina. Years later, when she was a slight, withered little figure living at Baton Rouge and poring over her papers with a powerful magnifying glass, Nannie recalled Varina's ardor for her task at this time. She would be sound asleep when Mrs. Davis would call to her in the night, "Wake up, Nannie; I've thought of something else." [7] Nannie would get up, light her lamp, and write as Varina dictated. Miss Smith had many memories of the

Davis family. She lived until 1938 and was buried beside Knox Taylor. This work entailed a fresh network of correspondence, of rounding up records, and checking facts. It was a repetition of what she had gone through with her husband's book, except that she was covering a broader period of time, and was writing a more human narrative, injecting a great deal more of the personal into it. She was aided in her work not only by Redpath, who had collaborated with her husband, but also by John Dimitry, son of the popular Professor Alexander Dimitry, of New Orleans.

While she threw out nets for fresh material, and kept close track of every move made by her collaborators, she had other and pressing worries. Her financial affairs were muddled and she was almost instantly threatened with material troubles after her husband's death. Brierfield was heavily entailed. She was so pressed for ready cash that she quickly sold her big carriage for forty dollars, keeping only her phaeton. The estate left by her husband was encumbered. His book had been a financial failure. Her income was small and depended almost entirely on returns from the plantation. She leaned heavily on Major Morgan for business advice at this time. "Our friendship has grown like Jonah's gourd, and now it shelters me & mine. I trust it will deserve to be withered by God's frown only when betrayal shall have rendered it unfruitful," she wrote.

On March 9 she called herself an "incompetent old woman" in a letter to Judge A. McL. Kimbrough, a prominent lawyer living in Greenwood, Mississippi, who had taken hold of her business affairs.[8] A group of her husband's friends had been trying to push through the sale of some land he owned in Arkansas to meet the liabilities of Brierfield. She was so confused about stock payments that she wrote she would obey him literally "and try to acquit herself well." Her transactions with the Belford Company, which planned to bring out her husband's *Brief History of the Confederate States of America* for school use that year, were cloudy too, and the competent Varina was finding it difficult to get her bearings with her husband gone.

There were heavy rains that spring. The north wind blew continuously. She feared for the planters on the bottoms and understood now why her husband had always been so weather-conscious. "*Dear me, I am so tired & so miserable,*" she wrote to Judge Kimbrough. "I seem to be making arrangements of a hurried kind for my taking off & am possessed all the while with a sense of coming dissolution."

Varina's anxiety about Winnie by this time had become so intense that she urged Fred Wilkinson to go abroad and see her. He readily agreed, and as he left she wrote to Major Morgan: "Youth is needful to prevent one from dying outright in the nervous state in which he is." Fred found Winnie a sick and tortured girl, much more broken down than he had expected. Her father's death had cast fresh uncertainties over their romance. All the panoply surrounding the funeral, the spotlight playing on her family again, the revived memories of the part they had played in the nation's history, were too much for her, even though she was far from the scene. Winnie's long period of depression had ended in a severe collapse, in which her love for her family, her loyalty to the Confederate cause, and her sensitive conscience, all were involved. Her own state of tension was such that Fred could scarcely handle the situation when he joined her in Naples. She no longer knew if she wished to marry him, although Varina was urging her to take this step.

She was staying with the Pulitzers at the Grand Hotel, and their yacht was in the harbor. Kate Pulitzer, who was devoted to Winnie, was sympathetic to her romance with Fred and tried to help her in every way she could. Fred stayed with them at the Grand Hotel and reported at once to Varina on Winnie's condition. He thought she should stay in Europe all summer but he would await the doctor's verdict in the matter. Varina suffered as she read his frank comment on her daughter's state.

Physically she is decidedly better but mentally she has some very depressed days—almost anyone else I should call morbid but it would be unjust to apply that word to her. She feels some days almost as though her heart were broken & looks forward to the future with little hope—& perhaps you will see from her letters better than from mine, how it is only a pain to talk to her of marriage or anything of the sort.[9]

Fred warned Varina not to mention their engagement when she wrote to Winnie. Mrs. Pulitzer was "kindness itself and she thought Winnie had improved greatly since coming to Italy." He was grateful to her for treating his fiancée "in the best & most sensible way, giving the care almost of a mother." He urged Varina to send her some good news, such as word that her newly published novel was selling well, "for she tortures almost everything into a cause for worry."

A week later Winnie wrote both to her mother[10] and to Major

Morgan, who was greatly interested in her romance with Fred. Joseph Pulitzer had been ordered by his doctor not to leave Naples, although the noise of cannon being tested in the Bay was driving him wild. Always abnormally sensitive to noise of any kind, he was trying for the second time to prevail on the Italian Minister of War to have it stopped on his behalf.

Winnie jested lightly that Fred, "as dear an old goose as ever," was watching what she wrote. The weather had been frightful and Kate would not let her go out. The water was dashing up against the sea wall "in such foaming masses that it reminds me of Undine's Uncle and even in here you can hear the sound of the waves like the report of great guns." Kate had been bilious but had recovered and "was looking as fresh as a rose this morning in her beautiful pink morning gown of brocade and crepe." Winnie ended her letter on an affectionate note, "Good-bye, dearest, do write, Devotedly, Varina Anne Davis."

At the same time Winnie wrote to Major Morgan saying she wished her mother had let her go back earlier, since now she would have to travel with "some unknown lady" for a chaperone. Everything depended, however, "on what mother wishes . . . as for myself I have very little joy in anything and would just as soon do her way as any." [11]

Again Fred wrote to Varina, this time disclosing that only now did he realize "how critical has been her condition." He thought it would take at least six months more, and probably "a year of care & tender thought to spare her in every way before we can say she is pretty well— but after that, I believe a few quiet happy years will make her as well as ever she was." [12] Fred wrote very seriously to Varina now. Because of Winnie's condition they had not been able to see Naples properly. They had managed Pompeii and hoped to get up Vesuvius. She was keeping a diary, which pleased Fred, since she showed so little interest in anything. They would be going on to Rome within the next few days, then would go to Florence and stay there until Mr. Pulitzer recovered. Fred expected "to say goodbye there to our girl, & see you soon after." He signed himself "Ever with more love, Your affectionate son, Fred Wilkinson." But Varina was angry now and scrawled a sharp comment across this letter: "Now the devil was sick the devil a saint would be." Obviously the romance was not flourishing on either side of the Atlantic, and Varina was disappointed that Winnie was showing such reluctance to come to terms with Fred.

That same day Fred wrote to Major Morgan that he wished he had come over earlier, since he believed his visit had done Winnie "an immense deal of good." [13] Mr. Pulitzer thought so, too. The bewildered Fred continued:

> She has depressed days of course but I hope they will be fewer & fewer, & when you have time do pray write her an occasional letter. You know she longs all the time to have her friends love her. She is in no condition however to hear about marrying or even having her engagement announced —so those things must just be *not* spoken of for months—I shall let her wait as long as she wishes.

Winnie had her father's overwrought temperament and suffered extremely under stress. None of these letters mentions the circumstance that must have loomed large in her mind at this time—the fact that Jefferson Davis was dead. Varina wrote to Grace King that she had tried "with might and main" to keep Winnie from coming home at that time.

Four days later Fred wrote again to Varina, and this time she scribbled another biting comment on the letter: "I laughed heartily over *this* letter." His earlier urgency had now changed to caution.[14] He was so alarmed by Winnie's condition that he suggested Varina herself come over and get her. He had changed his mind about her spending the summer in Europe. She should be brought home one way or another and it would be cruel to talk of marriage before the following winter. Fred was beginning to see the hopelessness of what he was up against.

> I understand how she feels so I shall say nothing more of that but shall do my best to take good care of her & save her every bit of worry between now & then. I understand better & better every day how sick she has been & what a state she is still in. The least little thing starts her off—for instance yesterday she asked me a question about my business & because I hesitated a few seconds before answering she thought I was trying to deceive her! Of course it took an hour to quiet her.

After receiving their letters from Europe Varina sent one of her hasty undated notes to her neighbor, Major Morgan, saying: "Well, Winnie & Fred are all right. Fred says he cannot under the circumstances think of urging her to marry until January, which means he has got a half way promise—he is coming home in three weeks & will come here at once & I hope you can see him. Burn all these letters at once after you read them." [15]

On Fred's return in April she formally announced their engagement. The newspaper reaction was sharp. In Syracuse Fred's abolitionist background was recalled and the story was treated for its dramatic values—the Daughter of the Confederacy engaged to the grandson of Samuel May. Varina and Winnie both were deeply troubled by the reaction in the South. On April 20 Varina wrote to General Early, giving a detailed account of Winnie's romance and saying that when Winnie met Fred four years earlier she thought "absence would efface the impression." [16] Her husband was bitterly opposed to the union at first, she said, and Winnie "was entirely submissive to our will on the subject, but her health gave way under the strain." Then Fred visited them and won him over.

. . . to my astonishment Mr. Davis became so mollified that he talked to him like one of our own people & invited him to come again to visit us which he did & my Husband seemed entirely reconciled & considered it a matter of course. Mr. Wilkinson was only six years old when the war began & neither knows or cares anything about it but sympathizes with our people as he is a States Rights Democrat as his grandfather, Judge Wilkinson, and his Father were before him.

Varina added that he was a graduate of Harvard, was "refined, handsome & as genuine a good hearted young fellow" as she had ever known. His income was five to six thousand dollars a year, and he could give Winnie every comfort. "Winnie had nothing but her fine character and herself to give him," she added. She hoped the wedding was a long way off, but she could not bear that anyone should know more of their family affairs than he, "our dear generous & faithful friend." Neither Winnie nor she would be happy about it if he disapproved, Varina concluded.

It would seem from this letter that Jefferson Davis had given his full consent to Winnie's marriage and that Varina now approved it, but in the next few months the situation went from bad to worse. Winnie's nervous condition and her indecision on her return from Europe in midsummer kept Fred in a state of uncertainty. In July his mother's "palace of a house was burned down . . . with the collections of generations of statuary and paintings of the finest possible kind and Fred and his brother came near being burned alive as their old servant was in fact," Varina wrote. Winnie's distress and reluctance were so marked by this time that in August her mother made a formal announcement to the press: "The marriage of Mr. Alfred Wilkinson, of Syracuse, and Miss Winnie Davis, daughter of Jefferson Davis, has been postponed until June 25, 1891, Miss Davis not desiring to be married until after a year of the date of her father's death."

After his mother's house burned down Fred learned to his chagrin that a prominent Mississippian had arrived in Syracuse to check on his financial and social standing, his ability as a young attorney, and his prospects. The failure of the banking house of Wilkinson and Company was closely investigated, and the visitor wished to know how much of the debt had been paid, and how the family had been supported since the collapse of their business.

Fred wrote angrily to Varina at this point, but she was not pleased with what she had learned, either. Fred was summoned to Beauvoir to explain why he had "written wildly" to her after Varina had dug up some old family scandal. He arrived "looking like a criminal and sat expecting sentence evidently." She asked him why he had written in so intemperate a fashion, and he defended himself and said that he had been quite frank about his family affairs when Varina accused him of concealing some of his family history.

When the interview was over the end had come for Winnie and Fred. Varina dashed off a hastily penciled card to Major Morgan, saying: "All is better than I expected. He behaved gently & tenderly & acquiesced quietly but with evident deep grief. I feel heartbroken about the whole matter & so is W."

She wrote to the Major in more detail on October 5, 1890, describing the difficult scene that had just taken place at Beauvoir. Fred insisted that he had laid bare his family condition to her.

He then said that he thought he had told me all about his Father, denied that he managed a bucket shop & oh me I felt wretched for him. I said, my poor boy, frankness is the only policy in life that succeeds if it is to be a family connection. I then told him I loved him & grieved over the sorrow to him. I found he had not maintained his mother, had nothing but his small salary & this year could not possibly have supported Winnie. . . . He did not want to see her, but she came out & after they had a very long & affecting conversation he went off on the 4 o'clock train looking about the same as he did when he came. She suffered dreadfully for awhile but is now cheery & eats more. He has written to her since a farewell letter in which he said he would never give her up. The correspondence has stopped however, & thank God it is over.[17]

On October 14, 1890, the *New York Times* quoted Fred as admitting that the engagement was broken. Various reasons were given for the rupture—Mr. Wilkinson's financial standing, Miss Davis's health, and the opposition of prominent Southern families. All Fred would say was that his fiancée's health had been poor for some time. She was little better on her return from Europe and "but a few weeks ago she expressed the wish of both herself and her estimable mother that the engagement cease." [18] Varina's public explanation was that the engagement was broken because of Winnie's ill health.

She was blamed quite generally for the collapse of her daughter's romance, but many other elements entered into the situation. Winnie had suffered acutely during the years she was concealing her love for Fred, and her health had broken down by the time her parents accepted the situation. She was extraordinarily sensitive to the opinion of her Southern friends, and her father's death made her situation seem unendurable for the time being. On top of this, her mother's anxiety for her to marry someone who could support her, and Varina's doubts about Fred's financial standing, cast a deep shadow over her relations with him. They had been desperately in love, and he was utterly bewildered by the doubts and fears that beset Winnie. Her mother's inquiries after the Wilkinson home burned down raised fresh doubts in the minds of both mother and daughter, and the curtain fell quickly after that.

All through the 1890's Winnie and Fred lived in New York, but there is no record that they ever met again, except once at the Pulitzers'. As she walked through the snowy park in her winter furs, or drove through the gaslit streets to the theater with Varina, she was sometimes pointed out as the Daughter of the Confederacy, the girl with the ill-starred romance who had fitted into the Victorian pattern of submission. Fred prospered in the world of patent law. He never married. Neither did Winnie. But his sorrowful face was noticed at the back of the church on the day of her funeral.

All through the summer, while Winnie's romance was heading for the rocks, Varina was working with some degree of desperation on her *Memoir*. She had to revise it three times for purposes of condensation. By the time her ailing daughter returned from Europe the manuscript was "all in a snarl," but Winnie was still too despondent to help her. Varina not only exhausted herself but she wore out her collaborators. Both Redpath and Dimitry found her exacting and fanatically industrious at her task. As he was about to leave Beauvoir,

Redpath wrote to Dimitry that he had not had a ten-minute recess to himself, as "Mrs. Davis has been at work herself and kept me at work, from morning to night." [19] She was taking a much more active part in the work than he had expected. "In fact, she works longer than, I fear, is good for her and certainly longer than I like. But she is so nervous and anxious about the book that of the two evils she has probably chosen the least." She had revised her collaborators' work sentence by sentence and "in most cases verified or modified or amplified our work at New Orleans." By the end of August, Redpath was "tired of the lonely drudgery," and Winnie walked into the study one day to find her mother in a dead faint from exhaustion.

Varina was deeply disturbed at this time by the publication in the New York *Sun* of extracts from letters purporting to be from her husband to Colonel Lucius Bellinger Northrop, his much criticized Commissary Department chief.[20] They were put into circulation by Eugene L. Didier, the newspaperman who had married Louise, the Colonel's daughter. The widow of Jefferson Davis felt that this was betrayal of trust.

The disputed correspondence quite frankly expressed the former President's opinion of Beauregard and Johnston, and accused them of "undermining the administration, electioneering with their troops and making a record for themselves." [21] One stated matters rather bluntly. "There can be no doubt of the venom of J. E. Johnston, Beauregard and his tool Jordan, and I have none of their conspiracy against me personally and officially, from an early period of the war, the misfortune is that it was not then discovered. . . ."

Another crisp opinion expressed by Davis was that "there never was so much credit given where so little was due, as in the case of Beauregard at Charleston."

In July she wrote to the General, demanding an explanation. She wished to know why letters "written with the freedom and intimacy of a 'brother' " [22] were published without giving her, the Davis literary executrix, the opportunity to express her opinion. On August 17, 1890, Louise Didier wrote to Varina from Baltimore that her husband had made the letters public "because they were a justification of Northrop's management of the Confederate Commissary Dept." [23] She felt that her father had been "treated so unjustly."

Varina became angrier still when she learned that the letters were up for sale. She now questioned their authenticity and, as her husband's amanuensis at the time, had no memory of "such epithets being applied to General Johnston" as appeared in the published letters. But Didier insisted that they were exact copies of the Davis letters. Varina sent several emissaries to Colonel Northrop, who had had a stroke and was living with his daughter in Baltimore.

Her first mediator was Thomas Lafayette Rosser of Charlottesville. She asked him to check the published copies against the originals.[24] He reported back that he thought them genuine and that he would dislike "to hear anyone apologize for anything the President might [have] written."[25] Varina promptly sent her old friend, Bradley T. Johnson, to interview the Colonel, giving him a personal letter to deliver in which she asked Northrop to withdraw them and "stop this shameful betrayal of trust."[26] She was not sure that her messages were reaching the ailing Colonel. In her accompanying letter to General Johnson she wrote:

> I am exceedingly anxious to get the letters, and would give a large amount of money for them if I had it rather than have this wretched penny a liner Didier hawking them about to magazines and newspapers as a "friend." What can I do? Will you if Genl. Northrop does not withdraw them see what they ask for them and if it is not over $500 buy them for me. Or take any legal remedy possible.[27]

But five days later General Johnson, having paid his visit and found himself in an impasse, wrote that he feared he could not stop the sale and publication of the letters, although he would exhaust all legal means to do so.[28]

Noting that Varina was heading into trouble, Jubal Early wrote to her, urgently suggesting that she omit from her book all references to the unpleasant relations that existed between Jefferson and General Joe Johnston or any other officer, since her husband had given his own views in his book.[29] He hoped she would not misunderstand his motives in writing. No one could have a higher veneration for her husband than he, the General assured her. Varina was unable to abide wholly by this advice, but she softened many angles along the way and the book shows little rancour.

Winnie was now a lonely figure, wandering along the beach without her father by her side. She missed him keenly in their old setting, and her final farewell to Fred that autumn further deepened her melancholy. Soon after their breakup Varina left for New York to correct her proofs and consult with her publishers. She left Winnie at Beauvoir. "She hardly gets her boxes unpacked on the Gulf coast before the climate makes her ill," Varina confided to Connie Harrison.

In October, Winnie was asked to represent Mississippi at the World's Fair, but she felt she might be a contentious figure and declined the honor. Her experience with Fred had made her doubly sensitive to the implications of her ancestry. "The things which would not be said to another Southern woman, would be said to me in a representative position and people who almost anybody else might meet on a neutral footing, it would be impossible for me to speak to," Winnie wrote to Major Morgan from Beauvoir on November 3, 1890. "I am too vulnerable to place myself in a position to be at once the source, and victim of contention." [30]

The Davises were never dead to the fact that their appearance anywhere in the North might have inflammatory consequences. Meanwhile, Varina had become quite ill at the New York Hotel, and for the next three months she had a succession of heart attacks "so numerous and unaccountable" that Winnie dragged herself out of her own sickbed to hurry north and nurse her mother. She was so conscientious about it that Varina told Connie Harrison "the poor child does not even go to the public table, which I think is being too nervous about me." By the spring of 1891 Margaret had made the first of many trips east to care for her mother. Both Winnie and Varina were invalids by that time, and she was of the opinion that her sister was too much confined to their quarters and was suffering from "severe nervous strain and anxiety" about their mother. [31]

But the *Memoir* came out that spring, and fresh interest came into Varina's life. Although essentially a history of her husband's life, it is also the best biographical source on its author. It is not an objective biography of Jefferson Davis but it is the most revealing. Although it is laudatory throughout, Varina's common sense and realism are also brought to bear to some extent on the high moments of her husband's career. But General Joe Johnston, General Beauregard, and General Nelson A. Miles emerge quite clearly as the villains.

There was much newspaper comment on the *Memoir*, and Kate Field nipped sharply at Varina in her paper, *Kate Field's Washington*, saying it was a trifle late in the day for Mrs. Davis to accuse General Miles of ill-treating her husband in Fortress Monroe. "Certainly Mr. Davis never went so far as this, and he was not at all given to underestimating his sufferings for the lost cause," she wrote. "Mr. Davis was sensible enough to recognize the reasonableness of his treatment. . . . There are times when hypercriticism is out of place; and hypercriticism that is 25 years stale is especially unsavory." [32]

Eugene Field attacked her in the Chicago *Morning News*. A Southern journalist had told him that Mrs. Davis had simply goaded her husband into resistance to the very end. "It was to the lasting credit of the man, said my informant, that he never uttered a word of complaint against the extra burden of sorrow and of suffering which a woman's vindictiveness entailed." The Brooklyn *Standard Union* commented on Field's dictum and found it unfair: "We do not doubt that Mrs. Davis had the courage of her convictions, but she is not to be held responsible for the misfortunes of her husband and the doom of the Confederacy."

In general the *Memoir* was mildly received and a few critics read with interest Varina's own appraisal of her husband's qualities, aside from its military and political values. None knew better than she how faulty his judgment about people had been at times; how he withered under dislike or criticism. She wrote of his piety, his courtesy, his reserve, his care of his person, and his disapproval of disorderly attire.[33] She described his sense of the ludicrous as being intense, his powers of observation close, and his memory phenomenal. Inclined to satire in his younger days, he never used it cruelly. Paradoxically, she considered him a shrewd judge of character, but also a ready victim of duplicity. "He was excitable, but not petulant, easily persuaded where to yield did not involve a principle, and was more stern toward himself than to any other. . . . To his family he was niggardly in nothing, denied himself all that our love permitted him to relinquish. He rarely made known a personal want." Summing up, Varina wrote:

Forty-three years of intimate companionship, from the beginning of his political career until the end, left me with the profoundest respect for his unswerving mental and moral integrity, his stanch adherence to principle, his self-immolating devotion to duty, his calm, invincible courage, his wide sympathy with mankind, and his unfeigned reverence for his Creator.

She believed that in the supreme effort of his life he failed from the "predominance of some of these noble qualities . . . he sacrificed the labors and ambitions of his life to the maintenance of his faith."

But the *Memoir* never found its audience. The Belford Company went into bankruptcy. Few copies were shipped out. Both mother and daughter were now faced with a serious financial situation. Winnie had inherited Beauvoir from her father's estate, but a series of floods at Davis Bend had cut off their annual income, and Varina was in a state of bewilderment about the family finances. Since neither felt well on the Gulf Coast they began to think in terms of settling in the North.

Margaret took them with her to stay at St. Elmo Cottage at Narragansett Pier in the summer of 1891. Varina delighted in the moss-covered sunken rocks of the Rhode Island resort and the play of her grandchildren. Many Southerners were there, and she was warmly welcomed. Winnie's health was better although she still had daily fevers. They had discussed a move to Colorado, but the altitude made this impossible for Varina. Robert, who had watched her children so faithfully when they were little, was now with Margaret's family.

Varina wrote from Narragansett on September 1 to Sallie B. Morgan, the Major's sister, explaining that she had been much too ill to attend the unveiling of the first monument to her husband, which Sallie had helped promote in Jackson, Mississippi.[34] She was smarting under criticism in a Mississippi paper, saying it was the only one that had attacked her either in the North or South. "If my going could have given one moment's stability to my husband's reputation or to the prosperity of Mississippi I would have gone, for life does not hold much for me with a hopeless disease, feeble and poor as death. . . . I have tried to do right in the sight of God and man, and if man does not approve God sees the motive. . . ."

For the next year they moved restlessly between New York and Beauvoir. They passed part of the winter of 1891-92 on the Gulf Coast but felt they could no longer afford to maintain the house. "Winnie has worked herself quite down in her efforts to straighten out the place," Varina wrote to her old friend, Mrs. Octavus Cohen, of Savannah. "This is a summer resort for fine people but there is no one here in the winter but us." [35]

The wash of the Gulf made her lonely now. The winter storms suggested desolation at her plantations. Her grief over her husband's death, her worry about Winnie, her months of illness in New York, the failure of her book financially, all contributed to Varina's depression. She encouraged Winnie to go in to New Orleans, to spend time with her young friends, to cultivate suitors. It was a new life for her daughter, who had always lived like a recluse, more prone to write verse than to dance, happier in a flower garden than a gaslit ballroom. Varina was anxious to see her well settled, and she encouraged the attentions of the handsome young men who were Winnie's beaux.

In the spring of 1892 she was Queen of Comus at the Mardi Gras.[36] Her Japanese silk costume with its jeweled sunburst, scepter, and crown, her jeweled belt and the golden cup presented to her on that occasion, may all be seen today in Confederate Memorial Hall. No Queen of Comus was ever more warmly cheered in the French Opera House than the Daughter of the Confederacy, or looked more pensive in her role. General Beauregard was there to honor the daughter of the man he had greatly disliked. A year later he, too, would be dead. Winnie had been a maid of honor for General Lee's daughter at the Mardi Gras of 1884. Thus her life spun round in circles, but she and Varina were soon to go north to settle permanently—a shocking move in the eyes of many of their Confederate friends.[37]

❦ 22 ❧

MRS. JEFFERSON DAVIS ON PARK ROW

THE Golden Nineties were in full swing when Mrs. Jefferson Davis became part of the New York scene. Her presence was almost unnoticed at first, but as the decade advanced her name appeared in the papers with increasing frequency. She was spotted at the opera, in the theaters, driving through Central Park in a carriage—looking extraordinarily like Queen Victoria with her flat ruched widow's cap and small black parasol tilted against the sun. Varina's cheeks were pendulous now. Her large fine eyes looked out wearily on the world from under drooping lids. But her conversation sparkled, her wit was keen, her observations as sharp as ever.

Soon she had her own Sunday *salon* where literary figures gathered, as well as the Old Guard from the South who had moved north after the war. She had taken on importance in her own right as the surviving symbol of the Lost Cause, and she used her pen to vindicate her husband's memory. She wrote articles for the *Sunday World* that ranged from the last Christmas at the White House of the Confederacy to a tribute to Ulysses S. Grant. The Pulitzers paid Varina fifteen hundred dollars a year and Winnie a similar sum to write exclusively for them in the newspaper field. The *World* used only a fraction of her output, but when a story appeared it was heavily played with the byline "By Mrs. Jefferson Davis."

Her own conception of her literary work was tempered by common sense and the realization that her value in this field lay largely in her name and memories. But she had always had strong literary interests and liked to circulate among writing people. Her work had clarity and strong opinion. Winnie was the creative writer, who busied herself with fiction, sketches, verse, and book reviews.

Winnie had been writing for years, beginning with an early poem addressed to the giant pines of Beauvoir, which appeared in the New Orleans *Times-Democrat*.[1] After that she wrote for the national magazines and newspapers on such subjects as serpent myths, the execution of Robert Emmet, life in Germany, the women of the South before the war, based on material supplied by her mother; and one of the most enlightening sketches ever done on her father. Her two novels were *The Veiled Doctor* and *A Romance of Summer Seas*.

Her daughter's literary future was one of the decisive factors in Varina's determination to settle in the North. They were worse off after her husband's death than anyone suspected, and she was too proud to make much of their poverty. In 1891 she disclosed to a friend that until she made her arrangement with the *World* her income was less than one thousand dollars a year.[2] But with the help of the Pulitzers and other literary friends she saw the possibility of making a living and at the same time of giving Winnie a chance to fulfill her unassuaged desire to write. The shift to New York involved much consideration on her part and she was astounded by the unfriendly echoes that reached her from the South after she had made the move. Varina's second reason—and a compelling one—was her health. For years she had felt unwell in warm or humid regions, and, with her increasing weight and her serious heart condition, this became an essential consideration.

In addition, she fitted easily into New York life at a time when dowagers thrived and life was formal and stately. There were some who thought that she viewed herself as a dethroned queen in exile. She enjoyed the social round, the literary claque, the concerts and theater, the stir of urban life, and the bright wits gathered around her. But it was not until the turn of the century that these things came her way. Her early days in New York were wretched enough, with poor health, little money, and a constant effort to keep up appearances. Tales sifting back to the South that she was living in high style and being lavishly entertained by Northerners had little foundation in fact. She and Winnie made their own way financially, as best they could, with the never-failing aid of Margaret and Addison. Varina summed up the situation in a letter to her friend Mrs. Kimbrough.

Some day in the future the hard battle I have fought with disease and poverty will I hope suggest itself to the people of the South, and the effort

I have made to sustain myself in dignified independence may be acceptable to them as not unworthy of my position.[3]

They lived at first in the Marlborough Hotel. Old friends from the South came to call. Burton Harrison now had a flourishing law practice. Connie was a sparkling hostess in ostrich plumes and fur-edged basques. She was writing novels and occasional pieces for the *Sunday World*, which was featuring Southern material heavily at this time. They were part of the social life of the city, and Theodore Roosevelt had backed Burton for the Century Club. "Being a 'Black Republican' I am not likely to be deemed to be swayed by party motives when I say as I always have said, publicly and privately, that a man's having played an honorable and distinguished part on the Confederate side ought simply to be a recommendation for his admission into the Century, or any other club," he wrote.[4]

In the early 1890's Varina was faced with a decision that caused her many sleepless hours—the ultimate resting place of Jefferson Davis. At the time of his death Mississippi, Virginia, Tennessee, Alabama, Georgia, and Kentucky all made overtures, but in the midst of her distress she was advised to postpone her decision. As time went on different loyalties tugged at her. She had asked her husband once where he would prefer to be buried.

He answered that he did not care—he would as soon be buried under one of the live oaks at Beauvoir as elsewhere, he said, "you must take the responsibility of deciding this question, I cannot—I foresee a great deal of feeling about it will arise when I am dead." This distressed me greatly and I did not renew the subject, hoping he would live after me.[5]

Varina took the responsibility as seriously as anyone could, and strong feeling developed over the ultimate choice, as Jefferson Davis predicted it would. Beauvoir, the only spot he had mentioned, was ruled out because of the low-lying land unsuitable for a permanent tomb. Varina seemed to lean to Mississippi, but she was not satisfied with the overtures that had been made and in a bitter statement which she left for post-mortem reading she made it clear that the state her husband loved so dearly had in some way failed to strike the right note with her about his burial. To many, Virginia, where so much of the war had been fought and her husband had served his presidency, seemed the logical place—among the other warriors buried in Hollywood Cemetery. And this was her ultimate decision. She addressed a letter to "The

Veterans and Public of the Southern States" from the New York Hotel on July 11, 1891.

Virginia asked for his honored remains because the most strenuous efforts of his life had been made upon her soil and in defence of Richmond as the capital of the Confederate States. . . . She urged the fact that he did not in the fulness of his fame belong exclusively to any part of the country. Every hillside about Richmond would tell of the valorous resistance which he initiated and directed with tireless vigilance as Chief Magistrate. . . . All these claims have touched my heart and contended together for the mastery. . . .[6]

Again Varina was in the limelight in the spring of 1893 when Jefferson Davis's body was removed for final burial in Richmond, and the Confederate States, slowly recovering from prostration, united again to do him honor. After a formal lying in state in Confederate Memorial Hall, New Orleans, a special train moved slowly on its way to Virginia, making stops along the way. Crowds assembled to watch the final journey of the Confederate chief, and bonfires blazed through the night. Children gathered at the stations to offer bouquets of magnolia and yellow jessamine to the guards. They strewed flowers along the track at Beauvoir, where a great storm came up suddenly and the dust of Mississippi blew across the train.[7] Wreaths hung on the little frame station, and friends climbed into the family car to greet Winnie and Margaret. It rained at Montgomery where the Confederate flag that had floated over Fort Sumter hung with a Buena Vista flag on the Capitol. Minute guns were fired, and ten thousand visited the bier of Jefferson Davis. At Danville the crowd gathered at the station sang "Nearer, My God, to Thee." Church bells tolled throughout the South.

Varina joined her daughters in Richmond. She was not strong enough to travel all the way with the train. Jubal Early paid her an early morning call on the day of the funeral and she rode with him under the burning sun in the long procession to Hollywood Cemetery. Like her husband, he had never ceased to wear his Confederate gray.

Jefferson Davis was laid to rest on an oval-shaped plateau slanted toward the James River. Varina was dimly conscious of the glitter of polished muskets and swords, of gold lace and tall plumes, of white horses drawing the funeral carriage, and tattered Confederate flags. The military bands played the familiar requiem. It was thirty-two years since Jefferson Davis had arrived in Richmond. A cannon boomed from one of the nearby hills. With the salute and three volleys, there was a rustling movement in the crowd and Varina, who had stayed in her carriage under the trees, now moved forward. She watched the slowly sinking coffin and her self-control deserted her. Her body trembled and she bowed her head. A group of veterans, watching her, cried like children. The few surviving generals at the graveside stood with bared heads, silvered now. A bugle sounded as Varina drove away, a drooping figure heavily shrouded.[8]

This revival of Confederate solidarity was viewed with comparative calm in the North and the New Orleans *Times-Democrat* of May 27, 1893, observed that "ceremonies like these have lost all political significance, and the sensible people of the North see nothing to criticize in our showing respect, devotion and admiration for our heroes." Papers that had virtually ignored the funeral ceremonies of 1889 ran columns now and the New York *Sunday World* paid tribute to Varina in a flattering editorial.

While her health is poor, her mind and her person are worthy of the great position she has held and still holds. She is one of those rare human beings who retain in age the brightness and strength of mind that usually pertain only to middle life. Apart from the respect which is hers from her high place beside her husband in Confederate history, she is in all worthy of love and admiration on her own account. . . . Her appearance and manners have all the dignity and grace of a queen. . . . With all the domestic virtues of Queen Victoria, she has a mind of masculine strength and culture. Her conversation shows learning and appreciation without any pretense. She has read and travelled and has studied human nature under all conditions. The long years of distinguished Governmental position of her husband gave her opportunities which she used as few persons do use them.[9]

By this time resentment over the wife and daughter of the Confederate President living in the North was showing clearly. Varina was wounded by stories that she had deserted the Confederacy and was living in affluence in New York. The burial of her husband in Virginia had repercussions in Mississippi. When word reached her that she and Winnie were reported to have Beauvoir on the market to the highest bidder she wrote indignantly to Mrs. Kimbrough: "How could they think that after all the sacrifices I have made for the South, born, bred in it, and indissolubly connected with it, indeed feeling daily the weight of the prejudices of our enemies against us—how could they suppose I did not love it? . . . I think I have earned the confidence and love of the Southern people. If I have it not I shall continue to feel, 'though they slay me, yet will I trust in them.' " [10]

Carefully explaining her financial circumstances, she pointed out that she and Winnie lived at the Marlborough for twelve hundred dollars a year and were about to move to cheaper quarters as the rates were being raised. It would cost them at least six thousand dollars a year to maintain Beauvoir, with all the visitors and strangers who flocked there.

Moreover, it was absolutely imperative for her to live within reach of a cool place, so that she could get away within a few hours when her "heart palpitations became severe." She could travel to Narragansett for a small sum, whereas it would cost her three hundred dollars to get from Beauvoir to the Virginia mountains. Her doctor had told her she might live for another ten years if she stayed in a cool climate, but might drop dead at any time if exposed to heat. So far her plantation had brought her nothing but debt and she did not see how she could maintain Beauvoir. All her other resources were now used up. She was approaching sixty-nine and had trouble rallying after an attack. "I am such an invalid that I seldom leave my rooms and am fallen so lame that I walk with great difficulty." But this was a temporary condition.

Varina's next move was to the Gerard Hotel on West Forty-fourth Street, in the heart of the theatrical district. At this time she maintained a voluminous and affectionate correspondence with Judge Kimbrough, calling herself "Your old woman friend"; and with his wife, Mary Hunter Kimbrough, whose great grandfather was appointed by Thomas Jefferson to lay out the territory of Mississippi. Only the Kimbroughs knew how badly off Varina was at this time and how great was her pride. The Judge helped her sympathetically in all her financial and legal affairs, and his wife worked ceaselessly that she should be duly honored in Mississippi, but the issue became contentious, with echoes long after Varina's death when Mrs. Kimbrough stunned a gathering of the United Daughters of the Confederacy at Gulfport in 1906 by reading a post-mortem letter that Varina had sent to Judge Kimbrough in 'the autumn of 1894.[11]

It was Varina's apologia, her justification. There was no intention that it should reach the press, but extracts were published in Richmond and the repercussions were severe. Some of the Daughters heard it in frozen silence. Others wept. "This is a voice from the dead," said Mrs.

Loudon of North Carolina. "Let us rise & with bowed heads receive it in silence." Mrs. N. V. Randolph, of Richmond, reported "great disturbance among the Mississippians" when Varina's letter was read. No action was taken on it. The whole affair was more or less suppressed, but it had focused much of the bitter feeling surrounding Varina. She was reported to have composed it after Mrs. Kimbrough had shown her a batch of unfriendly clippings from Mississippi papers, criticizing her for living in the North, and for having Jefferson Davis buried in Richmond instead of in Mississippi. Her own correspondence shows that she kept reminding Judge Kimbrough up to the time of her death that she wished the post-mortem letter used when the right time came.[12] Her need for self-justification was intense.

The controversial statement was signed on October 16, 1894, when Varina was staying at Green's Inn, Narragansett. It was addressed to Judge Kimbrough to be used as he pleased.

The abuse or criticism showered upon me in every quarter of my native state is so unreasonable and undeserved by me on the three counts generally cited, that I feel it due to myself to plainly state the whole truth, which I have hitherto withheld because I did not wish to blame Mississippi. The three counts seem to be in the indictment:

1st, that I gave my husband's remains to Richmond
2nd, that I did not write up Mississippi in my book
3rd, that I live in New York instead of there.[13]

Varina detailed at length the various overtures that had been made to her by different states after her husband's death, and the motives that had prompted her decision. Personal delegations had come from other states, but although she waited for Mississippi to make clear its claim she did not feel that the matter had been handled with the necessary dignity and consideration.

On the second count she explained that although "especially anxious to set forth Mississippi in as brilliant a light" as she could, her publishers had objected to the length of her book and had proposed cuts on Mississippi, telling her that she was not writing a history of the war but a memoir of Jefferson Davis, and he had already given much space to Mississippi in his book. She charged that the only "severe and abusive attack" made upon her was in Mississippi, and that a paper in Greenwood said she was too stupid and spiteful to be allowed to write a book.

Eleven years later, when she felt that death was close at hand, Varina wrote most emphatically to Mrs. Kimbrough, asking her to have the Judge have a "typewritten copy of the letter I intrusted to him to be published after my death, so if anything happens to one the other might remain, for it is in the nature of a death bed document and justifies me. Please do not fail to do this." [14]

In Colorado after her mother's death Margaret was deeply agitated over the publicity the post-mortem statement received. She was deluged with letters and clippings from the South. She wrote in severe tones to Mrs. Kimbrough, regretting the use she had made of the letter and asking to have it returned.[15] She had known about it, and in the spring before her mother's death had urged her to recall it as an ill-judged document. However, it was immediately after this warning from Margaret that strong-minded Varina wrote more determinedly than ever about it to the Kimbroughs.

Now Margaret wrote to Mrs. Kimbrough that the reading of such a letter at such a meeting in Mississippi, her father's best beloved State, was a grave mistake. "I have yet to find one person whose opinion is worth considering, who feels anything but tenderness & consideration & respect for the widow of their one & only President," she added.

In this same letter Margaret took occasion to deny stories of discord between herself and her mother. It was reported among their friends that sometimes they did not speak to each other for days on end. Varina had unquestionably become more autocratic with the years. Margaret was a handsome, clever, and capable woman whose marriage had been a happy one. Her children and her grandchildren had been trained to pay honor to Varina, when they were in the East, or were on their way to Europe. Addison was good to Varina in every way. She explained all this in her letter to Mrs. Kimbrough.

The impression exists, I understand, that she & I were estranged & not on intimate terms, & judging from the number of letters I get telling me her wishes, I presume some people may believe it. However those who saw us together know of the deep & tender love we bore each other, & the perfect understanding that existed, also of the devotion & care I gave her, and her appreciation of it. I spent more than half the months of the year with her of late years, & nursed her & cared for her with untiring devotion. She and I had long & intimate conversations on all the subjects nearest to her heart. . . .

During these same years of ill health and financial trouble Varina kept in lively touch with her surroundings and made an impression on all who met her. Two of her closest friends throughout the 1890's were Dr. John W. Burgess, Ruggles Professor of Political Science and Constitutional Law at Columbia University, and his wife, Ruth Payne Burgess, a well-known artist. They first approached her because Dr. Burgess was doing a book for Scribner's American History Series and wished to write about Jefferson Davis without prejudice, although he was not in sympathy with his states' rights theories. The interviews that followed led to a sustained friendship. "She was brilliant—charming and so interesting!" commented Mrs. Burgess.

Varina responded with enthusiasm to the professor's overtures. She hoped that her husband might "receive the tardy justice at his hands" [16] for which she had long hoped. She thought it difficult for contemporaries to write unbiased history, but enough time had elapsed since the war so that a "new generation has risen up who begin to look more coolly over the ground where the contest raged thirty years ago," she wrote.

Professor Burgess was captivated by Varina. They talked for hours. She gave him many of her husband's papers for study, feeling that his "absolutely honest clear conviction and devotion to the right, and his scholarly diction would declare themselves better thus than through any other channel." She wrote to him on May 29, 1893, proving herself a false prophet:

> I shall not live to see the end of this wide divergence of my countrymen, but I firmly believe the time will come when the blood of the martyrs North and South will be the seed of the States rights school of thought. There can be no perpetuity where centralization is the shibboleth. Congress is a "many headed monster thing" that to my mind is much worse and more dangerous than a king because there are so many heads to diverse usurpations of power. But at all events I feel that my husband's reputation is safe in your hands and thank you for pouring this oil upon my wounds now when I am "wild with all regrets." [17]

Varina was staying at the Rockingham at Narragansett Pier in the summer of 1894 when she wrote to Dr. Burgess that she had finally recovered from the bankrupt Belford Company the plates, cuts, and unsold copies of her *Memoir*. The matter had been in litigation for three years. She had raised two thousand dollars on a mortgage to put through the transaction and she would now try to sell them at less than the former price, but she was full of trouble "as the sparks fly upward." Varina confessed that she had bad luck in everything she undertook. "I hope that my death may break that curious charm which seems to affect everything that came from me. . . . Everything I undertake seems to fail." [18]

Professor Burgess brought Varina and Horace White together in his drawing room for a spirited evening. White was the Chicago *Tribune* editor and reporter who had covered the Douglas-Lincoln debates. They talked for four hours, and to the watching professor the encounter was "simply breathlessly fascinating." Varina was at her most eloquent. White knew Lincoln and his wife quite well. He had viewed some of their family spats at close range. After his encounter with Varina he said to Professor Burgess, "If Mr. Lincoln could only have had such a wife!" White added that he had never in his life so greatly enjoyed an evening with anybody.

Dr. Burgess was not only interested in Varina; he was influenced by her. In his *Reminiscences of an American Scholar* he wrote:

> In those years of friendly converse with her, I learned to appreciate fully the Southern view of the great struggle of 1861-65 and of the causes and conditions leading up to it. . . . Thus prepared and equipped, I addressed myself to the work of writing the history of a development, not a dogmatic criticism of sin or even error.[19]

But the old fires were burning down only slowly. Varina had been truly horrified to read the Northern headlines when Lee's statue was unveiled in Richmond in the spring of 1890. "Treason Glorified" said the *Mail and Express* of New York on May 29. "Traitors are on the March in Richmond." "Scene that All Americans Blush For." [20] She recalled that the Washington *Post* was the only paper in the North to give a full account of her husband's death.

Joseph Johnston had died in 1891 and Beauregard two years later. General Kirby-Smith was gone, and in 1894 Varina was mourning the death of Jubal Early. She had outlived them all. From time to time she and Winnie were drawn back to the South for official ceremonies. By the mid 1890's, thanks to the Pulitzer backing, things were slightly better for the Davises. Both were becoming quite well known in literary circles in New York. They were invited out with greater frequency, and Varina presided with dignity in her hotel apartment. Winnie, still frail in health but enjoying her literary labors, had become expert at gracing a public platform and responding to reminiscences about her father. Both went south in the summer of 1896 for the Confederate Reunion held in Richmond that year and were feted as the wife and daughter of the Confederate chief, and now in their own right, too.[21] Winnie was accompanied by her young nephew from Colorado Springs—Jefferson Hayes-Davis, who changed his name legally to honor his grandfather. The cornerstone of the Jefferson Davis Monument was laid on this occasion and there was a great parade. General Stephen D. Lee delivered the oration. Varina wept as Lee spoke of her husband. She drew her chair close to the derrick in order to have a good look at the foundation.

They were serenaded at the Jefferson Hotel and she sat on the balcony and listened to the bands play "Dixie," with memories of the war days in Richmond swamping her with regrets. A reception was held for Winnie and Mildred Lee at the Masonic Temple, and the gaslit ballroom shimmered with the silks and jewels and shining hair of the women who danced—a new generation now, the sons and daughters of the warriors of the Civil War. Varina was too tired to attend, but she held court at her hotel. She mustered strength, however, for the next event and stood before a huge audience at the veterans' convention while General Gordon, who had christened Winnie the Daughter of the Confederacy, led both her and Varina to the front of the platform and presented them again. The hearty General Gordon seized his old friend Varina around the waist.[22]

"And now, my comrades, I imprint upon her brow a kiss for every comrade," and General Gordon kissed Mrs. Davis while the audience roared its approval.

The White House of the Confederacy in Richmond was opened again to the public that year. It had been used for twenty years as a public school but was now taken over by the Confederate Memorial Literary Society and established as a museum.[23] Restoration began as the old oak staircase was replaced by a facsimile in iron, and the five chandeliers used in the time of the Davises were restored to their original settings. Varina held a reception in the familiar rooms, receiving old friends and their sons and daughters, and remembering the many occasions on which she had functioned from the same spot, surrounded by warriors whose names now were history—General Lee, Jeb Stuart, General Hood, General Bragg, Wade Hampton, and dozens more.

Her friendship with Mrs. Ulysses S. Grant was much discussed at this time, for since 1893 they had been on the best of terms. The sight of these two ladies together invariably evoked comment. Actually they had much in common. Julia Dent Grant understood the agricultural life from her early days in Missouri. Both had followed the fortunes of their husbands with great intensity during the days of the war, and neither Davis nor Grant had ever felt vindictive toward each other. Both women had soft, low voices. Both had portly figures and wore their hair parted in the middle and drawn down tightly over their ears. Both had the same sort of memories.

They met on a June day in 1893 at Cranston's-on-Hudson.[24] Varina had arrived to watch a cadet parade at West Point. Mrs. Grant had been staying there for some time and when she heard that Mrs. Jefferson Davis was a fellow guest she went to Varina's room to welcome her.

"I am Mrs. Grant," she announced, as Mrs. Jefferson Davis opened the door.

"I am very glad to meet you," Varina responded. "Come in."

After dinner they sat together on the piazza, and the other guests watched this curious tableau with interest. When Mrs. Davis went off to bed the widow of the Union General remarked, "She is a very noble looking lady. She looked a little older than I had expected. I have wanted to meet her for a very long time."

After that they met often and corresponded from time to time. They went together to Grant's tomb and Varina heard his widow say, "I will soon be laid beside my husband in this solemn place." [25] Varina dropped to her knees and prayed when she learned of Julia Grant's death in 1902. The *World* made the most of this association and featured a brief tribute by Varina to Grant in a special memorial number issued in April, 1897. " 'Let us have peace,' said the gentle-hearted soldier, and I believe every portion of our reunited country heartily joins in the aspiration," Varina wrote.[26] She was invited to the memorial services held next day in icy winds at Grant's tomb. There were men in the parade who had fought both with and against the Union General. President McKinley was present and paid tribute to Grant: "A great life never dies. Great deeds are imperishable; great names are immortal." [27]

All this made strange reading in the South, but gradually Varina assumed the aura of one who was helping to wear down prejudice between North and South. As the birthday of the General who had finally vanquished the Southern forces approached in April, 1901, readers of the New York *Sunday World* found a featured article in its columns entitled "The Humanity of Grant," written by Mrs. Jefferson Davis.[28] She maintained that the fact that she had been asked to write the piece was significant in itself of wounds that were healing.

"Even in the stress and heat of hostilities, military and political, the humanity of the man shone through the soldier's coat of mail," Varina wrote of the General who had battered hard at the defenses of Vicksburg, her home territory. Like other Southern women, she had viewed him as the Northern General who, above all others, had thrown with "relentless force and never flagging energy the masses of the armed hordes against our half-starved, worn-out little army, to whose depleted ranks we had not a man to add."

But the lengthening perspective of the years had enlarged Varina's vision if it had not abated her devotion to the Confederate cause. Grant's attitude to Lee at Appomattox had convinced her of his "kind heart and unwillingness to inflict needless pain." She now wrote that he "used his influence in Mr. Davis' interest in several directions" when he was in Fortress Monroe, and added:

. . . bitter prejudices and resentments have been much modified by intercourse, the inter-marriage and inter-education of the people of the two sections. . . . I hope there are people both North and South who are already looking above and through the smoke of battle to take the just measure of the statesmen and commanders who have left their fame unclouded by atrocities committed upon the helpless who fell into their power, and in this galaxy I think General Grant will take his place unquestioned by his former antagonists.[29]

But from all such lists Varina banished the names of General Butler, General Sherman, and General Miles, who aroused the most passionate anger in her to the day of her death. She was ever ready to champion the Confederate cause and would debate military points and strategy by the hour. The Northern generals were as prone to pay her honor as those of the South. General James J. Wilson, who had been so closely identified with the fighting in Mississippi and with her husband's capture, often visited her at the Gerard and enjoyed her conversation. He viewed her as a "proud, self-contained old woman, alert mentally, and with much conversational charm." [30] In the past he had been one of her severest critics but he found her persuasive in these postwar years.

General N. M. Curtis, a Congressman from Ogdensburg who had

met her years earlier at Vicksburg, described her at the turn of the century as a "most interesting woman" [31] who had kept well informed on all public matters for the last half century. He thought that by her "influence and power" both in the North and South she had helped to bring about "the harmonious relations which now happily exist among the people of all sections of the country."

Meanwhile, Winnie reviewed Mrs. Humphrey Ward's *Marcella* and Gilbert Parker's *The Seats of the Mighty*. Nellie Bly trained an elephant, argued with Susan Anthony, and talked of raising her own regiment for Cuba. Ella Wheeler Wilcox studied a murderess, and Kate Swan paddled through Hellgate and went down in a diving suit, all for the *Sunday World*. Varina was in curious company, but it did not dismay her.

In the late 1890's she and Winnie usually went to Narragansett Pier for the summer, seeing something of the Pulitzers while there. They stayed at the Rockingham or Green's Inn, and Varina went for daily drives and had many friends at the resort. Winnie, a splendid horsewoman, took up bicycling enthusiastically when it became fashionable, and could be seen whizzing along with encumbering skirts and high-collared blouses. But in the summer of 1896 she had a fall and sprained her ankle, and Varina wrote of the bicycle craze: "I do not know why girls love them so much." The following summer she tore the muscles of her knee and was quite lame for a time. By the spring of 1898 she was in poor health and she sailed for Egypt in February. Before leaving she made her will, bequeathing Beauvoir and everything she had to her mother except for remembrances to her cousin Anna Smith and her "dear old nurse Mary Ahern." [32] Her mother was to choose keepsakes for Margaret and her children. "I know she will know what I wish done," Winnie wrote.

She sailed in a depressed state. She was now quite familiar with the European scene and had made several trips abroad.[33] She was fluent in foreign languages and always thought she could pick up copy abroad. At this time she was weary from her long siege of nursing Varina and of being in constant attendance on her in a small hotel apartment. She had not forgotten Fred although she never saw him. Winnie never seemed to recover her spirits after her break with her Northern suitor, but she had many friends in the North and South and she worked quite hard.

On her return in May, after visiting Rome, Venice, Florence and Paris, she was still feeling far from well. In July her mother delegated her to take her place at a camp gathering of the Confederate veterans in Atlanta. She was later to reproach herself and call this Winnie's death warrant. On September 7, 1898, she wrote to Connie Burton that she had urged her to go against her will because she felt it was best for her not to lose touch with her father's friends. "She was parched by the July sun in an open carriage and a summer rain came up suddenly and wet her to the skin, yet she could not get out of the crowd to change her clothes," Varina wrote.[34] Winnie attended the grand ball at the Kimball House that night and then traveled back to Narragansett feeling desperately ill. As her mother described it:

> My Winnie is the most suffering person not to be dying that I ever saw. She has now been over six weeks *violently* seasick without any relief night or day. She cannot retain any nourishment except an occasional teaspoonful of cracked ice and raw white of egg, and even this she cannot assimilate. . . . She has wasted away dreadfully but she bears everything with fortitude and patience I have never seen equalled except by her father. . . .

Again fate was striking at Varina. Winnie was mortally ill with what the doctors, in the medical language of the day, described as malarial gastritis. As she grew steadily weaker she would press her mother's hand and whisper, "We shall have our carriage when my book sells." Harper's were bringing out her second novel that year. But Winnie died on September 18, 1898, at the age of thirty-three.

She had a military funeral in Richmond and was buried close to her father.[35] Services were held for her in St. Paul's, and all the Confederate camps had memorial gatherings. A chair was placed for Varina beside the grave, since she was unable to stand, and Margaret stood by her side with her arms around her. Burton Harrison, who remembered Winnie from the day of her birth, was present. There were many echoes of the past and a great outpouring of patriotic feeling throughout the South for the popular Daughter of the Confederacy. A palmetto from South Carolina was planted over her grave. Theodore Roosevelt sent a wreath. She was the fifth of Varina's children to die, but now she had grandchildren to comfort her, and Jefferson Hayes-Davis and Lucy Hayes spent that Christmas with her in New York, "so I am not alone," Varina wrote. "I love my grandchildren dearly."

She passed the following summer with Dr. and Mrs. Burgess at Montpelier, Vermont, in a small house adjacent to theirs, with a garden between.[36] Here Mrs. Burgess painted Varina and included the cane given her by the ladies of Mississippi, which she wished to have in the portrait. She had sat for A. Muller-Ury at his New York studio in 1895, and two years later Winnie had posed for him. He considered her a "sweet and wonderful character." [37] He paid tribute to Varina, too, saying that "nobody could help admiring the intelligence, grace and personality of Mrs. J. Davis."

Some Vermonters remarked on the oddity of Mrs. Jefferson Davis's being among them, chatting with them in their gardens, as if she had never known a slave or gone through the agonies of the Civil War. "She charmed everybody in that old abolitionist state," Dr. Burgess wrote of her. "Governor and ex-Governors, United States Senators and ex-Senators, Representatives in Congress and in the State Legislature and ex-Representatives, and most of the prominent men of the State paid her court and were all won by her courtesy, her kindness and her brilliant conversation." [38]

He used to take her driving over the neighboring hills and they would stop to talk to the farmers. By this time she was so extremely stout that he feared the springs of his buggy would break as they drove over rough country roads. One day as they neared the village of East Montpelier he heard a crack. A spring had gone. He jumped out and tackled a farmer raking leaves in his orchard. He asked for a piece of wire. "Mebby," said the farmer and went on with his work. He took his own good time and when he had finished raking up the leaves went off to get the wire. Varina was much amused. She had a fine understanding of the meditative ways of the farmers as well as of crops, the state of the trees and the live stock on the New England farms.

The Burgesses felt that Varina bore her grief over Winnie, as she did all the other catastrophes of her eventful life, "with unparalleled courage and uncomplaining serenity and cheerfulness." But her thoughts now ran along melancholy lines. The monument for her husband's grave was ready and "even to me it is satisfactory," she wrote to Mrs. Lizzie Cary Daniel of Richmond. It showed her husband in the uniform and cavalry boots in which he was captured. "Mrs. Davis hoped thus in enduring stone to refute a persistent slander," Nannie Davis explained. [39]

At this time the Daughters of the Confederacy were planning a monument for Winnie's grave, and Varina wrote to Mrs. Daniel that she thought it would "be unfortunate if my darling's tomb should overtop her father's in the lot." While at Montpelier she worried about the epitaph for her husband and asked John Warwick Daniel to suggest a hundred words of requiem. [40] For once, eloquent Varina was at a loss and appealed to several friends to submit suggestions, from which the most suitable would be chosen.

Varina had many Confederate affairs to attend to at this time. She was consulted about the various memorials planned in different parts of the South and wrote to Mrs. Octavus Cohen of Savannah on June 11, 1900, that she was anxious to have the "best work on our Confederate monuments that our scant purses can supply." [41] But she took a dim view of a memorial arch proposed in honor of her husband in Richmond. The thought of trolley cars clanking in its vicinity disturbed her. She wrote to Miss Emily Mason deploring the whole idea and to another friend she confessed that the Richmond papers had given her "an old fashioned setting down" and she feared that the "dreadful arch business . . . had destroyed the regard of the ladies for me who advocated its erection." [42] Once again Varina was in hot water.

The time had now come for her to scatter her own relics and at Beauvoir she took up this task wearily in the late spring of 1899. The ultimate distribution of most of the Davis treasures was to the Confederate Museum in Richmond, the White House of the Confederacy in Montgomery, Confederate Memorial Hall in New Orleans, and Beauvoir itself. Today all four are museums containing Davis mementoes.

Sorting their possessions for distribution was a difficult task for Varina, with countless intimate reminders of her husband and daughter. She broke down repeatedly as she came on the last shoes, hat, slippers, and dressing gown worn by her husband; his watch and chain; his pipes and cigar case; the thread case she had always kept fitted up for him, his toilet set and the tobacco pouches she had made for him under such stress. Grim reminders of his days in Fortress Monroe were the crown of thorns she had woven for him which hung over the picture of Pope Pius IX that he had received with a letter of sympathy from Rome, and his tin cup and eye mask.

There were several quilts to dispose of, including the treasured one made for her husband by the Confederate women, which Varina noted he valued so much "that once when he was sleeping under it, he recognized the fact and asked to have it taken off to be 'put away in lavender.' " [43] The familiar Meissen china ornaments from their drawing room in Richmond were returned to their original places on the mantelpiece, and the inkstand which their children had specially loved was sent to Memorial Hall in New Orleans. Each little figure on it was named for one of the children, and Jefferson Davis had made a plaything of it with his boys and girls. After the fall of Richmond an old man employed around the grounds saved it and sent it to Varina years later.

Varina could scarcely bear the sight of Winnie's schoolbooks, her scarlet satin-lined workbox, her paintbox and guitar, her driving whip and prayer book, the watch given her by Princess Charlotte, the apron she had embroidered for her in 1877 while she was still at the Institut Friedlander Zeugnis in Carlsruhe, her sketches and regimental badges, the canopied bed in which her children had slept, their tiny chairs and playthings—all painful reminders that they had died young. Among the more curious items was a doll in whose hollow body morphine and quinine had been smuggled and a bar of soap in which a secret message had come from England for Benjamin.

She was greatly worried over all the papers and documents, many of which were sent to the Howard Memorial Hall, today known as Confederate Memorial Hall in New Orleans. Her little bundle of *cartes de visite* which she called a "collection of my special friends in the Confederate Army," gave her concern. In sending them to the Confederate Museum in Richmond she wrote: "I fear their being lost or scattered in case of my death should I keep them until the last hour of my life." [44] At the same time she sent the Museum the "very rare and precious prayer book" that her husband had valued beyond price; the red prayer book which had belonged to young Jeff, sent him by his father when he was in prison and was thought to be dying, and Winnie's Bible which she used while in school, with every page showing "how constantly it was studied."

While they were in the midst of sorting out the family possessions Margaret wrote to Mrs. Carrie Phelan Beale, daughter of their old family friend Judge James Phelan, suggesting that the name "Jefferson-Varina Davis Memorial Library" be used at the White House of the Confederacy in Montgomery, to which they were sending a number of the family possessions with the stipulation that the President's bedroom should be recreated exactly as it was in his lifetime.[45] Margaret wrote with some feeling that "so little honor has been paid to my dear Mother's name, so very worthy of all honor, peerless woman, perfect wife, and tender mother as she is, and always has been."

Margaret continued in an illuminating vein:

It was always she who bore the burden and heat of the day, cheerfully and uncomplainingly, she who for forty years acted as amanuensis for my dear Father, often writing eight to ten hours to his dictation. When he wrote his book she alone could assist him, her memory was so clear, her style so graceful, yet so strong, and her mind so brilliant that her criticisms alone were valuable. With every womanly accomplishment added, her beautiful fingers did work I have never seen surpassed, as well as every useful work. Her works of charity and the good she has done have left her memory green wherever she has lived. In her home her individuality impressed itself on everything around her, making the most unpromising surroundings beautiful and graceful by the actual work of her hands. In sickness and sorrow no one could take her place, so tender, so wise and so devoted was she, I say, *was* only because she is now too old and feeble to do for others as she has always done. I know our Winnie would agree with me in wishing her name honored where she was beloved. Maggie.

But the effort Varina had made on this occasion upset her greatly. Her emotions were so stirred by these visible reminders of the past that she collapsed and had to go north to seek rest and coolness. Her capable daughter continued the work of dividing the family possessions and closing up Beauvoir. It was a clean cut with the past, and Varina now felt that her "life was not worth much, but there is much for me to do still and I am necessary to a few."

Among the few was their old coachman, James Jones, whom she was recommending for a job in the stationery room of the Senate in December, 1899.[46] She wrote to the Mississippi Senators on his behalf, vouching for his honesty and industry. At the same time she sent a note to Jim, who had roused them all in camp before their capture, saying she was glad to help him although she did not like to ask for personal favors. He was part-Negro and part-Indian, and had worked as a coachman for the St. Charles Hotel. He always said that having driven Jefferson Davis, he would never drive another President.[47] In distributing her belongings Varina sent him a walking stick with an elkhorn handle that had belonged to her husband. Like Robert, who had now gone to Colorado Springs with Margaret's family, Jim was one of their most loyal servants.[48]

❦ 23 ❧

CONFEDERATE COURT IN NEW YORK

VARINA considered writing a biography of her daughter after Winnie's death, but the effort made her so ill that her physician ordered her to stop. She struggled along with her newspaper assignments as well as she could, and coped with an endless round of correspondence. Sitting up in bed in the early morning, her white hair neatly coiled in a bun, the day's papers by her side, her mind as alert as when she was forty, she would write a score of letters in her neat, legible script. She insisted on answering them all, although she had no secretarial help.

To the end Varina sparkled with mental energy, and was always eager to open her mail, to receive calls, to study the news. She breakfasted early, Margaret bringing her a tray, and even on days when she could not get out of bed the busy round went on and she worked with extravagant energy.[1] Her letters came from many quarters. They raised strange and controversial points. They drove her back over the years with their insistence on settling old issues. She was asked to give, to recommend, to praise, to sponsor. Varina was charitable and invariably helped where she could. She asked favors not for herself but for others.

After her husband's death she had deliberately changed her name to Mrs. V. Jefferson Davis. She had always been erratic about her signature, shifting from Varina Davis to Varina Banks Davis, then Varina Howell Davis, and other variations. "I would not give up the precious name for anything," she wrote to Major Morgan soon after her husband's death. "I have hyphenated my name with Mr. Davis' first name ever since his death and so people know me best at the post offices everywhere as Mrs. V. Jefferson Davis, and this would find me anywhere," she wrote in 1901 to Mrs. Thomas Roach, whose husband was cashier of the State National Bank in New Orleans.

The authenticity of her husband's signature frequently came into question, and she wrote repeatedly to people explaining that he rarely used a pen in his later years. She had practiced copying his writing to where it was practically indistinguishable from the original.[2] In many instances she had even signed his checks for him, but she learned to put a period after the name when it was authentically his. Only she could tell the difference. Belated recognition of her substitution in this respect posed a problem for the collector when it was finally discovered, but her own letters support the theory that this practice developed largely at Beauvoir.

By the turn of the century Varina had mellowed, or else had found a certain measure of resignation. Except where the most sensitive areas of feeling were concerned, she had become comparatively tolerant and deplored that "most terrible scourge to society, one who listens to controvert." Yet she often found herself in that situation. There was always the astonishing moment when she would pick up a paper or open a letter and see that someone else—occasionally an old associate— was making statements about her husband that she must challenge.

One of her deepest wounds was inflicted by Theodore Roosevelt in 1900 when he wrote in *Thomas Hart Benton*, that the "moral difference between Benedict Arnold on the one hand and Aaron Burr or Jefferson Davis on the other, is precisely the difference that obtains between a politician who sells his vote for money and one who supports a bad measure in consideration of being given some high political position."

Varina made no public comment on this occasion, but her daughter Margaret indignantly protested the comparison of her father with Benedict Arnold. Roosevelt stuck to his guns at the time. Writing to George Brinton Harvey in 1904, he said that as a matter of "pure morals" he had been right in grouping Davis with Benedict Arnold and that Davis was an "unhung traitor." [3] The difference between them was one of degree, not of kind, he added.

In the summer of 1905 he declined to speak in the South on Jefferson Davis and confessed in a letter he wrote, but may never have sent, to Clark Howell of the Atlanta *Constitution*, that writing when he was younger he "used improper severity" in his comments on Davis, who had annoyed him with a "rather ill-tempered and undignified letter" which he had answered with "some acerbity." [4] However, he still felt that while he could speak of Lee, Stonewall Jackson, Albert Sidney

Johnston, and Joseph E. Johnston with the heartiest respect and admiration, he could not conscientiously speak in the same vein of
Jefferson Davis. He added, however: "It seems hardly worth while for
any person now to feel offended about what I said twenty years ago
of Jefferson Davis."

But Roosevelt softened by the time of Varina's death, and on
October 26, 1907, Margaret wrote to him from Colorado Springs,
thanking him for his "graceful compliment to my father, Jefferson
Davis, and his matchless Mississippi regiment" in a speech he had
made at Vicksburg.[5] She regretted that her parents had not lived to
share her gratification, for her father had loved Theodore Roosevelt's
mother very dearly, she wrote, and "even in your college days realized
that you were to be a man among men, a leader of those associated with
you." With some of her mother's forthright quality Margaret added:
"There are very few men with real courage enough to say 'I have
made a mistake and wish to make amends' and when I see such a man
he commands my admiration and respect."

At the time that Roosevelt made his comments on Davis, Varina
viewed herself as something of an oracle on matters military and
political. She had indeed become a legend, an institution. Her opinion
was sought on all manner of subjects, from contemporary manners
to freedom for the Philippines, which she approved.[6] Her encounters
with men of affairs were always stimulating. She never missed an
opportunity to laud her husband and Winnie as deified beings.
Varina admitted in one of her letters to a friend that she "liked to be
original." Spurts of her early spontaneity showed in her old age, as
she became more and more of a character. At times she recalled the
years when "the world was full of fiddlers for her." [7] Actors now gave
readings in her rooms. Her tea hour became fashionable.

The Southern colony in New York by this time was strong and
pervasive. There had been much intermarriage. Old friends of Varina's,
like Roger Pryor and Burton Harrison, had done well at the bar. The
Southern women were popular, and their children were now attending
Northern schools. Much honor was paid Mrs. Davis by her compatriots
from the South. Her apartment was well supplied with flowers. She was
remembered on birthdays and anniversaries. From the obscurity of her
early days in New York she had become a regal and recognized figure.

Varina, enthroned in New York as Queen of the Confederacy, was
often asked to place books and articles by Southerners because of her

literary connections. She always did her best for them but had a realistic appreciation of the writing craft. Her articles in the *World,* which continued almost until her death, usually aroused interest, and the paper sometimes called her "Our Southern Queen." But when Mrs. Kimbrough wrote asking her if she could have something published relating to her daughter, Mary Craig, Varina explained the difficulties of the craft.[8] Her own subjects were assigned to her and "if they do not like the article they throw it aside and I must write another," she explained, with a well-disciplined approach to the exigencies of Park Row.

Soon after this Mary Craig visited Varina in New York. She was a pretty and talented girl who eventually became involved with the literary set and married Upton Sinclair in 1913. Varina did not live to learn her ultimate fate, although she was one of many young girls whom she chaperoned and guided in their early teens. But in 1957 Mary Craig's autobiography, *Southern Belle,* published in her old age, told of the difficult route she had traveled since she first sought publication in New York of a book on Winnie Davis's romance, written with Varina's co-operation. Upton Sinclair deplored it. Some thought it too sentimental. Others felt it would be deeply wounding to Southern feelings. Mary Craig took the stand that Jefferson Davis had flatly opposed Winnie's marriage and that she had died of a broken heart. The book was never published.

When she felt well enough Varina usually attended Albert M. Bagby's morning musicales at the old Waldorf-Astoria, occupying a special chair and holding court afterward.[9] She greatly enjoyed the opera when she could afford to go, or when someone invited her and she felt equal to an outing. Her sage face was seen occasionally in the Golden Horseshoe. She lived strictly in the social traditions of the Victorian era and only succumbed to the horseless carriage shortly before her death in 1906 when she was staying at the Gramatan Inn in Bronxville. But she much preferred the victoria, and she and Winnie had planned to get their own carriage when they could afford it. Varina had always had excellent horses, and it irked her to have to rely on friends for a carriage drive, or to go to the expense of hiring hacks. As her doctors' bills and the cost of her medicines mounted, she felt she had less to spend for the theater and drives. Toward the end she dreaded train journeys. It was increasingly difficult for her to travel south. "Railway travel shakes me so that I feel as though my nerves were tied with strings and jerked violently," she observed in the autumn of 1902. Her friends from the South noted the change in her from year to year. Her once beautiful eyes that had seen so much of tragedy and intrigue were heavily hooded now, and their glance was brooding and weary. Her hair had turned snow-white. The line of her mouth had sagged. But she was as careful as ever about her dress and appearance. Margaret knew how she liked her hair dressed; how her tight corseting should be effected; how her ruche, her lawn cuffs, and bonnet ties should be adjusted. Her eyeglasses were latched to her bodice with a moonstone chain. She often wore a favorite cameo brooch. Her voice was rich and deep in her old age, with the liquid intonations of the South. All agreed that it was well worth listening to what Varina had to say.

She became well known by sight around New York, driving in an old-fashioned carriage, and when Mary Day Burchenal took her to an Old Guard ball she seemed surprised when the audience burst into applause as she entered her box.[10]

"What is all this noise about?" she asked.

"They have recognized you, Mrs. Davis," Mrs. Burchenal informed her.

Although she enjoyed her public role and took bows with ease she seemed to be genuinely surprised at this public demonstration on her unheralded arrival.

Varina liked afternoon tea, a daily drive when the weather was fine, a good game of cards, and a light novel, as well as heavier reading. It bothered her when she had to take ten doses of medicine a day, eat carefully, and stay calm. She was never tired of gossip, and kept up with all the family ramifications, but she shied away from scandal. Her friends from the South found her surrounded with familiar touches —photographs of Jefferson Davis and her sons; a painting of Winnie as Queen of Comus which hung prominently in her hotel apartment; her tea things and her souvenirs, although by 1900 she wrote to a friend that she had given away virtually everything and sometimes longed to have a few trifling reminders of her past. She gave dinners for such friends as Mrs. John P. Labouisse of New Orleans and they would talk of old friends on the Gulf Coast.[11] Varina was always tactful about subordinating her conversational interests to her guests.

She took a cool view of the growing agitation over woman suffrage in the early part of the century. Few women of her generation had wielded more subtle power than she, but she was not an advocate of votes for women. Her sense of convention was unshakable and she wrote: "A woman is no less a citizen because she has no vote, and can a good citizen have a higher duty than fitting a child to be the worthy head of a family?"

When Judge Howry asked her for advice on the education of his daughter, whom his wife wished to enter in a convent, Varina made an interesting comment on her husband. Suggesting compromise, she observed: "Now unlike my dear radical husband . . . I believe much is achieved by compromises." [12]

One of her great joys in her old age was the congregation of young people around her, whether she was in the North or South. As the years advanced and the number of her grandchildren increased, she became truly matriarchal. She was too intense in her family and intellectual interests ever to feel the emptiness of a lonely life. The young people enjoyed her somewhat acid wit and appreciated the fact that she was not sentimental. Her great-niece, Mary Stamps, spent a good deal of time with Varina, who scolded her and her sister Lucinda (later Mrs. Morgan B. More), for lacing so tightly and giving themselves hour glass figures.[13] She thought they should achieve a simpler effect at their age.

"Mary, you remind me of the lily," she said on one occasion.

Mary was delighted—the white, languid lily, epitome of the South. She thought she was being complimented.

"Yes, they toil not, neither do they spin," Varina reminded her.

She was a great worker herself and expected no less of others.

She often recalled for them the responsibilities of her own early years, and during the Spanish-American War she wrote sympathetically to her cousin, Mrs. Devereux Shields, when she read in a Natchez paper that her husband had been wounded in action and captured. This incident reminded her of the time her own husband was wounded in the Mexican War. There were no telegraph wires then and she had three weeks of anguish. "A great spot of gray came in my hair," wrote Varina, "but he came home, spent with pain and lame, and he lived forty-two years afterwards." [14]

Jefferson Hayes-Davis, attending Princeton, was a frequent caller at his grandmother's apartment in the Gerard Hotel. "She had great charm and her Sunday afternoon teas were attended by many famous and interesting people," he recalled half a century later. "When I brought friends from Princeton on week-ends they would rather spend their time with Mrs. Davis than go out in New York. Young and old were fascinated by her interesting sprightly conversation." [15]

His sister Lucy was to remember Varina at this time as a "most regal woman—five feet ten inches tall and always noticeable." [16] She could recall her singing folk songs to her as a child. She thought her artistic and musical, and her needlework superb. She could never forget the way in which she made her own designs, "embroidering them without drawing them, from the flowers we had picked."

Although Varina had tried at times to discourage her husband from brooding over every attack and answering them all in detail, she had now taken up the same burden with a vengeance. Early in 1901 she was plagued by a story that he had sent Prince de Polignac to offer the French Emperor land in exchange for aid. Writing to Colonel James Morris Morgan, of South Carolina, who had brought the matter to her attention, she observed: "That some thoughtless men might have collogued together to make such a suggestion is *barely possible*, but not probable as if we had been reduced to such a strait the French Govt. would have known Mr. Davis could not give France territory already on the eve of being captured from us, and such an agreement or offer would have been utterly worthless. This is a ridiculous mess, I suppose found by some pothouse statesman." [17]

Varina questioned Reagan about the matter. He was one of the last survivors of her husband's entourage, and he sent her a letter that seemed conclusive evidence to her "of the falsity as well as the absurdity" of the report. Sending it to Colonel Morgan, she wrote:

I am not troubled by such vague revelations of treason and stratagem as may be made as time rolls on and the acts in the awful drama pass away. The truth may be overborne for a time by fiction, but Mr. Davis' reputation cannot suffer by the utmost publicity being given to his official acts, and I do not fear the verdict of posterity upon him as a citizen or a man. Imputations cast upon him will fall pointless in the light of truth.

After one of these attacks Varina wrote to the Kimbroughs: "In my times of sorrow and suffering I have wondered for what use I was spared but suppose now it must have been to protect the blessed memory of my husband from misrepresentations against which he is powerless to defend himself." [18]

Even while he fought with her, as he often did, Richard Watson

Gilder, editor of *The Century*, enjoyed Varina and admired her. After spending a long evening with her he wrote appreciatively of the experience to James Calvin Hemphill from his summer home at Tyringham, Massachusetts. He and his brother Joe got up to leave at eleven but she held them spellbound and they stayed on listening until half past twelve while she talked about Winnie, whom he called Varina, and her husband—"I who would have hanged him how often on a particularly 'sour apple-tree'!" wrote Gilder.[19] Actually they had a "great time" with Mrs. Davis.

> She told us with enthusiasm of Wade Hampton—"the finest product" she said "of civilization"— and of Lee the handsomest man "of his coloring" she had ever seen—till he put on his masque—a beard. She talked about Fortress Monroe, praised her husband, referred with something other than praise to Genl. Miles,—and Gen. Sherman. And Varina! there we mingled our tears—for I knew long that lovely "daughter of the Confederacy!" and the mother is kind to me, and forgives my northern and Union sentiments for my love of Varina.
> I told her there was occasion for bitterness on our side as well as hers— as for instance, 'twas my own beloved wife's beloved youngest and angelical brother whose funeral was insulted in New Orleans!

Varina reigned as Queen again in the spring of 1902 when she went south and visited Jackson, Vicksburg, Natchez, Memphis, and New Orleans, holding receptions in each place. Although full of "neuralgia creeping out of my finger ends today and in and out of my temples" she sat enthroned in the Palm Garden of the St. Charles Hotel for a large reception given in her honor by the United Daughters of the Confederacy and other women's organizations. Mary Craig sat at her feet to protect her from handshaking, which she could not endure in her neuralgic condition. She was presented on this occasion with a diamond ring.

She met the children of her old friends and was saddened over the deaths of so many of her contemporaries. "I did not realize how long I had lived until I had seen the immense list of the silent majority of my old friends and neighbors," she wrote to Mrs. Kimbrough. She attended the opera and drove out to the Country Club and overawed the younger generation with her majesty, coupled with the warnings they had had that they must mind their "p's" and "q's" because Aunt Varina was coming.[20] She seemed more a personage than ever away from the shadow of their dearly beloved uncle Jeff. There was much ceremonial during her visit.

Another celebration was held in her honor in Memphis where a crown-shaped diamond and ruby brooch was presented to her. Her hostess was Mrs. Hugh M. Neely, an old friend from her days in Tennessee. In Jackson, Varina was entertained by Governor A. H. Longino and she held a reception in the state Capitol. Her visit to the capital of Mississippi was twofold in its purpose for she hoped to sell Beauvoir to the state.[21] But she was too sensitive to push the matter when she saw that there was no enthusiasm for the purchase. She had finally decided to sell the property, but she hoped that it might remain a memorial to her husband's memory and a home for veterans. Mrs. Kimbrough and her sister, Mrs. L. F. Yerger, had worked for eleven years toward this end, hoping that the state would take it over. When their plans failed Varina wrote consolingly to Mrs. Kimbrough that "if the sentiment of the people did not call for it I am satisfied, and as I do not owe anything, I am not worrying about the purchase money." [22]

By the end of the year she had sold it for ten thousand dollars to the United Sons of Confederate Veterans. She could have disposed of it over and over again, but she and Winnie had always cherished the hope that they could leave the house and grounds to the state as a gift, to be used as a soldiers' home.[23] In 1893 Winnie was offered ninety thousand dollars for it as a site on which to build a hotel. She rejected this proposal emphatically. The last offer of twenty thousand dollars was declined at a time when Varina wrote that she had not had a dollar of income for three years and was leaning on Addison for support, although his mining stock had not been doing well, he had a large family to support, and his health was precarious. Relatives of Mrs. Dorsey had tried to buy it for ten thousand dollars cash in 1896, "but I did not wish to sell it except as a home for the Veterans," Varina wrote to Judge Kimbrough on November 6, 1902. Least of all did she wish to sell it to anyone belonging to Mrs. Dorsey. She felt that the attempt had been made only to mortify her.

While in the South, Varina learned that a little group of women were determined to keep her name off the memorial. She was shocked over a proposal that it should be named the Davis-Dorsey house. She stipulated that no names other than those of her husband and children should be perpetuated there. She was indifferent about the use of her own name, and wrote:

Now the only two names I care to have inserted are my Winnie's whose house it is and her father's great name. . . . Confident in the memory of my almost lifelong service to my husband and to the country through him, I do not care in the least whether anyone mentions me at all or not. I shall know as I am known in the home beyond this world, and when the time is remote enough nobody amounts to much.[24]

Varina wanted to reserve sixty feet on the sea front and to furnish Winnie's room. She wished she could send "her blessed name from pole to pole," she wrote to the Kimbroughs on August 21, 1902. She signed the deed on October 10 for the house and eighty-seven acres of land as a "free and welcome home for all indigent ex-Confederate soldiers and sailors, their widows and orphans and servants." It was to be preserved as a "perpetual memorial sacred to the memory of Jefferson Davis, only President of the Confederate States of America and to his family and the 'Lost Cause.'" Varina stipulated that no material alterations should ever be made in the house or land, and that the two pavilions should be preserved, more specifically the one in which he wrote *The Rise and Fall of the Confederate Government.*

A year later, when a plan to name rooms after generals was considered, she bluntly stated in a letter to the Kimbroughs that she did not wish the names either of J. E. Johnston or Beauregard used in this way "but would not make a point upon anyone but Johnston's name."

The sale of Beauvoir helped little except that she no longer had to maintain it. Great storms raged that winter and her plantations were laid waste. Her crops were washed away and all the fences on both properties went with them. Forty-three houses "were torn to pieces" on the land and she had to spend seven thousand dollars for a new gin, "so I must darn my stockings, not indulge in candy, carriages or shows!" she noted, quoting from Vergil: *"Infandum, regina, jubes renovare dolorem."* [25]

But Varina was feeling unusually well that autumn after a summer spent in Canada. She had been with the Neelys at a Southern colony in Port Colborne, Ontario, twenty miles from Buffalo, and she had "enjoyed Southern ways greatly. My people are anchored in my heart and I never expect to slip the cable or drag the anchor," she noted.

Varina spent three summers in all at this Northern resort, which covered forty-five acres, was known as the Humberstone Club, and extended half a mile along Lake Erie amid a grove of pines and cedars. She automatically became the matriarch in this congenial colony, and the cool weather suited her.

Miss Florence M. McIntyre, of Memphis, whose father founded the club, has many memories of the dowager Varina and the three seasons she spent with them. Catching her one day as she set out wearing her bonnet and crepe veil, suggestive of Queen Victoria, young Florence asked if she might take her picture.

"What do you want with a picture of an ugly old woman like me?" Varina demanded.

When she told her on another occasion that she thought she looked like the Queen, Varina remarked with a twinkle in her eye, "That is not a compliment to either." [26]

She usually took a siesta in the afternoon. She always enjoyed a game of cards and was everlastingly ready for conversation, which she had long been accustomed to dust with Attic salt. She liked to talk of her early days in Washington and to tell stories of Daniel Webster and John C. Calhoun. But by this time she was reluctant to discuss politics for publication, and when a reporter arrived from a Buffalo paper she chose to talk of the huge hydrangeas that grew at the club, the newest books and the status of the married versus the career woman, a current subject of debate. Varina said quite frankly that she believed in the mental superiority of man, although women had no cause to be ashamed of their achievements. "They are advancing in the right direction when the circumstances are taken into consideration," she briskly observed. "The married life is the best and fullest for the woman—but the times have changed and complicated matters."

The reporter noted her snow-white hair, parted in the middle and drawn back gracefully on either side. She wore a *peau de soie* dress with tiny white dots, and had a thin shawl over her shoulders. This was her view of Varina at the age of seventy-seven:

> So we sat chatting about books and people past and present. It looked for all the world like a miniature court. In the middle sat Mrs. Davis, holding our unwavering attention, not by the prerogative of rank, but by the power of her extraordinary intellect which compels attention to all she says. Whether composed of the simplest commonplaces, or reminiscent of

the turbulent times of which she was not only an eye witness but a foremost participant, her conversation is superlatively interesting.[27]

Varina had her granddaughter, Lucy Hayes, with her on her third summer at the Humberstone Club. Lucy liked to sketch. So did Florence McIntyre. Varina insisted on both going out "to make use of what little God gave us." That same summer she was asked to write something for charitable funds that were being raised. Always responsive in such matters, she gave considerable time and thought to writing *The Grasshopper War*, based on a war between the Huron and Iroquois Indians. In setting up a flagpole at the Humberstone Club a large Indian burying ground had been discovered, with kettles, pottery, pipes, and wampum in the mound. Florence and her father collected the historical facts of the war and Varina wrote the little history, a five-page booklet, which is now a collectors' item, and may be found in the State Library, New Orleans.[28] Two hundred copies were bound in vellum and had limited circulation. Florence illustrated the cover with a life-sized grasshopper.

The year 1904 was a sad one for her in many ways. Burton Harrison died that spring. She had written to him a few days earlier, commenting on some observations in General Gordon's newly published book which seemed to reflect on her husband's relations with General Lee. "I am sure he meant no harm to Mr. Davis, and though I find in his book some '*implied*' criticism . . . I think nothing he has said is incompatible with allegiance and friendship for my Husband," Varina wrote.[29] Her last words to Burton were characteristic.

No two people if they are strong, or even active thinkers, agree with their verdict upon any actor's course, partly because the commentator has not been consulted. For my own part, had I been consulted about the cosmos, I should have criticized its parts with great vigor and complained about the result, in fact I, as "at present informed," should have resisted imposing Adam's society upon Eve as an infliction of boredom—not justified by a paternal government.

Varina was distressed by General Gordon's suggestion that General Lee hesitated at the end to let her husband know what he was doing. When challenged by Reagan, to whom Varina turned as the last survivor of these days, General Gordon blamed the interpretation on a typographical error and promised to have it changed in later editions. By way of apology he added: "There were the most complete cordiality and fullest conferences between President Davis and Genl. Lee as to all military movements and conditions." [30]

General Gordon assured Judge Reagan that General Lee's hesitation in the closing hours of the war "was not as to giving information in regard to all matters relating to the army and its operations, but that Lee hesitated to advise the civil authorities as to their duties in the trying exigencies of our situation." Gordon strongly suggested that both he and Lee had favored Johnston over Hood for the Western command and he reported glumly on Lee's eleventh-hour trip to Richmond when the war seemed over, quoting Lee's statement on his return that "nothing could be done at Richmond. . . . You know that the President is very pertinacious in opinion and purpose." General Gordon expressed the view in this book that Jefferson Davis and Joe Johnston were "cast in similar moulds and were of the most inflexible metal. The breach, therefore, once made, was never healed."

Instead of battling things out with her old friend whom she called the *"preux chevalier,"* Varina sent a letter to the *World* praising General Gordon and recalling that he was one of the first of her husband's friends to visit him at Fortress Monroe, that he threw his arms around him and burst into tears when he saw him, that they used deal boxes as seats for dinner in the casemate, reviewed the conduct of the battles and wound up with Gordon toasting Davis and Lee, "the complement of each other." [31]

. By this time Varina was a clever propagandist and she had coped with so many of these revelations that she had acquired some finesse. She drew Burton Harrison's attention to her letter in the *World* with the suggestion that it was better policy than some of her other communications. Three months later she was sympathizing with Connie as she closed up the home she had shared so happily with Burton. "When I went to shut up Beauvoir I counted my loss in such a desperately despairing way I can imagine how you are suffering," she wrote. Connie had borne four children—Fairfax, Francis Burton, Archibald Cary, and Ethel. She went abroad and lived in Cannes for the first three years after her husband's death.

John Taylor Wood, Zachary Taylor's grandson and Winnie's godfather, was the next to die, and on July 29, 1904, Varina was writing to Knox Taylor's sister, Mrs. Elizabeth Taylor Dandridge, that "few of the Confederates of this day even know his name which was among the brightest stars in our Confederate roster when it blazed with the great deeds performed by our naval men, hampered as they were by a too-powerful environment." [32] She recalled that he performed "prodigies of valor" and sank nine ships.

Forty years seem to have wiped out with the bitter tears of defeat many glorious memories and every now and then like "Old Mortality" I try to freshen the minds of our people to the glorious deeds done by these now "dead at the feet of Wrong." In dear John's death I feel sorely stricken for I loved him dearly.

Major Morgan died in the following year and Varina worried over his daughter Belle, who planned to contest his will. "Money certainly is the root of all evil as much as the want of it is," she wrote to Judge Kimbrough on October 20, 1905, saddened by these echoes of death and discord.

🎄 24 🎄

GENERAL MILES IS ROUTED

M Y CONTROVERSY with Miles is ended," Varina wrote on March 9, 1905, as the close of her own life approached. She had borne her grudge for forty years, remembering the indignities her husband had suffered at Fortress Monroe and the insults that had been offered her. She felt she had won the last encounter. At length she was satisfied and would "notice nothing more from him."

The final argument involved a letter he insisted Varina had written to him at the time of her husband's imprisonment, thanking him for his treatment of Davis. She challenged him to produce it. When he finally did, under much pressure, Varina pronounced him "unmasked." It proved to be a meaningless note written to Miles after she had begged knowledge of her husband when he was taken to sea under sealed orders on his way to Fortress Monroe, and before she knew what was happening to him. Varina wrote:

He answered by false assurances of Mr. Davis' health & comfort. Then I thanked him for answering and we steamed away in ignorance of what had happened in the four days my poor husband had been in his clutches. He meant to brag of the letter and believed I was as craven as himself and would be frightened by the clamor his announcement would bring about my head and he had not wit enough to see the production of the letter would prove him the abject liar he is, so he published it and it "unmasked him." [1]

Although she had first heard of the disputed letter in 1898 it was not until February, 1905, when Miles, having retired from the army in 1903, presented a general defense of his acts in a magazine article "My Treatment of Jefferson Davis," published in *The Independent*, that Varina exploded. She was desperately ill at the time, being treated with strychnine and nitroglycerin, and Margaret kept it away from her as long as she could, but once having seen the article, nothing could stop Varina. His defense that he had shackled Jefferson Davis lest he escape seemed merely ludicrous to her under the circumstances.

She took up Miles's case, point by point, tearing it apart—the fear that Davis would escape, the assassination charges, General Johnston's cartel. "Mr. Davis had not been covered by Genl. J. E. Johnston's cartel and did not care to be, though I do not think Genl. Johnston was anxious to provide for the President's safety," Varina wrote. She then stated her own view of the reason that General Lee was not taken prisoner—because "Genl. Grant said that he would resign his commission if such an act of bad faith was attempted. . . ." [2]

Varina sent Miles's attack and her answer to Walter Charlton, a Savannah lawyer, who drew up a statement for her, and she wrote to him on May 18, 1905, that when she received his "crushing review of Genl. Miles' interview at the *Herald* office" she was too ill to offer thanks and her eyes did not permit her even to read his "model denunciation of a vulgarian" but she pictured herself lying in bed "in almost mortal agony and having it read to her again and again." [3]

General Miles had been getting on in the world since these distant days, and Varina had watched his progress with interest and disapproval. He became a major general in 1890, fought in the Spanish-American War, and was a lieutenant general by 1901. To her he would always be a "vulgarian, a boor, a plebe," a man who had never heard of George Bancroft, the historian; and did not understand her allusion to Nessus' shirt. She wrote to her old friend Major Morgan in 1898 that "to have risen from the depths of ignorance and brutality in which he lived when I knew him shows he is adroit, ambitious, unscrupulous and persistent, but no man was ever more heartily despised by those under him." [4] Varina added scornfully: "I believe the creature has social ambitions."

She could never for a moment forget her husband's shackles or the personal affronts offered her at Fortress Monroe when Miles tried to have her quartered with the "camp women" instead of with the officers' wives. She could not understand why he had finally taken to the rostrum after so many years of silence. But Varina's railings now were ended. She was old and tired and ill and had endured much. The fires had burned themselves out at last. She deplored the whole matter in a letter written on March 15, 1905, to Dr. C. W. Chancellor, former

Confederate surgeon. "The controversy has not been of my seeking," she wrote.[5] When a reporter asked her soon after this if she still felt the same about General Miles, Mary Day Burchenal, who was with her at the time, heard Varina murmur, "Oh, my good man, there is no room in an old woman's heart for hatred." But her final word on the matter to Judge Kimbrough was, "I hope you saw and approved of the Miles controversy. I had to exculpate myself from his false accusations toward my husband."

Varina was her spryest self when she wrote to Walter L. Fleming on December 20, 1905, about the biography he was writing of her husband. She warmly denied the "absurd charge that Mr. Davis thought himself a military genius." On the contrary, Varina wrote: "He was devoid of every kind of assumption and never once did he by word or deed interfere with the generals conducting our unequal war against the North—Genl. Lee was his best friend, so was Genl. A. S. Johnston, indeed so were the generality of the leading officers of our army with the exception of Genl. Beauregard and Joe Johnston. This last wrote a book so full of egotism and misrepresentation seconded by poor old senile Genl. Longstreet's glaring misstatements that to answer them would be to blot out the whole of the two books." [6] In this same letter Varina charged that General Johnston had been "stabbing her husband ever since he found Genl. Lee ranked him in the army register."

Busy to the last days of her life, Varina collaborated with Campbell MacCulloch in a series of reminiscences for the magazine *Spare Moments*, published in Rochester, New York. It stirred her up to work on these final articles, and she wrote with feeling:

The silent ghosts of things that were, and the spirits of men who did and dared for the cause they believed in, file past in solemn review, and drag in their train events that have been well nigh forgotten; and memory rises upon memory and raises a clamant call that the truth be known.[7]

Varina wrote of the "startling absence of truth and fact in many of the tales that stand forth as history, of the inaccuracies that are painfully palpable, and personal memoirs that mislead are accepted as plain unvarnished statements of events as they occurred, while they are very far removed indeed from any semblance to actuality." Graphic in her own reporting, it is equally true that she could be passionately biased where her husband was concerned and although her *Memoir* preserves a balance her conclusions, as viewed through her letters and articles, were often affected by her own strong emotions.

Varina became desperately upset if the question of the disguise came up. In January of 1905 she was writing anxiously to General R. H. Henry to ask if the garments her husband had actually worn on that occasion were safely back in the deposit place she had chosen for them. She had permitted Margaret to give them for exhibition at the St. Louis Fair, and she now wrote: "The safety of these clothes is of more importance to us than much gold and silver . . . these are our irrefragable proofs of the falsehoods told by the enemy at that time." [8] They are in the Confederate Museum at Richmond today.

Varina was suffering at this time from her surroundings. The theaters had been encroaching steadily on the block where she lived, close to Sixth Avenue, and now the Hippodrome was being built, shutting out her light and air and bringing a strange assortment of sounds into her neighborhood. While she was doing battle with Miles in March, 1905, she was also writing with a touch of humor to Mary Craig that a "grand new Hippodrome *à la Paris*" had been built half a square from her. "On the front is 'Andersonville,' I suppose such a travesty of truth as *Uncle Tom's Cabin*." [9]

But things seemed to be dissolving around Varina. Her faithful maid, Margaret Connelly, was getting married after eleven years of companionship. Varina was at Ye Olde Greenwich Inn in Sound Beach in the summer of 1905, listening dreamily as the "sea laps the lovely beach not an hundred yards from us." Her fine handwriting was failing her at last. She had trouble with her spelling. The lights were dimming for Varina.

But she made her last public appearance at the wedding of her great-niece, Mary Stamps, to William Gaillard, in February, 1906. On this occasion she attracted almost as much attention as the bride. She was gowned in heavy white silk with lace, the dress in which she was later buried. Varina had always liked to dress in white, although for most of her later years she was somberly clad in black.

In July she was writing to Mary Craig from the Gramatan Inn that "I shall be no weaker when death knocks at my door." [10] She had been lifted in and out of her carriage by her daughter Margaret but now she sat all day "looking at the trees and enjoying the pure air." In her own words Varina was now taking "short views of life as Sidney Smith advises." She detested her incapacity and was deeply embarrassed when she tripped and fell flat on her face in the Church of Zion and St. Timothy when taking communion. She did not like being clumsy and later told her friend Mrs. Beale, "It is no disgrace to fall down in company, but even an accident smacks of a *faux pas* and is nevertheless a mortification." [11]

Mrs. Beale was Varina's close companion during her last few years. She was a lively and loyal friend, understanding the Dowager Davis to the full, sharing her passion for the South and her interest in the North. They went around New York together. They played cards, received their mutual friends from the South, and had long talks. Mrs. Beale was a bright and animated person in her own right and Varina had always liked good company. She found it more difficult to tolerate bores than any other type of person.

Her financial worries were eased at the end to some extent by the sale of the extra acres she had kept at Beauvoir. Judge Kimbrough disposed of this property for her in the autumn of 1905 for five thousand dollars.[12] Her first thought was that she could pay for the two stained-glass windows she had ordered from Munich as memorials to her husband and daughter, to be installed in the Church of the Redeemer at Biloxi. Now she could "square things and feel easy," she wrote. She was too ill to go south for the unveiling but asked Judge Kimbrough if he would take her place.

At this time she and Mrs. Beale were trying to arrange a joint living arrangement. Varina had decided to leave the Gerard and she finally took a four-roomed apartment at the Majestic Hotel. It was a major upheaval for her to move, since she had been in the one place for fifteen years and her rent would go up from twenty-five hundred dollars to four thousand dollars a year, but it "seemed to fill all requirements."

Her rooms looked out on Central Park. There were "nice influential people in the house" and she was to have the library always at her service as a public room for receiving guests. There was a concert once a week, a fete at Easter, a great Christmas tree for children and a good menu, Varina assured Mrs. Beale. They would be able to welcome the veterans when they droppd in. "Now when I think of them the tears well up in my tired old eyes . . . my Confederate feeling is a passion with me as I get older," she wrote.[13]

Margaret, who had nursed Varina most of the summer, went back west in July, leaving her at the Gramatan Inn. She warned her not to try moving without help, but Varina, feeling a little stronger, went straight ahead. She wrote that Maggie, "happy in her large family . . . will come whenever I write for her, but quietly I want to accomplish my move without letting her know until I am settled and then I will write to her." All her affairs were in order. She had willed everything to Margaret except her ten thousand dollar life insurance policy, and she had made bequests to her sister Maggie, to her maid Margaret Josephine Connelly; to her earlier maid, Margaret Elizabeth Bettie Hooks; to Mary Ahern, Winnie's nurse, and to various nieces. Varina was now prepared for death.

She caught cold moving to the Majestic, and before she had a chance to get thoroughly settled became seriously ill with pneumonia. She lingered for ten days and was still conscious when Margaret and her family arrived from Colorado on October 11. In a moment of lucidity her great mournful eyes turned to the daughter who so closely resembled her and she murmured, "My darling child, I am going to die this time but I'll try to be brave about it. Don't you wear black. It is bad for your health, and will depress your husband." [14] Her last conscious words were: "O Lord in Thee have I trusted, let me not be confounded."

She died at 10:30 P.M. on October 16, 1906, in a strange hotel room furnished largely with rattan pieces. Varina had not yet had time or strength to arrange her things or set out her souvenirs. Jefferson Hayes-Davis had come in from Princeton. Dr. and Mrs. Gerald G. Webb had come on from Colorado Springs with Margaret Hayes, the last of Varina's children. Mrs. Pulitzer was present at the end. So were Mrs. Charles E. Bateson and Carrie Beale.

The Rev. Dr. Nathan A. Seagle of St. Stephens Church, where Varina worshiped, was there to say a final prayer.[15] She had told Margaret all that she wished done at the end. A small service was held in the hotel apartment. Collects chosen by the family and the Twenty-Third Psalm were read. The hymn sung was "Guide Me, O Thou Great Jehovah." Robert E. Lee's daughter, Mary Custis Lee, was present to do Varina honor, and the Southern colony turned out in force to pay condolence calls on Margaret. President Theodore Roosevelt sent a wreath. So did members of the Vanderbilt and other old New York families. Both North and South combined at the end to pay tribute to Varina Davis. The Daughters of the Confederacy sent a large heart of lilies of the valley and American beauty roses. The governors of the Southern

States and many military organizations remembered the widow of Jefferson Davis.[16]

General Frederick Dent Grant, the son of her friend, Julia Dent Grant, sent a company of artillery from Governors Island to escort Varina's cortege through the streets of New York to the Pennsylvania Ferry, and the New York Camp of the United Confederate Veterans sent its own guard of honor. Park Row took note of this strange assemblage of North and South and of the fact that the Southern bands played "The Bonnie Blue Flag," "Dixie," and "Maryland, My Maryland" as well as the funeral march.[17]

Varina had a military funeral in Richmond. She had made her wishes clear on this. "Mother wishes every mark of respect and a military funeral such as Winnie had," Margaret telegraphed to Lieutenant Governor J. Taylor Ellyson, who was making the arrangements in the South.[18] Varina had spoken at the end in her old imperious way. A committee arrived from Richmond to accompany the funeral party south. The train drew slowly into Richmond on the morning of October 19. For the third time the city was in mourning for a member of the family that had lived so significantly and tragically in its midst. Again the bands played, the Confederate flags flew, and Varina received all honor in the city where her most triumphant and her saddest hours had been spent. The funeral procession passed through the crowded streets to St. Paul's Church, where she had attended so many war weddings and funerals, and where Jefferson Davis had received the message from General Lee that spelled the end of the Confederacy. The Richmond *News-Leader* commented on October 19, 1906:

Forty-five years and a few months ago Mrs. Jefferson Davis came to Richmond, the wife of the president of a new republic coming to the capital. The air was palpitant with enthusiastic faith and glowing hope and crowded with brilliant dreams. . . . Today, Mrs. Davis came back to Richmond to be buried, an old woman long widowed and bereft, who has been waiting these years for death. The Confederacy has gone, the hopes clustered so thickly and brightly about it have faded and gone, the dreams are vanished. The vast majority of the glorious, strong young men who answered the President's call so quickly, marching proudly to the centres of war from city, village, and farm-house, died on the field or have been borne away by the inexorable process of time and wear. But a few worn and aged veterans remain to represent them. . . . She was one of the last living mementoes of the Confederate Government, one of the last of all to die.[19]

Few of her generation were left to recall Varina's role in an intimate way on that autumn day as tinted light filtered through the memorial windows dedicated to Jefferson Davis and General Lee. It rained and stormed as she was buried in Hollywood Cemetery, and a mass of brightly colored autumn leaves swirled over the sodden ground around her grave. At the last moment Mrs. Beale strewed roses from the Richmond Capitol on her bier—a fitting touch for Varina, to whom the rose had always symbolized the crucial moments of life. James Jones stood sobbing beside the grave, his hat in his hand.

Varina was laid beside the husband she had loved so devotedly, and half a century later ivy grew on the twin graves and all the members of her family were memorialized around her. The tall monument to Jefferson Davis dominated the plateau. The sorrowing angel with laurel wreath that the United Daughters of the Confederacy had placed over Winnie's grave was beside it, and marble tablets marked the graves of Varina's other children, including the one put up by the children of Richmond over Joseph's grave.

Margaret chose the inscription she thought most suitable for the graves of her parents: "*Whom God hath joined together let no man put asunder. Lord Keep their memories Green.*" And for Varina alone: "*Beloved and faithful wife of Jefferson Davis and devoted mother of his children. 'Her children raise up and call her blessed; her husband also and he praiseth her.' 'She stretcheth out her hand to the poor; yes she reacheth forth her hands to the needy.' 'Give her of the fruit of her hands and let her own works praise her in the gates.'* "

Varina's turbulent life was over at last and she rested at peace on the quiet hillside. The White House of the Confederacy was within walking distance. The wooded hills, the meandering James, the church spires of Richmond, were all within easy range. She had rounded her eightieth year and had outlived her battle-scarred generation. She had developed strength and worldly wisdom and had figured more significantly in the history of the Confederacy than was recognized at the time. She had experienced such moments of crisis as come to few women in a lifetime, and had shared in counsels that involved the fate of a nation.

Varina had idolized one lonely man, and the vision had stayed with her to the end. Her critics called her vain, building up false images as bit by bit she added to the stature of Jefferson Davis. They thought her proud and pretentious, running a court in New York as in Richmond. Her more relentless enemies considered her ill-tempered, sarcastic, even vindictive. They identified her with many of her husband's mistakes and criticized her for Winnie's shattered romance. A touch of the truth may have lain in all these charges; but they were not the essential truth, as Varina's nature and history are revealed through her own letters and actions.

Her sufferings tempered the impulses of her strong nature and gave her understanding, as life slowed down for her in the still waters of endurance. The years changed and strengthened her character, even as her physical powers declined. Knowing her only in her old age, Dr. Burgess wrote of her:

It used to be said that she and Benjamin ran the machine at Richmond. However that may be, I can testify that she was capable of running that or any other machine, with or without Benjamin or anyone else. She was a personality with the instincts of a sensitive woman and the judgment of the strongest man. She was also endowed with tender feeling and indomitable will. Her powers of conversation and description were superior to those of any other woman I have ever known.[20]

Varina left an irreconcilable variety of impressions behind her. Both friends and foes conceded her intelligence, her influence, her stately manner, and her devotion to her husband and his cause, but she was the victim of many apocryphal tales. She had the critical temperament and was prone to analyze and appraise, with a sharpness that sometimes hurt. Those who knew her best considered her a warmhearted, generous and spontaneous woman, who suffered from her own impetuosity and her ready tongue.

She had formidable enemies as well as many friends, but the military men of the day, with few exceptions, respected her, and the statesmen and writers found her witty, thoughtful, and astute. She was a personage and a positive force, under the most trying circumstances, and although her life was filled with major tribulations and uncommon abuse she drew deep and lasting satisfaction from the warmth in her own home. The war years deepened and strengthened the bond between Varina and Jefferson Davis. Their letters reflect their growing appreciation of each other.

Varina undoubtedly emerged at her tenderest and best in the years immediately after the war when Jefferson Davis was in greatest need of the kind of comfort that only she could give him. This was a difficult time for her, since the task was overwhelming, with a man so sensitive to begin with, and then so wounded in spirit. His letters mirror what she meant to him in the crash of the Confederacy. It was harder to sustain the same high pitch during the rootless and wandering years that followed. Until they settled in Beauvoir there was no peace for either of them, but through these unhappy months Varina catered unceasingly to his shattered ego, tended his enfeebled body, went every step of the way with him in his slow recovery from the effects of the war, and harassed him only in being so gregarious a human being, so constant and insistent a talker, and in showing so marked an aversion to Mrs. Dorsey.

Varina understood the complex nature of Jefferson Davis as no one else ever did. He, in turn, profoundly influenced her, steadying her in the days of her immaturity and bringing out the best in her flexible nature. He saw her develop from an impetuous and self-willed girl into a woman of strength and purpose who fought a long and wearing battle on his behalf and gave him a wealth of love and fidelity that he recognized and cherished. To many beholders it seemed a form of worship, and at times it blinded her to the realities of their situation.

Varina liked to think that she had helped to bind up some of the wounds between North and South, and in her own way she was an able mediator, talking persuasively to the writing men and politicians of the day. She had moved to some degree with the times but to the end she remained intrinsically a rare old lady of Victorian vintage—a woman who had lived and suffered and loved beyond the common lot and was well aware of her own importance, yet could take ironic note of her imperfections.

NOTES

CHAPTER 1: A *Christmas Encounter*

1. Mrs. Lucy Hayes Young, of Colorado and Arkansas, granddaughter of Mrs. Jefferson Davis, to author.
2. Varina Davis, *Memoir*, I, pp. 191-93.
3. Mrs. M. E. Hamer (Lise Mitchell), Walter L. Fleming papers, Manuscript Division, New York Public Library; Isaiah T. Montgomery, *ibid.*
4. Mrs. Eron Rowland, *Varina Howell*, I, p. 61.
5. Varina Davis, *Memoir*, I, p. 191.
6. *Ibid.*, pp. 191-92.
7. Mrs. M. E. Hamer, *op. cit.*
8. Hudson Strode, *Jefferson Davis*, p. 130.
9. *Ibid.*
10. Mrs. M. E. Hamer, *op. cit.*
11. Robert W. Winston, *High Stakes and Hair Trigger*, pp. 36-37.
12. Varina Davis, *Memoir*, I, p. 199.
13. Mrs. Eron Rowland, *op. cit.*, I, p. 96.
14. Varina Davis's own notes on place and date of birth, given to author by her grandson, Jefferson Hayes-Davis, of Colorado Springs.
15. *Ibid.*
16. Mrs. Thomas Stone Howell, of Alexandria, Louisiana, to author.
17. Edith Rossiter Bevan autograph collection, Manuscripts Division, Library of Congress.
18. Jefferson Davis to Robert J. Walker, March 18, 1848, Manuscript Division, New York Public Library.
19. Varina Davis's own statement on family ancestry, Confederate Museum, Richmond.
20. T. C. De Leon, *Belles, Beaux and Brains of the 60's*, p. 68.
21. Mrs. Lucy Hayes Young to author.
22. Varina Davis, *Memoir*, I, p. 189.
23. Mrs. William Winans Wall, owner of The Briers, Natchez, Mississippi.
24. Mary A. Irvine to Walter L. Fleming, quoting Jefferson Davis in a letter written to her brother, undated, but shortly before Mr. Davis's death in 1889, Fleming papers, New York Public Library.

CHAPTER 2: *Wedding at The Briers*

1. Mrs. John W. Stewart, of Santa Barbara, California, great-granddaughter of Varina Davis, to author.
2. Mrs. Eron Rowland, *op. cit.*, I, p. 99.

3. Mrs. Harry Winston and Mrs. J. Balfour Miller, of Natchez, to author; *Early Memories of Natchez,* by Elizabeth Dunbar Murray.
4. Mrs. Elizabeth Taylor Dandridge, *New York Times,* October 20, 1906.
5. Charles Gibson, unidentified St. Louis newspaper, January 5, 1890, Fleming papers, New York Public Library.
6. Varina Davis to Major William H. Morgan, Nannie Mayes Crump collection, Jefferson Davis papers, Library of Congress.
7. Varina Davis, *Memoir,* I, p. 164.
8. *Ibid.,* I, p. 20.
9. Nannie Davis Smith, narrative on Davis family life, prepared for Dr. Robert McElroy, Manuscript Division, New York Public Library.
10. Jefferson Davis, *Belford's Magazine,* January, 1890. Biographical sketch prepared by Mr. Davis.
11. Varina Davis, *Memoir,* I, p. 202.
12. *Ibid.,* I, p. 204.
13. *Ibid.,* I, p. 203.
14. Isaiah T. Montgomery, *Boston Transcript,* February 16, 1902.
15. Varina Davis, *Memoir,* I, p. 175.
16. Mrs. M. E. Hamer, Fleming papers, New York Public Library.
17. Varina Davis, *Memoir,* II, pp. 301-5.
18. *Ibid.,* II, p. 304.
19. *Ibid.,* I, pp. 171-72.
20. *Ibid.,* I, p. 206.
21. *Ibid.,* I, p. 198.
22. Nannie Davis Smith, McElroy papers, *op. cit.*
23. Mrs. Eliza Davis to Mary Elizabeth Mitchell, September 15, 1845, Mary Elizabeth Mitchell papers, University of North Carolina.
24. Varina Davis, *Memoir,* I, pp. 209-15.
25. *Ibid.,* I, p. 216.
26. *Ibid.,* I, pp. 216-19.

CHAPTER 3: *Varina Meets Mrs. Polk*

1. Varina Davis, *Memoir,* I, p. 266.
2. Mrs. Eron Rowland, I, p. 162.
3. Varina Davis, *Memoir,* I, p. 229.
4. *Ibid.,* p. 253
5. *Ibid.,* pp. 253-58.
6. Mrs. Eron Rowland, *op. cit.,* I, p. 160.
7. Varina Davis, *Memoir,* I, 243-44.
8. Landon Knight, *The Real Jefferson Davis,* p. 39; *Memoir,* I, p. 245; Mrs. Roger A. Pryor, *Reminiscences of Peace and War,* p. 25.

9. Hudson Strode, *op. cit.*, p. 159.
10. Jefferson Davis to Varina Davis, August 16, 1845, Special Collections, Emory University.
11. Mrs. Elizabeth Taylor Dandridge, *New York Times*, October 20, 1906.
12. Varina Davis, *Memoir*, I, p. 290.
13. Jefferson Davis, *Belford's Magazine*, January, 1890.
14. Brierfield litigation: Davis vs. Bowmar and Smith, Mississippi Reports, annotated edition, LV; Wirt A. Williams, *Journal of Mississippi History*, July, 1947.
15. Varina Davis to Mrs. Robert J. Walker, September 4, 1846, New York Historical Society.
16. Joseph Davis Howell to Mrs. William Burr Howell, October 13, 1846, *Memoir*, I, p. 308.
17. Jefferson Davis to Varina Davis, October 5, 1846, *Memoir*, I, p. 307.
18. Varina Davis, *Memoir*, I, p. 310.
19. *Ibid.*, I, p. 311.
20. *Ibid.*
21. Joseph E. Davis to Jefferson Davis, December 16, 1846, Confederate Museum, Richmond.
22. Jefferson Davis to Varina Davis, February 25, 1847, *Memoir*, I, p. 316.
23. Varina Davis, *Memoir*, I, p. 352.
24. Thomas L. Crittenden to Joseph E. Davis, February 25, 1847, Confederate Memorial Hall, New Orleans.
25. Jefferson Davis's description of Buena Vista, March 2, 1847, *Memoir*, I, pp. 325-26.
26. Varina Davis, *Memoir*, I, p. 357.
27. *Ibid.*, I, p. 357.
28. Jefferson Davis to Varina Davis, September 30, 1847, Confederate Museum, Richmond.

CHAPTER 4: A *Zealot Scales Olympia*

1. John H. Reagan, *The Davis Memorial Volume*, compiled by J. William Jones.
2. Mrs. Clement C. Clay, A *Belle of the Fifties*, p. 68.
3. Varina Davis, *Memoir*, I, p. 283.
4. *Ibid.*, pp. 409-10.
5. *Ibid.*, p. 277.
6. *Ibid.*, p. 265.
7. *Ibid.*, p. 282.
8. William E. Dodd: *Jefferson Davis*, p. 109.
9. Varina Davis, *Memoir*, I, p. 414.

10. Jefferson Davis to R. J. Walker, March 18, 1848. Jefferson Davis miscellaneous papers, Manuscript Division, New York Public Library.
11. Varina Davis, *Memoir*, I, p. 262.
12. *Ibid.*, p. 418.
13. Zachary Taylor to Jefferson Davis, July 10, 1848, Jefferson Davis papers, Library of Congress.
14. Varina Davis to Jefferson Davis, January 25, 1849, Strode, *op. cit.*, p. 208.
15. *Ibid.*, January 24, 1849; Confederate Museum, Richmond.
16. Bess Furman: *White House in Profile*, pp. 148-49.
17. Varina Davis, *Memoir*, I, p. 412.
18. Mary A. A. Fry to Robert McElroy, September 22, 1937, Manuscript Division, New York Public Library.
19. Varina Davis, *Memoir*, I, pp. 442-43.
20. *Ibid.*, I, p. 458.
21. *Ibid.*, I, p. 463.
22. *Ibid.*, I, p. 439.
23. *Spare Moments*, 1906.
24. Mrs. Laura C. Holloway: *The Ladies of the White House*, p. 459.
25. Mrs. William Burr Howell to Varina Davis, quoting Dr. Samuel A. Cartwright, October, 1849, Jefferson Davis papers, Library of Congress.
26. Varina Davis, *Memoir*, I, pp. 469-70.

CHAPTER 5: *A Son for Varina*

1. George H. Gordon to Carnot Posey, June 9, 1852, Fleming papers, New York Public Library.
2. Varina Davis to Jefferson Davis, July 25, 1852, Jefferson Davis papers, Duke University.
3. Varina Davis, *Memoir*, I, p. 474.
4. *Ibid.*, I, p. 475.
5. Mrs. Eron Rowland, *op. cit.*, I, p. 276.
6. William Burr Howell to Jefferson Davis, January 31, 1853, New York Historical Society.
7. Mrs. William Burr Howell to Varina Davis, undated, but early in 1853, Jefferson Davis papers, Library of Congress.
8. Varina Davis, *Memoir*, I, p. 540.
9. Mrs. Clement C. Clay, *op. cit.*, p. 27.
10. *Ibid.*, p. 68.
11. Varina Davis, *Memoir*, II, p. 919.
12. Clifford Dowdey, T. C. De Leon, Morris Schaff, Douglas Southall Freeman, H. J. Eckenrode, Robert McElroy, Pierce Butler, Mrs. Mary

Boykin Chesnut, Mrs. Roger A. Pryor, Mrs. Clement C. Clay, Mrs. Burton N. Harrison, Mrs. D. Giraud Wright, Dr. John W. Burgess.

13. Mrs. Eron Rowland, *op. cit.*, I, p. 294.
14. Jefferson Davis to James Buchanan, July 23, 1835, Dreer Collection, Historical Society of Pennsylvania.
15. Ben Perley Poore: *Perley's Reminiscences*, I, p. 492.
16. Varina Davis, *Memoir*, I, pp. 545-46.
17. *Ibid.*, I, p. 548.
18. Varina Davis, *Memoir*, I, p. 555; Dunbar Rowland, *op. cit.*, VIII, pp. 1-10.
19. *Ibid.*, I, p. 536.
20. *Ibid.*, I, p. 30.
21. Varina Davis, *Memoir*, I, p. 538.
22. *Blackwood's Magazine*, September, 1862; Clippings in Fleming papers, New York Public Library.
23. Varina Davis, *Memoir*, I, p. 535.
24. Varina Davis, *Memoir*, I, p. 541.
25. *Ibid.*, I, p. 559.

CHAPTER 6: *Two Presidents Come Calling*

1. Varina Davis, *Memoir*, I, p. 571.
2. *Ibid.*, I, p. 223.
3. Jefferson Davis to Joseph E. Davis, August, 1857, Jefferson Davis miscellaneous papers, Manuscript Division, New York Public Library.
4. Varina Davis, *Memoir* I, pp. 575-78.
5. *Ibid.*, I, p. 581.
6. Varina Davis, *Memoir*, I, pp. 589-92.
7. *Ibid.*, I, pp. 593-94.
8. Boston *Morning Post*, October 12, 1858; *Memoir*, I, pp. 608-40.
9. William E. Dodd, *op. cit.*, p. 173.
10. Mrs. Clement C. Clay, *op. cit.*, p. 116; T. C. De Leon, *op. cit.*, p. 36.
11. Dr. John J. Craven; *Prison Life of Jefferson Davis*, p. 302.
12. Varina Davis, *Memoir*, I, p. 579.
13. Marian Gouverneur; *As I Remember*, pp. 276-77.
14. Mrs. Clement C. Clay, *op. cit.*, p. 134.
15. Mrs. Elizabeth F. Ellet: *Queens of American Society*, pp. 396-416.
16. Mrs. Clement C. Clay, *op. cit.*, pp. 30-31.
17. Mrs. Roger A. Pryor, *op. cit.*, p. 81.
18. Varina Davis, *Memoir*, I, pp. 557-58.
19. Mrs. Clement C. Clay, *op. cit.*, p. 62.
20. Varina Davis, *Memoir*, I, p. 574.

21. William Ernest Smith; *The Francis Preston Blair Family in Politics*, I, p. 502.
22. Varina Davis to Jefferson Davis, April 17, 1859; Strode, *op. cit.*, p. 329.
23. *Ibid.*, April 10, 1859, p. 326.
24. William Ernest Smith, *op. cit.*, II, p. 323.
25. Varina Davis to F. Philp, July 2, 1859, Manuscript Division, Henry E. Huntington Library, San Marino, California.
26. Varina Davis to Jefferson Davis, July 2, 1859, Strode, *op. cit.*, pp. 330-31.
27. Mrs. William Burr Howell to Jefferson Davis, July 14, 1859, Jefferson Davis papers, Library of Congress.
28. Mrs. M. E. Hamer, Fleming papers, New York Public Library.
29. Varina Davis, *Memoir*, I, p. 683.
30. Dunbar Rowland, *Constitutionalist*, IV, pp. 541-43.
31. Mrs. Clement C. Clay, *op. cit.*, p. 138.
32. Mrs. Elizabeth Keckley, *Behind the Scenes*, pp. 66-74.
33. Mrs. Roger A. Pryor, *op. cit.*, p. 111.
34. Gideon Welles: *Diary of Gideon Welles*, II, pp. 255-56.
35. Varina Davis, *Memoir*, I, p. 697.
36. Allen Tate: *Jefferson Davis: His Rise and Fall*, p. 7.
37. Varina Davis, *Memoir*, I, p. 698.
38. Dunbar Rowland, *op. cit.*, V, p. 44.
39. Varina Davis, *Memoir*, I, pp. 697-99.
40. Jefferson Davis to Franklin Pierce, January 20, 1861, Fleming papers, New York Public Library.

CHAPTER 7: *Birth of the Confederacy*

1. Varina Davis, *Memoir*, II, p. 19.
2. Major L. S. Daniel, *Daily Advocate*, Victoria, Texas, June 2, 1905.
3. Mrs. M. E. Hamer, narrative in Fleming papers, New York Public Library.
4. Mrs. Eron Rowland, *op. cit.*, I, p. 443.
5. Jefferson Davis to Crafts J. Wright (Original owned by Charles Gunther of Chicago), Jefferson Davis papers, Library of Congress.
6. Isaiah T. Montgomery, Jefferson Davis's departure for Montgomery, Alabama; Fleming papers, New York Public Library.
7. Varina Davis, *Memoir*, II, p. 20.
8. Katharine M. Jones; *Heroines of Dixie*, p. 13.
9. Varina Davis, *Memoir*, II, p. 33.
10. *Ibid.*, p. 34.
11. Montgomery *Daily Post*, February 18, 1861.

12. Mrs. Mary Boykin Chesnut: *A Diary from Dixie,* p. 12.
13. Original sketch by Varina Davis in White House of the Confederacy, Montgomery, Alabama.
14. *The Weekly Confederation,* March 10, 1861.
15. Montgomery *Weekly Advertiser,* April 17, 1861.
16. George Templeton Strong; *Diary of George Templeton Strong,* p. 113.
17. Varina Davis, *Memoir,* II, p. 37.
18. Mrs. Mary Boykin Chesnut, *op. cit.,* p. 20.
19. Katharine M. Jones, *op. cit.,* p. 20.
20. Mrs. Mary Boykin Chesnut, *op. cit.,* p. 39.
21. Varina Davis, *Memoir,* II, p. 80.
22. William Howard Russell, *My Diary North and South,* p. 62.
23. *Ibid.,* p. 97.
24. *Ibid.,* pp. 93-94.
25. Varina Davis to Jefferson Davis, April 11, 1865, Confederate Museum, Richmond.
26. William P. Trent; *Southern Statesmen of the Old Regime,* pp. 197-253.
27. Varina Davis, *Memoir,* I, pp. 410-11.
28. *Ibid.,* II, p. 70.
29. Clifford Dowdey: *The Land They Fought For,* p. 95.
30. Jefferson Davis to Crafts J. Wright, Jefferson Davis papers, Library of Congress; *Memoir,* II, p. 75.
31. Varina Davis to Clement Claiborne Clay, Jr., May 10, 1861, Clay papers, Duke University.
32. Mrs. Mary Boykin Chesnut, *op. cit.,* p. 50.
33. Mrs. Eugene McLean: "A Northern Woman in the Confederacy," *Harper's Magazine,* February, 1914.
34. Varina Davis, *Memoir,* II, pp. 73-75.
35. E. Merton Coulter: *The Confederate States of America,* pp. 109-10.
36. Mrs. Mary Boykin Chesnut, *op. cit.,* pp. 70-71.
37. Mrs. Roger A. Pryor, *op. cit.,* p. 166.

CHAPTER 8: *Women of Manassas*

1. Mrs. Mary Boykin Chesnut, *op. cit.,* p. 86.
2. Mrs. Eugene McLean, *op. cit.*
3. J. B. Jones, *A Rebel Clerk's Diary,* July 21, 1861.
4. Catherine Cooper Hopley: *Life in the South: from the Commencement of the War by a Blockaded British Subject.*
5. John S. Wise on General Joseph E. Johnston, *The Circle,* May, 1908; Wigfall papers, Library of Congress.

6. Mrs. Mary Boykin Chesnut, *op. cit.*, p. 96.
7. Varina Davis to Mary Boykin Chesnut, April 27, 1862, Chesnut papers, University of North Carolina.
8. Mrs. Roger A. Pryor, *op. cit.*, p. 173.
9. E. Merton Coulter, *op. cit.*, p. 112.
10. Mrs. Mary Boykin Chesnut, *op. cit.*, pp. 18-19.
11. Mrs. D. Giraud Wright, *op. cit.*, p. 57.
12. William Willis Blackford: *War Years with J. E. B. Stuart*, p. 15.
13. Varina Davis, *Memoir*, II, pp. 202-3.
14. Journal of Mary Elizabeth (Lise) Mitchell, 1842-1927, Mary Elizabeth Mitchell collection, University of North Carolina. (Original owned by Mrs. John G. O'Kelley, of Pass Christian, Mississippi.)
15. Mrs. Eliza Davis to Mary Elizabeth Mitchell, August 10, 1861, Mitchell collection, University of North Carolina.
16. Varina Davis, *Memoir*, pp. 198-201.
17. Varina Davis to George Barksdale, June 18, 1903, Valentine Museum, Richmond.
18. Varina Davis, *Memoir*, II, p. 162.
19. T. C. De Leon, *op. cit.*, p. 67.
20. *Ibid.*, pp. 196-200.
21. *Ibid.*, p. 67.
22. Richmond *Daily Dispatch*, July 20, 1861.
23. E. Merton Coulter, *op. cit.*, p. 110.
24. Charleston *Mercury*, August 17, 1861.
25. Constance Cary Harrison, "Virginia Scenes in '61," Burton N. Harrison papers, University of Virginia.
26. Varina Davis, *Memoir*, II, p. 152.
27. Richard Taylor, *Destruction and Reconstruction*, p. 26.
28. Jefferson Davis to Varina Davis, October 2, 1861, Confederate Museum, Richmond.
29. Mrs. Mary Anna Jackson: *Life and Letters of General Thomas S. Jackson*, p. 194.
30. Richmond *Whig*, "Caxton" article, September 30, 1861.
31. Richmond *Dispatch*, October 4, 1861.

CHAPTER 9: *Disasters Multiply*

1. Varina Davis to Mary Boykin Chesnut, April 27, 1862, Chesnut papers, University of North Carolina.
2. Notes on Mrs. George Washington quilt, Armistead Burt papers, Duke University.
3. Varina Davis, *Memoir*, II, p. 180.

4. Varina Davis, *Memoir*, II, p. 183.
5. J. B. Jones, *op. cit.*, I, p. 111.
6. Varina Davis, *Memoir*, II, p. 163.
7. Cincinnati *Daily Gazette*, February 27, 1862.
8. Varina Davis to Mrs. Charlotte Wigfall (Mrs. Louis T.), March 4, 1862, Confederate Museum, Richmond.
9. William Preston Johnston: *The Life of General Albert Sidney Johnston*, p. 14.
10. Jefferson Davis to Lucius Bellinger Northrop, April 29, 1879, Confederate Memorial Hall, New Orleans.
11. Katharine Jones, *op. cit.*, p. 122.
12. Varina Davis to Francis Lawley, June 8, 1898, Pierce Butler collection, Tulane University.
13. *The Living Church*, June 8, 1935; *Christian Advocate*, June 12, 1936; *Memoir*, II, p. 269, Fleming papers, New York Public Library.
14. Varina Davis, *Memoir*, II, p. 268.
15. Jefferson Davis to Varina Davis, May 13, 1862, Confederate Museum, Richmond.
16. *Ibid.*, May 16, 1862, Confederate Museum, Richmond; *Memoir*, II, pp. 273-74.
17. *Ibid.*, May 19, 1862, Confederate Museum, Richmond.
18. *Ibid.*, May 28, 1862, Confederate Museum, Richmond; *Memoir*, II, pp. 275-76.
19. *Ibid.*, May 31, 1862; *Memoir*, II, p. 279.
20. Scenes in Richmond during the Seven Days' Battles: *Recollections Grave and Gay: Heroines of Dixie; A Belle of the Fifties; Pickett and His Men.*
21. Jefferson Davis to Varina Davis, June 2, 1862, Confederate Museum, Richmond.
22. Varina Davis, *Memoir*, II, p. 321.
23. Jefferson Davis to Varina Davis, June 3, 1862, Confederate Museum, Richmond.
24. Edward A. Pollard: *Life of Jefferson Davis*, p. 154.
25. Jefferson Davis to Varina Davis, June 3, 1862, Confederate Museum, Richmond; *Memoir*, II, p. 294.
26. *Ibid.*, June 13, 1862, Confederate Museum, Richmond; *Memoir*, II, pp. 311-13.
27. *Ibid.*, June 23, 1862, Confederate Museum, Richmond.
28. J. B. Jones, *op. cit.*, I, p. 134.
29. Jefferson Davis to Varina Davis, June 25, 1862, Confederate Museum, Richmond.
30. G. A. Saussey to Walter L. Fleming, October 23, 1907, Fleming papers,

New York Public Library; Henry Thompson Stanton to Varina Davis, March 24, 1890; *Memoir*, II, p. 317; J. B. Jones, *op. cit.*, June 28, 1862.
31. Richard Taylor, *Destruction and Reconstruction*, p. 87.
32. Mrs. Mary Boykin Chesnut, *op. cit.*, p. 233.
33. T. C. De Leon, *op. cit.*, p. 176.
34. Katharine Jones, *op. cit.*, p. 173.
35. Varina Davis, *Memoir*, II, p. 204.
36. Gamaliel Bradford, *Wives*, pp. 176-77; Robert Winston, *op. cit.*, p. 193 (based on story told by the Rev. W. W. Page, of General Lee's staff); Mary Boykin Chesnut, *op. cit.*, p. 440.
37. T. C. De Leon, *op. cit.*, p. 69.
38. Varina Davis to Mrs. Laurence O'Bryan Branch, September, 1862, Laurence O'Bryan Branch papers, North Carolina State Archives, Raleigh, N. C.
39. Richmond *Examiner*, October 8, 1862.
40. J. B. Jones, *op. cit.*, November 1, 1862.
41. John S. Wise on General Joseph E. Johnston, *The Circle*, May, 1908.
42. Richmond *Examiner*, November 20, 1862.
43. J. B. Jones, *op. cit.*, November 8, 1862.
44. Jefferson Davis to Varina Davis, December 15, 1862, Confederate Museum, Richmond.
45. Joseph R. Davis to Varina Davis, April 22, 1862, Confederate Museum, Richmond.
46. Richard Taylor, *op. cit.*, p. 24.
47. John S. Wise, *The End of an Era*, p. 401.
48. Constance Cary Harrison, "Richmond Scenes in '62," *Battles and Leaders of the Civil War*.

CHAPTER 10: *Varina Practices Statesmanship*

1. Pierce Butler collection, Tulane University.
2. T. C. De Leon, *op. cit.*, p. 92.
3. Varina Davis to Francis Lawley, June 8, 1898, Pierce Butler collection, Tulane University.
4. *Ibid.*, April 4, 1897.
5. *Ibid.*
6. Varina Davis, *Memoir*, II, p. 207.
7. Varina Davis to Jefferson Davis, April 7, 1865, Confederate Museum, Richmond.
8. Mrs. Mary G. Billups to author, November 28, 1956.
9. Mrs. Samuel W. (Kate Lee) Ferguson to Walter L. Fleming, October 4, 1907, Fleming papers, New York Public Library.

10. Gamaliel Bradford, *Wives*, *op. cit.*, p. 176.
11. Jubal A. Early to Varina Davis, September 5, 1890, Confederate Memorial Hall, New Orleans.
12. Varina Davis to Dr. John W. Burgess, June 29, 1895, Confederate Museum, Richmond.
13. Varina Davis, *Memoir*, II, p. 529.
14. Mrs. Roger A. Pryor, *op. cit.*, "Agnes" letter, January 7, 1863.
15. *Ibid.*, undated letter from "Agnes," winter of 1863, p. 235.
16. Constance Cary Harrison, *op. cit.*, p. 127.
17. Mrs. Myrta Lockett Avary, *Dixie After the War*, p. 221.
18. Mrs. D. Giraud Wright, *A Southern Girl in '61*, p. 77.
19. T. C. De Leon, *op. cit.*, p. 215.
20. Constance Cary Harrison, *op. cit.*, p. 61.
21. T. C. De Leon, *op. cit.*, p. 117; Edward M. Alfriend; "Social Life in Richmond During the War," State Archives, Montgomery.
22. Constance Cary Harrison, *op. cit.*, p. 150.
23. T. C. De Leon, *op. cit.*, p. 197.
24. Mrs. Myrta Lockett Avary, *op. cit.*, pp. 28-29.
25. Mrs. Joseph E. (Lydia) Johnston to Mrs. Charlotte Wigfall, January 19, 1863, Wigfall papers, Library of Congress.
26. Mrs. Joseph E. Johnston to Louis T. Wigfall, March 16, 1863, Wigfall papers, Library of Congress.
27. Mrs. Johnston to Mrs. Wigfall, April 19, 1863, Wigfall papers, Library of Congress.
28. *Ibid.*, May 17, 1863.

CHAPTER 11: *A Plea for Bread*

1. Richmond *Examiner*, April 4, 1863.
2. Varina Davis, *Memoir*, II, pp. 374-75.
3. J. B. Jones, *op. cit.*, I, pp. 293-97.
4. Mrs. Mary Boykin Chesnut, *op. cit.*, p. 314.
5. Varina Davis, *Memoir*, II, p. 382; Jones, *op. cit.*, I, p. 321.
6. *Ibid.*, II, p. 383.
7. Mrs. D. Giraud Wright, *op. cit.*, p. 135.
8. Jefferson Davis to Joseph E. Davis, May 7, 1863, Mary Elizabeth Mitchell collection, University of North Carolina.
9. E. Macomber to his sister (unnamed), July 22, 1863, Electus W. Jones papers, Duke University.
10. J. B. Jones, *op. cit.*, I, p. 339.
11. Jefferson Davis to Robert E. Lee, August 11, 1863, *Memoir*, II, pp. 396-99.

12. Varina Davis to Mrs. Mary Boykin Chesnut, undated but soon after Gettysburg, Chesnut papers, University of North Carolina.

13. *Ibid.*

14. Mrs. Johnson to Mrs. Wigfall, August 2, 1863, Wigfall papers, Library of Congress.

15. Mrs. Johnston to Mrs. Wigfall, July 5, 1863, Wigfall papers, Library of Congress.

16. Varina Davis's *cartes de visite*, Confederate Museum, Richmond.

17. Mrs. Mary Boykin Chesnut, *op. cit.*, p. 317.

18. Richard Taylor, *op. cit.*, p. 44.

19. Varina Davis, *Memoir*, II, p. 451.

20. Mrs. Mary Boykin Chesnut, *op. cit.*, p. 329.

21. Jefferson Davis to Crafts J. Wright regarding attempt on his life, Jefferson Davis papers, Library of Congress; Davis Memorial Volume; *The Life and Death of Jefferson Davis*, edited by A. C. Bancroft, pp. 132-33.

22. Henry Stuart Foote: *A Casket of Reminiscences*, pp. 148-49.

23. Mrs. Mary Boykin Chesnut, *op. cit.*, p. 328.

24. *Ibid.*, p. 357.

25. *Ibid.*, pp. 335-36.

26. *Ibid.*, p. 344.

27. Richmond *Examiner*, January 20, 1864.

28. Mrs. Mary Boykin Chesnut, *op. cit.*, p. 352.

29. James L. Orr to James H. Hammond, January 3, 1864, James H. Hammond papers, Library of Congress.

30. Mrs. Roger A. Pryor. Letter from "Agnes," January 30, 1864, *op. cit.*, p. 263.

31. Mrs. Constance Cary Harrison, *op. cit.*

32. Mrs. Mary Boykin Chesnut, *op. cit.*

33. Richmond *Examiner*, January 21, 1864.

34. Varina Davis, *Memoir*, II, p. 217.

35. Official War Records, Series I, 51, McDowell to Stanton, May 4, 1862.

36. Mrs. Lucy Hayes Young to author, April 4, 1957.

37. Miss Nannie Mayes Crump to author.

38. Varina Davis, *Memoir*, II, p. 201.

39. *Ibid.*, II, p. 206.

40. Captain Robert E. Lee, Jr., *Recollections and Letters of General Robert E. Lee*, p. 287.

41. Judith Brockenbrough McGuire, *Diary of a Southern Refugee*, pp. 116-17.

42. Varina Davis, *Memoir*, II, p. 206.

43. Mrs. Clement C. Clay, *op. cit.*, p. 206.

44. Mrs. Mary Boykin Chesnut, *op. cit.*, p. 400.
45. *Washington Daily Morning Chronicle*, April 10, 1863.

CHAPTER 12: A Small Boy Dies

1. Varina Davis, *Memoir*, II, p. 496.
2. Mrs. Mary Boykin Chesnut, *op. cit.*, p. 405.
3. Mrs. Constance Cary Harrison, *op. cit.*, pp. 181-82.
4. Varina Davis, *Memoir*, II, p. 498.
5. *Ibid.*, pp. 499-503.
6. Edward A. Pollard, *Life of Jefferson Davis*, pp. 361-62.
7. Mrs. Johnston to Mrs. Wigfall, June 26, 1864, Wigfall papers, Library of Congress.
8. Mrs. D. Giraud Wright, *op. cit.*, pp. 185-86.
9. Varina Davis to Mrs. Lizzie Cary Daniel, December 10, 1898, Confederate Museum, Richmond.
10. Varina Davis to Mrs. Chesnut, A *Diary from Dixie*, p. 453.
11. Official War Records, Series 1, #78—464, 479, 488, 501.
12. Mrs. Mary Boykin Chesnut, *op. cit.*, pp. 437-40.
13. Varina Davis to Mary Boykin Chesnut, two letters, November, 1864, A *Diary from Dixie*, pp. 446-49.
14. Mrs. John W. Stewart to author, May 29, 1957.
15. Emma Lyon Bryan, *Reminiscences of Emma Lyon Bryan of Harrisonburg, Virginia*, Fleming papers, New York Public Library.
16. J. B. Jones, *op. cit.*, p. 360.
17. Varina Davis, "Last Christmas in the White House of the Confederacy," New York *Sunday World*, December 13, 1896.
18. J. B. Jones, *op. cit.*, II, p. 384.
19. William Ernest Smith, *op. cit.*, II, p. 304; Richmond newspapers through January, 1865.
20. Edward A. Pollard, *op. cit.*, p. 437.
21. *Harper's Magazine*, Vol. 124, 1911-12, p. 103.
22. General Wade Hampton to Louis T. Wigfall, January 20, 1865, Mrs. D. Giraud Wright, *op. cit.*, pp. 222-23.
23. Mrs. Johnston to Mrs. Wigfall, January 22, 1865, Wigfall papers, Library of Congress.
24. Louis T. Wigfall to General Joseph E. Johnston, February 27, 1865, Henry E. Huntington Library, San Marino, California.
25. Joseph E. Johnston to Louis T. Wigfall, March 14, 1865, Wigfall papers, Library of Congress.
26. Mrs. Mary Boykin Chesnut, *op. cit.*, p. 508.
27. Mrs. D. Giraud Wright, *op. cit.*, p. 241.

28. Varina Davis (with Campbell MacCulloch), "Last Days of the Confederacy," *Spare Moments*, October, 1906.
29. Varina Davis, *Memoir*, II, pp. 575-78.
30. Amelia Gorgas to Walter L. Fleming, March 16, 1908, Fleming papers, New York Public Library.
31. William E. Dodd, *op. cit.*, p. 355; Constance Cary Harrison, *op. cit.*, 207-19; *Memoir*, II, 582-83.
32. Mrs. Roger A. Pryor, *op. cit.*, p. 356.
33. Mrs. Constance Cary Harrison, *op. cit.*, p. 216.
34. Avary, Pickett, Pryor, Pollard, Harrison; Official War Records; Charles A. Dana to Edwin M. Stanton, April 5, 1865, Stanton papers, Library of Congress.

PART TWO

CHAPTER 13: *Flight*

1. Jefferson Davis to Varina Davis, April 23, 1865, Confederate Museum, Richmond.
2. Varina Davis to Jefferson Davis, April 28, 1865, Confederate Museum, Richmond.
3. Jefferson Davis to Varina Davis, April 5, 1865, Confederate Museum, Richmond.
4. *Ibid.*, April 6, 1865.
5. Varina Davis to Jefferson Davis, April 7, 1865, Confederate Museum, Richmond.
6. Joseph R. Davis to Jefferson Davis, Vol. 25, Stanton papers, Library of Congress.
7. William E. Dodd, *op. cit.*, p. 357.
8. Robert E. Lee, Jr., *op. cit.*, p. 157.
9. Burton N. Harrison to Varina Davis, April 12, 1865, Stanton papers, Library of Congress.
10. William Preston Johnston to Varina Davis, April 12, 1865, Stanton papers, Library of Congress.
11. Official War Records; Dodd, p. 387; Pollard, p. 516; T. Harry Williams, *P. T. G. Beauregard*, p. 255; *The Rise and Fall of the Confederate Government*, II, pp. 678-81; Stephen R. Mallory, "Last Days of the Confederacy," *McClure's Magazine*, XVI, 1901, pp. 240-42.
12. Jefferson Davis to Varina Davis, April 14, 1865, Stanton papers, Library of Congress.

13. Burton N. Harrison, private narrative written for his family, Burton N. Harrison papers, Library of Congress.
14. Wade Hampton to Jefferson Davis, April 19, 1865, Stanton papers, Library of Congress.
15. Varina Davis (with Campbell MacCulloch), "The Last Days of the Confederacy," *Spare Moments*, December, 1906.
16. Jefferson Davis to Crafts J. Wright, May 11, 1876, Library of Congress.
17. Varina Davis, *Memoir*, II, p. 611.
18. Mrs. Eron Rowland, II, p. 418.
19. Varina Davis, *Memoir*, II, pp. 610-12.
20. Varina Davis to Jefferson Davis, April 19, 1865, Confederate Museum, Richmond.
21. Varina Davis, *Memoir*, II, p. 615.
22. Varina Davis to Jefferson Davis, April 24, 1865, Confederate Museum, Richmond.
23. Jefferson Davis to Varina Davis, April 23, 1865, Confederate Museum, Richmond; Stanton papers, Library of Congress.
24. Varina Davis to Jefferson Davis, April 28, 1865, Confederate Museum, Richmond.
25. Burton N. Harrison, narrative, B. N. H. papers, Library of Congress.
26. Varina Davis to Jefferson Davis, April, 1865, Confederate Museum, Richmond; Dunbar Rowland, Vol. VI, p. 590.
27. Eliza Frances Andrews: *The War-Time Journal of a Georgia Girl*, pp. 191-93.
28. Mrs. D. Giraud Wright, *op. cit.*, pp. 243-44.
29. Varina Davis to Francis P. Blair, June 6, 1865, Gist-Blair papers, Library of Congress.
30. Varina Davis, *Memoir*, II, pp. 625-26.
31. Burton N. Harrison, narrative, B. N. H. papers, Library of Congress.
32. Varina Davis to Jefferson Davis, April, 1865, Dunbar Rowland, VI, p. 589.
33. Edward A. Pollard, *op. cit.*, p. 520; Mrs. Myrta Lockett Avary, pp. 59-60.
34. John H. Reagan to Walter L. Fleming, May 1, 1899, Fleming papers, New York Public Library.
35. Varina Davis to Francis Lawley, June 8, 1898, Pierce Butler collection, Tulane University.
36. Varina Davis, *Spare Moments*, October, 1906, to March, 1907.
37. Mrs. M. E. Robertson to Walter L. Fleming, Fleming papers, New York Public Library.
38. Varina Davis, *Memoir*, II, p. 617.

39. Jefferson Davis: *Rise and Fall of the Confederate Government*, II, pp. 700-5.
40. Burton N. Harrison, narrative, B. N. H. papers, Library of Congress; *Recollections Grave and Gay*; "Last Days of the Confederacy," *Spare Moments*; F. R. Lubbock, Fleming papers, New York Public Library.

CHAPTER 14: *A President Is Captured*

1. Varina Davis to Francis P. Blair, June 6, 1865, Gist-Blair papers, Library of Congress.
2. Jefferson Davis, *The Rise and Fall of the Confederate Government*, II, pp. 700-5.
3. Varina Davis to Francis P. Blair, *op. cit.*
4. Varina Davis, *Memoir*, II, p. 641.
5. George Templeton Strong, *The Civil War—1860-1865*, p. 598.
6. Jefferson Davis, *op. cit.*
7. Detroit *Sun*, May 13, 1899.
8. *Confederate Veteran*, May, 1907.
9. Capture of Jefferson Davis: *The Rise and Fall of the Confederate Government*; Varina Davis to Francis P. Blair, *op. cit.*; Jefferson Davis to Crafts J. Wright, April 18, 1878, Library of Congress; Burton N. Harrison's private narrative, Library of Congress; William Preston Johnston to Major W. T. Walthall, July 14, 1877, Confederate Memorial Hall, New Orleans; Diary of John Taylor Wood, 3 vols., University of North Carolina; Jefferson Davis to the Rev. W. M. Green, Fleming papers, New York Public Library; *Recollections Grave and Gay*, p. 227; Howard T. Dimick, "The Capture of Jefferson Davis," *Journal of Mississippi History*, Vol. IX, 1947; Nannie Davis Smith, McElroy papers, New York Public Library; *Complete Works of Abraham Lincoln*, edited by John Hay and John G. Nicolay, pp. 269-74; William E. Dodd, *op. cit.*, pp. 363-64; papers and clippings on capture, 1865-1899 in Jefferson Davis papers, Library of Congress; Varina Davis in *Spare Moments*; *op. cit.*; James H. Parker, Portland *Argus*, and his statement on attire when captured, Confederate Museum, Richmond; *Davis Memorial Volume*, pp. 404-7.
10. Varina Davis, *Spare Moments*, January, 1907 (appeared posthumously).
11. Varina Davis, *Memoir*, II, p. 642.
12. *Ibid.*, p. 644.
13. Mrs. Clement C. Clay, *op. cit.*, pp. 256-57.
14. *Personal Memoirs of Ulysses S. Grant*, edited by E. B. Long, p. 524.
15. Mrs. Eron Rowland, *op. cit.*, II, p. 445.
16. Varina Davis, *Memoir*, II, 645.

17. *New York Times*, May 22, 1865.
18. Varina Davis to Francis P. Blair, June 6, 1865, *op. cit.*
19. Charles A. Dana to Edwin M. Stanton, May 23, 1865, Stanton papers, Library of Congress.
20. Richmond *Times Dispatch*, February 12, 1905; Mrs. Clement C. Clay, *op. cit.*, pp. 264-66.
21. Varina Davis, *Memoir*, II, p. 650.
22. Varina Davis to Captain of English Man-of-War, May 23, 1865, Confederate Museum, Richmond; Stanton papers, Library of Congress.
23. Varina Davis to Dr. John J. Craven, October 10, 1865, *Prison Life of Jefferson Davis*, p. 331.

CHAPTER 15: *Savannah*

1. Dr. John J. Craven, *op. cit.*, p. 335.
2. Gideon Welles, *Gideon Welles Diary*, II, pp. 314-15.
3. Thurlow Weed to Edwin M. Stanton, May 29, 1865, Stanton papers, Library of Congress.
4. Dr. John J. Craven, *op. cit.*, p. 59.
5. Captain Jerome B. Titlow, narrative on shackling, Fleming papers, New York Public Library; Dr. Craven, *op. cit.*, p. 39.
6. Varina Davis to Dr. Craven, June 1, 1865, *op. cit.*, p. 88.
7. *Ibid.*, July 2, 1865, p. 169.
8. *Ibid.*, October 10, 1865, p. 331; *Memoir*, II, pp. 708-17.
9. Burton N. Harrison to Francis P. Blair, May 22, 1865, Library of Congress; Dunbar Rowland, *op. cit.*; Vol. VII, p. 20.
10. Varina Davis to Francis P. Blair, June 6, 1865, Gist-Blair papers, Library of Congress.
11. Francis P. Blair to Varina Davis, June 12, 1865, Gist-Blair papers, Library of Congress.
12. General Montgomery C. Meigs to Edwin M. Stanton in indirect response to Mrs. Davis. *The Trials and Trial of Jefferson Davis*, by Charles M. Blackford, read before Virginia Bar Association, July 17, 1900.
13. Varina Davis to Horace Greeley, June 22, 1865, Confederate Museum, Richmond.
14. George Shea; *A Letter from George Shea*, London, 1877.
15. Varina Davis to the *Metropolitan Herald and Vindicator*, July 9, 1865, Henry E. Huntington Library, San Marino, California.
16. Varina Davis to William H. Seward, July 10, 1865, Confederate Museum, Richmond.

17. Varina Davis to George Shea, July 14, 1865, Confederate Museum, Richmond.
18. Gideon Welles, *op. cit.*, II, p. 339.
19. Varina Davis to Dr. John J. Craven, October 10, 1865, *Memoir*, II, pp. 708-17.
20. Varina Davis to Octavus Cohen, August 3, 1865, Confederate Museum, Richmond.
21. Varina Davis to Mrs. Martha Phillips, August 18, 1865, Jefferson Davis family papers, Library of Congress.
22. *Ibid.*, September 17, 1865.
23. Varina Davis to Lise Mitchell, December 7, 1865, Lise Mitchell correspondence, University of North Carolina.
24. Varina Davis to Mrs. Martha Phillips, August 22, 1865, Jefferson Davis family papers, Library of Congress.
25. *Ibid.*, September 17, 1865.
26. Varina Davis to Joseph E. Davis, September 5, 1865, Mitchell correspondence, University of North Carolina.
27. Varina Davis to Mrs. Howell Cobb, September 9, 1865, *Correspondence of Toombs, Stephens and Cobb*, edited by U. B. Phillips, II, pp. 667-68.
28. Varina Davis to Mary Boykin Chesnut, September 20, 1865, Chesnut papers, University of North Carolina.
29. Varina Davis to William Preston Johnston, October 3, 1865, Howard Tilton Library, Tulane University.
30. Varina Davis to Dr. John J. Craven, October 10, 1865, *Memoir*, II, p. 708.
31. Varina Davis to Armistead Burt, October 20, 1865, Armistead Burt papers, Duke University.
32. Varina Davis to Mrs. Clement C. Clay, October 29, 1865, Clay papers, Duke University.
33. Mrs. Clement C. Clay: *A Belle of the Fifties*, pp. 346-48.
34. *Ibid.*, p. 311.
35. *Ibid.*, p. 301.
36. Varina Davis to Armistead Burt (undated), Armistead Burt papers, Duke University.
37. Dr. John J. Craven, *op. cit.*, p. 175.
38. *Ibid.*, pp. 126-28.
39. *Ibid.*, pp. 172-73.
40. *Ibid.*, p. 194.
41. *Ibid.*, p. 150.
42. Jefferson Davis to Varina Davis, October 11, 1865, *Memoir*, II, pp. 720-22.

43. *Ibid.*, November 21, 1865; *Memoir*, II, p. 729.
44. *Ibid.*, December 7, 1865, *Memoir*, II, p. 736.
45. Varina Davis to President Andrew Johnson, May 5, 1866, Johnson papers, Library of Congress.
46. *Ibid.*, May 12, 1866.

CHAPTER 16: *Washington Revisited*

1. New York *Tribune*, May 28, 1866.
2. *Memoir*, II, p. 757; Robert McElroy, *op. cit.*, II, p. 562.
3. New York *Tribune*, May 26, 1866.
4. Dr. George E. Cooper to Mrs. Jefferson Davis, March 23, 1866, Confederate Memorial Hall, New Orleans.
5. Burton N. Harrison to his mother, June 13, 1866, B. N. H. papers, Library of Congress.
6. Mrs. Clement C. Clay, *op. cit.*, p. 352.
7. New York *Tribune*, June 9, 1866.
8. Varina Davis to a group of Richmond mothers, June 16, 1866, Confederate Museum, Richmond.
9. Varina Davis to Nora K. Henley of Liberty, Virginia, June 13, 1866, Confederate Museum, Richmond.
10. Burton N. Harrison to Varina Davis, June 28, 1866, B. N. H. papers, Library of Congress.
11. Varina Davis to Burton N. Harrison, August 2, 1866, B. N. H. papers, Library of Congress.
12. Varina Davis to Burton N. Harrison, August 9, 1866, B. N. H. papers, University of Virginia.
13. Varina Davis to Mrs. Howell Cobb, August 2, 1866, New York Historical Society.
14. Mrs. Clement C. Clay, *op. cit.*, p. 30.
15. Varina Davis to Reverdy Johnson, July 19, 1866, Confederate Memorial Hall, New Orleans.
16. Mrs. Montgomery (Minna) Blair to Varina Davis, September 9, 1866, Confederate Museum, Richmond.
17. Mrs. Joseph E. Johnston to Louis T. Wigfall, July 26, 1866, Wigfall papers, Library of Congress.
18. Varina Davis to William Preston Johnston, Howard Tilton Library, Tulane University.
19. Mary Day Burchenal, *Holland's Magazine*, October, 1931.
20. Varina Davis to Mrs. Martha Phillips, April 16, 1867, Jefferson Davis papers, Library of Congress.

21. John R. Thompson to Varina Davis, October 16, 1866, Confederate Museum, Richmond.
22. Varina Davis to Horace Greeley, September 2, 1866, Manuscript Division, New York Public Library.
23. *Ibid.*, October 16, 1866.
24. New York *Tribune* editorial, November 9, 1866.
25. Varina Davis to Horace Greeley, November 21, 1866, New York Public Library.
26. Jefferson Davis to Gordon L. Ford, April 20, 1888, Jefferson Davis papers, New York Public Library.
27. Richard Taylor to Varina Davis, November 10, 1866, Confederate Memorial Hall.
28. Correspondence regarding Jefferson Davis in John W. Garrett papers, Library of Congress (Courtesy of Robert Garrett of Baltimore); Interview with John W. Garrett, Baltimore *Sun*, May 28, 1866.
29. Varina Davis to Jefferson Davis, March 23, 1867, Library of Congress.
30. *Ibid.*, March 28, 1867.
31. Burton N. Harrison to Constance Cary, May 13, 1867, B. N. H. papers, Library of Congress.
32. Richmond *Enquirer and Sentinel*, May 13, 1867.
33. Court proceedings; Richmond newspapers, New York *Tribune*: Burton N. Harrison to his mother and his fiancée, Constance Cary, May, 1867, B. N. H. papers, Library of Congress.

CHAPTER 17: *Dispossessed*

1. Varina Davis to John W. Garrett, May 3, 1867, John W. Garrett papers, Library of Congress.
2. Robert E. Lee to Jefferson Davis, June 1, 1867, Dunbar Rowland, *op. cit.*, VII, p. 110.
3. Varina Davis to Mrs. Howell Cobb, September 6, 1867, New York Historical Society.
4. Virginia Frazer Boyle's manuscript, including Steven S. Cummins's recollections of the Davis family, Confederate Museum, Richmond.
5. Varina Davis to Burton N. Harrison, November 1, 1867, B. N. H. papers, Library of Congress.
6. Varina Davis, *Memoir*, II, p. 800.
7. *Ibid.*, p. 799.
8. Jefferson Davis to Joseph E. Davis, July 22, 1867, Fleming papers, New York Public Library.
9. Varina Davis, *Memoir*, II, p. 804.
10. Mrs. M. E. Hamer, Fleming papers, New York Public Library.

11. Nannie Davis Smith, narrative, McElroy papers, New York Public Library.
12. Jefferson Davis to Judge Charles B. Howry, February 8, 1868, Howry papers, Library of Congress.
13. Sue Tarpley Carter, *Confederate Veteran*, May, 1903.
14. Varina Davis to Mrs. Howell Cobb, July 6, 1868, Toombs correspondence, *op. cit.*, II, pp. 698-99.
15. R. E. Blackwell to Walter L. Fleming, August 17, 1910, Fleming papers, New York Public Library.
16. Jefferson Davis to Howell Cobb, with postscript by Varina Davis, Toombs correspondence, *op. cit.*, July 6, 1868, pp. 698-99.
17. Nannie Davis Smith, *op. cit.*
18. Varina Davis to Mrs. Howell Cobb, *op. cit.*
19. Varina Davis, *Memoir*, II, p. 806.
20. Liverpool newspaper clippings, State Archives, Montgomery.
21. Varina Davis, *Memoir*, II, p. 807.
22. Varina Davis to Mrs. Howell Cobb, October 22, 1868, Toombs correspondence, II, p. 704.
23. Varina Davis correspondence with British friends, Confederate Museum, Richmond.
24. Varina Davis correspondence with British journalists and authors, Confederate Museum, Richmond.
25. Varina Davis, *Memoir*, II, p. 809.
26. Margaret (Pollie) Davis to Jefferson Davis, November 14, 1869, Confederate Museum, Richmond.
27. Billy Davis to Varina Davis (undated but in 1869), Confederate Museum, Richmond.
28. Theodore Roosevelt, *Diaries of Boyhood and Youth*, p. 16.
29. Edward A. Pollard, *op. cit.*, pp. 154-55.
30. Henry Stuart Foote, *op. cit.*, p. 241.
31. New York *Tribune*, July 16, 1869.
32. Edward A. Pollard, *op. cit.*, p. 157.

CHAPTER 18: *Memphis*

1. Varina Davis, *Memoir*, II, pp. 812-13.
2. Stephen Rice Phelan, of Memphis, to author, December 2, 1956.
3. Varina Davis, *Memoir*, II, p. 916.
4. Varina Davis to Dr. Robert P. Myers, October 8, 1882, "The Family Sorrows of Jefferson Davis" by Arthur Marvin Shaw, *Alabama Historical Quarterly*, Vol. IX, 1947; *Memoir*, II, p. 814.
5. Varina Davis to William Preston Johnston, August 7, 1874, Howard Tilton Memorial Library, Tulane University.

6. Mrs. M. E. Hamer, narrative in Fleming papers, New York Public Library; Davis vs. Bowmar and Smith, Mississippi Reports, annotated edition, LV; Wirt A. Williams on Brierfield litigation, *Journal of Mississippi History*, July, 1947; *Memoir*, II, p. 815.

7. Mrs. M. E. Hamer to Walter L. Fleming, New York Public Library.

8. Bible with inscription on view in Confederate Memorial Hall, New Orleans.

9. Varina Davis, *Memoir*, II, pp. 821-22.

10. *Ibid.*, p. 824.

11. Marcus F. Cunliffe: *Notes on the Dorsey-Stanley Correspondence* (1871-1873), John Rylands Library Bulletin, Vol. 36, 1953, Manchester, England.

12. Mrs. Sarah A. Dorsey to Major W. T. Walthall, May 1, 1877, Mississippi Department of Archives and History, Jackson, Mississippi.

13. Varina Davis to Major W. T. Walthall, January 6, 1878, Confederate Memorial Hall, New Orleans.

14. Varina Davis to Constance Cary Harrison, November 7, 1877, B. N. H. papers, Library of Congress.

15. Varina Davis to Jefferson Davis, April 18, 1878, Confederate Memorial Hall, New Orleans.

16. M. J. Crawford interview, New Orleans *Times-Democrat*, May 11, 1902.

17. Jefferson Davis to Colonel Lucius Bellinger Northrop, April 9, 1879, *Jones Memorial Volume, op. cit.*

18. Mrs. Eron Rowland, *op. cit.*, II, p. 506.

19. Varina Davis to Major W. T. Walthall, September 8, 1878, Confederate Memorial Hall, New Orleans.

20. Jefferson Davis, Jr., to Jefferson Davis, September 19, 1878, Confederate Museum, Richmond.

21. Mrs. Merrill Parrish Hudson, of Memphis, to author.

22. Margaret Hayes (Mrs. J. Addison) to Varina Davis, October 15, 1878, Confederate Museum, Richmond.

23. Varina Davis, *Memoir*, II, p. 828.

24. Copy of property deed, February 19, 1879, Jefferson Davis papers, Library of Congress.

25. Mrs. Sarah A. Dorsey's will, January 4, 1878, copy in State Library, New Orleans.

26. Varina Davis statement, April 21, 1902, Kimbrough collection, Jefferson Davis papers, Library of Congress.

27. Jefferson Davis to Mrs. Samuel W. Ferguson, September 5, 1879, Fleming papers, New York Public Library.

28. Varina Davis, *Memoir*, II, p. 829.

29. Mrs. Eron Rowland, *op. cit.*, II, p. 504.
30. Margaret Hayes (Mrs. J. Addison) to Mrs. Carrie Beale, April 6, 1899, White House of the Confederacy, Montgomery.
31. Varina Davis, *Memoir*, II, p. 826.
32. Judah P. Benjamin to Jefferson Davis, February 15, 1879; *Harper's Magazine*, Vol. 124, 1911-12, pp. 102-3. Fleming papers; Dunbar Rowland, *Constitutionalist*.
33. Mrs. Mary Boykin Chesnut, *op. cit.*, p. 285.
34. Jefferson Davis to Colonel Lucius Bellinger Northrop, Dunbar Rowland, *op. cit.*, VIII, pp. 437-39.
35. Varina Davis to J. C. Derby, April 15, 1880, Historical Society of Pennsylvania.
36. Varina Davis, *Memoir*, II, p. 830.
37. Varina Davis to Constance Cary Harrison, April 5, 1880, B. N. H. papers, Library of Congress.
38. Constance Cary Harrison, *Recollections Grave and Gay*, p. 281.

CHAPTER 19: *Beauvoir*

1. Mrs. Myrta Lockett Avary, *Dixie After the War*, pp. 415-16.
2. Robert Douthat Meade, *Judah P. Benjamin*, p. 356.
3. Mrs. Samuel W. Ferguson to Walter L. Fleming, October 16, 1907, Fleming papers, New York Public Library.
4. General George W. Jones, Dubuque *Herald*, June 20, 1883.
5. Chiles Clifton Ferrell, "The Daughter of the Confederacy," Publications of the Mississippi Historical Society, Vol. I, 1898.
6. Varina Anne (Winnie) Davis article on Jefferson Davis, New York *Herald*, August 11, 1895.
7. *Ibid.*
8. Varina Davis to Dr. Robert P. Myers, October 8, 1882, *op. cit.*
9. Varina Davis to J. C. Derby, January 9, 1881, Henry E. Huntington Library, San Marino, California.
10. Mrs. William Fayssoux to author.
11. Poultney Bigelow; *Seventy Summers*, II, pp. 221-25.
12. General George W. Jones, *op. cit.*
13. J. William Jones, The Davis Memorial Volume, pp. 432-41.
14. Alexander K. McClure's "Recollections of Jefferson Davis," *World's Events Magazine*, December, 1906.
15. Catharine Cole, *Davis Memorial Volume, op. cit.*
16. Minnie Reese Richardson, Montgomery *Advertiser*, June 4, 1916.
17. Steven S. Cummins, *Confederate Veteran*, March, 1929.
18. Mrs. Ralph Wood, of Biloxi, to author.

19. Jefferson Davis to General Josiah Gorgas, Confederate Memorial Hall, New Orleans.
20. Mary Boykin Chesnut to Varina Davis, June 15, 1883, Confederate Museum, Richmond.
21. Burton N. Harrison to C. C. Buel, March 24, 1887, B. N. H. papers, Library of Congress.
22. Jefferson Davis, *Confederate Veteran*, December 10, 1888.
23. Jefferson Davis to Crafts J. Wright, February 12, 1876; Varina Davis to Captain C. B. Winder, January 9, 1869; *The Rise and Fall of the Confederate Government*, II, p. 419.
24. Jefferson Davis to Jubal A. Early, September 14, 1888, Early papers, Library of Congress.
25. Jefferson Davis to the Rev. Edward Bailey, June 15, 1886, Dreer Collection, Historical Society of Pennsylvania.
26. Jefferson Davis address before Mississippi Legislature, March 10, 1884. Dunbar Rowland, *Constitutionalist, op. cit.*
27. Jefferson Davis to Crafts J. Wright, February 12, 1876, Library of Congress.
28. Varina Davis to Mrs. M. E. Hamer, October 20, 1885, Fleming papers, New York Public Library.
29. Jefferson Davis to Mrs. M. E. Hamer, February 7, 1884, *ibid.*
30. *Ibid.*, January 7, 1882.
31. Isaiah T. Montgomery, Boston *Transcript*, February 18, 1902.
32. New York *World*, April 4, 1886.
33. Winnie Davis, New York *Herald*, August 11, 1895.
34. Mrs. William Fayssoux, of New Orleans, to author.
35. Mrs. Stamps Farrar, of New Orleans, to author.
36. Davis family album, Confederate Museum, Richmond.
37. Major J. J. Hood, tribute to Mrs. Davis, jotted on copy of Jackson *Daily News*, June 2, 1908, State Archives, Montgomery.
38. Jubal A. Early to Jefferson Davis, April 30, 1885, Early papers, Library of Congress.
39. *Confederate Veteran*, December 10, 1888.
40. Gamaliel Bradford, *Wives*, p. 192.

CHAPTER 20: *Death of Jefferson Davis*

1. New Orleans *Picayune*, June 8, 1886.
2. Varina Davis to Constance Cary Harrison, December 20, 1886, B. N. H. papers, Library of Congress.
3. *Ibid.*, December 23, 1886.
4. Syracuse press clippings, Fleming papers, New York Public Library.

5. Varina Davis to Jubal A. Early, May 8, 1888, Early papers, Library of Congress.
6. *Ibid.*, May 23, 1888.
7. New Orleans *Picayune*, June 3, 1888, birthday interview with Jefferson Davis.
8. Varina Davis to Major William H. Morgan, June 9, 1888, Nannie Mayes Crump collection, Library of Congress.
9. General John M. Read to Varina Davis, August 20, 1888, Confederate Museum, Richmond.
10. Varina Davis to General Jubal A. Early, August 6, 1888, Early papers, Library of Congress.
11. Varina Davis to Major Morgan (undated but in September, 1888), Crump collection, Library of Congress.
12. *Ibid.*
13. Mrs. Margaret De Vore, of Vicksburg, to author.
14. Fred Wilkinson to Winnie Davis, Crump collection, Library of Congress.
15. Mrs. William Fayssoux, of New Orleans, to author.
16. Varina Davis to Major Morgan, November 30, 1889, Crump collection, Library of Congress.
17. Varina Davis, *Memoir*, II, p. 930.
18. Stuart A. Weiss scrapbook with assorted clippings on death of Jefferson Davis, Confederate Museum, Richmond.
19. Varina Davis, *Memoir*, II, p. 932.
20. *The Davis Memorial Volume, op. cit.*; Weiss scrapbook, *op. cit.*, *Memoir*, II, pp. 932-39.
21. New York *World*, December 6, 1889.

CHAPTER 21: *Daughter of the Confederacy*

1. Varina Davis to Major Morgan, February, 1890, Crump collection, Library of Congress.
2. Varina Davis to Grace King, December 18, 1889, Department of Archives, Louisiana State University.
3. Varina Davis, *Memoir*, II, p. 934.
4. *Ibid.*, p. 933.
5. Varina Davis to Mary Day Burchenal, December 25, 1889. (Courtesy Charles D. Burchenal, Brooklyn, N. Y.)
6. Varina Davis to James Redpath, December 28, 1889, Howard Tilton Library, Tulane University.
7. Nannie Davis Smith, narrative in Robert McElroy papers, New York Public Library.

8. Varina Davis to Judge A. McL. Kimbrough, March 9, 1890, Kimbrough collection, Jefferson Davis papers, Library of Congress.

9. Fred Wilkinson to Varina Davis, February 23, 1890, Crump collection, Library of Congress.

10. Winnie Davis to Varina Davis, March 1, 1890, Crump collection, Library of Congress.

11. Winnie Davis to Major Morgan, March 1, 1890, Crump collection, Library of Congress.

12. Fred Wilkinson to Varina Davis, March 1, 1890, Crump collection, Library of Congress.

13. Fred Wilkinson to Major Morgan, March 1, 1890, Crump collection, Library of Congress.

14. Fred Wilkinson to Varina Davis, March 4, 1890, Crump collection, Library of Congress.

15. Varina Davis to Major Morgan, March, 1890, Crump collection, Library of Congress.

16. Varina Davis to Jubal A. Early, April 20, 1890, Early papers, Library of Congress.

17. Varina Davis to Major Morgan, October 5, 1890, Crump collection, Library of Congress.

18. *New York Times*, October 14, 1890.

19. James Redpath to John Dimitry, August, 1890, Mayes-Dimitry-Stuart papers, State Archives, Jackson, Mississippi.

20. New York *Sun*, June 22, 1890.

21. Dunbar Rowland, *Constitutionalist.* Jefferson Davis to Lucius Bellinger Northrop, April 24, 1879, VIII, pp. 380-83.

22. Varina Davis to Lucius Bellinger Northrop, July, 1890, Confederate Memorial Hall, New Orleans.

23. Louise Didier to Varina Davis, August 17, 1890, Confederate Memorial Hall, New Orleans.

24. Varina Davis to Thomas Lafayette Rosser, August 26, 1890, Confederate Memorial Hall, New Orleans.

25. Thomas Lafayette Rosser to Varina Davis, August 29, 1890, Confederate Memorial Hall, New Orleans.

26. Varina Davis to Lucius Bellinger Northrop, September 6, 1890, Bradley T. Johnson papers, Duke University.

27. Varina Davis to General Bradley T. Johnson, *ibid.*

28. Bradley T. Johnson to Varina Davis, September 11, 1890, *ibid.*

29. Jubal A. Early to Varina Davis, September 5, 1890, Confederate Memorial Hall, New Orleans.

30. Winnie Davis to Major Morgan, November 3, 1890, Crump collection, Library of Congress.

31. J. Addison Hayes to Varina Davis, April 20, 1891, Confederate Museum, Richmond.
32. Press comment on *Memoir*—Kate Field, Eugene Field, Brooklyn *Standard Union*, sundry clippings, Fleming papers in New York Public Library.
33. Varina Davis on Jefferson Davis's characteristics, *Memoir*, II, pp. 918-25.
34. Varina Davis to Sallie B. Morgan, September 1, 1891, Kimbrough papers, Library of Congress.
35. Varina Davis to Mrs. Octavus Cohen, January 7, 1892, Georgia Historical Society, Savannah.
36. Souvenirs in Confederate Memorial Hall; contemporary press clippings.
37. Mrs. Eron Rowland, *op. cit.*, II, p. 530.

CHAPTER 22: *Mrs. Jefferson Davis on Park Row*

1. Chiles Clifton Ferrell, *op. cit.*
2. Varina Davis to Mrs. Sallie B. Morgan, September 1, 1891, Kimbrough papers, Library of Congress.
3. Varina Davis to Mrs. Mary Hunter Kimbrough, October 16, 1894, Kimbrough papers, Library of Congress.
4. Theodore Roosevelt to Burton N. Harrison, March 23, 1891, B. N. H. papers, Library of Congress.
5. Varina Davis to Judge Kimbrough (for post-mortem reading), October 16, 1894, Kimbrough papers, Library of Congress.
6. Varina Davis to "The Veterans and Public of the Southern States," July 11, 1891, Fleming papers, New York Public Library.
7. Nannie Mayes Crump to author, February, 1957.
8. *New York World*, June 1, 1893; New Orleans *Picayune*, May 29, 1893; Richmond papers, May 28-June 3, 1893.
9. New York *Sunday World*, editorial on Mrs. Jefferson Davis, May 28, 1893.
10. Varina Davis to Mrs. Mary Hunter Kimbrough, November 12, 1894, Kimbrough papers, Library of Congress.
11. Mrs. N. V. Randolph correspondence with Mrs. Mary Hunter Kimbrough regarding Mrs. Jefferson Davis's post-mortem statement, Confederate Museum, Richmond.
12. Varina Davis correspondence with Judge Kimbrough, 1894 to 1906, Kimbrough collection, Library of Congress.
13. Varina Davis to Judge Kimbrough, October 16, 1894, Kimbrough papers, Library of Congress.

14. Varina Davis to Mrs. Mary Hunter Kimbrough, October 1, 1905, Kimbrough papers, Library of Congress.
15. Margaret Hayes (Mrs. J. Addison) to Mrs. Mary Hunter Kimbrough, December 11, 1906, Kimbrough papers, Library of Congress.
16. Varina Davis to Dr. John W. Burgess, April 26, 1893, Confederate Museum, Richmond.
17. *Ibid.*, May 29, 1893.
18. *Ibid.*, June 29, 1894.
19. Dr. John W. Burgess, *Reminiscences of an American Scholar*, p. 292.
20. New York *Mail and Express*, May 29, 1890.
21. Richmond *Times*, July 4, 1896.
22. *Ibid.*, July 2, 1896.
23. New York *World*, March 1, 1896.
24. New York *World*, June 25 and 26, 1893.
25. Mrs. Eron Rowland, II, p. 544.
26. Varina Davis tribute to General Grant, New York *Sunday World*, April 25, 1897.
27. New York *World*, April 28, 1897.
28. Varina Davis article on General Grant, New York *Sunday World*, April 21, 1901.
29. *Ibid.*
30. Randall Blackshaw, *Putnam's Monthly Magazine*, November, 1906.
31. Southern Historical Society papers, edited by R. A. Brock, Richmond, 1900.
32. Winnie Davis, copy of will in State Library, New Orleans.
33. Varina Davis to Mrs. Florence Hayward, April 1, 1898, Missouri Historical Society, St. Louis.
34. Varina Davis to Mrs. Constance Cary Harrison, September 7, 1898, B. N. H. papers, Library of Congress.
35. *Armstrong's Magazine*, January, 1899; *The United Daughters of the Confederacy Magazine*, July, 1954; Richmond and New York newspaper clippings.
36. Mrs. John W. Burgess to Miss Susan B. Harrison, April 29, 1931, Confederate Museum, Richmond.
37. Adolfo Muller-Ury to Miss Susan B. Harrison, July 1, 1918, Confederate Museum, Richmond.
38. Dr. John W. Burgess: *Reminiscences of an American Scholar*, pp. 292-93.
39. Nannie Davis Smith, narrative in Robert McElroy papers, Manuscript Division, New York Public Library.
40. Varina Davis to John Warwick Daniel, June 19, 1899, John Warwick Daniel papers, Duke University.

41. Varina Davis to Mrs. Octavus Cohen, June 11, 1900, Georgia Historical Society, Savannah, Georgia.
42. Varina Davis to Miss Emily V. Mason, April 2, 1903, Confederate Museum, Richmond.
43. Varina Davis to Mrs. J. Taylor Ellyson, January 3, 1895, Confederate Museum, Richmond.
44. Varina Davis to Mrs. Lizzie Cary Daniel, May 29, 1899, Confederate Museum, Richmond.
45. Margaret Hayes (Mrs. J. Addison) to Mrs. J. D. Beale, April 6, 1899, White House of the Confederacy, Montgomery, Alabama.
46. Varina Davis to James Jones, December 8, 1899, University of Louisiana.
47. Mrs. Lucy Hayes Young to author.
48. *New York Times,* June 11, 1911.

CHAPTER 23: *Confederate Court in New York*

1. Varina Davis to Mrs. Mary Hunter Kimbrough, January 4, 1901, Kimbrough papers, Library of Congress.
2. *Confederate Stamp Album,* 1956.
3. The Letters of Theodore Roosevelt, edited by Elting E. Morison, IV, pp. 947-48.
4. Theodore Roosevelt to Clark Howell, June 12, 1905, Manuscript Division, Library of Congress.
5. The Letters of Theodore Roosevelt, *op. cit.,* pp. 674-75.
6. *The Arena,* January, 1900.
7. Varina Davis to Mrs. L. G. Young, August 15, 1903, Emory University, Georgia.
8. Varina Davis to Mrs. Mary Hunter Kimbrough, January 4, 1901, Kimbrough papers, Library of Congress.
9. Mrs. Eron Rowland, II, p. 548.
10. Mary Day Burchenal, *Holland's Magazine, op. cit.*
11. Mrs. John P. Labouisse, of New Orleans, to author.
12. Varina Davis to Judge Charles B. Howry, spring of 1903, Howry papers, Library of Congress.
13. Mrs. M. B. More, of New York, to author.
14. Varina Davis to Mrs. Devereux Shields, October 16, 1900 (Letter owned by Mrs. Judy Stone, of Natchez).
15. Jefferson Hayes-Davis to author.
16. Mrs. Lucy Hayes Young to author.
17. Varina Davis to Colonel James Morris Morgan, March 2, 1901, James Morris Morgan papers, South Carolina Library, University of South Carolina.

18. Varina Davis to Judge Kimbrough, July 8, 1902, Kimbrough papers, Library of Congress.
19. Richard Watson Gilder to James Calvin Hemphill, July 5, 1904, Hemphill papers, Duke University.
20. Mrs. Stamps Farrar, of New Orleans, to author.
21. Varina Davis to Mrs. Lizzie Cary, February 9, 1902, Confederate Museum, Richmond.
22. Varina Davis to Mrs. Mary Hunter Kimbrough, March 8, 1902, Kimbrough papers, Library of Congress.
23. *Ibid.*, April 30, 1895.
24. Varina Davis to Judge Kimbrough, May 10, 1902, Kimbrough papers, Library of Congress.
25. *Ibid.*, November 6, 1902.
26. Florence M. McIntyre, *Art and Life*; also correspondence with author.
27. Buffalo *News*, July, 1903.
28. Varina Davis to Mary Craig, February 1, 1904; McIntyre book, *op. cit.*; Meigs O. Frost in New Orleans *Times Picayune*, January 13, 1935.
29. Varina Davis to Burton N. Harrison, February 19, 1904, B. N. H. papers, University of Virginia.
30. General John B. Gordon, *Reminiscences of the Civil War*, p. 393.
31. New York *World*, February 7, 1904.
32. Varina Davis to Mrs. Dandridge, July 29, 1904, J. E. Buchanan papers, Duke University.

Chapter 24: *General Miles Is Routed*

1. Varina Davis to Judge Charles B. Howry, March 9, 1905, Howry papers, Library of Congress.
2. Varina Davis statement prepared for Walter Charlton, of Savannah, February 20, 1905, Emory University, Georgia.
3. Varina Davis to Walter Charlton, May 18, 1905, *ibid.*
4. Varina Davis to Major Morgan, June 30, 1898, Kimbrough papers, Library of Congress.
5. Varina Davis to Dr. C. W. Chancellor, March 15, 1905.
6. Varina Davis to Walter L. Fleming, December 20, 1905, Fleming papers, New York Public Library.
7. Varina Davis (with Campbell MacCulloch), *Spare Moments*, 1906.
8. Varina Davis to General R. H. Henry, January 3, 1905, Kimbrough papers, Library of Congress.
9. Varina Davis to Mary Craig, March 26, 1905, Kimbrough papers, Library of Congress.
10. Varina Davis to Mary Craig, July 12, 1906, Kimbrough papers, Library of Congress.

11. Mrs. Eron Rowland, *op. cit.*, II, p. 549.
12. Varina Davis to Judge Kimbrough, August 18, 1906, Kimbrough papers, Library of Congress.
13. Varina Davis to Mrs. J. D. Beale, September 6, 1906, White House of the Confederacy, Montgomery, Alabama.
14. Mrs. Eron Rowland, citing Carrie Beale, *op. cit.*, II, p. 554.
15. New York *World*, October 17, 1906; Richmond *Times-Dispatch*, October 17, 1906; New York *Tribune*, October 17, 1906.
16. New York *Tribune*, October 19, 1906.
17. Mrs. Eron Rowland, *op. cit.*, II, p. 556.
18. Margaret Hayes (Mrs. J. Addison) to J. Taylor Ellyson, Richmond *News-Leader*, October 19, 1906.
19. Richmond *News-Leader*, October 19, 1906, editorial on Mrs. Jefferson Davis.
20. Dr. John W. Burgess, *Reminiscences of an American Scholar*, p. 292.

BIBLIOGRAPHY

ABELE, RUDOLPH VON: *Alexander H. Stephens.* New York: Alfred A. Knopf, 1946.

ALFRIEND, FRANK H.: *The Life of Jefferson Davis.* Cincinnati and Chicago: Caxton Publishing House, 1868.

ANDREWS, ELIZA FRANCES: *The War-Time Journal of a Georgia Girl.* New York: D. Appleton and Company, 1908.

AVARY, MYRTA LOCKETT: *A Virginia Girl in the Civil War 1861-1865.* New York: D. Appleton and Company, 1903.

———: *Dixie After the War.* New York: Doubleday, Page and Company, 1906.

BADEAU, ADAM: *Grant in Peace.* Hartford, Connecticut: S. S. Scranton and Company, 1887.

BIGELOW, POULTNEY: *Seventy Summers.* New York: Longmans, Green and Company, 1925.

BANCROFT, A. C., edited by: *The Life and Death of Jefferson Davis.* New York: J. S. Oglivie, 1889.

BLACKFORD, CHARLES M.: *The Trials and Trial of Jefferson Davis.* Paper read before Virginia State Bar Association, Old Point Comfort, July, 1900.

BLACKFORD, WILLIAM WILLIS: *War Years with J. E. B. Stuart.* New York: Charles Scribner's Sons, 1945.

BRADFORD, GAMALIEL: *Wives.* New York: Harper & Brothers, 1925.

BREMER, CHARLOTTE, edited by: *Life, Letters and Posthumous Works of Fredrika Bremer.* New York: Hurd and Houghton, 1868.

BREMER, FREDRIKA, edited by Adolph B. Benson: *America of the Fifties.* New York: The American-Scandinavian Foundation, 1924.

BURGESS, DR. ROBERT W.: *Reminiscences of an American Scholar.* New York: Columbia University Press, 1934.

BUTLER, BENJAMIN F.: *Autobiography and Personal Reminiscences of Major-General Benjamin F. Butler.* Boston: A. M. Thayer and Company, 1892.

CATTON, BRUCE: *This Hallowed Ground.* Garden City, New York: Doubleday, 1956.

CHESNUT, MARY BOYKIN, edited by Ben Ames Williams: *A Diary from Dixie.* Boston: Houghton Mifflin Company, 1949.

CLAY-CLOPTON, VIRGINIA, edited by Ada Sterling: *A Belle of the Fifties.* New York: Doubleday, Page and Company, 1904.

COIT, MARGARET L.: *John C. Calhoun.* Boston: Houghton Mifflin Company, 1950.

COLE, CATHARINE: *Catharine Cole's Book.* Chicago: Way and Williams, 1897.

COMMAGER, HENRY STEELE: *The Blue and the Gray.* Indianapolis: The Bobbs-Merrill Company, 1950.

COULTER, E. MERTON: *The Confederate States of America.* Baton Rouge, Louisiana; Louisiana State University Press, 1950.

CRAVEN, BVT. LIEUT. COL. JOHN J., M.D.: *Prison Life of Jefferson Davis.* New York: G. W. Dillingham Company, 1905.

DANIEL, JOHN W.: *Life and Reminiscences of Jefferson Davis.* Baltimore: R. H. Woodward and Company, 1890.

DAVIS, BURKE: *Gray Fox.* New York: Rinehart and Company, Inc., 1956.

DAVIS, JEFFERSON: "Andersonville and Other War Prisons," *Belford's Magazine,* Vol. IV.

————: *A Short History of the Confederate States of America.* New York: Belford Company, 1890.

————: *Calendar of the Jefferson Davis Postwar Manuscripts.* Louisiana Historical Association Collection. Confederate Memorial Hall, New Orleans, 1943.

————: *The Rise and Fall of the Confederate Government,* 2 vols. New York: D. Appleton and Company.

DAVIS, VARINA: *Jefferson Davis, A Memoir by his Wife,* 2 vols. New York: Belford Company, 1890.

DE LEON, T. C.: *Belles, Beaux and Brains of the 60's.* New York: G. W. Dillingham, 1907.

DIMICK, HOWARD T.: *The Capture of Jefferson Davis.* The *Journal of Mississippi History,* Vol. IX, January-October, 1947.

DODD, WILLIAM E.: *Jefferson Davis.* Philadelphia: George W. Jacobs and Company, 1907.

DORSEY, SARAH A.: *Recollections of Henry Watkins Allen.* New York: M. Doolady, 1866.

DOWDEY, CLIFFORD: *The Land They Fought For.* New York: Doubleday and Company, Inc., Garden City, 1955.

ECKENRODE, H. J.: *Jefferson Davis, President of the South.* New York: The Macmillan Company, 1923.

ELLET, MRS. ELIZABETH FRIES: *The Court Circles of the Republic.* Hartford, Connecticut: Hartford Publishing Company, 1869.

————: *The Queens of American Society.* New York: Charles Scribner and Company, 1867.

FERRELL, CHILES CLIFTON: *Varina Anne Jefferson Davis*. Atlanta, Georgia: Library of Southern Literature, Vol. III. The Martin and Hoyt Company, 1907.

FOOTE, HENRY STUART: *A Casket of Reminiscences*. Washington: Chronicle Publishing Company, 1874.

FREEMAN, DOUGLAS SOUTHALL: *The South to Posterity*. New York: Charles Scribner's Sons, 1930.

————: *A Calendar of Confederate Papers*. Richmond: Confederate Museum, 1908.

FURMAN, BESS: *White House Profile*. Indianapolis: The Bobbs-Merrill Company, 1951.

GARLAND, HAMLIN: *Ulysses S. Grant, His Life and Character*. New York: Macmillan Company, 1920.

GAY, MARY ANN HARRIS: *Life in Dixie During the War*. Atlanta, Georgia: Constitution Job Office, 1892.

GORDON, ARMISTEAD C.: *Jefferson Davis*. New York: Charles Scribner's Sons, 1918.

GORDON, GENERAL JOHN B.: *Reminiscences of the Civil War*. New York: Charles Scribner's Sons, 1903.

GOUVERNEUR, MARIAN: *As I Remember*. New York: D. Appleton and Company, 1911.

GOVAN, GILBERT E. and JAMES W. LIVINGOOD: *A Different Valor. The Story of General Joseph E. Johnston*. Indianapolis: The Bobbs-Merrill Company, 1956.

GREEN, HORACE: *General Grant's Last Stand*. New York: Scribner's Sons, 1936.

HARRISON, CONSTANCE CARY: *Recollections Grave and Gay*. New York: Charles Scribner's Sons, 1911.

HAY, JOHN, and JOHN G. NICOLAY: *Abraham Lincoln, A History*, Vol. X. New York: The Century Company, 1890.

HOLLOWAY, LAURA C. (LANGFORD): *The Ladies of the White House*. Philadelphia: Bradley and Company, 1883.

HOPLEY, CATHERINE COOPER: *Life in the South: from the Commencement of the War by a Blockaded British Subject*. London: Chapman & Hall, 1863.

HOWARD, DR. EWING FOX, and W. A. EVANS: *Jefferson Davis, His Diseases and His Doctors*. Reprinted from the *Mississippi Doctor*, June, 1942.

JACKSON, MARY ANNA: *Life and Letters of General Thomas S. Jackson*. New York: Harper & Brothers, 1892.

JOHNSTON, WILLIAM PRESTON: *The Life of General Albert Sidney Johnston*. New York: D. Appleton and Company, 1878.

JONES, J. B.: *A Rebel Clerk's Diary*, 2 vols. Philadelphia: J. B. Lippincott & Co., 1866.

JONES, J. WILLIAM: *The Davis Memorial Volume; or our Dead President Jefferson Davis, and the World's Tribute to His Memory.* Richmond: B. F. Johnson and Company, 1890.

JONES, KATHARINE M.: *Heroines of Dixie.* Indianapolis: The Bobbs-Merrill Company, Inc., 1955.

KANE, HARNETT T.: *Bride of Fortune.* Garden City, New York: Doubleday, 1948.

KECKLEY, ELIZABETH: *Behind the Scenes.* New York: G. W. Carleton and Company, 1868.

KEYES, E. D.: *Fifty Years Observation of Men and Events.* New York: Charles Scribner's Sons, 1884.

KING, GRACE: *Memories of a Southern Woman of Letters.* New York: The Macmillan Company, 1932.

KNIGHT, LANDON: *The Real Jefferson Davis.* Battle Creek, Michigan: The Pilgrim Magazine Company, 1904.

LEE, CAPTAIN ROBERT E.: *Recollections and Letters of General Robert E. Lee.* New York: Doubleday, Page and Company, 1904.

LONG, E. B., edited by: *Personal Memoirs of Ulysses S. Grant.* New York: The World Publishing Company, 1952.

LYON-FREMANTLE, SIR ARTHUR JAMES: *Three Months in the Southern States: April-June, 1863.* New York: J. Bradburn, 1864.

McGUIRE, JUDITH BROCKENBROUGH: *Diary of a Southern Refugee During the War.* By a Lady of Virginia. Richmond, Virginia: J. W. Randolph and English, 1889.

McINTYRE, FLORENCE M.: *Art and Life.* Memphis, Tennessee: S. C. Toof and Company, 1952.

McELROY, ROBERT: *Jefferson Davis, The Unreal and the Real.* New York: Harper & Brothers, 1937.

MEADE, ROBERT DOUTHAT: *Judah P. Benjamin.* New York: Oxford University Press, 1943.

POORE, BEN PERLEY: *Perley's Reminiscences; or Sixty Years in the National Metropolis*, 2 vols. Philadelphia: Hubbard Bros., 1886.

PICKETT, LA SALLE CORBELL: *Pickett and His Men.* Atlanta: The Foote and Davies Company, 1899.

POLLARD, EDWARD A.: *Life of Jefferson Davis, with a Secret History of the Southern Confederacy.* Philadelphia: National Publishing Company, 1869.

————: *Southern History of the War*. New York: Charles B. Richardson, 1866.

PRYOR, MRS. ROGER A.: *Reminiscences of Peace and War*. New York: The Macmillan Company, 1904.

RANDALL, JAMES G.: *The Civil War and Reconstruction*. Chicago: D. C. Heath and Company, 1937.

RICHARDSON, E. RAMSAY: *Little Aleck, A Life of Alexander H. Stephens*. Indianapolis: The Bobbs-Merrill Company, 1932.

ROOSEVELT, THEODORE: *Diaries of Boyhood and Youth*. New York: Charles Scribner's Sons, 1928.

————: *Thomas Hart Benton*. Boston: Houghton Mifflin Company, 1899.

ROWLAND, DUNBAR, edited by: *Jefferson Davis Constitutionalist, His Letters, Papers and Speeches*. Jackson, Mississippi: Printed for the Mississippi Department of Archives and History, 1923.

ROWLAND, ERON (MRS. DUNBAR ROWLAND): *Varina Howell, Wife of Jefferson Davis*. New York: The Macmillan Company, 1927.

RUSSELL, WILLIAM HOWARD: *My Diary North and South*. New York: Harper & Brothers, 1954.

SALM-SALM, PRINCESS FELIX: *Ten Years of My Life*. New York: R. Worthington, 1877.

SCHAFF, MORRIS: *Jefferson Davis, His Life and Personality*. Boston: John W. Luce and Company, 1942.

SHAW, ARTHUR MARVIN: *The Family Sorrows of Jefferson Davis*. Alabama Historical Quarterly, IX, 1947.

SCHMIDT, WILLIAM A.: *The Last Days of the Lost Cause*. Clarksdale, Mississippi: Delta Press Publishing Company.

SCHURZ, CARL: *The Reminiscences of Carl Schurz*, Vol. II. New York: The McClure Company, 1907.

SHEA, GEORGE: *Jefferson Davis, A Letter from George Shea*. London: Edward Stanford, 1877.

SIMKINS, FRANCIS BUTLER, and JAMES W. PATTON: *The Women of the CONFEDERACY*. Richmond: Garrett and Massie, 1936.

SMITH, WILLIAM ERNEST: *The Francis Preston Blair Family in Politics*, 2 vols. New York: The Macmillan Company, 1933.

STRODE, HUDSON: *Jefferson Davis*. New York: Harcourt, Brace and Company, 1955.

STRONG, GEORGE TEMPLETON, edited by Allan Nevins and Milton Halsey Thomas: *The Diary of George Templeton Strong, 1860-1865*. New York: The Macmillan Company, 1952.

STRYKER, LLOYD PAUL: *Andrew Johnson*. New York: The Macmillan Company, 1929.

TATE, ALLEN: *Jefferson Davis: His Rise and Fall.* New York: Minton, Balch and Company, 1929.

TAYLOR, RICHARD: *Destruction and Reconstruction.* New York: D. Appleton and Company, 1879.

THOMPSON, JOHN R.: *Extracts from the Diary of John R. Thompson.* Lippincott's, 1888.

TOOMBS, ROBERT, edited by Ulrich Bonnell Phillips: *The Correspondence of Robert Toombs, Alexander H. Stephens and Howell Cobb,* 2 vols. Washington: Ninth report of the Historical Manuscripts Commission, 1913.

TRENT, WILLIAM P.: *Southern Statesmen of the Old Regime.* New York: Thomas Y. Crowell and Company, 1897.

————: *Alexander H. Stephens.* New York: Alfred A. Knopf, 1946.

WAGERS, MARGARET NEWNAN: *The Education of a Gentleman.* Lexington, Kentucky: Buckley and Reading, 1943.

WATTERSON, HENRY: "Marse Henry," Vol. I. New York: George H. Doran Company, 1919.

WELLES, GIDEON: *Diary of Gideon Welles,* Vol. I. Boston: Houghton Mifflin Company, 1911.

WILLIAMS, T. HARRY: *P. G. T. Beauregard.* Baton Rouge: Louisiana State University, 1954.

WILLIAMS, WIRT A.: "Jefferson Davis Lawsuit for Brierfield." *The Journal of Mississippi History,* July, 1947.

WINSTON, ROBERT W.: *High Stakes and Hair Trigger.* New York: New York; Henry Holt and Company, 1930.

WISE, JOHN S.: *The End of an Era.* Boston: Houghton Mifflin Company, 1902.

WRIGHT, MRS. D. GIRAUD: *A Southern Girl in '61.* New York: Doubleday, Page and Company, 1905.

Newspapers

Birmingham *Weekly Age-Herald*
Boston *Morning Post*
Boston *Transcript*
Brooklyn *Standard Union*
Buffalo *News*
Charleston *Mercury*
Chattanooga *Daily Times*

Chicago *News*
Christian Science Monitor
Cincinnati *Daily Gazette*
Congressional Globe
Dallas *Morning News*
Dubuque *Herald*
Jackson *Clarion Daily Ledger*

Jackson *Daily News*
Jackson *State Times*
Louisville *Courier Journal*
Memphis *Commercial Appeal*
Metropolitan Herald and Vindicator
Montgomery *Advertiser*
Montgomery *Daily Post*
Nashville *Banner*
National Intelligencer
Newark *Star Ledger*
New Orleans *Item*
New Orleans *Picayune*
New Orleans *Times-Democrat*
New York *Herald*

New York *Mail and Express*
New York *Sunday World*
New York Times
New York *Tribune*
New York *World*
Philadelphia *Weekly Times*
Portland *Argus*
Richmond *Dispatch*
Richmond *Enquirer and Sentinel*
Richmond *Examiner*
Richmond *News-Leader*
Richmond *Whig*
Washington *Chronicle*
Washington *Post*

Magazines

Alabama Historical Quarterly
Armstrong's Magazine
Belford's Magazine
Blackwood's Edinburgh Magazine
Christian Advocate
Confederate Stamp Album
Daughters of the American Revolution Magazine
Harper's New Monthly Magazine
Harper's Weekly
Holland's Magazine
Journal of Mississippi History
Journal of Southern History
Leslie's Illustrated
North American Review
Putnam's Monthly Magazine
Sewanee Review
Southwest Review
Spare Moments
Sunny South

The Arena
The Century
The Circle
The Collector
The Confederate Veteran
The Index
The Living Church
The Metropolitan
The United Daughters of the Confederacy Magazine
Tyler's Quarterly Historical and Geological Magazine
World's Events

INDEX

in Warren Co., 12; firmness of purpose demonstrated, 12; memories of The Briers, 17; brothers and sisters, 21; solitary pleasures and brooding, 22; reading as pleasure of married life, 25-26; knowledge of Indian tribes, 26; respect for Varina's opinion, 27; indebtedness to Joseph, 27; rides with Varina, 28; nervous tension, 28; mother's death, 28; speaks before Varina for first time, 30; life in Washington in early days, 34; elected to House of Representatives, 34-35; contempt for "illiterate clamor," 35; confirmed insomniac, 35; talk with Tyler, 36; skirmish with Andrew Johnson over military service, 37; commands First Mississippi regiment in Mexican War, 38-39; urges use of Whitney rifle, 40; dispute with Joseph over property rights, 41; gallantry at Monterey, 42; leave of absence to see Varina, 42-44; wounded in battle of Buena Vista, 44; on extension of slavery, 44; returns on crutches to Natchez, 45; chronic illnesses following Mexican War, 46; serious eye trouble, 46-47; appointed to Senate in 1848, 48-64; "icy shell of coldness," 48; increasing political importance, 53; quandary over support of Taylor, 56; refuses to lead Cuban revolutionary force, 59; fight with Henry Foote, 59; camaraderie with Taylor, 60; eulogy on Calhoun, 62; debate with Foote, 63-64; severe eye trouble, 64; defeat by Foote, 64; campaigns in North for Pierce, 65-68; advised to rest by Dr. Cartwright, 68; congenial work in War office, 70; physical appearance in 1853, 70; help from Varina in political rise, 72; highly constructive work in Washington, 1853-54, 72-73; as Secretary of War, 68 ff.; strong censure of General Scott, 75; plan to use camels in America, 77; interview with Pierce on Kansas-Nebraska bill, 77-78; grief at son's death, 78-79; dislike of William L. Marcy, 79-80; respect for Pierce's feelings, 80-83; activity in Senate, 83-84; becomes spokesman for South, 84; laryngitis and eye trouble, 1857-58, 84; "speaks from conviction," 85; threatened duel with Sen. Benjamin, 85; trip to New England, 1858, 86; defense of slavery in Faneuil Hall speech, 87, 94; upholds secession, 87; impressions of Buchanan's "court," 89; happiest phase of marriage, 95; heart condition, 95; frees Maryland soldiers, 96; 1860 resolutions defending slavery, 97-98; denounced by Douglas in Senate, 98; fatigue over secession movement in 1860, 98; first thought of Presidency, 99; cold-shouldered by Buchanan, 100; ambiguous position on secession, 100; illness and sorrows, 101; departs from Senate, 101-103; named commander-in-chief of Confederate Army, 103; chosen as President of Confederacy, 104; chronic ill health, 105; trip to Montgomery, 1861, 105-106; inaugurated President, CSA, 106; as "Lord Davis," 110; reaction to fall of Fort Sumter, 111-112; described by Russell, 114; appoints cabinet members, 115-116; prostrated in Montgomery, 120, 124; orders Johnston to aid Beauregard at Manassas, 124; patches up differences with Wigfalls, 128; illness following heavy newspaper attacks, 133; reluctance to mingle with people, 136; dispute with Gen. Johnston, 138; described by Stonewall Jackson, 140; faces military disasters, 142 ff.; abnormal sensitivity to disapprobation, 144; joins Episcopal Church, 146; loneliness in Richmond, 147; on battle of Seven Pines, 150; as "most uxorious man," 151; uncertainties about Confederate generals, 151-152; exposed to fire at Richmond, 154; inaccessibility of, 159; familiar figure on horseback, 159; nepotism charges against, 162; friendship with Benjamin, 165; attends theatricals in Semmes home, 173; snubbed by Wigfalls, 175; ill health and eye troubles, 180-182; scathing rebuke to Gen. Johnston, 184, 187; attempt on life, 188; called a "dictator," 189-190; visited by Lee, 194-195; proclaims day of fasting and prayer, 197; careworn and troubled, 198-199; abuse for removing Gen. Johnston, 204; proposal to use slaves in army, 206; illness and neuralgia, 207; last message to Confederate Congress, 213; flight after fall of Richmond, 219 ff.; hopes for rescuing Confederacy after fall of Richmond, 221; gives up last vestige of hope, 226; reaction to news of Lincoln's assassination, 227; "betrayal" of by Gen. Johnston, 236; attorney general, 238; deserted by Cabinet, 238; reaches Varina at last, 240; captured by Union troops, 243 ff.; "petticoat disguise" incident, 244-245; protests petty pillage, 247; alleged participation in Lincoln's assassination, 250; separated from family, 253-255; lampooned and caricatured, 258; shackled in irons, 258; reported in dying condition, 259; rapid decline in health at Fortress Monroe prison, 265, 273; talks with Dr. Craven, 276; tributes to Grant and McClellan, and to Confederate officers, 276-277; reading at Fortress Monroe, 277; reunion with Varina and Winnie at Fortress Monroe, 279; examined by McCulloch, 284; money raised for, 285; visits from old friends, 292; Greeley's editorial on, 293; released from Fortress Monroe, 296-297; case against dismissed by U.S., 299; heads for Canada, 300; man without a country, 301-302; sails for Havana and New Orleans, 304; warmly received at Jackson, Miss., 306; falls downstairs, 306; trip to England, 307; entertained by British peers, 309-310; visit to Paris, 311; to Scotland, 312; presidency of insurance company, 313, 319; death of brother Joseph, 319-320; 30 years of married life, 321-322; new financial difficulties, 322; second visit to England, 322-323; final haven at Beauvoir, 323; begins history of Confederacy, 323 ff.; stunned by death of son Jeff, 330; bequeathed Beauvoir estate by Mrs. Dorsey, 330; finishes history of Confederacy, 332; daughter Winnie as companion, 336; literary tastes, 1880's, 336-337; peaceful days,

return to Memphis, 317 *ff.*; poor health, 318; death of son Billy, 318; mounting debts, 319; at Brierfield property trial, 320; 30 years of married life, 321-322; second visit to England, 322-323; moves to Beauvoir, 323; eye trouble, 324-325; returns to Memphis, 325; animosity toward Mrs. Dorsey, 326 *ff.*; 331; inner melancholy, 334; lets burden slip to daughter Winnie, 336; life at Beauvoir in 1880's, 338; visit from Oscar Wilde, 340; on prisoners of war, 342; long illness, 1883, 344; as husband's amanuensis, 347; growing feebleness of husband, 352; opposes Winnie's engagement, 356; death of husband, 358-360; at burial ceremonies, 362; returns to Beauvoir, 363; transactions with publisher of Davis's history, 365; announces, then postpones, Winnie's engagement, 369-370; end of engagement, 371; heart attacks, 374; attacked by Eugene Field, 375; life in New York, 378 *ff.*; literary work, 378; as "dethroned Queen" in N.Y., 379; joins daughters in Richmond, 381; editorial in *Sunday World*, 382; moves to Gerard Hotel, N.Y., 383; postmortem letter to Judge Kimbrough, 1894, 383-384; close friends, 1890's, 386; serenaded in Richmond, 1896, 388; friendship with Mrs. Grant, 388-389; writes "The Humanity of Grant," 390; death of daughter Winnie, 392; moves to Vermont, 392-393; Confederate affairs, 1900, 394; changes name, 397; resents T. Roosevelt's comparisons, 398; becomes legend and institution, 399; as Queen of Confederacy in N.Y., 399; old age, 401; visits South in 1902, 404; summer in Canada, 406-407; appearance at 77, 407-408; dispute over Lee, 408-409; articles for *Spare Moments*, 413; gradual decline, 1905-06, 414; moves to Majestic Hotel, 415; death, 1906, 416; military funeral in Richmond, 417; final assessment, 418-420; criticism of, 419

Davis, Varina Anne ("Winnie"), daughter, 203, 255, 266, 285, 287, 290-291, 296, 306, 313, 322, 333, 335 *ff.*, 340, 345, 348, 355, 366-368, 376, 400, 418; christened "Daughter of the Confederacy," 349; collapse of romance, 371; engagement to Fred Wilkinson, 369; literary work, 378-379; lonely figure, 373-374; public speaking, 388; "Queen of Comus," 377; secret romance, 351-352; severe breakdown, 358; trip to Europe and death, 391-392

Davis, William Howell (son), 141, 318
Davis, Bend, 14, 305, 320, 344, 376
Day, Capt. Selden Allen, USA, 291
Day, Mary (Mrs. Burchenal), 291, 364, 401, 413
Delafield, Maj. R., CSA, 75
De Leon, T. C., 71-72, 109, 136-137, 158, 166-167, 194
Democratic party, 10; split in, 84, 97
Deslonde, Marie Mathilde, 91
Diary from Dixie, A, 341
Dickens, Charles, 57, 93, 268
Dickinson, Julia G., 246
Didier, Louise, 372
Dimitry, Alexander, 365
Dimitry, John, 365, 371
Disraeli, Benjamin, 29
Dix, Maj. Gen. John A., USA, 90
Dorsey, Mrs. Sarah Anne Ellis, 323, 328, 330, 405, 420
Dorsey, Samuel Wentworth, 324
Douglas, Stephen A., 49, 77-78, 84, 97-98, 100
Douglas, Mrs. Stephen A., 89, 171, 275
Dowdey, Clifford, 72, 101
Dred Scott decision, 83, 100
Dreux, Capt. Charles D., CSA, 107
Dumas, Alexandre, 346

Early, Gen. Jubal A., CSA, 169, 343, 347, 352, 355, 373, 381, 387
Ebbitt House, Washington, 78, 91, 276
Eckenrode, H. J., 167
Eliot, George, 93
Ellis, Thomas G. P., 323
Ellyson, Gov. J. Taylor, 417
Elzey, Gen. Arnold, CSA, 180, 189, 234, 238
Emancipation Proclamation, 159, 193
Emory, Dr. Thomas, 352
Emory, Gen. William H., CSA, 352